There's a disco ball between us

There's a disco

a theory of Black gay life

ball between us

Jafari S. Allen

Duke University Press *Durham and London* 2022

Printed in the United States of America on acid-free paper ∞
Designed by Aimee C. Harrison
Typeset in Portrait Text Regular and SangBleu Kingdom
by Westchester Publishing Services

Library of Congress Cataloging-in-Publication Data
Names: Allen, Jafari S., [date] author.
Title: There's a disco ball between us :
a theory of black gay life / Jafari Allen.
Description: Durham : Duke University Press, 2021. |
Includes bibliographical references and index.
Identifiers: LCCN 2021013522 (print) | LCCN 2021013523 (ebook)
ISBN 9781478013662 (hardcover)
ISBN 9781478014591 (paperback)
ISBN 9781478021896 (ebook)
Subjects: LCSH: Gay culture. | Gays, Black—Social life and customs.
| Gays, Black—Conduct of life. | Queer theory. | BISAC: SOCIAL
SCIENCE / Black Studies (Global) | SOCIAL SCIENCE / Anthropology /
Cultural & Social
Classification: LCC HQ76.96 .A454 2021 (print) | LCC HQ76.96 (ebook)
| DDC 306.76/608996—dc23
LC record available at https://lccn.loc.gov/2021013522
LC ebook record available at https://lccn.loc.gov/2021013523

Cover art: Jim Chuchu, "Pagans IX" from the Pagans series, 2014.
Courtesy of the artist.

To our "epidemic dead, and the living. Remember Them."
—MELVIN DIXON, "AND THESE ARE JUST A FEW"

& To the Children.

For Phillip: "Long may we live to free this dream"
—ESSEX HEMPHILL, "AMERICAN WEDDING"

contents

an invitation

Dear Reader,

There's a Disco Ball Between Us was expressly written to my students and to friends of my mind—some of whom I have never met, and among whom you may be counted. This account may seem to you a peculiar re-narrativization of a small story that you have never heard before, or something of a refraction, rather than a reflection, of what you already know. Perhaps you too feel called or curious—or *assigned*. Thank you. You are welcome to join this conversation, whether you find your experiences here, sit in silence struck by strangeness, or furiously jot your disagreements in the noisy, crowded margins of this book, chatting back with many others. Perhaps you have come only for the promise of Black bodies glistening in night light: swinging. In any case, you are invited to look again and to listen closely.

It is true: the stakes are, literally, life and death for African (descended) nonheteronormative and gender-variant individuals—not only in the global South, which is often labeled a homophobic place out of time with the "en-lightened" North, but also in "developed" states. In many nations of the world they face criminalization of "sodomy" and "cross-dressing." In extreme examples, rumor and innuendo—perhaps plastered on the front page of a newspaper—are enough to cause one to be beaten, jailed, or killed for "being" homosexual or gender nonconforming. Nationalist rhetorics that cast lesbian, bisexual, gay, and transgender rights and recognition as foreign attacks on tradition or sovereignty resonate with fundamentalist religious rhetorics in the former colonial world and in the metropole. An assortment of players—from Muslim clerics in northern Nigeria, Christian fundamentalists and racist white nationalists in the US federal and state governments, to parliaments of Western Europe and the Caribbean—imagine a great moment before the recognition of same-sex desire and support the installation or continuation of "antigay" legislation.

Racist and transphobic disenfranchisement, employment discrimination, and the lack of targeted public health interventions for LGBTQ individuals whose secondary and tertiary marginalization find them more vulnerable are widespread. Moreover, as they perform a celebration of sexual diversity, North Atlantic nations continue to deny the Black and Afro-hyphenated within their borders, affirming that their lives do not, indeed, matter. *Not to mention* those who lose their lives on the seas and over land, trying to get in or away. This all inarguably demonstrates that marginalization is in fact compounded and intersectional, as Black feminist work has averred from the beginning. It is also dynamically reiterative. Police violence, high and disproportionate incidence of HIV infection, cultural exclusion, and other forms of social suffering experienced by Black lesbian, gay, bisexual, transgender, queer, and *same-gender-loving* individuals are global. Contrary to the protestations of commentators who have hailed the end of the state, all minoritized and historically disenfranchised individuals and communities remain both dependent upon and vulnerable to *state power*, which has been steadily disinvesting from social welfare and reinvesting in various forms of police apparatus since at least the 1970s. Although there are certainly differences in intensity, formal political structure, and material resources throughout the world, we must make no mistake: whether state power is held by a democratically elected head of a nation-state, stolen by a crime syndicate, or administered by what Richard Iton called a "duppy state," propped up and animated by global capital headquartered elsewhere, it still largely and uniquely determines what Ruth Wilson Gilmore has aptly termed the "state sanctioned and/or extralegal production and exploitation of group-differentiated vulnerability to premature death": her definition of racism.[1] Of course, nonstate actors such as religious and cultural organizations, and families, often *see and think like the state.* The shared project of these strange bedfellows—driven by class, racial, and/or ethnic heteronormative respectability—is to discipline individuals into particular forms of subjectification, or nonexistence. Certainly, these push factors set Black/queer flowing. Nonetheless, we are more than the calculus of our compounded vulnerabilities. We create worlds that are yet unthought in pre-narrativized discursive dramas.

This is a book about desire: Black desire for political empowerment or autonomy, fun and carefree play in the face of social suffering, and erotic desire for one another. It is also one instantiation of an authorial desire to write the experiences and imagination of blackness into the record in another way. But dear reader, you likely want to hear about how imperiled and sick(ened) we are, or how always already dead we are. Perhaps you are convinced that there is no *we* at all: simply a nothing. With nothing between us. Or your orientation may be to resist alignment in any case: to throw off any affiliation with failed projects (and "failed" peoples). Admit that you think these academic positions are not only smarter but also more satisfying to your scopophilic drive. Although all of this is important to think with, we hope you will also consider other ways of seeing, listening, and sensing.

This ethnography of an idea emerges in *conversation* with those with whom I stand shoulder to shoulder (and shoulders joined to the hoe!) across miles and seas and continents, listening to and in conversation, still, with our dead. This register—that is, this way of speaking directly to you, with and about a variety of respondents, artists, scholars, and activists, whose names are sometimes written in the familiar first name and other times more formally—is essential to the structure (of feeling) and mode of engagement of this work. Citational practices are key to the rigor, structure, politics, and feeling of any work. Here I have chosen to sometimes efface, for example, the status of "theorist," "scholar," "poet," "DJ," "activist," "respondent," or disciplinary description in order to render everyone as an equal part of the conversation. In other cases, in the mode of Black vernacular English, I mark generational difference to indicate a particular regard for elders. Your author does not think at arm's distance from "Lorde," "Baldwin," "Alexander," or "Cohen," for example. By citing first names, I am attempting to reflect and invite the intimacy of invested conversation between intellectual forbearers/ancestors, colleagues, and/or friends (and indeed those who are friends only in the head of the author). Here's an important caveat: my (imagined) intimacy with these conversation partners has developed and deepened over many years of demonstrated respect for and intense study of their works. If this is not your experience, "do not try this at home."

All of this speaking out loud and directly to or about the living and our dead is an attempt at a live remix of a conversation in Black gay space time: here and there, then and now. Savoring the sweetnesses of this moment precisely because we know the bitterness too well. We know how easily any of us (all of us) can slip into the ether. As the author, I want to reconstitute and renarrate in languages and styles that reflect *how we do* (at least how I understand

and do how we do): our sensing, sound, and meter, our frames and paces and rubrics—our values, which include and sometimes messily spill over what some of us understand as scholarly "rigor." Or ease of "accessibility." You will hear this referred to as constitutive of a *Black gay habit of mind* or a Black gay aesthetic. The *voice* here is my own, as much as can be countenanced by astute peer reviewers and decently managed by generous copy editors. It is heard/read best if you imagine talking with a passionate friend from Southeast Queens who went to an HBCU as the sort of not-so-raw material they like to turn into leaders and Race Men. Imagine that he had an Afro-centric awakening followed quickly by a gay awakening, the compounded complexity of which prompted this author, your passionate friend, to drop out of school to be professionally Black and gay and political (which also meant catering and serving and being fired from a lot of restaurants). Your narrator, who by now was learning many ways to see, went back to school with more very smart Black folks after a while, then quickly off to graduate school, which found him listening-watching-doing in one new language on a new island, then writing about it in another. This traveling witness—still your passionate friend from Queens—became a professor who revels in the promise of Blackfull futures.[2]

There is much talk about *writing in a way that your grandmother can understand*. We ought to remember that Toni Morrison was a grandmother. The paradigm-setting theorists of my scholarly fields fit in the age cohort of Black and Latinx grandmothers. Yet this is not what or whom you imagine when you invoke the Nana clause. If you are not careful, your admonition to use simple language for Granny may unintentionally efface her wisdom. What might we hear if, instead of merely seeking to "explain to" or "write to" her, we listen carefully? Learn, as Black gay speech registers evidence, from grandmothers' sophisticated and highly elaborated intellectual practice of critical conversation. Depending on the sharpness of our reading/listening practices, the depth of our interest or attention, or in fact whether we are ready to engage, we may not be able to easily appreciate Grandmother's vast knowledge, intellect, wisdom, or artistry if our ears are not properly attuned.[3] Observers of Black women's rhetorical styles will tell you that it is not always perceivable on a shallow level. Her theoretical turn may be put to you in the form of a sly aside, a joke, or a one-word exclamation (even a look/gesture) that leaves it to the skill of the conversation partner to discern whether it is interrogative, declarative, or imperative.

Listen for what is quickly mentioned or elliptical or parenthetical (which an attentive conversation partner would never mistake as insignificant), and that which is repeated in the author's attempt to "complete the line."[4] In this book some streams of the main argument should nearly imperceptibly come together, gain saliency, and then diverge again, finding rich new rivulets of particularity before spilling out toward other streams and swells in other parts of the work. Some longer quotations are set off, perhaps louder or in spotlight, and others remain in the main flow of conversation. Epigrams are whispers in your ear, asking "Put a pin in this." The endnotes and index here make me smile because they provide another set of voices that intervene in or signify on the narrator's voices and priorities. The conversation partners with the receipts. Meant for all readers, not just researchers, these endnotes are provocative pursed lips and raised eyebrows pointing to the object being discussed, perhaps without the subject knowing they are being "objectified." Like endnotes, good indexes complement and extend the main text. There's evidence and heritage there. A practice of not only expertise, but also community and friendship. This index, compiled by archivist Steven G. Fullwood, is a rich finding aid for further Blackfull reading and research.

No reckoning allowed
save the marvelous arithmetics
of distance[5]

Joseph Fairchild Beam (Joe) was my first. He was for a lot of us. But like my deep, forestalled adoration—meeting his intense gaze from the back cover of *In the Life* but never in person—his status as everyone's imaginary movement babydaddy would find him feeling lonely and dying alone, if his letters and the testimony of many who knew him are accurate. Here's a stumbling start to one story, retold: in the harsh Atlanta sun, when I temporarily lost sight of the grace I could hold, I imagined it was Joseph Beam's voice that first called me by my new name before putting his lips on mine, his hand in mine. Years passed until I confessed my schoolboy crush. I learned I would never meet Joe. He had been gone for two years by then. This *poem* (therefore) is for Joe.[6] Of course, Joe created the anthology that called brothers together: recruiting, cultivating, culling, and editing *In the Life: A Black Gay Anthology*. But it was also that skin. Those lips. Mustache and dimpled chin. The work, the man I imagined I could *become*, and one I could *have* collapsed and conflated with my nascent intellectual, political aspirations: all libidinal. Driven by desire, not shame. This is neither an apology nor a confession, and this author is not alone. It is more of a description that may make what Black gay men were doing clearer and perhaps also generalizable for liberation projects of the living. They followed Black gay women—lesbians—who had already authored the project and politics of Black liberation in the context of radical socialist feminism, but only partly down the road, and they fought alongside Black gay men and women who today might name themselves as transgender. All these folks are our Black gay *epidemic dead and living*[7]—anthological world makers whom we refuse to let go. They also deserve more critical parsing and what Essex (Hemphill) called "ass-splitting" truths.[8] Audre (Lorde) offered in "Dear Joe" that "Nobody here will lean too heavily on your flowers / nor lick the petals of a lavender gladiola / for its hint of sweetness,"[9] but here we intend to lean heavily and greedily lick the sweetness. Here we are gathered together.

Today, the children are voguing in Paris and in Port-au-Prince, and Audre's words are on lips and hearts all over the world. US Black gay parlance and gesture—the snap, the read, the side-eye, and the intonation—have entered the realm of global mass culture, mostly out of context and poorly performed. Even as some of the affect and style of Black gay are mechanically reproduced, the politics of it is elided in mass culture and inadequately understood by scholars. Moreover, while the once and would-be Black LGBTQ movement in the United States has very little material connection with the activist work of Black "brothers and sisters" around the world today, the political sensibilities and aesthetics of this earlier period continue to resonate. This resonance or recurrence (perhaps reflection too?) is caused by both social and poetic forces. First, the habits of mind that we pursue here reemerge, taking on particular localized shapes because the global political-economic structuration that compelled it continues. The panoply of "romantic" visions can be seen in strongly held myths of "the Black family" as either always-already deracinated and broken (through de-gendering) *or* defiantly upstanding, "traditional," and heterosexual—led by a "strong (endangered/dangerous) Black man" with the help of a "strong (long-suffering and devout) Black woman" in the face of forces that would see "our men" "emasculated." This is narrative doxa in a variety of contexts: from conservative Islam, Christianity, and other religions to Black nationalism and various nativist, ethnic, and national movements in sites around the globe. In Africa, South and Central America, and the Caribbean, something similar is at work: Eurocentric "development" rhetoric that supplants local analyses and solutions. This policy-making framework is resonant with the popular drama in which the global South is cast as a fallen Eden (singular intended, as "the tropics" are undifferentiated in this fantasy) to be consumed all-

xiv / An Invitation

inclusive style via cruise ships, theme parties, and porn and sex work, but not taken seriously as complex geopolitical sites populated by people who strategically read and advocate their own vexed translocal positions. Note here the "First World" romance that holds the global North as the site of progress and ease, to which traffic dependably flows. But unbelonging is, paradoxically, powerfully constitutive: a Black radical "antiromance" orientation toward "home" inheres in translocal Black gay habits of mind.[10] Some of the most nettlesome or intractable political issues and methodological and theoretical conundrums that Black folks face can be illuminated by careful attention to this understudied intersection of race/place(lessness), gender, sexuality, and time(lessness) rather than relegation to the margins of Black studies, already at the margin.

There's a Disco Ball Between Us is based on more than three years of tracing various routes of works and flesh through field research in Trinidad and Tobago, Rio de Janeiro, Nairobi, and the internet, and other research travel to London, Bridgetown, Toronto, Paris, Ocho Rios, Miami, Vienna, and New York City. The excursions narrated here explore how legacies of enslavement, colonial oppression, heterosexism, and the well-worn routes that these legacies have created condition predictable itineraries and expected arrivals. But not all trips go as expected. Notwithstanding this fieldwork, the book is not a travelogue. Nor does it set out to offer a thick description of the lifeworlds of any particular place. As I wrote and revised (reiterated and revised again and again . . .), what emerged was much less a multisited ethnography of places but rather a work that reaches toward a new form: *ethnography of an idea*. Rather than hold fast to the conventions of ethnographic methodology and writing, this work deploys an *ethnographic sensibility*, or attunement with the social and the intersubjective, to pursue the politics and historicity of Black gay and Black/queer habits of mind. Archival work was undertaken in the Schomburg Center's In the Life Archive (formerly the Black Gay and Lesbian Archive), the Sharing Tongues collection at the London Metropolitan Archives, private collections, digitized internet archives of the Caribbean International Resource Network virtually housed at the Digital Library of the Caribbean, digital holdings of the New York Public Library and Lesbian Herstory Archive, and online curation of archives by public scholar/activists and artists Tourmaline and Alexis Pauline Gumbs.

The book holds and examines a variety of subjective motivations, scenes, and scales through an interrogation of "minor to minor" texts and social interactions analyzed in a relational and interstitial framework. Here we trace power and differential agency in the lives and works of desiring (and desired) subjects across borders of geography, nationality, class, gender, sexuality, and citizenship—re-narrativizing the flows and friction of the idea of Black gay (and Black/queer). The book offers selfies, art reflecting harsh realities and fantastical visions, self-love as political practice, local activism, and travel as key sites for the exploration of desire, autonomy, and sociality. It is attentive to the legacies of slavery and colonialism, and to the current creeping neoliberalism that disproportionately affects the poorer, darker, and less powerful throughout the world. Some of the sites that the book visits are rarified, such as international conferences, high art, film, scholarship, literature, performance, formal archives, and the everyday lives of elites and their organizations and international meetings. Others are "low" sites of everyday expression and entertainment in the lives of nonelite subjects and their political struggles and quotidian pursuits. This includes digital activism and attempts at connection in cyberspace, which offers circadian circuits of professional and do-it-yourself pornography, local and international news, and interpersonal communication. Each of these new scenes—often with old scripts—provides exciting and potentially far-reaching new challenges and opportunities for scholars, artists, and activists. But we must be willing to take a new trip and to "seek beyond history" for something new and "more possible."[11]

I hope that you will be moved to allow me to bring you out to the club.

Your eyes may take a moment to adjust to the quality of light inside: the various flickers of experience, sensual movement, and rousing sound. Each chapter of the book, and movements within chapters, combines multiple methodologies or ways of seeing, invokes different disciplinary traditions and investments, and contains a wide range of close readings as well as quick observations. All of this is grounded in what I call an "ethnographic sensibility." I am aware that the world that we have re-narrated here, or created through narration, may be unfamiliar to most. Below, I offer incomplete orientation notes for the uninitiated. Still, these are merely the lowest bass frequencies of music that escape through the club walls and the momentarily opening doors. Only a few furtive glimpses of folk tipping in and others, only occasionally, stumbling out. Soaked. This gesture cannot capture the ineluctable experience of reading fully. There is much more in each chapter (self-consciously almost "too much") than listed here. For the more adventurous, I recommend simply turning to the Introduction now.

The Introduction will help readers come to understand the structure of the book's argument and evidence through discussion of our modes of attention and engagement. We introduce concepts of "Black gay time," narrative theorizing, "resonant reading," and the image of a kaleidoscopic disco ball. Beginning with acknowledgment of a conflation of the intellectual, erotic, and political in the work of Black gay men, including the author, this chapter reads "generations" and genealogies of Black gay (lesbian, transgender, bisexual, and gay male) politics and cultures through visual art and theorization from the dance floor, poetry, Black feminist theory, and historiography. There are three parts to the book: "A Stitch in Space Time. The Long 1980s," "Black/Queerpolis," and the "Conclusion. Lush Life (in Exile)."

"The Anthological Generation" is the book's first chapter. It inaugurates the sort of genealogical analysis that will recur throughout and introduces the central concept of the *anthological*. After situating the historical and conceptual foundations of radical Black lesbian feminism and the foundational importance of *Conditions Five: The Black Woman's Issue,* the chapter moves to discuss the long-1980s "endangered Black male" discourse, the Blackheart Collective's first two issues, Joseph Beam's *In the Life,* and critical political supplements offered by trans activists Marsha P. Johnson and Sylvia Rivera.

The short chapter "What It Is I Think They Were Doing, Anyhow" begins an exploration of the habits of mind of Black gay men writers of the long 1980s, beginning with Joseph Beam. Here we witness Joseph Beam's, Essex Hemphill's, and Melvin Dixon's conceptualizations of home/belonging, inheritance, and blackness move beyond contending paradigms, including the foundational work of James Baldwin. The chapter ends with an extensive experimental reading of Charles Lofton's short film "O Happy Day: The Early Days of Black Gay Liberation."

"Other Countries" offers a granular exploration of the confluence of Black masculinity, desire, diaspora, and Black gay sociality. It begins with setting the scene of Gay Men of African Descent (GMAD), then moves to Melvin Dixon's rarely analyzed diaspora theorization before new readings/re-narrativizations of Assotto Saint, Marlon Riggs's *Tongues Untied,* Audre Lorde's "Tar Beach," *Gary in Your Pocket,* Essex Hemphill's *Ceremonies,* less remarked-upon works by Lorraine Bethel, *This Is Not an AIDS Advertisement* by Isaac Julien, and commentary on porn/erotica by Isaac Julien and Kobena Mercer. Salient themes of political organizing, intra- and interracial sexual desire, and transphobia and trans recognition are discussed here. The chapter ends with an autoethnographic scene in which race, class, and desire collide.

Speaking of music and dancing: the "Disco" chapter is an example of how this work invites the reader to participate with their imagination. It begins a transnational political-economic analysis of the contingency of Chic's 1979 proposition that "These. Are. The. Good. Times"; narrates a nostalgic dance through personal experience of "passing strange" from bridge and tunnel address to cosmopolitan subjecthood; and performs a musical analysis of performances of gay men's sibilance and the assumed stridence of Black women. We listen to works by Diana Ross, Grace Jones, Chic, Ashford and Simpson, Loleatta Holloway, and Luther Vandross. Extended close readings of Sylvester ("You Are My Friend," "Over and Over") and Carl Bean ("Born Gay") parse embodied Black gay ethics.

"Black Nations Queer Nations?" takes its name from the historic Black Nations/Queer Nations Lesbian and Gay Sexualities in the African Diaspora: A Working Conference, documented by filmmaker Shari Frilot. From the vantage of the author as a participant in the 1995 event, it offers an analysis of salient concepts of Black(ness), nationality/nationalism, queer (which makes its conceptual debut in this chapter), and finally, "Black queer counterpoise." Returning to Essex Hemphill's notion of "standing at the edge of cyberspace," we take up transnational meanings and circulations of art, porn, and self-made images in the digital present. This chapter closes out the temporal frame of "the long 1980s."

"Bonds and Disciplines" is the first chapter in part 2: "Black/Queerpolis." The preface proposes and defines the term, which seeks to supplement *diaspora, Afropolitan,* and *pan-African,* all of which are inadequate to the task of capturing the experiences and literatures invoked in *Disco Ball.* Here we turn to the contemporary moment, after the establishment of Black Queer studies in the US academy. The author reconstructs a transcript of the opening of the 2009 Black/Queer/Diaspora symposium—outlining theoretical, methodological, ethical, and genealogical (or rhizomatic) conundrums. Multivocal, the chapter proceeds as a mediated conversation with participants Natalie Bennett, Fatima El-Tayeb, Lyndon Gill, Rosamond S. King, Ana-Maurine Lara, Xavier Livermon, Graeme Reid, Matt Richardson, Colin Robinson, Omise'eke Natasha Tinsley, Rinaldo Walcott, Michelle Wright, and guests George Chauncey and Calvin Warren.

"Archiving the Anthological at the Current Conjuncture" extends this section's pivot toward the constitution of Black/queer study and Black/queer memory. It is also the first of a sort of triptych of methodological chapters. After discussing the "archival turn" and its prospects for Black queer memory, we visit the contested archive of Black lesbian activist Venus Landin ("another Venus") via the theorization of Saidiya Hartman, M. NourbeSe Phillip, David Scott, Matt Richardson, and others. Then, staging another conversation—this time between far-flung Black queer archival projects, drawn from a "virtual roundtable" (with Steven G. Fullwood, Ajamu Ikwe-Tyehimba, Zethu Matebeni, Matt Richardson, Colin Robinson, and Selly Thiam)—we engage an array of international archivists and leaders of archival projects themselves, including Alexis Gumbs and Tourmaline. Appended to this is an invaluable short guide to Black (queer) archives indexed in this work, compiled by archivist Steven G. Fullwood.

"Come" analyzes transnational Black queer sociality and introduces some of the pitfalls of traditional ethnography, moving from critical reflections on embodiment, belonging, and inheritance in Rio de Janeiro to an ethnographic vignette set in Nairobi, Kenya. Drawing distinction between Black/queerpolity and uncritical formulations of "global gay" and "gay international," this argument takes us from East Africa to Rio, to Paris, and Ocho Rios. The chapter considers tourism, (im)migration, sex work, exile, self-discovery, transnational curiosity, and solidarity (sometimes without travel), departing from clubs and romantic relationships to literature, ethnography, social theory, and Thomas Allen Harris's film *E Minha Cara*.

The final part of this methodological triptych, "'Black/Queer Mess' as Methodological Case Study," contributes to ongoing discussions of ethnography of Black subjects and fieldwork practices by exploring concepts of "cognate," "stranger value," and "native anthropology" through the author's reconsideration of an unpleasant email exchange with friends/collaborators in the field. Here we query the limits of the project of transnational social science research and collaboration by resituating key formulations of "diaspora," "Afro-Modernity" (Michael Hanchard), "incorrigibility" (Charles Taylor), "ethnographic sincerity" over "authenticity" (John L. Jackson), "outsider within" (Faye Harrison), Brackette Williams's analysis of Zora Neale Hurston's famous "skinfolk not kinfolk" formulation, and Ted Gordon's activist anthropology. Returning to Marlon Riggs's definition of anthropology as "the unending search for what is utterly precious," we argue for the central inclusion of radical Black feminist lesbian formulations of transnational outlaw status (M. Jacqui Alexander), deviance as resistance (Cathy Cohen), and recognition of difference and status as "a relative" (Audre Lorde) as crucial interventions in these perennial ethical and intellectual dilemmas.

Whereas the final chapter of this section, "Unfinished Work," is named in honor of a poem by the long-term Trinbagonian activist/writer Colin Robinson and begins with an excerpt of Essex Hemphill's "For My Own Protection," this is the chapter that will be most readily identified as "about politics" (although I hope that readers will find that the entire book is political and elaborates *a politics*). The chapter follows currently unfolding political dramas in Guyana and Trinidad and Tobago, where activists are shaping a new political agenda; the United States, where we grapple with the consequences of the "NGOization" of HIV/AIDS services and what once was a Black gay *movement* (beginning where we leave off in part I); and East Africa, where we meditate on Afropolitanism and pan-Africanism, and read writer Binyavanga Wainaina in tandem with the political organizing underway in Kenya.

The tripartite concluding section "Lush Life (in Exile)" explicitly upends "romantic" and masculinist discourses of diaspora, travel, fugitivity, "vagabondage," and militancy through making good Black gay sense of these recurring freedom dreams of the Black radical tradition. First it re-situates "exile," then introduces readers to my good friend Nehanda Isoke Abiodun. Her story and my memories bring us briefly back to Special Period Cuba, then to Harlem—both pre–Columbia University expansion, then gentrified Harlem—on the occasion of the posthumous "return" of the New Afrikan freedom fighter. This (believe it or not) finds us making some explicit prescriptions for Black studies, which (no surprise) returns us to the anthological epidemic dead, and the living, of the long 1980s! There's music here, and more dancing.

Please also note that the "Acknowledgments" section reads more like a short chapter focused on literally acknowledging what (professional considerations and intellectual discoveries) and who shaped this particular work. Addressed in a way that emerging scholars or readers/seekers may begin to see how they might navigate their own routes, and for my mentors, predecessors, and conversation partners to understand how their work and their way shaped my thinking here, this is another gesture toward "resistance to containment" to traditional forms.

JAFARI S. ALLEN

Introduction

Pastness Is a Position

The disco ball is not made of a single mirror, but numerous tiny mirrors. Each reflects and refracts light at different angles, showing different colors of the spectrum—seemingly in a different time too, shifting on the walls, on the floors, on the face of dancers at different points in space and depending on where you stand. Relatively. So too are my readings (and yours) deictic and relational. Isn't that always the way, no matter how many accounts claim universality and precise authority? Defying funhouse-mirrored representation, and not seeking unified reflection, this account is characterized by generative flashes of nows in which pasts are present. I see W. E. B. Du Bois showing us how to create a portrait of *Black Folks Then and Now*. Closer in time, St. Clair Drake strongly echoes in space, responding to Du Bois by writing a testament of *Black Folk Here and There*. Then Michel-Rolph Trouillot intervenes with a deeply ethnographic sense of historicity that we intend to explore here: "But nothing is inherently over there or here. In that sense, the past has no content. The past—or, more accurately, pastness—is a position. Thus, in no way can we identify the past as past."[1]

This book's title, *There's a Disco Ball Between Us*, is borrowed from a friend: artist Wura-Natasha Ogunji. In *Oyibo versus Herself (That's not the Atlantic. There's a disco ball between us)*, Wura visually initiates a conversation about

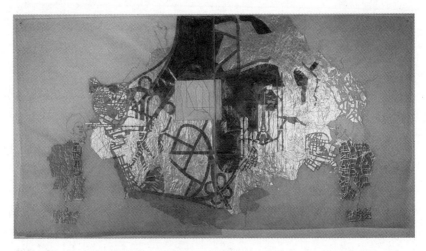

I.1 Wura-Natasha Ogunji, *Oyibo versus Herself (That's not the Atlantic. There's a disco ball between us)*. 2013. Mixed media (thread, graphite, ink, colored pencil) on tracing paper with video projection. 2 panels (25 inches high × 24 inches wide each).

Black (un)belonging and sociality that this book joins, following disparate itineraries and tracing the contours of Black gay (and Black/queer) politics and culture through scenes of Black folks relating to one another in and between several places around the globe (see figure I.1). In Wura's piece, *Oyibo* (the titular "stranger" or "white woman") is the artist herself: a Black woman of Nigerian and Jewish American background. The meeting of two hemispheres of rice paper constitutes her cartographic sea terrain drafted with streets and symbols. Her armless body(ies) made of red fragments and rivulets, estuaries, and roads, is topped off by a rendering of Wura's head. Each figure projects a narrow metallic laser-like gaze at the worlds before her and calls out on either side of the almost sculpted, metallic center. This reflective space Wura imagines is "not the Atlantic," she tells us (but of course it can be if it needs to be!), but a disco ball. It is an aerial rendering of islands in her father's birthplace (and now her home), Lagos, Nigeria, as well as her native St. Louis, Missouri. Stepping back, I see a face in profile on the right side of the work, which is more recognizable in the blue light of video projection. The eyes of this Ife-head-sculptured-face are cast down. To the left and center, I see a keyhole or a window, or a door (of no return?). In the exhibition space, lights flicker, and beginning in this center, ocean blue light begins to fill the space of the work while Chic plays "Le Freak." Of course, dancing ensues: arms in the air, asses shaking, lips bitten as flesh travels the space of the gallery/dance floor and beyond. Wura says: "That space between Africa and the Americas is often imagined as an abyss, a space of loss or disconnection. With this work, I am imagining the sea as a collection of mirrors which are constantly reflecting and refracting, much like a disco ball. In the space of the nightclub anything can happen. Our futures are not (pre)determined by the past—be that history, or even memory."[2]

Our futures are not (pre)determined by the past. "Pastness is a position," Michel-Rolph (Trouillot) has already told you. And/nevertheless there is still much to navigate within that position. Indeed, *Oyibo versus Herself* is a visual example of what Dionne Brand might appreciate as a kind of *ruttier* (map) "for the Marooned in Diaspora."[3] This poetic, layered, navigational work of memory is a kind of multidimensional chart capable of imagining and plotting time and space travel. For us, the metaphor of the disco ball also refers to the theorization of Kevin Aviance—legendary performance artist and impresario—meditating on the final lowering of the disco ball at Club Palladium, at the moment in which northern LGBTQ urban milieux were transformed by conjunctures of "Race, Violence, and Neoliberal Spatial Politics in the Global City."[4] Kevin reflects:

> What I remember at the closing night at the Palladium [was] the disco ball being brought down to the floor. And looking inside the disco ball, and seeing all my girlfriends who had died. Seeing all their faces and realizing that that time was over for me. It was over. But they were all like this [*applauding slowly*]. I remember looking in that disco ball and I saw all their faces, and I gagged because I saw all my girlfriends. [*pause*] I may have known—this is a rough number—maybe three million faggots in my lifetime—known or seen that many. [*pause*] What is really fucked up is that number has gotten smaller because girls have gone on or died or passed on or whatever. And so, when I see this disco ball, which they don't have a lot in clubs anymore—that's when I see all those people again. I can see them, I can feel them, I can talk to them, they wave to me. I know this sounds really crazy—but that's the only time I can see those people again, and it's really amazing. An amazing time for me.[5]

Generative flashes in which pasts are present. Both Wura and Kevin reimagine loss in their understandings of the disco ball. Their memory making refracts violence, death, and disconnection. That is, it bends and can break it apart—or perhaps merely resides in that kaleidoscope of the break/wake.[6] The sanctity of the dance floor is upheld here. The audaciousness and vulnerability of our flesh: made, acknowledged, and remade holy in Black gay time.

Black studies scholars and artists have engaged in a number of memory projects in recent years, many turning to the Middle Passage as the constitutive moment of blackness and Black being.[7] You may think of this as another project of "recovery," or perhaps more precisely (re)constitution or (re) articulation—not of a "lost" or "absent" culture but of strategies and formulae, techniques, forms, and agenda needed to withstand recursive material attacks in the present. And, of course: recovery of warm, wet, sticky affect. Kisses, for example, can be adhesive. Bodily fluids, constitutive. What if we were to follow each for a spell—turning to Black folks then and now and here and there, all at once, and through the lenses of those only occasionally and conditionally invited to the margins of Black studies? What is the promise in an archive that sees "the spaces where others ought to be" on the dance floor at the club?[8] What remains in mourning's memory, recollected stories, and the ache (or the *aché*, small axe, or the *axé*?) of yearning lodged in our bodies (and our) politic(s)?

Black Gay Time

On the night that he recalled the lowering of the disco ball at Club Palladium,[9] what would be Kevin's eyebrows, had they not been shaven already to give full effect to his beautifully painted eyes, rise. He nods after softly squinting: "It was cute. . . ." Eyes to the side. Shoulders hunched. Filmmaker Wills Glasspiegel is interviewing Kevin for his film on the techno song "Icy Lake" that had been performed on the closing night of the Palladium.[10] Kevin turns his head and lifts his shoulders, preparing a rise in inflection to be delivered with the next line: "It was cute." This rising inflection is key to the transmission of meaning. There is a world of difference between what is "cute" and what Kevin later invokes as "the carry-on and the ki-ki" of Black gay sociality. "Yes. The 'Icy Lake' was icy dry. It was a very dry song," he tells Wills—a bit breathless and *verklempt* after his moving toasts and reunion with old friends. To say it was *cute* is at once to (begrudgingly) countenance a bit of value—tolerating another (flawed) perspective while pointedly holding a privileged space for something else that one values more. Kevin gives that side head movement that says "Perhaps." He goes on: "But it wasn't . . . *A Little Bit of Bass*. It wasn't Loleatta Holloway. It wasn't Diana Ross. It wasn't, you know, real *real* dance music." There it is. Holding the line on what is authentic in his estimation (and authentically Black cultural production). Songs like "Icy Lake" had sounded a loud atonal death knell for the house-music club (which continued the disco project) as Black and Latinx folks and others in urban centers of the global North had experienced it. No soul and no gospel riffs. Not even the fresh high-energy danceable European electronica of a Kraftwerk or George Kranz, for example, which Larry Levan and, later, Frankie Knuckles mixed into the house-music canon. "But at that time and at that place . . . ," Kevin continues. There, again, is Black gay deicticity: recognition of relativity, contingency, and context, but also clearly not a concession. Although there is certainly what looks to some like resignation here—perhaps an analysis or recognition that this is the prevailing market—attend also to how he understands this as (merely) a temporal-spatial blip. It has not been always, is not everywhere, and will not be forever.

The twirling, cruising, and artistic production that emerged from the clubs of downtown New York, Chicago, and London in the 1980s and 1990s had been made possible by the (temporary) desertion of these urban centers, following the 1960s urban "unrest" or uprisings in the United States, which came to London in the late 1970s and 1980s, then to various places around the world. Gay folks created oases of nighttime revelry in daytime commerce deserts facing criminalization and violence and/but/also creating art, fashion, culture, and of course income in formal and informal markets. But developers realized that today's "blight" can equal tomorrow's low or no tax. In short order, they began transforming the inner city to havens for a global elite. By the late 1990s, it was clear that capital required the space of the city to be returned to its service by both day and night. Like many other clubs, bars, and small businesses felled by the changing New York real estate market (including, in this case, New York University, which built a dormitory on the site), the Palladium closed its doors.

This state of at once exceeding and belonging irreducibly to (one's) time invoked and enabled by the disco ball represents a Black gay temporality and sociality (time and ways of being together) that are processual, not teleological.[11] Within Black gay time space, one can cut into the past and project or imagine a future in which we are still dancing with friends and lovers gone too soon to the ethers of the dance floor and the flickers of the disco ball light. This temporality is one of time collapsed or at least reconfigured from "straight time" in which, for example, what is most important happens in the day, or in which one "grows out of" same-sex "play" or finally "settles down" into heteronormative or homonormative sociality. This excessive temporality spreads out broadly behind us and in front of us in the pursuit of an elaborated litany for thriving. In this space we claim family and children not merely from biological or legal means but by a process of nourishment and nurture. Audre (Lorde) gave us this vision of work, love, and struggle many years ago, and I have repeated and remixed her words many times since:

> For those of us who cannot indulge the passing dreams of choice
> . . . seeking a now that can breed futures
> like bread in our children's mouths
> so their dreams will not reflect
> the death of ours. . . . [12]

Black gay is out of time. So much so, dear reader, that you may wonder why many of us (still) insist on identifying and self-identifying at all. It seems anachronistic to some. Certainly, *dépassé* in the academic-industrial complex in which folks are tripping over each other in a rush to denounce what they understand as "identity politics." The excessiveness of socialities that include and spill promiscuously over heterosexually reproduced families, crisscross polities, and could not care less what critics think of what and how they call themselves requires new ways of seeing. Black gay be *extra*. Often doing too much (for you to see with limited range). Black gay is outside bourgeois time, outside of nation time, ahead of time in culture—language, art, and fashion, for example—but also in many ways just out of time. Long ago, James Baldwin reminded us of how one passes time and passes on, with "coffins piling up around you."[13] Black gays be dying early, still.

Jack (Halberstam) defines queer time as occurring "once one leaves the temporal frames of bourgeois reproduction and family, longevity, risk/safety, and inheritance."[14] This is good to think with: the (white) queer temporal imperative celebrates the release of normative expectations and responsibilities. That is in fact what is most "queer" about it. It is the "turn away" from normativity and the negation of futurity. But *we* do not (get to) simply turn—we twirl, arriving inevitably out of sync with these expected bourgeois temporalities (if we are not permanently "detained," never to arrive at all). This is not to suggest that Black LGBTQ folks cannot be bourgeois or, on another register, *bourgie*. My point is the reckoning of time, value, and access within those systems. In the current moment, lives are differentially valued by their ordered relation to capital, aiming for the narrow bull's-eye of the "charmed circle" of (heterosexual or homosexual) monogamous marriage, home ownership, child rearing, long life, and bequeathing to children the means by which their trajectories find them within that charmed—that is, privileged, illusive for most—circle of putative security. This is certainly about material resources that can provide enough privacy so that the smoke and mirrors of this particular gag seem like moral triumph rather than inherited ascription and luck. Black gay habits of mind are inexorably bound to this space-time orientation of living in the present, powerfully conditioned by history, but also attuned to radical possibility. They straddle the now and *the ether*. Imagine the ether as the space of transition, into which the dead pass and in which those who are not yet born await. Dynamic and simultaneously here and there—sometimes disoriented(ing). Always moving.

I cannot help remixing this nostalgic time travel once again: "Is It All over My Face?"[15] We stumble, gracefully, out of the blue-black club light. The eternal night of the club, with the flicker of the disco ball keeping suspended time. Walls painted with black acoustic tile and heavy velvet blackout curtains have cocooned our nascent comings, goings, and carryings on. "We are exhausted / from dreaming wet dreams / afraid of the passion / that briefly consoles us," Essex (Hemphill) said.[16] This is, of course, partly about my own nostalgic longing. What and whom has passed before my own eyes. But unlike discrete, individual melancholia, my longing is connected to that of a number of Black gays and other queers of color anthologized in books, archives, and treasured memories of friends, families, and lovers: "In the harsh glare of leaving that space and forgetting, we get distorted glimpses of our present. And I wonder about this current moment—half-past, or thirty 'til. This time fifteen, twenty-three, thirty-five years too late? And I wonder. I want to look for what we have forgotten, inside."[17]

Thomas (Glave), in a different moment of reflection and reassessment— the 2002 Fire & Ink Black Lesbian and Gay Writers' Festival—also turned to Essex. Addressing Essex-in-the-ethers about the inheritance he has left for the children who follow, as much as to the writers and activists and scholars who were assembled in the flesh, Thomas does not address whether one should or can turn away. Talking to Essex-in-the-ether, he offers this: "Our futures would without question be imperiled, you told us, if, sometime discarding vigilance, we dared curtsey to that enduring U.S. mind-altering favorite, ahistoricism. . . . In the fierceness of this now, it is exactly the radical art and life-effort of conscientious remembrance that, against revisionism's erasures and in pursuit of our survival, must better become our duty. Memory in this regard becomes responsibility; as responsibility and memory both become us."[18] In this elegant arrangement of future, peril, historicism, and urgent demand, Thomas reaffirms that we are made and marked by our responsibility to not be erased from the past or from the present. Damn. This is the Blackest conjuncture of all, is it not? A lot of work. Always at once arriving, emerging, and preparing for unpromised futures in uninvited spaces: "imprinted with fear," "like bread in our children's mouths," indeed. And/but I hear the children asking. They are clamorous and quite dubious by now: when? Audre-in-the-ether, Essex-on-the-other-side and *just above my head*: when will it be my time to "indulge the passing dreams of choice"?[19] So in a process of conscientious and critical remembrance, it is now of the utmost importance to remember what and who bring us to a singularly Black gay understanding of this conjunctural moment.

This "theory of Black gay life" tracks practices and habits of mind that emerged during *the long 1980s*. Just as the smoke of the 1970s had begun to clear, the devastation of AIDS dawned harshly. Folks first began to dance, fuck, organize, and make art under the banner of "Black gay" in the 1980s and 1990s. Autonomous organizations arose to demand recognition and acknowledgment of the presence and contributions of lesbians/gay women and gay men within Black communities and within nation-states, and folks debated where the modifier should be placed—whether Gay *black* or Black *gay* would be the term of art—supposedly emphasizing gays who just happened to be Black or Blacks who were also gay, respectively.[20] The *idea* of Black gay (and, later, Black/queer) emerges directly out of the political, artistic, and activist work of radical Black lesbians of the 1970s who had cut their teeth in civil rights, Black power, peace, labor, antiapartheid, reproductive rights, and radical feminist movements—in the United States primarily but also connected to anticolonial liberation struggles and the organized Left around the world. This work happened mostly out of the view of professional academics, who rarely understand community organizing, archiving, academic work, sex parties, and the literature and art of Black lesbian, gay, transgender, bisexual, and *same-gender-loving* people as all of a piece and constitutive of a distinct politics. I draw the long 1980s roughly from 1979—the year that *Conditions Five: The Black Women's Issue* was published, months before the first cases of what we now call HIV/AIDS were identified and the globally consequential neoconservatism of Ronald Reagan and Margaret Thatcher first began to coagulate—to around 1995, when Black Nations/Queer Nations? Lesbian and Gay Sexualities in the African Diaspora: A Working Conference took place, at the same time that disco balls were lowered in cities across the North Atlantic as capital reclaimed urban space and scholars belatedly began to decry the "neoliberal moment."

Anthological Habits

Our re-narrativization of Black gay and Black/queer inaugurates a form (of critical ethnography) that builds upon the Black feminist imperative to produce purposefully embodied narrative theory, the queer mandate to resist or subvert normativity (including sometimes tactically performing it), and the ethnographic warrant to poetically represent lived reality. Elsewhere, I have described the radical Black gay habit of mind that produces this as "relational," following Glissant; "nomadic" or "rhizomatic," after Deleuze and Guattari; or simply "promiscuous." Still, dear reader, you want an accounting of this author's textual stroll: "cruising" theories, as dear José (Esteban Muñoz) exemplified.[21] Now, with more force, I want to offer this as an *anthological* habit of mind. The mode of attention in this book—that is, its research methodology, theory, politics, and the aesthetic intentions supporting rearrangement of various modes of interdisciplinary inquiry—is anthological, meant to honor the often circuitous but also convergent temporalities, themes, sites, texts, and individuals represented. At the start of the long 1980s, the explosion of the poetry broadside, the reimagination of long-standing urban Black tradition of soapbox preachers and corner philosophers, and the expansion of popular poetry and spoken word to various sites within Black communities fomented new intellectual and political spaces and innovative thought. It is in this rich intellectual-creative environment that the anthology—not the academic journal, single-authored academic or trade book, or press-mediated reader—became the major repository of Black political philosophy of the long 1980s. In this anthological tradition the editor is not a single author or even necessarily the most important. She is, rather, a sort of arbiter, consensus builder, keen observer, and laborer—as well as shaper of discourse.[22] Multivocal anthologies such as *The Black Woman; Homegirls: A Black Feminist Anthology; This Bridge Called My Back: Writing by Radical Women of Color; In the Life: A Black Gay Anthology; Brother to Brother: New Writing by Black Gay Men; Other Countries: Black Gay Voices*; and *Afrekete: An Anthology of Black Lesbian Writing* are central to the Black gay intellectual "canon" and were essential to my own intellectual foundation. In the *anthological tradition* a collection purposefully makes a multivocal statement of the political and aesthetic commitments of a group of artists and/or scholars engaged in what they—or at least the editor—believe is a collective (that is, not necessarily "unified" but rather harmonious) project. This is how we compose a theory of Black gay life. One generous way to read this ethnography of an idea is to think of this book and its author as part of the anthological tradition.

"A Necessary Theater"

Margaret Walker Alexander's "I Want to Write" inscribes the at-once scholarly, political, and deeply personal motivations of this author. In it, the poet not only expresses her desire to, for example, "write the songs of my people" but also demonstrates that to write, one must also listen to them "singing melodies in the dark / . . . floating strains from sob-torn throats," searching and shaping. Following Dr. Walker, I too endeavor to "frame" and "catch" what she describes as fugitive "sunshine laughter in a bowl." This classic Black *ars poetica* does not pose the intellectual-artistic project as sweatless or effete or dilettantish—there is work here. In the last lines she makes the dexterity needed to undertake this evident: expressing her own desire (brilliantly fulfilled in her illustrious career) to not only "fling dark hands to a darker sky"—that is, perhaps, to the ether from which more light emanates—but also to "then crush and mix such lights till they become / a mirrored pool of brilliance in the dawn."[23] Yes. "A mirrored pool of brilliance in the dawn" feels a lot like a disco ball. Like a sparkling ocean. Or a puddle we jump over—for example, on our way to the corner store in Queens. "I Want to Write" betrays my own perhaps unfashionable affection "for my people."[24] To explain "how"—derived from what methodologies, critical habits, and quality of sight, I turn, venturing a bit of reverential creative license, to Elizabeth Alexander. Here is her "Ars Poetica #100: I Believe"—for a moment trying on "ethnography," where she so beautifully and precisely placed "poetry."[25] For this occasion, I might, in part, read Elizabeth's poem this way:

> [Ethnography], I tell my students,
> is idiosyncratic. [Ethnography]
> is where we are ourselves,
>
> . . .
>
> [Ethnography] is what you find
> in the dirt in the corner,
> overhear on the bus, God
> in the details, the only way
> to get from here to there.
> [Ethnography] (and now my voice is rising)
>
> . . .
>
> (here I hear myself loudest)
> is the human voice,
> and are we not of interest to each other?

A fusion of the modes, genre, and habits of mind of ethnographic methodology and writing with the practice of poetry would more precisely name the writerly and political commitment to *see* and *say* reflected in this book. After all, Audre already told us that "the quality of light by which we scrutinize our lives has direct bearing on the product which we live. . . . This is poetry as illumination . . . givi[ng] name to the nameless so that it can be thought."[26] One of the central meta-theoretical impulses in this book is to try to faithfully caress in between the material and affective: listening intently and occasionally showing the work, allowing the seeming messiness and unseemliness of everyday life to be felt, but also often economizing the language—sometimes only obliquely naming. Telling it elliptically (like we do). We are reaching for an "ethnopoetics" that seeks not only to describe or theorize Black gay poesis and sociality but also to perform it on the page. To *be it*. Following Sylvia Wynter: "Ethnopoetics can only have validity, if it is explored in the context of sociopoetics where the social firmly places the ethnos in its concrete historical particularity."[27] Naming sociopoetics, Professor Wynter insists that we ground ourselves in the high stakes of social and historical interaction. Aimé Césaire saw it this way:

> . . .
> In the current state of things, the only avowed refuge of the mythic
>   spirit is poetry.
> And poetry is an insurrection against society because it is a devotion
>   to abandoned or exiled or obliterated myth.
> . . .
> The vital thing is to re-establish a personal, fresh, compelling, magi-
>   cal contact with things.
> The revolution will be social and poetic or will not be
> . . .
> I'm calling upon the magician.
> . . .
> I'm calling upon the Enraged.[28]

The sociopoetics engaged here emerges from an intellectual tradition and aesthetic created by and for Black gays—bisexuals, lesbians, transgender, and gay men—that emerged within the "epidemic time" of *the long 1980s*. We will offer a fuller accounting of this soon, but, for now, meditate on Assotto Saint's manifesto "Why I Write"—in some ways remixing Monsieur Césaire's earlier Black social/poetic/revolutionary articulation:

> Right from the start, my writings . . . became what I call *a necessary the-
> ater*. I was cognizant of the wants and needs of our emerging commu-
> nity; my writings needed to serve its visibility and empowerment. Most
> revolutions—be they political, social, spiritual, or economic—are usually
> complemented by one in literature. . . . The best answer to the question

of who we are resides in our experiences; from whence our strongest writings are derived. While we map out this new wilderness of our experiences, we must also bear witness. Like archaeologists, we have to file those reports in the form of our finely crafted poems and plays, which we then make available to the world.

. . . We must strive before it is too late to realize this creative wish: that the writings of our experiences serve as testaments to those who passed along this way, testimonies to our times, and legacies to future generations. . . . [29]

Here is where I enter. This is where our conversation begins. Assotto issues a methodological mandate that we take up as our work in this book. A "necessary theater" composed of "testaments, testimonies . . . and legacies." *There's a Disco Ball Between Us* inaugurates an ethnographic register that aspires to represent the particularities of Black gay social experience in a "poetic" way as well as track the poesis, or *making*, of Black gay (and later Black/queer) here and there. Assotto assigns us, "like archaeologists," to keep finely crafted field notes that we "file and make available to the world." After all, Marlon (Riggs) has already redefined anthropology as "the unending search for what is utterly precious" in his *Tongues Untied*.[30] They understood. And they were prescient—this is precisely the anthropology we pursue here. Perhaps we can name this "*Ours* Poeticas?" *Ambas Poeticas*? The peregrinations and *makings* are, after all, at once those of respondents and conversation partners, their works, and the author. Here "the native" is neither noble nor savage: not insolent, and not merely a hapless victim, but rather a complex agent with a limited repertoire of actions, doing the best they can in a world structured in and through late-capitalist white supremacy and heteropatriarchy. This work given by Assotto, in service of testaments, testimonies, and legacies, is not easy. In some ways what I am offering can be read as a counterhistory in the way that Saidiya (Hartman) or Robin (Kelley) or Vincent (Brown) has shown us. But with a difference. *Something else.* Hall, the brother/narrator in Mr. James Baldwin's *Just above My Head*, may provide a productive way to see what we reach toward here. At the end of the novel, Hall summarizes:

To overhaul a history, or attempt to redeem it . . . is not at all the descent one must make to excavate a history. To be forced to excavate a history is also to repudiate the concept of history and the vocabulary in which history is written, for the written history is, and must be, merely the vocabulary of power . . . power is history's most seductively attired false witness. And yet the attempt or necessity to find the truth about oneself—to excavate a history—is motivated by the need to have power to force others to recognize your presence, your right to be here.

. . . Our history is each other. That is our only guide.[31]

Saidiya has contributed similar insight. She writes: "The history of Black counter-historical projects is one of failure, precisely because these accounts have never been able to install themselves as history, but rather are insurgent, disruptive narratives that are marginalized and derailed before they ever gain a footing."[32] In previous works I have attempted to describe and historicize the efforts of a preceding and continuous generation of decolonizing scholars (in anthropology) and have followed pathbreaking anthropologists' onerous labor to try to install "insurgent, disruptive narratives" as authoritative anthropological knowledge. This book does neither of those things. What we pursue here is a complementary but distinct project. I have no desire to force recognition of our right to be here, precisely because "our history is each other." It occurs to me that this is another way to ground the poetic in the sociocultural. In sociality. How we do. This work is therefore comfortable with permanent "disruption," as one would experience in a spirited conversation among intimate friends. Toni Morrison's educative insistence to turn away from the "white gaze"—her insistence and example that we (Black folks) already have aesthetic and intellectual traditions to attend to and refine, and that we are keen observers, participants, critics, and narrators of Black experience ourselves—pushes past the impulse to create exceptional heroic figures to rescue, revindicate, or "humanize" our folks. She teaches us that the truth, told as beautifully and meticulously as one can manage, is vindication enough for those who are already human and recognized as such among one another.

To be sure, *There's a Disco Ball Between Us* owes a tremendous debt to theoretical (and countertheoretical) interventions, after The French, to render a "writerly" Black gay work.[33] These theorists follow nomadic trips to capture and convey the complexities and ambiguities of everyday intensities through feeling, difference, embodiment, "nondualistic thought," "reparative reading," "weak theory," and "low theory."[34] Still, it would be ahistorical— treasonous, really—to not acknowledge the foundational work of Frederick Douglass, W. E. B. Du Bois, Zora Neale Hurston, Katharine Dunham, and St. Clair Drake, for example, which set the terms of engagement of anthropology of the Black world as we practice it today.[35] Largely uncredited work in the long Black intellectual tradition inaugurated what we now think of as affective scholarship long before it became sexy. *There's a Disco Ball Between Us* therefore surges with Black gay flow: simultaneously here and there, then and now—reaching toward (re)connection and grounded in Black intellectual and aesthetic traditions that accent (even severely limited and contingent) Black agency and value nonlinearity, capaciousness, and serious play. What we offer in this work honors Faye Harrison's notion of and steadfast commitment to "reworking anthropology" to meet the demands of the twenty-first century,[36] but one of these demands must be to take seriously the critiques of Magubane and Faris, Ted Gordon, and others who have advocated abandoning the disciplinary enclosure altogether, or as Ryan (Jobson) has recently provoked, "let[ting] Anthropology burn."[37] Finding myself equally as engaged in *doing* the work as I am uninterested in the disciplinary enclosure in which it is currently entangled, I would be pleased if this "ethnography of an idea" contributes to the further decolonization and transformation of anthropology. Better would be the creation of something "more possible" (emerging from its ashes).

The anthropology of LGBTQ subjects has pushed queer studies significantly away from less empirically grounded theorization, attempting, as Tom (Boellstorff) has averred, to *anthropologize* queer studies—that is, not only to provide empirical grounding and humanistic context of "over there" but also, more fundamentally, to advance understanding of the inescapable social character of human beings.[38] Still, without the critical supplement of Black feminism's signal contribution—thinking gender, sexuality, race, class, and nation simultaneously, as it is lived—we cannot understand the dimensions of the social character of human beings. Note the full stop and lack of qualification here. Today, if you are not thinking intersectionally, you cannot see society. So we need to make this move to attend to Black gay and Black/queer desire in the context of here and there, not only because Black people have been viewed through jaundiced lenses but also because it is now clear that standard frameworks and optics do not allow us to see anyone or anything fully enough or clearly enough. We must attend to what folks are listening and dancing to, and reading, whom they desire, and who their people are. Some self-imposed limits of social science research would enervate this aspiration. Primary among those limits, we have needlessly dichotomized our research ambits: dividing affective desire, "tacit subjectivity," and "erotic subjectivity" in one bloc of study; and material suffering and HIV/AIDS, violence, and discrimination in another—engaging disparate and in some cases mutually illegible methods, theoretics, and writerly strategies. Previous work, including my own, has not sufficiently attended to the breadth and heterogeneity of practices, modes, and uses of desire. *There's a Disco Ball Between Us* grapples with Cathy

Cohen's entreaty to more carefully draft lines of intention to resist and her demand that we contend with the political reality of motivations and practices that cannot be read as resistance at all (yet).[39] For example, a few of my respondents seek their versions of freedom through contradictory (re)incorporation into the neoliberal nation-state and into often-unreconstructed cultural institutions and families. Some fashion themselves as citizens, tourists, and consumers and others as advocates on the inside of local governments and international organizations. The lines of lived experience are seldom straight, precise, or elegantly drawn. Upon close reading, these may be constitutive of practices and habits that may light our way to possibilities, potentialities, and forms of freedom that we have not yet recognized.

Open Your Umbrella

We are aware, dear reader: you will demand that we show our papers. *Black* (especially capitalized, as we insist here) never escapes suspicion and surveillance. "Define blackness," some will have already interjected in these margins. *What is this Black* in "Black gay" (and "Black/queer")? We offer this orthographic note: you may think of it as a capitalized line in soft white sand, via Ms. Gwendolyn Brooks. Here, "Black is an open umbrella."[40] The impulse toward parsing the particularities of difference had been mostly salutary in the beginning, as a correction of the unfounded notion of blackness as monolithic, which had been promoted by a few streams of Black nationalism. These streams regrettably and self-servingly misread assertions of ethnicity, nationality, women's autonomy, and—later—gay and lesbian identity as politically enervating "disunity." Since then, this lie has been uncritically and clumsily extended by individuals and movements that see themselves as the heirs to (one stream of) Black radicalism. Still, by now the incessant demands to continue to "deconstruct" blackness have gone well beyond this important critical caution against "essentialism," raised during the long 1980s by Black British cultural critics, Black feminists, and Black gay artists, activists, and scholars. They represent important contending streams of the Black radical tradition that are no less vital than the stream that has come to be identified, oversimplistically, as radical "Black nationalist." So clarion calls to antiessentialism well after *anti*-antiessentialism had already been theorized warrant a stern caution, a correction, and our refusal to capitulate to the diminution or erasure of blackness.[41] This to say nothing of how "whiteness" still floats innocently, remaining "a tale told . . . full of sound and fury." *Signifying.*[42] Calling the po-lice. And voting.

Language often fails, and the process of renegotiating more precise language is a worthy project. At the same time, too often the one thing that scholars and pundits who know nothing about blackness, or Black folks, (think they) know well is that it is not essential, transhistorical, or easily trafficked across borders. The fact that this is true is utterly beside the point here. Race (if you prefer it: "race"), like ethnicity (like gender, like nationality), is always constituted by and through particular political projects and conjunctures (everywhere). And "biology"—that is, genetic heritage and phenotype—though important, does not singularly determine blackness or any other social formation. I have argued elsewhere that no term, even those that may seem self-evidently autochthonous or "traditional," can be perfectly stable or synchronous with dynamic self-identification on the ground. Moving a bit further, allow me to offer this account: here "Black" refers to a set of complex and deeply held translocal historical, political, and affective ties among individuals, movements, and works—to, from, and beyond Africa and constitutive of and spilling over hybridity, Creole(ization), and national hyphenations and color designations. To focus on everyday Black-fullness as we do here is to offer a dynamic, textured, enduring feeling of common union among African (descended) peoples that is not only and not merely a condition of biology, history, global political economy, or common vulnerabilities. In some cases, it is all of these. In others, only the inescapable conjuncture of personal and global histories adhere. Here we see this unfold as what Michel-Rolph Trouillot named a "fragmented globality" played in a minor key.[43] It is perhaps a minor pan-Africanism. A blackness of both feeling and of objective political condition.

Put Your Body in It

You may have noticed that this groove is intramural. Here we are among friends, and our mode of intellectual engagement is a dance. Cue Stephanie Mills's 1979 invitation and command: "Put your body in it."[44] Picture yourself on a pulsating dance floor or in a comfortable spot among friends or fellow partyers at a tightly packed fete. (I hope that you have experienced this feeling of safety, generosity, and deeply embodied pleasure.) What we do here, moving through one theoretical position to the other, one disciplinary commitment, interpretation, or intellectual habit to one that might fit better or more precisely for the moment, is that ever-so-gentle hand on your back, hip, or shoulder. Unobtrusive, without disturbing your rhythm, it suggests/invites/impels: this way, please. We unconsciously move aside to let another—stirred by the DJ or on the way to the bar—pass on their way. Straighter texts brusquely "push past" the writer whose pen precedes it. Not here. Our engagement is not a "sidestep" or "dance around." It is something more intimate and mutual. The gesture is in tandem if not syncopation. After all, this groove is not about supplanting or imitating other formulations, or strictly "arguing" our own (although some moves and positions will become apparent). This follows other modes of intellectual generosity, like Carole (Boyce Davies)'s "critical relationality"—likewise, a Hurstonian hermeneutic is at work/in play here—but this is much sweatier. It is perhaps more embodied, erotic, and taken over by the shared experience of feeling the bass in your chest. Sometimes the intimacy is less "personal"—simply a respectful sharing of space. Other times it inspires a little shimmy or reciprocated touch. In a few cases in our conversation the move will resemble that more suggestive furtive touch on the small of the back ("a tiny piece of perverse heaven," Yolanda called it). But most times we will simply waltz our way through from one end of the dance floor (conversation) to another.[45] I understand that some (in increasing numbers, it seems) prefer to haunt the perimeter of the party—perhaps suspicious of the laughter and what may look like intramural ease or fluency. Seeing these merely as gestures of everyday aliveness may allay your reticence to come closer. These are attempts at connection. Whether you dance or not, you too are an important part of this communion (assembly, if you prefer).

Like "critical relationality," this is an intellectual strategy of deep listening and conversation marked by going "a piece of the way" with one theoretical framework or discourse, then with another, knowing that the length of fellow traveling is contingent on how effectively (and affectively) it takes one where one wants to go. Farther north, and across the Atlantic, this is resonant with Stuart Hall's understanding of the function of theory—to "get a bit further down the road." Carole's "critical relationality" saunters elegantly along long, winding, and often rocky roads of the sort of critical/ethical stance we want to invoke here. One can almost hear the clink of her gold bangles and the smile in her warm, lilting voice: "Critical relationality . . . is a process and a pattern of articulation. . . . A way of relating to visitors or difference is embedded in this approach." She wants to "engage . . . a number of theoretical models, including feminism, postmodernism, Afrocentricity, nationalism, etc. as visitors."[46] To honestly engage in this way we must also eschew opportunistic shifts in scholarly fashion, in favor of more capacious and fluid models, including those that have been overlooked or misunderstood. I intend to follow Carole's generative and intellectually honest approach:

here at the fete, on the parkway, in the basement, on the dance floor, perhaps up on the sweaty wall: blue lights, laughter, and flickering lights in the dark. Fellow dancers, not only visitors.

So, what sort of moment is this in which to raise these questions?[47] Today, the political landscape is stony and contradictory, the economic outlook is dire, and there are "new" reminders every day of the banal denial of Black beauty, Black dignity, humanity, and life. That is, we are living through technologies of the changing same. As I complete the final revisions, another devastating pandemic has laid bare the murderous inequalities we have lived with for numerous generations. "Everything has changed." Again. Still, we make work and make love and make mistakes every day in ways that must be traced, vetted, and sometimes celebrated. Finally, and most importantly, real fists hit actual flesh. Material jails—those with physical bars and state-sanctioned torture from which some materially profit—imprison living human beings guilty only of poverty and desire. Right at this moment—near and far. This is no metaphor. And what is more, although writing a book will never un-punch or de-rape, and may not reverse the court decision or legislation, people deserve study and a record of some of the highlights and performance of their freedom. Thus, out of political-economic and cultural crisis, and precisely to stage the inauguration of "a new and more possible meeting" of disciplines, commitments, aesthetics, geographies, and temporalities, this work offers another way—exceeding the current limits of social science scholarship. You may think of this book as an uninvited new iteration of the Black radical intellectual tradition: re-narrativizing sociocultural analysis through an insistence on and/both, intersections and compounds, hyphens, strokes, parentheses, and messy interstices of real life and audacious imagination. Understanding that our Black interiors are neither inviolate nor completely destroyed, nor hollowed of humanity that reaches out to one another. Yes, that we have interiors. That we are. ("We out here!" I hear my students shouting in the streets.) We be. Let this confirm what we who live through this nadir already know and must remind ourselves: together, we add up to more than the calculus of our compounded vulnerabilities.

Quality of Light

These habits of mind in service of sociality, friendship, love—and yes, recognition of incalculable loss—reach toward connection across difference and across multiple borders. The current disciplinary divisions of academe are not capacious enough to hold these important contradictions of everyday experience, or the ways that my colleagues and I are researching, living within, and narrating them. So how do we best *see* and *say*? What "quality of light"[48] shall we employ here? This is especially poignant in the current moment. Narrative theorizing is not only about the professional or vocational production of "texts" but also about the practice of everyday life among those who, though least authorized to produce "theory," create and enact theory in their works of art and representation, everyday language, and on-the-ground practices. Anthropologists often call these folks "respondents," but they are just as often the one who initiates/calls the question. Literary and cultural theorists may see their lives as "texts" to be bracketed and deconstructed. Here we are most interested in "grounding," as Walter Rodney would have it—narrating experiences and imaginaries, and vetting creative and programmatic solutions that emerge from those grounds.[49] As C. L. R. James has already told us, "Every cook can govern."[50] Everyone must therefore certainly be capable of telling their own story—of theorizing from experience, expertise, and practice.

Our understanding of Black subjects as complex, often contradictory agents emplaced within and negotiating multiple deeply consequential translocal political-economic dramas, and of the ethnographer/author as a fully participating, observant, coauthoring witness, comes from the "decolonizing" stream of Black anthropology. Faye (Harrison)'s groundbreaking *Decolonizing Anthropology: Moving Forward toward an Anthropology for Liberation* (alas, another anthology!) did not merely initiate a transformation of anthropology through the assertion of a generation of anthropologists who identify with or as "Third World" and shift what was "Afro-American anthropology" to a focus on the global problem of racism, rather than on "the problematic Negro," by centering Black agency. Moreover, this stream of work pursues practices that resist or critique modern projects of (post)colonialism, neoliberalism, and state racism.[51]

Owing a great debt to anthropologists who have challenged orthodoxy and provided provocative new frameworks, *Disco Ball* also significantly departs from them in a number of ways. Unlike St. Clair Drake's two-volume vindicationist masterwork, *Black Folk Here and There*, this book does not take on the heady authorial tone that unproblematically insists that we can deeply know another *there* (in Professor Drake's case, just as importantly drawn from archives of the distant past as from a contemporary field site), then return, *here*, to explain it all to an audience of monolingual elites, even from what he calls "a Black perspective." Still, I emphatically claim a similar politics of Black agency bequeathed by Professor Drake's work. It is part of my intellectual inheritance.[52] As is Clifford and Marcus's *Writing Culture* and Ferguson and Gupta's rethinking of the boundaries of "the field" (if perhaps more problematically).[53] My respondents and their works are variously mobile, polyglot, slippery, and agentive. Some are self-consciously fugitive. As an ethnographer, a "native" participant in some of these lifeworlds, and a privileged holder of immense internet bandwidth and a US passport, this author can work or "be" more or less easily, and sometimes instantaneously, both *here* and *there*. This author is no wallflower/fly on the wall, and the words of my respondents are not magical or inerrant: they do not go unchallenged or escape the intentional framing, curation, and narrativization of the author. "How else . . . ?" (We hear the voice of Barbara Christian again.[54]) Black gay folk have always practiced "flipping the script." Rewriting it or merely acting the part—rehearsing lines with a very different feeling, for example. *How else* and how other than through transformative narrative theoretical practice could one withstand the multiple violences inflicted upon gender-insurgent or same-sex-oriented Black people? Thus, we do not aim to compose a "self-portrait" of Black globality as John Langston Gwaltney claimed for "core Black culture" in the United States in his enduring tour-de-force, *Drylongso: A Self-Portrait of Black America*. Instead, here the author has intentionally composed a mixed-media *collage* with respondents, collaborators, conversation partners, and their texts of representation found in archives, museums, and libraries.

Narrativization must simultaneously hold in tension several theories, methods, reading practices, disciplines, and writerly positions. This re-narrativization is not merely about restructuring just-so stories, single-issue politics, or old-school analyses. The world we live in now calls for an expansive engagement rather than jealous guarding of theoretical or disciplinary borders. It calls for a re-disciplining of the intellect, the widening of reading practices, and the political commitment to "master" particular methods and theoretical frameworks, and then loosen our possessive investments in them. This anthological mode of work is new in academe (and perhaps also confounding or frightening to some), but it has a longer history in Black feminist, Black gay, and queer-of-color activist work, artistic practice, and art of living life. This reflects my intellectual and political inheritance from paradigm-shaping radical Black gay lesbian feminist and Black gay male poets and essayists whose forms function to affect, inspire, and enact. After all, long before their emergence, Monsieur Césaire had admonished that "the revolution must be social and poetic, or it will not be."[55] It is the human voice and human interaction that is of interest and up for analysis here, whether we find it at a beach fete, stubbornly sticking to us like sand, or overhear it on the minibus, on an activist listserv, or in the business class lounge at DeGaulle: "The only way to get from here to there."[56] If this mode of interaction is the only way to travel, perhaps an accounting of the excursion should mirror this—that is, it should employ conversation as a mode of presentation as well as inquiry. *There's a Disco Ball Between Us* invites you to enter a conversation that began before I arrived and that will continue long after me. We have attempted to retain the conversational quality of our encounters and to include voices other than that of the author.

In a conventionally disciplined book, or one in which the strategy was to perform the sort of interdisciplinarity that privileges disciplinary "tradition" while filling in with the color or flavor of feminists, queers, poor people, or "natives," for example, who is topping whom in the intercourse of high culture and low culture, or of interpellation and self-making, would be easily apparent and unremarkable. Not so here. We will stroll the road a piece with one, then the other, flip-flopping rather promiscuously, shamelessly, and, we hope, generatively. Doubtless, findings that I had already anticipated made their way into this account, along with the systematically researched and unexpected. And like all privileged travelers, this author *carries on* with a few bags and pre-chartered maps (along with a chic navy-blue passport embossed with a sad, worn, and shamefaced golden eagle). Like every work of scholarship, this book reflects the author's particularly constituted poesis, and this book consciously traces and reflects the author's particularly constituted Black gay habit of mind. Not unlike M. Jacqui Alexander offered of her work in the Bahamas, despite a number of personal and political connections, in most instances this author also writes as an outsider, "neither a national nor citizen," of most places I studied.[57] That is, despite at points abstract and at other moments expressly materialized solidarity, this researcher/sojourner is not only (at least theoretically) outside the repressive reach of those states but holds at least symbolic imperial power of his own emplacement as one sort of conditional "American" and one sort of unstably/precariously bourgeois or "elite" subject. Further, the consequences of being disloyal to heteropatriarchy certainly fall differently, if in any way I may consciously register in any given situation, on my adult cisgender male body than on the bodies of others—especially the trans and cisgender women I engage.

Although gatekeepers who claim to know better than the rest of us what systematically derived generalizable frameworks for understanding (or "theory") should look like, Black bisexual lesbian transgender gay and queer critics, and other Black radical theorists—mostly outside of academe but also within—have taken the mantle of developing reading and writing practices that refuse both positivist science and postmodern "theoritism," which suggests that knowledge is not situated (everywhere) but lodged somewhere far from where Black folks live. In this work we highlight grounded theorization, suggesting that concepts are no less powerfully incisive and analytically bridging when we read them over borders and seas, speaking different languages, from strategy meetings to dance floors to texts of representation, to the author's own experiences, practiced habits of mind, and sensibilities. "For people of color have always theorized," Barbara Christian has already told us. "How else have we managed to survive with such spiritedness the assault. . . . My folk, in other words, have always been a race for theory—though more in the form of the hieroglyph, a written figure which is both sensual and abstract, both beautiful and communicative."[58] Riffing on her theme, I have already offered that "if in fact my people of color are a 'race for theory,'" Black gay is made up of sensual, abstract hieroglyphs *in motion*, seen best in black light: disco balls mirroring and refracting their complex facets. The poet's visions, the artist's eye, and the dancer's movements represent our courage to imagine a grace that would transcend stultifying hegemonies and abstractions that pretend to tell us who we are. Especially, in fact, if the answer is no one, absent(ed) in the Symbolic, connected to no one and nonpolitical.[59]

Our commitment in this work is to attempt to finally register more than "an encounter with power . . . [or] merely a sketch of existence," as Saidiya Hartman offers (after "a famous philosopher") regarding redressing the violent archives of Black subjection.[60] It inaugurates a critically engaged ethnographic practice that grows out of a radical Black lesbian feminist habit of mind. Through careful attention to both the praxis and poetics of everyday life, you will come to know and feel my respondents, conversation partners, and those whom Melvin Dixon called "the epidemic dead, and the living" as complex agents centered in global, deeply consequential political-economic dramas.[61] You will come to know the author as an observant and fully participating coauthoring witness—invited to the party, in on the joke, as deeply committed as my respondents and conversation partners to addressing the savagely uneven stakes of our encounters here and there, and as unavoidably implicated in this savagery (as are you, dear reader).

And if we lose? Hortense Spillers has already illuminated this in her examination of the consequences of another brand of discursive "beaching" of "ungendered," silent, yet hypervisible Black subjects.[62] Think about the real and rising stakes of continuing to rehearse old narratives of unchanging, immobile, long-suffering blackness (often without redress or apology, and certainly without justice) on one hand and liberally consuming, antisocial queerness or conservative imperial settler colonial gayness on the other. What if "Africa" were to discursively remain the locus of inalienable "tradition" or "backwardness" or the Caribbean figured only through television commercials that promise neocolonial romance or blog comments that guarantee a machete to your queer neck should you step foot on one of those sandy shores? Now nearly thirty years after the original controversy, can you imagine questions of Black masculine desire continuing to be framed through a thirsty one-way white-only gaze, or Black women through oversimplified bimodal (neo)liberal feminist frames of "objectification" *or* "empowerment"—"leaning in" with a measure of confidence only to experience . . . la même chose? Of course, Hortense would emphatically agree that Audre's notion of "losing" is about much more than controlling images, psychodramas, patronymic rehearsals, and competing calypso, dancehall, and hip-hop lyrics. The stakes are not only discursive (queer) failure that may in fact point toward more capacious scholarly frameworks.[63] "If we lose . . . ," Audre tells us, "someday women's blood will congeal upon a dead planet."[64] Dear reader, look around at the blood already spilled. Now pooling.

I

A stitch in space time
the long 1980s

1   The Anthological Generation

CONSIDER ANOTHER OF Kevin Aviance's theorizations, please. Now on the raised platform of the club floor. He stands, commanding, in a fitted one-shoulder gold lamé column gown. Obviously well-cocktailed, Kevin reads the children present for mishandling their nomadism.[1] To Kevin, the girls had failed to meet *what must better become their duty* to carry on. The children had failed in their suturing work and needed reminding of the *stitches* that had fashioned them and by which they—we—are held together. (Don't we all need reminding sometimes?) His toast provides a rich archive through which we can feel the *tabanca* of this moment: the intense otherworldly feeling of loss, longing, and blues all at once.[2] In this toast to the excessive Black gay now, at the gala New York birthday party for the father of the House of Aviance, Kevin Aviance shifts from his previous disco ball theorization of beloved dancers in the ether to the flesh and blood assembled at the club in 2012:

> Children! I am overwhelmed with all the drama, the hoopla, the kiki, and the carry-on that is in this room tonight! [*pause/applause*]. It gags me to know that you children have not gathered together like this recently. And it gags me to know that you children have not been together, living and loving, and being each other's [*pause*] you know, *stitches* in life, darling. [*pause*]

So from this night forth: if you aren't carrying on like this, [*pause*] then what's the motherfuckin' point, girl? I mean, I am from New York City! Are you from New York City?! I mean—when music, art, fashion, kiki, carry-on, faggotry, and all that comes together to bring you *this* [*positively appraising the crowd*] and you are not doing this every day? Then what's the motherfuckin' point, girl? Go somewhere else.

For the young kids that are here, I am so sorry that you are so freaked out right now. [*laughter, approval, and applause*] I am so sorry that you don't seem to understand what's going on in here tonight. But you have to understand one thing: some of us have known each other for like 20, 25 years, girl, OK? [*pause/huge applause*] You don't hear me. Y'all don't understand what I'm saying, girl. Some of us have known each other for 20 years, girl. And we *live for the carry-on and the kiki!* [*pause/the crowd goes up*].

What I don't understand is why all you i-generation-phone children [*snatch/purse lips*] don't know your history, girl. Because if you think you're going to your future, you can't, girl. OK? You cannot at all. Because you got to know where I come from. And I come from another queen. 'Cause I come from another queen. 'Cause I come from another queen. And that queen comes from another queen. And that queen comes from another queen. And that queen comes from another queen. And that queen comes from another queen. [*pause*] You weren't the first to wear that, OK bitch? [*pause/pearls clutch/edges snatch*] No girl, you weren't, honey. It's all part [*now, in silence, Kevin is making a stitching movement with his right hand*] it's all a part of the same kiki, carry-on, hoopla, la la, ga ga trala la lalalala [*the crowd goes up!/pause*]. OK, let me get off my soapbox. Hi, y'all! W'sup, girls?! What's going on!?

"Back to the middle and around again."[3] If "I come from another (butch)queen" who comes from a bulldagger or punk who comes from another (femme) (welfare) queen who comes from one whose name was misspoken or misgendered, deadnamed or perhaps unknown, my stitches are blood-soaked. One injury or triumph always indexing a number of other, perhaps deadly, more sedimented ones. I hear Vanessa Agard-Jones's formulation of the materiality of accumulative and accretive toxicities—of soils, sands, (lack of) waters—in which she convincingly argues we are all "entangled" and compelled to "endure," worldwide.[4] We live for it. Yes, and (Vanessa tells us) we also live through it—endure its tangles and layers—making our worlds from/within this.

Thomas (Glave) had already recounted for the children the importance of "radical art and life-effort of conscientious remembrance . . . against revisionism's erasures and in pursuit of our survival,"[5] yet according to Kevin, these iPhone-generation children had forgotten. Or they did not know, and believe their carrying on to be an innovation. Worse, they mistook their carrying on as an option rather than a high sacrament. Do not be mistaken. You cannot understand "Black Gay" without accounting for this. Kevin's use of Black gay vernacular and performance of instructive shade in his analysis provides nuance—like the addition of a more intensely plum hue of purple to lavender eye shadow, perhaps. Just as in Alice Walker's famous definition of womanism, the difference between purple and lavender is significant.[6] Affect can be constitutive and effective too. Here, *shade* is not just added accent, but content. Hear and heed the queen. Kiki, carry-on, hoopla, la la, and ga-ga (emphatically no relation to the pop star) are as constitutive to Black gay praxis as the blues and juke are to the larger Black American tradition, as liming and calypso are to English-speaking Caribbean traditions. We could go on throughout the Black world recounting the centrality of compounded kin spaces of sociality that we create and transform. Kevin has told us that this is all of a piece—underscoring the fact that *being each other's stitches* is essential in a world in which one's peace is too often casually torn apart. The gag is that the histories and political-economic connections between these are often ignored or left uninterrogated, or devalued just as casually: that is, *you don't know your history, girl.*

Our story begins in medias res, when the conversation becomes explicit: the long 1980s. The long 1980s is the Black gay classical period—during which Black lesbians, trans folks, bisexuals, and gay men first self-consciously re-named themselves and made art, organized, danced, and fucked under the sign of "Black Gay." At the same time that David (Scott)'s incisive appraisal of anticolonial epistemologies may be a bit too "straight" for this story, in terms of its reliance on fixed "generations" that unfold in stricter age and inheritance cohorts than our queer story evidences, my thinking here is conceptually indebted to his formulation that "each succeeding generation constructs anew out of its inheritance and its own experience the relation to the formative events of the past that have organized the imagination of the future."[7] Allow therefore a gentle hand as we glide to another part of the dance floor—still dancing to the same music. Here we begin our exploration of some of the ways a variety of folks—activists, artists, filmmakers, DJs, drag queens, and impresarios among them—made sense of the upheavals that the global losses of the 1970s Atlantic revolutions, and the settling in of neoliberalism, Thatcherism/Reaganism, AIDS, and crack had wrought to inaugurate *Black Gay.*

"This Poem Is for the Epidemic Dead and the Living. Remember Them?"

"For the living, there is no constituency as formative as the dead. . . ." Dagmawi (Woubshet) tells us this in the opening line of his book *The Calendar of Loss: Race, Sexuality, and Mourning in the Early Era of AIDS*. Dag continues, offering that this is "a fact I learned growing up in 1980s Ethiopia, where loss governed time and temperament."[8] Loss does seem to govern (the) time (we have together), although I must reject (social and actual) death as nonbeing. Temperament seems to me to be a more elastic matter. Among others, Colin (Robinson) speaks to this painful and necessary memory/forgetting as the caskets pile up. Your work becomes focused: first, stay alive. Do not allow your collective past to be erased. Safeguard, as you can, those pieces of your experience that may be kept for the children. For posterity ("Everything is useful," Audre said, *for each of us*[9]). In an epidemic one cannot *let the dead bury the dead*, yet of course in some ways, one must.[10]

"Look to your children!" the Louisiana Bayou priestess/counselor Elzora says to Mme. Roz Batiste. The Creole lady is dripping pearls, perched in silk dupioni, with hair impossibly coiffed in the steamy marshland of *Eve's Bayou* (in Kasi Lemmons's film of the same name).[11] Elzora is embittered and disheveled (but, of course, also ever Diahann Carroll). Her head turbaned and face covered with *efun* (powder), Elzora casually delivers her counsel in a produce stall by the market. She can command futurity—that is, know what will happen in three years and demand the turn/look "to your children"—only via death: dead cat bones, shells of long-departed cowrie mollusks, and everyday communion with what and who has already passed on to the ether. Elzora divines and mediates from resonances, just like any other conjurer, priestess, or counselor. The dead are not only with us; they also communicate. My therapist asks about my parents, and James, and Saba. Looks deeply into my eyes. Witnesses my body language as I remember. Girlfriends, Kevin Aviance insists, wave to him from facets of a disco ball. The face of Wura's father presents himself again and again as an Ife head in her artwork. This motif flies across the Atlantic, leaps above a creek in Austin, and is stitched into a piece destined for a museum, a gallery, or your wall: sitting just so, your gaze connecting to other memories.[12] Now, here in this chapter, we look to the epidemic dead of the long 1980s and the living who carry on. For the children.

The epidemic dead are subjectifying political subjects. We the Black gay living do so in *epidemic time*. This eerie temporality demands that we read and live in multiple directions. Epidemic time accounts for vulnerabilities and mounting and compounded loss while valorizing and prioritizing moments of Blackfull vitality and intensity. In the movement to come, rereadings, remembrances, and a hint of provocative annotation of texts and contexts attempt to remember and revise a Black gay politics that may be necessary for our futures. To command any future at all in which a *we* survives, this conjuring by the water's edge must proceed. The time, space, and materials we gather here are as queer as cat bones and cowries. The methodology is a counterpoise against erasure and toward better politics.

Another cinematic Creole woman is germane to this conversation: Mozelle Batiste, the equally poised and pulled but apparently more earthy, lusty, and dangerous sister-in-law of Mme. Roz. Mozelle is essentially in the same business as Elzora. However, she receives her respectable clients in the parlor of her fine home. They discreetly leave their gratuity on a porcelain bread plate that sits on a Chippendale side table (after quiet and prayerful spiritual advice), not the mason jar stuffed with dollars that the older teller demands. Mozelle has taken to her bed, despondent, after burying yet another husband. Her niece Eve—the daughter of Roz but clearly more like Mozelle—lovingly places irises on the graves of the three dead men before arriving at her aunt's bedside, then beckons Mozelle awake with the last flower. The child keeps her company as Mozelle attempts to gather herself. In a reverie, she tells her niece that "I loved them [all]. I swear I did," as the flash of the chifforobe mirror projects from her mind's eye an image of her three deceased husbands standing silently side by side. Later that summer afternoon, dressed in a fitted black dress with her hair beautifully combed into place, Mozelle languidly sips sherry and smokes as her niece dusts the fireplace mantle (as altar) in her dressing room. Three handsomely framed photographs of three beautiful Black men sit on a pressed-white-linen mantilla as elegant white tapers burn, giving light to the dead. A crystal goblet of cool water is, no doubt, nearby. Freesia become incense. When the girl child asks, "Who did you love the most?" Mozelle tells her that "they were all different . . . [from] the handsomest man I had ever seen [to] . . . the sweetest, and . . . the one who loved me most." Declaring that Eve is too young to understand, Mozelle begins talking about her former lover, Hosea, who killed her second husband. With him, she said, "It was like my whole body was burning. I'd come home and would have to rub ice on my face and neck to cool down." That is, like Essex (Hemphill), Mozelle bears a sort of "burdensome knowledge of carnal secrets." All of these lovers offered what

Essex named "sacred communion." My *we* was conceived in epidemic, dear reader—unchaste and holy. Essex has already told it:

> For my so-called sins against nature and the race, I gain the burdensome knowledge of carnal secrets. . . . It often comforts me. . . . At other moments it is sacred communion, causing me to moan and tremble and cuss as the Holy Ghost fucks me. It is a knowledge of fire and beauty that I will carry beyond the grave. When I sit in God's final judgment, I will wager this knowledge against my entrance into the Holy Kingdom. There was no other way for me to know the beauty of earth except through the sexual love of men, men who were often more terrified than I. . . . Men emasculated in the complicity of not speaking out, rendered mute by the middle-class aspirations of a people trying hard to forget the shame and cruelties of slavery and ghettos.[13]

Here is an invitation to read a fictional early-1960s Black/Creole femme heterosexual woman as a Black gay man (especially but not exclusively in the 1980s).[14] An invitation to push beyond reading reparatively but also to read and imagine for resonance, across blacknesses. Mozelle, the psychic counselor, is unapologetically sensual. And she pays the price of desire with a collection of dead lovers and husbands. Described as "crazy" and (more upper-class appropriate) "eccentric" by family members, and by a brave new lover called "wounded," for her own part Mozelle describes herself as "barren" and "the same" as her philandering brother, "except I have no children to catch me!" she says. Though clairvoyant, Mozelle tells her niece she had been "blind to my own life" like all of us, regarding her inability to see the string of tragedies that would have Elzora label her the cursed "Black Widow." Now on the porch of the large Batiste family home, wearing a polka-dot dress with a portrait collar exposing her beautiful dewy smooth brown skin and highlighting her breasts, high cheekbones, and (unmissable Debbi Morgan) dimples, Mozelle is communicating with that other world, absently staring into the blackness of the Spanish moss-covered evening ("A hundred midnights in a cypress swamp" comes to mind[15]). She tells us—or tells Eve or no one at all: "Life is filled with goodbyes, Eve, and it hurts every time. . . . Sometimes it feels like I have lost so much, I have to find new things to lose." A litany. An address book of names crossed out. A *calendar of loss*—Dagmawi has already said it. This sort of grief—three husbands gone—multiplied by the number of lovers, friends, trade, tricks, and neighbors now gone or infected, the calculus of the specter awaiting you, and the knowledge that "no one cares"[16] begins to capture what it feels like to live in *epidemic time*. My *we* was conceived in epidemic, dear reader. Here is an excerpt from Craig G. Harris's "I'm Going Out Like a Fucking Meteor." Receive this as more than "moving" and evocative writing, but also critically astute theorization. This short essay stands as one of the most potent and comprehensive statements of social life in the long 1980s:

> After completing the calls, I turned on the television set hoping to find something other than coverage of the war in the Middle East which our country had entered into thirteen days earlier. I had no idea that I would find President George Bush delivering his State of the Union Address. I . . . he tried to assure us that adding to the devastation in the Persian Gulf was what made the United States a great country—the greatest! President Bush dedicated only a short potion of his speech to domestic issues. Somehow he managed to work AIDS, illiteracy and homelessness into one sentence and indicated that the government really couldn't solve these problems. . . . Bush suggested that U.S. citizens become a thousand points of light to tackle these dark, despairing, social ills, and recommended that each American visit a person with AIDS. . . . I'm not waiting for a cure. I'm not looking for a miracle. I am not resisting the inevitable. I will die. I will die much sooner than I would like to accept, and there is little I can do about this fact. Kubler-Ross can call that acceptance if she wants, but in doing so, I believe she minimizes one's will to fight. It is precisely because I know I will die that I work even more diligently for the causes I believe in. . . . I have made a commitment to relinquish control only as a last resort. I want to live the rest of my life with an energy that ignites and irritates, burns and bubbles, soothes and inspires until it bursts from the atmosphere, dissipating into the cosmos.[17]

Remember, "For the living, there is no constituency as formative as the dead." Mozelle bears burdensome knowledge and is communicating the burden to Eve—that is, to us (the children) gifted with sight and this *magnificent arithmetic of distance* offered beyond sight, if we learn and innovate disciplined (re)memorial that makes memories mean something, including and beyond the personal. Here is Robert (Reid-Pharr): revealing and shading simultaneously. As if counseling over tea, he says,

> It is profoundly difficult to remember and memorialize heroic victories and pitiful defeats while bombs continue to fall and pestilence steadily seeps from subway sewers; strange to contemplate the relics of a glorious past while steadily negotiating the rigors of an inglorious present.

No matter. The masters gave careful instructions in how to overcome obstacles and salve the marks of defeat. We are continually reminded to relinquish the self-interested desire to celebrate solely the content of our productions. Instead our focus must ever remain on form. Neither my name, nor yours for that matter, is likely to be etched in granite. We can, however, work to reproduce the technique of the artisan who takes the chisel into his hands.[18]

"No matter," Robert says, interrupting his own litany for survival. ("I am nothing if not practical," he told Kevin and me.) You can feel him rushing you along. Yes, this is the reality. Yes, it is fucked up. And "the masters" have not given an antidote for the seeping pestilence or even a preemptive antiballistic strategic defense or prophylaxis for the falling bombs. Just "salve" and "instructions." I wish I could offer more. Marcus, a brilliant young friend and former student, insists that we need a vision of "normative Black/queer politics." Our languages and methodologies differ, yet the desire is the same. Here we shall attempt to critically assess, celebrate, and "reproduce the technique."

And I Come from a Black Lesbian. SisterLove.

Arguments among those engaged in adjudicating the proper intellectual genealogies and practicable uses of intersectionality, or whether Beyoncé may be or claim to be a Black feminist, rage on. Still, the broad outlines are well known (or should be by now): Black women from various walks of life, many who were students or well educated and many of whom had also been involved in civil rights, antiwar, Black Power, labor, abortion rights, antiviolence, and anti-forced-sterilization activism, came together to articulate their multiply constituted, "interlocking" positions at around the same time that the larger and overwhelmingly white middle-class "second wave" of feminism began to swell with the recognition that *the personal is political,* also gleaned from the work and experiences of Black and other "Third World" women. This occurred just ahead of wide international circulation of English translations of French poststructuralist theory's enumeration of the diffuse discursive workings of power, and alongside the critical mash-up of gender and race at Birmingham's Centre for Contemporary Cultural Studies, whose orientations to discursivity focused on contemporary material struggle. To be sure, "Black women had never been fools," as Barbara (Smith) had already averred and as Dr. Guy-Sheftall details in "The Evolution of Feminist Consciousness among African American Women."[19] In speeches, writing, and activism, at least since battles over (white women's *or* Black men's) voter enfranchisement in the United States, Black women had demonstrated that their liberation must be built on more than *either* race *or* gender *or* class. "(We didn't want to fix the system) We Wanted a Revolution!" succinctly captures the intellectual and political impetus of radical Black feminism as it was expressed from the early 1970s.[20] Barbara (Smith) says to Keeanga-Yamahtta Taylor, "I think our first goal was to make a political space for ourselves. . . . We needed to have a place where we could define our political priorities and act upon them. . . . We were not saying that we didn't care about anybody who wasn't exactly like us." Crystalline. All of this precedes the growing critical mass of Black women in the academy of the long 1980s that would ignite what we now know as academic Black feminism. Patricia Hill Collins's crucial articulation of a "matrix of domination," which emerged conterminously with the concept of intersectionality, for example, "demonstrates Black women's emerging power as agents of knowledge."[21]

"Intersectionality" is a central and urgent concept, yet Black feminism—which is currently the most vital stream of the long Black radical tradition—cannot be reduced to this alone. Theorization of the interlocking and/or interstitial and/or intersectional has a much longer, deeper, and traceable intellectual and political history than critics often discuss. A number of fine works review and assess this.[22] A few also offer important theoretical and sociohistorical framing to understand subsequent streams of Black feminism and womanism in the United States, such as militant, neoradical, cultural, academic, transnational, hip-hop, queer, liberal, and that which can best be described as ludic; as well as sister movements of Caribbean feminism, (pan-)African feminism, Black British feminism, and other local and translocal expressions. Moreover, much ink has been spilled parsing the genealogies of intersectionality. We will not rehearse these here but rather offer a re-narration that highlights radical (and) lesbian expressions in the United States. All streams of Black feminism insist that we move beyond simplistic formulations and dichotomous thinking. For example, here is an important and/both formulation that some of the recent criticism either misses or willfully mischaracterizes: whereas the recognition that intersectionality is an embodied concept or politics is not to "limit" it to the bodies of Black women; the conceptual framework of intersectionality should not be invoked without referencing the Black women who coined and developed this. That would evacuate what Jennifer (Nash) rightly refers to as "the fleshy materiality of Black women's bodies" (regardless of the circumstances of gender assignment at birth).[23] We must have it both ways because the reality works in at least both ways. And because you seem to easily forget Black women. There would be no need to remind and insist that we #Sayhername and #CiteBlackWomen if this were not true. There is a long, consistent history of trying to "walk off with all of [their] stuff." In this case, "walking off" seems to include a common practice of casual citation of the Greatest Hits of Black Feminism without study, renaming without attribution, and enervating one's own argument by passing over (that is, *walking by* rather than walking off with) radical Black lesbian feminist theorization.[24] I hear Ntozake Shange's Lady in Green speaking, in a pivotal moment of her choreopoem:

> i want my own things / how i lived them / & give me my memories /
>   how i waz when i waz there
> . . . / waz a lover i made too much
> room for/ almost run off wit alla my stuff
> & i didnt know i'd give it up so quik
> . . .
> . . . / my stuff is the anonymous ripped off treasure
> of the year / did you know somebody almost got away wit me?[25]

Black feminism is rooted in the historical, political, and socioeconomic realities of everyday Black life and is expressed, with very few exceptions, through the organizing, art, and scholarship of Black women. But Black feminism is not a unitary intellectual tradition or monolithic politics. Today, the word *intersectionality* is on the lips of think-piece authors, (would-be) activists, Twitterers, and political organizers all over the world. Perhaps having imbibed the surface, instrumental ways it is deployed in (the last weeks of) a number of women's studies courses, folks often poorly or only symbolically perform its real meanings and constitutive politics. Many seem to miss the fact that intersectionality is not only a metaphorical illustration of compounded subjectivities and experiences but is more pointedly an expression of where Black women are located: in the crosshairs. Shifting battlefields of the same war, Audre already told you. Like earlier Black feminist theorization, such as Frances Beal's 1969 naming of the "double jeopardy" of Black women, critical race theorist Kimberlé Crenshaw's formulation of "intersectional" is more substantively about the compounding of specific forms of institutional political-economic harm. These concepts complement, but are not identical to or mutually exclusive with, for one example, Hortense Spillers's formulation of "interstices."[26] Whereas the intersectional approach advanced by Kimberlé and others is more specifically about juridical structures that are rearticulated by groups and individuals toward particular remedies, "interstice" suggests, for the literary theorist, structuring grammars and deep wells of consciousness. Out of this, interactions emerge from the "great (discursive) drama" in which *the Black woman* (yes, in this case discursively singular in her radical discontinuity) "became the principal point of passage between the human and the non-human world . . . therefore making Black . . . vestibular to culture."[27] Of course, the Combahee River Collective statement, which for me is the most powerfully succinct definition of the politics of radical Black lesbian feminism, holds that "we are actively committed to struggling against racial, sexual, heterosexual, and class oppression, and see as our particular task the development of integrated analysis and practice based upon the fact that the major systems of oppression are interlocking."[28]

These should be settled questions. One can argue, for example, whether Black feminist theory or practice is effective, or smart, or even possible, given the obstacles. Still, the most common indictment or epithet deployed against it contemporarily—that it is "essentialist," or that it is *identity politics*, par excellence (with scare quotes around identity politics as if it really meant what detractors claim it does)—is clearly falsified by both the way the women who created it describe their intentions, then and now, and the actual work that radical Black feminists took up and continue to practice.[29]

Radical feminist Black woman Cellestine Ware's *Woman Power: The Movement for Women's Liberation* was published in 1970—the same year as *The Black Woman*. Her radical philosophy is clearly aligned with that of radical Black feminists such as the Combahee River Collective, though addressed largely to and for the wider women's liberation movement. The frontispiece of this influential work begins: "Radical feminism is working for the eradication of domination and elitism in all human relationships. This would make self-determination the ultimate good and require the downfall of society as we know it today."[30] Clear as day. Women from the Pat Robinson Work Group, Third World Women's Alliance, and other activist-intellectual groups and individuals were clear that neither gender nor race should be viewed as a superordinate category. With distinct emphases, they each claimed that the material position of Black women at the nexus, double, interlock, compound, interstice, matrix, et cetera, provides a powerfully clarifying way to analyze the operations of each component and how they interact. The objective of radical Black feminism is the eradication of all forms of domination and elitism. This does not mean that there is no methodology to meet their ends. The erudite and practical early reading of what we now think of as US heteropatriarchal racial capitalism by the Pat Robinson Work Group, for example (identified as a collective of Black women community "theoreticians" ranging from "welfare recipient" to "housewife" to "worker" to "psychiatric social worker" from New Rochelle and Mt. Vernon, New York), does not insist on simultaneous work on all fronts but prescribes an order of work. In one of their contributions to *The Black Woman*—"Poor Black Women's Study Papers"—they conclude: "At this point in our history many Black and white women are forming their own class and historical analyses of capitalism. The poor Black woman is the lowest in this capitalist social and economic hierarchy. First, we must smash the myth of white supremacy. Then together we can work toward smashing imperialism and capitalism."[31] This method does not mean that the analysis is *privileging* class or race. The work group had likely recognized disparate positions and interests represented in their cross-class collective of Black women. Likely, their order of work emerges from this, and their experiences with whiteness. It is a clearly understandable practical matter, to help ensure that the white supremacist acculturation of white women—only "a few [of whom] are beginning to see their oppressors as those who mean to keep them barefoot and pregnant and ignorant of male oppression"[32]—would not enervate, co-opt, or upend the possibilities of alliance and accomplice toward poor Black women's racial and class liberation.

"The Blacker the Berry, the Sweeter the Dyke"

The Combahee River Collective began as a chapter of the National Black Feminist Organization (NBFO), founded in 1973. It remained a chapter until about 1976, when the collective broke off from the national organization, citing its desire to concentrate on the grassroots issues and consciousness raising that collective members had long worked on in the Boston area. Combahee disagreed with what it believed to be NBFO's aspiration to model itself after the "electoral focus" of the National Organization for Women (NOW). In *How We Get Free: Black Feminism and the Combahee River Collective*, Keeanga-Yamahtta Taylor engages in invaluable conversations with members of the Combahee River Collective (Barbara Smith, Beverley Smith, Demita Frazier), Black Lives Matter Network leader Alicia Garza, and scholar-activist Barbara Ransby, reflecting on the Combahee River Collective statement's lasting importance and influence on current Black feminist and Black liberation movement(s). As Barbara (Smith) tells Keeanga-Yamahtta, "It is difficult to explain what we were up against . . . in that historical moment citing the constant and banal ridicule, debasement, and insults against Black women organizers in that moment. . . ."[33] The networks, publications, retreats, and campaigns that the members worked on were part and parcel of saving their own lives in ways that some perhaps find it hard to imagine today. But those who cannot imagine must have found a way to dissociate from the present. News of anti-Black and *misogynoir*[34] violence (both "symbolic violence" and material physical injury and death) is so common that it is perhaps merely ambient for some. As Barbara pointed out, "The thing that I want you to keep in mind . . . is that we [Combahee River Collective, but it can also be said of organized Black feminists more broadly] were organizing in the context of a race war. . . . So, a major question was racial politics. And then the one that was right next to it was class and economic politics. So, the first is the fact that we were socialists. We were a part of the organized left."

I am "guilty." In some ways I do "look to intersectionality's past in order to enable the analytic," as Jennifer (Nash) has warned against.[35] Here, we attempt, as any good student would with a concept as useful and clarifying as intersectionality and its cognates, to do this judiciously. In her conversation with Keeanga-Yamahtta, Barbara Ransby wisely reminds us that "sometimes we talk about these empowering important historical moments, and we are looking for blueprints or road maps. Unfortunately, history does not offer us that. We have our own work to do in our own time." She is certainly correct. Complicating this further, Barbara avers that "in many Black feminist circles, Combahee River Collective Statement is seen as a sacred text, and I say this as a pretty committed secularist."[36] This author is "guilty" on this score as well, and I hear Jennifer calling for perhaps more ecumenicism than I am prepared to embrace. Still, *sacred* does not mean inerrant or above questioning. It is, rather, something *not to be defiled or dishonored*. As one who is perhaps not as committed to secularism as Barbara Ransby is, I certainly agree that blind fidelity—dismissing what I think of as one's god-given intellect/ intuition/*orí*, innovative thinking, creativity, or new research for the sake of orthodoxy—is itself *unholy*. We can all agree that blind fidelity is a fascistic, anti-intellectual invention to which we need not capitulate. Still, there is so much that is sacred that is not well known or has yet to be completely unburied. This does not seem like a moment to turn too quickly or decidedly away from what is "original." The photo in figure 1.1 is one small example. There is much more research ahead to narrate the profound significance of the Black Lesbian Caucus (of the New York City Gay Activists Alliance, before breaking away from the GAA in 1971). These women are directly and indirectly linked to a number of projects and important successor groups, representing among the oldest Black (and/or) Latina lesbian organizations in the United States (African Ancestral Lesbians United for Societal Change [AALUSC], Las Buenas Amigas, Salsa Soul Sisters), which published *Azalea: A*

1.1 Black Lesbian Caucus of the New York City Gay Activists Alliance.
Photo: Bettye Lane, 1973.

Magazine by Third World Lesbians and *Salsa Soul Gayzette*. Why not regard oral histories, journal copies, and reports of the various organizational splits and reconstitutions along fault lines of language, class, ethnicity/nationality (and more) as sacrosanct and/or worthy of exhumation for current use?

It does seem clear that the current moment demands better reading practices (toward understanding works created under very different conditions), as I hear Jennifer eliciting. Still, inasmuch as paid academics (like me) debate these issues in elite spaces, with or without connection to work on the ground, we also need more careful attention to historical and institutional connections and commitments of early authors and exponents—for example, to Black Power, civil rights, socialism, antiwar, lesbian separatism, and the organized Left more broadly. And we need to read with more generosity. Jennifer is an honest Black feminist scholar invested in launching a critique of intersectionality and how we remember and deploy its origins. I agree with her that we must "remain open to both the fact that analytics transform move, wane, develop, and morph, and to the fact that analytics' movements are political and institutional questions." At the same time, I affirm other Black feminists' impulse to attempt to "defend" sets of politics that are embedded in the larger project of Black feminism and orbit the analytic of intersectionality. These need not be oppositional impulses. It seems quite possible, in what Jennifer calls "originalist claims" of "early work" in her well-argued appraisal, for impulses toward "originalism" to be tempered by a critical jurisprudence. That is, good scholarship—close reading of the work or text, alongside critical engagement with the conditions of its production and political conjunctures on the ground at the moment of its production. One can—must, if one is to be an honest interlocutor—read closely and follow genealogical strands without being doctrinaire. These are not dependent variables. For example, this includes practices of historicization and providing nuanced understanding of the context of the current conjuncture, sensitive genealogical probing, and what we have come to understand as an *archaeological* method of inquiry.[37]

Yes, there is suspicion of criticism of Black feminist thought. I believe there ought to be (just as there must be principled critique of the work itself). We are each accountable to respond to the question "What is the politics of your question . . . (or critique, or insistence on discursively unburying the epidemic dead)?" My own understanding of the ethical stance of Black feminism demands that I situate myself and the stakes of my critique on both affective and material registers as well as intellectual ones, to demonstrate a progressive critical demeanor.[38] I hear Barbara in my head saying "Black women have never been fools," and those who raised me raised no foolish

Black gay boy. The suspicion and perhaps ambient pessimism of those who seem to be defending what they (and the author herself) understand as the original meaning and proper interpretation of Kimberlé's "intersectionality," as well as Black feminist theory and practice more broadly, likely also spring from witnessing very real practices of misrepresentation, willful misreading, and historical reconstruction. For example, Barbara's contention that "we need more dialogue about the history and the ongoing organizing of people who claim and share these politics" is not evidence that she is policing the borders of what is acceptable today or that she is positing an "originalist" claim. She is, rather, clarifying the record regarding the politics that she and other Black women defined for themselves, which various folks now claim, invoke, seek to understand academically, or indeed merely find opportune. Moreover, given the alreadyness of contingency, interstices, intersections, interlockings, and so on created by Black feminists (and) Black LGBTQ folks, I must take exception with the sleight-of-hand targeting of Black feminism as the poster child for poorly defined "identity politics" used in some works— that I have not and will not mention here—to magically erase the theorization and the groundwork of radical Black feminists. Perhaps these writers, who will go unnamed in this work, consign them to meager footnotes or make slight changes to the analytic formulations not in a conscious attempt to silence Black women who are trying to protect themselves and what they and their elder sisters have created, but for some other, unconscious reason. No matter. I suspect that a few of these critics of intersectionality, Black feminism, and identity politics have chosen what they see as an easy target and cheap entrée or recirculation within an academic marketplace of ideas in which Black women's intellectual and artistic labor is already devalued.

Christina Sharpe parses the word *opportune* as one example of what she calls the "orthography of the wake." In her illuminating discussion of the willful misreading of and disuse of one Black mother's narrative, Christina says that "they see in her an opportunity (from the Latin *ob* meaning 'toward.' And *portu[m]* meaning 'port.'). . . . She is the ejection, the abjection, by, on, and through, which the system reconstitutes itself."[39] Thus, although healthy, invested critique is of course necessary and salutary, academic opportunism must not stand. The effect of this would be the "reconstitution" of an epistemic system in which radical Black women, and all those they carry with them, are once again assumed silent or in need of translation (in scholarly literatures). And this too is worth considering, even elliptically: how, in what has become a cottage industry of reassessing intersectionality, did radical Black *lesbians* (and/or the fact of their lesbianism) become consigned to footnotes in so much academic writing in an intellectual tradition that they had first articulated and *worked* in their organizations? In some instances, critics of intersectionality, Black feminism, and/or what they call "identity politics" reconfigure the theoretical work Black women have done without the putatively unsophisticated bothersome and loud Black women themselves. Especially without highlighting the fact that many were and are Black Lesbians—here capitalized, per the Combahee River Collective statement, in which lesbian identity is affirmed a number of times, including in the last powerful declaration: "As Black feminists and Lesbians we know that we have a very definite revolutionary task to perform and we are ready for the lifetime of work and struggle before us."[40]

The intersubjective, nomadic, destabilizing, interrogative, radical Black feminist stance that we argue characterizes the habit of mind we pursue throughout this book emerges from what Audre Lorde named global "racism, destruction, and a borrowed sameness" with respect to the state's disposition toward Black and brown folks, both here and there. As the band WAR told us in 1972, *The world is a ghetto*. Barbara (Smith) continues: "Our involvement with the antiwar movement . . . characterized the politics of Combahee, which was our internationalism. This is not a part of our politics that has been uplifted widely, but that's where we were coming from. We considered ourselves to be Third World women. We saw ourselves in solidarity and in struggle with all Third World people around the globe. And we saw ourselves as being internally colonized within the United States."[41] This version of Black feminism insists that interlocking or intersectional politics is also in large part a commitment to work with and to follow Black lesbians, and to listen closely to others who find themselves vulnerable to the deadliest calculus of compounded power.

In a succinct poetic challenge constituting the core of the politics of the Black transnational sensibility that we explore here, Audre likewise held that "self-preservation demands we involve ourselves actively in those policies and postures," with the understanding that the *self* to which she refers here is at once local and/but an intersubjective self, connected through history and materiality, as well as deeper ethical bonds with other Black and brown folks living throughout the world:

The battlefields shift: the war is the same. It stretches from the brothels of Southeast Asia to the blood-ridden alleys of Cape Town to the incinerated lesbians in Berlin to Michael Stewart's purloined eyes and grandmother Eleanor Bumpers, shot dead in the projects of New York.

We are gays and lesbians of color at a time in [this] country's history when its domestic and international policies, as well as its posture toward those nations with which we share heritage, are so reactionary that self-preservation demands we involve ourselves actively in those policies and postures.[42]

Black trans gay bi and lesbian writers, visual artists, and others have engaged these questions historically and contemporarily; activists have in some cases taken on the very challenging work of creating sustained cooperative or co-alitional projects. However, it seems that many scholars have abandoned advancing the "same war/same battlefield" formulation to focus only on historically particular specificities. We will take this up in chapters to come.

In her 1980 "Revolution: It's Not Neat or Pretty, or Quick" speech, Pat Parker draws important spheres of socialist internationalism, anticolonial-ism, and feminism together, calling out liberal feminism and challenging nationalist (and other) liberation movements to grapple more seriously with gender inequality and heterosexism. Cheryl Higashida proposes that "Black internationalist feminism challenges heteronormative and masculinist ar-ticulations of nationalism while maintaining the importance, even central-ity of national liberation movements."[43] Her term *nationalist internationalism* seems apt to describe the complex position of those of the Black anticolonial Left, like Pat, who championed self-determination for all oppressed nations, including *Black America*. Pat said: "Each time a national liberation victory is won, I applaud and support it. . . . We know and understand that our op-pression is not simply a question of nationality. . . . At the same time that we must understand and support the men and women of national liberation struggles—the Left must give up its undying loyalty to the nuclear family."[44]

In contrast to sometimes uncritical calls for the state to honor the citizen-ship rights of properly respectable and/or exceptional, and thus putatively "worthy" Black non-gender-binary, gay, lesbian, and transgender citizens in the United States and throughout the world rather than insisting on human and ecological integrity in any case, listen to Pat's first line. In "Where Do You Go to Become a *Non*-citizen," she begins: "I want to resign. I want out." In this poem, the speaker's response to Audre's global "racism, destruction, and . . . borrowed sameness" is a principled refusal. Written in 1978, her typi-cally biting and chillingly current "Tour America" not only illustrates global borrowed sameness but also presciently articulates ecological concerns of the natural environment and viral risk, along with police occupation of Black communities. Beginning "Tour America! / a t.v. commercial said. / I will . . . ," Pat goes on to list a number of things that she will need (her PPE, as it were) to visit various urban centers of the United States, including "gas masks," "face masks," and shields against petty community "hustlers." Finally, after citing sites in the North, South, Midwest, and West, Pat wonders whether abolishing the nation-state would be better than touring it, calling, in the last instance, for "Bullet proof vest and helmet / to protect me from police /—everywhere."[45]

To follow Pat is to recognize what she and other radical Black lesbian feminists had been saying (to [neo]liberal feminists) since the mid-1970s: there are instances in which we all must be prepared to give up something, even if it is the chimera of acceptance, or visibility. Or inclusion in the project of US statecraft and global expansion. At the 1980 "Becoming Visible: The First Black Lesbian Conference," Pat laid down a radical challenge to single-issue liberal feminist politics: "If the passage of the ERA means that I am going to become an equal participant in the exploitation of the world, that I am going to bear arms against other Third World people who are fighting to reclaim what is rightfully theirs—then I say fuck the ERA." The "fuck you" to the ERA was a refusal to be party to empire, even as liberal feminism invites some women to the table (or the editorial board, executive staff, academic department, or deanery). Black US American Pat Parker's poetic invective is an example of the *politics of accomplice* that radical Black lesbian feminism demands. Alliance is crucial. We must have allies who will support from a distance at which their own privilege might be leveraged as a resource, but this is not what I mean by accomplice. (Stephanie Mills said, "Put your body in it.") Accomplice requires one's batty on the line. Hands dirty and at risk. Regarding the costs of acknowledging this intersubjectivity or kinship, Pat speaks plainly in the *I* and *we* to those in the global North who would call themselves "Third World" people and allies: "The rest of the world is being exploited in order to maintain our standard of living . . . as anti-imperialists we must be prepared to destroy all imperialist governments; and we must realize that by doing this we will drastically alter the standard of living that we now enjoy."[46] Consider the global political-economic truth of this which seems rarely highlighted (perhaps because of what it seems to demand). Pat's most famous poem, "Where Will You Be?," calls us (out) to recognize the various ways we attempt to provide measures of safety and proximity to power or respectability, even as she insists that these identities and pretentions "won't matter . . . when they come." Listen closely.

Anthological Women

Including literary luminaries and foremothers of Black feminism and womanism alongside and among new and emerging voices, editor Toni Cade's *The Black Woman: An Anthology* was published in 1970. The first of its kind, *The Black Woman* not only makes way for the anthological generation inaugurated by *Conditions Five*, but following the example of the Harlem Renaissance journal *Fire!!*, it is also one of the finest early examples of the Black anthological tradition. Eleven years after her publication of *The Black Woman*—writing a foreword to the Kitchen Table Press classic *This Bridge Called My Back*—and after becoming Toni *Bambara*—Toni underscores the importance of these works of literature and criticism beyond the burgeoning literary archive and scholarly canon waiting in the wings. Recalling *This Bridge Called My Back,* she could easily also be talking about the groundbreaking *The Black Woman* when she writes: "Quite frankly, *This Bridge* needs no Foreword. It is the Afterward that'll count. The coalitions of women determined *to be a danger to our enemies,* as June Jordan would put it. . . . And the personal unction we will discover in the mirror, in the dreams, or on the path across This Bridge. The work: To make revolution irresistible."[47] Just briefly, witness a few lines of now-legendary introductory essays by the progeny of *The Black Woman,* laying out the stakes and prospects of the work in strong terms that in many cases verge on manifesto:

> "Qué hacer de aquí, y cómo" ("What to do from here, and how?" Gloria Anzaldúa, *This Bridge Called My Back: Writings by Radical Women of Color*)
>
> "There is nothing more important to me than home" (Barbara Smith, *Home Girls: A Black Feminist Anthology*)
>
> "All the protagonists are blond; all the Blacks are criminal and negligible. By mid-1983 I had grown weary of reading literature by white gay men. . . . I was fed by Audre Lorde . . . Barbara Smith . . . Cherríe Moraga . . . Barbara Deming . . . June Jordan . . . Michelle Cliff. . . . Their courage told me that I, too, could be courageous. I too, could not only live with what I feel, but could draw succor from it, nurture it, and make it visible" (Joseph Beam, *In the Life: A Black Gay Anthology*)
>
> "Welcome to a birth. . . . Other Countries is . . . a vision: a brave and sometimes difficult journey into new territory and the simultaneous excavation of a past that has been lost, hidden, stolen. It is an homage to our forefathers . . . a recognition of our pioneers . . . a pride in

our immediate parentage in *Blackheart*, and a resolution to use this legacy to go beyond . . ." (Other Countries, *Black Gay Voices*)

Yes, the word made flesh.[48] Again, not hard to understand. Take for a brief example, another reprinted essay published in *The Black Woman*—"Who Will Revere the Black Woman?" by legendary jazz artist and actor Abbey Lincoln—first appearing in 1966 in *Negro Digest* (which became *Black World* in 1970).[49] Ms. Lincoln's trenchant personal essay is a sort of jeremiad. As one writer of a subsequent letter to the editor stated, this intervention was "painfully, bitterly, dead on target."[50] Writing *as* and *for* "the Black woman," to whom she sees no reverence extended, Ms. Lincoln's last line forlornly avers metaphorical and actual vulnerability and injury as she asks: "To whom will she cry rape?" In her bold title, *The Black Woman*, Toni (Cade Bambara) sought to encompass the differences among class, education, and temperament of a plurality of Black women belied by the singular moniker. "Who Is the Black Woman?," its frontispiece asks, answering: "a college graduate . . . a drop out. . . . A student. A wife. A divorcée. A mother. A lover. A child of the ghetto. A product of the bourgeoisie. . . ." Still, in 1970 *lesbian, gay, bisexual* (and certainly not *trans*) could not speak their names out loud within these pages, despite the inclusion in the collection of women who were living openly at the time. Who (indeed) will revere the Black lesbian, gay, or trans woman? *Revere* is a funny word: from French *révérer*, it is derived from Latin *revereri*—"revere, fear." The *re-*, intensive prefix+ *vereri*—means "stand in awe of, fear, respect"—from PIE: "perceive, watch out for." This may also limn *regard*, which thanks to Christina (Sharpe), I hear in recombination with "care." So I read in turn, over again, together, or at their interstices: *Who cares?* Who regards (has your back/watches out)? Who will R-E-S-P-E-C-T? And perhaps closer to Ms. Lincoln's original meaning: who will look up to and honor the Black woman herself, and her works in the world (and be awed by her honor)?[51]

Published in that pivotal year that our particular Black gay story begins, 1979, *Conditions Five: The Black Women's Issue* inaugurates a long-lasting tradition of Black Lesbian publishing. The issue is the forerunner to *Home Girls: A Black Feminist Anthology*, published by Kitchen Table Press. Kitchen Table is, of course, foremother to Lisa C. Moore's RedBone Press, as well as journals and zines such as *Azalea* and *Venus*, which we will turn to later. Nine years after the watershed *The Black Woman*, and longer still since Black women writers' broadsides and pamphlets began to circulate—narrativizing Black women's lives and their activist work—Barbara Smith was invited to guest-edit an edition of the radical feminist journal *Conditions*: "a magazine of writing by women with an emphasis on writing by lesbians."[52] Barbara asked Lorraine Bethel to collaborate, and they named the issue "The Black Women's Issue." Lorraine and Barbara's work to create this special issue reflects a maturing discourse that was self-assured and beginning to codify around a radical Black lesbian feminist politics that insisted on diagnosing and rearticulating heretofore silenced or falsely dichotomized issues. This is also to say that Black lesbian cultural production and habits of mind and body of the long 1980s enthusiastically responded to Ms. Lincoln's question "Who will revere the Black woman?" with "Sister, we will" (as "levelly human," the Combahee River Collective might add). Even a cursory look will show that Black lesbians have most enthusiastically and consistently shown up for the signal honor to revere (other) Black women. And among lesbians, those self-described as dykes—the first to be baited and targeted for antilesbian *misogynoir*—are often at the forefront. "Dykes" and "bulldaggers" do not easily or comfortably fit into commoditized slots of lesbian chic, bourgeois intellectual, or Black femme earth mother. Thus, their embodiments and politics can sometimes make *everybody else in the room feel so uncomfortable* (in my Drake voice). I am making a point here about the costs of unapologetically and unreservedly choosing Black women (femme, soft butch, butch, and otherwise). Let us be clear: those perjured as or self-identified as Black bulldaggers and dykes built this tradition. Anthologized themselves into spaces of multiplicity and productive, messy, sexy difference, not fracture or disaffiliation. And/but this is never "easy, or quick, or pretty," as Pat already told you. To be anthologized is to be called and culled together under one cover. The title may not fit easily for each of us or for each of our genre choices, styles, or languages. But we consent to be gathered together to at least explore our common through-lines—our *stitches,* Kevin Aviance would say—hoping for generative connections to our individual projects. Maybe those culled/called into or through a tradition, or gathered together in a text/work, write to each other and other works as much as to readers. After all, maybe one of the unique elements of our sociality is that this sister love and Black men loving Black men is, as Audre wrote to Pat, "like being in a relationship with a beloved part of my own self. . . . There are conversations we need to have, Pat, each for her own clarity, and neither of us has forever."[53] How many times have we each had this longing for conversation, dear reader? *For our own clarity?* Pat and Audre's exchanges in *Sister Love* not only chronicle the intimate relationship of two key figures but also remind us that the essential lifesaving bonds that folks have with one another are also often delicate: brittle. They require nurturing. Pat responds—months later, although it is not clear whether they spoke on the telephone in the interim—"Audre, too often in the past I have put letter writing off because I thought whatever free time I had had to go to those survival things, and any energy left over would go to writing. However, it does occur to me that letter writing is both a survival thing and writing, plus it is so important to me to continue our conversation. It's always been so difficult to love you from afar, and so costly to come in close."[54] A few years later, Audre includes these few lines of her "Sister, Morning Is a Time for Miracles" in her landmark essay "Eye to Eye: Black Women, Hatred, and Anger," which had been published around the same time she and Pat had been regularly corresponding:

> and in case you have ever tried to reach me
> And I could not hear you
> these words are in place of the dead air
> still
> between us

Of course, Audre had also made this the epigram to "Dear Joe: For Joe Beam."[55] As we turn, presently, to rethink some of the ways Black gay men have chosen to apotheosize our fallen brothers, and launch another *defense of the dead* and the living through re-memory—her words are particularly apt. Think of this book as one more gesture to replace the "dead air / still / between us" with some fresh air of critical reconsideration. Audre's poem to Joe begins bracingly:

> How many other dark young men at 33
> left their public life becoming legend
> the mysterious connection
> between those we murder and those we mourn?
>
> Everyone here
> likes our blossoms
> permanent
> the flowers around your casket
> will never die
> preserved without error
> in the crystals between our lashes
> they will never bang down the phone
> in our jangled ears at 3:30 AM
> nor call us to account for our silence
> nor refuse to answer
>
> . . .

down the street
at the Pathmark Pharmacy
a drag-queen with burgundy long-johns
and a dental dam in his mouth
is buying a straight-razor.[56]

Endangered Black Hearts.
"I Have to Ask My Gay Brothers Some Questions"

Black gay men writing and doing community and cultural work in the early
1980s were among the first of many to adopt radical Black lesbian feminists'
refinement or elaboration of the mantra "The personal is political."[57] Im-
provising a politics to save their own lives—toward re-memory and against
erasure—Black gay men did not, however, widely adopt the anticapitalist
politics of the radical stream of the Black feminist movement. You might
argue, dear reader, that the default for many (not all) was a sort of liberal accent on personal freedom.[58] Perhaps what Black gay men wanted and fought
to achieve—evidenced by their writing and organizing and by observation of
how folks lived their lives—was not far from what white men wanted *restored*
to them. Primarily working toward an end to the AIDS crisis and against antigay legislation and policies that threatened to block white men's privileged
access within mainstream racial capitalism, the (white) largely cisgender
middle-class leaders of gay rights in North America and Western Europe have
been surgical and single-minded, not ecological or intersectional, in their
approach. One could say more. However, our point is to draw a comparison
to what Black gay men were, and are, doing (and what we ought to do better). And to suggest, at least to think with, the proposition that because the
central mode of Black gay men's political work during the long 1980s was
largely focused on visibility, mobility, and recognition—increasingly toward
an end to AIDS—their politics, in large, did not expand and connect beyond
the immediate life-or-death crisis in ways that radical Black lesbian feminists had. For example, returning from the National Conference of Black
Lesbians and Gays in Los Angeles in 1987, Pat said that she had "listened to
Black gay men tell, with a great deal of anger, of their battles with white gay
men over who should control the pitiful allotment of AIDS funding." Later,
she put her challenge bluntly: "I have to ask my gay brothers some questions.
Instead of organizing and marching for people with AIDS or ARC, why not
instead organize and march for a national health care system so that any person needing medical care can get it in this country? And if tomorrow I call

for a march to raise funds to fight cancer—which is decimating my lesbian community—will the gay men be there?"[59] She politely states these concerns as interrogatives instead of the declarative indictment that could have been made against a lack of reciprocal care between Black men and women (political and otherwise). Pat's questions about the strategy of working toward a national health care system and the dubiousness of Black gay men's solidarity in the fight against cancer are crucial. (We hold provisional answers in abeyance until part 3.) Still, to be clear, Black gay men were far from complacent privileged subjects awaiting sudden politicization by AIDS. Black "homosexual," bisexual and trans men, have participated in every aspect of Black life, including civil rights, labor, and Left politics in the United States and elsewhere, toward Black "uplift" and/or "liberation," alongside and often ahead of prominent straight Black men and women.[60] Moreover, they lived these struggles, most often closeted, holding an open secret, or compelled to be *discreet*. In part 2 we will attend to how Black gay men's work and forms of political identification shifted from the early 1980s to the middle years of the AIDS pandemic. Although radical and indeed revolutionary Black gay voices were also at work (that is, the classical nonmetaphorical sense of overthrowing one form of government for another), the loudest voices were righteously single-mindedly focused on saving their own lives—both literally, working to prevent death from AIDS as well as in the sense of preserving (or "saving") a record of their lives against what Melvin Dixon called "double cremation."[61]

Citing *Black male unemployment, imprisonment, and homosexuality* in one breathless litany throughout the long 1980s, social scientists, policy makers, and various observers of (and within) Black communities bemoaned not only the *problem* of Black masculinity but more pointedly the problematic Black man himself. This popular and academic discourse seemed to find Black men a different species altogether, designating them "endangered" (even before AIDS and HIV). Although breaking masculinist silence on the particularities of Black men's experiences was a much-needed turn, this attention was not only belated but also baiting. Of course, Black feminists had already called for (at least) a thoroughgoing reevaluation of the intersections of race and gender. Moreover, widely ignored in mainstream scholarly and popular discourses, Black gay men had already begun their trenchant critiques of masculinity, which were quite opposed to mere reconstruction or rehabilitation of racialized heteropatriarchal models of respectable male leadership uncritically offered as the solution to the "problem" of the so-called disintegrated Black family.[62] The Blackheart Collective organized the first Black gay men's writing collective in 1980, amid a significant worldwide eruption of structural political-economic "crisis" (which we can identify as racial capitalism—certainly not a new phenomenon).[63] Scholars, policy makers, and pundits exploited and intensified the material difficulties with caricatured, perverted versions of Oscar Lewis's "culture of poverty" thesis, promoted by Daniel Moynihan and reified in innumerable ways since.[64] International discourse on "the crisis of the endangered Black male" and "endangered Black masculinity" very quickly devolved to something quite unhelpful and doggedly persistent. It still negatively affects our ability to talk about Black men both in the United States and transnationally. This discourse has many lives and still resonates today without adequate critical attention to the myriad ways it is yet another example of what Stuart Hall and the Centre for Critical Cultural Studies had named "policing the crisis"—that is, the exploitation and spectacularizing of conditions expressly to manufacture consent for harsher surveillance, external control, occupation, and incarceration.[65] Discourse of the "crisis of the endangered Black male" was everywhere in the long 1980s. Today, it should not be hard to imagine the ubiquity of the chatter and how the media exploited material conditions Black folks had faced for hundreds of years, which were re-coagulating in new ways by the 1980s. Real political-economic and sociohistorical issues were reduced to simplistic recriminations: whether Black "males" had been fairly treated by "their women," including mothers responsible for whether they became punks or thugs; whether Black males themselves were taking enough responsibility for communities they were putatively meant to lead, only by virtue of their status as male; and or/thus—whether Black males were irretrievably broken, except their sex. Note that brothers are stripped of humanity here—not *men* (cisgender or trans) or persons, but "males"—like any other animal. Certainly, much of this owes to white supremacist heteropatriarchal notions of what a "man" is and what should be expected of him, both of which it constructs as fungible—that is, discretionary to meet the needs of capital. After all, by the 1980s the global economy needed less of the factory or farm-laboring "male" and began demanding a differently trained and perhaps differently (dis)embodied party to feed the emerging global economy. Imagine twenty-first-century workers seated, politely and quietly, in a transnational call center, or repairing electronic components or expensive specialized technology that requires advanced technical training and delicate, nimble fingers. Imagine jobs that require no human body: no flesh at all. This is a far cry from what had been previously imagined as or for a *Black male*. In the long 1980s it became fashionable in both social science literature and the popular press, throughout the English-speaking world, to uncritically accept various iterations of essentialist thought that find Black men fundamentally disabled by "masculine failure" *and/or/thus* perpetrators of various forms of violence and prime vectors of disease: HIV/AIDS most prominently. Typically, these "studies" focus on ideas of Black men's individual and group pathology. They often blame Black female "success," an effect of the emasculating Black matriarch that Moynihan created.[66] Other studies foreground "decency" and illuminate various forms of (alternative) respectability.[67] So the Black "male" *remained*—though not precisely "beached." Black men's verbs—well rehearsed among talking heads, scholars, and preachers, for example—were (and are) neatly dichotomized between the hard rock of endangerment/dangerous and the hard place of respectability and exceptionalism.[68] The ubiquity and force of the "endangered Black male" discourse has weakened the potential of Black masculinity as a legitimate locus of critical enunciation; so far, it has disabled the development of a field of corresponding Black feminist or otherwise nonhierarchical Black masculinity studies. There is much more to say about this discourse that directly relates to the story we are telling here about the epidemic dead and the living in the long 1980s. However, for the moment consider this: no one—no prominent scholar or pundit or preacher, imam, celebrity, or talk-show host—offered sharper analysis of and "solutions" to the so-called crisis than that which Black gay men produced in their own artistic and activist work and by the examples of their own lives. Following the success of Black lesbian and feminist writers, editors, and collectives, and Calvin Lowry's Black gay newspaper, *Moja*, Isaac Jackson, Fred Carl, and Tony Crusor founded the Blackheart Writer's Collective "to publish Black gay writers and graphic artists." In a 1984 interview in *Gay City News*, Blackheart Writer's Collective cofounder Fred Carl exposed the lie that the endangered Black male/endangered Black masculinity discourse promoted:

> Black gay men are as many different things as there are Black gay men. Just in terms of sensibility. We have a lot of different voices. . . . Inside of that common thing, we have our own particular kind of identity and it's important that people begin to . . . really understand what Black gay men are, who Black gay men are as a group. Right now, there's nothing existing to even express that difference. [Isaac Jackson added] "We're either totally invisible or we're some stereotype."[69]

Black gay men, like Black lesbian (and) feminists, exposed the vulnerabilities and violence that unbelonging foments. In a corrective challenge to "endangered Black male" discourses and as a complement to burgeoning Black feminists, these artists, writers, and activists articulated *another way*.

Something else. Situated as the driest, kinkiest, and most inflexible knot within the artificially and extrinsically manufactured "tangle" of so-called Black "pathology"—putatively hypersexual and at once "hypermasculine" but/also/and missing the essential qualities of manhood—Black gay and bisexual men had a privileged epistemological vantage point (not unlike Black women, posed by Moynihan as the "emasculating matriarch" who set this in motion). Black gay men's literary and organizing works, focused as they were on their own experiences at the cold-blooded intersections of deviant gender, race, and sexuality, provided a lens to read what perhaps could not have occurred to Black, white, elected, self-appointed, unlettered, and lettered demagogues who appeared in an endless parade of talking heads on news programs and tabloid media that began to appear during the long 1980s (and now have become normalized and digitized in innumerable forms). None offered, as a policy proposal or ethical stance, what Black gay men like those in the Blackheart Collective and others did: *Love your sons, gently. Nurture the softness as well as the hard. Hug them and let them hug. Consider how your class (aspirations) and expectations affect gender roles. Gay and bisexual experiences or identities* (and *trans*, although this was not explicitly part of the conversation, as we will discuss later) *do not detract from their blackness, or readiness for anything other than to fit into categories that have never served our communities.*

The name "Blackheart" was therefore apt for the collective. According to Carl (who described his background as "mixed"—Caribbean and United States!), Blackheart is "a term that's borrowed from the West Indies. A blackheart man is a wise person, someone who is a little bit tuned into things that most people aren't."[70] The blackheart is essential to community but also stands a bit outside or *to the side*—offering critique and counsel that many folks often do not want to hear. When journalist Charles Michael Smith (also published in *Brother to Brother* and various other outlets) asked about Blackheart's thoughts on the women's movement, the collective acknowledged its admiration for Black lesbians who had "a strong institution of writing, of putting out literature whereas Black gay men have a much stronger tradition of partying." Carl's observation of the prospective galvanizing function of everyday oppression aligns with what the sisters themselves have said about writing and organizing to save their own lives: "Women's oppression operates every single day of their lives. . . . They have to deal with it constantly. They go home, they don't get a break, . . . [which] means that you take something like that and you make it mean something."[71]

Significantly, the first issue of the Blackheart Collective's journal was titled "Yemonya" in honor of the Yorùbá mother/nurturer deity whose storied attributes include protection of men who have sex with men. The second issue was conceived thematically as "The Prison Issue." Fred said that this issue of the journal was meant to "give voice to Black gay men in prison, to proclaim their existence . . . to connect people on the outside with people on the inside." Issue 2 attempted to articulate rarely discussed personal experiences of Black gay prisoners and what we have now come to understand as a carceral system with/in which all Black folks are discursively engaged or implicated, but for whom those "on the inside" suffer exponentially because of the distances that those of us on the outside maintain. This formulation seems to have reemerged and begun to gain momentum in scholarship and public discourse only recently. Although Blackheart Collective's "Prison Issue" contains many of the same metaphors that we read in subsequent Black gay works—masks, kidnap, organic growth versus cyborgs, inauthentic machines, lynchings, and white men with "a God complex"—here they convey the particular experience of being physically incarcerated, not metaphorically "imprisoned" like so many works by Black gay men who felt confined or "imprisoned" by heteropatriarchy and silences. Continuing the work of collective writing support and publishing after personnel changes and shifted priorities, the Blackheart Collective gave way to Other Countries. In 1986, the same year as the founding of two other vitally important New York Black gay organizations—Gay Men of African Descent (GMAD) and Adodi—Daniel Garret invoked Mr. Baldwin in his invitation to Black gay men to attend the first writing workshop of Other Countries with these words from his recently published *Just above My Head*: "Our history is each other. That is our only guide."[72]

The anthological generation not only is made up of activists who were also poets, artists, writers, and teachers but also includes activists who were drag queens who entertained for money, criminalized trans folks, "transvestites," "cross-dressers," and others who traded sex for money in a context in which they could scarcely earn money doing anything else. Lest we forget, it was the "girlies"—like those who worked 40-deuce and 14th Street in Manhattan—who first introduced prison (abolition) work to the queer liberation movement. We will soon turn to Marsha P. Johnson. Some six years before the Blackheart Collective's prison issue, Marsha's close friend and collaborator, legendary Latinx activist Sylvia Rivera, read for filth at the Christopher Street Liberation Day celebration. The first Christopher Street Liberation Day demonstrations, which would later morph into the corporate "Pride" celebration parades we know today, terminated at the West Village Women's Detention Center, where folks who understood the interlocking violence of state repression shouted "Free our sisters! Free ourselves!" At the 1973 rally, however, after literally fighting her way on to the stage to boos and jeers by the largely white crowd, reportedly having been attacked by white gay and lesbian organizers, Sylvia—cofounder, with Marsha P. Johnson, of STAR (Street Transvestites [now Transgender] Action Revolutionaries)—had the following to say. Not only is Sylvia's righteous anger instructive here, but also her championing of radical anthological-cum-intersectional politics at this historical moment illustrates the antagonisms between these politics, and an emerging LGB movement that would soon shift focus from liberation to integration and end in the early twenty-first century with "celebration." Read this excerpt from her incisive political praxis out loud, dear reader, in a loud angry, raspy rant. Some who have defended the abuse of Sylvia that day have alleged she was under the influence of alcohol and/or drugs, but no matter. Her reasoning and politics are obviously unimpaired:

> Y'all better quiet down.
>
> I've been trying to get up here all day, for your gay brothers and your gay sisters in jail! They're writing me every motherfuckin' week and ask for your help, and you all don't do a goddamn thing for them. Have you ever been beaten up and raped in jail? Now think about it. They've been beaten up and raped, after they had to spend much of their money in jail to get their self home and try to get their sex change. The women have tried to fight for their sex changes, or to become women of women's liberation. And they write STAR, not the women's group. They do not write women. They do not write men. They write STAR, because we're trying to do something for them. I have been to jail. I have been raped and beaten many times, by men, heterosexual men that do not belong in the homosexual shelter.
>
> But do you do anything for them? No!
>
> You all tell me, go and hide my tail between my legs.
>
> I will no longer put up with this shit.
>
> I have been beaten.
>
> I have had my nose broken.
>
> I have been thrown in jail.
>
> I have lost my job.
>
> I have lost my apartment for gay liberation, and you all treat me this way?
>
> What the fuck's wrong with you all?
>
> Think about that! . . .
>
> That's all I wanted to say to you people. If you all want to know about the people that are in jail—and do not forget Bambi L'amour, Andorra Marks, Kenny Messner, and the other gay people that are in jail—come

and see the people at STAR House on 12th Street, on 640 East 12th Street between B and C, apartment 14. The people who are trying to do something for all of us and not men and women that belong to a white, middle-class, white club. And that's what y'all belong to.

REVOLUTION NOW![73]

The anthological generation included perps and prisoners. Resonant with Sylvia, Kenyatta Ombaka Baki, who had been engaged in a pen-pal relationship with Joe Beam for a number of years by the time the Blackheart Collective's prison issue was published, appeals to allyship in the shape of extending unmasked humanity to the prisoner:

I have been taken away from you, my family. I have been denied the right of all humanity—to watch my tree grow. They are trying to force my feelings into a "mettaloid" of being and I find myself searching for a smile in the mirror. . . . Around me, people are wearing masks. Some remove them during visiting time. But I can't seem to get mine off. My mask causes visitors feelings of guilt which they hide. . . . Are you still there or are you cowering behind your barred doors from the abused people that you have hidden behind the cement walls and steel bars, and forgotten? Can you stand to see beyond the walls that you have built and readily pay taxes to build higher? Did you know that your taxes are being used to create people who will keep you in fear? Of course, you didn't know that. You are helping breed anti-social people who are bitter and disillusioned with laws that you pride yourself in having legislated. When was the last time you paid a visit to the people behind bars just for a friendly chat?[74]

B. Nia Ngulu[75] contributed a poem called "Guardians of the Flutes" to the "Prison Issue," referring to the ritualized homosexuality practice of the Sambia, in Papua New Guinea. Ngulu imagines an escape from the confines of the prison for him and his lovers/brothers/friends. This transformation of commonly mediatized homosocial fantasies of prison sex and sexual assault draws together a far-flung sort of diaspora of deep homosexual traditions, from Oceania to the Siwan of Egypt (who reportedly revered men who had sex and relationships with men and practiced homosexual marriage):

we named our cellblock
"the East Bay"
(of Melanesia)
and we named ourselves
"the Siwans"

and the prison guards didn't know nothing
about Black-sexual anthropology

But the stories of the imprisoned are not the sort of romances we imagine
when we genuflect at the altars of Joe, Essex, and Marlon, notwithstanding
this poem by Ngulu. Many of their stories, rife with elements of the strictly
disreputable, not only show a side of Black gay men's experience often not
discussed but also index how even "in the life" in which one is hustling to survive, the real taboo is having sex with another man. As Darnell Tatem writes,

> I am an African. I was brought up in the streets . . . mainly on my own. My
> outlook on life was all that was needed to survive, mainly at the expense
> of another. So I pimped, strong-armed, did stickups, broke into houses,
> sold drugs, ran long and short cons, sold slum jewelry, and was a male
> prostitute. . . . All this time I was going in this manner there was main
> talk about how fucked homos were, out one side of their neck, how they
> were no good. I even read a note by one of the groups that stated all fag-
> gots need to be killed, etc. Then on the other hand, all would sneak and
> get their dick sucked or would speak on another prisoner walking down
> the hall whose ass was big, about how they would like to get into their ass,
> etc. . . . I also could never get out of my mind that if there was a change in
> power and these people were in control then most likely I would die along
> with all the other homos, no matter that I put my life on the line, etc. So,
> this left me not knowing if I should just forget about all this revolutionary
> shit . . . I think I don't catch hell because I am Catholic, Muslim, Baptist,
> etc., but because I am African. Then I add to it the new understanding I
> have gotten about sexual oppression and I come to the fork in the road.

A fork, an intersection, and interlocking gate. Darnell's prescience about
the way that the new carceral studies, in the wake of Angela Davis, Ruth
Wilson Gilmore, and Michelle Alexander, for example, are conceiving the
prison as part of the continuum of slavery and a carceral state is not precisely
"uncanny"; it is more specifically what Fanon would call *the lived experience of
the Black* ("l'expérience vécue du Noir," most often (mis)translated as "fact of
blackness").[76] Experience. In his essay "A System of Slavery in the Real," Darnell says that "the courts are the most racist aspect of the nation. This is not
a statement made by a crazed prisoner who read this in a book, but by a man
who has been in since Ford was president. I have dealt with the criminal justice
system in this land ever since I was seven years old. It's the system of slavery
in the real." Like Ombaka, Darnell returns our "outside" gaze with a challenge

from "inside." Like Pat Parker, he warns us of the inescapable mutuality of "hard times" from which we cannot turn away. Darnell, the African born and raised largely by himself on the streets of Connecticut, is hipping us to the tea: the neoliberal order had already taken hold in the United States by 1984. I hear June Tyson and Sun Ra again: "(It is already after the end of the world). Don't you know that, yet."[77] Darnell says that "while people are looking up in the sky for the bomb, the bomb has already gone off right in their front yards. Because of revolutions in other countries, that has meant an end to cheap labor and goods. Those on the other side of the wall have come on hard times." This makes it harder for those on the inside. Alliance and solidarity are stretched:

> So who is there to fight with and for the prisoner? How can this be done? Yes, I have to fight for sexual freedom because we are all human and this is just. Yes, I must fight for the end of the criminal justice system because it is a slow death for us all. Yes, I must be about the business of standing with the oppressed of the world over, and I hope I'm able to come out of self-exile and move on. . . .

He does not end here. The gag is this: "But after I have written all this, still the bars will be full on the weekend, there will be parties and joy expressed all over by those who will not understand."[78] Having been released several years after publication of the Blackheart Collective Prison Issue, then returned, Darnell Tatem remained in the Connecticut prison system.

Reproductive Failure?

In the fall of 1980, I did not know that one of every four Black men would experience prison in his lifetime. Nor did I know that my motivations for writing to prisoners arose from a deep sense of my captivity as a closeted gay man and an oppressed Black man rather than as an act of righteousness. Finally, I had no idea that such a correspondence would become an integral part of my life and a place for dreaming.
—JOSEPH BEAM, *IN THE LIFE: A BLACK GAY ANTHOLOGY*

"Gone too soon" and "cut down in their prime" are at once clichés and apt descriptions not only of the personnel of the long 1980s Black gay arts and political movement but also of some of the ideas and politics. Joe and Ombaka supported each other through their respective writing practices. Exchanging letters between 1980 and 1987, they intended their correspondence to appear in a book ("a book of our friendship," Joe wrote). Later, referring to his now-classic essay "Brother to Brother: Words from the Heart," which appears in *In the Life* and lends its title to the follow-up edited by Essex, Joe wrote to Ombaka that "it really is about us." What if? What might have become of our politics if this project had been published? And if, following Joe, we had centrally included in the struggle for visibility and survival those (yet *living!*) who had already been declared socially dead? In *In the Life*, Joe had attempted to show a diverse cross-section of Black gay men, following Blackheart's desire to demonstrate that "Black gay men are as many different things as there are Black gay men."[79] Interventions such as "'Color Him Father': An Interview" follow Phillip Robinson's "When I Stopped Kissing My Father" and Donald Woods's "A Poem for Eric." "Brother, Can You Spare Some Time?," an interview with a "a closeted Black man" who volunteered as a companion and caretaker to people living with AIDS, exposed the lie that all bisexual (or "DL") brothers are predators or are hiding from their "true" homosexual identity. Inroads to understanding and including rural experiences were made by publishing "'Emmett's Story': Russel, Alabama." These works represent a few of the myriad aspects of the US Black community to which Joe refers to in his famous theorization of the Black counterpublic. After opening with an epigram from Audre and illustrating his own anger and need to speak ("I, too know anger . . . it is the material from which I have built my house . . .") in the second paragraph of "Brother to Brother," Joe writes that "when I speak of home . . . I mean . . . the Black press, Black church, Black academicians, Black literati, and Black Left . . . ," where he finds invisibility and silence, and to which he cannot return as an "out" Black gay man. This mirrors the sort of ethnographic sensibility that Joe displays as he illustrates various Black men later in the essay: on the corner, in the corporation, turning away from Joe's greeting at the doughnut shop, "walking down Spruce/Castro/Christopher Street," traveling to "Atlantic City, or Rio or even Berlin. . . ." He invokes the club and his "warm brown" Bajan father, boy-man Bryan, Vietnam vets, and lost high school buddies before turning to his dreams. Citing Malcolm and Martin as dreamers, Joe offers that "dreams are what propel us through life, and allow us to focus . . . I dare myself to dream that our blood is thicker than difference." So here's how to read Joe—and to recast for a refinement of his sterling visionary "daring to dream" that "Black men loving Black men is the revolutionary statement of the eighties."[80] The question for us in the now is this: what do we do when the dream that is also perhaps a kind of romance is also our politics?

2

"What It Is I Think They Were Doing, Anyhow"

I HAVE ALREADY TOLD YOU THAT Joe Beam was my first. He was for a lot of us. Toward more critical parsing and what Essex called "ass-splitting" personal truths, here we lean more heavily and greedily lick the sweetness.[1] Steven (Fullwood) and Charles (Stephens) showed us one way to do this work in their crucially important anthology, *Black Gay Genius: Answering Joseph Beam's Call.* Talking to Barbara (Smith) in one of the early chapters, Steven says that he and Charles wonder why Joe does not figure more in the "new Black queer studies." Barbara ventures that scholars are "not that interested, necessarily, in people who operate on a kind of grassroots level. The academy, as far as I can judge, is ever more removed from the day to day struggle of our lives."[2] These are strong words and a fair indictment, and/ but there is more to consider. Perhaps there is not more of the kind of work Charles and Steven have done for the reasons that Jennifer cites, regarding intersectionality "originalism." Some of the children would rather move on, and in languages and styles that seem more academic or more sonorous with contemporary high art or high theory. Perhaps it is also an effect of our (academics', that is) critical impulse against reducing the scholarly enterprise to a "project of recovery of the lost tribe of Black gay exceptionals," as Cathy has warned against, and toward a politically engaged (research) agenda that Barbara, and Joe himself, might have engaged and supported.[3] Although many seem to need icons to retain a burnished glow, hagiography is not critical inquiry. *Black Gay Genius*, of course, engages both critical inquiry and critical memory-recovery work. Barbara continues, homing in on how academic scholars research—identify and mine archives, respondents and sites, read closely, and "write up"—"Maybe they don't know where to put him," she says.[4] Where to put him, yes. And also, *how* to put him. How to see Joe and *say* Joe in a way that is accurate and fair-minded: affecting and perhaps lasting, or at least instructive. Knowing that we are here to do more than deconstruct and dissemble (our) culture, the politically engaged among us might also ask: *How does Joe help us to stage an intervention? Black Gay Genius* provides provocative archival and theoretical arrows. Multivocal, at turns blindingly brilliant and imperfect, with contradictory and complex stories gathered and held in place by an editorial vision committed to critical commemoration, the collection celebrates, parses, and at times mediates messiness through personal reflections, scholarly assessments, and personally held archives. There is no place more appropriate to begin this work than in an independently published anthology. In the opening conversation, Barbara offers a framework to understand Joe's life and works. Like her, many of the contributing artists, scholars, and activists knew Joe personally. Still, Colin (Robinson) says, "I am afraid of remembering."[5] Friends of Joe can no more coolly and with detachment talk about their dead friend/collaborator/brister/lover than I can about mine. Why should we? Criticality does not require what folks used to call "objectivity" before we all knew better than to think that it was possible or desirable. Melvin asks and implores: *Remember them.* Cathy adds that this remembering "should also lead to reconsideration and reconceptualization . . . [and] the reconstruction and reemphasis of standard narratives [in Black studies] rooted in ideas such as deviance and agency, and not exception and inclusion."[6] We can do both, and more. In *Black Gay Genius*, Robert (Reid-Pharr) challenges us to take on the work of "attention to the quality of the discursive artifacts . . . living and endangered documents."[7] You will remember his entreaty to focus on form and technique of the masters. Below, Essex (Hemphill) is speaking to his Black gay contemporaries in the anthological generation, but his words also urgently reach beyond the ether to speak to those of us today who try to do our work with love and rigor and no lack of style. Trying hard to rebuke the demons of shade and lack of self-regard that often find us seemingly so ready to greet another's pain with our own. Essex assigns a worthwhile agenda:

What we must do now, more than ever is nurture one another whenever and wherever possible. We *must* focus our attention around issues of craft and discipline in order to create our very best literature [research, policies, programs], . . . look closely at revealing the full extent to which Black gay men have always participated in positive and nurturing roles in the structures of family within the African American community, . . . look closely at intimacy and the constructions of our desire and bring forth from these realms the knowledge that we are capable of loving one another in . . . productive relationships. . . . We must begin to identify what a Black gay sensibility is; identify its aesthetic [social and epistemic] qualities and components; identify specific constructions . . . and then determine how this sensibility . . . aesthetic [and epistemology] relates to and differs from African American literature [life, studies, politics] as a whole.[8]

The brackets are mine because my own sensibility is also ethnographic. (What, I wonder, is in your bracket, dear reader?) Anthropological in the ways that Assotto and Melvin and Marlon have already named. By this, I mean that the "particular contexts" Robert cites are prime for my spyglass. "Living and endangered documents" read alongside "the rigors of an inglorious present" are the bread and butter of an ethnographer, even one haunting archives, sensing affect, and poring over secondary sources. Our (Zora Neale) Hurstonian "spyglass" even occasionally turns inward, remains attuned to all of this, even courting incommensurability (or "irresolution," to invoke Matt Richardson's expansive theoretic) toward trying to "begin to identify what a Black gay sensibility is" as part of the work that Essex left for us.[9] This, even if I must leave the work of naming a Black lesbian and gay aesthetic to those like Robert and Charles (Nero) and Matt and Omi and Kevin and Dagmawi and Darius (Bost), who are trained and invested in formal literary study. Here we accept as our undertaking the parsing of the "communal genius" of anthological bulldaggers, *masisi*, and libidinal Black genies.[10] Joe, yes. And the genii to which we all have access. This is the gleaming glittery center of what I mean by the Black gay *habit of mind*.

Still, I have come to find that my dear NorthStar brother, Joseph, was wrong about a few things. Or at least he had miscalculated. Perhaps more precisely, it is the uses we have put to Joe (and Essex and Marlon and Assotto and Melvin) that have been too meager. As the 1980s wore on, we learned, tragically, that "visibility" is emphatically not "survival." Survival is. Visibility works to prevent erasure, but it is not survival. Visibility also does not necessarily require legibility. To be seen does not automatically conjure positive relationality or solidarity.[11] Most importantly, even though survival—even "pending revolution," as the Panthers used to say—is an important tactic, it is not an elaborated politics or vision of what happens on the other side of survival. And this too must be said: although *Black men loving Black men* is a powerful and necessary statement, only *revolution* is revolution. Ours certainly requires *Black men loving Black men*. Still, it is hardly the only revolutionary statement we need. It should be clear from Joe's life and work that brothers must (at the very least) embrace a kind of love that extends to Black women, girls, boys, and Black folks who refuse gender binaries. Otherwise, we (Black gay men) ought to merely enjoy Joe's call as a warm homosocial embrace, brother to brother, and forget hanging our political futures on it. This is one way to enter a discussion of where we would look to progressively shape our politics in the now/toward futures. Although we enjoy each other's company and find it essential to have spaces in which to ground with our brothers and love them in as many ways as we choose to manage, to create a critical locus of enunciation—a counterpublic, an alternative politics, and/or a movement—requires growing our project with our cis and trans sisters and with those of our brothers who understand the precarity and "magic" of being raised as Black girls. It requires nimble transits between our people in different class positions, and it requires us to learn new languages and to try to listen beyond borders and beyond received or expected grammars. Please do not misread this as a reversal or as a critique of what you call identity politics, dear reader. I invite you to look more closely. This is not a critique of naming and defending a political space and critical locus of articulation, and it is surely not a slight to my own Joseph Fairchild Beam. I am calling for a necessary assessment of the ways we read him (and the ways we read Marlon Riggs's luminous films that remix his words). There is no reason to extinguish your Joseph Beam 7-Day Candle, or to quit scattering the ashes of American flags on Assotto Saint's grave. Do not take this to mean you should not revel in Melvin Dixon's erudition, true mastery, and expansive intellect and in Essex Hemphill's lyrical genius. Quite the contrary. The call here is for a refocused accounting. Still libidinal. Desire for love and clarity but also moving decidedly toward freedom-winning revolution and new societies. Perhaps this is close to how Melvin intended us to read these lines for Joe: "This poem is for Joseph, Remember Joe? Whose longing / For the language of Black men loving black men / became our lore?"[12]

We do not like to think of his work as "lore." And our lure. It has become us. We want a living and usable set of Blackprints, and/but Barbara Ransby reminds us that we all "have our own work to do." It is "in the technique," Robert offers.[13] Beyond the seductive iconography of Joe in his chambray work shirt or staring longingly from the back cover of *In the Life*, Barbara Smith counsels that if we want to emulate Joe, "emulate . . . the value system . . . integrity . . . compassion and the kindness." Joe was "extremely Black identified," she says.[14] He followed and was inspired by Black and women-of-color feminists. Are these emulatable or educatable techniques of the self? Is this a *politics*? A methodology? Surely this is part of the discernible Black gay habit of mind. But is it *enough*?[15]

"River, Remember Your Source"

If Joe is our untouched dreamlover-martyr-philosopher, Melvin Dixon is the one whom many of us did not know we deeply needed. Steven asks, "Why not Joe?" I wonder, "Why not Melvin?," especially given the literary bent of Black queer studies. One would assume Melvin should be the model for Black gay scholars looking for an accomplished ancestor: a cosmopolitan, polyglot Black diaspora critic, a fine poet, and a gifted novelist. Erudite and poised, he meets our gaze with classic good looks and gorgeous almond eyes in his Robert Girard portrait. In this, the most widely circulated of few photos, like Joe he gives squared-jawed eighties-mustachioed Butchqueen, with the bonus of enviable academic bona fides and critical literary acclaim. So where is Melvin? There is no hagiography of him (yet). The remaining *Tongues Untied* cohort does not dine out on Melvin stories as they do Essex, Joe, and Marlon— or even Assotto (whom we will turn to next). It is harder to find casual stories and remembrances beyond formal archives. Does being situated in academe make one less accessible or desirable as an object of adoration? (Don't answer that!) Could it be temperamental? Or is the seeming distance caused by his own bourgeois remove? After all, folks seem to like their heroes and icons scrappily bootstrapped. Melvin "was our generation's Black literary treasure, cut off too soon," according to Dwight (McBride), whose *Melvin Dixon Critical Reader* is a precise example of the sort of work that Melvin had called for: recovering "endangered documents."[16] As a novelist, there are few contemporaries to whom he can be fairly compared. Moreover, Melvin's grounded critical work was unique in remaining unmoved by the powerful pull of postmodern theory and writerly performance that was newly in vogue in the long 1980s, which Barbara Christian so cogently read in her essay "The Race for Theory."[17] His incisive readings and careful translations of French and Spanish texts make him a singular Black studies figure of the long 1980s. And his singularity stands today. Yet his work is not often taught in our undergraduate classes. He is certainly "somewhere listening for [his] name."[18]

In his aptly titled article "Rivers Remembering Their Source," Melvin argues that each distinct literature of the New World at once "remembers" the source—the continuous presence of African oral traditions—retaining particular historical and linguistic features of its original terrains while continuing to move, finding new streams and new ground. His point of departure here is the Negritude movement, which he calls "the single most resounding literary achievement of international scale in the twentieth century . . . through which an entire continent renamed itself, and by [which] . . . generations of Blacks dispersed throughout the world reclaimed a part of their identity as members of the African diaspora."[19] Melvin critically parses and celebrates African-derived oral and movement traditions that he finds in the work of French-, Creole-, Spanish-, and English-speaking writers. For him, what connects Black cultural workers is therefore not merely "an identity of passions or a racial feeling" (advanced by Aimé Césaire, who of course did promote a perhaps politically limited but also strategically useful and beautifully wrought aesthetic essentialism). Melvin argues that the work of Black diaspora writers "reveals the challenge that modern Black writers have faced—the creation of . . . a language that expresses the acculturation of traditional African and European forms and the dynamic transformation and reinvention of self that results."[20] He writes, "Black writers of the Caribbean, North America, and Africa confront European civilization on the cultural level, not merely on the level of feeling or passion. The form of their response to acculturation has been to combine the best of traditional African oral heritage with the most useful European vocabulary. African languages in motion and in contact with Spanish, French, and English have created something new: not a pidgin or dialect version but a language that seeks within its national oral foundation a synthesis based on racial characteristics and allegiance."[21]

In this essay Melvin quarrels with Ralph Ellison and James Baldwin, who he says "mistakenly separate feeling from form and from their essential interaction in culture or art."[22] Most often, Mr. Baldwin and Mr. Ellison either report on their encounters with African and Caribbean writers with ambivalence or pose the injuries of slavery, colonialism, and continued anti-Black racism as our only sources of connection. According to Melvin, for Mr. Baldwin and Mr. Ellison this is "feeling," unrelated to the form of their works. As our dear, peerless bard Mr. Baldwin writes, "They face each other, the Negro and the African, over a gulf of three hundred years—an alienation too vast to be conquered in an evening's good will, too heavy and too double-edged to be trapped in speech. . . ."[23] Mr. Baldwin highlights distinctions to stunning and convincing affect. In his classic essay "Encounter on the Seine," he writes of the African student in France: "His mother did not sing 'sometimes I feel like a motherless child'; and he has not, all his life, ached for acceptance in a culture which pronounced straight hair and white skin the only acceptable beauty."[24] Gorgeous and achingly resonant. But the Black American exceptionalism that he narrates so well just *ain't necessarily so*. Especially these days. More than a casual look around the Caribbean and Latin America and across to Europe and the continent of Africa reveals that, while it shows up differently in various locales, this sorrowful "ache for acceptance" caused by a white standard is common.[25] Our histories are unique but not dissimilar. With respect to Afro-American ontologies, similar modes of expression, similar spiritual and metaphysical schema, and ethics of how to treat a stranger or to regard children, for example, have similar elements throughout the Americas, and many are common across the shiny mirror of the Atlantic. Black Americans from the United States are not exceptional with respect to Black folks in other locales. Although breathtakingly argued, Mr. Baldwin's stance is partial. It also reflects, perhaps, a missed opportunity for the sort of pan-African or diaspora sociality and politics celebrated and practiced by Negritude writers, for example. We will return to this in part 2.[26] This is one example of an "internationalist" stance that Mr. Baldwin occupied—distinct from Melvin's diasporic or transnational view, in that he sees, and seems to engage and invest, only in siloed national groupings. But our histories are more complex than additive accounting. The main exception of Black Americans from the United States, Mr. Baldwin finds, is the problem of the lack of a reliable name by which his great-grandfather could be called, other than that of the white man, *Baldwin*, who held pretentions to "own" him. Of course, Hortense Spillers's "'Mama's Baby, Papa's Maybe': An American Grammar Book" has brilliantly elucidated the epistemological consequences of chattel enslavement and the British colonial practice of *partus sequitur ventrem* (mandating that the status of offspring—whether they are to be free or enslaved—depends on the status of the mother), racializing patriarchy from the jump.[27] This is the "drama of words" that Mr. Baldwin conjures in his 1969 speech in front of a group of West Indian and African students in London, in which he lucidly discusses his perspective on the key distinction between the American Negro and the West Indian and African in the United Kingdom, captured in the title of the marvelous Harvey Ové film that chronicles it: *Baldwin's Nigger*.[28] Here is his wish (our wish) to be more than a possession reflecting only nonpersonhood. Still, "West Indians"—a misnomer many now correct with "Caribbean," which is also historically flawed nomenclature—have no more of a proper patronym than mainland North, Central, or South Americans. Add to this the history of internal colonialism and slavery on the continent, the spread of Islam and Christianity by force and by choice, European colonialism throughout the world, and the fact that not all cultures pass on family names (patrilineal or matrilineal) the same way: it is clear that the vast majority of our names are "not our own" in the way that Mr. Baldwin imagines his perhaps unknowable fathers' fathers' fathers' . . . name. What would it be like to call ourselves by the name our mothers called us by/into being? That is, to count our generations via a line of active *mothering*? Remember and revere the mother(s) lost, and at the same time keep our focus on work and love in the alive, self-defining, perhaps coldblooded, but Blackfull present.

In "Rivers Remember," Melvin is arguing for recognition of enduring socio-linguistic traditions, following and revising anthropological assertions of Black cultural retentions, continuances, routes and roots, as opposed to total deracination or disconnection.[29] One need not reduce Black/African diasporic connection (between individuals or between Black/African/Creole cultures) as something "inherent," wholly biologically heritable, or "essential." Neither is Black connection with, fluency in, or transformation of European cultural forms "inauthentic" (or even oppositional in all cases). Black cultures that are created in the violent clash are at once historically particular, most often shaped by similar political-economic imperatives (that we have come to understand as racial capitalism), and deeply and lovingly held, practiced, and connected across geographies and time. Melvin, our doyenne of Black diaspora letters, once again named this dynamic work *in tradition* in his brief introduction to a reprint of Mr. Baldwin's "The Preservation of Innocence" in the popular LGBT journal *Out/Look*: "What, then, could I ever hope to tell on the mountain but the tremoring cadence and mystery of my own name or identity, which is the most difficult task any writer must face," he asks.[30] The task involves observing, participating, and narrating one's identity as a mystery, toward reconstructing oneself with clues often far-flung and written in different tongues at different points in time. Eschewing dichotomous thinking that would pose blackness as noncultural and based on injury alone, Melvin offers instead "a language that is the danced speech of its people." One that has tremendous cultural value and political potential.[31] Here he models a Black diaspora fluency and criticality that, while certainly a feature of the long Black intellectual tradition, would not become widespread until Black British and Caribbean scholars' notions of hybridity and creolité, respectively, circulated more widely in the nineties and beyond. Note his accent on "the creation of . . . a language . . . and the dynamic transformation and reinvention of self that results."[32] Sounds like Audre and Joe and Essex and Assotto and Colin. This accent on speech tied to visibility and creation of new sociocultural space and political projects became the center of Black gay ideology and political practice in the long 1980s, following Black feminist theorization and praxis. It is the insistence on Black LGBTQ belonging, even highlighted by a celebration of gender and sexual difference and the creation of new relations, languages, and grammars (as well as perverse recitations of old ones). Cultural tradition and memory therefore inhere in my notion of Black gay habit of mind but do not determine it. The distinction is perhaps slight, but it is important to retain the crucial aspect of historically specific difference and dynamism within sets of tradition. As Wura insists, "Our futures are not predetermined. . . ." *Rivers remember*, yet they continue to find their own level, and to flow, undulate, and sometime flood in unexpected excess! My notion of Black gay *habit of mind* acknowledges the pull of well-worn routes but does not require identical itineraries.

Narratively innovative and beautifully and emotionally precise, Melvin's *Vanishing Rooms* is a sterling model for "the Black gay novel." In it, the Black gay protagonist embedded in concentric Black worlds where race, gender, class, and sexuality interlock must manage the action and the weight of these histories with distinctly compounded agency and limits. This of course follows Mr. Baldwin's gleaming *Just above My Head*, published in our year of long-1980s inauguration, 1979. Given the centrality of white rescue figures in previously published works with Black gay protagonists, what makes *Vanishing Rooms* racially "transgressive" is the fact that we learn by page 12 that the protagonist's white lover, Metro (Jon-Michael Barthé), is dead.[33] This after the narrator has offered an expertly drawn preliminary portrait of the protagonist, Jesse Durand, and his (Black) world. *Vanishing Rooms* is set in the mid-1970s as recent college graduates Jesse and his lover Metro begin their lives together in New York City. The novel, which we will return to later, is told in two parts and narrated by three characters: Ruella, a Black woman dancer who befriends Jesse; Lonny, the young white assailant whose savage, coerced gang rape and murder of Metro sets the taut emotional drama in motion; and Jesse himself. Therefore, this novel is also *anthological* in a way as it presents the points of view of multiple narrators in concurrent time frames as a sort of counterpoise to the violence of a single-trajectory "history." The long 1980s was the height of poststructuralist reconsideration, after all. Like *Just above My Head* and the long-1980s works of Toni Morrison and Alice Walker, *Vanishing Rooms* celebrates and "exploits the fundamental dishonesty of linear narrative storytelling."[34]

Despite having his works published and favorably reviewed, Melvin understood that his (our) recent arrival and nascent *evidence of being* could be easily erased. During his keynote speech at the 1992 Out/Write Conference, Melvin reveals the most profound fear pushing the cultural production of Black gay men in the long 1980s: "the chilling threat of erasure." He is speaking here and elsewhere against what he called "double cremation": the total evisceration of one who is already in many ways invisible, illegible, or (socially) *dead*. Melvin likely shocked some in the audience by beginning his address to the largely white crowd of queer writers with "As gay men and lesbians we are the sexual niggers of society. . . ." and I believe this is an uncharacteristically imprecise statement. Although reminiscent of Mr. Baldwin's bracing exclamation that "the Algerian is the nigger in Paris," Melvin's phrase made a false equivalence, whereas Mr. Baldwin had deftly analyzed racial capitalism's need to manufacture a "nigger" in the United States and everywhere else that hierarchies needed to be concretized for capital to exploit more efficiently.[35] In any case, Melvin's point was to dramatically elicit solidarity from partial identification. He continues: "Some of you have felt a certain privilege and protection in being white. . . ." Two years earlier, Essex (Hemphill) had addressed this conference in a different register but spoke to a similar point. Whereas Melvin seemed to be speaking more broadly about gay and lesbian cultural production, and his reference to "sexual niggers" was meant to shock the conference-goers into recognition of their own vulnerability, Essex had given an emotional and direct talk at Out/Write, but one addressed to other Black gay men, as this was a version of his introduction to *Brother to Brother*. Their strategic choices were each well executed and effective to a degree. Melvin is more politic and perhaps both more invested in preserving his connections to (well-meaning) liberal white gay men and their networks and more engaged with moving them to action than Essex seems. But no matter. Melvin's message to the audience is clear: despite your privilege, *you too may have to go this way*. You too may face erasure. Of course, as his poem "And These Are Just a Few" attests, by 1992 Melvin had already said good-bye to many lost to AIDS, including his life partner. He said: "In my former neighborhood in Manhattan, I was a member of the 4H Club: The Happy Homosexuals of Hamilton Heights. Now, it is the 3D Club: The dead, the dying, those in despair. I used to be in despair; now I am just dying."[36] That for some the 3D Club has recently been shuttered is certainly reason to celebrate. Yet HIV surveillance data tell a very different story for Black folks. 3D is in full effect throughout the world as a result of, at least, disparate access to adequate health care. Perhaps folk heard Melvin's "some of you have felt a certain privilege and protection in being white" in a different register than he meant it. Suffering from the condition of *premature jubilation,* in the 1990s more than a few prominent white gay pundits chose to announce the end of the AIDS crisis, rather than interrogate the relationship between gentrified expansion of 4H "happy homosexual(ity)" among white gay men and the continuation of 3D—"death, dying, despair"—among Black and brown folks throughout the world. Although US statistics that put the likelihood of a Black man who has sex with Black men contracting HIV at about 50 percent in many major cities seems to invite consistent reification of blackness as the vector of disease, these horrifying numbers also clearly falsify the widespread lie that "the AIDS crisis is over."[37] It seems that the CDC and other agencies can find no other way to sound the alarm other than through deeply troubling "dark continent" references. Still, the commonality of lack of access to an affordable and sustainable health-care infrastructure—that is, HIV prophylaxis and treatment, basic health care, adequate housing and nutrition, and sexual education—experienced by Black folks both in among the poorest and richest nation-states in the world constitutes another form of kinship that we must not overlook. The concurrence reminds us that we have structural vulnerability *between us,* as much as we do enjoying authentic jollof rice in Atlanta, a perfect recitation of Lùcumí in London, or favela funk in Toronto.

Today, many erudite scholars ask us to consider Black social death as the paradigmatic scene or condition of impossibility for Black personhood in the afterlife of slavery. But Melvin's Black gay time found him writing within what we can describe as a time-compressed *posthumous futurity.* What to do when there really is *no future?* When death and nonbeing are imminent realities and not profound theorizations and understandable reflections of depressed public affect? Feel deeply. Fight to be seen for the future. And love fuck hate rage laugh work and twirl, *alively,* in the present. Check your technique and innovate for the present crisis and future horizons. Admonish friends, accomplices, allies, and all who may listen, in whatever now they inhabit, to pick up your tools to finish the work toward an unpromised future freedom. Melvin knew his death was imminent. Projecting himself to this moment in which he speaks to us through his works, from the ether, alive and anticipating his demise, he insists: "You, then, are charged by the possibility of your good health, by the broadness of your vision, to remember us."[38]

(*In Your* Shaft *Voice*) "Beautiful, Baby.
That's What I Want to Hear!"

Charles Lofton's short film, "O Happy Day! The Early Days of Black Gay Liberation,"[39] begins with a beauty shot of two Black Panther men wearing standard gear, whetting our desire for turtlenecked black-bereted and leather-jacketed masculinity—along with our righteous desire for revolution. They are not in military formation, but are seated back to back with their shoulders touching on one side. The brother in the center of the frame has sensitive eyes, full lips shaped like the Kiss icon, and a square chin. Not exactly smiling, he seems satisfied. The second brother—goateed and more intense—is captured in profile, looking to his left, vigilantly. They are ready. And I imagine they are in love. Perhaps the sister in charge has called the attention of goatee Panther, and it is this couple's turn to serve breakfast to the Black schoolchildren or to deliver acupuncture for sisters and brothers working to kick the "white horse" or the "white girl." "O Happy Day!" allows us to confront and pleasurably consume recontextualized images of "Black macho." It concentrates Black gay jouissance in a six-minute experimental film.

Fade to black. We hear young women chant "Revolution has come!" Clap! Clap! And the film's titling corroborates: "Revolution has come!" The first words we hear are from Black Panther Party heartthrob par excellence, Chairman Huey P. Newton. The chairman is extolling the fact that not only does *nothing necessarily preclude a homosexual from being a revolutionary* . . . as Fidel Castro, in the face of his Cuban government's homophobic policies, had equivocated a few years before. Moving beyond Fidel, Huey affirmed that "maybe a homosexual can be the most revolutionary."[40] At least in Charles's imagination, revolution is happening both in the ways imagined by Joe and them—Black men loving (and fucking) Black men in the context of Black communities and cultural idioms—and as organized Black revolutionaries such as the Black Panther Party for Self Defense (BPP) practiced it, with Black communities nurtured and protected by a dedicated cadre of Black women and Black men: hot breakfast served, health care delivered, and rifles at the ready.[41] Charles deftly plays with and deploys a variety of 1970s images, using a long-1980s sensibility that we might describe as *reassembled anthology*. The film interpolates slowed-down familiar scenes of Black Panthers in formation, chants of "Revolution Has Come," clips from *Sweet Sweetback's Badass Song*, home-movie footage, Tommie Smith and John Carlos giving the Black Power salute at the 1968 Olympics, Third World Lesbian and Gay Caucus demonstrations, and vintage Black gay porn. A handsome muscular Black man looks into the camera with those Joe Beam–like eyes and thick Melvin Dixon–like mustache. He caresses his chest, nipples erect, and concentrates on his own pleasure. The shot is steady on his torso as his hands go down. More exuberant chants singing: "Black is Beau.ti.FULL! [*clap.clap.*]" Indeed it is. Brothers embrace. Then, beginning with the familiar gospel chords, Dorothy Morrison-Combs and the Edwin Hawkins Singers lift their voices in praise: "Oh, Happy Day!" Of course, it is: "He washed my sins away." They sing as we hear shouts of "Gay Rights Right Now!" and the title appears against a black background ("Gay Rights Right Now!"). Fade to a very handsome and familiar Black man in a cashmere turtleneck sweater, dialing the telephone in a nicely appointed room: at two minutes and forty seconds into the odyssey, Shaft (Richard Roundtree) enters from the big screen of the eponymous 1971 film. He is not wearing a beret, and his turtleneck is cream colored, in contrast to the black ones of the Panthers and the bare chest of the self-pleasuring lover in the previous scenes. In Charles's reassembled narrative, Shaft is more than the "Black private dick / That's a sex machine to all the chicks."[42] He embodies all of the foregoing representations. I turn to this elaborate description—or re-narration of the reassembled anthology—to attempt to "reproduce the technique" of Charles Lofton's "discursive artifact" in my own way. And to revel in it. Celebrating the singularity drawn from a number of what may appear to be disparate influences, references, and traditions, we want to invite more juxtapositions and comparisons, and to mark resonances and clapbacks of other works, authors, and themes.

In "O Happy Day!" John Shaft—"the man / who would risk his neck for his brother, man"—rescues sweet Bernard (actor Reuben Greene), the lone Black man and seemingly only an ex officio member of the band in the controversial 1970s film *The Boys in the Band.* Bernard suffers both from his youthful unrequited love of the scion of his mother's white employer and his loneliness as the proverbial "fly in the buttermilk" within the sad shady gay sociality depicted in the film. In what I read as a clever, elegant nod to the work of talented novelists Larry Duplechan, Stephen Corbin, and Melvin Dixon, and to Marlon's classic filmic treatment of the white boy as sexual prize/salvation/curse to the gay Black man, Charles's editorial choices produce a cinematic exhale. You may recall that in *The Boys in the Band,* the catty host of the birthday party at the center of the film sadistically insists that his "friends" play a game in which they call an unrequited (read: straight) love. This is dangerous territory, especially in 1970. "Go on, call Peter Dahlbeck, that's who you'd like to call, isn't it . . . ?" Bernard's "friend" says, explaining to the others that Bernard has known the family "since he was a pickaninny."

Perhaps handsome Bernard is really as nonplussed by the pickaninny comment as he seems. In any case, he behaves as if he is lonely in this band. Although his tight maroon turtleneck, tight dark slacks, and flawless midsize afro are on point—his gold medallion swinging as he dances confidently on the 1 and 3 after pouring yet another drink (his boys stay on 1-2-1-2)—his eyes meet only the recurring bottom of his red wine glass. "Get that liar on the phone!" the disdainful host, now united in a project of outing heterosexual privilege, tells Bernard. In silence, Bernard takes a long drag of his cigarette, picks up the heavy rotary telephone, and dials. (Dials! It is 1970.) He knows the telephone number by heart. Bernard hangs up. Further cajoled by the host, he dials again. A dial tone. The birthday boy derisively quips "Hateful" from the other side of the otherwise silent living room, referring to the host's treatment of confounded Bernard. The other boys watch—rapt. When Dahlbeck's mother answers, Bernard, his face now softer, frightened, boyish, says "Mrs. Dahlbeck, [this is] Bernard, Francine's *boy*. . . ." "*Son*, not boy!" his friend quickly chides, apparently guarding Bernard's racial pride. Perhaps racist barbs are to be shared only between intimates.[43] Bernard winces at his slip. Peter is not in. Bernard is crushed after the call and wonders why he capitulated. Finally, the host assesses this first volley of his sadomasochistic parlor game: "Two points—terrible." But in Charles's hands there is redemption. His quick edits in "O Happy Day!" find Shaft on the other end of Bernard's desperate call instead of Mrs. Dahlbeck. "The cat that won't cop out when there's danger all about" will bring a smile to Bernard's face. You may see this filmmaking/storytelling strategy as a sort of redaction and annotation of textual evidence: Shaft dials and says "Hello, baby." Bernard answers (still sheepishly—soft, boyish. Not frightened): "Hello?" Shaft answers— smiling confidently: "I'm ready, baby. Can you dig it?" Dashing. Ready for revolution! Bernard may be self-conscious of the smile that Shaft is eliciting from his worried face: how Shaft might hear it and whether his band can see it. "Yes," Bernard says curtly, unable to contain it completely. Shaft assures him: "That's what I want to hear, baby."[44] Finally, Charles borrows the last chords of Isaac Hayes's famous opening song (how could he resist?) to resolve this *Black men loving Black men* rescue romance with soulful strings. As the Edwin Hawkins Singers continue to take us further *in*, the last third of the film continues to interpolate various representations of Black masculinity in film, from the BPP to a topless, smiling Jim Brown, brooding Melvin Van Peebles, and less explicit portions of a Black gay porn film. In the final shot, which appears to be culled from what we used to call a "home movie," two Black men lovingly and playfully embrace, allowing us a rare privileged view of a tender moment they share at an outdoor gathering. Other folks mill about in the background. Children play. A sweet ear nibble. O Happy Day! Fade to black.

Sweet, single Neil was born after *Black Nations/Queer Nations*. Unlike Bernard, the boys and girls, girls who used to be (mistaken for) boys, and various combinations of resplendent gender self-assertion in his twenty-first-century band are mostly Black. Neil had sent me a text complaining about the Black gay men in his town who he thought seemed to have impossibly high demands for a Black boyfriend (postgraduate-educated, attractive, sex-positive, body by God, financially independent . . .). For a white boyfriend, Neil surmised that the criteria were "white? Check! Alive? Check!" My fabulation of Charles's reimagined rescue of a pre–*Brother to Brother* brother reaches back to 1970s "blaxploitation" visions of virile, *suave* Black masculinity, which certainly include a number of "problematic" representations (and an impossibly high standard of sartorial splendor while routing out corruption and fighting "The Man"). Still, what my millennial friend—ensconced among Black bristas and sisters as a Black gay man (platonically) loving other Black folks—longs for is at least one who will call him the way Charles edits *Shaft*, calling heretofore unrequited Bernard: "I'm ready. Beautiful, baby!"

3	Other Countries

IF JOSEPH BEAM WAS MY FIRST LOVE and Melvin's scholarly contributions prefigured what I would later hope for my own, GMAD (Gay Men of African Descent) was the first to invite me to begin to compose the self that I have come to cultivate in adulthood. GMAD was created in New York in 1986— the year I graduated high school. My first Friday Night Forum, which must have been in 1987, demonstrated to James (Jefferson) and me that we were not alone, that there was a *community* just a Long Island Railroad ride and four quick subway stops away from Laurelton. Que Chaka: "*Chaud sont papillon,* we were very young / Like butterflies, like hot butterflies / Chaud sont papillon, we had just begun."[1] Like yours and mine, dear listener, Chaka's memory trip is induced by archival evidence. She cites "a faded photograph I mailed to you / with feelings I don't want to face / And a love song of surrender in blue / . . . I remember when you took my breath away. . . ."[2] I have already told a piece of this story, rhetorically stumbling—hopefully with a bit of grace—out of the blue-black club light, or out of a Friday night GMAD forum, to find what I may have missed from this moment of incipience.[3] Still, as Colin (Robinson) has said, it is painful to remember too much. James, for one personally hurtful example, is not here to tell the story the way it ought to be told.[4] Thankfully, Donald (Woods) had already written this snapshot of our friendship when he wrote: "shoulder to shoulder sissies / on the crest of manhood / twirling like tomorrow is certain. . . ."[5]

Masc Black Gay Man 4 Mask Black Gay Man?

If James were here, he could better tell you how I behaved at the GMAD-sponsored premiere reading of *The Road before Us: 100 Gay Black Poets*, where I met Donald Woods for the first time.[6] Donald towered that evening: languid, lean, and elegant in language and body. Brilliant and sibilant. I remember attempting amateurish come-hither looks. Donald declined graciously, with a warm *nice try little brister* look-away. I swoon(ed) (I would not have known what to do next if he had responded otherwise). Black gay men, longing for a mirror made of flesh, saw ourselves for perhaps the first time in the literature of the long 1980s. But what of those reflections? Were they aspirational? Honest? Were they just? And how did these reflections—whether honest and affirming or not—serve as blackprints for the movement fomenting in tandem in organizations such as GMAD? The erotic is certainly constituting, but it can also breed deeply consequential exclusions. The poetic *Brother to Brother* confession of Cary Alan Johnson, whom I first met at GMAD and to whom I personally owe a great deal for his mentorship in the early nineties, predates my own, just as his globe-trekking African diaspora do-gooding as a professional human rights activist modeled my own early career goals. In "Hey Brother, What's Hap'nin'?" Cary wrote that "everybody wants to be the boy next door and *have* the boy next door. And I am no exception."[7] To me, this typifies the structure of feeling at GMAD in the early years. (See figure 3.1.) The fact that everyone seemed cute and educated (or on their way) and middle class (or aspiring) was a lure and lubrication for sociality among those who thought of themselves likewise ("and I am no exception"). Tragically, this also proved to be a trap, or—more precisely—a lack of political consciousness around what to do with this confluence of class, sexual, and gender desires and performance is the trap. In the early 1990s, GMAD's transformations had as much to do with the perceived shift in class positions, education, looks, and presentation of the folks who increasingly accessed the services of the organization and populated the Friday night forums as they were a result of the vagaries of national and municipal HIV funding.

Today, the work of Fatima Jamal, creator of the film *No Fats, No Femmes*, calls me to account for a finer distinction between the making we do, the masc (putatively "masculine" performing) we feel internally and/or are called to be by our communities, and the masks we often create for ourselves, simply

3.1 L to R: Cary Alan Johnson, Colin Robinson, Olubode (fka Shawn) Brown, B. Michael Hunter, and Donald Woods at Cary's Washington apartment before an Other Countries reading. Thank you to the Estate of Bertram Michael Hunter.

to be seen. I am learning from a different angle, as I attempt to peek over the artist's shoulder to see what she sees and how she sees it—how desire shapes politics and who we want to become. What I imagined as my own possibilities emerged from the seventeen-year-old self that was coming together at the time—using the body, background, sensibilities, capacities, and geographies available to me. And strictly limited by the same, to be sure. Had any of this been significantly different—had I been trans, fat, poor, non-English-speaking, a son of the elite, more butch, more femme, from a rural place, or streetwise, for example, my experience would have likely been very different.[8] I have often joked that in my early twenties I tried several times to exchange my *youthful exuberance* for sexual attention from Allen, Donald, Len . . . all to no avail. Especially Len—our chats at Keller's Bar about his trips to Brazil fascinated me and educated my desire to travel. I thought about him as I found myself there some fifteen years beyond that moment. Chronically unrequited as a lover by the (slightly) older brothers I desired, however, middle-class intellectual and political types at least did seem to *see* me. I am deeply grateful to have been seen.[9] I now understand that the failure to be recognized and affirmed results in nettlesome and consequential issues later.[10] Could they have seen me if I had towered over them in stilettos? Might I have clawed my way, like Duncan Teague's brilliant gemstone alter-ego Amethyst, for recognition of my substantial gifts to offer the community? I learned a great deal from Duncan's community work in Atlanta over a number of years before I returned to New York—working with him in the African American Lesbian Gay Alliance (AALGA) and later the Coalition of African Descent (CAD), which we helped create alongside Archie Freeman (without whose mentorship and care I might not have ever broken free of the confines I had created for myself), Joan Garner, Maurice Franklin, Venus Landin, and my good friends Craig Washington and Lance McCready, among others. In E. Patrick Johnson's remarkable oral history, *Sweet Tea: Black Gay Men of the South*, Duncan (now the Reverend Duncan Teague) describes himself to E. Patrick as "a flaming queen . . . occasionally a vicious Miss Thing . . . and sometimes in Drag."[11] I also know Duncan to be whip smart, loving, and/but with a fierce tongue that can cut deep. In my memory he engaged legendary quarrels with Atlanta "dick politics"—my shorthand for how attractive, well-spoken, typically masculine cisgender gay men are recruited, expected to, and often do take up disproportionate room in Black LGBT and queer spaces. When I was in my early twenties, I did not see the consequences of dick politics—only that I wanted to be around the men whom Fatima would call butchqueens, who now occupy binders in my memory and my field notes. They still speak to me from anthologies, chapbooks, films, and fevered memories.[12] Through watching how and to whom Atlanta Black (and) gay communities listened (or did not), I realized that Duncan's Amethyst tongue had been sharpened through sometimes striking stoned silence and needless exclusions.

Returning to that night at the 100 Gay Black Poets reading, Carlos Segura's poem "Classified," collected in the anthology, put middle-class (aspiring) "masc 4 masc" dick politics right on the line—way ahead of AOL chatrooms, Craigslist, and innumerable apps that glibly provide headlines that anticipate the inevitable question "What (whom) do you like/what (whom) are you into?" In my mind I can still hear Carlos reading. He starts out seductive and romantic: "wanted: a man / to hold me / during thunderstorms / so I won't shiver anymore / fuck / through blizzards / so I could keep warm. . . ." I remember the place went up when he delivered the next stanza at the standing-room-only reading: "white men need not apply." Then Black mask romance turns again here: "knowledge of snap-finger theories /

girlfriend language / or cha-cha queenologies / need not apply." Essentially, "no femmes." As if writing the 2009 Morehouse College Appropriate Dress policy to come some twenty years in the future, a perfect storm of Black bourgeois anxieties that made "women's clothing and accessories," sagging jeans, and grills each verboten and imagined as of a piece, the sexy Black gay Dominican poet from Brooklyn pushed further: "philosophies of / be-bopism / dick holdism / or home boy talkism / not required. . . ." Note, "not required," but this poetic erotic job advert suggests that, unlike the white boy or the femme, a dick-holding homeboy is already trainable for employment in Black gay romance (coming with something extra). Homeboy to Black Boho Homo. We went up! Hollered laughed clapped cheered—and some certainly also snapped. However, there is an ethical—that is *political*—danger in this pleasure that I did not recognize at the time. It is hard to hear the wisdom of the accented diva over the deafening rhythm of one's own masked blood beat.

This author is unashamed of his desire for and to become Joe or Cary or Len or Maurice . . . (or Melvin, if I had been paying attention). Still, we must question both the presumption of butchqueen leadership of "the movement" and how masculinity moves us. To where? Why do the intimately entangled class, gender, and sexual desires that form our choices and aspirations so often also reinscribe pre-scripted exclusions that make our folks more vulnerable? Today, we demand more honesty and forthrightness of our critical activist-intellectual project(s). There is work to do that may be less sanguine, romantic, and nostalgic: to undo what has been riddled with poor or no translation, spatial displacement, missed opportunities, and regret. Dwight McBride has already wisely cautioned us that "it is the narrowness of the vision for what is constitutive of . . . community that is most problematic. . . . 'Community,' regardless of the modifier which precedes it, is always a term in danger of presuming too much."[13] This is well taken.

You will not be surprised, dear reader, that Essex had already theorized some of the contradictions and complexities of dick politics in poems such as "Family Jewels," his epic "Heavy Breathing," and perhaps most directly and complexly implicating the speaker/himself and all of us caught in the "irresistible" allure of complex contradictory Black masculinity: his stunning "Black Machismo." Here, Essex begins with one already-faceted aspect of debilitating dick politics:

> Metaphorically speaking
> his black dick is so big

when it stands up erect
it silences
the sound of his voice.
It obscures his view
of the territory, his history,
the cosmology of his identity
is rendered invisible.[14]

Here the metaphorical mass of "his black dick"—the legend and stereotype and promise of putatively excessive Black masculinity—becomes a self-disabling appendage. It renders *him* silent and effectively blinds *him* (affectively blinds *us*). In the second stanza, Essex's speaker fares no better than the subject (him/his) of the poem. The drama of the flaccidity of "his big black dick"—now "a heavy, obtuse thing, / his balls and chains" is too disorienting and loud for the speaker. Of course, Black gay men may choose to identify as both the besotted/disappointed speaker and/or the disabled and larger than life him/his, who is expected to have no identity, history, or voice: "clattering, making / so much noise / I cannot hear him / Even if I want to listen."

"Even if I want to," others are inured to Black men's voicelessness and lack of subjecthood, even if he—we—were to suddenly be able to speak, the poem's speaker finds. Struck voiceless when erect/hard and drowned out by obtuse, clattering, noisome softness! Damn. Consciously not choosing the popular language of "emasculation" or pathology, Essex presents us with a complex and heartbreaking analysis of a masculinity, which in "Heavy Breathing" he describes as "rumpled"—"this threadbare . . . perpetual black suit / I have out grown."[15] This is to say, in short, that Essex's theoretically and ethnographically astute poetic observations light the way toward radically new Black masculinities. *How else*? How else could we imagine relationships between Black men, given the impossibility of "Black machismo" that Essex parses in this work (for just a moment holding in abeyance the profound conundrums that Black feminists had already vividly detailed regarding our relationships with Black women and children)? In "American Wedding," Essex's speaker says that "we need each other critically . . . I assume you will always / be a free man with a dream."[16] That is, the man-to-man (cock)ring exchange ceremony that Essex imagines in the poem requires and assumes "voice," "view," "identity," "history," and "visibility." Something other than impossible or pathological, the anthological generation of brothers imagined radical or revolutionary futures that they knew would be difficult (yes—*something else*). As Isaac Jackson first said in Other Countries'

Yemonja, "Being a Black man who loves . . . Black men is a radical statement in these United States in 1981."[17]

Butchqueen, Listen!

What happens when we attempt to re-narrativize and reconceptualize those who, as another globally important diva of this era, Sylvester, said of himself, are not easily conceptualized *but are the very concept*?[18] Marvin K. White makes this plainer and more beautiful than I could, so hear this extended excerpt of his homily preached on the thirtieth anniversary of Sylvester's transition, arguing at the historic progressive Glide Memorial Church in San Francisco, where Marvin is minister, for Sylvester's beatification:

[1] In the beginning was the Queen, and the Queen was with God, and the Queen was God.

[2] Yes, "THAT" Queen. That same Queen was in the beginning with God, teaching God how to tuck and contour and nurse drinks and pass for a top.

[3] All things, all stunts, all costumes were made by him; and without him, without sequence, there would be no sequins, was not anything made that was made.

[4] In her we got our life; and the life was the spotlight on us.

. . .

[6] There was a Queen sent from God, whose name was Willi Ninja, was Tatiana, was named Carmen, was named Brandy Martell, was named Eddie, was named Peter, was named

. . .

[10] This Queen was in the world, and the world was made by her, accessorized by her, and the world knew her not. But she was not having it!

[11] She came into her own, and her own received her not.

[12] But as many as received him, to them gave she power to become the sons and daughters, the queer and the questioning, the trans and the bisexual, the A-sexual and the Gender Non-Conforming Children of God, even to them that believe on her name:

[13] Which were born, not of blood, nor of the will of the flesh, nor of the will of Queens, but of God.

[14] And the Queen was made flesh, and dwelt among us, and dwells among us (and we beheld her glory, the glory as of the only begotten of the Mother of the Disco, Sylvester), full of grace and truth.

Amen[19]

There are precious few voices of or reflections on gender-non-conforming (GNC) or trans existence in the most widely circulated of Black gay works of the long 1980s. It is not likely that Audre, Essex, Joe, Marlon, Pat, *and them* appreciated the distinctions of gender performance and identity in the more sophisticated ways that circulate today thanks to the self-advocacy of trans and GNC folks.[20] In fact, one senses negative tension, especially in some lesbian feminist work. Before moving on to think more specifically about Assotto and his depiction of Marsha P. Johnson, I want to briefly mark the appearance of two silent GNC Black folks in Marlon Riggs's film *Tongues Untied*. The film does not reveal how (or whether) they identify their genders, and we will sit with this silence here. They may have presented or described themselves variously and contingently as transsexuals, drag queens, cross-dressers, transvestites, transgender, or simply as a woman or a man with a difference they prefer not to parse. All of these ways of describing gender identity or rejecting gender were defined at the time within the larger category of gay. Although silent, the fact that they are represented with resonance at a pivotal transition of the narrative—not played for a laugh or outrageous quip—is significant and worthy of consideration. You will of course recall that in the film, Marlon (the speaker, or the filmmaker's *biomythographic* avatar I will call "Marlon") narrates his move to Hephzibah, where white folks' insults of "nigger go home" and "coon" give way to Black folk joining them in calling him "faggot," until all the epithets are interlocked, compounded, and repeated ad nauseam. This is followed by a vignette featuring a voice-over by Essex depicting a night of cruising turned to violent attack: "Summer full moon started with the rhetorical chant, 'hey faggot' (then ending) . . . in a bloody pool / he waited for the police, ambulance, the kindness of brethren, or Jesus, to pick up his messages." Separated by one beat from this "Black-on-Black violence," it is a white boy who shows Marlon kindness. Roberta Flack's voice dissolves in, singing "The first time ever I saw your face."[21] The blonde, blue-eyed boy's high school photo fades in, interrupting the black screen, and the curtain rises on the controversial interracial sex drama (to which we will attend later). The lyrical composition of *Tongues Untied* could have gone in various directions from here. Marlon could have chosen a number of vignettes that would have followed a more obvious trajectory toward the money shot that we know and love: his invocation of Joe's "Black men loving Black men is *the* revolutionary act." Instead, his choice was to pivot to a silent but visually powerful interstice. Remember that before announcing that he had "quit the Castro," Marlon's arresting direct address to the viewer was about images and exclusions: "In this great gay Mecca, I was an invisible . . . I had no shadow no substance no place no history no reflection. I was alien unseen unwanted." The next scene responds with shadows playing on the subject as they give summer-in-the-city beauty. Billie Holiday sings "Lover Man, Oh Where Can You Be." Poised in a headband, they quietly contemplate the park scene smoking a cigarette. Consider (the limits of) visibility, voice(lessness), and representation: the title of the film promised that *Tongues* would be *Untied*. There are no other sustained silent subjects in the film and no other places where women's voices (and two of among the most iconic of Black women's voices) take center stage. Fading in next, a woman dressed for evening saunters along Lake Mead in daylight. Essex makes multiple references in his poems and essays to cruising and carrying on in parks, in which one might *get their life* or get their life taken. This sort of meeting at "The Tomb of Sorrow" illustrates just as significant a place of gathering as the club. In fact, these hidden-in-plain-sight public spaces of parks, rambles, lakefronts, and piers were often (before gentrification) more easily accessible and democratic, demanding no monetary entry fee. These are the margins of the margins, where gender-non-conforming folk have more reliable access, although access does not make it safer. In *Tongues Untied*, Nina Simone sings "Black Is the Color of My True Love's Hair"[22] as they saunter, and Essex in voice-over recites his elegy for Star, who had been found shot to death in Washington, D.C., on January 8, 1982, at age twenty:

> Grief is not apparel
> Not like a dress, a wig
> Or my sister's high heeled shoes.
> It is darker than the man I love
> who in my fantasies comes for me
> in a silver, six-cylinder chariot.
> I walk the waterfront/curbsides
> In my sister's high-heeled shoes. . . .[23]

Assotto Saint pens a beautiful and ethnographically astute portrait of the travails of the sort of street life many trans women endure(d) in order to survive, in his "Miss Thing / for Marcia [*sic*] Johnson." The subject/protagonist is his friend and legendary activist model sex worker and revolutionary Marsha P. (Pay It No Mind) Johnson. Miss Thing (Marsha) is also a character in one of Assotto's plays, *Rising to the Love We Need*. The cofounder (with Sylvia Rivera) of Street Transvestite (now Transgender) Action Revolutionaries (STAR), Marsha was a founding member of the Gay Liberation Front, Gay Activists Alliance, and ACT-UP (AIDS Coalition to Unleash Power). The essay begins: "Had you been driving on the West Side Highway by 10th Street last Thursday, you would have seen Miss Thing turning it out at 4:00 a.m. . . ." In "Miss Thing," Assotto describes Marsha's creative makeshift wardrobe as "flawless" and "sexy," inspired by the pages of *Vogue*: "For an entire week, she had slaved over the outfit / the gold fringes & the paillettes were her own touch. . . ." Describing the process of premiering this fabulous outfit on the streets where Marsha hustled money for survival—"she had to support a silicone & hormone treatment / s.s.i. just wouldn't do / she was no queen made up for the night / drag was her life / 'honey,' she'd tell you, 'this shit's a trip!'"—Assotto affirms Marsha's drag as not merely for your entertainment any more than were Joe's chambray work shirt and quilted vest, or Melvin's black cashmere turtleneck. All drag. *Honey, this is a trip*, indeed. All gender is "dysphoric," from the jump. If not also appropriately dynamic, ambiguous, and *nonconforming* (perhaps amounting to "Pay It No Mind"), the end of Marsha's interview "Rapping with a Street Transvestite Revolutionary" gives some important and incisive clues about what pronouns or identifications Marsha might choose today (because commenters on social media sites continue to speculate): "Lots of times they'll tell me 'you're not a woman'! I say, 'I don't know what I am if I'm not a woman' . . . let me tell you something. You can either take it or leave it . . . if they take me, they got to take me as I want them to take me. . . . Because no woman gets paid after their job is done. If you're smart, you get the money first."[24]

There is plenty more to say about this rich and at the same time problematic collapse of womanhood with sex work here. Marsha is affirming her gender for herself and in the context of the occupation she was forced to choose, but also against extrinsic definitions of any kind—she says, "as I want them to take me." Moreover, she is signifying on the commoditization of femininity. The cheapening of it to something that can be traded for only enough money for a hot meal or a room for the evening. This therefore rhymes with the analysis of radical feminists and Marxist theorists, even as there seem to be little resonance on the surface (especially given today's encampments). Meditating on Marsha's words, I hear Black Arts performer Hattie Gossett's glorious café performance at the 1992 National Black Arts Festival in Atlanta: the "Pussy and Cash Suite." From my memory of that evening, her refrain was "it all comes down to pussy and cash." Perhaps to some also coarsely put, her incisive poetic and musical commentary, which today's City Girls, Meg tha Stallion, Cardi B, and others echo, is not alien to Marsha. The violent ambience described in Assotto's essay in which Miss Thing is a sort of street trans Everywoman is one in which violence is not merely a threat or possibility but is assured: coming from the police, and/or abusive or cheap or mean johns, and most reliably from symbolic violence of cisgender lesbians and gays who refuse to recognize them as kin. Of course, the most palpable sense in Assotto's piece is of an author writing about an adored friend and comrade. Assotto's overlooked long-form poem/essay conveys Marsha's resourcefulness and self-sufficiency as one with no band of allied-community support re-narrativizing, publishing, and advocating on her behalf (at that point). This despite Marsha having hurled beer bottles and attitude at the Stonewall Rebellion and serving queer communities since the 1970s. Today Marsha P. Johnson stands as a gleaming symbol—yet another icon—thanks in no small part to Tourmaline. We will turn to this later. But Marsha was also a flesh-and-blood sister whose reflection is not adequately represented in the Black lesbian and gay movement of the long 1980s despite her signal contributions. For example, as Tourmaline remarked, Marsha "laid out a really queer anti-assimilation freedom dream" in this interview:[25]

> We want to see all gay people have a chance, equal rights, as straight people have in America. We don't want to see gay people picked up on the streets for things like loitering or having sex or anything like that. . . . STAR is a very revolutionary group. We believe in picking up the gun, starting a revolution if necessary. Our main goal is to see gay people liberated and free and have equal rights that other people have in America. We'd like to see our gay brothers and sisters out of jail and on the streets again.
>   . . . I think if transvestites don't stand up for themselves, nobody else is going to stand up for transvestites. I guess a lot of transvestites know how to fight back anyway! I carry my wonder drug everywhere I go—a can of Mace. If they attack me, I'm going to attack them, with my bomb.
>   [Interviewer asks]: "Did you ever have to use it?"
>   [Marcia]: Not yet, but I'm patient.[26]

Assotto ends his poetic reflection this way: "she stared for a long time at her reflection in the water / the wind blew unkind / as she raised her head looking dead-ahead. she sang."[27] Marsha's body was found in the Hudson River off the West Village Piers on July 6, 1992. She was forty-six. Although the city ruled her death a suicide, friends maintain that Marsha was not suicidal and point to the long history of uninvestigated murders of Black and Latinx trans women. Assotto's haunting piece leaves this an open question, in any case turning the focus to his loving observations of the life she led. Although the "water blew unkind," Marsha continues, in this tribute, to sing and look unflinchingly ahead.

"Haunted by the Future". *Èske Ayisyen Rèn nan pale?*

Assotto Saint (née Yves François Lubin) and I were born on the same day—he eleven years my senior. Assotto seemed larger than life when I caught glimpses of him at poetry readings or on the street. A full-blown multidisciplinary artist diva, Assotto took up space in a fearsome way. Like the awesomeness of a burning bush, or the intensity of *aché* that makes one turn to the side, eyes bulging from the power.[28] A tall, lithe, powerfully built dancer, Assotto moved through space in a self-possessed way that only (someone I thought of as) a queen could. Perhaps it was in the Libra stars Assotto and I share that I could one day be that fierce? Still, I did not (dared not?) aspire to this.

There are (butch)queens—most of whom would bristle (at least) at the thought of being considered a queen at all—and then there are Queens. Those whose twirls leave errant glitter all over anyone fortunate enough to find themselves in casual proximity. Having left behind notions of passing—voluntarily, or as a matter of inevitability for their own safety—he or she or they cannot suffer fools or easily grant a compromise or pardon. For Black gay letters, the dominant presumption of an eccentric, "fabulous!" queen who decorates the margins of our archive but remains largely silent—even in the face of productivity that outstrips most of their contemporaries—must be accounted for if not falsified altogether. Perhaps more of a tired tactical heteropatriarchal habit than a particular strategy, the silencing of the queen (and masking of those who would be queen) nonetheless represents a tragic failure of imagination that we must now confront and reverse. In "Can the Queen Speak?," written at the emerging edge of Black queer studies, in 1998, Dwight exhorts: "As a community of scholars who are serious about political change, healing Black people, and speaking truth to Black people, we must begin the important process of undertaking a truly more inclusive vision of blackness (wherever we find it)." And "I mean this critique quite specifically," as Dwight did in his original passage.[29] Dwight's wise words take on new meaning—that is, *it hits different* today, after the recent emergence of Black trans scholarship, artistry, and activism. We are in an exciting moment in which the most visible and relevant popular cultural avatars of Black queer life are trans and/or non-gender-conforming. It is past time to confront our desires and fears.

I do not remember (and there are no journals to attest and, alas, no James with whom to confer), but I believe I must have been frightened. I believe many were awed by the Haitian diva and "impossible Black homosexual."[30] Today, our narratives are enervated by missing, partial, and poor readings of Assotto. Unlike Marlon and Essex and Joe, his icon is not burnished by the children's devoted caressing. It rather sparkles, sequined. His icon is a drapeau: a Voudun flag with flashes of color and light and dense meaning-filled veve whose signs may transport you to another time-space. Attending to Assotto also insists that we challenge presumption that our ethnicity and language should be uniform, despite the ways that Melvin had already showed that we, in Colin's words, "pervert / the language"—every language—to creative ends throughout the Black world.[31] Do we imagine the long-1980s cultural and political movement as strictly bound to the United States and Black gay restricted by Black United States nationality? The travel itineraries and transnational connections of many of the architects of the movement tell a different story: Audre's Barbadian (Bajan) and Grenadian heritage and extensive travel to Germany and the Caribbean; Joe's Bajan father; Colin wearing his Trinbagonian alterity as a purple velvet cape on Yale's Cross Campus green and his self-reported "too bright West Indian smugness";[32] Cary writing from West and Central Africa, and making connections between far-flung organizations and individuals; and Essex's travel to the United Kingdom and plan to live there are just a beginning.

"Haiti. A Memory Journey"

So, *what about Yves*: Assotto/Assoto, who described himself as at once the "Haitian Queen Diva" and "loud low life bitch," and bequeathed to himself the abbreviated patronym of the Haitian liberator (Tous*Saint*) and took a sacred Voudun drum (*tambou assoto*) as his first name—changing the spelling when he felt he needed an additional "t" as his own T cell count fell to nine? Assotto's autoethnographic essay "Haiti: A Memory Journey" was first published in the special "Heritage of Black Gay Pride" supplement of the biweekly gay and lesbian newspaper *New York Native* on March 3, 1986. The special supplement was edited by Craig G. Harris, a formidable Black gay AIDS activist, writer, editor, cofounder of Other Countries Black Gay Writers' Collective, and close friend of Yves/Assotto.[33] The supplement featured an introduction by Craig ("Lesbian and Gay Voices of the Diaspora") and essays by Robert Reid-Pharr (at the time "a twenty year old Black gay activist living and studying in Chapel Hill, North Carolina"), Anita Cornwell ("Portrait of the Artist as a Young Black Dyke"), Barbara Smith ("Working for Liberation and Having a Damn Good Time"), and, sharing the "Gay Life in Haiti and Africa" section with "Haiti: A Memory Journey," Cary Alan Johnson ("Inside Gay Africa"). Although the essay has been anthologized in Assotto's posthumously published *Spells of a Voodoo Doll* and in collections by prominent

Caribbean writers Thomas Glave and Edwidge Danticat, this full context of the original publication is not noted in any of these works.

This lack of background represents a significant loss of an opportunity to demonstrate the inextricable articulation of blackness, Haitian nationality, gay sexualities, and *dyaspora*. Moreover, in these works the essay is abridged by nearly half. Andia Augustin-Billy's rich description of the piece alerted me to the fact that what I had read in the collections was incomplete.[34] The editing—or redaction—of details of Yves's experience as a gay Haitian in *dyaspora* at this historical moment is unfortunate. Embodying half of what the US Centers for Disease Control (CDC) called the dreaded "four Hs" of putative AIDS risk (hemophiliacs, heroin addicts, Haitians, and homosexuals) in the early 1980s, Assotto was situated between the Scylla of direct effects of racialized US imperialism in Haiti and the Charybdis of its neocolonial reverberations in the belly of the beast. Instead of the deeper and complex truths the longer essay expresses and indexes, in the redacted essay the reader is left with a more-or-less pat story of *sexile*. I believe this was inadvertent. Editors certainly saw value in adding Assotto's unique powerful voice to these important anthologies, and we are grateful. Still, I note this extratextual story here because it calls the question of archival, editorial, and publishing authority. First, what "testimonies" and "legacies" are we looking for in archives and libraries, and toward what ends? Archival and narrative power combined is not only the power to save and categorize things but also to decide to whom one gives access and how to shape the "finding aids" of a life. What are the critical functions of the archivist, the curator, and the editor? You must know by now: these are archival questions we must answer (and to which we will soon turn in part 2). How do collectors, holders, and interpreters of archives relate to family members and executors who decide what stories of the dead may be told, and where? *What is between us?* How do we who are perhaps "lesser kin" remember those we are seeking? In any case, the unfortunate clipping of Assotto's fierce, prolific tongue makes me wonder, "*Èske larenn lan pèmèt yo pale?*" pace Dwight (and Gayatri Spivak): Can the Queen Diva speak, after all? Here we attempt to displace the abridgment of Assotto Saint's "Haiti: A Memory Journey" toward hearing and heeding *Larenn* (the Queen).

We like the image Assotto draws at the opening of the essay: "Early Friday morning, February 7, 1986, drinking champagne and watching Haitian President-for-life Jean-Claude Duvalier flee for his life," because it seems indicative of personal triumph—the ability to watch your enemy being vanquished as you sip champagne from afar. This seductive scene seems to make the end of an evil dynasty of dictators that abused and stole from the people of Haiti for some thirty years all the more delicious (alas, if not also ephemeral). The same Libra moon under which Yves François Lubin (Assotto) was born also dawned on the initial election of promising former Negritude writer, vodouisant, and physician turned notorious dictator François ("Papa Doc") Duvalier. Assotto's life in Haiti and flight from it were thus marked by the intergenerational US-supported dictatorships of both Papa Doc and his son, Jean-Claude (Baby Doc) Duvalier. But the road to the opening of this essay was not easy or unproblematic. And it was not the end of Assotto's engagement with his birthplace.

The first half of the essay requires more context and detail; otherwise, it simply reinscribes the North as the space of unproblematic freedom where the only adjustments to make are "snow, muggers, homesickness, alien cards," learning English, and some abstract notion obliquely referred to as "racism." Assotto is saying much more in the complete version of this important essay. The abridged "Haiti: A Memory Journey" concludes with Assotto discussing the details of his conception and the standoff that becomes his relationship not only to his father but also to Haiti: "Accusations were made and feelings hurt. Each one's decision final, they became enemies for life." To stop at this juncture of Assotto's bittersweet childhood memories of local privilege, sexual discovery, and contested paternity serves to privatize his family history and tell only a small part of a complexly layered story. Young Yves, who found comfort and purpose in Catholic pageantry and whose class and color privilege in Haiti and the Haitian dyaspora structured a more relatively protected life for him than most other *masisi*, thus had a difficult decision to make: whether to leave the comfort of his home in Les Cayes, with his prominent grandfather and aunt, or join his single working mother who had recently left a job in Switzerland and moved to Queens, New York. His depiction of the moment of childhood decision is cinematic. At the end of his first visit to his mother, while riding the subway to Coney Island "two effeminate guys in outrageous shorts walked onto the train and sat in front of us . . . my mother said this was the way it was here. People could say and do whatever they wanted; a few weeks earlier thousands of homosexuals had marched for their rights."[35] To be sure, young Yves's migration to the United States brings up dramatic contrasts between the menacing rise of Papa Doc in Haiti and the liberties of 1970 New York City. Like many bi, lesbian, trans, and/or gay immigrants from nonurban places such as Les Cayes in the global South who travel to the urban global North, there are certainly elements of sexile in Assotto's story. This might have been different if he had migrated from more densely urban Port-au-Prince. The slightly expanded opportunity for privacy and perhaps anonymity in the (northern or southern) metropolis can also lead to the creation of new communities and affinities. At the outset of the *New York Native* essay, Assotto had admitted that "for years now, Haiti has not been a home but a cause to me. . . . Many of my passions are still there." But the first half of the abridged anthologized essay can only locate those passions in a hazy romance. The second half speaks more directly to this passion and desire, which frames the essay and its politics:

> Having seen, so many times during this AIDS crisis, Haitian doctors, and community leaders deny the existence of homosexuality in Haiti . . . I am duty-bound to come out and speak up for the thousands of Haitians like me, gay and not hustlers, who, for one reason or another, struggle with silence and anonymity yet don't view ourselves as victims. . . . *Haunted by the future,* I'm desperate to bear witness and settle accounts. These are trying times. These are times of need.[36]

The second half of the essay opens with Assotto/Yves arranging a meeting with his father and traveling to Haiti, where he attempts to reconcile his relationships with his father and his fatherland amid suspicion, fear, deep love, and longing (which appears largely unrequited). He writes that "I went to discover some meaning and understanding of myself, my mother, him, I went out of hunger and wonder. I went to break new ground." A part of the "new ground" the author hoped for was a renewed and informed relationship with his homeland and its people. Assotto admits that in the past, "I did my best to distance myself from the homophobic Haitian community in New York . . . bury painful emotions in my accumulated memories of childhood." After all, it was not just his sexuality that had caused the rift between him and the middle-class and middle-class-aspiring Haitian communities in New York. At first, Yves François Lubin had been a dutiful adherent to the preferred new immigrant script: from Jamaica High School in Queens to the premed track at the City University of New York's Queens College, which has ushered tens of thousands of Black and brown immigrants into medical professions. But it was his love for and talent in art—dancing professionally with the renowned Martha Graham Dance Company and immersing himself in music and literature—that shaped a life in which artistic expression became his medicine. Throughout many years of writing and performing, Yves/Assotto also maintained long-term employment with Health and Hospitals Corporation of New York, until the final weeks of the life of his lover, Jan.

US citizenship is not the ultimate goal of all immigrants to the United States. After living in the country as an "alien" for many years, in the original essay Assotto says he decided "last summer, after traveling to Greece . . . to become a US citizen." Assotto took this decision to become a US citizen not to add his colors to the "beautiful mosaic" or to dissolve into a "melting pot" of assimilated red, white, blue, and beige, but "decided to become an American citizen because I could then speak out, lobby legislation, vote, and open American eyes to what their government is doing in Haiti." He dispenses with the usual effusive thanks to the United States for being the "only place in the world" where he could be "free" to pursue his "dreams." Acknowledging the United States as "the symbol of democracy," he uses this moment in the essay and in his writing life to critique the United States' long-standing support of "dictators like Somoza, Duvalier and Marcos, and [its] prevent[ing] other democracies from establishing themselves." It must be noted here that a number of activists had engaged (and continue to engage) in HIV/AIDS activism and Black gay activism despite their status of being alternatively documented or undocumented/out of visa. Assotto's situation was acutely affected by the peculiar status of Haiti as a perennial target of the US Immigration and Naturalization Service. He would have been aware, of course, of the regular extralegal internment of Haitian refugees at the Krome Detention Center in South Florida.

The *New York Times* called Krome "an isolated stockade deep inside the Everglades." Today it is still essentially a jail for immigrants, administered by US Immigration and Customs Enforcement (ICE). In 1981 Ronald Reagan intensified anti-Haitian US immigration policy by ordering the interdiction of boats carrying Haitian passengers. For the next ten years, Coast Guard ships returned any seized boat carrying Haitian refugees to Port-au-Prince, flouting time-honored international human rights conventions.[37] McAllen Detention Center, in Puerto Rico, also began operating in 1981, detaining Haitian refugees. By 1983, the Reagan administration had composed its "Mass Immigration Emergency Plan," requiring that ten thousand immigration detention beds be located and ready for use at any given time. Then and now, Haitians are reliably denied asylum without a hearing and held without criminal charges being brought. Fleeing the politically motivated brutality of the *tonton macoute* (the Duvaliers' murderous police force), the ambient politically motivated violence that the Duvaliers sowed, and deep material privation, Haitians were nonetheless often summarily ruled as "economic" migrants by the former Immigration and Naturalization Service, not political escapees worthy of refuge. This is controversial in international human rights law, and a glaring contrast to the "dry foot" preferred immigration policy that has been accorded Cuban refugees. Cuban immigrants literally need only arrive on dry land—that is, make it to sandy ground or a pier in the United States or its territories—to be welcomed and processed, prima facie, as political refugees on the road to citizenship. Of course, the mass-exodus Mariel boatlift—markedly the first mass influx of poor Cubans, many of whom were Black—challenged the warm triumphal affect of this welcome policy of the US state and the US Cuban "exile" community.

Assotto's drapeau—his flag and icon—therefore constitutes a transnational call to arms. Arms to tightly embrace his homeland. Nèg Mawon (the "Unknown Maroon") sounding the conch! In the unabridged "Haiti: A Memory Journey" we also see echoes of the great Haitian poet Moriso (Félix Morisseau-Leroy), who championed Haitian Kreyol as a language for the entire country (not just spoken by those locked out of French-only education) and as an expressive tool for literature in a "sincere Haitian tongue."[38] Assotto's pride and implicit Haitian exceptionalism (as the first/only free Black republic in the hemisphere) are reflected in Moriso's famous poem "Mèsi papa Desalín," a paean to the formerly enslaved revolutionary who became the first leader of the new independent Haitian nation, Jean-Jacque Dessaline (Jan Jak Desalin, in Kreyol). Feel the resonance with the revolutionary refusals of Black gay cultural production, articulating the personal and political import of radical negativity. That is, "hell no" to white supremacist interpellation and "hell no" to self-alienation. The attributes adopted by radical Black feminists are part and parcel of a long, deep, and wide inheritance held throughout the Black world:

> Thank you, Dessalines
> Father Dessalines, thank you
> . . .
> It is you who taught us to say: NO
> . . .
> Some Negroes try to explain
> That today does not resemble yesterday
> And that now,
> Human fraternity,
> Humanity, civilization,
> All that is gibberish!
>
> All I know is Dessalines!
> I say: Thank you, dear father
> . . . .[39]

The personal reportage in Assotto's essay—from the description of his father and himself as "carbon copies" their dramatic confrontation, and his calculations and insights—is not only remarkable in content but also in context. To Assotto, life in his hometown, Les Cayes, had stood still for the most part: "The roads were in better shape, but the mentality and the routine hadn't changed much." This is a common (mis)perception of the returning emigrant who at once longs for signs of progress from their own point of view but desires a recognizable "home" to which they can return. He looked for his childhood friend Pierre, near the surf of Les Cayes that held the secret of their mutual sexual initiation. Assotto wondered what became of him: whether he was gay, whether he had migrated to Port-au-Prince or abroad, and whether Pierre remembered him. The personal dramas of Assotto's visit also parallel the tumultuous political moment in Haiti. The confluence of the two shape his perspective and new commitments. After sharing the fact that he is gay with his father (Dr. Mercier), Assotto reports "pandemonium. Tears flowed . . . he said that my gayness was God's punishment upon him. . . ." Dr. Mercier's well-earned suspicion of white foreigners "didn't register until later," Assotto said, referring to his father's "tirade about how foreigners should stay out of Haiti, how Americans had ruined the country and given it a bad name." Perhaps Dr. Mercier mistook Assotto's European lover, Jan, for an American. However, it was the thinly veiled homophobic comment after an altercation between Jan and Dr. Mercier that caused Assotto to bodily throw his father out of the room: "He told me with friends like Jan, he wondered what kind of person I was." Later, after another attempt at reconciliation on his part, Assotto reports receiving a terse, formal note in lieu of a second visit from his father. Rejected again, after a lifetime of his father's abandonment, Assotto writes: "I crushed that note in my hand and imagined it was his heart."[40]

The 1985 referendum vote on whether Baby Doc Duvalier should become president-for-life (as his father and a few other US-puppet presidents had been in the past) "finalized my decision [to become an American citizen]." He certainly would have known that this so-called election and result of 99 percent in favor were fraudulent. Still, he writes that he was "saddened that so few had dared to say no, including my own family, who should have known better, having travelled abroad. . . ." He says that he "gave up on [his] people . . . gave up on Haiti," until they rose up to oust Baby Doc six months later. Then, as if to prevent the people of Haiti from seizing the spotlight in his story, Assotto reports: "I tore up my application for US citizenship, which I had neglected to mail." Now in a "hurricane of thoughts, a storm of patriotic emotions," he promised that "I will go back and vote in that presidential election. For the first time, I will cast my ballot with renewed pride, I will go back for at least a year or two to help and rebuild Haiti. Jan understands my commitment. My closet door is open too wide for me to contemplate staying in. So, I will go back as an openly gay man, and attempt, once again, to make peace with my father."[41] The pull of nation and family is strong. I hear Moriso: "Some Negroes try to explain / that today does not resemble yesterday. . . . Thank you, dear father."[42]

You may dismiss Assotto's dramatic flourish of a promise to return to Haiti in the wake of Baby Doc's overthrow as the naive pronouncement of an immigrant in the grips of heady nostalgia, or momentary jubilation at another of Haiti's successful people's revolutions, if you like. However, I see this as just as profoundly held and sincere a desire as Essex had expressed about his own community: "I *am* coming home. There is no place else to go that will be worth so much effort and love."[43] If Assotto had survived, we can see him returning to Haiti, as Colin did to Trinidad and Tobago, where he serves and leads with skills sharpened working in HIV prevention and the arts in the United States. He too could have forged a transnational life and practice as a number of other artists, intellectuals, activists, and entrepreneurs have done. While Essex's address "I am coming home" is to mothers, Assotto's father and the fatherland find confluence here again. At the end of the essay that references Assotto's birth name for easy identification with his family, as well as the name he gave himself, Yves/Assotto seems to at once issue a nationalistic call to arms (to enfold the nation) and a personal message to his father. Remixing Essex's promise and plea to "return home" to the Black community before there is no home left after the ravages of violence, drugs, and HIV, and beautifully recasting uninformed narratives of the Caribbean as the *most* homophobic place on Earth, Assotto promises that "our gayness is not a burden, but a blessing."[44] He understands how homophobia and AIDSphobia were inherent in the rhetoric of activists who had worked to expose Duvalier. Still, in this essay he is determined to return to help rebuild a democratic society. Jan, he says, "understands." Regrettably, we do not hear of the experiences of any other LGBT folks in Haiti in this essay: those "thousands of Haitians like me, gay and not hustlers, who, for one reason or another, struggle with silence and anonymity yet don't view ourselves as victims" that Assotto has rhetorically invoked.[45] But, of course, this is not their narration. This is Assotto/Yves's story to tell. Was he aware, for example, of those in Haiti who had used their skin color, economic privilege, status, or shelter within the more accepting spaces of Voudun religion to shield them from the worst effects of homophobia at home—developing their own formulations of resistance or accommodation practices to avoid "victimization"? His "internationalist" call to those like himself in dyaspora is resonant with the work of emigrants whose regular barrels full of supplies and remittances also come with the understanding that they are helping to stave off disaster but may not be able to engage in the day-to-day life of "home."

The way this transnational Black (and) gay counterpoise works is that there are no elegant transitions between strolling the piers, frolicking in the surf of Les Cayes, fucking, making art, and dying. Each seemingly disparate scene or moment is as intimate as one breath to another. A flash/flicker. Or a change in drumbeat, as if we were communing with the *lwa* of *Ginen* around a peristyle. Let us briefly consider that the coffins that piled up among and alongside that long-1980s generation were likewise borne on their shoulders and through their words. Assotto attending to the epidemic dead and the political contexts of the response-able living is legendary: he stages then poetically journals this famous scene at Donald Woods's funeral, in which he explicitly challenged the sanitized version of the brilliant poet and arts administrator being funeralized, while understanding the layers of complexity of the moment in which the community resolves:

> to stand up together to a bewildered father needing a stiff drink
> as he comes to grips with his son's faggotry
> to stand together to a desperate mother who must safely deliver
> to paradise her baby closeted in a Pandora's box coffin[46]

These were "the same imperatives of mourning, of reanimating the queer dead, that AIDS political funerals carried out in the streets . . . (against posthumous disposal of queer life)," Dagmawi tells us.[47] Assotto's lover, Jan, died in March 1993—a few weeks before the historic 1993 LGBTQ March on Washington. In his obituaries, contribution to the Names Project, and participation in direct action in Washington, Assotto reanimated their fleshy reality—not only as lovers, but as taxpayers to a system that had ignored their dying and deaths. In his poem "The March on Washington" Assotto wrote this:

> from championing
> those dying
> of a virus
> our government
> neglects . . . wishfully thinking

we've finally
"arrived" in a town
of backstabbers
even on blinding days
of sunshine.

Marlon Ross observes that in his tributes to and three-part obituary of his lover, Jan Holmgren, which he titled "No More Metaphors,"[48] Assotto "reduce[es] to triviality the calls for shame in his portrait of gay love ... [and], seek[ing] to reduce the slurs against interracial love, [composed] a beatific portrait of a Black gay man holding his dying white lover in his arms."

Halves of a Whole

In class, Troy has that look on his face. He and a few other undergraduates had been talking about this for hours after our previous class. Reading blog posts and think pieces. Arguing and gossiping and trying to wrap their heads around it. He asks (for the group): "So, Prof: what are we to make of the fact that Riggs and Dixon and Saint were all into white men, and Beam seems to not have had anyone? You said they were 'paradigm builders': "is 'Black men loving Black men' a fictional paradigm"? By his tone, Troy seemed also to mean *fraudulent* paradigm. Cary Alan Johnson had anticipated this in 1990, and Essex rose up and clapped back in Marlon's defense.[49] Crestfallen in my classroom, I took a breath. I explained that the context of Joseph Beam's essay and the conditions of his editorship of *In the Life* show that he was making a broader statement about a sort of communitarian love, *philia*, between Black men of every description, not necessarily about sexual or romantic coupling, and that Marlon Riggs reappropriates this *movida* ("Black men loving Black men") at the end of *Tongues Untied*. I had punted. The powerfully erotic structure of feeling of this work speaks for itself. Sexual and romantic love is at the center of it, and Ketlie excitedly reminded me that "Eros is still all over it!" She is dubious, and it strikes me that my unwillingness to go where these students need me to go with them not only undermines my authority in this classroom but also more importantly threatens our precious intellectual intimacy. I could have told them, "Stay out of grown dead people's business—it's rude." I could have said, "Love is love." I might have said that published works cannot cover the entirety of one's erotic history and desires, that archives go only a few steps further, and that full accounts are rare. My pedagogy could have leaned old-school literary: just focus on the works themselves (but these students are being close critical readers—deeply engaged, they are searching for motivations beyond those readily apparent, even looking *under the author's clothes*). I could wax academic about the artist's prerogative to not completely identify with their speaker, or especially how the personal freedoms of the individual artist must not be wholly defined by the community. Each of these may be correct in a way, and in the past I may have taken every one of these convenient truisms as an "out." Still, I would never insult their intelligence or hurt their tender hearts by admonishing them for "nationalism" or "essentialist thinking" or "identitarian sexual politics." Troy really wants to know how his heroes could have, at once, skillfully exalted a mirror image of him—promising love, sex, loyalty, and revolution wrapped in rhythmic meter, but also live-and-die realities that Troy feels would have excluded him. Of course, at the same time, Troy is thinking about the person he likes—or would like, if they would at least return his gaze when they see each other at the library, in front of Af-Am, or passing on Crown Street, where they temporarily blend into the mass of other Black and brown folks in New Haven. Ketlie "comforts" him: "Dr. Allen, you asked us to meditate on erotic subjectivity." [*She turns to Troy*] "I feel you. As a straight cis Black woman. . . . Yale is . . . training me for the professional world where I will most likely not be seen." Again. "I don't know," she says. "We have to focus on other things."

If it is discussed at all, we usually talk about sexual partner choice as if it is only about deep psychological motivation—self-love versus self-hate—or concrete political identification: cosmopolitan versus narrowly nationalistic, interracialist versus Afrocentric, as if any of this really was this simple. Here, "I am asking the question, not answering it."[50] Others hold that these questions are beside the point—arguing that the only important thing is unreservedly loving whomever one *happens to* love and desiring whomever one desires with no guilt or recrimination—or reflection. But then there is that spyglass of social inquiry that critical intellectuals claim, that problematizes "happens-to" propositions and that which we think of as *just so*, "natural," or common sense. It troubles our neat suppositions and concrete positions, and insists that our choices are fair game for conversation. Here the anthropological spyglass is not a disciplining panopticon. These notes must not be mistaken for either a blotter or a ledger. Rather, they are a collage attempting to show patterns and outlines by aggregating experiences and texts. We have questions (that we seem to avoid, except in the shadiest or messiest ways). Why folks care who chooses or ends up with whom is a legitimate question and one that warrants careful attention. Are we not of interest enough to one another to wonder, really, how our most intimate choices relate to our politics? Can we listen past our assumptions toward a truer politics—or questions that will get us further along?

Of the serious reflections on Black men, "white dick," "marketplaces," "snow queens," and "dinge," the best of these—by Darieck (Scott), Dwight (McBride), and Robert (Reid-Pharr)—do not capitulate or cop out with notions of "natural" or "neutral" common sense, or the suggestion that "love is love," or that any questioning of (interracial) desire is therefore pathologizing.[51] This would be as unacceptable as shaming individuals for their consensual romantic, sexual, and partnership choices. Darieck has troubled the facile supposition of the "utopic Black gay bedroom," and Robert has shifted our understanding of how primary recognition of Black beauty and desirability might reshape the discourse by recasting the pejorative "dinge."[52] Dwight recasts this in terms of a marketplace situated within a "white man's world." Here we follow each, *a ways*, in conversation with others, and offer a retrospective meditation on Gary Fisher. Another invested re-narrativization is overdue—especially for Troy and Ketlie, and for all of us who still have questions. We must confront and reconsider how we reckon availability and appropriateness, and how partner choice can be viewed as another effect (affect) of ambient cultural understandings—for example, of what and who is beautiful and valuable and desirable for what (and whose) purposes. You can certainly tell, dear reader: I am attempting to (too) cautiously navigate these "dingy" waters. At a similar place in his collection of essays *Why I Hate Abercrombie and Fitch*, Dwight confides that for him "in many ways this is the most difficult chapter of this book to write. . . . It means articulating painful lessons learned about your value—or lack thereof—in the dominant logics that fuel that same marketplace. . . . I come not to this work as a fearless explorer, outfitted to take on the rough, uncharted terrain of which I speak."[53]

Assotto's blunt words may provide a perverse *ruttier* that can be followed to help us ride the swells more directly. Assotto talked about his interracial relationship more often and more forthrightly—in first person, autoethnographically, as well as "bio-mythographically," to follow Audre's *Zami*—than any of the other shapers of Black gay cultural arts.[54] Others created flawless literary records of Black men loving Black men exclusively, while silent about what was actually happening in their bedrooms (piers, parks, backrooms, saunas . . .). This is also likely one of the reasons he is often forgotten among them. In this excerpt we confront a more complex lived experience than simplistic name calling and division into camps would allow. Offering "no justification" of his interracial (and intergenerational and international) relationship in his "The Impossible Black Homosexual (or Fifty Ways to Become One)," here the speaker (whom we can fairly name "Assotto") provides, in third person, an (auto)ethnographic inventory of formative daily realities, in ways thirty-one through thirty-five:

> the one with the white lover whom he met in a backroom bar
> white lover twenty years his senior
> white lover he's lived with for over a decade
> the one who in the midst of this crisis
> still celebrates vicious officious cocks
> the one who yells at his white tricks
> "i'm gonna fuck you with this big black dick"
> the one who yells at his black tricks
> "yeah, fuck me with that big black dick"
> the one who even after extended one-night stands
> always crawls back to his nuclear lovers' nest
> in Chelsea[55]

There is much to explicate and unpack in "The Impossible Black Homosexual." Let us consider only two, for now: the narration of raced sexual division of labor between "Black tricks" and "white tricks" and the resolution of the drama: his return to the "nuclear lovers' nest / in Chelsea," where, offstage, the white lover twenty years his senior whom he has loved for more than a decade is presumably waiting. Assotto leaves old tropes of Black rapaciousness and the irresistible BBD (big black dick) firmly in place here—topping the white ones and bottoming with Black tricks. We are not told what the speaker's tricks yell, if anything—this is not their poem. Nor is it his white lover's story to tell. The clarity and directness of the litany—and recipe, as it is also a "how to"!—requires us to merely sit with and witness the desires and antics of "The Impossible Black Homosexual." Likewise in Adrian Stanford's poem "Yeah, Baby" in his remarkable 1977 book of poetry—which as far as I can surmise is the first time *Black* and *Queer* show up together in a title of a publication—the speaker does not elicit our opinions. Beyond the quality and verve of his work (his beautiful and taut "In the Darkness, Fuck Me Now!," anthologized in *In the Life*, is among my favorites in that exceptional volume), we do not yet know much about Adrian, who is among the earliest out Black gay writers to publish a poetry chapbook with these themes. His "Yeah, Baby," which reminds one of Robert's "Dinge" in both its insistence on training our attention to Black beauty and agency, and its humor, bears full rendering here:

yeah baby

i've had them roll up in chauffeured limousines
swing open the door and beg "please get in" .

i've been approached, followed, waited for, hung onto,
and groped by all those staid white queens that
don't like *colored* boys.

and certain nigger fags (who don't want nothin' but blonde
hair around the cocks they suck), have more than once pushed
their fat asses my way !

you think all this has gone to my head; made me some kind
of valentino—lena horne queen bitch ? (yeah baby !)[56]

Pushing the matter further, here is Assotto carefully explaining his "personal choice" to use "Gay Black" in the title of his landmark *The Road before Us: 100 Gay Black Poets*, rather than "Black Gay":

I have never labeled myself either Afrocentrist or interracialist. From reading or seeing my theater pieces, many might characterize me as an Afrocentrist; but others might immediately characterize me as an interracialist because I have loved and lived with a white man for the past eleven years. Although I make no excuses or apologies for the racially bold statements in my writings, I also owe no one any justification of my "till-death-do-us-part" interracial relationship. . . . "Who are gay blacks and black gays? Halves of a whole. Brothers."[57]

As if responding directly to Assotto, Cary (Alan Johnson) reveals a conundrum that it seems we are still working through today, perhaps less explicitly in literature (although this is a constant conversation on social media, for example). Talking to Kevin (McGruder) about the organization of the Other Countries Collective, but also more broadly about the scene of Black gay cultural production in the long 1980s, Cary says that "there were definitely two camps. Those of us who were doing Black identified, Black lovers, Black, Black, Black. And those of us who were more identified in the white gay community. And there were a few in the middle, like Fred [Carl]. We were all struggling with the issue, not terribly tolerant of the other point of view, trying to figure out what being Black and gay and self-aware meant in the eighties."[58]

That this issue was such a central part of the discourse warrants our current retrospective "trying to figure out what being Black and gay and self-aware meant in the eighties." Let us follow Darieck a bit, in a shift from pathologizing "snow queens," and in his view, uncritically celebrating what he cheekily calls "the utopian Black bedroom," toward honest conversation. Cary's phrase here goes directly to some of the tensions. Perhaps "more *identified* in the white gay community" is less helpful than we would like. It smacks of the presumption of knowing where someone's deep "identification" lies or whether *gay* modifies *Black* or *Black* modifies *gay* in the grammatical hierarchy. At the same time, we must also make a critical shift that I have not seen foregrounded in the handful of serious commentaries on this nettlesome multipronged question of who's fucking whom (and why do we care anyway). Here I insist that the "doing a Black identified, Black lovers, Black, Black, Black" formulation and feeling be taken seriously—rather than dismiss those who celebrate or participate in endogamous Black male sexual and romantic relationships as unsophisticated nationalist Afrocentrics taken in by "essentialist" or slippery identity politics. Sincerity requires, or at least works best with, reciprocity. It has become conventional to uncritically pose folks referred to in the long-1980s literature as "Afrocentrists" (putatively as opposed to "interracialists") as big bad kente-cloth–wearing blackness police who indict and silence the set-upon cosmopolitan queers who have bravely dared to step outside of racialist thinking and racial boundaries to find love. This liberal assumption is not only ubiquitous but also lazy and dangerous. To be sure, the summary dismissal is itself a dangerous example of antiblackness. Consider suspending the articles of faith of (neo)liberal intellectual discourse to think about whether the debate and everyday practices among Black transgender queer bisexual lesbian and gay scholars and cultural workers may have shifted in thirty-plus years.[59] Consider a new sort of abolition: no identity police and discursive political imprisonment, just (perhaps difficult) sincere family conversations.

Economies of Racial Desire

Black British filmmaker and avowed "snow queen" Isaac Julien agreed—but in a very different register—with my students, and Cary, that Marlon Riggs's representations of desire in his films throw up a contradiction. Though astutely qualifying his statement with the observation that "the economy of racial desire is [not] always fixed," Isaac correctly cites what Troy noticed as one of the "unspoken economies of inter-racial desire at work in the signifying practices of gay cultural production . . . that these Black artists have all been 'snow queens.'"[60] Isaac averred that Marlon's (and others') reticence to discuss interracial relationships and show this in his work made him and others prime targets for gossip and charges of charlatanism. Isaac felt doubly stigmatized because other Black gay men with white lovers seemed to be publicly closeted. He told Bruce (Morrow):

> [Marlon] was a filmmaker whom I greatly admired, even though we had our differences. Some people would say it was like being with two divas, our meeting. Marlon "read" everybody—including me. I think our differences pivoted around questions of interracial relationships as he would go on to visually portray them. I felt at times quite lonely in terms of being what I would call a proud "out" snow queen. But we did share quite a lot of things—anger being one of them—at the indifference we face as Black gay men.[61]

Recalling the dreamy fade-in of Marlon's white boy savior/curse, Isaac confides to Bruce: "I have always been disappointed that this representation of interracial desire was then undermined by the tape's Afrocentric gay ending, reinforced by one's 'extra-filmic' knowledge of Riggs's longtime relationship with a white boyfriend. . . . Opposed to that, I am insisting, against any such readings or representations, on the fact of inter-racial desire, its very transgression of racial boundaries."[62]

But do interracial desire and relationships necessarily and exclusively "transgress" racial boundaries? I think not. We can certainly also think of examples in which interracial desire and relationships may reify or celebrate or rigidify roles, stereotypes, and boundaries, if we pause long enough to trouble "romantic" assumptions of interracialism as always progressive. Another question: for whose pleasure or benefit are the boundaries transgressed, and what are the relative costs and benefits? This is not to say that one should measure the worth of their relationship (or lack of one) against a standard of whether or not or how it is transgressive. This is a losing proposition. What good does labeling one mode (or "camp") as transgressive and the other as "undermin[ing]," unsophisticated, and anachronistic do? "Afrocentric readings" certainly did not invent "pathologized racial identities" and have no power to "reverse racism" by saying *no, thank you* to (a) white lover(s). One need not "active[ly] avoid the psychic reality of black white desire"[63] to engage what Cary called a "Black Black Black" sensibility and sexual dance card. Recalling the effective (but also perhaps unimaginative) GMAD chant— "We're Black! Black! Black! Black!; Gay! Gay! Gay! Gay! We Won't Have It No Other Way!"—"Black Black Black" communicates a joyful excess. "All Black everything," the young people say today (do they still?): "Blackity Black."

Moreover, desires are not necessarily static. Are we to assume that although sexuality and gender are understood to be fluid, being an "interracialist" or "Afrocentric" is etched in stone? Or that Black or white are the only options on offer! Desire is certainly also educated by sociocultural and political-economic forces. For example, briefly reconsider millennial Neil's quip: "White? Check! Alive? Check!" as his assessment of the disparate standards of hooking up, dating, and partnering in his community of young queer professionals, artists, and academics of color. After I had encouraged him to find and employ a bit of an arm's length *sociological remove*, for the sake of his heart and self-esteem, regarding Black men who avert his gaze, Neil posed this question to me in a more recent text: "Do Black people in the academy who have white partners realize the ubiquity of interracialism in this profession? Or do they find the fact that everyone has a white wife/husband unremarkable? Like maybe they don't even notice. It's a little outrageous to me (see how I had to assign value to it while pointing it out?).... And my peers are training to fit right in...."

Isaac's queries and challenge to Marlon push us to reconsider a rich diversity of perspectives and experiences between us. Let us reflect on a few that have not been aired. If, as Isaac avers, we are all snow queens or, more precisely, "we have all grown up as snow queens," we are all caught (regardless of gender or race or class) in the thrall of white supremacy and racialized patriarchy—many of us born and raised in its crucible and all of us subject to its imperial logics. In that case, shouldn't racial capitalism also emerge as a lens through which we ask who among us loves fucks marries dates covets white partners/tricks/lovers or spouses?[64] Thinking anthropologically—that is, about how the sociocultural and political-economic puzzle pieces fit together within white racist heteropatriarchy—access emerges as an important driver. And not only access to the kindest or most adoring ("vicious" or "officious") lovers, partners, or sexual playmates, those with the best bodies or best minds or best hearts. But also access to this board and that foundation. To restoring some color correction to the departmental potluck. Perhaps also access to assuaged fears of neighbors and colleagues that you are not *that* different and your tastes and politics and values are not *that* far away from their own. Whiteness has value: symbolic, material, and apparently also psychic. Dear reader, please take a breath. We are still in the realm of Darieck's insistence that we think through the discursive limits of "white dick and the utopian Black gay bedroom." Within white racist heteropatriarchal capitalism, interracial coupling looks like relative potential material advantage to Black folks with white partners. We can also turn to discursive or representational advantage within the cultural ambiance of anti-blackness. After all, taking Isaac's "we have all grown up as snow queens" seriously—and psychoanalytically—could also mean, after Fanon, that we all desire whiteness for and as ourselves. To crib Hortense Spillers's reconsideration of the foundational drama of US blackness, Black/white interracial coupling could therefore be imagined as the Black person's wish for a legitimate patronym. A white father with an agential political-economic phallus. A white mother—alma mater—whose ventrem may result in the sequitur of freedom? (Remember the law for enslaved people and other chattel—*partus sequitur ventrem* [offspring follow the condition of the mother]?) You may clutch pearls, or simply shrug, dear reader, and/but consider the sociocultural implications. I am still following Darieck here: his lucid argument dismantling the old Black nationalist sense of what Black men are doing with white dick is intriguing. I am presenting some educated political-economic and psychoanalytic conjecture for our conversation. And please note that I am, throughout this discussion, holding in abeyance the question of love and fleshy desire. Not because it does not matter. The way your blood beats matters in the most elemental way. I hold it in abeyance because the way yours goes is none of my business. Try to think of the personal only in the most critical way: *close* and/but at half an arm's length of ethnographic, or nonjudgmental, distance.

It would not have been difficult to walk my students through the sociological implications of Melvin's novel *Vanishing Rooms*. Young people beginning their romantic and sexual lives are keenly attuned to the prospective impacts of partner choice, and some of the key literary and cinematic characters referencing interracial romance are twentysomethings. Recall our earlier brief discussion of the novel. We may wonder, but need not parse, whether in beginning a relationship with Metro in college, Melvin's *Vanishing Rooms* protagonist, Jesse, was attempting to forget the silliness of the brothers and sisters of the Black Students Association who ridiculed Jesse's choice to be a dance major. They found him therefore *suspect*, as sophomoric youth often do. But this is important background. Moreover, there is no evidence that Jesse hated himself or (his) fine Black skin or (his) fine Black body(ies). What if Metro, his white southern lover, had not been killed by a mob of white thugs (driven by a murderous combination of racial and sexual self-hatred)? What would it mean for Jesse—the talented emerging Black dancer without resources or family connections to rarified and elite spaces—to travel in circles with Metro (that is, Jon-Michael Barthé, of the Louisiana Barthés) as opposed to another struggling talented Black dancer without resources or family connections to rarified and elite spaces (whom he begins seeing after Metro's death)? How might they be perceived? How would you, as the artistic director of this dance company or that theater production firm, rate their intelligence, training, "taste," "deportment," or even attractiveness, without an authorizing white imprimatur, mater, or patron? . . . Honestly, now. What might their material circumstances be? Deep breath. There is more. If we project the fictional couple into New York City putatively "after the AIDS crisis," we know what the materiality of their vulnerability to sexually transmitted diseases might look like. HIV vulnerability is one in two for Black men.[65] We are asking questions.

So here's something else to consider: what if the more radical or so-called transgression of racial boundaries is, in fact, the so-called Afrocentric or "Black Black Black" image and narrative that Marlon Riggs (and others) chose to portray and promote? Are works that depict interracialism more sophisticated or beautifully wrought simply by virtue of the inclusion of the reality of—that is, "insistence on"—interracial desire? After all, as I might have explained to Troy and them, we can all agree that the artist is under no particular indenture to represent the *truth* of their own lives. They often choose to invent or promote other worlds that communicate the truths they are bound to by their conscience and their muse—that is also to say, their politics—to create. Still, Isaac's challenge is interesting to think with. What work would an alternate director's cut of *Tongues Untied* (or *Black Is/Black Ain't*), in which Marlon explored this, have done? What a complex pivot it would have been, at the end of his short films "Anthem" and "Affirmation," to show supportive white lovers of one or two of the demonstrators walking home with the director or to a Black and White Men Together meeting? Cinema verité? One can clearly see how this might serve as an important personal affirmation or acknowledgment—an exhalation for those who have craved this recognition of their experience.[66] It would add another complex layer upon a number of those intersecting issues already dealt with in the works. What if Marlon had included his lover in his films? What iconicity would this recall or serve to upend?[67] Precisely what would be transgressed—why, and for whose purposes?

We are taking Isaac Julien's critique seriously here. Let us also briefly consider this short example of his important and influential image making. The auteur of the gorgeous lyrical meditation *Looking for Langston*, which became the first transnational Black gay cause célèbre when the estate of the Great Man of Black Letters refused to allow Isaac to use some of Hughes's poetry in the film, Isaac also made history with his *This Is Not an AIDS Advertisement* (1987)—in his own words, Britain's first "pro-sex advertisement for gay desires." He said he wanted to "make a less didactic tape as compared to ACT-UP's more vigilante tapes which came out during the mid-1980s. . . ." Painterly and impressionistic, like his films made for the big screen and more recently for museum installation, Isaac's televisual short film *This Is Not an AIDS Advertisement* begins in black and white, with excerpts of Simon Turner's score for the film *Caravaggio* complementing shots of gently moving water and a watery view of a Roman relief of a man—by his robe, a citizen— then a modern man, white. Next there is a gondola, then a shot of Isaac and the white man embracing cheek to cheek while holding a bouquet of flowers together, gesturing toward/offering it to the viewer. The repeated shot of water broadens, and we recognize the Grand Canal of Venice. An illuminated door appears, now with the face of the white man superimposed, and a shot of a cemetery—the man blindfolded and still. We now see the relief shown earlier in a wider shot, confronting a skull in a hooded robe: death. Part 2 of the video shifts mood and location. It is inaugurated by strings giving way to synth music (Larry Steinbachek of Bronski Beat) and the darkening of the water. Eighties models pose and smolder for the camera as earlier repeated images of men slowly walking the streets (of London and Venice?) take on new meaning. Toward the end of the second half of the short film, Isaac and (his lover and collaborator) Mark Nash's slow rap over the eighties synth music becomes the crucial text animating the visuals, underscoring or shifting their meanings. This is a piece about HIV/AIDS, but it also constitutes a response to critics by the interracial couple. The audio insists: "(This is not an AIDS advertisement.) Feel no guilt in your desire." More complexly expanding the transnational range of their commentary beyond recognizable signs of European cultures, the rap and video continue, with shots of the models—white, save one we see only in profile—interpolated with dark watery background and other scenes:

Parting glances

buddy's friend . . . Meet between the gaps between mirrors and turned away eye [*a new image—tropicalesque, with a dark figure wearing a fez in the foreground, with a minaret(?) and tall palm tree in the background*]

The civilizing pleasure-seeking mission tourist.

Black boys bought for a package of cigarettes

That exotic other might just translate/ How a small disease in a Third World domain became a First World problem, with a little name

This is not an AIDS advertisement

[*Black men appear, superimposed with the water. We hear Mark's voice more clearly.*] "Feel no guilt in your desire." [*Then Isaac slightly revises "The Rose" in the last lines.*]

"Don't say love it is a razor/ That leaves your soul to bleed . . . ," [*ending with*]

"I say love, it is a flower/ And you, its only seed.

[*Finally, the coda.*]

"This is not an AIDS advertisement. Feel no guilt in your desire."

The sort of representation of interracial desire that Isaac may have wanted to see, including meaningful relationships between white, Black, and other people of color—which, for example, were portrayed in Rikki Beadle-Blair's vital and exuberant UK hit *Metrosexuality* in the early aughts—would have had a very different valence in the United States in the long 1980s.[68] The history of African descendants in the United Kingdom is divergent in a number of ways from the United States, and the works of Marlon Riggs are Black US American works. The ways we talk about or elide representations of interracial desire in each national context are varied. Race is "lived as class" differently in each place, finding Black white and other working-class and poor Britons in proximity in housing estates in ways that we do not often see in the United States, for example. This is certainly not to say that Black Britons and Black Europeans do not experience racial terrorism—clearly, they do. Their "forgotten" or "silenced" histories are now being exhumed.[69] The relative size of the populations certainly has had a hand in the differences. The proportion and total number of Black people is much smaller in the United Kingdom. The fact that many Black folks (certainly not all) immigrated to the United Kingdom with and following the Windrush generation (1948–1971) means that patterns of segregated settlement and housing are less historically entrenched than in the United States. Nor do I suggest that there is or should be a monolithic US response or "camp." But while "Black Is Beautiful" certainly bloomed throughout the world, in the United Kingdom the rhizomatic ethic did not take root in ancestral soil that Black Britons understand and continue to experience as the very terrain on which their ancestors were bought and sold as Black Americans do. One's potential playmates and partners may therefore be understood as direct local material beneficiaries, and potentially current executors of white supremacy, not merely abstractly racially "privileged." The movements for civil rights, Black Power, and Black Arts that raged in the sixties and seventies in the United States were transformative. How, therefore, still in the hazy Afrosheen afterglow of "Black Is Beautiful!" could the incipient independent statement of Black gay men of the 1980s have proclaimed "Black men loving Black men . . . *as friends is great, and/but 'white boys are so pretty'*"?[70] Imáginate!

Marlon and Joe before him are not alone in their self-conscious construction of a vision of profoundly transformative Black gay romantic relationships. In fact, they are following Audre's lead. Biomythography, the form that Audre Lorde invented in her 1982 *Zami, A New Spelling of My Name*—combining elements of history, biography, and myth—names an aspect of the anthological generation that they each embody.[71] Assotto, Pat, Barbara, June (Jordan), and others had also said this in various ways—they were re-creating lore/myths Blackprints and normative (that is, illustrative) narrative theory to supplant old texts of antiblackness. They were each telling a truth that they believed conveyed what we needed to learn or hear—perhaps what they felt deeply themselves and wanted to create but not necessarily reflective of their experiences at the moment. In "Tar Beach," the short story that is also the gorgeous and stunningly detailed climax of *Zami*, it is Afrekete (Kitty for short)—a hip soul sister years before the celebration of soul sisters—who aids the transition of (the biomythographic character we will call) "Audre" from the downtown gay girl scene of mostly white women, mystically delivering her to new understandings of herself. You will recall Audre and Afrekete's legendary meeting in that brick-framed house in St. Albans, Queens, in 1957 and their subsequent reunion, after Audre breaks up with her girlfriend Muriel, a white woman. Afrekete's Harlem tenement apartment and its roof become a psychic transport hub to a different ("Black Black Black!") consciousness for Audre in this erotically charged section of the work. Tropical fruits are involved. Earlier in *Zami*, the avatar "Audre" allows:

> During the fifties in the Village, I didn't know the few other Black women who were visibly gay at all well. Too often we found ourselves sleeping with the same white women. We recognized ourselves as exotic sister-outsiders who might gain little from banding together. Perhaps our strength might lay in our fewness, our rarity. That was the way it was Downtown. And Uptown, meaning the land of Black people, seemed very far away and hostile territory.[72]

We are not accustomed to thinking of Audre as an "exotic sister-outsider" very far away from those she considers "hostile" Black people. Resonant with Marlon's confession at the end of *Tongues Untied*—that previously, while "immersed in snow" in the Castro, he had been blind to his brother's beauty and his own, but now sees, Audre writes: "Afrekete taught me roots, new definitions of our women's bodies—definitions for which I had only been in training to learn before." She went there—to "root working" as authorizing deep Black women's knowledge! Audre italicizes the romance in beautiful erotic prose: *"And I remember Afrekete, who came out of a dream to me always being hard and real.... She brought me live things from the bush, and from her farm set out in cocoyams and cassava....* West Indian markets along Lenox Avenue ... or the Puerto Rican bodegas.... We were each of us both together ..." on the "tar beach" of the Harlem tenement rooftop. Audre sees the roof as "the beaches of Winneba or Annamabu, with coco palms softly applauding and crickets keeping time with the pounding of tar-laden, treacherous, beautiful sea."[73] The author reserves this intensely florid language for this story at the end of *Zami*. She is telling us something specific here. By the long 1980s, time was overdue for Black people centered in Black stories in Black spaces. No matter that some read them as "just-so" romances—these narratives necessarily celebrate affirmation of Black as good and sexy and smart: desirable and transformative beyond disgust and/ or fetishization and/or fashion.

Lorraine Bethel published her "what chou mean *we* white girl? or, the cullid lesbian feminist declaration of independence (dedicated to the proposition that all women are not equal, i.e., identical/ly oppressed)" in *Conditions Five: The Black Women's Issue*, out of frustration with

> talking to others
> translating my life for the deaf, the blind ...
> educating white women ...
> on the job, off the job, in bed
> in bed ...
> while we wonder where the next meal, job, payment on our college
>   loans ... archives ... press, forty acres and a mule
> or national conference
> are going to come....

Her poem is a manifesto of independence and *Black Black Black* self-regard that takes aim at the labor the Black woman speaker is asked to do for white women:

> ... on the job, off the job, in bed
> in bed

Lorraine's direct serious play lets us have it—each stanza valorizing what she sees as authentic Black women's space and working toward Black woman–identified institutions and other spaces. This is the "they" to come. She assures her audience of Black and other women of color:[74]

> They will come.
> From us loving/speaking *to* our Black/Third World sisters, not *at*
>   white women.
> They will come
> When we separate the Third World woman–identified Third World
>   Women
> From the white woman–identified Third World women
> when we Black woman–identified Black women leave the
>   white woman–identified Black women
> those who can't come to their Black female senses
> who won't deal with real sista love
> way behind
> you know the ones
> who don't really like themselves or other Black women
> the ones who've accepted and glorify in myth roles
> Black bull dyke stud or Black lesbianfeministgodesstokenstar
> Of the white women's community. . . . [75]

This is not polite. Some of it borders, shadily, on ad hominem ("You know the ones," as she threatens naming names). We can grant that if you like, dear reader. How do we know who does or does not like themselves, or what investment another person has in their kinks, or what look like "myth roles" to those who are not having sex with them? You may understand this as the sort of "essentialist" rhetoric that folks have railed against. Still. Listen. Hear her—viscerally and unvarnished. Read closely and listen. Among other things, Lorraine is expressing her love for Black women and her passion for revolution that will find her and her people liberated from poor, reduced life chances. We can disagree or suspend whether there is, somewhere out there, a Black woman Self with singular "Black female senses." We might even criticize Lorraine for thinly veiled allusions to the bedrooms of specific sisters and the ways she casts aspersions (albeit clever, I think—and it certainly must have been a relief to say this out loud!). Still, her frustration must not be ignored or unaccounted. For real: what is it about sista love that makes it so (hard) (great) (impossible) (remarkable beyond an assumed "colorblind" love)? What is it that makes many of us have feelings about, comment upon, or resent the sexual, romantic, and/or contractual choices of others? Why does it feel *personal* to many of us? Is this another post-slavery traumatic disorder? Investment in community, perhaps? Or something else? You may find that I am making a leap here along with Lorraine. Although I cannot speak for her, my *cosmetic intuition* (to borrow a phrase from Marsha P. Johnson) is that these individual feelings are connected not only to widespread anti-Black historical structuration but also to daily experiences in which we see antiblackness everywhere and creeping still: from what and who is beautiful to who and what is true. From a carefree drive or jog, selling of loosies on the corner, or evening at home . . . to no breath at all. From a twenty-year jail sentence to no charges brought. From who is a theorist to what makes a discipline or language or a religion or a neighborhood or a man or a woman. To *who gets what when where and why*—which is just a handy definition of formal politics, after all. Would you argue that the personal is not, in fact, political? Or that our personal choices and our very persons—our bodies and their desires—emerge, innocent and untouched, within a vacuum? Would you contend, dear reader, that many of us—regardless of whom we desire sexually—are not addicted to constantly looking outside of blackness for affirmation and acknowledgment?[76] Essentially, my concern, like sister Lorraine's, and quite possibly yours too, is this: how can we live best, within (perhaps multiple) communities of support and kindness, toward total liberation?

Oh, Gary . . . ("I Hope He Smiles")

Here we briefly turn to 1979 once again. Just briefly, to the then-private journal of eighteen-year-old Gary Fisher, who has recently returned to the United States from Düsseldorf, where his father was serving in the US military. Gary's journal entries span most of the long 1980s (until 1993): the last part of his tragically short life.[77] Readers of *Gary in Your Pocket: Stories and Notebooks of Gary Fisher*—the posthumously published collection edited by Gary's former professor and friend, Eve Kosofsky Sedgwick—encounter these 151 pages of journal entries after a number of Gary's previously unpublished short stories and story fragments. On November 7, 1979, Gary writes (to himself, or perhaps to posterity/to no one): "With all these white friends I think in many ways I am white or not the Black stereotype that Blacks and whites alike have of Blacks. I like it, that's all that matters." Dwight McBride offers that Gary's "do[es] not fit easily into any pre-packaged, normativizing, easily respectable understanding of Black identity, of Black life, or even of

Black gay life. His honesty—his at times deep commitment to that, above all other considerations—is enough to leave any variety of readers both vexed yet profoundly fascinated."[78] Dwight is right that Gary's story does not fit easily, yet his experience is distinctly Black. And *me vex,* indeed, reading this profoundly saddening account. A story that Eve tells in the conclusion exemplifies why. When Eve mentioned to Gary's sister that toward the end of his life, Gary told her that he felt "impaled by the stigma" of his Kaposi's sarcoma lesions, his sister replied: "I think that's how Gary experienced being Black too."[79] He was impaled by the stigma(ta) of blackness. Gary's sister confirmed that he saw in (his) blackness a deep debilitating wound and mark of shame. My sadness and wish for re-narrativization is not focused on his s/m kink, public sex, or the fact of his interracial desire, therefore—none of which is shocking, cringeworthy, or unknown to me. Like the 2002 version of the "pornotopic fantasy" novel *The Mad Man,* by our polymath, Samuel Delany, and Delany's earlier horror novel of rape and torture, *Hogg, Gary in Your Pocket* certainly also leaves us to grapple, if we dare, with what Robert called "what lies just beneath the surface of polite, 'civil' American race talk."[80] Still, for me there is more to consider. It is this inescapable sense of deep woundedness—a stigmata of disregard that Gary evidently carried— that is so vexing and haunting. He might have dealt with the accretive weight of this in many ways. His journals suggest that one externalization was Gary's relentless search, over nearly twenty years, for (mostly consensual) humiliation and abuse by the words and silences, hands, fists, dicks, steel-toed boots, excrement, guns . . . of white men and their friends.[81]

I am thinking again about Essex. This time, my attention is piqued by his less-remarked-upon story of sexual initiation, in which one of the rituals in his Southeast DC "oasis of strivers" was sex with George. Our dear sterling Black Black Black Essex writes (and we read but rarely critically consider the brother's assertion): "George was a white man. My initiation into homo sex was guided by the hands of a white man."[82] He goes on to say that in the summer of his fourteenth year, he "poured [his] adolescence into" the at-least-forty-something-year-old shopkeeper. Essex reports: "My dick did not fall off in [George's] mouth. I did not turn green from kissing him. . . ." Essex enjoyed it. He does not remember this as exploitative or negative, even while some may bristle today at what looks like (at least) inappropriate sexual contact with an adult when he was a minor. He dismisses this. Essex's deep and compounded regret or missed opportunity was: first, "that [the young Black men in the neighborhood] were never able to talk about our visits to George [and] that we were not able to sexually explore one another in the same ways that we allowed George to explore us."[83] Compounding this was that the weight of the secret he shared with George, and against the neighborhood boys who insisted on silence, seemed to require his dragging an unsuspecting Black girl into this messy drama among boys (and a man) as a shield from being accused of being a faggot. An adolescent also reaching for sexual exploration and companionship, what she found was disregard as an accessory. Try, perhaps, to feel the weight of all this loss, dear reader, or the intensity of this anger. You too might be vexed (and perhaps less apt to indict this author on charges of being sentimental, normativizing, or simply uncool for finding Gary's story so overwhelmingly sad).

Kevin Quashie confides: "Actually, the words weren't quite 'I love you' but something nastier, something thrilling and delicious. And they were whispered in a walk-in cooler at McDonald's where I had started a job days before I turn sixteen, weeks before my senior year. I am a boy in full blossom and ready for a whisper. . . ."[84] I will leave it to you to decide whether George's whispers to Essex while he pretended to browse the store's shelves were qualitatively different from the sweet-nasty-nothings whispered by Kevin's coworker. He remembers:

> His name is Carlton and he's a co-worker, skinny, dark brown, probably twenty-five years old. His voice is deep (me and these deep-voiced men) and his lips glisten as if they have just been licked. This seems impossible but it is also how they are every time. From early on, Carlton smiles at me; sometimes he winks.
>
> I don't know what he knows; I want to know what he knows
>
> . . .
>
> He wouldn't have known I was sixteen. And we are, in this moment, both living in urban Miami in 1987 where regard for gay young Black men is low and the ravages of AIDS are high. We, this man and I, are living surrounded by a discourse that disparages homosexuals, Haitians, Africans generally, drug users, sex workers. It is less than seven years past the Overtown/Liberty City riots. In our churches and homes and schools—never mind elsewhere—there is not much concern for Black boys like us. We live encircled by the dominance of fear, silence, and hate.
>
> In the freezer that one day, he said the most explicit thing, something about wanting my ass but the language was more poetic than that, more determined, phrasing so new to me that I'd never heard it before and can't remember its precision now.
>
> I melt still in recalling this thing I can't recall properly.[85]

I am most interested in stories like this Blackfull Miami tale not because it "fits easily" or is "pre-packaged . . . normativizing." It is neither. Moreover, there is a "fierce [re]articulation" of gender, nationality, class, and ethnicity in this short essay, as well as in Essex's under-read essay and Audre's classic "Tar Beach." We each contain multitudes—even in the back of a Southeast DC grocery store, Harlem rooftop, or an Opa-Locka McDonald's—negotiating the ambient disgust of most of the fry guys and the utter uninterest of Kevin's cashier colleagues, the fascinating Black girls who pay him no mind as they "radiate fabulousness." I reflect on stories like these and tarry at the *biomythos* and lived experience that Marlon and Audre and Essex, Mr. Baldwin, and others have crafted. (Troy *and them* loved, for example, the brotherly affection and romance of Arthur and Crunch, touring with the Trumpets of Zion in *Just above My Head*!) I revel in and revere hard-won real-life evidence of this thick Blackfullness, as well as the Blacklight flickers of this kind of love and desire valorized in reflexively imagined literature. I reach for manifestos of independence and *Black Black Black* self-regard, whether in romantic love or friendship or political solidarity. I wish for Gary—although out of time—this re-narrativization in the ether.

The Other Ferragamo Drops

At the end of my discussion with Troy, Ketlie, Me'lisa, and them I pivoted— not exactly a punt—to class. Here is a story that may in some ways pervert Manthia Diawara's notion of the "Black good life" as I experienced it as a student at NYU Africana studies in the late 1990s. The first part takes place after a memorably fancy Africana studies event at which Toni Morrison and Wole Soyinka were honored guests. Afterward, I glided past Washington Square Park and down Christopher Street to a bracing realization. I remember the manicure I had sat for that day so that the fresh high buff of my nails would shine resplendently. I tied and untied my bow tie several times to have the perfect suggestion of serious whimsy (insouciance was not appropriate in this company)! And I was wearing the Ferragamo shoes that I had scored at 70 percent off on the last day of the Barney's sale (despite what I imagined my nemesis, Sallie Mae, would think of the expenditure). Once at the Hangar on Christopher Street, I perched at the far end of the bar, near the pool table. Still glowing from being close enough to touch the hem of Toni Morrison's garment (I resisted) and having shaken the hand of Wole Soyinka as if genius could be passed on through touch, drinking good wine in the company of my Africana studies friends and professors, I was still in a sort of bookish Black bourgie nirvana. One drink, I thought, before heading one block to my PATH train. Almost immediately, an average-looking white man offered me a drink and an intense stare. I smiled, politely. After drinking half of the cocktail, I asked "Why me," indicating the other men, of various ethnicities, at the bar. This had been one of the standard questions I put to men I recruited to a (failed) ethnographic study on interracial desires, prompted by my (non-monogamous) former partner Sacha's incredulity that I had never had sex with a white man by what was then my advanced age of twenty-seven.[86] AOL White Men for Black Men (WM4BM) and HX adverts seeking and describing WM4BM and BM4WM offered pages of narrative that comported to boring stereotypes and racial fantasies that seemed unremarkable. I went on a few dates, but nothing transpired that I thought was ethnographically compelling. However, it was the stark contradiction between how I saw myself (and the facts of my experience) that night and my cocktail benefactor's fantasies that fascinate me still. To my question "Why me?" he said, as if rehearsed: "Because I can tell you're from the streets and can take me in the back and really fuck me hard and dirty." Streets!? Did this dude not notice the precision of my manicure? Although I had loosened my silk bow tie, was the glowing penumbra of Black genius from being in the orbit of heavenly literary bodies not apparent to him? What about my leather knapsack led him to believe that it contained only a depleted MetroCard and a change of clothes? I was stunned. Impressed by the intensity of his fantasy and sensing, finally, a significant ethnographic moment, I attempted to get him on the record. The spell was broken when I asked the dude if he would repeat what he had said for my tape recorder (standard issue for ethnographers in training).

I did not know then that days later the other auto-ethnographic Ferragamo would drop. At the newly renovated Harlem brownstone of an attractive Black gay architect, I am smitten by another brother. A Bronxite, I think, whom I had not seen before in the clubs or in this widening private circle of mostly professional Black gay men. Sadly, it seems I took no notes that night. I cannot say what we talked about, but it lasted a while. I remember that he was fine. Just as the telephone number exchange was about to happen (or so I thought hoped deeply desired), we shook hands: a quick standard handshake transitioned to a slow, warm, brotherly salaam: between our chests, our fists intertwine thumb over thumb, as we embraced, left hands over right shoulders. Deep Inhale/Deep Exhale. I was besotted. I remember our extended holding of hands and the look of incredulity on the brother's face as we let go the shoulder embrace—now, with his left over mine, feeling my hand with both of his. I loved the touch but was confused by the look on his face. "Damn!" the brother said, "you don't do *no* work! Do you?" Laughing it off, I weakly protested that reading, writing, and facilitating therapy sessions and group interactions were, in fact, work. The softness of my hands had already betrayed me, however. The evidence was overwhelming: exceptionally bourgie even in a room full of middle-class men. Read as effeminate and effete. I am from Queens: home of the hardworking. I am a native and enthusiastic speaker of Black vernacular English. If I had assessed the situation differently, I might have had a little Henny or Courvoisier. I can drink cognac—or even pop an occasional 40 ounce—with the best of them (OK—I did it once). But the body can give away one's desires—mine, to be supple and gentle, "refined" in my own silly way. (I hear my older Cuban respondents grasping for a way to opt me out of the lowest category of *negro*—coming up with *negro fino*.) No matter. I—or my party avatar—was not who (or what?) this brother wanted in his bed (in my bed, in the park, on the subway platform . . .) that night. This handsome Bronxite, unlike my cocktail benefactor, could project his desire/fantasy only so far, and there were still a number of willing screens yet available at the impeccably restored brownstone. Perhaps my hands indicated to him other softnesses that this brother could not abide. He may or may not have misread me. But at least I was dismissed only after he dutifully collected information, I rationalized. No matter. I booked no telephone number from him that night. Just a (sexy, heart aching) head nod and "a'ight" from him, and a (fake) smile, head nod and sincere "peace" from me.

4   Disco

I propose that disco was a medicine, disco was a balm, and disco was a healing. That disco saved our lives. That the moment we started dancing, we were healed in our bodies of all kinds of stigmas and oppressions. You don't have to be cured, to be healed.—From "Theology of the Discopocene" by MARVIN K. WHITE

HERE'S WHERE WE RETURN, briefly, to the music. To disco—which is much more than what they say it was—to ask *what does it sound like at the end of the world?* Of course, answering this question will also require a re-narrativization of the historical and political-economic context. We undertake this here by mixing on at least two decks, hoping you will dance. Grounded in multi-vocal blacknesses—funk and gospel and reggae, rock and roll and rhythm & blues—with new technologies and new arrangements, the disco we follow here contains multitudes. No part of which is corny or anachronistic. Our disco later came to be called Garage (after the Paradise Garage), or club music, then House (in honor of the Warehouse), with its numerous streams. But disco, like Black gay, cannot be confined to one moment or trajectory. And of course, it is also (a) space: disco the club the basement your beach or rooftop a loft or the Loft (one of the earliest discos), for example. Shelter. Most easily understood as music meant for social dancing, like hip-hop, disco emerged through the innovation of selectors, or DJs working in public halls, gay bars, community centers, and later businesses known as discos or clubs, but never lost the feeling of a good juke joint, bashment, or rent party.

Disco is cosmopolitan. At the edge of the end of the world, disco sounds like the Black British funk band Cymande's "Bra," released in 1972 and sampled and spun on dance floors ever since. With one of the hottest breaks of all disco breaks (that cowbell at 2:49!), "Bra" conveyed its message in the music and in the lyrics ("But it's alright, we can still go on").[1] The edge of disco must have sounded like Bob (Marley) prophesizing in "War" but assured victory in "Positive Vibrations." Donny and Roberta sounding prophylaxis or conjure medicine for what was to come, exhorting each other to "Be Real Black for Me" and bringing couples to the dance floor for the extended remix of "Back Together Again." Manu Dibango making the continental connection, and your pretension to dance cute flies out the window when the Cameroonian beat hits and you are commanded: "Soul Makossa." Then (more recognizable to you as disco) a reminder as you cook out with the family, lime on the beach, stop at the side of the road, or chill with the smart set at the Loft: "Love Thang" by the trio First Choice. Yes, this is certainly as much about class and place as it is about race. Stuart (Hall) has already told you.[2]

In the 1960s and early 1970s (the edge of disco), revolution had seemed palpably imminent and liberation an attainable goal. Both political revolutions and ideological "revolutions" had already occurred. For example, the sexual revolution *freed the asses* of millions, and some *minds followed*, suggesting that George Clinton's acid-tripping pronouncement may be valid in both directions.[3] Various national revolutions, with their roots in 1950s movements for self-determination in Asia, Africa, and the Caribbean, had already won political independence from European colonial powers by the late 1960s. Among the earliest, Cuba had triumphed in 1959, in its third revolutionary war of independence. This time, not from the Spanish colonial master but from neocolonial structures that found the country controlled by a small Creole elite with intimate ties to US corporations and modes of intelligibility. It is not just an accident of history, but a feature of a peculiarly recurrent US miscalculation, that one of the rebellious members of this Creole elite, Fidel Castro, would insist on more concessions to their at-first friendly relationship than the United States would allow. The 1959 revolution did not end "friendly" relations between Cuba and its powerful neighbor to the north. Cuba's subsequent insistence on its autonomy did. Señor Ferrer taught me a great deal about the sort of indignities he had faced in the old world "before the revolution" in Cuba. For him, this world ended when Fidel and the 26th of July Movement emerged from the Sierra Maestra Mountains and former dictator Fulgencio Batista fled the country. For Ferrer, the world in which human dignity was assumed for the white(ened) Creole elite and often extended to their poor white(ened) cousins when necessary, but withheld by law and custom from the blackest of their kith and kin, had ended. Still, as I showed in my book ¡Venceremos?, in which the interrogative (?) replaces the standard exclamation of victory (!)—this "just-so" story of revolution as panacea is too pat and incomplete. In various sites in the Caribbean, including Cuba, national elites—prominent families who were generally more well educated, connected to mainstream Christian institutions, lighter-skinned, and having "been to" their putative "mother" countries through travel or local acculturation—began their own Creole rules in the 1960s and 1970s. They were perhaps naive about the fact that perpetuation of colonial common sense—that is, patriarchal domination of one's "lesser" brethren and (especially) sistren—would foment new battles if not new revolutions. They seem to have been unaware that perhaps unlikely transnational alliances would soon threaten the uneasy "peace" of their hegemonies. During the long 1980s new waves of immigration to European metropoles brought *citizens* in their own right, not just the colonial subjects of previous waves. This slightly shifted and intensified the already tense situation within global centers such as Paris, Amsterdam, and London, with respect to these denizens of the empire "striking back" daily by going to work, raising their families, paying taxes, and thus participating in daily life as something other than a forgettable offshore specter from which the empire could draw raw materials.[4] For Black Americans, "revolution" would have to remain merely a shining chimera. The revolution, in the fashion that folks had seen sweep the Third World and that seemed possible to some in the United States and Canada in the 1960s and 1970s, never came to North America (or has not yet). As Assata Shakur remarked, "There is no Sierra Maestra" in the urban centers of the United States. The police state increasingly expanded as the welfare state retreated throughout the late 1970s and early 1980s.[5] Revolutionary disappointment began to set in as neoliberalism settled. Black gay folks began to make sense of the detritus of the pre-AIDS days of patchwork-jeaned, Afroed free love on the piers and rooftops and tenements of the urban United States. After all, it was already "after the end of the world (don't you know that yet)?"[6]

"Revolution is a time when everything can—and sometimes does—go wrong" for David (Scott). He says that our current political time is marked by mourning the failure of total revolution that seemed belated, but perhaps still possible in the early 1980s, which I previously defined as the (continuing) temporal space of "after revolution, before freedom." Like the long-1980s stream of Black gay works, David's recent scholarship and theorization of Grenada's New Jewel Movement is also preoccupied with "the aftermaths of political catastrophe, the temporal disjunctures involved in living on in the wake of past political time, amid the ruins. . . ." Offering the framework of tragedy to illuminate this moment, David argues that "revolution and tragedy . . . have between them an uncanny but nevertheless adhesive intimacy [that] perhaps what our present solicits from us most urgently is an attunement to tragedy, to the sort of appreciation of contingency, chance, *peripeteia,* and catastrophe."[7] Although he eruditely parses this moment as one caught in the throes of a great tragedy, and Afro-pessimist theory resonates, pointing out the impossibility of Black people launching a Gramscian war of position in any case, to my reading the catastrophes of the long 1980s, marked by seeming reversals of the gains of the decolonizing generation of the 1960s and 1970s, seem to also evidence what Pat Parker reckoned as "imperialist forces in the world . . . finding themselves backed against the wall; no longer able to control the world . . . and they are getting desperate. . . ." She calls fellow travelers throughout the globe toward revolutionary action.

On January 22, 1979, the four largest public-sector unions in the United Kingdom called on their 1.5 million members to strike to protest the British government's attempt to create a pay-increase ceiling of 5 percent. This national unrest as a result of the demonstrations is widely understood as a prime factor leading to the election of Margaret Thatcher, following her twin pledges: to end the economic crisis through "small government" and to stem the tide of Black (that is, Asian, African, and Caribbean) immigration. Writing in the moment as a way to make good critical sense of the new times, the New Right (including what he named "Thatcherism"), and its articulation to race, immigration, and class, Stuart stated in his classic essay "Race, Articulation and Societies Structured in Dominance" that "race is the modality in which class is 'lived,'" the "medium through which class relations are experienced, and the form in which it is appropriated and fought through."[8] This is of course stunningly resonant with radical Black lesbian feminists' formulation of inescapably "interlocking" structuration. Revolutionary changes were taking place in the global South—or the Third World, as it was called. The apparent cultural ascendancy of other Third World peoples was aligning in 1979 as Thatcherism ascended. This set many people flowing, along with their ideas and ideas about them. Uganda's Idi Amin was overthrown in 1979. St. Lucia became independent of the United

Kingdom; Rhodesia officially became Zimbabwe. The People's Revolutionary Government (PRG) was proclaimed on March 13, 1979, after the New Jewel Movement overthrew the oppressive puppet government of Grenada; the Sandinista National Liberation Front triumphed in Nicaragua. The Soufriere volcano on Montserrat erupted, destroying much of the island in the same year. In the United States, similar local and international tensions heralded Reaganism, caused likewise by deep economic crisis, which must have seemed business as usual for most Black folks.

Remember that in 1979 the world was still reeling from the revolutionary shifts over the previous decade. There was also fatigue and national disenchantment in the US after the catastrophic, but also in a way "anticlimactic" defeat in Vietnam in which Black soldiers were disproportionately killed: no V-Day, no cataclysmic atom bombing like Hiroshima demonstrating the perverse humanity-ending power of the United States. Today, we can read Stevie Wonder's political commentary more particularly and specifically, not only as a comment on typical pre-1980s anti-Black racism, but now also in terms of Black working-class fears of competition for the lowest-paid dead-end jobs by immigrants from Mexico, Central America, and the Caribbean, beginning in the late 1970s in such places as Miami, New York, and Los Angeles.[9] This seemed especially galling to Black Americans, given recent history. As Stevie sang, "They had me / Standing on the front lines / But now I stand at the back of the line when it comes to gettin' ahead." We know, of course, that "getting ahead" is overstated here. Although differentiation between Black folks of various nationalities may have been chalked up to negligible "cultural" differences in the past, the rising pitch of "culture of pathology" discourses that particularly targeted Black US Americans (or United Statesians) also weaponized national and ethnic difference by the 1970s. Cathy (Cohen) reminds us that Ronald Reagan was elected on a platform that highlighted and targeted the "moral deficiencies" of the "undeserving poor" and "welfare queens": "Black Americans . . . can point to, at best, a mixed record of economic, political, and social progress under advanced systems of marginalization. The 1980s during the Reagan administration was just such a difficult period where few if any gains were made at the national level. . . . Reagan was elected (and reelected) without significant support of African Americans."[10]

The "epidemic" of crack cocaine made its appearance in the early 1980s, devastating Black and poor communities. It would not be the health effects of the drug on individuals that alone caused devastating and enduring sociocultural damage in the United States, however. More consequentially, Reagan wielded crack and cocaine as a central piece of both his domestic and foreign policies.[11] Regarding the former, through strategic targeted deployment of the "War on Drugs." This was an initiative by US President Nixon in the early 1970s that allowed Reagan to extend and intensify the reach of the federal government's powers, which effectively became a war on Black and brown people, marked by mandatory incarceration for often long terms including nonviolent drug offenses: from 50,000 convictions in 1980 to 400,000 in 1997.[12] There was constant chatter about the "War on Drugs," including Nancy Reagan's disdainful "social inoculation" gesture: "just say no." In contrast, it was not until September 17, 1985—after more than six thousand people had died in the United States—that Reagan mentioned the term *AIDS* in public.[13]

Trans, gender-variant, bisexual, homosexual, and same-gender-oriented individuals have always existed in Black communities throughout the world: sometimes occupying spaces of silence or tacit understanding, sometimes taking up awesomely power-filled and/or hyper-vulnerable statuses of explicit difference, and at other times marked without value distinction. Recently, scholars have begun to elaborate the histories and social functions of far-flung same-gender-oriented, homosexual, bisexual, and gender-non-conforming key figures, cultural roles, and historical figures in precolonial Southern and Central Africa and the precolonial Americas, and of course now well-known exemplars of the Harlem Renaissance, civil rights, Black arts, and other important periods in the United States and Canada, for example. Still, the evidence we have now shows that the explicit arrangement of a Black gay community with signal Black gay politics did not emerge until the mid-1970s. Thanks to the political articulations that Black women made in the 1970s in their lesbian feminist work as radical Black folks, a translocal Black gay public sphere began to emerge as among the most vigorous sites in the Black world, finding its apogee of political and cultural expression in the mid-1990s. You might find, like David Scott, that "the historical experience of my own time, is a disenchanted world, a world defined precisely by the loss of that promise of revolution, a world of temporal aftermaths."[14] I feel this too, dear reader. But then I remember: Black gay abjures permanent loss (we must). Never promised nothin', our "aftermaths" exist within the flicker of the disco ball and in the unseen rhythm that moves the dance floor as one organism. Remember your "stitches, darling." Speaking to an audience of radical Third World women, Pat said, "We are facing the most critical time in the history of the world. The superpowers cannot afford for us to join forces and work to rid this earth of them."[15] Consider the "us" Pat references and whether everyone she called to could hear her. Of course, this was already belated in August 1980 when she gave this speech (*didn't we know that yet?*). Still, demonstrating the pragmatic untimely timeliness of Black/gay, she insists: "We cannot afford not to." By the 1980s, even those who wanted to recuperate the (would-be) (Black) nation would have to contend with the apparent failure of many revolutionary projects in the face of rearticulated capital and its police apparatus, largely headquartered in the United States. Moreover, heterosexism seems, after all, a structural flaw built into the system of newly independent nations of the Caribbean, South Asia, Africa, and Oceania, as well as in Black Power and other movements in the global North. (Why should they be different than the nations they aspired to stand alongside?) This conditioned and precipitated numerous breaks and cleavages. But the connection between these two things—the failure of revolutionary movements to bring about a totalized new world, against the global reach and strength of neocolonialism and white supremacy, and the failure of the imagination of these movements to see strength in differences between "mens womens some that is both some that is neither"—is rarely read in the same frame.[16] However, it seems clear that intersectional analysis and "seeing each other" undergird a politics of accomplice that might have made us (all) freer.

In the long 1980s Black folks began to identify and make way to a something else that we are currently struggling through. And today, we increasingly understand better that the dividing and enervating force of heterosexism and *misogynoir* within revolutionary or otherwise Left movements—and within intellectual discourses and practices—exacerbates and perpetuates conditions of tragedy and impossibility. We cannot afford not to heed—to listen and *move* this time to—Black gay disco.

Chic

I was ten years old when Chic's second album, *C'est Chic*, was released. Before presenting myself at the club six years later, where I eagerly traded the cool elegance and glamour that I thought I desired for what the club promised, it was the "sophisticated" look and sound of Chic that called to me. In my basement. In my bedroom mirror: "I want your love." The carillon chime chords pealing the melodic line (*"iwantyourlove* / I want. Your love") combined with the singularly funky bass line, defining disco. Although my adolescence occurred at the exciting beginning of the rap era in New York City, I had no desire to go to hip-hop jams at Montebello Park on Springfield Boulevard or the forested Brookville Park (each equal walking distance from my home), and I certainly never entertained a long double-transfer bus ride to Queensbridge or bus and subway to the Bronx. Cue Ashford and Simpson's 1977 instrumental classic "Bourgie Bourgie."[17] Phillip reminds me that the sound that Ashford and Simpson employ on "Bourgie Bourgie" feels like our favorite depiction of utter Black elegance (and conspicuous consumption), the Emerald City scene in *The Wiz*. I invoke it here as a classic example of a late-seventies/early-eighties disco aesthetic. Horns blare, awaiting word from on high. *The color is green*: "You got to be seen. / Green. / To show that your stuff's / laid. If you're not seen green. / you better be wearing / jade." The lyrics in that scene of opulence offers a searing, true-to-experience critique: "Oh, you've got to be seen green / Don't tell them your cupboard's bare / That you gave up one week's feed / To pay for your colored hair. . . ."[18]

The fantasy that Chic (and early-disco-era Ashford and Simpson) promoted so well sounds like a highly stylized version of polished New York urbanity, even amid epic unemployment, garbage strikes, legendary crime, and/but the feeling that New York is the center of art and culture in the global North. This just a couple years immediately preceding the time we were *imprinted with* (a new) *fear* as the first cases of what we now know of as AIDS surfaced in 1981. Disco timing seems out of sync with political economy. So-called carefree partying and acquisitiveness as white folks were just a couple years out of major economic recession in the global North, and Black and other people of color, and poor people continued to push through hard times and "structural adjustment" all over the worldwide ghetto. "Good Times?"[19] Really?

Do not be misled by the steady beat and fresh looks: the politics of dancing is multivalent. Perhaps, if we consider what was to come in terms of the changing same of Black political-economic conditions of precarity (and of course thinking of the *"weary years* [and] *silent tears"* of enslavement, Jim Crow, and colonialism), could we now entertain considering that these were in fact relatively good times at the edge of AIDS? In 1979, when Chic sang those infectious lines proclaiming that "these are the good times" and enjoined us to "put an end to this stress and strife" and "to live / the sporting life" of "clams on the half-shell and roller-skates," the wage gap between Blacks and whites in the United States was 18.1 percent. According to Valerie Wilson and William Rodgers of the Economic Policy Institute (EPI), "Black-white wage gaps are larger [in 2016] than they were in 1979, but the increase has not occurred along a straight line. Since 1979 median hourly real wage growth has fallen short of productivity growth for all groups of workers, regardless of race or gender. At the same time, wages for African American men and women have grown more slowly than those of their white counterparts. As a result, pay disparities by race and ethnicity have remained unchanged or have expanded." The report continues: "During the early 1980s, rising un-employment, declining unionization, and policies such as the failure to raise the minimum wage and lax enforcement of anti-discrimination laws con-tributed to the growing Black-white wage gap." The EPI found that the racial wage gap has little to do with access to education, disparities in work experi-ence, or where someone lives, but rather discrimination and growing earn-ings inequality in general. As the authors summarize, "Race is not a skill or characteristic that should have any market value as it relates to your wages, but it does."[20] This is also more widespread and deeper than wage earning. The 2018 report "What We Get Wrong about Closing the Racial Wealth Gap" shifts from the important issue of earned wages to the related, more long-term structural issue of wealth and wealth distribution in the United States. Addressing persistent myths about remedies to close the racial wealth gap, they argue against, for example, the pernicious and unrelenting *misogy-noir* propaganda promoted as central to the "endangered-Black-male" dis-course that "Black family disorganization is a cause of the racial wealth gap"; the more nuanced yet dangerously shortsighted view that follows William Julius Wilson's formulation of the "truly disadvantaged" touting improved "soft skills" and "personal responsibility" to increase the "employability" of Black men; and popular appeals to "emulate successful minorities" or to look to the success of Black celebrities who are said to prove postracial op-portunity. Instead, the economists conclude that "addressing racial wealth inequality will require a major redistributive effort or another major pub-lic policy intervention to build Black American wealth." Given the typical disciplinary conservative bent of economists, their advocacy of a "major re-distributive effort" and "another major public policy intervention"—namely, reparations for enslavement (and racial discrimination)—is momentous.[21] We should hear and respond to this as it is intended: an urgent plea. Of course, nearly two generations ago radical Black feminist groups such as the New Rochelle Working Group and the Combahee River Collective had already qualitatively analyzed the conditions of their own lives and that of their communities—finding connections with others, worldwide. The "major re-distributive effort" they called for was socialism.

Disco moves like the unequivocal classic "Love Is the Message" by MFSB.[22] An example of felt time-space compression inside the party, it can be re-mixed and played for hours, and sometimes was played on and on and on. In one of the most poignant episodes of its first season, the television show *Pose* illustrated Black gay time compression through the demand of elder and ball commentator Pray Tell to incessantly play "Love Is the Message" at the ball, as he grieved the recent death of his lover. In this profoundly affecting episode set in the early 1980s, for Pray Tell just a few years before, pre-AIDS, felt to him like "another era."

My Paradise Garage debut, at the tender age of seventeen, was in the 1985 season. Already after the end. One of the last of the storied clubs.[23] I was an unlikely club-goer. James—worldlier than I—first heard about it. He was much braver than I was, but my determination to dance was stronger. The central questions in Queens to determine whether one "got down (like that)" were not only *who you be with*—that is, who your friends and acquaintances and companions are—but also *where* they are. If the answer was "the city" (Manhattan), you would be "sus" (suspected) to be gay. In the Sharing Tongues archive by the London group Rukus! one can likewise hear folks coming from the Midlands, Croydon, or suburbs to London or Manchester as similar spaces of temporary gay relief. In Paris, to be Black and caught in the Pigalle, or more recently the Marais (before gentrification), suggested that you were *in the life* in some way. Among rural and exurban communities, the very notion of a city might be enough to raise concern—to make one sus. After all, those individuals who offered cosmopolitan connection to the latest in music and fashion and literature might also be precisely the older men and women that you had been warned about. Cue the pool party scene in which French expatriates creepily watch young Malians enjoy the upper-class ambience, in auteur Djibril Diop Mambety's *Touki Bouki*—a scene that seemed to be reproduced at gatherings I witnessed in Sint Maarten, Brazil, and Kenya some thirty years later. Still, I had to dance.

The glimmer of the disco ball called to me. I do not remember hearing the instrumental version of "Bourgie Bourgie" before I first stepped into the Paradise Garage. Listening to it now, I am transported and (still) feeling the fantasy: Upper East Side, 5th Avenue with my friends! Tea dance at the Pines! Concord to Paris! A yacht to Bermuda! The sound of the strings is expansive. At 2:40 the bass drum asserts itself before receding again for the one-two preparation for the hustle-arm extension to a vuelta—a turn. We can thank Puerto Rican, Cuban, and Dominican dancers for the return to partnered dancing in the clubs of New York (mostly boy/girl, butch/femme) because they had never abandoned this practice. But my extensions—hip flexion, arms in arabesque, fluid with the music—called for solo. Unlike the nasty, deeply libidinal bass-heavy grooves that I took to so organically once Better Days (NYC), Tracks (NY, DC), Paradise (Baltimore), Traxx and Loretta's (Atlanta), and Sugar's

(Miami) had taken hold of me in the most elemental and irresistible ways, it was only my feet that had been turned out. In first position. Extending. Then twirling. "Bourgie Bourgie" has the most delicious, lush orchestration. Elan! Even today, the flute sounds to me like a white linen suit with tailored pants and espadrilles. Expensive ones. "A what, wow!" I imagined Sister Sledge dressed in pale-pink Stephen Burrows gowns would exclaim when they saw me. Was their Nile Rodgers and Bernard Edwards 1979 lyric "He's the Greatest Dancer" about me, as my shoulders kept time to the bass line, my feet the drums, hands articulating and gesturing, melodically?[24] Or ("a what, wow!") was it the men? The legion of fine-ass dancers I was afraid to touch beyond the boundaries of the club floor, suspicious and frightened even of the ubiquitous sweat? We believe Nikki Giovanni: "Black love is Black wealth."[25] Still, HIV/AIDS uniquely challenged how we would love, under what conditions, and what consequences might come.

Sibilant and Strident Modes of Futurity

Of course, we are not so naive to imagine that there has ever been a carefree time for Black people or that AIDS is the only long-1980s experience worth talking about. Still, coming of age in the long 1980s conditions in me a feeling of tabanca for a relatively fabulous Blackfull "happy, carefree ... and gay" world, a past that we were never able to participate in because AIDS had already imprinted.[26] Here we take seriously Tina Campt's entreaty to "make modes of futurity audible" through a Black feminist mode of attention that she aptly describes as "listening at lower frequencies."[27] Perhaps this listening will reveal something about why important voices seem to be ignored or why some folks' ears seem attuned only to the most obvious major chords, losing what may be the most important grooves of experience or texts. I am thankful to Tina for her lesson in sensing frequency. At her Barnard Center for Women talk, she offered a table that describes the first octave as "the human threshold of hearing, and the lowest pedal notes of a pipe organ," moving to the second through the fifth octave, at which "lower upper bass notes" lie. The rhythm frequencies, which can be felt more than heard. The fifth to seventh "define human speech intelligibility," but/and the eighth to ninth octaves are described as "giv[ing] *presence to speech, where labial and fricative sounds lay*." What I am most interested in during this seeming departure, dear listener, is the tenth octave, which Tina tells us is marked by "'brilliance'—it is the sounds of bells, the ringing of cymbals, *and sibilance in speech*." I get it. This is certainly the queer octave. Is this why they (still) cannot hear us? Brilliance and ringing brass and bells. Sounds like ceremony. Looks like a shiny ocean, a flash of experience. A disco ball. The assumed sibilance of Black gay men's sound. A bit of a "lisp," or what you hear as a dramatic or elongated *s* or *sh* sound when you might not expect the tongue so close to their hard palate, or so intimately directing air out of his mouth.[28] The putative stridence of the Black Lesbian—perhaps the best example of which is the sound of a woman of any sexual identification saying "No!" Unvarnished expression. The ringing of trans bells you thought were merely quiet symbols, now brassy cymbals and cowbells keeping a different time. Believing your convictions and making them forthrightly can define stridence, in one register. Sibilants are a higher-pitched subset of the stridents. "Stridency" refers to the perceptual intensity of the sound.

We are taught by music theorists that all sibilants are also stridents. Of course, this comports with the long-standing stereotype of feminists (and therefore baited as lesbian) as being strident or humorless. All women are subject to lesbian baiting once they too declare their erotic autonomy, susceptible to being likewise tuned out as inaudible (or redundant). Stridency is deep. Remember the poems of Lorraine Bethel? Pat Parker? June Jordan? Let us consider, briefly, the audio recording of June's "A Poem about My Rights," which ends with a manifesto:

> I am not wrong: Wrong is not my name
> My name is my own my own my own
> and I can't tell you who the hell set things up like this
> but I can tell you that from now on my resistance
> my simple and daily and nightly self-determination
> may very well cost you your life.[29]

Hear the genius of her stridency. Her serious Black woman resolve to self-defend. Listen to the entire poem and check your uncertainty of (June's) bisexual capacity to make runs between octaves. Taken together, these are the sort of "uncomfortable" performances that made a mob big enough for a stadium blow up a crate of records during "Disco Demolition Night" on July 12, 1979, at Chicago's Comiskey Park. After all, when they said "Disco Sucks," they were (are) really saying: "You are wrong, and ought to be silent—and still, not dancing." "Shut the fuck up already!" "Go back where you came from!" "All lives matter!" They were trying, preemptively, to "make America great again."

Think about how a perhaps dramatically elongated vowel or a sing-songy quality of everyday vocal performance is often marked as effeminate. In phonetics, sibilants are fricative consonants of higher amplitude and pitch, made by directing a stream of air with the tongue toward the teeth. Think also of a local accent that has circulated promiscuously outside of the five boroughs of New York: (not sibilance at all, but) the nasal vocal performance of New York Black gay sound. This is significant not only because of the fact that New York in the long 1980s has been the popular gay cultural touchstone since *Paris Is Burning* and now *Pose*. But also think of dear talented Leroy, from *Fame* (Gene Anthony Ray). His brilliant New York faggotry burned too hot to be extinguished by heterosexual story lines in both the film and television series. I hear the voice of multiple Tony Award–winning actor Andre De Shields turning in tour de force performances in *The Wiz* and *Ain't Misbehavin'* in the long 1980s: "Tsso you wanted to meet / The Wizaaaa'd!" For another example of audible modes of sibilant futurity, also consider the multiple levels of "Lush Life's" Black gay genius—sung in Andy Bey's unmistakably Black gay diction and intonation, saying so much so beautifully: the orchestration that complicates what folks think of as a "sad song" (lyrics written by sixteen-year-old Black gay phenom Billy Strayhorn).[30] Described as annoying and unpleasant, examples of sibilants include hissing and hushing. A related feature is *glissando*, also called a "bent" note. Moving up and down a scale, melisma is defined as singing a single syllable while moving between several notes one after the other, as opposed to in syllables. This is also called vocal *riffing*, or playing with a word, breaking it down into several parts. Can you imagine the long 1980s without Luther Vandross riffing and bending ballads, creating (re)new(ed) forms? Perfect for the roller rink (an extension of disco space) we were first captured by and fell in love with Luther and his sibilance in "In the Glow of Love." Hear the *s*-sounds in *sflowerS* and gorgeous *Ssseems.t'Sssay*. Every *s* hitting and pronounced New Yorkese nasality that the kids imitate when they want to "talk gay" today (whether they know it or not): "Flowers bloomin', mornin' dew / And the beauty seems to say / It's a pleasure when you treasure / All that's new and true and gay. . . ."[31]

The stridency of women singers typifies disco frequencies. In 1977 Evelyn "Champagne" King arrived on the scene with "Shame," but she is not talking about the affect that animates (white) queer theory. The speaker/singer in this bop is unashamed of her sexuality. Rather, she is lamenting, in 4/4 time, the possibility of losing a relationship that keeps her "burning . . . [her] whole body yearning." It is the dissonance between libidinal impulses (which she does not question here) and social expectations that has her "so confused / It's a shame." After all, "Mama just don't understand / How I love my man."[32] This will certainly preach in the club. People who have been bludgeoned with the lie that their desire is a cause for shame will shake their asses in alleluia. Likewise, in 1976 the Boss, sighing, whispering, and coyly vamping through live strings and rich orchestration, told everyone in her #1 *Billboard* hit, "Love Hangover":

> If there's a cure for this
> I don't want it . . .
> If there's a remedy
> I'll run from it
> . . . I don't want a cure for this.

Indeed. It had been only three years since the American Psychiatric Association had controversially removed the diagnosis of "homosexuality" from the second edition of its *Diagnostic and Statistical Manual of Mental Disorders*. In the break, Ms. Ross lets loose. Those listeners enamored of the famous French philosopher's preoccupation with disciplinary institutions of the church, the medical establishment, and the mental institution will find it hard to not hear him invoked when she uncharacteristically *rasps*: "Don't call the doctor / don't call my momma / don't call the preacher / No! I don't need it. . . . If there's a cure for this, I don't want it."[33] Think also of the fierceness and power of Loleatta Holloway—her directness: "Yes I'm gonna mess around / Cause that's the way I want to be / Gonna try to get it down / Before I let it get to me / Don't want your love / Don't need it / That's the way I see it / Oh! Run-a-way!"[34] Strident. And you cannot say she did not warn you. "Nightclubbing" is only one of too numerous to cite examples from the oeuvre of "Jamerican" legend Grace Jones, who earned her icon status in gay communities. It not only burned the dance floor as it was spun by DJs worldwide, but killed at the Garage and other clubs in live performance.[35] You would do well to arrive late and be prepared for body paint and high drama. Evidencing another form of stridence, Grace transformed this song written by David Bowie and Iggy Pop using a rhythm section grounded by Jamaican legends Sly & Robbie, giving it a reggae and dub feel. Her vocals are more laid back than usual, à la New Wave. We can still hear the reggae influence and her nods to the Jamaican selectors in studio—chatting with engineers as she vamps *in*: "Louder . . . can you hear me?" So it is art pop, New Wave, a bit dub, one type of inventive reggae. And disco. Yes. All disco. "Is it all over my face?"[36] (Hell yeah! is the only acceptable response, dear listener.) "You caught me love dancing." These are blueswomen for the long 1980s. Like their foremothers in the Great Migration, women performers on the cusp of the epidemic 1980s were facing a heretofore unimagined reality and the tangible possibility of erotic autonomy that they were creating in the "tense of possibility" to which we will turn to reconsider in part 3.

"I'm Happy. I'm Carefree. And I'm Gay"

The significance of the disco—the club or the bar—for Black gay communion in the long 1980s cannot be overstated any more than can the centrality of the Black Christian church in the United States' long civil rights movement. The limitations are similar too: not everyone attended these institutions, and certainly neither is a perfect model of accessibility and democracy, despite the fact that many of us were (re)formed by them and insist on waxing rhapsodic about the institutions. It is also true that we run the risk of hiding other experiences if we overemphasize these centers. Still, the club/disco/bar was the central meeting space of what folks thought of as a community. Here's Audre commenting on the drylongso gay sociality at the club/bar back in the day: "Sometimes there was food cooked, sometimes there was not. Sometimes there was a poem, and sometimes there was not. And always, on weekends, there were the bars."[37]

I remember Better Days on Fiftieth Street in Manhattan. Five-feet-tall neon dicks were painted on the walls.[38] Men grinding on the dance floor to Shep Pettibone's mixes threatened to disrupt the comfortable domesticity that I had briefly escaped via the Long Island Railroad and a nervous subway ride two stops uptown, hopefully to finally impart "burdensome knowledge of carnal secrets" I longed to know.[39] This was the first time I heard "I Was Born This Way," (now Archbishop) Carl Bean's 1977 gay anthem. A few facts of its production warrant closer consideration. Written at the height of the "disco era" by Bunny Jones, a straight Black woman beauty-salon owner who sold the original self-published record from the trunk of her car, "I Was Born This Way" has the distinction of being the first openly gay-affirming song to hit the charts. Ever. The peppy original, sung by Black gay Broadway actor Charles "Valentine" Harris, garnered the number-one spot in the United Kingdom in 1975, and Bean's version rose on Black music and dance charts in the United States.[40] Legendary radio personality of the local Black radio station WBLS, Frankie Crocker, "the chief rocker," was the first to air it, to widespread approval. That the song was produced and distributed by Motown Records and was successful among Black listeners in the late 1970s evinces the dynamism of Black US attitudes toward sexuality, pre-AIDS. Imagine this today, nearly two generations later. What I heard at Better Days was most likely the Bruce Forest and Shep Pettibone Better Days mix. It starts a capella. Recorded for a large club, the sound feels as if the archbishop is whooping from his pulpit after a long service. The gospel veteran has that pre-rasp. A voice that has been working:

(w)Oh / OOOh / OOOOOOh / O.OOOOO.Oh / At last I can be free.ee
Yeah [*a significant exhale here . . .*] ListennnnnnN. I MeeAn. I really.
    Can.be. Meeeeee
[*Echo. Eight-second silent pause (intense foot stomping in the club ensues).*]

I'm happy. [*inhale*] I'm carefree. And I'm gay/ [*inhale*] I was born this
    way [*echo*]. . . .
[*strings only*]
From a little bitty boy. yeah. Yeaayyyh. / I was born this way/ heah eah.
I gotta tell the world about it / yeah / I was born this way. . . .
[*electric gospel piano*]
I feel good. I feel good yeah yeah. I . . . I . . . I'm . . .
From a little bitty boy / [*cymbal sweeps*] Knew. Something about me
    had changed. . . .
[*Four-on-the-floor bass drums and all. Going in.*]
You. You / You may not understand / But I was born this way.
[*By now the whoop is a melodic wheeze at the end of his run.*]
I want the world. To know / I'm just. / Ordinary folk yeah yeah
    yeah.

In this version the backstory of the insult does not occur until you have already broken a full sweat and heard a million turns of "I'm gay/I/I/I'm gay. . . ." An electronic string pentatonic progression introduces the return to the archbishop's voice at 3:38:

You / Laugh at me / And you got the nerve / to criticize / (yeah)
If I were you / I would sit down. And consider. What. You're doin'.
Love me. Like I love you / And together / Ain't no telling / What
    we'll do. / Yeah / Born.
I said it. Yeah, I was born this way. . . .

This is liberation theology, requiring zeal and evangelical-level stridency:

Proud to tell you. Proud to tell it / Yeaayh I was born this way!
Run and shout it / Tell the world about it / Hey gay. gay. hey . . .
    Born! / Born! / Born! / Born! / Born! / Born. This way.

The archbishop has sung himself happy. No turning away from this Pentecost: "You don't have to be cured to be healed." Seemingly modulated up, at 5:07 the instrumental break emerges. Here's where the children *per-form*, honey—accompanied by electronic cymbals/tambourines/*shekeres*! With the piano at 6:05, it gets more serious. There are multiple breaks in what Kevin Aviance calls "real *real* dance music." Like a singer using melisma or runs or changes in phrasing, the DJ can surprise you with new possibilities and breaks in sequence and time that are not in the original recording, but what they intuit and improvise. Remember Wura: "Our futures are not predetermined." We twirl. Cut. Scratch. Repeat. Long play. Extend.

Congas! Right around the 6:59 mark on the remastered Shep Pettibone mix feels like the point I leaped to the top of the speaker at 688, the short-lived "mixed" club that was across from our regular Friday and Saturday night club, Loretta's, in Atlanta. It was someone else's graduation celebration in 1990—the year that I was supposed to *walk* but danced instead. Most of the Morehouse and Spelman folks we knew had left by this late deep-house/disco portion of the evening. Several months before, devastated, I had sadly broken up with my girlfriend and did the thing that people call "coming out" for the first time. Temporarily breaking through my dance-floor fugue at the end of one long instrumental piece, my friend Amy—one of the few that remained after this drama—joined me on top of the speaker (as we often did). *I will not forget*: her braids flying, Amy sing-shouted affirmingly along with Archbishop Bean: "You're gay! you're gay! You're my gay troll, and I love you!"

You Are My Friend

Graciously, before beginning his now-legendary March 11, 1979, San Francisco War Memorial Opera House performance of "You Are My Friend," Sylvester says to the audience "This song is dedicated to all of you. . . ." But this communion certainly sounds more like dedication and love between Sylvester and his friends and bandmates Izora Rhodes and Martha Wash (collectively Two Tons of Fun, later the Weather Girls).[41] A flute and slow steady percussion. Then he says, "It goes like this. . . ." Midrange hums. Sylvester begins gingerly: "You Are My Frien." The *d* has faded. Sibilant. Glissando: "I never knew 'til then, my friend." Tongue poised at the top of the hard palate articulating that "gay sound": "ooooh, when you hold my hand," singing three different colors in the melismatic "oh." Reaching higher before approaching falsetto. The upsouth accent. Watts, cum Arkansas, from where his mother and her people had migrated. Sylvester, now the epidemic dead, lives and gives life in this song: "You made me re-a-lize / the fu-ture / is bright. . . . I been around." Melismatic trills and runs. Martha's descant punctuates the harmony: "You know I been lookin' around. . . ."

"I been lookin' around, and you were here all the time. . . ." All three are blended from the first as "one voice" reflecting the best of church training. Martha's ethereal melisma. You can hear Sylvester moving away from the mic, like Sarah Vaughn does—like Lucumí drummers turning their heads or caressing their drum: "Everything I needed . . . is right here all the time." Then Sylvester speaks: "You see these girls . . . Martha and Izora. [*applause*] I met them three years ago . . . [*aside*] was it February, Martha?" [*she answers*] "February." "Three years ago . . . a little audition we held on *Sissthx* [Sixth] Avenue and Judah—I will not forget. . . ." Sylvester's speaking voice has a nasal quality that is not detectable in singing. Clock the fricative gesture made with pursed lips. Can you sense the Black gay verbal performance here? "We had our first rehearsal in a *Volkswagen* on the way to Marin County. And these girls have stuck with me all through everything, y'all, and they're here right now. I want you to know that." The audience goes up. Biggest and longest applause yet. The background instrumentals continue: "You see . . . [*interrupted by swells of applause, Sylvester teases*] I don't know if y'all have noticed it or not, but these women can t*hsing* [sing], y'all! Honey, your ear has to be in yo' foot, to not hear these women can t*hsing*! They don't need these dresses. They don't need them jewrie*ss* [jewelry]. They don't need that hair. These women can t*hsing*, y'all!" They take the mic and prove Sylvester correct, each demonstrating her own virtuosity. Martha first. He sings, "Martha, you've been around . . . girl, I know that you've been around," and she responds with color and control: "I've been around. And you were here all the time. . . ." The response of the crowd seems perfectly attuned as the band modulates. By 4:42, she is hollering! Spirit has descended, and she will not let it go. The band is in tandem, with the crowd swelling with applause; then they seamlessly modulate down and play more softly. This is the end of a historic and triumphant evening at the august San Francisco War Memorial Opera House. To add further significance, the name of the album on which it appears (and from which this listening account draws) is *Living Proof*. The (church/club) opera house is enraptured. One can hear the breathlessness of the audience as they cheer. "I hope y'all understand that we love each other, y'all," an obviously *verklempt* Sylvester says at around 5:41. The feeling in the music is languid and generous. Then Sylvester sing-invites Izora: "Izora, you been around . . . girl, I know you been around." "I been lookin . . . ," she sings from her low register and scales up each word: "you / were / here / all / the / time. . . . I been many places. Seen a lot of faces. But, oh, when I needed someone / you were here all the time / Round! Oh, round / yeah!" She seems to step away from the microphone to not overpower it. The crowd is worked into a frenzy by 6:50. The three are going around and around and around like the lyrics. This could go on all night. You can hear the live audience on their feet. The tripartite magic of Sylvester—he and Izora and Martha together—is on display here in this song originated by Patti Labelle. Sylvester's powerful highs, Izora's ancestrally deep tones and church growls, constructing a framework for Martha's rich coloratura flirting beautifully in between, reaching upper registers with Sylvester, then falling back to allow the diva his due. The tight-ass band with those crisp drum hits and bass hits. This performance is coalition work. If this were a church building and not an opera house, we would expect the drumming to speed up now—aisles clearing for running and fainting and prophesizing.

Find Yourself a Friend

The invocation to ceremony takes place in one abrupt drum clap. Eleguá needs no introduction. The opener of the way and guardian of crossroads in Yoruba spiritual tradition. Brass blaring. Four-on-the-floor drums. Then, Erzuli—the coquette and apothecary, a dangerously seductive party girl—arrives, laughing, gleeful squeals and hollers in the background: it is a party from the first bar. "Over and Over" is funk sped up.[42] Tambourine shaking. Then the strings, indicative of "disco" for most folks, enter. Repeat. It's hotting up. And that voice:

> Over and over / time and time again. Over and over and over / time and time again.
> You can't be nobody's lover, you can't be nobody's lover . . . somebody's friend
> I love you / [*Izora co-signs* Well] to me you're a shining star / First you gotta find out / [*Martha co-signs* yeahyeahyeah] just who you really are
> And you can't be nobody's lover, you can't be nobody's lover . . .
> Until you're somebody's friend [*repeat*].

I have already suggested that a friend is one who shares in our individual process of knowing and becoming. Friendship instantiates *una tierra desconocida* and is a ground that is inevitably one of discovery.[43] Jacqui (M. Jacqui Alexander) has told us that "no one comes to consciousness alone, in isolation, only for herself, or passively. It is here we need a verb, the verb *conscientize,* which Paolo Freire used to underscore the fact that shifts in consciousness happen through active processes of practice and reflection . . . the fact of the matter is that there is no other work but the work of creating and re-creating ourselves within the context of community."[44]

Four-on-the-floor bass, plus a relentless tambourine doing double its time. The stamina! Guitar frets barely hold on in the guitar solo. It is in the pocket with the bass and drums, strings on top. Disco, yes, and/but it is better to just call all of this Black music. The designations disco or funk, dance pop or gospel at the club, do not necessarily serve. At the same time, we do not want to concede or diminish the *space* of disco. It is a righteous container for this sonic Blackfullness. Ashford and Simpson had already recorded a beautiful version of their song "Over & Over" in 1977 on their *So So Satisfied* album. The narrative gist of the song follows one of the winning themes of Ashford and Simpson's brilliant partnership: a romantic couple affirming that friendship is necessary as the foundation for a romantic relationship. Sylvester queers this in his version. We understand from the orchestration, vocal performance, and production that the accent here is friendship of many kinds that may or may not involve coupledom. The entire song is in congregation: a party with requisite hoots and hollers and signifying. The mandate, in case you cannot hear it repeated *over and over* again, is "Find yourself a friend." Then the break. Bass drum drops, and you might hear the gender-variant Fon deity, Sogbo, appear suddenly like a crack of thunder. Holy Ghost most certainly descends. The comforter. "Sing, Children!" Martha cries. There are more voices, all in the studio together. The multivocality is necessary to anthologically drive home this coda, punctuated with hand claps:

> Find yourself a friend
> Find yourself a friend
> Find yourself a friend
> Find yourself a friend. . . .

Now soaring strings try to catch up, encircling the percussion. There's a box drum around 6:20 with vocalizations that commence at about 6:34. Sylvester, Izora, Martha, and them are not ready to give up the mic. They cannot. The spirits have descended. All of them. And there is more to convey on this frequency. At about 7:20 the High Priest(ess) is strident, melismatic, and sibilant, all at once. Hollering "People!" with the urgency of a word that will save their lives. The children are deep in this break/wake/kaleidoscope, carrying on. Someone shouts "Sing Children!" (is it me?) as Martha and Sylvester run up and down the scales, *singing in tongues*. Izora joins their seemingly effortless vocalization. Pentecost in the studio. *Find yourself a friend.* The voices are almost indistinguishable in one moment; then each is perfectly singular. The tambourine reasserts. My ear was not trained as early or as finely as Ashon (Crawley)'s to hear the breath and the break.[45] As a Presbyterian kid, it was only through this so-called secular music that I first learned the polyphonic triple-beat hand clap, dear dancer. But blackness is not really "secular" at all, is it? From *voudun* ceremony to *bembe* (Cuban Yoruba religious gathering in which drumming is central) to dance floors on four continents, I now know when to fall out and holler. "Hold my mule!" I hear E. Patrick (Johnson) shouting from the dance floor at Traxx, Atlanta.[46] Marvin is right: "Disco is a medicine, disco is a balm, and disco is a healing." Sylvester and them "pervert the language," break it down into morphemes of sung conjure medicine: "Go out and find yourself a friend. Go out and find yourself a friend, my friend, my friend. . . ."[47]

5   Black Nations Queer Nations?

Open Ellipsis. Brooklyn, New York, 1995

Mudcloth. On the opening day of the Black Nations? Queer Nations? conference, I wore the mudcloth I had purchased at the Kwanzaa Expo at the Jacob Javits Center a few months before. It was stunning. Wrapped simply around my waist and falling to my combat boots in Afrocentric butchqueen seriousness, it was printed with an orderly, but not staid, geometric pattern in shades of coffee tobacco and a bit of cream. I am pretty certain I paired this with a heavy black turtleneck. Recalling this without the benefit of field notes (a practice that I would not be introduced to until I began to take graduate classes, one year later) is easy because that is the way I always wore my mudcloth wrap in New York City—with combat boots and not a small amount of "out" late-twenty-something triumphalism. That year my mudcloth wrap was four seasons, as I pummeled the streets of Manhattan, Brooklyn, and downtown Jersey City where I lived. Had it ever made it to Laurelton, Queens—on the Long Island Railroad I took on trips home to see my family—my mother would have surely judged this outfit a chuckle-worthy "get-up." For me, batik pants, tie-dye shirts, cowrie chokers, and wax-print remnants tied as belts had been de rigueur in the late 1980s and 1990s, but I thought that the wrap was a bit much for Laurelton. One late afternoon in Brooklyn, leaving Island HIV Family Services, where I had facilitated a staff training session, I noticed the sun was beginning to set. It was only then that I realized that I was in Bed Stuy (pre-gentrification), essentially wearing a long skirt that impeded my ability to run quickly, and combat boots whose heaviness and association suggested the lie that I was prepared for a physical altercation. On my way to the office, I had not noticed folks in the street noticing me. (After all, the vacant look of a runway model reflects one absorbed in his own imagined fierceness. I was giving it to them, but) I did not notice what the streets were giving. Now, with my heavy leather backpack and mudcloth, walking those seven unsure blocks of turns—and now very aware of my own inevitable twists—I see brothers assembled on the corner. Certain types of ethnographers love to write about brothers who seem to magically appear on corners like these, as if awaiting a sociological questionnaire or an "inner city" intervention. These brothers looked to me like stalwart habitué—all-season corner boys. These days, only rarely are dark-brown young men like these seen chilling on the corner, as they were that day before "community policing" surveillance promoted stop-and-frisk harassment as the center of so-called protection services in New York City and other cities around the world. Since the early aughts, this same block has been heavily trafficked by Black and brown women from the Caribbean and Southeast Pacific who push an endless parade of prams, bursting with white babies. Anyway, the brothers noticed me. I mentally check my twist— deciding (at least I hope had a modicum of courage and self-determination *to decide*) that there is now no use in trying to hide the slightbop.*twist*. slightbop.twist of my booted bloodbeat stride. Breathe in.

Our experiences are marked by various levels and intensities of precarity. A slightbop/twist is not a languid runway saunter. It is not a stonebutch swagger, a ballroom duck walk, dip, or spin.[1] I look at the brothers, about five of them, in the eyes. There were two crinkled brown bags, each holding forty ounces of ice-chilled *Olde E*. Sensimilla shared among them wafted around us all. A natural mystic blowing. I ritually Black man head nod: never gesturing downward in submission to the brother, always up, led by the chin in acknowledgment of equality. One brother (the one with those lips I still remember) turns his head decidedly away. Breathe out. What will they do—especially he who stands in profile, occupying the center-right soloist position in this tableau posed as if they were in a Blackstreet or Soul 4 Real video? I must have taken another deep breath. Having been raised to love not fear my people, but also aware of the pain we inflict on the different, softer among us—those wearing skirts long or (too) short, or perhaps unable to run fast enough (to where? Really). Breathe deeply. Nostrand Avenue is now only perhaps one-and-a-half blocks away. Step.step.stepstep. step. step.*slight*twist/bop. My right arm likely swung a bit, as my left clutched the backpack strap on my chest, exposing the cowrie-shelled leather band on my wrist. Step.step.stepstep. step.step.slighttwist. "A salaam alaikum, brother," the soloist says seriously, while attempting without success to hide his paper-bagged treasure behind the back of another (the one with those eyes). "Wa alaikum salaam, brother!" I return, enthusiastically. Step.step. slight twist/bop. slightbop. Twistbop. Twistbop to the train station.

We have reached the end of the long 1980s. M. Jacqui Alexander greets us:[2] "Welcome to this partnership of energy building thinking working loving laughing and struggling. We have come from many places for this conference ... as far away as South Africa from London from Canada ... from various places around the US, ... and we could name it all. So we welcome you to these three days of work. It's serious work that has brought you here and work that you will do beyond," she promises/demands/invites.[3] You will remember, of course, that at the start of the 1980s, Black feminists had already charged us to be accomplices with the most vulnerable and to be responsible to the past and to the present. Black gay men assigned archaeological unburying and an "unending search for what is utterly precious," warning that we would be eviscerated from the record if we dared not heed. And now that promise again here—work—"here and work ... beyond." I hear it all at once: the playful entreaty "wuk" of soca and calypso indexed for me in Jacqui's Trinbagonian accent, and the blues-filled songs of chain gangs and blueswomen. That plaintive command *"werk!"* on the dance floor or just off the runway. What our ancestors and some of us do today: from can't see to can't see. The labor of it all. The struggle/*la lucha. No es fácil* (it ain't easy). A lot of work. But she offers partnership too: in energy building, thinking, loving, and laughing.

The work of Black LGBTQ individuals, organizers, and movements had been ongoing since at least the mid-1970s, but the mid-1990s represents the apex of explicit and organized Black gay and lesbian public expression. The year 1995 was indeed a crucial historical moment. The Black gay 1980s began to give way to the decade that would end the twentieth century and usher in Black *queer*. We tarry here at Black Nations/Queer Nations? Lesbian and Gay Sexualities in the African Diaspora: A Working Conference, and the film that so evocatively captures it—to begin to frame the problematique of Black recognition, intersubjective regard, and solidarity across various types of borders, at the moment in which the conversation emerges. This is demonstrated through the multiple interrogations and interarticulations of *Black? Nations? / Queer? Nations?*

As our own dear and *late-too-soon* Vincent Woodard asserted in his astute review of the historic and influential 2000 Black Queer Studies in the New Millennium conference, the 1995 Black Nations/Queer Nations? "was the first to pose the Black queer question in an academic setting. . . . The conference's critical attitude towards naming reflected its conscious awareness of the power dynamics inherent in language creation, usage, and dissemination, a mode of inquiry cultivated and foregrounded in the work of radical Black feminists."[4] It is more than significant that this first explicit invocation of Black/queer—notably ambivalent about *queer* from the first—was made in the context of national and ethnic multiplicity, trans/inter-nationalism, and diaspora. Of course, the language of the conference was meant to be provocative, and it cannot be separated from paradigm shifts that had been recently forced by a few streams of related scholarly, activist, and artistic work that had emerged in various places around the world since at least the middle of the 1970s. The interrogative and often contradictory meanings and politics of each term—Black, queer, nations—are pluralized to signal multiplicity. The articulations and tensions among them are signaled by the stroke (/), making this formulation a potentially destabilizing and generative heuristic, with global resonance. The *Black? Nations? / Queer? Nations?* formulation sutures (or makes coherent) the in-between idea that we pursue throughout this book.

Shari Frilot's evocative and rich true-to-life film, *Black Nations/Queer Nations?*, begins in silence, with an invocation of the memory of Essex Hemphill, who had died of AIDS and passed to the ether eight months after his pivotal interventions at the conference. This is followed by a brief scrolling description in which the end statement issues a lofty challenge, taken up since then in scholarly, artistic, and activist work in various corners of the world: "What results [from this conference] will shape debates around race, gender, sexuality and sexual practice well into the next century."[5] Then an Audre Lorde statement appears from her essay "The Transformation of Silence into Language and Action," which reads in part: "The fact that we are here is an attempt to break silence and bridge some of the difference between us, for it is not difference which immobilizes us, but silence. And there are so many silences to be broken."[6] The frame fills with the faces of a variety of individuals who appear in their various shades of brown and cream, multiple ways of saying, styling, and signifying on gender, speaking in English with various regional and national accents. They say, in tandem:

Black Nations Queer Nations? is a working conference. Our work is to analyze the political, economic, and social situations of lesbians, gay men, bisexuals, and transgender people of African descent. . . . This conference comes at a crucial historical moment. Over the last decade, the visibility of our cultural work has blossomed. We have worked to build and solidify our own grassroots organizations. We have organized against oppressions of many different kinds. We have fought for the right and dignity to live work and love.[7]

In the frame following the conference description (1.16), adding to the litany, writer and activist Jacquie Bishop begins with "We have fought for the right and dignity to live," and then is joined in split-screen duet with another woman, as they add "work," before the two are joined by the face of a child: "and love" all three say. As an invocation of Black/queer futurity, the child—with a collared shirt, short hair, and new teeth!—appears between wispily mustachioed Jackie, who is soft spoken and wears a leather cap and leather vest, and the sister with long dreadlocks pulled into a ponytail. This image incites a reading of a queered "nuclear option" for Black/queer familyhood (well before "gay marriage" took center stage) and is especially significant, anticipating the next line: "Notwithstanding, we are still threatened by daunting challenges: homophobia, sexism, racism, poverty, physical violence, unemployment, exploitative working conditions. . . ." Next, with "Moreover," the litany of current vulnerabilities deepens: "Our communities are being disproportionately ravaged by HIV/AIDS, cancer, and the inaccessibility of health care. These threats are made more horrific by the growing power of the not-so-new right, xenophobia, and ethnocentrism; as well as the resurgence of many reactionary forms of nationalism—globally and in the United States. Given those challenges, we must challenge those forces which restrict our lives, and threaten the survival of our many communities."[8]

Cut to the opening session of the conference in which we are greeted by Jacqui Alexander's warm invitation to *la lucha*. Then Wahneema (Lubiano) intones, as if to speak directly to the project of critical analysis in which the participants and the viewers of the film (and now you, dear viewer) are being invited to participate. Shari's camera cuts in to Wahneema's plenary panel presentation as she provokes: "Who is being addressed, by whom, to what end? What is identity? Who answers to a specific identity? What gets constantly revived in the answer? What is stabilized, for example, in the question and in the answer?" Here Wahneema and her colleagues on the plenary panels set out an initial exploration of what would become among the central critical questions of Black queer studies to come.

The first interrogative is nation: *whose* nation? Constructed out of what histories and political economies and relating to what other nations at particular moments in time? Jacqui had already made significant contributions to this discussion in her academic work. However, like Cathy (Cohen), another co-organizer of the conference, Jacqui's importance to movement politics and radical Black queer organizing in New York City went well beyond her scholarship. For example, before reading a word of their work, I was impacted and inspired by the way Cathy and Jacqui's presences in discussions—like the marathon meetings during which New York activists pursued the finer points of the mission statement of what would become the Audre Lorde Project: A Lesbian, Gay, Bisexual, Two Spirit, Trans and Gender Non-Conforming People of Color Center for Community Organizing—contributed (eventually!) to conceptual clarity. At the opening of the conference, Jacqui noted that although, in fact, it is difficult to imagine anticolonial struggle without nationalism, "I am discomforted by the nation and I am perennially suspect of it. Whether it is queer nation, lesbian nation, white American imperial nation, or Black middle-class nation. It poses a big problem," she said, and the audience applauded enthusiastically.[9] Knowing. In 1995 this audience of largely Black folks and other people-of-color activists, artists, and intellectuals were already poised to be suspicious of the United States and a number of nations of origin. The public prominence of ACT-UP and Queer Nation seemed recently to begin to fade from the center of the LGBTQ activist stage, as more homonormative gay rights organizations and discourses seized the spotlight. By the mid-1990s, the GLB (civil rights) movement was inviting gays and lesbians to imagine themselves as husbands, wives, and US soldiers—*just like everyone else*—to serve (semi-)openly as part of the global police apparatus that Pat Parker had already rejected and given us colorful language to resist a dozen years earlier, and to enter into civil partnerships in advance of the right to marry. Of course, the ever-elusive promise of (homo)normativity creates a very powerful pull for Black people, who have been offered very few opportunities to exhale the atmospheric poison of antiblackness and inhale the rarified air of acceptance. *When can we finally just breathe?* But as Jacqui's countrywoman, Carole Boyce-Davies, contends, "Going all the way home with . . . nationalism . . . means taking a route cluttered with skeletons, enslavements, new dominations, unresolved tensions and contradictions."[10] Both of these scholars had been shaped by Trinidad and Tobago's own nationalist movements and exclusions. The eminent historian and first prime minister of independent Trinidad and Tobago, Eric Williams, brilliantly theorized that "Massa Day Done" in his rousing 1961 speech. He held that "Massa" is more than a personage: "the owner of a West Indian sugar plantation, frequently an absentee . . . dominating his defenseless workers by the threat of punishment or imprisonment, using his political power for the most selfish private ends, an uncultured man with an illiberal outlook. . . ." More than this, according to Williams, Massa is also a "racial complex [that] stunted the economic development of our territories . . . standing for degraded labour . . . racial inequality [and] . . . colonialism." His postindependence Afro-Creole government pushed against detractors as "Massa['s] . . . stooges, who prefer to crawl on their bellies to Massa, absentee or resident."[11]

But Williams's party, like all of the others in the nations of the Americas in the long 1980s, also traded on the consolidation of patriarchal heteronormativity to purchase conditional inclusion in the fraternity of sovereign nation-states. With this as historical context, Carole recently brilliantly theorized her own movements within the United States and between the northeastern United States, West Africa, and the Caribbean—both the actual archipelago and the imaginative lived experiences and invocations of the Caribbean elsewhere—as movement between "Caribbean spaces" and escape from "twilight zones" of exclusions and cultural anomie in the United States.[12] And/but lesbian, transgender gender-non-conforming, gay bisexual, and queer folks live within spaces/zones that are qualitatively different from Carole's. These are made through compounding multiple transnational twilight displacements. To illustrate this, here, quoted at length, is how Jacqui famously begins her essay "Not Just (Any) Body Can Be a Citizen," published in *Feminist Review* the year before the Black Nations/Queer Nations? conference:

> I am an outlaw in my country of birth: a national; but not a citizen. Born in Trinidad and Tobago on the cusp of anti-colonial nationalist movements there, I was taught that once we pledged our lives to the new nation, "every creed and race [had] an equal place." I was taught to believe "Massa Day Done," that there would be an imminent end to foreign domination. Subsequent governments have not only eclipsed these promises, they have revised the very terms of citizenship to exclude me. No longer equal, I can be brought up on charges of "serious indecency" under the Sexual Offences Act of 1986, and if convicted, serve a prison term of five years. In the Bahamas, I can be found guilty of the crime of lesbianism and imprisoned for twenty years. In the United States of North America where I now live, I must constantly keep in my possession the immigrant

(green) card given me by the American state, marking me "legal" resident alien; non-national; non-citizen. If I traverse any of the borders of twenty-two states even with green card in hand, I may be convicted of crimes variously defined as "lewd unnatural; lascivious conduct; deviant sexual intercourse; gross indecency; buggery or crimes against nature. . . ."[13]

At the conference, the audience went up at Jacqui's perennial suspicion and problematizing of *any* nation because we know all too well how "home" is often the first zone of dissociative twilight and constrained space. Moreover, there are "new dominations" or perhaps "unresolved tensions" that find Black (would-be) citizens still ineligible: without franchise or shelter within their nations of origin and when they attempt to leave or return from here to there.

Interrogating the category *Black* (and Black "nation") proved to be more controversial than *nation*. The terms under which folks accepted—or were accepted *as*, strategically deploy, or *feel Black*, and their various wishes to (be) organize(d) or (be) understood as a subject of or to the power of any racial category—were in (now permanent) upheaval. In the long 1980s, "racial hybridity" was the trend in race studies—often with "race" significantly set off in scare quotes to underscore its constructedness. Influential Black British critics Paul Gilroy and Kobena Mercer, along with various critical cultural studies acolytes, not only problematized but assiduously wrote "against race" and for recognition of various iterations of hybridity.[14] Other modes of teasing out what was unthought in uncritical bipolar dichotomies North/South, white/Black, US/Mexico, for example, began to proliferate in the late 1980s. For example, Anzaldúa's invocation of "*la conciencia de la mestiza*" beautifully harmonizes and riffs off Du Bois's "double-consciousness" toward the recognition of the creation of a new consciousness at the border/crossroad of Native and European, South and North. But "mixedness," which is imagined as something other than Black, is too often positioned as a virtue and/or a desired end in itself.

Although some scholars and critics, like Manning Marable, continued to hold Black self-identification as distinct from interpellated racialization and emphasized connection and similarities between Black folks (mainly in the United States), the trend in the elite academy was toward "deconstruction" and distinction. Following Jacques Derrida and others, the salutary point was to undermine the unquestioned or unthought "just-so" understanding of social relations, as one would do in a scholarly deconstruction of a text. Much of this work is important and enabling, but I have already cautioned that we ought to be more attentive to how this may (perhaps unintentionally) reify blackness as a singularly stable sign in a universe of hybridity, most pertinently regarding Black US Americans. Although it was likely not his intention, in one example in the film Raúl Ferrera-Balanquet's panel comments illustrate how concepts of hybridity can also unintentionally be (mis)used to diminish Black identification. Invoking the Yorùbá/Lucumí word for divine power, Raúl offered, "Mestizáje . . . was my aché, it was my power. . . . It was very difficult for African-Americans to understand that the African diaspora covers a very large territory. . . . We are mixed people. That idea of being Black is a very reductionist idea that always keeps us linked to the colonial power, and it won't be until the moment that we realize we are mixed [*applause. Inaudible*]. We have from the beginning have been mixed . . . different African ethnic groups and they mixed themselves . . . from the beginning, and we have to take power from that mixture." I believe that Raúl wants to argue against "race" here, or at least against colonial racism. But what he actually says takes aim at "the very reductionist idea" of being Black. The immediate, then suddenly scattered audience applause pattern in the film also seems to indicate agreement with what we believe the sentiment is, but knowing that there is something else happening in the elocution. I raise this to demonstrate how easily concepts that are not critically challenged for their potential for antiblackness can collapse and degrade, among friends. From where, precisely, do we imagine the "power" of mixture is drawn? Does it empower one side from or to another partisan of the mix? I have shown, in the Cuban context, that focusing on hybridity—or color Cubano—does not necessarily get us further along the road but often merely predictably retreads well-worn antiblackness. That is, another way to read mixing discourses is as one of many alchemical imperial projects that provide expanded forms of whitening, for some, while rigidifying that which or who is cast as unalterably black.[15]

Ibrahim Abdurrahman Farajajé (née Elias Ferajaje-Jones), or Ibrahim Baba, as his students and protégé affectionately called him most recently—the Black queer bisexual multiracial theologian and mystic who transitioned to the ether in 2015—clarified and pushed the conversation significantly forward. A superb thinker and teacher, drawing from his experience as Howard University faculty at the time, Ibrahim beautifully and graciously discussed Black diversity and attempts to exclude queer Black people from full Black identification: "And that raises for me the issue of multiplicity of blacknesses"—he stressed the plural, and the audience responded with applause and approbation—"that as Black people we speak many languages and have many religious and spiritual paths and nationalities, etcetera, but . . . somehow we have a deep-seated fear of the so-called 'real Blacks' and . . . we buy into the dichotomous way of thinking that says we cannot be both queer and really down with the revolution." Here Ibrahim nimbly argues against discourses and practices that aim to diminish blackness, while also launching a critique of those who set themselves up as the arbiters of correct blackness. That is, he cautioned against diminishing blackness by claiming both/either that blackness is "reductionist," as Raúl erroneously and likely unwittingly did, or to diminish it by claiming that blackness is monolithic, easily or simplistically drawn, or noncultural. Today—now that a diminished view of blackness has become de rigueur in scholarly circles—we must add that our real "deep-seated fear" is not only of the "so-called real Blacks," who in any case had only limited and symbolic power to draw boundaries around a category in which there was already narrow investment or purchase. Even more fearsome and pernicious than these inimical would-be patriarchs (now caricatured as "Hoteps" or "No-Teps") and Queen Mother matriarchs are scholars and policy makers who regularly dismiss, perjure, and attempt to diminish the idea of blackness and who dismiss those who would revise and defend blacknesses. Antiblackness is still real and ubiquitous today—as ever, compounded by classism, xenophobia, heterosexism, and misogynoir. In contrast, a Black gay habit of mind upholds a version of blackness that seeks to invite, seduce, repatriate, and recover our folks lost to various versions of antiblackness.

The year 1995 is in the recent past—interned in some ways. Sadly, this retelling and rereading must also continue a litany of our brave brilliant dead who nonetheless continue to speak to us. In the film the next to appear onscreen holding forth on the concept of blackness is the late South African activist Simon Nkoli. Perhaps anticipating your practiced suspicion of the category and your rigorous, gleeful deconstruction of blackness, Simon's panel commentary provides a clear answer. Whereas here we emphasize the agency of Black self-identification, it is no less true that blackness is (also) because of what white supremacy does and has done. His incisive analysis, based on the specific context of South African apartheid, is also deeply paradigmatic. That is, how black racialization is lived as class in a number of places (nearly everywhere) around the globe. The materiality of the matter could not be stated more directly or more incisively than this:

> Even when you want to ignore the fact that you are Black, you will be kept on being reminded by the government. The system. [*pause*]. I knew I was Black at the age of three. And it didn't come to me as a surprise. [*knowing giggles erupt from the audience*]. Because we had our little ghettos where we were pushed in.... "Don't come here and stay with us. The

only time you can cross the line is when we need your labour. When you can come and make us tea in the morning and then tidy up these little towns of ours, and then go back to the townships."

The first bars of the Staple Singers' "I'll Take You There" plays in response in a quick cut. Perhaps *there* to a nonnational space. Perhaps the space that Mavis and them want to take us to is not a physical place at all but a psychic or spiritual one. There, "ain't nobody cryin' / ain't nobody worried / ain't no smilin' faces, lyin' to the races" *there*.[16] In the next frame a visual of Earth from outer space appears, then moves closer to the atmosphere, to the old CUNY Graduate Center building where the conference was held. We are in midtown Manhattan at BN/QN? The scene opens to the door of the conference and candid scenes of friends and colleagues—many of whom have been gathering for work and events for many years—reacquainting. The conference call for panels and presentations had promised it would "bring together workers, intellectuals, political organizers, scholars, artists, students and everyone committed to the struggle of gay, lesbian, bisexual and transgender people of African descent to claim and live our lives . . . [in] an environment which will facilitate collective discussion and analysis across the many communities of the diaspora where we actively struggle toward our own empowerment."[17] This was a suitable event for the first outing of my Kwanzaa Expo mudcloth *lapa*, which I had bought to rock here as I prepared to lead one of the conference breakout sessions, "Defining Ourselves for Ourselves: Developing Community."

Out of Our Names

Although the word *queer* was already burgeoning within the US academy and some activist networks, guests in our home in town for the conference were still stridently arguing over the use of *gay* even then—in 1995. Our early ambivalence with *queer* (or "quare," as E. Patrick insightfully mediated years later[18]) would have seemed *so late* to (white) queer studies academics. But we are on our own time for our own reasons. Many of us still have not signed on. The most forceful of critics of the Black gay moniker is Cleo Manago, a very-well-known *same-gender-loving* community worker and founder of the AMASSI Institute and Black Men's Exchange. Cleo's coining of the phrase *same gender loving* (SGL) to replace *gay* and *queer*, which he maintains are "white names," is a poignant example of both the utter necessity of his point of view and the serious shortcomings of his intervention. Cleo is right that naming is crucially important. We ought to self-name and self-determine.

He and I—and the vast majority of Black gay, Black queer, and SGL intellectuals and activists—would agree that there is less overlap between the everyday experience of middle-class white gay men and poor Black homosexual, bisexual, trans, or nonbinary people than there is between Black folks of any sexual or gender expression or identity. And who would argue with "love" as a term of identification? Still, as I read the use of the term, its brightly divided gender lines; lack of attention to lesbian, bisexual, and trans experiences; and refusal to engage critical Black queer, Black LGBTQ, and Black feminist formulations that raise generative cautions to the name or category *same gender loving* weaken it. I worry that SGL really signals "typically or passingly masculine cisgender Black men, who prefer not to give up the sliver of contingent privilege that their gender presentation affords, whose sexual attention and political affiliation is geared toward others just like them." Of course, this is not what everyone means when they use it, like any other term. My reading may be too influenced by what I hear in public discourse/social media as the loudest voices employing the term. So, because of the resonance many find in this term, regardless of its faults, I sometimes use it, sparingly and in context, as a descriptor for those who prefer it. Let a thousand flowers bloom. There is transformational potential if we stay in conversation.

This is more generous an allowance than Cleo has afforded me. After the 2013 announcement that my alma mater, Morehouse College, would offer my course "Genealogies of Black LGBTQ Culture and Politics" (the second to be offered at an HBCU, after Dr. Layli Phillips's course at Spelman in the early aughts), Cleo wrote a scathing repudiation on his Facebook page of what he saw as the "white gay perspective" that the course and the instructor would bring to Dear Old Morehouse. I had not yet released the syllabus, although even the shallowest appraisal of my previous work would not leave a reader with the expectation of a "white gay perspective." To Kwame Holmes's Facebook query, "So, to be clear, you critiqued the class before seeing the syllabus?" Cleo responded, "Of course, Dr. Allen will be filling the white queer frame work he's bringing to Morehouse with Black voices." This baiting is familiar, of course: positioning those who disagree as aligned with or parroting "Massa." Cleo continues to push a popular and perilous form of cultural nationalism that would simply uncritically celebrate a great African past, imagining a time before difference constituted vulnerability for any Black person. This is a dangerous fantasy. Essex had already cheekily exploded this myth and repeated it during the BN/QN? conference. He checked the racial imperialist fancy of an African past in which some imagine we were all kings and queens. Warning "Y'all not going to like this" (as he laughed),

Essex informed us: "*Somebody* had to clean the temples . . . somebody had to carry water from the river. Somebody cooked the dinners that were served in the temples!" We chuckled and nodded and cosigned this truth, even as many of us in the conference auditorium were perched regally in mudcloth and wax prints, with braids, cowries, dreadlocks, Africa medallions, and new proud African names we had chosen ourselves (like "Jafari"). The fact that I had used "LGBTQ" in the course title was enough for Cleo: evidence that I had capitulated to categories of white gay existence. But "same gender loving" does not do the trick either. And it has not protected him from the virulent attacks of hate mongers who would put him and me in the same category—and in front of the same so-called Black nationalist firing squad—regardless of our differences.

Calling its post an "emergency alert," War on the Horizon posted a longish homophobic diatribe called "Haitianists, PanAfrikans, & Black Nationalists Beware: The Faggits [*sic*] Are Coming!" on its blog. The rant takes aim at Cleo as the most dangerous "white-sex offender." Here, the purported author of the YouTube video "The Effeminization of the Black Male," which regularly circulates on Facebook to alternate cheers and jeers, charges that "there is an international phenomenon threatening to destroy our people before we get the opportunity to launch our next movement. It is the international push to 'homosexualize' Afrikan people."[19] Their thinly veiled threats of violence are chilling. They spew (verbatim, and with no editorial correction on my part):

> The newest and boldest of these "Black Nationalist" imposters is a white-sex offender named Cleo Manago . . . one cannot be a white-sex offender and a good Afrikan anywhere in the world. . . . white-sex offense is a product of racism white supremacy, thereby making our participation in it treasonous. Blackskinned white-sex offenders are traitors by definition, and Afrikans must permanently remove this decadent element of our Race from all positions of influence and power. They must feel the threat of Black male aggression in its most righteous form. The day will come very soon when white-sex in Afrika will be a crime punishable by certain death. . . .

Then, pointing out what they see as the fallacy of the term *same gender loving*:

> He is a very bold and sophisticated white-sex offender who is trying to force his way into the back door of the Black Nationalist community. (That's one thing about homos, they're always trying to get into back doors.) At any rate, he is trying desperately to present himself as a strong

Black man, while at the same time, he's a salacious "homo." We should probably refrain from calling him a "homo" since he prefers to be called, "Same Gender Loving (SGL)." But, we will just call him a salacious "homo." We describe him as sophisticated because he does things like replace the terms fag, "homo," queer, stinky boy, etc . . . with a term like "Same Gender Loving." I love both of my Brothers who are the same gender as me. Does that make me Same Gender Loving? But I do not want to have sexual contact with them. That's a job perfectly suited for their wives. But with new terms like this hitting the market, malicious fagdom can be reduced in the minds of otherwise civilized people to a person's "personal preference."[20]

According to War on the Horizon, "a 'homosexual' or 'faggit' is a male who enjoys putting his penis in the mouth and/or anus of other males and enjoys having the same done to him." The conundrum of Cleo's disapproval of me and my fellow travelers reminds me of Elias's entreaty: "Somehow we have a deep-seated fear of the so-called 'real Blacks' and the extent to which we buy into the dichotomous way of thinking that says we cannot be both queer and really down with the revolution." These days, each of our lives may depend on confronting that fear that makes us turn away from listening and carefully and lovingly reading one another.

So, Finally. *Queer*

Readers can plainly see that Black lesbian, transgender, bisexual, and gay scholars most often perform a sort of ambivalence toward the concept of "queer," resonant with Kevin Aviance's conditional tolerance of the industrial/techno incursion into the clubs of the 1990s. It is therefore not a stretch, for example, to imagine a mash-up of E. Patrick Johnson and Kevin Aviance. After all, they are both fierce and now-legendary North Carolinians who found the vocation of shaman pathbreaker and diva in the big city. "Dr. E. Patrick Aviance" might quip that *queer is cute. It's cute, it's a cute theory . . . but it ain't "quare"! It ain't Cathy Cohen or Jacqui Alexander or Gloria Wekker or Cheryl Clarke. . . . It's not real critical race/gender theory!* Honestly, perhaps we were just never that into queer theory—even (Teresa) de Lauretis, (Judith) Butler, and (Eve) Sedgwick, from whose singular glittering contributions I have learned a great deal, but do not hear daily in my head as I hear Essex, Audre, Pat, Joe, Barbara, and Sylvester. For myself, and a number of fellow travelers, stellar (white) queer theory arrived on our bookshelves only after we had already imbibed the political and poetic nectars of intellectual activism and intersectional politics offered by Black trans, bisexual, lesbian, and gay poets, essayists, activists, and scholars. Thus, this author does not feel partisan to "Queer Incorporated." To be sure, like most Black/queer scholars, I have not been offered an ownership share in the ongoing concern. I am, instead, merely an interested observer of the drama that Jack (Halberstam) playfully reimagines. With tongue in cheek—and, typically, with no small amount of keen provocation and shade—Jack likened the various streams of current queer studies to the great houses of the popular HBO drama *Game of Thrones*.[21] So, allow me to project backward—reimagining the *Game of Thrones* ficto-historical medieval moment through Afrocentric historiography: I imagine my people a long way south of the known world of Ice and Fire. Having already circumnavigated the globe, building foundations of art and architecture and medicine in Africa, the Americas, and Oceania. After inventing higher mathematics and charting the stars, beating their faces with galena and kohl, and sailing strategically around the foolishness of the Seven Kingdoms, my people would not be vying for a throne of swords dripping with blood. If I could, I would warn them about the disastrous consequences of remaining too long in, or identifying too closely with, any kingdom of the North.

On its own—that is, outside of the creative reworking it continues to undergo in the hands of critical race, "of-color," decolonial, indigenous, Black studies and disability theorists in the arts and activism as well as in academe—*queer* may never include a more capacious co-articulation of a number of embodied and embodying categories, as some defenders claim it was always meant to do. Despite this, as I have already announced, following José (Muñoz), I also find the concept worthy of revision and supplement toward a truly disruptive and capacious hermeneutic. Though emerging from a very particular place and time (yes, of course), thoughtful invocation of *queer* in scholarly work not only describes the sense of the nonnormative status of those who identify with or are identified as homosexual and those whose gender self-identification or nonidentification is not resonant with the sex assigned to them at birth; but also, more pointedly, queer can be an aspirational way of seeing and saying. To borrow José's brown lens, "We may never touch queerness. . . . Queerness is a structuring and educated mode of desiring that allows us to see the future beyond the quagmire of the present. . . . [It is] essentially about . . . an insistence on potentiality or concrete possibility for another world."[22] It is to be found *in the break*.[23] Still, please do not mark me or my fellow travelers in the "queer camp." Black/queer does not do camping. It is unsettled by history, choice, and necessity—all at once. The articulation I have offered—the stroke (/) connecting Black to queer—signals at least a critical repositioning, if not also a novel take altogether. It reasserts the concept and experience of blackness complexly and even contingently— but never apologetically, secondarily, or in lowercase.

Standing at the Threshold of Cyberspace

Essex offered this, in the historical moment of the 1995 Black Nations/Queer Nations? conference, at the dawning of cyberspace:

> The texture of my hair and the color of my skin are just two of the pre-requisites for visibility and suspicion. I am profoundly perplexed by this continuing adversity and the unnecessary loss of life that occurs as a result of being seen. . . . I remain the same in the eyes of those who would fear and despise me. . . . I stand at the threshold of cyberspace and wonder, is it possible that I am unwelcome here too? Will I be allowed to construct a virtual reality that empowers me? Can invisible men see their own reflection? . . . As always, I am rewarded accordingly when I fulfill racist fictions of my aberrant masculinity. My primary public characteristics continue to be defined by dread of me; myths about me; and plain old homegrown contempt. All of this confusion is accompanying me into cyberspace. Every indignity and humiliation, every anger and suspicion. It is not easy loving yourself as a Black person—a Black man living in America. It is not any easier for our sisters either. . . . Don't be confused: racism doesn't go better with a big dick, or a hot pussy, or a royal lineage. . . .

We return to Essex with new questions borne of new technologies and new conditions. Today we are in a better position to query precisely what "confusions, contempts, dread" and possibilities accompany Black bisexual, gender-non-conforming, lesbian, trans, and gay people around cyberspace— which is currently the ultimate space of de-territoriality and also one kind of diaspora. Who is the gazer, in the context of the internet? Is the object thereby no longer a fetish and now a subject? Or, what does it feel like to be an object looking at a fetish? At the beginning of the twenty-first century, the motives for and forms of *minha cara* recognition (remember? "It's my face"!) and representation are various and mostly "undisciplined." Black queer individuals and groups make themselves legible to one another and to world-wide publics in myriad ways and with a variety of intentions. Four figure most prominently: first, to the state and powerful corporations to appeal for inclusion, redress, or welfare; second, to signal membership in far-flung polities and affinities and to address these fellow travelers as prospective allies whose differently situated voices can be brought to bear on local projects; third, to make appeals and announcements to perhaps say directly to their nation, church, family, or no one in particular in the impersonal intimacy of the internet: "We been here, we are here, and we are not leaving"; and finally, the exponentially most common use of cyberspace technology: folks make themselves available as potential friends, lovers, and objects of admiration or desire on various social media platforms and work as curators of and respondents to various individual sites—narrating, positioning, and framing themselves for transnational erotic literacy, legibility, and consumer consumption. New routes condition and support new socialities on the expanding threshold of cyberspace that we now inhabit. And like any black hole, the possibilities on the other side are infinite. Increasingly, even those without direct access to this virtual travel are "networked" nonetheless, albeit at a much slower speed and without the defining "new" characteristic of unmediated instantaneity. The newly mediated internet provides a powerful space for the creation of anonymous intimacy and various forms of queer becoming—in which, for example, races, genders, and sexualities are rehearsed, discussed, researched, applauded, and of course also derided. People trade porn, gossip, sweet and/or nasty nothings, barbs, bad translations, and urgent political news through these media.

Marcelo is one of a few respondents with whom I communicated in real time in a virtual space in which we could not only see and hear each other but also have access to (poor-quality) online translation software in cases in which our lingua franca of serviceable Spanish or "Portuñol" (an improvised mix of Spanish and my mostly terrible attempts at Portuguese) left too far a gap in legibility. Marcelo, who described himself as middle class, had access to the internet at his university in Brazil's interior, where he kept up with the goings on of Brazil's Black movement and cultural events in cities such as Salvador do Bahia and Rio de Janeiro. Moreover, in contrast to the majority of my students in the United States (queer and otherwise, Black and non-Black) who are largely monolingual and seem less apt to engage the world (wide web) beyond what English-only algorithms bring them, young people in the global South seem engaged, especially with the North, as if this is an important measure of their sophistication. I hear Rinaldo (Walcott)'s reproof about what he calls the "sexual/textual economy" and "unequal exchange" by which "Black diaspora queers find African-American queers, yet the reverse always seems impossible . . ." echoing.[24] Marcelo learned about the murder of Trayvon Martin and the arguments of Black gay and lesbian activists for gay marriage (which he understood as *tático* [tactical] for US politics) on the internet. His understanding of Black America had not just been shaped by Hollywood films, mainstream hip-hop/pop, and a couple of African American novels translated into Portuguese. He also read news and opinion blogs such as *Love B Scott* and *Rod 2.0* and viewed pirated copies of *The DL Chronicles* and *Noah's Arc*. Viscerally, more embodied and of the flesh, his vision, or way of seeing *there*, had been shaped by these cultural products, Facebook profiles, and pornographic videos that explode linguistic barriers · by performing a sort of male sexual desire Esperanto—a plain-text erotics that leaves intentions bare. This "visibility" and visual narration enable the *minha cara* feeling—allowing one to appreciate the resonances of race, gender, sexuality, and class (aspirations)—even with the sound turned down. Another respondent—in the Caribbean, with less dependable internet service—stays current through real-life networks of friends and neighbors and acquaintances: I text my friend, who calls our acquaintance in common via Digicell, but must wait until she has money to retrieve the messages. If we are lucky, my friend will see her at a meeting or a party and convey the message. Or they can go to the home of a more well-heeled acquaintance to Facetime or Skype from there to here.[25] Commodities of information, relationships, and objects do not stay embargoed within closed class networks, but the goods or values are circulated through variously networked nodes. Cyberspace provides a wide virtual berth for a variety of potential interactions and (dis)connections. In the case of the relatively very privileged who enjoy twenty-four-hour access to the internet—most commonly, via smartphones—what we will explore in the next section as *Black/queerpolity* is represented as a virtual global space of unregulated and instantaneous potential fulfillment of desire in the form of porn and dating websites, Facebook pages, Skype or Orkut, various dating apps and quick payment-enabled apps, and Instagram, all navigable from almost anyplace. The anthropologically minded may think of the value that is generated by circulation of this media from the networked to the less networked or nonnetworked as another form of *hau*: the invisible penumbra of privileges and obligations of exchange attached to "the gift."[26] The trade here is often in the currency of beauty, youth, willingness (or a combination of these), which can leverage access. Following Essex, however, this so-called access may still prove "perplexing" on this "other" side of the threshold of cyberspace.

Brother with No Suit

Essex's queries about what cyberspace would mean for Black people were prophetic. He muses, "Will I be allowed to construct a virtual reality that empowers me? Can invisible men see their own reflection?"[27] Continuing our reconsideration of these questions in the digital age, let us first briefly consider his criticism of the representation and consumption of an analog representation of Black skin and Black bodies that became one of the major skirmishes of the "culture wars" of the long 1980s. Essex found resonance in Kobena Mercer and Isaac Julien's essay "True Confessions," on photographic representation of Black male bodies, such as the well-known portrait of model Milton Moore, a lover of the famous white US photographer who named the (in)famous composition "Man in Polyester Suit" in his *Black Book*.[28] You will recall that this black-and-white image of a Black man wearing a three-piece suit caused controversy not only among those who saw it as "pornography" and therefore putatively not art but also among close readers of the studied and beautifully composed portrait who noted that the figure is headless and heartless: cropped at chest level. The star of the composition is situated at the center of the frame. A very large semierect uncircumcised penis juts out protuberantly from an open fly. Was this a comment on the ill fit of Black men in the corporate world—savage dicks unable to stand the discipline of corporate slacks, attempting to inappropriately insinuate themselves into the polyester world of corporate America? Or perhaps it is a statement of the photographer's (and the viewer's) desire for the only thing that could be of value or desirable from the Black man, given the fact that there is no head (and therefore no "eyes to the soul," or no soul indeed) in the frame and no shoulders (to cry on, or even to put to a hoe!). The hands in the photo are empty. Caught as if Milton was just about to gesture meaningfully (we cannot hear him, of course. He has no mouth), the camera denies him— denies us—any action. The singular focus of the work is the big Black dick, now so commonly referred to that it has been codified as BBD. But, of course, this is more specifically *Milton's* Black dick.

Milton Moore said that "I think he [Mapplethorpe] saw me like a monkey in a zoo." While I have no interest in the artist's intention at the moment—it is the subject of the work and the act of objectifying him that I am interested in—Milton was not far from the mark. The photographer had expressed complex feelings of what he described as love for Milton alongside zoological curiosity, reportedly telling friends that he found Milton to be "a primitive."[29] It is likely that enough has been said about the talented late white American photographer and fetishist whose lighting techniques and style Rotimi Fani-Kayode cited as inspiring his own works. He hardly needs another citation here. Contemporary Black photographers such as Ajamu Ikwe-Tyehimba, Lyle Ashton Harris, and Cuban Rene Peña, as well as his contemporary, Rotimi, have already entered into visual and textual conversation with their own beautiful and impactful riffs of the now "iconic" bodily gestures, methods of light and dark, stark and nuance that he employed and popularized.

In his introduction to *Brother to Brother*, Essex invoked "Man in Polyester Suit" as further evidence of white gay men's possessive desire and consumption of Black men's bodies (and dismissal of their minds).[30] Kobena and Isaac's critique of the photographer begins with their ambivalence about erotic and porn images of Black men. They hold that "a certain sexual liberalism of gay (white) men assumes a 'freedom of choice' to consume various types of porn. . . ." They write that distinct from the white gaze, as Black gay men "we want to look, but do not always find what we want to see," not just in the work of the artist in question but also in pornographic representations of Black men by white men. The uneven transnational erotic trade between Black men was left unremarked upon at that time. This Black gay looking reveals another channel of what Black men might want to look at but not want to see. This time below the surface of their own sexual desire—perhaps to a transnational political-economic discussion of sex work, pornography, and representation. They—we—are implicated in many ways as Black men. We will turn to the global political economy of who desires whom, for what, and under what circumstances later. As if to provide a coda to essays by Essex, and Kobena and Isaac, nearly thirty years later, on the occasion of an original print of "Man in Polyester Suit" selling for nearly a half million dollars, an official at Sotheby's quipped that "you either have to write an 800-page dissertation about [the photo], or you have to look at it as a kind of perfect joke and laugh."[31] For Sotheby's, the stakes of representation are negligible. Not even small change. Especially relative to its latest windfall on this trade.

What is striking to me about *Black Book* today is Ntozake Shange's beautiful and complexly contradictory foreword, in which she claims the men in it as "irrepressibly bronze, beautiful, and mine" in the title of the poem she pens in dialogue with the photographer, and I believe more so with the subjects of the work.[32] Shifting from a white gay male gaze (and not just any white gay male) to the voice of a cis Black woman who had loved and longed for Black men since she was a child necessarily complicates and expands our discussion. In the foreword the author and the photographer share a moment of perhaps pleasurable confusion or lack of awareness of the distinctiveness of the men. A "(little) black book" is of course also shorthand for a listing of past and perhaps future romantic trysts. Ntozake said that she had looked for a former lover of hers among the photos in *Black Book*: "I can't seem to find him now, but I know he's there somewhere." She says the photographer lifted his head slightly with a telling half smile: "I know what you mean, I can't find mine either."[33] They liked each other instantly, she says. There is in this exchange—especially noting the possessive celebration in her poem's title—a hard-to-read playfulness around authentic or sincere affinity with, or ownership of Black men here, along with a mutual recognition of desire and of lives lived as free sexual beings. Dedicating the poem to performance artist Ana Mendieta, in this foreword the late-too-soon Ms. Shange writes of a family friend who looked after her:

> all my life they've been near me these men
> . . .
> my eight-year-old
> precocious soul was hankering
> for days to come with one
> one of them colored fellas
> who'd be mine/on purpose/not
> just some cause of pigmentation
> problem/or grandfather clause.[34]

Among other things, the poem speaks to strong bonds with irrepressibly bronze, beautiful Black men who play various roles in the speaker's life, and/ but most especially longing for one of her own. "One of them colored fellas" who would be with her, not as a default or seeing her as facsimile, but (the poet is heartbreakingly precise here) "on purpose." Later, after the speaker is "grown," she teases/demands "bring it on baby," holding that phrase offset at the top of the page. A few stanzas before this, she had shifted language— addressing/commanding a *maldito negro hermoso* (damn beautiful Black man), in his own language, to see her. The speaker looks beyond routine places and recognizes the depth of the humanity of the Black men in her poetic frame, as well as the vulnerable space that her declarations find her occupying. The complex Black love of "irrepressibly bronze, beautiful, and mine" is transgressive placed as the preface of the famous white photographer's *Black Book*. For me, this recalls an antipodal example of Black gay representation and (mis-recognition): an emotional and perhaps nervous Essex Hemphill at the 1990 Out/Write conference, sharing what was to be his introduction to *Brother to Brother*. He spoke of how Black gay men who were shunned in middlebrow white gay cultural and political spaces were celebrated as consumer goods—sometimes by the same men—in backrooms, bookstores, and saunas: "At the baths . . . certain bars . . . Black men need only whip out a penis of almost any size to obtain the rapt attention withheld from him in other social-political structures. . . . These sites of pleasure were more tolerable of the presence of Black men because they enhance the sexual ambiance, but the same tolerance did not always apply when the sun began to rise."[35] Pursuing this further in his panel comments at BN/QN?, Essex asserts, "Don't be confused: racism doesn't go better with a big dick, or a hot pussy, or a royal lineage. . . ." Still, today a number of folks seem to have found measures of affective and material utility in, for example, a BBD and/or a hot Black pussy—or more precisely the representation or virtual interweb performance of possessing or consuming these. Internet-based technologies enable the circulation of a huge number of professional and amateur gay porn images—much of which is free and available to anyone with access to a computer or smartphone and adequate bandwidth. However, it is striking that with the internet's wide variety of genre, themes, interests, and formats, images of Black men (and those racialized as Black) seem to fit only a limited number of pre-narrativized frameworks.

Consideration of a selfie that I found on the internet around 2012 and like to call "Brother with No Suit" because of its uncanny similarity to the $478,000 photo of Milton Moore and his BBD might open this up more purposefully to the now. I have not been able to trace the precise provenance of this evidently self-made image, although it is safe to say that it has been shared, (re)blogged, (re)posted, and "liked" several hundred times around the world (and counting). I can say with certainty that it has "traveled" to at least four continents and has been used as bait for "catfishing"—that is, using an image or images as the basis for a false or assumed identity—on at least three occasions, including in the popular practice of racialized "cuckolding," in which Black men serve as exogamous sex partners for non-Black women in heterosexual couples as their non-Black partners watch or receive reports of the superior sexual performance of the BBD (of course "superior"—the game would not be coherent without confirming the assumption of excessive Black virility). Unlike the studied sculptural studio image of the more famous portrait, the anonymous brother here appears, like many contemporary selfies or "dick pics," to be snapping a quick shot of himself. His dick is semi-erect but already formidable and seemingly unable to be contained by his tight jeans. It is glistening moist, as Black bodies are often portrayed: working or ready for *wuk*. "Brother with No Suit" stands in poetic comparison to "Man in a Polyester Suit," revealing in retrospective juxtaposition that "the object" in "Man in a Polyester Suit" is, in contrast to the dick pic, contained or "tamed" by the photographer's framing and authorship. The object of the gaze in "Brother with No Suit" is polymorphous: at once playful and dangerous. The unnamed brother is likewise unzipped and putatively available, at least for gazing. But also, playing the trickster, here the image—or the imago—does not necessarily answer back to the actual person in the photo, the photographer/author, or the original poster. Again, no head is shown, but this follows internet dick-pic selfie convention, likely for privacy and semi-anonymity. That is, the missing head here represents the author's/model's refusal of a casual consuming gaze. As one of my early internet respondents said about their raft of body and dick pics, "They don't need to know my name or see my face or think that they know me. . . ."

Racism might "not go better with a big dick, a hot pussy, or a royal lineage," as Essex said, but does authorship of one's own image make one a subject? Is the action of gazing at, consuming, or "owning" another's image always objectifying? As the same internet interlocutor put it, completing his thought, "They will see what I want them to see, when I want them to see it." Is there a *we* that can hold both the Black desired object and the Black desiring/consuming viewer subject? What does consumption of images of other Black men—perhaps those that Essex, Joe, and others imagined as a mirror-image brother with whom they promise our act of loving as Black men would make the revolutionary statement of the 1980s—say about our own fantasies across the often brutally uneven terrain of nationality, class, and age? Including fancies that might be described as "colonial"? Later, our exploration of tourism may shed some light on this. What does gazing upon or fetishizing others (or a character that one "creates" through catfishing), or displaying one's body for comparison with ready-made imaginaries of the Black body *do* for Black folks? What meanings do people make of a "royal" lineage that calls up particular sites or scenes of iconic or imagined blackness? The internet's relatively inexpensive and accessible technology has ushered in an explosion of DIY erotica and porn. But even with all of this self-representation, we must still hear Essex asking "Is this a virtual reality that empowers me?" and "Can invisible men (women, and GNC family) see their own reflection?" Our questions echo through the time space of Black/queerpolis.

A Black/Queer Counterpoise

> Counting t-cells on the shores of cyberspace,
> my blessing is this: I do not stand alone,
> bewildered and scared.

Director Shari Frilot closes the film *Black Nations/Queer Nations?* with Essex's end. He slipped into the ether, dying of "AIDS complications" eight months after sharing this truth, above, on the dais at BN/QN?. In a tragic comment on Black/queer time, Essex died at the threshold of new anti-retroviral drug cocktail treatments that inhibit viral enzymes critical to the HIV replication cycle, essentially suppressing progression of the infection.[36] Standing on the cusp of new technologies "on the shores of cyberspace," the speaker's condition is compounded by the condition of loneliness, but he is redeemed (even fleetingly) by companionship. Romantic love and close friendship are his "blessing." This formulation goes well beyond a poetic rumination on living and dying with AIDS. Riffing on Audre's earlier notion of "those of us who live at the shoreline / standing upon the constant edges of decision / crucial and alone," here Essex sets out a life-and-death conundrum just as provocative as the seemingly still intractable "twentieth-century" problem of "the color line" that W. E. B. Du Bois had put forward in the "forethought" of his foundational *The Souls of Black Folk* in 1903.[37] The life-and-death struggles of global AIDS and the cofactors of lack of access, poverty, and state disinvestment that feed it constitute the color line compounded and viralized. It is raced, sexed, gendered, and territorialized. Black/queer poesis—elaborating the uses and pleasures of Eros while understanding and at times embracing its inevitable shadow, Thanatos—is a Black/queer counterpoise. Essex does not aver that there is nothing to cause fear or bewilderment. The facts and vulnerabilities are clear. Still, sociality—not standing alone, even perhaps virtually—is the grace. This is of course resonant with a number of Black/queer poetic theorizations of living *in the life* and living through to see possibilities beyond nonbeing. Alively. Stuart Hall already told us that there are *no guarantees.* Still. According to Audre, "It is better to speak, re-membering. . . ."[38] Claude McKay's classic antilynching poem may read like a paean, but it is not about unqualified winning. His title, after all, carries the conditional mandate of Black death: "If we must die." Active, alive, and with an eye toward what future Black/queer children will say of us (or even if they will survive at all to *conscientiously remember, in pursuit of their own survival, in relation to the formative event of our passings*), McKay demands, "O let us

162 / Chapter Five

nobly die!" The great bisexual Jamaican communist of the Black Renaissance charges us to heroically return "one death blow" to the thousands of blows from the "murderous lot": "Pressed to the wall, dying / but fighting back."[39] Even pressed, "sounding an ordinary note of care."[40] In this *ambiente*.[41] So our focus is not on paradigmatic violence but rather on the extension of cool drinks of water like the one Dionne Brand conjures in *In Another Place, Not Here*: the sweetnesses one may be able to "thief."[42] This by no means diminishes other ways of making sense and/or making moments of respite and/or/ thus making a way toward freedom. Indeed, this Black/queer way embraces another vision of *hold*.[43]

Black/Queerpolis

All discourse is "placed," and the heart has its reasons.—STUART HALL

"All discourse is 'placed,'" Stuart has already told us in his classic essay "Cultural Identity and Diaspora." "And the heart has its reasons," he finishes, elegantly.[1] Those of lesser analytic power, or less self-reflexivity, might have missed this articulation entirely. Stuart's understanding of place, "diaspora," and identity was both deeply studied and embodied in his own experiences, commitments, and disavowals. Still, "diaspora" leaves us reaching for something else. Here, we propose *Black/queerpolis* as a supplement.

After the Atlantic revolutions and Maurice Bishop, after structural adjustment, after Reagan, Thatcher, AIDS, and crack (and of course there is no closure to any of these "afters"), after "diaspora" but before reparations and before freedom, there is Black/queerpolis. It represents the ongoing process of composing a distinct and instructive global counterpublic articulated through "worlds in motion." Here a triangular trade of affect, materiality, and historicity is held in tension by the force of desire. I propose this supplement as a corrective to conceptualizations that might require "straight time"; limit archives, language, speed, or modes of intercourse and (re)generation too strictly; or constrain possibilities within "white space." *Black/queerpolis* is not meant to displace *pan-African, diaspora,* or *Afropolitan* but rather to push each significantly forward in the various directions that Black people are moving and through which we *become*. Black/queerpolis is always now. This is not to say that it is ahistorical. Rather, it represents a queer temporality that is processual, not teleological. That is, the notion of Black/queerpolis offers a rhizomatic conceptualization of relations, space, and time, enabling a rerouting of old teleologies of heteronormative natural "progress" from a single root or (family) tree. The rhizomatic includes and exceeds tradition and memory: it is creative, promiscuous, multiple, sometimes deep in dark muck, and often contradictory.

Even *in place*, Black lesbian, transgender, bisexual, gay, queer, or same-gender-loving people can hardy escape the transnational flow of Black desires (to say nothing of the desire for Black bodies and Black cultures by others). This has never been truer than in the current moment. Well-informed, or with an intransigent ignorance of their Black (and) LGBTQ "other," Black LGBTQ, queer, or same-gender-loving folks continue to participate in un-even global exchanges, whether with their bodies or merely by a mouse click engaging their imaginations. Black people, even (when) *still*, do not merely await extrinsic definition of verbs or simple translation of their experience, they live and die, here and there, relatively. And collect the evidence of their living in archives of their own making. Some folks move fairly easily (and a number of them quite elegantly) within and between translocal spaces in Africa, Europe, North America, and the Caribbean. Whether "born there" and returning, on business, or decidedly for pleasure, they report particular strategies of *safer mobilities* between North and South. Paradoxically, these include ways to avoid misrecognition as a local/native by police, other state functionaries, and hospitality staff (lest you be treated "like a native" on holi-day), while they proliferate tactics to encourage recognition by Black and Af-rican (descended) local individuals as a (solidary, mutually respect-worthy, and, at times, privileged) "diasporic subject" or Black "sister" or "brother." In northern metropolises with Black cosmopolitan neighborhoods, daily trips to local restaurant offerings of chicken roti or jollof rice, the sounds of favela funk blasting from the speakers at the club, or culturally "accented" lovers and friends inform the local imaginations of those "Black others" one might meet *there*. In all cases, there are dramatic differences, not only in affect but also in access to various forms of respect and mobility, depending upon whether one is a brother or a sister—and whether one is clockable as one or the other, or as a nonbinary, transgender, or gender-queer person whose self-presentation explodes those murderously limiting boundaries.

6　　　　　Bonds and Disciplines

I begin my reflections on the state (history) of Black feminist criticism(s) with this memory because it seems to me we so quickly forget the recent past. Perhaps some of us have never known it. Like many of us who lived through the literary activism of the sixties, we of the eighties may forget that which just recently preceded us and may therefore misconstrue the period in which we are acting.
—BARBARA CHRISTIAN, "But What Do We Think We Are Doing Anyway"

BLACK/QUEER STUDIES was literally created and necessitated by our "epidemic living and dead." We have indeed quite directly and very recently *come—treading our path through the blood* of our *slaughtered* AIDS, violence, and cancer dead—into academe, into executive positions in community-based organizations, into libraries and archives, think tanks, publishing, punditry, and think-piece stunting. Thus, the politics of Black/queer/diaspora extends well beyond the terms of debates within what emerged in the long 1980s, separately, as queer studies and (a newer version of critical) Black studies. Black gay artists and activist intellectuals of the long 1980s provided the foundation and impetus for Black queer studies, which, following the popular movement's insistence on claiming space, "animates the dialogic/dialectic 'kinship' by mobilizing the tensions embedded in the conjunction of 'Black' and 'queer,'" as E. Patrick (Johnson) and Mae (Henderson) aver in the introduction to their pathbreaking 2005 collection *Black Queer Studies*, continuing the anthological tradition.[1] One of the most salient moves at the outset of what we now understand as Black queer studies was to claim and even celebrate blackness and Black self-identification as a sort of kinship— significantly in counterpoise to and seemingly out of time with the academic moment in which the identity-politics pendulum had swung in the direction of a postmodern retreat that asked us to abandon kin, familial connection, and futurity in the name of antiessentialism.

M. Jacqui Alexander—the foundational transnational feminist theorist whose recent turn toward indigenous plants, spiritualities, healing modalities, and nonsecular historicity is both an extension of the roots she has nurtured and a poetic return—has already cautioned us that we would need to "keep company with each other as we visit the terrors that . . . disavowals produce."[2] The very particular "we" explored here—already making the "keeping of company" problematically constrained and the prospective disavowals multiple—is a small group of scholars, activists, and artists that had begun self-consciously contributing to the shaping of Black/queer/diaspora discourse in the early aughts. In 2009 I invited these folks to engage in a conversation and explore collaborations. As an invitation for you to join the ongoing conversation, I have re-narrated an edited transcription of our opening conversation and reframed fragments from two published conversations between Omise'eke Natasha Tinsley and me. Here we shift from aestheticizing Black/queer/diaspora studies, and our relationality of love and friendship, to revealing methodological, theoretical, critical, and professional conundrums: plainly and unvarnished, in the words of conversation partners, toward new forms. In the introduction of what became the initial public record of our encounter, I claimed that "Black/queer/diaspora constitutes a heterotopic love." That is, the sort of love that does not overidentify with the other in ways that efface differences or uneven vulnerabilities. I said, "This is a love that announces itself ready and willing to embrace and be embraced—to listen and to negotiate."[3] I stand by this today. I still believe that love is the *movida* and that friendship is the technique. Thus, our intellectual work is both a labor of love and evidence of it. It is the driver of the habit of mind we follow. And/but it is also true that I owe a richer accounting of different and sometimes contradictory voices, sensibilities, and disciplinary investments in the work. Moreover, I owe an account of the real difficulties of collaborating, or even conversing, across intellectual, professional, and personal/political differences. We offer this sort of anthology of voices here to respond specifically to Jacqui's entreaty and promise that "as teachers we can stage a set of collective conversations in which we map the genealogies of our own disavowals."[4] Here is one attempt at such a collective conversation. Before this, however, consider a couple more love letters—this time between Omise'eke Natasha Tinsley and me, published in a recent public conversation looking backward at Black/Queer/Diaspora ten years after our workshop, on the occasion of the twenty-fifth anniversary of the journal *GLQ: A Journal of Lesbian and Gay Studies*.[5]

Dear Jafari,

So wonderful to hear your voice coming through the car yesterday. Since we never catch each other by phone more than twice a year, what a gift to write this together—because it means we *had* to find time to call! And because the only time I had was driving with Matt to pick up my diva-esque daughter, your goddaughter, Matt got to be in on the call too. (He wanted me to remind you of his *undying devotion*. Very insistent on that phrase.) You're endlessly missed in Austin, you know, and sometimes when I'm having a bad day I fantasize: what beautiful thing is Jafari wearing today, that makes the world a better place just by existing?

When Marcia and Jennifer generously asked us to think about the impact of *Black/Queer/Diaspora*, I plucked my copy off my shelf for things most crucial to writing *Ezili's Mirrors*. But I never got past the table of contents. I ran my eyes down authors' names stacked in bold—Jafari, Omise'eke, Lyndon, Xavier, Vanessa, Ana, Matt—knowing I should be thinking about us as a scholarly field but thinking about us as friends. About searching for roti and gay clubs with you, Xavier, and Matt in London, at the conference where Matt presented work that made it into GLQ and Xavier shocked folks with descriptions of gay sex. About CSA in Curaçao where Lyndon introduced me to Vanessa and I first got to hear the paper that became her article and we sat by the pool proclaiming black femme Pisces solidarity.

In other words, all I could think about is the ways *Black/Queer/Diaspora* came out of and built so many personal/professional relationships that have made this generation of black queer scholarship possible.

Because I never made it past the contents before our call, you had to remind me how the introduction evokes this scholarly practice of black queer friendship, kinship, and love. "For black queers, survival has always been about finding ways to connect some of what is disconnected, to embody and re-member," you wrote. "The conventions of our guild—steeped in cool reason—avoid love as a *movida*. It is nevertheless evident in the works featured here and in the passion-filled (not easy, uncomplicated, or necessarily romantic) relationships between many individuals who do this work."[6] This passage is marked by Matt's handwritten note "<u>Love</u> as a methodology," framed by flowery, vèvè-esque arrows.

Maybe you remember it differently. But I remember April 2009, when you convened the Black/Queer/Diaspora Work(ing) Group at Yale, as a time when the world felt full of promise. I was four months pregnant with Baia. Obama was just inaugurated. Young black queer scholars were being hired at prestigious institutions—Yale, UT—and many of us would soon be tenured. But as I write in early 2018 it feels like this promise has crumbled. I've had four miscarriages. Trump blustered into another year of transphobic, xenophobic, anti-Black madness. Academic institutions haven't been able to force black queer faculty out, but undervalue and undermined us in ways we never foresaw. Why was Yale hemorrhaging black queer faculty by the time Baia started kindergarten? Why did UT just promote a professor whose work attacks queer families while those of us who live in them remain underpaid? Why does a next generation of black queer scholarship feel less possible now than ten years ago, and why have some in our field attacked friends when we have common enemies to fight?

It's impossible to look back on *Black/Queer/Diaspora* without sinking into how much I love the people in it. But it's equally impossible to read our names, think our stories together without mourning the ways black queer love has failed to make change in the academy. I look back and ask myself, what did we do wrong? Did our thirst for queer sociality lead us to underestimate institutions' racism, misogynoir, queerphobia? Don't forget, I'm a Pisces: I have to learn over and over again how the search for love makes us vulnerable.

Maybe you're thinking: *Omise'eke, you're a black lesbian writing a love letter to a black gay man to publish in* GLQ. *You're not afraid of vulnerability and you haven't given up on black queer love!* Of course, of course I haven't. Black queer love has failed this generation in academia but it's also the only thing that's worked for us. I'm not still in this profession for my health. I'm here because you, Lyndon, Xavier, Vanessa, Ana, Matt and so many others are here too, and I love seeing our black queer impossibility reflected in your disco balls and black sands. Remember Barbara: "What I write and how I write is done in order to save my own life. And I mean that literally. For me, literature is a way of knowing that I am not hallucinating, that whatever I feel/know *is*. It is an affirmation that sensuality is intelligence, that sensual language is language that makes sense."[7] You, Jafari, and our writerly black queer sistren and brethren are that affirmation—that push toward remaking the world—that feels, tastes, moves like survival to me.

You mentioned *Sister Love: The Letters of Audre Lorde and Pat Parker,* so I rushed to buy it. I thought of us when Pat wrote: "Too often in the past, I have put letter writing off, because I thought whatever free time I had had to go to those survival things and if any energy left over would go to writing. However, it does occur to me that letter writing is both a survival thing and writing, plus it is so important to me to continue our conversation."[8] It's painful to read this knowing neither sender nor receiver *did* survive cancer. But because Pat took time to write Audre, this book now sits beside me as a map for what black queer sociality can—and can't—do. Right now, I want to take you really seriously and imagine: what if we take these letters as a model for what black/queer/diaspora scholarship does now? How can we care about black queerness in ways that are concrete, embodied, personal, sustainable? How might the tools we've relegated to the last century—tools we thought we could put away with in the post–Civil Rights, post-Stonewall era—serve us in this moment?

Sister love,
Omi

Oh, Sister Love!

I am grateful to Marcia and Jennifer for inviting this conversation. Perhaps these love letters will inaugurate another way to mine our pasts and current feelings, for what is usable and sustaining. Let our letters be the beginning of starting the dance, again—a recursive "(re-)situat(ing)of our work through *conjunctural moments.*"[9] Your words are always inspiring to me. On time, especially when I feel out of time. *Thiefing Sugar*[10] came out one year before ¡*Venceremos*?[11] "Black Atlantic/Queer Atlantic" provided a framework for us to begin our conversations in 2009. Last year I read galleys of *Ezili's Mirrors,*[12] breathless and awed, while my own second monograph awaited my courage to turn it in.

Yes! The letters between Pat and Audre are striking in their dailyness—making a living and doing the work; illnesses, romances, children, shady editors, and Audre's too-familiar drama in academe—but also the sometimes very long intervals between. They remind me that I have to do better. Moving to Miami was supposed to be about "reclaiming my time." Still, I find there is much work to do, everywhere. And, as I keep rediscovering, not all of this work is "my work." You asked "what happened . . . ?": certainly, some of what we set out to do is somewhere buried under somebody else's agenda. While many of us get worn down by marginal employment in academe's precariat, for those of us you call "our writerly black queer sistren and brethren" situated in the Master's house of the tenured professorate, it is *adminstrivia* that threatens to take us out.

In any case, what is on my heart most urgently, is to say I am so sorry that I was not there to lift your spirits or hold your hand through much of the pain you have endured—even with a note or a phone call. Matt's letter is coming, presently.

We have learned that while our love is not enough, it is what allows (some of) us to survive. Essex wrote, "Counting t-cells on the shores of cyberspace, my blessing is this: I do not stand alone, bewildered and scared." He doesn't aver that there is nothing to cause fear or bewilderment. The facts and vulnerabilities are clear. Rather, not standing alone—even perhaps virtually, is the grace. *Black/Queer/Diaspora* emerged from relationships and could not be sustained without them—from pitching the idea to Ann, to the grace of all of you showing up—sanctifying that Anthropology conference room one semester after I had arrived from UT. Faculty meetings in that room provided an often violent but invaluable education. But when I convened my classes there—smudged with incense—it is our engagement that I tried to model. *Friends,* we had come to work. It's a queer, Black thing that we find each other and convene in institutional spaces that (re)shape and sometimes mangle us, but as Christina reminds us, "We are not only known to ourselves and to each other through and by that force."[13]

Re-reading the introduction—written at one "current conjuncture" that has given way to another—I am struck at how unsettled we are. De-territorialized. Some in generative ways, and in others, merely perhaps *without portfolio*. *Ezili's Mirrors* provides a beautiful model toward understanding and inhabiting unsettled and generatively de-territorialized space-time. I too have responded with the unsettled—traipsing very Black and queerly across continents and themes, re-narrativizing the idea of Black/queer in clips, cases, vignettes, and memories. I am trying to offer an accounting of our habits of mind in *There's a Disco Ball Between Us.* Isn't this how we build a future for Baia, Georgia Mae, and our students? A palimpsestic "litany toward survival"? Now, thriving is another question. What must we do? Who must we be, inside, for ourselves and to one another, to really win?

You invoke mourning. Is my private-public feeling mourning? Is it *tabanca,* or lovelorn? I'm hearing "Earth Wind & Fire" and Paul Gilroy in stereo: "After the Love is Gone." Cha, my references are old (classic!). I know the insistence on (r&b) love seems hokey to many. Still, I believe that with everything that is wrong, "Every night / somethin' right / Would invite us to / begin the dance."[14] Don't we have to continue to dance? Beginning again, (and again . . . certainly). Sometimes less or more elegant or funky, but dance. I do not want to be mistaken here, especially because I think some may mistake our love ethic and the insistence on Black/queer sociality in our issue as a description of a club of folks who co-sign and adhere to the same politics. We know that's far from the truth. Agreement is not sine qua non of love. Nor is proximity, really. It is our willingness to begin again, even when "something happen(s)"—violence, loss, forgetting, for example—"along the way."

. . .

The introduction to the issue ends: "Here, the threads of our mourning clothes are laid down/bare."[15] I don't remember writing this, but it is there. Perhaps it is a love note from then, to us now. If we take off our mourning clothes, what do we put on? The bareness of our vulnerability? The beauty of our multihued Black flesh (that dances . . . *here in this place*[16])? I look forward to meeting y'all in the clearing to find out, Sister.

—Love,
Jafari

New Haven, 2009

During the first session of the Black/Queer/Diaspora Working Group symposium, we sought to warm up our time together by bringing our individual interests, projects, and locations to the table. After tea and a short introduction of the individuals present, we settled in to sherry and sweets while we listened to short presentations by Omise'eke, Matt (Richardson), and Rinaldo (Walcott), which moved from Dionne Brand's image of waters coming together beyond the canons, to a call for rhythmic re-harmonization, renaming, and re-gendering, to conceptualizing a project that pushes not only beyond the boundaries of revindication and queer of color critique but necessarily also beyond disciplines. I suggested then:

Our task is to mind only the canons and methodological conventions that move the work forward, and to mine those particular disciplinary frameworks, pushing significantly beyond them. These are also questions of ethics. Since we are clear that what we call ourselves, others, and things, have consequences: how does the work of those of us who define, create, save and represent—artists, archivists, and scholars—intersect with, complement, or hinder social justice work? One of the points of our gathering, I hope, is to think about how these projects—both coming together, and in fact pointing out the dissonance or brokenness—are based in folks' everyday material and metaphysical practices.

Taking Jacqui seriously, I must begin by asking what and whom I had already disavowed—and/or disallowed—in the process of orchestrating a conversation on Black/queer/diaspora in the spaces I staged it.[17] The first and most obvious thing to consider is the limited invitations I extended to the conversation and the even more circumscribed list of authors in the special double issue of GLQ that resulted. At the time of the invitation, I was thinking of folks who were working on the culture and politics of Black gender insurgents and same-sex-oriented folks outside of the United States—pushing forward concepts of diaspora and the transnational, and Black national and ethnic difference.[18] I knew that space had already been beautifully taken up by folks making tremendous contributions to US Black studies. But what about the wider Black world? On top of limits to resources, time, and logistics, there were many considerations. How many from particular disciplines? What parts of the world are represented? How can we achieve a productive mix of academic seniority and avoid gender imbalance? Further, although brilliant colleagues and friends represent some of the wider Black world in this issue, Black queer scholars working in languages other than English and those working outside of the elite North Atlantic academy were sadly not represented here—some because of travel expense and visa concerns, and some because of my own ignorance of their work, or how intimately that work relates to those gathered. There were other limitations to the conversation. Among these, a few participants were not published in the collection for various reasons—mostly their own preference but in one case because of negative reviews from peers we asked to evaluate the essays. This a peculiar "terror" of academic life that could not be resolved in the time we were allotted (and not by an untenured guest editor!) but that I wish I could have mitigated.

Omise'eke began remarks on her influential essay "Black Atlantic, Queer Atlantic: Queer Imaginings of the Middle Passage" by invoking Jacqui's contention that "water overflows with memory . . . emotional memory, bodily memory, sacred memory." This is one way to express the need to further develop Black feminist epistemologies that uncover submerged histories, which traditional historiographies had not, cannot (shouldn't?), or would not validate.

"Black Atlantic, Queer Atlantic" breached the levees of Black diaspora studies and queer studies by forcefully bringing together powerful streams of US and Caribbean Black feminist narrative theorizing. Our terrains and seascapes expanded and enriched in its wake. But Omi herself sits still. Rather more like a deep river of secrets turning golden with the dawn than a roiling ocean. At one conference—the one at which we met (the 2007 Race, Sex & Power at the University of Illinois, Chicago), it was her thigh-high black leather boots that intrigued me, even before reading and falling in love with her masterful work *Thiefing Sugar: Eroticism between Women in Caribbean Literature*. Months after this, we (Omi, Matt, and Xavier) presented together on a conference panel in London (the 2008 Race in the Modern World at Goldsmith's College, University of London), where Omi announced that she was pregnant with Baia and Xavier introduced me to the joys of peri peri chicken. In New Haven she explained that "'Black Atlantic/Queer Atlantic' started really as kind of a long-term interest in the 90s when I was a graduate student." Of course, during that time Black diaspora studies was consumed by its love/hate relationship with Gilroy's formidable 1995 *Black Atlantic: Modernity and Double-Consciousness* and other metaphorical and historiographic uses of oceans and seas, whereas

> on the other hand there was a lot of even more metaphoric work in queer studies about gender and gender fluidity, right? And yet never, never the two seemed to meet at the time. And so, that was kind of in the back of my mind when in about 2000 there was this kind of space, of Black Queer Caribbean novels that started dealing with the Black Atlantic and the Caribbean as queer spaces. And so, Dionne Brand's *A Map to the Door of No Return*, Nalo Hopkinson's *The Salt Roads*, Ana-Maurine Lara's novel, *Erzulie's Skirt* . . . it seemed like it was no coincidence, right? That these two vocabularies of fluidity were meeting in these works. And I was also particularly interested in why this was happening in fiction. Why wasn't it happening from within what was traditionally thought of as theoretical work? And taking very seriously Barbara Christian's idea of the novel as a place of theorizing, particularly in African Diaspora scholarship, I wanted to turn to these novels and see what alternative theoretical spaces were being imagined as well as what other materialities were being evoked.

Omise'eke reminds us of Sylvia Wynter's critique of the divisions of academic disciplines that split apart, colonize, and hierarchize knowledges that are in fact powerfully connected: knowledges of what she calls the human, which span art, biology, sociology, and on and on and on, but which the academy atomizes. As we gathered, my mind went to the graduate colloquy that Matt (Richardson) and I taught together at the University of Texas–Austin. He and I struggled with including Professor Wynter—that is, not *whether* to include her, but rather how. One cannot be sure that even the brightest students have an "advanced" grasp of even the "greatest hits" of Black feminism. The work of choosing from the impressive and growing corpus of works for our class—called the Combahee River Collective Colloquy on Black Feminist Theory and Praxis (yes, what else would we call it!?)—and team teaching across discipline and genre proved an invaluable experience that deepened my teaching in ways I could not have come to alone, or with a partner less brilliant and generous than Matt. Likewise, a number of related questions of methodology came up during the initial discussion at the symposium. On one hand, for Hortense Spillers, "first-order naming" seems to happen through perhaps more traditional social science and history, not literature or art. On the other, frontally challenging this false dichotomy of what is real and primary, which finds Black queers and insurgent Black women "word poor" in the academic realm while we have so much word wealth in our communities (perhaps not invested well?), has emerged as a priority.

Natalie Bennett is currently director of the Women's Leadership and Resource Center at the University of Illinois, Chicago. At the time of the symposium, she was an assistant professor at DePaul University. "I will just make a couple of comments," Natalie says as she reclines just slightly after having been near the edge of her seat during Omise'eke's presentation. Her right hand hooks another stitch on the soft wool destined for her growing son's neck—a loving gesture of security against the harsh winds of Chicago. Natalie's lips slightly purse as she raises her chin a bit to speak with that glint/sparkle in her eyes. The trees outside the leaded-glass windows are turning golden, with glints of red, and the wood-paneled Gordon Parks Conference Room in the Department of African American Studies is warm, despite its vaulted gothic ceilings. I sense we are really about to get started:

> I was thinking about the way that Jafari introduced everybody in terms of our individual biographies, and it raised the question: what does interdisciplinarity mean in the production of Black queer theories? Or Black queer studies proper? I am thinking about all the stuff that I teach in genders and sexualities in the Caribbean: although I trained as a sociologist, I have always used novels to do particular things. But I am also finding that we seem to be moving very quickly towards novels and fictional works, because it allows certain kinds of thinking and imagining. Part of what has been happening, and I think it is happening in our individual work,

is a retreat—or perhaps what I mean is more like a fleeing to fiction—a particular kind of imagining—and away from making the material conditions of Black queer lives more central to our thinking and theorizing. I wonder if some of those questions, or what it is that we are using literature to do, cannot also be reproduced in other kinds of spaces. Is it only in the context of fiction that we can really do the kind of Black queer theorizing that we are talking about here?

Sometimes, when a group gathers, it does not take long to get to the salient questions. Emanant brilliance. Knit one, purl two. Each other's seeded stitches, indeed.

Colin (Robinson) extends Natalie's proposition. This is the same Colin we met in the long 1980s: a cofounder of Other Countries, a producer of *Tongues Untied*, first executive director of Gay Men of African Descent (GMAD) and New York Black Gay Network, cofounder of Caribbean Pride and Coalition Advocating Inclusion of Sexual Orientation (CAISO, which we will turn to in subsequent chapters), HIV activist, writer, collaborator, and friend to Essex, Marlon, Joe, Assotto, Craig . . . we could go on. As a paradigm shaper, Colin is central to the Black gay narrative and therefore intervenes in every chapter of this book. At the table, he offers: "I guess I am having similar epistemological troubles as Natalie. The fact that you reference the notion of archives as opposed to ethereal realities is interesting enough because there is no imaginary necessary, not in the same way. And that was one of the things that was striking me as well, as someone who is not in the academy; about the metaphorizing on the one hand and materiality on the other." He was especially interested in pursuing this notion of the market given contemporary notions of "global queerness," agreeing that we should try to inject as much as we can of that kind of discussion to consider for the rest of our time together.

I have known Rosamond King, associate professor of English and director of the Ethyle R. Wolfe Institute for the Humanities at Brooklyn College, for many years. A poet and performance artist as well as a literary scholar, she and I met in what students called the "living room" of the Africana studies program at New York University, while she was a comparative literature graduate student and I was a returning undergraduate Africana studies office work-study student. Offering another perspective on disciplinary border crossing, Rosamond, who has traveled and studied in the Gambia and elsewhere with folks whom ethnographers have yet to engage, offered:

I know that for myself I would probably benefit more from the discipline of sociology because I come from [disciplines] where I did not have the opportunity to do things like that [ethnographic inquiry]. I do not know how to do that. And how many other people are going to have the opportunity . . . to, for instance go to Gambia [as I have]. So if I had the opportunity, I should take advantage of it, and yet I don't want to do it badly, right. . . . So I find myself in this interdisciplinary role, and yet not quite sure of what I'm doing.

At this point, Rinaldo (Walcott) and I—ironically taking the mantle of social science officialdom—interrupted her to say "Don't worry about that," and "Just get the stories documented." Rinaldo, director of the Women & Gender Studies Institute at the University of Toronto, trained as a sociologist but works interdisciplinarily as a critical social-cultural studies scholar. After directing social scientists to read more novels, Rinaldo helped to bring together some of the streams that had been flowing in our discussion. And although this discussion was about methodology, it was always also about theory and about ethics. Rinaldo said that the kind of work that he wants to imagine he is doing and the kinds of questions that he wants to ask are in large part material and embodied. We all agreed. He offered:

And so . . . what is at stake in theory, what is at stake in conceptualizing this term, this word that way . . . seems to call for a range of different kinds of methods, and a range of different kinds of objects of study. In some of them we are going to sit down and talk to real live people, and in some of them we are going to retreat to the novel, the poem, the play, music, and some of them we're going to retreat to spirituality.

Rinaldo is a devotedly secular theorist. And there is that "retreat" again. He may have meant this in a different register than Natalie had. He continued:

But it seems to me that all of them have to be on the table in different kinds of ways at different kinds of times, and we have to be juggling with them. I always say to my students, if you are going to be an interdisciplinary scholar, it means you have given yourself the most difficult job in the academy to do. You have to do all of that. You have got to account for all of it.

Do not mistake this commitment to "account for all of it" and stretching beyond the bounds of formal training and credentials to new forms of expertise, as adding up to mere "interdisciplinarity." Moreover, you must not receive interdisciplinarity—another freighted invention that came to prominence in the long 1980s—as somehow innocent. Professor Wynter's formulation of the human depends on us both unmasking Enlightenment constructions of "man" and attending to the discursive machinations that Enlightenment thinking makes to accommodate capital. This foundational debate, whose common historiographic and theoretical language owes to Hortense, Jacqui, Dionne, and Professor Wynter, has a lot to do with how each of us has come to our intellectual habits and politics. As Roderick (Ferguson) details in his *Reorder of Things*, "Power would attempt to invest the radical aims of antiracist and feminist movements of the sixties and seventies with another logic (replacing or supplementing Enlightenment), capitalizing those movements and their ensigns, cataloging them in the very institutions that those movements were contesting." Rod persuasively argues that "as both agent and effect of institutionalization, interdisciplinarity represents not only an obstacle for and a challenge to dominance, but the expansion and multiplication of power's relays. Interdisciplinarity . . . becomes the episteme that organizes the regimes of representation for academy, state, and capital."[19] During our subsequent one-on-one conversation, Omise'eke expressed agreement with Rinaldo about accounting for multiple disciplinary and epistemological modalities:

And, but—my agreement comes only if we're willing to expand our idea about "disciplines" of knowledge, and maybe even change that "d" word to something else. Instead, I like to think of deepening currents of knowledge and then, creating crosscurrents between them. And to decolonize the epistemologies we're crosscurrenting, I think it's crucial to think of *orisha* stories and *veves*—of ring songs and shouts—of hair braiding and barbering—yes, of growing okra and working herbs—as currents of knowledge that need to be brought into the cross, in order to more fully articulate all the possible ways we (we, people of African descent, we, just plain people) have of knowing the world. To me, that's no retreat; and, since I can't deal in teleologies, it's no advance, either. To me, it's an ocean-blue circle coming back around, and fuller this time.[20]

A doctoral student in anthropology and African American studies at Yale at the time of our New Haven conversation, the writer, activist, and anthropologist Ana-Maurine Lara—now assistant professor of women's gender and sexuality studies at the University of Oregon—offered her differential insight on ways of knowing:

Today I come to the table as an artist and novelist and scholar. . . . I'm thinking mostly in terms of performance and this idea of the griot aesthetic within theorizing in anthropological or ethnographic terms. What does it mean to collect stories from . . . bodies as a site of information, as a site of memory, and then to, on the next level, understand the aesthetics of that story . . . and what does it mean to not only read literature as theory but to read sociology as literature? What kind of critique of knowledge production can happen there?

Readers can see the consistent set of commitments that Ana has brought to her varied postgraduate publications.[21] Omise'eke adds:

> Another question that I think it might be interesting to think more about as we're together is: what is the role of literature in particular, and art in general, in . . . African diaspora social justice movements and resistance. . . . I mean these contemporary novelists that I'm talking about are very involved in social justice movements, so . . . how do those two things intersect, and why? Because for me I don't see it as an either/or. I see it as two things that are necessarily going together.

"Well, you know also the way in which Notisha [Massaquoi] entered the academy," Rinaldo interjects:

> She runs the only health center for women of color in the entire country of Canada. She's been around for a long time, and people kept coming—all women of color, Arab women, Africans, women of South Asian descent— people kept coming and saying "I'm going to study your patients, because there's nothing else like this, and you do this so much better. . . ." They have psychological counselors, they have physical health care, prenatal care, all kinds of things, and most of the people who work there are of color. And these mostly white counselors who are coming in and have no consent whatsoever, and are stealing the souls of the people who they have been working with for 10–15–20 years, and that was actually how she ended up applying to get a PhD. She doesn't plan on leaving her position. She plans to publish her research and so on, but it's a different kind of a model in terms of creating knowledge, and trying to get work that's already being done recognized.

Returning to Omi's critique of Paul Gilroy and how sexuality disappeared and other materialities appear/disappear from the Black Atlantic, Matt (now associate professor of feminist studies at UC Santa Barbara) offered that he is "very interested in that question of *how*"—taken up in his book, *The Queer Limit of Black Memory: Black Lesbian Literature and Irresolution*:

> What is that mechanism by which Black queer people disappear from Black memory in and of itself? How does a person become so queer as to not

even be recognized by Black people anymore? How do Black queer people try . . . to work ourselves back into Black memory? Spillers argues that the Middle Passage strips Black people from their gendered bodies and made their flesh into cargo, ungendering the Black captive. Misnaming is crucial to the process of domination; however, self-naming is integral to speaking a truer word concerning oneself. What does it mean for Black people to use the power of personal naming for the function of the pronoun? . . . One of the ways that I've decided that we have been trying to work our way back into Black memory as a whole is through fiction, and through these pieces of historical fiction that try to rewrite Black history with the Black queer involved. So I am so glad to see archivists here. The archives are a crucial part of this, so I'm suggesting that knowing and seeing that there is a gap in Black historical memory and in the physical archives that we create—that Black (and I would specifically say Black lesbian) writers create an alternative archive from which to reconstruct Black memory. . . . The novels for me are critiques of the archive, and critiques of historical methodology. So they are historiographical texts in and of themselves. They point to a kind of misplaced archive, or places where there has been an emphasis, one emphasis, but other places have been completely forgotten.

Historian George Chauncey, who was the director of lesbian and gay studies at Yale at the time, graciously joined us for the first conversation of the symposium. Reminding us that these questions of historiography are not limited to Black queer historical studies, George shared some of the reservations that Natalie and Colin expressed earlier on. Agreeing with Matt that fiction, literature, filmmaking, and performance art suggest new imaginative possibilities and nodes of community formation, he pushed further on what he called a "tougher epistemological question." Giving the example of Detroit in the 1940s and the 1950s again, he asked, "How do you start adjudicating truth claims being made by various accounts of that scene?" That is, he asked how one can reimagine a historical narrative and framework, and argue different or contradictory interpretations, through fiction: "I do not know how to begin to do it when fiction becomes a source for thinking about that history, that reality," he said. Moreover, like Rinaldo and me, George worried about letting social scientists off the hook—agreeing that we ought to push historians and ethnographers to do this work as well. Having read what he described as "amazing stories about Detroit in the forties" and brilliant research there, George said that he presses for specificity and distinctiveness in his own research interviews, in part because looking at Detroit in the forties and fifties makes one rethink constructing Black queer history from only a few, and particular, slices of Harlem in the twenties. Responding to George's query regarding competing truth claims of historical narrative and fiction, Matt returned:

> I hope that fiction writers really push the historians. I hope that one of the reasons why there exists some research about Detroit in the forties and fifties is because Cherry Muhanji wrote her novel (*Her*), and that pushed historians to think about other locations. And maybe following Jackie Kay (*Trumpet*), somebody's going to look at Glasgow. Even though I'm a literature person, one of the things I do is go to these sites and interview people. I interviewed Black lesbians in Glasgow, and I collect oral histories because I think they are incredibly important, in general, to find out what was happening. . . . The novel suggests that there are all these people that fall through the cracks of the archival nation-state. Birth certificate, death certificate, many of those things do not tell: what kinds of bodies did they have and what kinds of genders did they have? So I'm hoping that the novel pushes people to rethink these archives and these places, and do different kinds of discoveries . . . that it leads to other kinds of archives, right? It's not just a kind of, an absorption of culture and cultural forms, but a reformulation of them for their own reworking.

By this point in the conversation, Michelle (Wright) had set the sherry bottle a little closer to herself: "Right now, I am focused on disturbing dominant epistemologies in the academy," she said. Michelle's questions are big. After her *Becoming Black: Creating Identity in the African Diaspora* elucidated how the counterdiscourses to Enlightenment philosophies produced by Fanon, Du Bois, Senghor, and other Black thinkers worked toward "a synthesis of the Black Other and the existence (or possibility) of a Black subject" that requires a patriarchal Black nation, she turned to Black ontics in her second monograph, *Physics of Blackness*. At the time of the symposium, she had recently joined Northwestern University's African American studies faculty. She is now the Longstreet Professor of English at Emory. Positively appraising her glass, Michelle offers a way to resituate history, its uses, and its status:

> What I mean (by disturbing dominant epistemologies in the academy) is the fights that I think we have all had when talking about curriculum or hiring, and how, whether some of our colleagues say it explicitly or

implicitly, quite often what they suggest is "I don't need to know any-thing about minority studies because there is nothing to know outside the fact that 'Yes, I get that you all are equal,' and therefore let's get back to the real study which is located within white Western philosophy, white Western sciences, these true objective forms of knowledge." I think a lot about that when I teach, and I always go back to a poster a good friend of mine had in college of Malcolm X, where he says that history is the most important of all disciplines. As a literature person I even agreed with that. And I think possibly that may be because I see history as so many different things. It is a narrative, it is a series of facts, it is a way of re-imagining. . . . African American literature has to operate as a kind of social science even as it is an imagining, because you are aware that you are writing to a dominant group, and you have to negotiate these knowledges. Quite often I send my students to archives—they go to libraries, and they start digging up the histories, so that when we read the literature, they can see the literature in conversation with these historical moments, and then that in turn pushes us to think about questions of agency: the ways in which dominant epistemologies are quite often illogical, the way in which heteronormativity insists upon certain ways of being that simply cannot exist, the way in which Jehosephat begat Jeboth begat . . . and men "giving birth" to men, and gee, oh that doesn't make sense, or the notion that the civilization we have today all starts in ancient Greece, and they had no influences from the outside and somebody realizing, oh gosh, that doesn't make sense either. And also, even more complex, the way in which you can occupy a minority identity and still have privilege and fail to notice it; and that leads us to start talking about how the academy is really dominated by bourgeois epistemologies, and I'm bourgeois, so these are my people, and we really control the knowledge and what counts as knowledges. So quite often for me I bring up queerness not as you all do, but in a much more simplistic form I think, in terms of saying it forces us to rethink the assumptions that we have made, and to move into more complex pat-terns of thinking. . . . And in that way it encourages my students to think a GLBT course isn't simply about learning how GLBT people needed to be treated as equal, too. But GLBT really highlights paradoxes in hetero-normative bourgeois epistemologies—sometimes not the bourgeois part, sometimes just the heteronormative part—that are wrong and need to be rethought.

Blackness and "Diaspora" Redux

The sherry is nearly finished. More tea is steeping. As if anticipating your own query, dear reader, Natalie posed a second provocation:

> Then I had another question, and again this is also a methodology question: Does "diasporic" embody some transnational, transhistorical, framework, or cultural product, if you will, that we all are supposed to identify with, and recognize as inherently diasporic? For example, even though Matt is using jazz to talk about synchronicity, and not claiming that it is always about producing harmony, it seems that one of the reasons why we always take up jazz is because we have a sense that part of what we are looking for is harmony. And so how would we think differently about this queer transnational or diasporic subject if we used hip-hop as the mode or the form to understand sexualities? What if we use dancehall?

I waited for Xavier to reply with some examples of Kwaito, which relies more on bodily dexterity than harmony, like disco/house, or the blaring horns of Afro-pop, or highlife, in which the meter is different—dynamic in a way that resonates with other forms (for me, with Cuban *charanga*, for example— likewise brassy and exuberant) but is distinct. Natalie presses: "Does the form that we choose inherently tell us what it is that we are looking for, looking to say?" Matt offered, "I found the term reharmonization is [also] about . . . dissonance . . . the deep familiarizing process of being able, instead of embracing what we already know, to create something different, and having dissonance be able to exist in time." Rosamond responded:[22]

> Part of what you're bringing up . . . is the idea of ethics. And the idea that we need to constantly be aware of who gets left out, and the conversations that don't happen and the voices that don't get heard. And I am using "black" [lowercase for my own editorial emphasis, as I believe this is what Rosamond meant] and "queer" as shorthand, because I also work in areas in which those terms are not necessarily applicable, or useful, or embraced. And it can be both kind of beneficial in some ways or also very problematic in other ways. And this happens within Black studies and queer studies—when it is useful to have some exoticism, you can bring up the fact that there are black people outside of the US, but also: "OK, you said black, well, you meant African American." . . . It is important for us to constantly think about those things, not in a way to hamstring our work, but in a way to really be site specific, in terms of how they are

applicable in that situation and whether in fact they are useful in other situations. I think that the people who spoke did a very good job in terms of being specific about who it is you are talking about and the theories that you are coming up with.

Xavier Livermon had been quiet for most of the early part of the discussion. Studying popular Kwaito music in South Africa provides him a rich perspective on quotidian culture, transnational Africanness, and embodied transgression, evidenced in his recent book:[23]

So I have two things I want to say about the conversation. Let me start with music, and then I'll get to Africa. As someone who works on music, I don't feel like music can be discussed outside of materiality. That's how it circulates, that's how it gets produced, and so I can't really imagine one discussion without the other. That being said, for me I'm really interested in how other kinds of Black music circulate. As Matt mentioned, jazz and blues . . . circulations . . . lay a groundwork for further kinds of circulations or different kinds of networks. And I'm particularly interested in the way in which more electronic music is coming from Black people and circulating. . . . How that imagines things in different kinds of ways. . . . As far as the discussion of Africa in Black diaspora studies . . . there is also always this tendency to save the muddiness and complexity of Black identities for what happened after the Middle Passage, without recognizing the complexity of African identities before that point, or without stopping to historicize Africa at that moment. So that the way in which we can talk about Africa is . . . always at this point of origin from which everything streams. In my own work, I'm trying to push diaspora scholars to think about the ways in which that relationship didn't just sort of break historically, but continues. What does it mean to actually seriously think about the African continent as a very active, viable, and contemporary part of our discussions of African diaspora? What does it mean to think about the ways in which African identities affect and change how we think about blackness and then with that being said, thinking about what it means to then refocus the African continent away from this hyper-heterosexualization of it, what that then means for imagining all of these various forms of Black queer identities, as they've sort of arisen both historically and contemporarily, in our contemporary times. So . . . what does it mean when the patronymic is not from the master, per se (or when it's not necessarily always a patronymic, but that is another question), but still functions in a way that it's heteronormative or negative. And racialized in particular ways that are very limiting?

Anthropologist and human rights activist Graeme Reid, who was a lecturer at Yale on sexualities and masculinities in Africa at the time and is now the director of the LGBT Program at Human Rights Watch, had the ironic distinction of being both the only continental African, by nationality, and the only white invitee among us. Graeme had been struck by Matt's comments around the erasure of queerness from Black history. In the African context, likewise, opponents pose homosexuality as essentially un-African:

> In South Africa, where my current research is on same-sex marriage, this question of what it means to be African is constantly linked to homosexuality being un-African. Within South Africa this has been such a complex issue because the sexual orientation process and institutions are a litmus test of the success of constitutional democracy. So this question of sexuality has again been given an elevated status within a constitutional framework, and at the same time is used as defining what it means to be African. . . . And then also looking at . . . the way in which South Africa is positioned as somewhat uncomfortably aligned with the West within regional politics, and the evidence pointed to are the kinds of liberal attitudes in politics towards homosexuality.[24]

Working in the same nation-state, Xavier found that

> what is also really fascinating about South Africa is the way in which Johannesburg has become the site for a sort of new African "diasporism." . . . Or also the way in which Johannesburg also functions for a lot of my friends who are elsewhere on the continent, as this sort of Black queer utopic space. That is, they are able to experience being African and queer on the African continent itself, and not have to see Europe or North America as that space. Johannesburg has become this really interesting space, and to a lesser extent Capetown, for Africans elsewhere on the continent to imagine queer identities that are very much racialized as Black in some ways, but also very specifically African. This is in dialogue with larger Black queer identities elsewhere, in very interesting ways.

In his *Blackness and Sexualities* essay ("Somewhere out There: The New Black Queer Theory"), Rinaldo had already argued that "diaspora . . . is about processes of identification around which, at particular moments, various kinds of Black folk might gather around, in fleeting moments. . . . But it is also in reference then to a kind of, for lack of a better phrase, a deeper history that animates forms of contemporary blackness. . . ."[25] During our conversation at 81 Wall Street, he continues: "So one of the things for me, is that not unlike queer theory, diaspora discourses have to live up to the notion of contradiction. We need to develop the theory of contradiction to do this work." Yes. Contradictions abound, and this *ethnography of an idea* is my (perhaps faltering?) contribution to and re-narrativization of (a theory of) contradiction—or deep complexity—that Rinaldo explicitly calls for here and that all of us seem to be orbiting in this discussion and in our individual work. For some—perhaps you, dear reader—my own insistence on capitalized transnational multi-hyphenated contingent vital Black becoming is one of those contradictions. Colin's efforts to push us toward ways we (I) might reconsider this from various locations—and perhaps with an eye toward racial plurality—came in the form of what he posed as "the challenge as somebody who is viewing blackness in a site where I think blackness is much more complicated in relation to nation—in Trinidad and Tobago." Certainly, constituted not only by his view from Trinidad and Tobago but also from living and working in the United States for decades, he asked—not only on this day but on other occasions as well—whether our (my) notions of "Black" and "queer" were in fact "imaginary in some ways. To what extent is it material?" he asked.

Aligned with Colin's challenge to Black (imaginaries and) identification, Fatima (el-Tayeb) was coming from yet another queer space farther from the New Haven *here* we shared in the spring of 2009. Working on Black Germans and inspired by the idea of queer-of-color critique, Fatima had increasingly felt that notions of "nation" and "blackness" were not useful in the contexts in which she was working. Citing "what Jackie Kay does in challenging this erasure of blackness from the Scottish tradition," she told us that

> the notion of Europeanness excludes blackness or any people of color in a way so fundamental that it cannot be talked about.
>
> Race has not developed a vocabulary in Europe, even though most of the vocabulary of race has developed in Europe. But for me, this inability creates connection between racialized groups that may expand or perhaps question the notion of blackness. For example, the Roma, better known as "Gypsies," are defined and self-defined traditionally as "black" . . . it's not like Europeans think Gypsies are Black people, but you have parallel and interacting notions of blackness that can't really be approached in the same way as it is in the Americas. I'm working on a notion of "European of color" identity that is very new, and is very much inspired partly

by Audre Lorde because she was in Europe a lot involved with Black feminism there, and partly also by hip-hop because it is obviously a way for people who could not express themselves as members of the nation to assert an identity. But it's also something that is not really expressed in European literature. The people working in this field use poetry, hip-hop, performance, but literature is something that they do not have access to, because of material conditions.

Fatima later demonstrated this new territory of "interacting notions and analogues" in her *European Others: Queering Ethnicity in Postnational Europe*, published in 2011. As she spoke, my mind also went to another interacting analogue: the history of political, rather than heritable, black identification in the United Kingdom in the late 1970s and 1980s. Asian, Caribbean, and African (descended) immigrants and native-African-descended Black Britons drew the outlines of local blackness to be, in effect, defined by nonwhite Britishness in Thatcher's United Kingdom at a time in which the violence of empire "at home" was met with various forms of resistance, including this novel experiment to reconceptualize blackness. Of course, in the United States it seems that as a general orientation, Black studies scholars do not seem to cotton to "parallels" or analogs to blackness. In fact, many begin (explicitly or implicitly) with the supposition that blackness is without analog or fair comparison. I must admit that there is a fatigue that many US Black American Black studies scholars experience: having to always and at once concede the historically particular constructedness of race (if you like, "race") in a number of sites and at the same time point out its bloody/ied materiality, here (and there). You have certainly noticed: we struggle to find better language (adverbs and adverbial phrases?) to more carefully render *Black, black, African (descended), Black (and) Creole, Afro-/Afri-*, and various hyphenations as appropriate. They all seem at once insufficient, to the degree that various groups around the world who are interpellated by others as any of the descriptions invoked here may refuse or only temporarily sign on to the sort of connections that this author narrates. Still, each of these self-identifications is also "material," if by material we mean, for example, how one's livelihood and life (and death) are conditioned by racial interpellation, and, on the other hand, how some individuals appreciate, and perhaps celebrate, a lived (that is also a material and embodied) experience of historical, political, and affectual Black *being*. This can also be glossed as self-identification. Here the keens, breaks, and fissures are therefore only a necessary part of the story of connection. Not an alibi for atomization or diminution of blackness. Rinaldo took up related contradictions in his conceptualization of organizing and creating within diaspora in his short presentation to the group. In 2009, reflecting on *Queer Returns*, he began:

> So in the piece, I actually spend a little bit of time trying to make a case for why I think by the 1990s discourses around Pan-Africanism recede and discourses of diaspora, if you will, return to the conceptual stage. And part of it, I argue, had a lot to do with the ways in which at least two events allowed for Black people to begin to think about themselves as globally connected again but also needing to have to address the very local or national circumstances of that connection. So the first, even though you can't find the word *diaspora* attached to any of these particular moments, the first for me was around the antiapartheid movement. This was about kind of forms of global blackness and connection, but all of those forms of global blackness and connection had to take their action quite locally, whether at the national level in terms of the divestment movement and so and forth, and the second—HIV/AIDS and the stigma in its initial moments in the eighties around Haitians and Africans. Again, it produced a particular kind of diasporic connection, but it was a connection that only made sense in relation to how people responded to it at the local/national level. . . . If you look at the body of work of Isaac Julien, in the films and . . . the work he's doing in galleries, but if you look at "Looking for Langston," if you look at the "Darker Side of Black," you'll actually see those diasporic fissures; you'll see those antagonisms.

The hard work of reconciling contradictions, or merely sitting them side by side. Translating across languages and sensibilities, struggling at intersections—the fissures, antagonisms, and deep looking-again that Fatima, Colin, Isaac, Rinaldo, and others demand—this is part and parcel of the project of Black/queer/diaspora.

At the end of the day, we moved on to Q&A. Calvin Warren, then poised to complete his dissertation in African American and American studies at Yale, joined our discussion. He brought us back around to consider the distinctions and varied uses of the discursive and the material. Some of the intellectual commitments reflected in his query to the group find elaboration in his recent book, *Ontological Terror: Blackness, Nihilism, and Emancipation*:

> In some of the comments I thought I was hearing a subtle distinction between materiality and the literary or the metaphorical, and I'm wondering in Black queer theory, is there an archive or a cultural object that exists

outside the discourse or beyond the bounds of discourse, and if it is, what is it? I'm wondering if there is a particular function for the distinction between the material and the literary or metaphorical within Black queer theory. If there is a particular functionality for preserving that distinction, what is it? Does that distinction preclude or impede other sources of epistemological development? Or is that distinction not accurate . . . ?

Michelle responded:

> The object that stands outside Black queer discourse is the same one that stands outside of almost all discourses, and that is the body. The body constantly interrupts, and every time we try to frame it through discourse it escapes us once again. Materiality disturbs us even as we are hellbent on showing that it does not have an essential core to it. That it is something that is constructed. And that *here it is, there we are,* and it seems that so much of what we're talking about is the imagining of bodies in different spaces and having different relationships to one another. And then trying to find the discourses and archival material evidence of those bonds.

This is also an incisive answer to Colin's important question challenging the materiality of blackness or our imagination of blackness: the *reach-grasp-escape* (repeat) dance. I hear echoes of Melvin here too, speaking to us from the ether on the "tremoring cadence and mystery" that we have set out to explore, interrogate, or move to—toward dynamic transformation and reinventions of self.[26] Here (it is) and there (we are): our bodies moving—inviting us to begin the dance. Again. Lyndon (Gill), who explores the reinvention of self and/within community, through art and the arts of activism, in his *Erotic Islands: Art and Activism in the Queer Caribbean*, had been dutifully taking notes. He finally broke his uncharacteristic silence at the end of the conversation:

> Just quickly, and this is just the first part of your question, Calvin, what I hear is an implication that there is no outside of discourse, that we must enter in the discourse in order to interact, and that's sort of the classic philosophical . . . linguistic theory informed way of understanding human interaction. And I wanted to make a point about discourse and epistemological intervention that can go in a different direction. But just to propose one thing that lies outside of discourse is, going back to Jacqui Alexander: the metaphysical.

As I read Lyndon's words, my mind returns to Jacqui's "Pedagogies of the Sacred: Making the Invisible Tangible" in her *Pedagogies of Crossing*. In it she recounts how she earned access to Kitsimba—a formerly enslaved woman who not only *exists outside the discourse or beyond the bounds of discourse*, but also speaks: narrating her own story and refusal "to be cluttered beneath an array of documents of any kind, whether generated by the state, by plantation owners, or by [Jacqui]." Here Jacqui pushes us beyond the secular traditions and expectations of academe. She avers that wrestling with the disembodied presence of ancestral knowledges and histories requires us to profoundly challenge our methodologies, asking *which tools and technologies enable access*?[27] Lyndon continues:

> So precisely the place where the physical fails, where language fails, where there is an inability to talk about something that is not material—the metalinguistic perhaps, where it's not able to enter into the linguistic chain through which we are able to conceptualize it—then the metaphysical is what stands outside of discourse to a certain extent, although we try to draw it in every opportunity we get. But perhaps the best way to speak about it is knowing that you'll never have the language to be able to speak about the metaphysical. . . . Lorde is perhaps the nexus that allows for this relationship between the spiritual and the physical, between the social sciences and literature. As Professor Tinsley indicates, a lot of those novelists . . . who are also activists, who are also to a certain extent collecting histories, oral histories—their physical body functions as this bridge. There is a theoretical intervention that is happening in the very being of these individuals, and part of that intervention is a spiritual intervention, which is a part of what discourse cannot manage, what discourse is not yet able to address. . . . And I like Professor Bennett asking us to bring in the social sciences . . . what is that contribution? . . . Maybe this ability to think those things together, to work those things together, to live, write those things together, is part of the Black queer epistemological intervention. So that life on the ground is interesting, yes, but there is also a theoretical intervention that is happening in the very being of these individuals. . . . Is maybe the Black queer epistemological intervention the possibility of thinking, at once, that which we're thinking about in disconnect?

Here, dear reader, is a demonstration of the value of conversation. We could not manufacture a more apt coda than this (or a better preface to the triptych of chapters to follow). With that, we adjourned to more warm greetings and readied for more conversation, food, drink ("work . . . partnership of energy building thinking working loving laughing and struggling . . . here and beyond"[28]).

Archiving the Anthological
at the Current Conjuncture

One thing we know as Black feminists is how important it is for us to recognize our own lives as herstory. Also, as Black women, as lesbians and feminists, there is no guarantee that our lives will ever be looked at with the kind of respect given to certain people from other races, sexes or classes. There is similarly no guarantee that we or our movement will survive long enough to become safely historical. We must document ourselves now. One function the letters have served is to make us real to ourselves. And each other. To write a letter to another Black woman who understands is to seek and find validation.—BARBARA SMITH AND BEVERLY SMITH, 1978

IN THIS CHAPTER we extend our pivot toward the constitution of Black/ queer study and Black/queer memory to the archive—the *ether* in a material form. This certainly constitutes another crossing that requires accounting of our values and our disavowals. Critical reassessment that both takes the *archive* seriously as more than a building and deeply considers "how to" or why we say (or not) what we have found in them has come to be termed "the archival turn." But as Matt (Richardson) said, riffing on the French, "Black people have a fever for the archive," which is not new.[1] Today we face a conjuncture of burgeoning interest in Black LGBTQ history, wildly differential access to evidence of Black LGBTQ pasts, and disparate—often contradictory—politics and positionalities. I hope that the elliptical conversation we engage here will generate a different sort of narration in which we can finally put away false dichotomies of yesterday *or* today, action *or* reflection, mind *or* matter. Through brief examples of current archival practices and conversations among a few projects that propose to "save" culture, "share tongues," and put things "on record," this chapter offers a usable assessment of our possibilities. A portion of what follows is in the words of archivists, curators, and leaders of archival projects who have taken up this work (Steven G. Fullwood, Ajamu Ikwe-Tyehimba [also/formerly known as Ajamu X], Zethu Matebeni, Matt Richardson, Colin Robinson, and Selly Thiam) taken directly from a "virtual roundtable" that Matt and I compiled and originally conceived as a conversation across diaspora to be included in "Black/Queer/Diaspora."[2] We had hoped to provide a sort of "archive of archives" or elaborate finding aid, uninterrupted by our interventions. Portions of this idiosyncratically curated record of work to document and (re)discover contemporary and historical perspectives of folks *in the life* in various sites around the globe are finally included here, with brief intrusions of my authorial analysis. Before this, please allow a bit of curatorial framing, then brief commentary on two archival objects. The first is reconsideration of (another) Venus and of a "girl"—three, in fact—in a very different affective relation. Then we briefly engage Marsha P. Johnson once again before finally turning to our belated transnational conversation on projects that deploy meticulous vigilance, and a set of provocative arrows toward (your) future work.

The work of Black bisexual, transgender, gay, and lesbian archival projects is aligned with Michel-Rolph Trouillot's project to uncover and reanimate submerged histories, and with the first and second generations of autodidacts of the Black radical intellectual tradition, such as C. L. R. James, who tracked down facts, rearranging them through study to create archives of knowledge. Think also of Black feminists whose excavations, before this recent scholarly "turn," demonstrated the methodological and political stakes of moving beyond recovery and revindication toward unearthing more-nettlesome questions. For example, Hazel (Carby) has given us the incalculable gift and example of historicity as a foundational critical sensibility. Multisided and often multisited, historicity and conjunctural thinking—as a habit of mind.[3] Not "history" as merely a discipline or a method or a fashion, but more fundamentally as the way to think, see, and say. Recall Alice Walker, for example, who literally went in search of the grave of a then "little known Harlem Renaissance writer" and, alongside the scholarship of Cheryl Wall and others, recirculated

Ms. Zora—not quite "commemorating," but something like it—the singular figure of Zora Neale Hurston as she and her work *remained*, un(re)marked—in apparent final silent repose, far removed from her imagined grand "Cemetery for the Illustrious Negro dead . . . something like Pere la Chaise in Paris" that Ms. Zora had proposed to W. E. B. Du Bois.[4] One way to think about archives, from what a dear senior colleague would call a "deep Negro history" perspective—I remember her proposal each time I walk into a Black studies/ cultural center museum or library.[5] Matt, whose exploration of compulsory heterosexuality in Black memory entreats us to hold or suffer "No More Secrets, No More Lies," has already shown us that Black/queer memories and lives left "inconspicuous forgetfulness," as Ms. Zora had worried, are often less "lost" or "forgotten" than excised, mis(re)membered, and misgendered.[6] Precisely and emphatically not "illustrious," celebrated, or saved. After all, Craig (G. Harris) has already poignantly illustrated a glimpse of the double cremation that awaits if we are not vigilant. His "Hope against Hope" constitutes a powerful litany, or calendar including this scene:

> When he stopped writing
> His mother discarded the pen,
> Folded his hands,
> Donated the journal
> To the church
> With the condition
> It be cloistered
> And stored his memory
> In Woodlawn cemetery[7]

In 2011 I did not know that there was a name for the work Lisa (C. Moore) had done to reissue *In the Life: A Black Gay Anthology* and *Brother to Brother: New Writing by Black Gay Men,* from which the lines above are excerpted, and which had been poised to fall out of print. I did not know that I was really talking about an archival practice when I wrote in the new introduction to Lisa's RedBone Press reissue that *"Brother to Brother: New Writing by Black Gay Men* indexes our collective injuries in blood, cum, fire and tears." I imagined myself writing in the well-worn margins and between the lines of Essex's original introduction, when I wrote to my brothers and sisters in the new edition:

> We would be remiss in this re-consideration and re-reading . . . not to reflect on how our stories are endangered, at risk of revision, reversal and erasure; whether by the ravages of time on paper notebooks in a dank

basement; the best intentions of lovers and friends holding on to genius journals, rolled up paintings, recordings, cocktail napkins, xerographs or out-of-print books. These stories are also endangered by our own complacency, poor reading, self-appointed divadom and lack of vision. . . . We do not have to begin anew as if we have no intellectual genealogy, no aesthetic and political "tradition" to treasure, critique and push forward. After all, not only is "our loss . . . greater than all the space we fill with prayers and praise," but what we stand to gain from picking up the weapons and wands of our mothers, fathers, sisters and brothers may make all the difference in preventing more loss. We are worth more than "piles of nothing."[8]

Reissue is an act of rescue—a queer sort of rebirthing that requires returns to the archives of original writers and their survivors or descendants. Thus, our conversation is not only about "collecting" or "saving" the materials of our lives. It must also be about insisting upon according respect (at least to ourselves and our experiences) in spite of not being regarded by some as "safely historical," or deemed worthy of saving, consideration, and study, as Beverly and Barbara Smith tell us.

My encounters with the Black Gay and Lesbian Archive at the Schomburg (now the In the Life Archive) changed the way I think of the archive and how I *do* ethnography. Not only did I "discover" gems from the recent past—and my own life—but I began to see the "evidence of being" as field notes or journals detailing what was utterly precious to others. I encountered Black folks and others who have come to sit quietly to commune with what had been saved. This researcher learned about the risks of revision, reversal, and erasure of the scholarly record both through ethnographic and literary engagements, and from tuning my ears to occasional "behind-the-counter" talk of archivists, curators, and librarians I might overhear. Moreover, I have held unpublished genius in my own hands: coffee-stained and rescued from a dusty yard sale. I have sat with students as they puzzled through the trauma of poring over sadistically detailed notebooks of plantation overseers found at Yale's Beinecke Library, or the eeriness of finding rare or assumed lost materials that they could not find "at home" in the global South, available only at Yale, University of Texas, Archivo General de Indias, or the British Library. Earlier, as an activist and a student, I lived the "canon wars" of the long 1980s without realizing that I had been riddled with shrapnel of old ideas about evidence, method, discipline, and rigor—until the opportunity to reflect and produce my own original dissertation research forced me to return to what had brought me to the academy in the first place. What I had thought of as my method, as an ethnographer-in-training, was to run the streets (*la calle*) in order to be in the action, to hear stories of the living and watch them unfold. Still, the "data" collected—the experiences of Black Cuban revolutionary subjects remixing the ideologies they had been given—demanded to be told in context and forcefully against much of "the literature." I had to ask critical questions of the previous literatures and of the archivists and institutions in which they reside, as well as the materials I found and the stories I heard. What is important to collect and why? Who collects them, and why does it matter? What stories and images and ways of posing or narrating those stories, images, and objects can be authorized (by academe, by a state, by a discipline, for example)? What is foreclosed and concretized in each retelling or inaugurated or expanded in a re-narrativization? For me, Marlon's evocation of anthropology as the "unending search for what is utterly precious" finds expression at this convergence of the street, the archive, the library, and the classroom.

I came to understand archival practice as fundamental to an ethnographic sensibility only belatedly. In Cuba I tried to balance the time I spent at kitchen tables, at CDR meetings, during rum-fueled consciousness-raising circles, and on dance floors and barstools with looking at primary works in the Archivo Nacional de la República de Cuba (the Cuban National Archive) in Havana and later the Archivo General de Indias in Seville and the Benson Collection at UT–Austin, in an attempt to ground what I witnessed *en la calle* and read in historiographic and literary works "before the revolution." What I know now, for sure, is that our futures require fine, nimble, capacious readings of both "the archive and the repertoire."[9] It is one thing to be told, as Kevin Aviance already said, that someone "come[s] from a queen who comes from a queen. . . ." We also need to understand the conditions under which he made this utterance, the histories/herstories out of which it emerges. They are inextricably bound. Utterances, performances, and gestures must not float out of context. The archive shapes and provides the foundation and scaffolding for various claims and knowledges and histories/herstories. It sets the condition of possible statements that demand accounting. The double move that the Smith sisters advocate—"recogniz[ing] our own lives as herstory [and] document[ing] ourselves now"—requires meticulous vigilance.

Another Venus

A well-loved leader in the Atlanta lesbian and gay community, Venus Landin nurtured and served as an example to young Black lesbian and gay activists, including me. Encountering Saidiya's title "Venus in Two Acts" for the first time, fifteen years later, my mind flashed immediately to Venus and Bisa. Then to Venus and Charlene. First Act: in 1993 Venus's former lover, Bisa Niambi, shot and killed Venus before killing herself. Entr'acte: in 2005 Venus's close friend Charlene Cothran—entrepreneur and founder of the successful Black lesbian-focused events-producing company Hospitality Atlanta—created a Black gay lifestyle magazine and named it in Venus's honor. One year later, however, the Second Act: Charlene announced that she had been "delivered" from "the gay lifestyle" and made *Venus* magazine a vehicle for gay conversion. Poignantly and heartbreakingly, Charlene narrates Venus's murder and Bisa's suicide (as part of her own conversion testimony):

> Mercy had indeed covered me during those dark 1993 days when my good friend Venus Landin, for whom this magazine is named, was shot and killed. I recall how I went with her to her ex-lover's home to recover her things, how the woman had built a fire using Venus' precious journals as fuel, how she burned her clothes and how the flames and debris had fallen out of the fireplace's box and were ablaze along the carpet.[10]

As Saidiya (Hartman) laments, "Hers is the same fate as every other Black Venus: no one remembered her name or recorded the things she said, or observed that she refused to say anything at all."[11] No reliable witness. No participatory observer. No smartphone trained on the po-lice with the gun and the DA and the grand jury in his pocket, or on the white lady outraged at the magic of your Black *being*. No blog think-piece-of-the-day automatically "archiving" for posterity your hot take of the moment. No monument to the accretive toxic violence that can—as it so often does—undo a sister. This time it undoes a sister/lover, who then kills the sister she purported to love. Then, compounded undoing: a sister/friend incinerates a shared revolutionary statement of the long 1980s in the same blaze into which she has cast her "old life." The fragmented record now witnessing how the trauma of violence reverberates: a fire of "Venus' precious journals . . . the flames and debris . . . ablaze along the carpet."

"What else is there to know?" Saidiya asks. And that is also to ask "How can we remind ourselves of what we have forgotten and what we have been asked (or required) to disavow, and/or/thus what we might repair, to know in a different way?" "The woman had built a fire using Venus' precious journals as fuel." Indeed. In "Notanda," the short preface to her Black Atlantic epic, *Zong!*, M. NourbeSe Philip quotes from the famous French philosopher's meditation on his contemporary, in which "he talks of mourning, the specters of the dead, and the need to know the exact place where the bodies

7.1 Marsha P. Johnson hands out flyers in support of gay students.
Photo: Diane Davies, 1970.

and bones lie: there is a similar desire on my part for the bones [she writes],
I want the bones. . . . 'Give me the bones,' [she] say[s] to the silence that is so
often what history presents to us."[12] The material and/or ethereal evidence—
burnt shards, traces of the violence: your playlists, meeting agendas, eviction
notices, and the first draft of your grant proposal. "Habeas the corpus!" the
ethnographer exclaims. We want to see it! "Hers is an untimely story told by
a failed witness," I could say, after Saidiya and alongside many others who
attempt to reproduce in our own ways her meticulous "critical fabulation."
Dear reader, I want to say more than this. We reach to create that which will
finally do more than "recount the violence that deposited these traces in
the archive . . . without committing further violence in my own act of narration."[13] I want to *see* more than "meager sketch(es)." I want us to see and
say and keep safe something true that re-members, incites, helps, and heals.
Therefore, this is also a kind of love letter to Steven, Alexis and Julia, Ajamu
and Topher, Zethu and Zanele, Matt, Colin, Tourmaline, Selly, and them
(and some of you)—for their precious gift of meticulous vigilance.

The photo of Marsha P. Johnson (see figure 7.1), found on the blog of
Black trans artist and activist Tourmaline, speaks eloquently from the ether
to the current moment. To Marsha's left is New York University's Bobst

Library. Bobst, like most elite university libraries, is more than a library; it also houses the NYU archive. In this photo taken by Diane Davies on the campus of NYU, the scene looks toward the Silver Towers (left background, with the terraces). This tower of faculty (administrators and others) in "NYU Village"—a "superblock" in Greenwich Village—is mostly ivory. The most celebrated of its faculty are rewarded with higher floors and better views. This is to say that the archive, the professorate, and the market are intimately, even inextricably, bound. We cannot reckon the long-1980s changes in New York City without considering New York University's real estate moves, for example. Still, the cherubic, curly-haired protester in the trench-coat (right), whose bright white sign contrasts with Marsha's fashionable fur swing coat, hopes to interrupt a wholly bourgeois, liberal understanding of this knowledge *keep* and place of knowledge production. They hold a placard that insists "Come Out [!!!] of Your [Gay] Ivory Towers and into the Street!" Are they talking to me—to us? And are they also talking about the books, pamphlets, photos, journals, newspaper clippings, unfinished manuscripts, and ephemera housed in Bobst—the fortress-like library/archive and administration building—calling this knowledge out into the street and into the light of day? Can this move in both directions: calling our unarchived pasts from various streets into towers of our own creation where they can be shared, referenced, and kept—where our cultures may be "saved"? I am not suggesting that the politics of recovering, saving, and reanimating archival pasts can replace a mass Black/queer movement. We take this up in the final chapter. In this one we describe one example of what is—that is, another living practice of the Black gay habit of mind. Here we attempt to at least provoke more reflection and research on its political potential, if not also the intentional proliferation of more projects. So consider this naive question, sincerely asked toward usable truths: in what specific ways might the practices of those who "save" our lives through interdisciplinary, genre-bending, border-crossing anthological habits of meticulous vigilance really *save* us?

Placing and Saving

If "all discourse is placed"—and I have full confidence that Stuart-in-the-ethers is correct—it must be placed somewhere. We make our today and project our (non)futures partly out of pasts that others have lived and that someone "saved" someplace. Audre said—or, more accurately, Alexis tells us that Audre said this, for Audre did not publish these instructions from the ether kept in her 1974 diary: "When I have been dead four and a half seasons, dry my words, seek the roots where they grow, down between the swelling of my bones. . . ."[14] Alexis was able to find instructions from Audre-in-the-ether to prepare the rhizome that will bloom brilliantly and make good medicine because Audre left them to be saved at the Spelman College Archive at the Women's Research and Resource Center.[15]

Remember that Assotto pushed us to work like archaeologists and that Marlon defined anthropology as an "unending search for what is utterly precious." Steven has called this "saving culture." Each of their projects is distinct and cannot be collapsed under one heading, but this search and saving are precisely the work that Selly, Alexis and Julia, Steven, Ajamu and Topher, Tourmaline, Zethu, Zanele, and them are doing. This work gives us ways to remember and to think about remembering, and frameworks through which to (re)offer our (re)narrativizations for projects of the living and those who will outlive us. It is good medicine distilled from those dried bones. Evidence that needs to be unburied. As David Scott offers, "On this view, memory is at once conserving and a condition of criticism, revision, and change."[16] If so, this effectively constitutes much of what is generally thought of as a politics. The "stony contradictory ground" of our current conjuncture makes it necessary to recall, engage, and attempt to transform the present.[17] Work saving yesterday's pumps and placards and philosophies, binders of another queen who comes from another bulldagger, for unpromised and likely also problematic futures toward "bread in our children's mouths / so that they will. . . ."[18] This profound work and psychic commitment is therefore not merely an exercise in remembering or commemorating but also, more pointedly, about creating "countermemory." Here I follow David's beautiful reconsideration of the "Archives of Black Memory" of archivists themselves and the institutions they build toward crucial questions of the "relation between the idea of an archive, the modalities of memory, the problem of a tradition, and practices of criticism."[19] That is, we are meditating on the relationship between the practices of archiving and the politics of a Black/gay habit of mind. Steven (Fullwood) told us:

> I founded the archive in 1999 to aid in the preservation of Black queer culture and history. Arturo Schomburg's quest to create a collection of Black materials was inspired by the lack of Black history in his homeland, Puerto Rico, and the belief that people of African descent did not have a history, nor contribute to civilization. The inspiration behind the BGLA [Black Gay and Lesbian Archive] comes from a similar perspective; that the prevalent belief was that there was not Black queer community,

or communities, and therefore no Black queer culture and history. After working in the field for several years and researching archival institutions throughout the US, few institutions were actively collecting and preserving Black queer materials.[20]

If "all discourse is placed" before we first encounter it, it must be carefully placed by *someone*. David (Scott) could easily be talking about my dear friend Steven when he says of Robert Hill (founder and curator of the Marcus Garvey and Universal Negro Improvement Association Papers Project at the University of California) that

> it is not simply that these are all documents he has personally tracked down, one after the other, and brought together (though there is that too); it is rather that in doing so he has developed a distinctive relation to—I should more properly say sensibility toward—the very idea of an archive. Documentary records . . . do not have a merely instrumental validity; they are not simply means to an ulterior end; they are not just empirical windows, or data, through which a separable and more real past is glimpsed. Rather, they are for him, above all, *a fundamental discursive reality in their own right*. . . . "Collecting" . . . is at once an art and *a mode of intelligibility*.[21]

The italics are mine. Do you hear it again, dear reader? *Werk! Work! Wrq! Wrk! Wuk! Wuk!* Labor to shape a paradigm—to create a way for folks to reckon, to frame, and to order—in this case against the prevailing order of (at least) Eurocentricity, antiblackness, heterosexism, transphobia, and *misogynoir*.

"Saving" Culture

"There's a lot of stuff which isn't nice, which doesn't sit easily in museums and community events. And doesn't sit easily with our memories either. It was not some kind of halcyon trajectory from invisibility to visibility. It's born out of a struggle," Ajamu and Topher offer. Citing their proximity to the in-your-face, DIY ethic of the punk generation of London's long 1980s, Rukus! Federation and Rukus! archive founders Topher Campbell and Ajamu Ikwe-Tyehimba said that "there's always a bit of mischievousness in us. Rukus! is the finger up at the same time as the embrace and the kiss. 'Love and lubrication' is our sign-off at the same time as 'Fuck off, we'll do what we want.'"[22] A number of organizations have emerged in the United Kingdom—mostly in England—since 2000, such as Outburst UK, UK Black Pride, and BlackOUT UK. Rukus! Federation is an early important and active part of this emergence.

A project of Rukus! Federation, the archive, launched in 2005, "generates, collects, preserves and makes available to the public historical, cultural and artistic materials relating to the lived experience of Black LGBTQ same gender loving and gender non-binary folx in the UK."[23] Although Black included Asian and other nonwhites in the expansive multicultural anti-Thatcher UK politics of the 1980s, Rukus! focuses on people of African and Caribbean descent. It is Europe's first dedicated Black LGBTQ archive. Eschewing some of the polite language and perhaps aestheticized concerns of academics, artists Ajamu and Topher are clear on the need to remember and collect what is partly "a very unpalatable history. . . . The history of Brixton cottage, the sex parties, of violent and difficult relationships, of relationships between different Black communities, and of what's now been called gay racism, which is what the white community has done, systematically, to disempower Black clubs and to stop the Black presence happening."[24]

An exchange between Topher, Ajamu, and Mary Stevens, who interviewed them for "Love and Lubrication in the Archives," reveals the importance of the vision and dedication of the archivist/archaeologist/activist to champion the collection and presentation of culture, despite the lack of awareness or lack of support of many cultural producers and community members. This work was not a priority for most people. "The idea for the archive actually came about in 2004, when we got planning our exhibition, 'Family Treasures,'" they said. This first exhibit began from their personal collections, borne out of "very small, very sporadic representations" and of some photographs of Black gay men who were "no longer around" that Ajamu had photographed at Gay Pride events from the 1990s onward. Topher says, "We tried to get 'Family Treasures' off the ground by writing to people like Dennis Carney, and Dirg [Aaab-Richards], and various other people who had been active. We were asking 'What have you got?' And nothing came back. Nothing came back." Ajamu: "Nobody responded." Allow Steven to interject: "The Black LGBTQ community has demonstrated (at least in the past) that it has little interest in building its own, self-sufficient archival institutions. Mostly, our energies have focused on (and rightfully so, as a mandate of the times) creating and sustaining social service and ASOs [AIDS services organizations] rather than archival institutions. This is a perspective that I'd like to see change in the next 10–20 years."[25] Topher says to Mary and Ajamu, "People were working in a very minority maelstrom—a maelstrom which had no mainstream recognition at all. It is very tiring to work in that way, whether you are a community activist, or a DJ, or a club promoter. And then you move on, you get older, and somebody comes along and says, 'That was really valuable what you did,' but at the time nobody was telling you it was valuable."[26] In the eye of this maelstrom of necessary lifesaving work, our virtual roundtable considered competing interests and limits of time and resources of folks engaged in community work. As Steven said,

> Overall the response has been good to projects like the BGLA, None on Record and Rukus, but the resistance for Black LGBTQ people to archive themselves is a glaring problem, particularly when the main point of organizing is visibility. I generally attribute this oversight to activist fatigue, but for me it points to a lack of vision, which I too am guilty of particularly when I associate myself with people and institutions with whom I share some politics, but fundamentally disagree on how to get to where we all say we want to go. . . .

Colin (Robinson) responded: "Hmm . . . isn't how to get there the politics?" Steven answered:

> I have worked with both Selly and Ajamu and Topher, and it's interesting to consider where we are now as "gatekeepers" in our work. Selly owns None on Record. Ajamu and Topher have recently partnered with the London Metropolitan Archives to house their archival collection. . . . We all work with individuals and organizations and researchers from all walks who have and/or seek info about Black LGBTQ life, sometimes uncovering it, sometimes creating it. This is a very new moment for the Black LGBTQ individual, one that many people like Audre Lorde, James Baldwin, Ron Simmons, and Colin Robinson, just to name a few, helped to create by doing their work.

In response to an earlier quip about the relative import of "saving" culture, Steven had said to Colin, "Unfortunately, people like you, Colin, who offer a great deal in the way of theory and analysis, do not do this work regularly or at all. Folks like yourself sit on great information and often complain about the lack of work out there, which is frustrating to say the least." Colin has since donated a portion of his own papers to the In the Life Archive, and has made plans to donate other materials to institutions in Trinidad and Tobago and the US. The organizations he co-leads actively archive their ongoing work. His reply at the time is instructive and compelling in another way:

> Haven't I repeatedly said to you, Steven, when you come at me with this: "Get me a fellowship!?" I don't think I was complaining so much as suggesting we think about strengthening opportunities for our activists to

think and theorize. Bannerman and Revson and a few US and international social entrepreneurship fellowships do offer something akin to this. I was just wondering if university-affiliated folks could also create more opportunities, e.g. for activist chairs, for hiring activists on grant projects, or for making activists more central to activities like the seminar Jafari convened that generated the roundtable project.

Colin had attempted a few provocations toward crucial self-reflexivity that not everyone cared to take up during our virtual roundtable. He began:

> And I was deeply curious about how identities and migration and education and privilege shape the work we do. I was also curious about our politics, especially Steven's political statements that BGLA is not a social justice organization, as if interventions in power, production and access related to knowledge isn't some of the most critical social justice work.

Steven replied:

> I think my tendency to demark my work differently from those who call themselves social justice workers or workers for social justice is a lazy one, clearly with implications when called out in a conversation such as this. I was not always in the streets carrying banners and passing out flyers, but since 1998 I was the one collecting the banners and flyers and archiving them for self and then the community. This is what I mean by lazy because it doesn't highlight or represent the complicated relationship I have to activist work and archiving. With the exception of wanting to save Black LGBTQ culture so that generations would have the benefit of their ancestors' experience, or the fact that the name has to change to reflect the diversity of the community [he renamed it In the Life Archive in 2013], I had not thought very critically about the BGLA, nor had I been challenged to do so. Perhaps this moment of self-reflection will help change that. Of course, collecting an underdocumented and disappeared culture—until recently—is a social justice act, and allows for many to rethink history and culture from other points of view. It is absolutely an intervention, a very necessary one. I have to think about my own sensibilities with respect to this work and my own reluctance to align my work within a social justice framework.

Colin said:

> I want to push back a little, Steven, on this notion of "an underdocumented and disappeared culture," which seems a little overstated. Apart from resisting the self-pathologization we often revel in with regard to our

communities and cultures, I think that while we are all doing work that struggles against institutional erasure and exclusion, we are also engaged with rich oral and other historicist traditions that help guard against our cultures' disappearance.

Selly (Thiam), the founder of None on Record—what she recently described as "an African LGBT media organization," now including the *AfroQueer* podcast—would likely disagree that the notion of "underdocumented" and "disappeared" is overstated, at least in the context of continental Africa. During the early days of her work collecting oral histories of Africans on the continent and abroad, an African asylee that she interviewed in Chicago unwittingly gave Selly the name for her project. During the interview she asked him whether there was a name to describe lesbian, gay, bisexual, or transgender people in his indigenous language, and he said (after a very long pause and careful rumination), "I have none on record. . . . Yes, none on record." Selly told Matt and me that

> None on Record exists to archive a living history of African LGBT people . . . in the first-person narrative format instead of through a second or third party. None on Record is rooted in the idea that LGBT Africans are able to talk about their lives in their own words. We have challenged ourselves to collect a large number of stories from lesbians, bisexual and transgender people who do not have the same access to political space [as MSM/gay men who often find some financial support through international HIV/AIDS charities] due to a lack of funding and community support and therefore can be harder to locate because they do not fit into the funding narratives of these organizations.

In her "Navigating Epistemic Disarticulations," Grace (Musila) engages a discursive space marked by various iterations of what she calls "epistemic disarticulations," which also seem to reflect the material conditions to which many of the oral histories of "None on Record" attest. There are very high "costs of epistemic disarticulation when these multiple knowledge systems are overlooked." Grace thus argues for attention to multiple ways that Africans conceive of themselves as individuals within a number of competing epistemes and institutions, rather than referring to what she calls "anthropological common sense" or "discursive debris of received knowledge."[27] Selly continues:

> The work of None on Record is as much about building a comprehensive archive/record of LGBT African people as it is about empowering LGBT communities and combating isolation and violence through the power

of the first-person narrative. When a person speaks about what they have seen and experienced, what has been done to them because of who they are, it galvanizes the community. . . . Even though this is a period in which some African media openly call for violence against LGBT people, we combat that by taking control of our own narratives and eventually forcing a change in the public discourse.

For example, None on Record has documented the experiences of organizers of the first Gay Pride march in Africa, which took place in Johannesburg in 1990, followed up by an *AfroQueer* podcast that reflects on the history of Johannesburg Pride and the ugly and/but instructive events of the 2012 Johannesburg Pride. Black lesbian and GNC activists with the One-in-Nine campaign had hoped to bring awareness to the widespread problem of so-called corrective rape and murder of Black lesbians in Johannesburg, with signs that read "Stop the War on Women's Bodies" and "No cause for celebration," for example. They staged a "die-in" across the festive corporate-sponsored parade route by lying in the street in the path of the parade, requesting that the revelry be quieted for one minute of silence to acknowledge the ongoing rapes and murders. Instead of extending even performative solidarity, organizers and onlookers yelled, taunted, dragged, threatened, and enlisted police to arrest the score of protesters, with one parade participant threatening a dog attack, recalling the long-held apartheid strategy.[28] In 2010 None on Record documented LGBT organizing in Kenya that preceded the vote for the new Kenyan constitution and began offering workshops to other East African groups and individuals to follow suit with self-documentation and production of digital media toward public education.

None on Record was founded as a response to the murder of FannyAnn Eddy, a lesbian activist from Sierra Leone. Selly, a Senegalese-American journalist, filmmaker, radio producer, and writer, told us, "Because of the lack of accessible information surrounding her murder and her organization, I became increasingly interested in the experiences and organizing of LGBT Africans around the world and how these experiences were documented. . . . I began to interview LGBT Africans in North America." In a very early story Selly did on FannyAnn, Notisha (Massaquoi), whom Rinaldo had raised as an example of emerging scholar activism, reflected on what FannyAnn's death had provoked in her: "I felt that my silence allowed her to be murdered in that way." Selly continued:

In the first year most of the interviews were recorded in the US and Canada. By the second year we began collecting in South Africa and have spread to Senegal, Gambia, Kenya, and the Ivory Coast. . . . We have collected stories in Wolof, Zulu, Xhosa, French, English, Swahili, and Luo. The stories are housed in an online archive at noneonrecord.com and at physical archives, with our largest collection at the GALA Archives at the University of Witwatersrand in Johannesburg, South Africa. The struggle for LGBT equality in African countries has been going on for decades, long before None on Record's existence. The growing visibility of the movement on the African continent made a way for us to continue None on Record's work of documenting.

Ajamu said that their influences and collaborators came "from both heterosexual and queer cultural criticism in the 1980s onward," such as "Audre Lorde, Essex Hemphill, Marlon Riggs, and in the UK this includes Kobena Mercer, Isaac Julian, Professor Stuart Hall, the Black Arts movement and . . . Autograph ABP."[29] Although wider Black publics were important to them, Ajamu and Topher focus on documenting and keeping safe their own particular UK experiences and perspectives, proclaiming their presence as Black Britons, much in the style that Black critical cultural studies scholars had in the long 1980s. The banner text for their first exhibit came from Stuart (Hall): "The past cannot exist without its archives" (which rings harmoniously with "we cannot live without our lives"). Think of Paul (Gilroy) cheekily announcing "There Ain't No Black in the Union Jack!" in 1987 (twenty years before *The Black Atlantic*). Local institutions and media were not always on board. Ajamu avers that "*The Voice* had an article on Black Gay Pride in the States. And their offices were just down the road from Stepney Green (where their exhibit was held), and there was nothing in there whatsoever about what we were doing." Today, recent works, such as those published by Rikki Beadle-Blair's Team Angelica Books, with anthologies such as *Black and Gay in the UK* and *An Anthology of Writing about Same Gender Loving Women of African/Caribbean Descent with a UK Connection*; Frankie Edozien's Afropolitan memoir *Lives of Great Men: Living and Loving as an African Gay Man*; and a number of creative works such as *Fairytales for Lost Children*, by Diriye Osman, also continue this work of illustrating specific Black British and Black diaspora experiences and imaginaries. Ajamu and Topher seem to agree with Steven and Selly on the need to urgently document and place our stories on the record. Another archival impulse is to correct the record. Although the transnational UK-led "Murder Music" campaign directed at the homophobia in reggae lyrics "was seen to be led by Outrage!, a white gay group that was dogged by assertions of cultural incompetence and racism . . . ," Ajamu says, "we wanted to make clear that this campaign started back in 1992 with Black Lesbians and Gays against Media Homophobia."[30]

Escrevivência

If any among us have internalized Beverly and Barbara's charge "We must document ourselves now," gender nonbinary, trans, and gender-non-conforming (GNC) folks have certainly taken up this challenge. They are documenting themselves and excavating a past that had been erased not only by police violence, criminalization, and HIV/AIDS but also and perhaps most centrally by political betrayal by gay men, bisexuals, and lesbians. These efforts to be seen, heard, remembered, regarded, documented, and archived are all potent examples of what Dora (Silva Santana) aptly calls "escrevivência as an archive of transitioning."Escrevivência is a Portuguese portmanteau of escrita (writing) and vivência (living) borrowed from influential Black Brazilian writer Maria da Conceição Evaristo de Brito. Dora writes that "escrevivência is the woven tissue of unsubordinated writing of our living, writing as our living."[31] As the explicit Black trans discursive formation emerges in this current moment of new and rapidly expanding media, for Black transpeople escrita is of course also filmmaking, think-piece stunting and stanning, WhatsApping, blogging, vlogging, Snapchatting, and more. Think of all those mainly anonymous selfies. Hundreds of thousands of images of folks perched and posed—at turns sexy, humor-filled, sad, and/or serious—perhaps raw and vulnerable in their bathrooms, dorm rooms, in the wings or/of a subway platform before a performance, at the gym and triumphant, documenting their gender (transitions). Some also complexly and/or contradictorily claiming to want to end gender altogether. All of these representations announce, at any time they care to show the world, that they are enough as themselves and becoming more of themselves still. My mind goes to Fatima Jamal, whom I have written about before, beautifully inviting us to reckon with beauty and value and ovahness through her work as a media maker and as a model, activist, and It girl. (That very construction right there is new-ish for us too, is it not?) Think also of the innumerable house ball videos that circulate, nimbly performing expanded visions of gender, genderfuck, or the end(s) of gender. What about the mediatized demands to free CeCe MacDonald and her own self-representation and activism, or the urgent "wake work" that keeps the names of murdered sisters on our newsfeeds and our hearts (although "thoughts and prayers" of hashtag activism are not an end in itself)?[32] Another part of this litany is the up-to-date alerts on every move Laverne Cox and Janet Mock make, *en vivo*, from what might have been their private lives if they had not already been pressed into service as glittery exemplars. The trans, nongender binary, and gender-non-conforming children are documenting themselves, down. And they must. Quite unlike the long 1980s, during which Black bisexual gay and lesbian creatives and creativity were cute for a short while in highbrow art circles, but never quite pierced the PBS/museum/coffeehouse/academic bubble, Black trans images and cultural products today circulate widely and often wildly out of context. Just ask any of the cisgender non-poc kids on SnapChat, Instagram, YouTube, and TikTok who imitate the language and makeup tips of their favorite *RuPaul's Drag Race* queens, duckwalk, dip (erroneously called "death drop") during cheering competitions at their exclusive, segregated schools, or blithely misuse Black gay idioms following the solecisms and poor performances of "Atlanta housewives" or random white gay celebrities ("Yaaas, queen! No honey, you betta get your life! The house down boots!" as it were). A generation ago, Madonna cut, diluted, and mechanically reproduced cultural elements of the Black and Latinx underground house/ball scene of working (and) poor GNC people in the long 1980s for global masses who mainlined it for a short while. The kids who found a measure of marketable "exposure" working for her, and those featured in Jennie Livingston's classic *Paris Is Burning*, were not co-executive producers or writers of their own mass-mediatized images. Yet they are solid entries in the easily accessed popular "archive." Today, although not always under the control of or for remuneration to Black trans, gender-non-binary, or GNC people themselves, prominent transwomen like Angelica Ross, Laverne, and Janet, whose poise and carefully crafted images, utterances, and performances hew closely to Black and people-of-color GNC community values and standards, seem to consciously reach toward balancing image control, toward both self-interest, social justice, and posterity. The longtime goal to become legendary or "iconic" can be tested today by whom one can find in a Google search—photos, names, and "knowledge panels" serve to illustrate and define. Of course RuPaul, the global Black gay male drag queen mogul (yes, another new construction), whose steady and doggedly determined rise since the long 1980s very rarely found him publicly supporting radical causes or collective Black self-determination, assertively markets a number of aspects of Black gay culture. But "Mama Ru's" wares are also accompanied by tired reiterations of "glamour" that are always read as white (note the ubiquitous blond wig)—with the exception of hat tips to the exceptional Diana Ross—juxtaposed with the so-called funnier side of street life, Black Vernacular English colloquialisms, and cheap stereotypes played broadly and too often without a *wink* or *nod* to Black folks.[33] Note that we are still talking about archives, dear reader/collector. The most easily accessible and perhaps influential in-the-moment archives are those digitally available: internet streaming on computers, on televisions, handheld devices, or by order online for next-day delivery.

Rikki Beadle-Blair's dramedy *Metrosexuality* made history when it appeared as a short-run series on the BBC in 2001, with its multiracial, multi-gendered, and pansexual cast: equal parts high camp and emotional sincerity. Like the FX series *Pose*, *Metrosexuality* was a mass-media entertainment breakthrough that stood in for public education and/but also took this challenging reality seriously.[34] Janet (Mock)'s creative and editorial hand is apparent in *Pose*—balancing entertainment with a sincere sense of (OK, perhaps sometimes loose) historicity. The images and narratives entering the mass-mediated "archive" through this fictional television show are carefully drawn and performed. From the position of the uninitiated—most of the world—the most important and impactful aspect of its wide viewership is the careful and apparently necessary ethical pedagogical work it does: the *Pose* camera seemed to teach millions of viewers *here's how to care, here are the questions to ask and how to ask, here's where to look at us. Here is where you must look within.* Where, one asks, are transmen and masculine-of-center GNC folks in this emergence? One answer is in film—for example, in Kortney Zeigler's short documentary "Still Black" (2008) and feature films *Pariah* (2011) by Dee Rees and *Stud Life* (2012) by Campbell X. Commenting on the international reception of the film, Campbell said they were concerned about whether the broad London accents and specific cultural references of their characters would be understood and appreciated by an American audience, later noting that it is "interesting to see something so local to have that . . . common language of experience that can be shared across continents, and I was really happy with the response."[35] Likewise, there was an exuberant response to Campbell's multiracial short, "Desire" (2017), described as "a short jazz meditation on queer masculinity" at Miami's Third Horizon Film Festival in 2018.[36] Chanelle Aponte Pearson's *195 Lewis* (2016) also premiered to huge audience approval at the festival. Like Hanifah Walidah's *U People* (2011), which was eventually regularly broadcast on LOGO, *195 Lewis* offers a slice of life that includes an array of gender expressions, Brooklyn style. There is more to say about the Brazilian film *Bixa Travesti*, its place in the archive of representation, and its reception at the film festival and other outlets that is beyond this current intervention. I loved seeing Black Brazilian artists Linn da Quebrada and especially Jup do Bairro on the big screen, *faze musica por*

um arma . . . musia por me proteje ("making music as armor, for my own protection" from the violences inflicted on Black transpeople in Brazil). And
I loved hearing the searing favela funk I grew to appreciate in Rio, or especially Salvador—wishing I were in one of those pulsating airless clubs or
dancing under the stars, immersed in blackness—and not sitting in a theater.
But as an archive of representation, this performance documentary left me
longing for more expression *em Pajubá*—in the language and style of a mixture of Portuguese and Yorùbá that Linn, Jup, and other Black Brazilians
use to communicate discreetly to those in the know (apparently not me,
struggling with my very limited Portuguese!) and to otherwise strategically
obscure compromising views or to dissemble. In short, I am discomfited (annoyed, that is) by the white Brazilian anthropological gaze evident in the
film.[37] This is a nettlesome issue of linguistic and cultural access that we deal
with in other sections and that Watufani (Poe) and Jordan (Rogers) take up,
in different ways, in their dissertation projects. Speaking to African influences in contemporary Brazilian Portuguese spoken by Black Brazilians and
finding its way into standard Brazilian Portuguese, as Black English and the
musicality of Black Cuban Spanish have, Watufani schooled me on the notion of *pretugues*. Melvin already told you: "Rivers, Remember!"

Academe is having a similar moment of Black trans emergence, and Black
trans scholars are working to shape the formal scholarly archive before it is
whitened, caricatured, and/or politically sanitized. This savvy intervention
is precisely derived from lessons learned from previous evisceration, misgen-
dering, and "forgetfulness." In the introduction to their special issue of *TSQ*,
"The Issue of Blackness," Treva (C. Ellison), Marshall (fka Kai Green), Matt
(Richardson), and C. Riley (Snorton) read the current moment of emergence
of trans studies with the benefit of historical or conjunctural analysis, as they
analyze emerging images and statuses of Black trans folks and Black trans
intellectual and cultural production perhaps being put to the same old uses:

> We are in a time labeled the "transgender tipping point," a period charac-
> terized by the scaling up of legal protections, visibility, rights, and politics
> centered on transgender people. The contemporary visual landscape is
> populated with the bodies of Black women. How does the language and
> discourse of the tipping point elide the presence of a saturation of Black
> bodies? In academia this elision has taken the shape of the expansion and
> institutionalization of transgender studies as a discipline. . . . Though the
> popular representation of fabulousness and the crises of the trans subject
> are represented primarily by Black transwomen and transwomen of color,

the field of transgender studies, like other fields, seems to use this Black subject as a springboard to move toward other things, presumably white things.[38]

Riley set out similar intentions in his pathbreaking book, *Black on Both Sides: A Racial History of Trans Identity*, "an attempt to think more precisely about the connections within Blackness and transness in the midst of ongoing Black and trans death and against the backdrop of the rapid institutionalization of trans studies. . . ."[39] Thus, the most intentionally created-for-posterity representations or formally *archival* submissions among the current "scaling up" of representations continue the Black/queer habit of mind of foregrounding the stakes of representation, and digging/archiving/unearthing and critically analyzing, to avoid the formidable forces of "double cremation" through Sankofa-gazing backward while moving forward. Dora says: "The Black queer/trans work of love is . . . the work that fills our passion for living and assures our survival, but doesn't forget the dead."[40]

"I Call My Name into the Roar of Surf / And Something Awful Answers"

In our earlier discussion of disappeared and endangered stories and prospective archival materials, Colin clarified:

> I guess what I was trying to articulate, Steven, is that I was struck by how much there is a concern with the first person and capturing the authenticity of Black queer voices in others' work and vision. I was contrasting that to the primacy of imagination and performativity in my work and politics, and a sort of "fundamental anti-essentialism"—a politic (for those of you who know my poem "Unfinished Work" in *Voices Rising* and *Anthem*) that "rearranging syllables is revolution"; that as Daniel Garrett writes, we create ourselves, and that our struggle is to re-embroider and re-imagine ourselves in relationship to power and value and purpose. I was reflecting that maybe in my organizing work I need to respect the authenticity of my community's experiences for a moment, let those experiences be themselves for a few beats before I run off being the griot/ organizer and refashioning rotten syllables and metonyms of pain. That I need to decenter my "organizing" of others' experiences more often for the sake of the experiences. I was reflecting that I don't archive so much as I interpret.

Of course, archiving and interpreting are not mutually exclusive. And a number of archivists are also artists. In fact, for Steven, Ajamu, Topher, Alexis, and Tourmaline, these two activities seem inextricable.

Before the titling in Tourmaline's lyrical short film "Atlantic Is a Sea of Bones," starring ballroom legend Egyptt Labeija and costarring Fatima Jamal, Labeija—still beautiful though unadorned—stands stories above the West Side Highway, chatting in an expansive open room/gallery overlooking starkly diminished pilings that used to hold up part of "the Piers" on Manhattan's lower Hudson River, in Greenwich Village. Egyptt remembers for us:

> I literally lived on that pier that's no longer there. I lived there in a hut. See, that last one that's no longer? I lived on there. And I've slept on this thing right under there [edge of the pier] because I was homeless. And I had to make money and I had nowhere to go. . . . [*pause*] Oh my god, I've never seen it from this angle before. So, it's a lot. I don't want to cry. [*pause*] Well, I can cry now, I don't got no makeup on. [*Laughing. Verklempt, Labeija turns to the camera. Shifting to her announcer diction, she provides an apt coda.*] The times of the Village, from 14th Street to Christopher Street. The memories. People should not forget where they came from.

Tourmaline cannot help being archival: thinking past and present, aware of her work not only as art (and education) in the present but also as an important entry in the record—powerful words and images to be (re)dried and distilled for use long after she and everyone else involved have gone. Egyptt narrates her experiences of the Village at the end of the long 1980s, along the same river in which Marsha, who was neither the first nor the last to meet this end, was found dead. Lucille Clifton wrote, "I call my name into the roar of surf / and something awful answers" in her 1987 "Atlantic Is a Sea of Bones." The title of Tourmaline's film, borrowing from Ms. Clifton's poem, is not accidental.[41] In the next scene, from high above, we see a construction site on the edge of the Hudson. Graceful hand choreography gives way to a shot of Egyptt Labeija as audiences are more accustomed to seeing her: painted, coiffed, bejeweled, and up in an elaborate sequined gown. This time, on the roof deck of the new Renzo Piano–designed Whitney Museum in the Village, overlooking the West Side Highway. The Hudson and transforming North New Jersey skyline in the distance. In the next scene, blue light gorgeously frames the brown skin of Egyptt's character as she bathes. As she sinks into the luxurious milky white bath, it turns 1990s Hudson green, then Atlantic blue-green, and a memory trip ensues: Fatima's character emerges out of this murky past water, *efun* (white powder) faced. Eyes like *Beloved*. I do not

y

Archiving the Anthological / 213

wish to summarize or decipher the lyrical and moving film here, and Tavia (Nyong'o) gives a more thorough short reading of the film.[42] I will say this: for the homeless, marginalized, and thrown away, "for the embattled," the West Village—14th Street to Christopher Street—is and was indeed, in Toni Morrison's words, "spiteful."[43] As Labeija has already told you, "The times of the Village, from 14th Street to Christopher Street. The memories. People should not forget where they came from." Ending this short work of archive and imagination full of meaningful snippets of a dreamscape, Tourmaline's camera returns Egyptt's character to the Whitney rooftop. With her back to the camera—hair done and "that pier that's no longer there . . . that last one that's no longer" to her left—Egyptt Labeija slowly and elegantly raises her left arm: a salute of bittersweet triumph of one not meant to survive.

Zanele (Muholi) holds that "my own long-term vision as a visual and lesbian rights activist is to work towards creating a Black lesbian archive in South Africa." Even after South Africa ratified its new progressive 1996 constitution—including sexual orientation in its Equality Clause—the issues that dominated LGBTI legal struggles rarely addressed the complex socio-cultural issues and economic struggles faced by Black lesbians. In "Mapping Our Histories: A Visual History of Black Lesbians in Post-Apartheid South Africa," Zanele chronicles her own work to date, which shifts the presumptive gaze from the assumed white, well-heeled, rarified gallery viewer to the Black lesbian South African herself (and we can also imagine extending to her diasporic cognates/cousins). Zanele avers that "visual activism can be employed by socially, culturally and economically marginalized women . . . to not only return the gaze of our colonizers, but to develop what bell hooks has called a 'critical gaze' into heteropatriarchal constructions of Black women's bodies and their sexualities."[44] As critical scholar Zethu (Matebeni) averred, Zanele's question "What do we see we when look at ourselves?" invites "a deeply challenging introspection, [requiring] Black women in particular to reflect on the ways in which history has made us not look at ourselves, but be looked at."[45] How is one to become a subject—assert her own subjectivity—without self-reference and regard? Zanele's documentation work celebrating and memorializing Black lesbians, femmes, butches, and others constitutes an archive of blackness confident of its beauty and worthiness, which as the artist has said promotes "reflection as opposed to an interpretation." In her *Faces and Phases* (2006–2011), Muholi photographed more than two hundred portraits of South Africa's lesbian community: "The portraits are at once a visual statement and an archive, marking, mapping, and preserving an often-invisible community for posterity. . . . And the kind of violence that I show, that I talk about, it's the kind of violence that exists all over the world. I am not just looking at it from a South African perspective, because the same applies to other countries, including America."[46]

In 2002 Zanele, Zethu, and others cofounded South Africa's national, nonprofit organization Forum for the Empowerment of Women (FEW) for Black lesbian women to have a safe space to go to organize for the opportunities to access services such as health care, education, employment, and housing without being judged or discriminated for their sexualities. As Zanele wrote, "Experiences of being sensationalized, researched, and written about left me feeling disempowered and exploited. I then reached a point in my life where I told myself we can do it for ourselves. In fact, I began to understand at the gut level that if we are to survive as a community and to build our dignity as Black lesbians, we had to tell our own stories and create our own histories."[47] Zethu had told us in our virtual panel that FEW "aims to articulate, advance, protect, promote the rights of Black lesbian, bisexual, and transgender women [LBT]," celebrating their diversity by operating in many of the South African languages and showcasing art, poetry, music, academic writings, and archive collections during their Pride and Heritage festival week, where artists and scholars get together to share with communities some of the works that have been produced. This work is connected to the community-action programs run by FEW whereby visits to various townships were undertaken to interact with and document the daily lived experiences of lesbian, bisexual, and transgender women in the townships, which led to a number of national activist campaigns, such as the One in Nine campaign, which was launched on February 13, 2006, in response to the infamous State v. Jacob Zuma rape trial, which Zethu said had "embodied what we as women's rights organizations and HIV activists are aware of: reporting rapes, getting fair treatment and representation in rape trials and being respected for women's fight for their right against sexual violence is no less than an uphill battle."

Often overlooked, our archives sometimes circulate well beyond us and often without proper attribution—perhaps leading to citational "credit," financial remuneration, or an authorizing imprimatur for other individuals and communities. Materials are also used or routinely read as if uniquely freely accessible for any use and untethered to specific Black politics or the labor of particular Black folks. Although Black women scholars, and especially Black women cultural workers and activists, contribute lavishly to discourse—"word rich," to invoke Hortense Spillers—prevailing citational politics too often find them citation poor. To wit, these days "part of the story of an archive is of how the statement landed on the Internet," as Tourmaline has said. In response to the publication of a zine that compiled work from STAR, which she had posted on her blog, Tourmaline wrote that she was glad that the work was out and circulating. She acknowledged that the work does not belong to her, "and it needs to be shared as part of Sylvia and STAR's legacy." She writes:

> But I'm saddened when an anti-authoritarian press with a wider distribution reach (because of how oppression works) takes material that I worked hard for years to make accessible to the world and doesn't credit the labor that went into gathering it. I unearthed this material thru hustling my way into spaces that are historically inaccessible to Black trans women. . . . This was labor and like the stories of Marsha and Sylvia, the labor I put into this isn't even considered labor but something new, exciting, and revolutionary. Why not just use your distr(ibution) reach to link back to the people already doing that work?

Tourmaline signs off the message above: "still here." After facing foul backlash from anonymous commenters, she writes: "There is too much at stake not to name ourselves in the stories we pass down. Because *this is our time, this is our life*."[48]

Here it is again. Black/queer time (collapsed). Black/queer life fleeting, endangered, yet vital and here/now. Black/queer responsibility to fight double (triple?) cremation. And Black/queer labor that other folks often do not appreciate as labor (is it because we look so good doing it?). Some of the statements on and by Sylvia Rivera and Marsha P. Johnson in *Disco Ball* are drawn from the archive that Tourmaline recomposed from her primary work at the Feminist Herstory Archive, the New York Public Library, and Tourmaline's personal interviews. This work was done under very different conditions from my own relatively smooth entrée to archives, which is always mediated by my academic credentials, institutional affiliations, personal relationships with other professionals, physical ability, and cisgender presentation.

As scholars, teachers, activists, ritualists, and artists, Alexis and Julia (Roxanne Wallace) bring sacred words in the form of poems, lessons, and rituals to constitute a "mobile homecoming." One of their central projects, "The Eternal Summer of the Black Feminist Mind," is, in their words, "part of a biodiverse ecology of Black feminist interactive and immersive archival projects, root sources, and life-cycle participants." In "Seek the Roots," Alexis also generously offers "a resource list for any scholar wanting on-the-pulse information about the directions and directives of contemporary Black feminists. It is evidence of a crucial strategy of survival: the transformation of information and communication into access, power, community, and visionary practice."[49] The work that Alexis and Julia do to democratize materials and put them to use is clearly a wave of the future, notwithstanding ownership and privacy issues with some types of materials and the cost and sheer labor. Internet servers and digital platforms on which new media are cast and created also provide frameworks for sharing. Likewise, the Caribbean International Resource Network (IRN), an independent "network that connects activists, scholars, artists and other individuals and organizations who do research and work on issues related to diverse genders and sexualities in the Caribbean," has been pursuing digital humanities and organizing in ways that both preserve and make works available to wider global audiences. It was instrumental in contributing the Gay Freedom Movement in Jamaica (GFM) collection to the Digital Library of the Caribbean. In 1974 the GFM became the first organization to be formed to openly advocate for LGBTQI folks in the English-speaking Caribbean. GFM General Secretary Larry Chang safely kept records of its activities over many years, until Jamaica Forum for Lesbians, All-Sexuals and Gays (JFLAG) and Caribbean IRN arranged to have them digitized and transferred to the Digital Library of the Caribbean, which made the collection available on its online platform. Since this initial project, Caribbean IRN has curated and produced a number of online multimedia editions, including *Theorizing Homophobias in the Caribbean: Complexities of Place, Desire, and Belonging* (www.caribbeanhomophobias .org); *Love Hope Community: Sexualities & Social Justice in the Caribbean* with *Sargasso Journal*; and *Write It in Fire: Tributes to Michelle Cliff*, along with other materials and resources, including a helpful digital map of Caribbean LGBTI organizations. Although nineteen years is practically eons in the past, if we measure time by the march of new technology, Stuart (Hall) was prescient in his 2001 article "Constituting an Archive," in which he offered that "the question of technology, of access and therefore inevitably of funding . . . [is] as central to a 'living archive' as the aesthetic, artistic and interpretative practices" or "the corpus" of what is being archived.[50]

Responding to questions about community accountability and ownership in our virtual conversation, Steven had said this:

What I have witnessed is that most Black LGBTQ writers create poetry and fiction, and nonfiction is often left to academics, who, 98 percent of the time, do not have or seek a solid grounding in Black LGBTQ history, and their institutions don't know, so they cannot hold them accountable.

Thus, helping to develop or maintain a community of theorists and analysts of our own is a necessary yet difficult task. There has been, and continues to be, a great deal of mistrust and incompetence in Black LGBTQ organizing communities. . . . Yet there is also a remarkable collaborative spirit that has remained a hallmark in cultural efforts that seem to be coming even stronger (e.g., Alexis Pauline Gumbs and her Mobile Homecoming Project, which is collecting and disseminating stories among generations; E. Patrick Johnson's "Sweet Tea," a testament to the gay male in the South; the transatlantic work undertaken by Ajamu Ikwe-Tyehimba to connect generations and to provide the BGLA with materials about the life of UK's black queer culture; and the sexuality work that both Herukhuti and LaMonda Horton-Stallings are currently engaged in).

Colin reminded him:

Yeah, but you and I created a model for not leaving the nonfiction to academics in *Think Again*. . . . I came to writing because it was a way to think on paper and because I wanted to be heard. It is something I have to do because I need to communicate with others. By doing so I was eager to enter the larger conversation that has been going on forever about the whats and whys about the world we live in. This tongue has got to confess.[51]

Archival Recovery Writing

Resonant with the *Small Axe* issue "Archives of Black Memory," our Black/Queer/Diaspora convening also concluded that although archives are a point of departure, "scholars must turn to creative methodologies to intuit and imagine narratives of Black [women's] freedom: a freedom that has remained an impossibility in official discourses but that must be invented where it did not exist in the past, in order that it might exist in the future."[52] And we also found that the effort to account for it all—the experiences and visions, freedoms and "unfreedoms"—also requires a vigilant exploration of the archives of everyday experience and methodical accounting of this. In "Archives of Black Memory," NourbeSe tells Pat (Saunders) that "I think we've been using the master's tools (to use Audre Lorde's powerful metaphor) to dismantle the structures that hold us fast and that what is happening [now] . . . is that we are beginning to fashion new tools to do the work. . . . The master's tools . . . always hold within their very form and function the content of our denial."[53] Jacqui might call this one of the elements of a long litany of our "disavowals."

As Saidiya said, "It is a story predicated upon impossibility—listening for the unsaid, translating misconstrued words, and refashioning disfigured lives— intent on working toward an impossible goal: redressing the violence that produced numbers, ciphers, and fragments of discourse, which is as close as we come to a biography of the captive and the enslaved."[54] This is some queer magic. Is it "magical thinking" to believe that we can, as NourbeSe suggests, "conjur[e] something new from the absence of Africans as humans that is at the heart of the text"?[55] Matt and Omi say this is not impossible, not really. Jacqui tells us, after Kitsimba, to look elsewhere, beyond the formal archive and its disavowals and beyond secular epistemologies and the rules of evidence bequeathed by "the white fathers" who divided body from mind and mind from spirit and named this fragmentation the sine qua non of civilization.[56] One form of archival writing therefore "saves" and distills, not to "recover" words from damp, dusty basements or complete erasure, but rather from lifeless academic theoretism that threatens the "spirit" that drove the production of the original (taking Jacqui seriously, we understand spirit both figuratively and literally here—those in the ether who *walk with you*).[57] Still, I imagine Saidiya asking herself and all of us, earnestly, "Can beauty provide an antidote to dishonor, and love a way to 'exhume buried cries' and reanimate the dead?"[58] Hard-core social scientists seem to sternly reply, *No!* The question remains, following Professor Wynter, who encourages us to employ a "deciphering practice" that asks what does the work do?[59] Afro-pessimists—both the original continental writers and filmmakers and the new erudite theorists—shrug. It does not matter—they have seen these attempts to valorize Black humanity "fail" time after time, and they call upon us to not make the same discursive moves. Some of the Black gays (many now more comfortable with or resigned to being called Black queers)—perhaps convinced of their own conjure medicine or *carrying on,* still, with another trans man who comes from another dyke, who had been mis-gendered and dismembered yet who still glitters, *alively,* from disco balls—insist that we use everything we have. Invent new ways to do so. And that we find ways to gather all evidence and usable modes of intelligibility. Even "against the wall . . . fighting back."[60] The anthological Black gay habit of mind requires us to gather the social and the poetic (yes, "or it will not be," Aimé has already told you).

But we have not paid enough attention to the social part of the vision. I believe Omi's instruction to creatively "intuit and imagine . . . and to invent . . . where it did not exist." Pivoting also to the social science of Black studies would provide ways to account for what does exist and facets of the disco ball that we have not considered. This is the important work that Hortense (Spillers) called "first order." After all, our work must not be discretely enclosed in what they call the humanities, as if this is not also a set of disciplines/divisions with its own disavowals, limits, and silences. To constitute an us at the present conjuncture requires re-membering and (re)discovering together, with all our tools. For one short example, consider the fact that we have not yet fully grappled with what Cathy (Cohen) convincingly argues was the breakdown of Black politics in the long 1980s. Cathy specifies, enumerates, and qualifies as well as argues regarding a social and empirical understanding of what Alexis calls "our present apocalypse."[61] Consider how *The Boundaries of Blackness: AIDS and the Breakdown of Black Politics* exposed and analyzed how the US state and Black US civil society both deepened the multiple vulnerabilities of Black LGBT individuals and individuals infected with HIV. In an essay whose (unofficial) subtitle is "All the things you could be now, if Jacqui Alexander and Cathy Cohen were your . . . ," I have argued that Cathy and Jacqui's scholarly work—as Chandan (Reddy) said, "bookending Black Nations?/Queer Nations?"[62]—uniquely presents us with both a set of nettlesome political problems and a theoretical puzzle across the Black diaspora: is there any place where the benefits and recognition of citizenship can accrue to the unruly—the "prostitute," the homosexual, the "welfare queen," the transgender person, or the Black person? And what calculus emerges when these gendered, raced, and sexed categories of nonnational, deviant, nonethnic/racial subject, or merely "other" are compounded? We will return to consider this from another angle in the last chapter.

8   Come

Rio de Janeiro. June 2012

I sit here in Brazil—Black diaspora central—reflecting on a recent interaction that illustrates the fact that these excursions, conversations, and re-narrations are at once about affect and material effects: "roots," futurity, place, and space. Time collapsed. Kin (dis)engaged and keens drawn and deepened.

A Brazilian social work professor who is also an Ekedi (Candomblé official) addresses graduate students from Brazil and the United States who are also activists, along with three others: the activist professor who has brought all of us here, along with his upright bass and growing child making this trip back home with him; a biracial/binational artist from the United States, fresh from a trip to Nigeria, where she left imprints of her body in the red earth of her father's dilapidated dream; and a professional sojourner/witness, who has spent his time in Rio de Janeiro looking for evidence of Black men's desire for Black men. Breaking dawns can find him preparing boats he fashions from watermelon rinds, which he sets gliding into the surf and then the roaring Black sea, with offerings of molasses and silver change. The Ekedi, a well-respected scholar/activist, speaks in slow, clear, Portuguese, which the sojourner/witness understands almost miraculously.

He is convinced that diaspora diglossia is real: receiving her Portuguese as if it were that clear Telemundo Spanish, not the swift and treacly sweet, half-swallowed Caribbean tongue to which he was once accustomed. He easily finds cognates. Before she begins, following custom, Professor/Ekedji/Activist/Social Worker/Black woman asks permission to speak from the oldest person in the room. No doubt, cool water has been spilled already. She then asks all of us to introduce ourselves. After which, her lecture challenges the ways we name ourselves and trace our lineages. She asks us to recognize how our "choosing" to accept Western ontologies effaces other kin. One Brazilian student, a Catholic priest, shuffles nervously in his chair. Days later, the artist and the sojourner/witness (now a teacher/teller) take over this course in Black diaspora. Wura demands that we "ground ourselves in our bodies . . . breathe into (our) center." The visual and performance artist, lecturing on Afro-futurism, is now a Black femme yogi, calling us to our own momentarily forgotten corporeality as we sit in the modernist/brutalist classroom of the State University of Rio de Janeiro. Rising above the busily transforming streets of Rio (pre–World Cup and pre-Olympics), the buildings seem to promise an ordered, rational escape from bodies. We resist this pretension of escape, at Wura's insistence. Rise from our chairs. Rearrange our seats. Look at each other in the eyes. And breathe.

Dear Reader: Please stop reading for a moment. Take a few deep breaths.

Queerly, Wura asks us to draw, in silence and with our weak hands, "where you come from." The witness/scribe wonders whether his drawing of his lover, whom he misses during this faraway research trip, will do justice. To not scandalize the room, he draws a simple house instead. Trees and plants in greens, yellows and orange. Two parents looming large with smiles. One wears a blue halo, emanating gold (now, in this moment of compounded loss, my mind's eye draws a silver one over the other, with white light); four stick figures, with suitcases; and at the center, a small stick-child, figured akimbo and with an orange flower, smiling.

Giving respect to the elders, I will, however, not ask permission to speak. I must speak whether permission is given or not. The ethics on which my witnessing is based demand that I speak. Yes, Lorde: "Even if [my] voice shakes. Even if I am afraid. Even if I feel I will not be heard, or appreciated, or understood. It is better to speak."[1] And I will not return to silence. My permission to speak comes from a communion of heretical dead saints, on whose foundations of love and work I sail/stand/glide. Their resonance is no

less powerfully felt today. Although queer theory's insistence that we disas-
semble our ties to biological heredity and expose the kinship we are taught is
"natural" to be wholly constructed is useful to think with, Black gay (Black/
queer) more complexly goes a step further. All our kin—chosen, given,
forced, or coerced—are kin. Even those who must be placed in parentheses
or an explanatory endnote. Even if we must, as Sharon Bridgforth writes,
"take their names off of us"[2] at some point: they help construct the locus of
critical enunciation from which we speak (and from which we listen, with
neither judgment nor compulsion, to their whispers and stirrings within us).
Then, as to whispering and stirring, the research questions I have brought
with me—the sojourner/witness/scribe—now recur: *"Do Black sexual minorities and gender insurgents share common ideologies, practices, identities, and communities across borders and languages? Is the development of a transnational Black/queer
theory and praxis appropriate, useful, or desirable? To or by whom?"* Finally, this
meditation on the roads/shoulders/wave crests/gentle creek shores on which
I have been borne, rested, and poised to take off ventures an answer: "Yes,
well, let us see. It is possible."

Nairobi, 2013

Nicole says that her heart sank into her gut as the high iron gate of the
condominium complex slowly opened. The security guard stared at her in-
credulously as she prepared to leave the premises after midnight on a Thursday night. She was alone, and by this time all of the other gatehouses in this
upscale enclave of Nairobi had already shut their lights. The "inquisitive,
meddling, gossipy" guards had begun to nod off or have their own fun in
the small guard post near the gate—automatic guns slung on their backs.
Safe and comfortable indoors, her colleagues in the team of Canadian management consultants with whom she had undertaken this three-month assignment slept soundly, with no idea that she had left. Earlier, Nicole had
generously tipped their usual driver, then dismissed him for the evening. His
job was to arrange safaris and evenings out at the tonier restaurants and bars,
and shuttle the consultants from site to site in this bustling international
city bursting with expatriates, returnees, and UN workers who pull in extra
pay to work in this "troubled" East African capital. On one of those evenings
out, she and her colleagues casually met Nallah. Only she and Nicole knew
that their so-called chance meeting was anything but. It was the orches-
trated result of a two-month internet conversation. Having been "virtually"
introduced through friends of friends, these young women who live their

lesbian lives out of sight of employers, colleagues, and most family members arranged the encounter in the most discreet way possible. For Nicole, regular quick trips from her home in Toronto to Detroit or New York also require quick changes of currency and fashion—from the Canadian to the US dollar for tipping, and from the corporate togs she wore as "fashionable armor" to cashmere hoodies, low-slung jeans, and carefully collected snapbacks and diamond stud earrings, punctuating her cultivated soft-butch style. For Nallah, moments of respite to live openly as a lesbian require even more complex international machinations. She takes infrequent "mental health" treks to Malindi or Lamu, off Kenya's coast, with friends from other East African countries or even less frequently to London, where she went to graduate school and where Nicole said she felt at once "sexually free and utterly invisible." In London, Nallah had been unable to fully express, in the flesh, the freedom she had there to walk in Piccadilly hand in hand with another Black woman, because smart, attractive, and "well-brought-up" Black women were the very small change of the British sexual economy.

One might assume that at home in Kenya, Nallah's class status would make her more sought after, but it also conditioned vulnerabilities that made being open about her sexual desires impossible for Nallah, Nicole told me. Exposure would likely mean loss of her job and a debilitating erosion of the prestige that accords her family material privilege and protection. Nicole is the daughter of working-class small-island Caribbean people who migrated to Canada from the United Kingdom several years before she was born in the mid-seventies. She says that the presence of open Black lesbian and gay people in Toronto is no mean comfort to her, as she is the only Black person, and one of only a few women professionals, working at her level in her multinational firm. You will not find her hanging out on Queen Street or Bloor in Toronto's gay village. Nicole told me that she "refuse[s] to make [her]self a triple minority" and reports being "discreet" about a lot in her life, not just her sexual desires and orientation. So Nicole and Nallah found each other in cyberspace, through friends of friends. On this Thursday evening, Nallah had arranged a driver, who picked up Nicole at her huge iron gate. Just a click away, Nicole joined her for the starry velvet sky ride to a beautiful compound on just the other side of Kilimani.

To be sure, this scene could have easily served as a cautionary tale. Perhaps a Lifetime (Television for Women!) melodrama advising "discreet" Canadian women traveling alone to stay cozily inside their ample walk-in (and out) closets. Of course, it is not: Nicole's story is like many others I have heard and have experienced myself. Significant and intense, the scene is also by now ethnographically hackneyed, I am afraid. Nearly all of the descriptors one could use to describe the party at the compound of Nallah's friend—the moist air, the bass in the music, the scent of jasmine in the air (or was it jacaranda?), the sway of the hips of the women assembled, and the heavy laughter of their temporary freedom—echo what I had seen and written about in Havana and likewise have witnessed in Kingston, Washington, D.C., Salvador, Paris, and a number of other sites. Re-narrativization is, after all, palimpsestic. It means at once re/overwriting stories and/or writing into the record some of those who would have been mischaracterized or misread otherwise, but also, just as significantly, it means allowing others, whose fugitivity is intentional, to remain in the margins and shadows of the work. And all of this requires the sojourner/witness, now also the confidant and would-be scribe, to rethink the narratives I have already coconstructed.

"This could have been ten years ago in Havana," I told Nicole, referring to a scene I tried to re-create in my first book, which itself had reminded me so much of Audre's bio-mythographic recollection of meeting Af-re-ke-te! (a snap after each syllable). Was I reading too much into this? Romanticizing too much? There is certainly a bit of *sodade*, as the Brazilians or Cape Verdeans or Angolans might sing, or *nostalgia*, as Cubans would say. That is, there is an intense force of longing present in Nicole's recollection of her first trip to Nairobi a few years before—here, as we sit together taking tea in the courtyard of the Nairobi Fairmont Hotel among white European and North American guests readying for safari and Black African guests and locals conducting business. There is, I am afraid, still a bit of "adventure" to the story as I recount it here, dear reader: twice removed, retold with distance, as ethnographic "data," and in full knowledge of your judgment and its consequences. Is this what Audre meant by "if we win / *there is no telling*"? That winning means that writing our lives—*telling it*—can be so uncertain and contingent and maybe as ephemeral as our other life-affirming pleasures? This is an ethnographic conundrum as well as another dimension of the archival questions we discussed in the previous chapter: How are we reading the archive? What can really be said, given its limits, and what *should* we say? Ethnographers—many of us as much secret keepers as storytellers—consider and reconsider this often. What stories are important to tell? (How) *should we* represent? To what end and to whose or what purposes? Must ethnographic practice result in an *ethnographic monograph* or *thick description* of stories? Whatever the case (*no matter . . .*), Nicole's experience and the fact that she shared it with me in a multidimensional field of resonance remains. She simply had to get there—to Nallah or someone like her, yes, but most directly—to the spot. The club. Among her first considerations when approached with taking on a new travel assignment was finding connections to other women who might be able to introduce her to women who love women. "I had to find my people," she told me, then laughed nervously: "Not in that Black American way of going to West Africa and weeping at the site of a slave castle," she continued. Not ghosts or cultural remains, she said. "Yes," I told her. "Word: flesh."

The spaces where folks *get their life* are sometimes on the edge of a larger urban gay village but are more reliably in marginal places, in the bottoms (the low, or the bottom, is the queer sweet spot, after all). Or they can also be like the spot Nallah and Nicole fled to near Kilimani—behind a beautiful vine-covered high barbed-wire wall. In places like these the smart set assemble and arrange themselves from carefully controlled guest lists to produce a "discreet" structure of feeling characterized by what my Jamaican acquaintance Regina called "mutual assured destruction" among the mostly High Brown elite homosexuals and bisexuals on the island. To be invited to a gathering uptown, one must have just as much to lose as other highly placed educators, government officials, clergy, business leaders, and artists one will meet there, seemingly a world away from the fetid gullies downtown, in which young femme gay and trans youths survive on the margins of the global margin, after having been thrown away by their families and forgotten by the nation-state. In both cases—high vined/wired walls or low corners of the dutty bottom—this space among those who are unseen or do not want to be readily recognizable to the glaring gaze of various forms of power, interpellated as "suspect" or "other," is where you will most predictably find sexual minorities and gender insurgents in the Black world. They are largely unaccounted for. But some folks choose to live under the radar of appraising gazes, which are rarely accompanied by any true solidarity or material help. To be underreported is in some cases, therefore, also to be a bit less surveilled. These under-the-radar spaces and intentionally private postures are quite often where one can find common union. I have described elsewhere a scene that could have easily been Nicole's: "Getting our lives (together), the night and the club provide an essential and unique space to lose the minds one uses all week. To find small cracks and crevices to call home."[3] Travelers also seek out these *homespaces* when they visit because, as Juana (Rodriguez) dances across the page, "recognition, like survival itself, is a gesture—fleeting, flirtatious and precarious, that stretches out her hand and utters the word, come. . . ."[4]

(Read in Your Ten-Foot Club Floor Speaker Voice)

As Nicole and I talked about her party in Nairobi—trading stories of flesh that dances—I recounted my favorite spot in Rio de Janeiro: Buraco. I would not mention the club here by name if it had not already closed. At a talk in Berlin in 2014, a kind audience member suspected that my veiled references to "the club" in Rio were to Buraco and delivered the bad news. The steady march of global capital killed yet another "disco." This time in preparation for the 2016 Olympics. Therefore, I suppose that this is yet another sort of memorialization. There are a number of celebrated gay and lesbian clubs in Rio's upscale tourist zone, where the thump.thump.thump.thump. of "gay international" can sound and feel identical to what one would hear and feel in Buenos Aires, Berlin, Paris, or Los Angeles. However, Buraco was different. Cue the favela funk version of *Berimbau*.[5] Although another name (Star Club) was listed in the gay party magazine, along with a stern (dog whistle) warning about the lack of safety in that club frequented by "locals," the Portuguese name (*buraco*) literally means hole in the wall (for scorpions). There was a walk of several blocks from the subway, outside of the tourist zone, and some of those blocks were dark and deserted at the late hour you would be traveling, to be greeted at the door by a quick patdown and a chit for free *caipirinhas* made of the stuff that promises blindness. The experienced Black queer traveler will realize *Sim! Esse deve ser o lugar!* (Yes! This must be the spot). Buraco hosted the largest number of visibly Black and dark-brown people you would see in any gay club in Rio and certainly more than one finds in any popular representation of Brazil not related to African religions, sports, crime, or pornography (or indeed combinations of these!). Unlike most Brazilian media representations, Buraco was not pre-scripted to represent a so-called racial plurality in which the lightest of Brazilians are grossly overrepresented. I certainly could tell a number of stories of what may look like the sort of phenomena that Dennis Altman and various proponents of "global gay" observed from a distance—that same thump.thump. thump.thump. emanating from speakers at gay bars and clubs across the globe—but this is not at all what you would find at Buraco or at other spaces of Blackfullness around the world.

Although the thump.thump.thump.thump—which I have taken to appreciate as the vigorous heartbeat of global capital—is certainly alive and well, the deeper and more significant story is how various sets of individuals experience this. What distinct dances are folks doing to this perhaps deafening rhythm? Might we also hear a different, more polyphonic beat, right around the corner or across town—toward other pleasures, distinct meanings, or ends? How do we find it, and what happens along the way? In early lesbian and gay studies scholarship, observers too often oversimplified what they saw as "globalization," the seeming homogenization of culture, because too often they could not see us very clearly from their office chairs in the North, or they followed only one expected and perhaps more comfortable trajectory in only one direction. They, and their acolytes, mistook the common beat as an indication of a single trajectory in which the rest of the world would eventually evolve from "closeted" to "out" to liberal rights (to express, to assemble, to marry, for example, with no mention of clean water, health, or education) with the attendant rainbow flags. But Black/queerpolis is out of "gay international" time and outside of "global gay" space, both of which are burdened by tiresome and by now (at least) impracticable whiteness. Despite enticing popular travel advertisements and scholarly literature celebrating its so-called unifying gaze, "gay international" has its discontents. They are manifold: beginning with feminist critics who had already criticized the gendered logics of tourism.[6] Black migrants and citizens pushed to the margins of northern centers to accommodate perceived "safe" tourist zones where visitors are less likely to encounter Black folks, or anyone wearing a headscarf or turban, or who may be visibly poor, may participate in the tourist economy that fuels gay international in the back of the house but must remain unseen. In contrast, Black "natives" of the global South, represented in pre-scripted folkloric settings and as at-once easy sexual prey and rapacious brutes, figure prominently in the ambiance of "global gay." They too are included in the manifold discontented in many cases, although also conditionally afforded access as workers or "exceptionals," along with well-resourced Black male travelers, who are not always afforded full access to all of the accoutrements of "gay tourist," especially in northern metropolises. Black women travelers do not figure in the equation at all: the wide-ranging economic power of Black women of many classes, once again erroneously read as very small change. We will hear from some of these folks in the next sections of this movement. Here we turn decidedly away from this, toward Black/queerpolis.

The allure of Black/queer spaces *in the life* is not just the music and the bodies (although there is always music and always bodies moving). There is also intense (if also sometimes vague) curiosity and solidarity, tearful migration, and sometimes split-second exile and the specter of never returning (or finding) home. Black/queerpolity is my formulation of global Black LGBTQ/ same-gender-loving sociality and polity or, put another way, how we live in various places around the world and how we imagine each other, find each other, and relate. This has little to do with the fantasy of "global gay" and "gay international." In fact, you may appreciate it as its opposite, dear traveler. Black/queerpolity is a condition and a space we make with our movements and our imaginations of each other even when we are still. For Black folks, the desire to go *get your life* by indulging in far-flung socialities or migrating in search of a dream or a "cool drink of water" occurs alongside loss and deadly serious *run-for-your-life* sorts of travel.[7] There are long historical shadows here, of course: how we find each other and under what conditions. How we translate, share, host, and extend hospitality is not only fraught, but also weighted with the past and a hope for deeper connection or "recovery" of lost or attenuated connections in Blackfull futures.

Thomas Allen Harris's meditation on desire and displacement in his lyrical film *E Minha Cara*—at once perhaps romantic, nostalgic, and yet also critically self-aware—seems to stretch the limits of "diaspora" to include recognition and desires of many kinds. Shot in beautiful and evocative Super 8 film, Thomas gives us ancestral desire for recognition and evidence of being, articulated to and expressed as the auteur's spiritual desire to "find [his] *orixa* [orisha]" in Salvador, Bahia. *E Minha Cara* opens with the story of Harris's family's life in Black United States, grounded by his grandmother's propriety and religiosity. The filmmaker's mother became politically aware in the 1960s, however, with Black power and Black beauty being expressed in a wide diasporic community of activists and intellectuals, expanding the borders of where she found family. Eventually, she moved with her sons to Tanzania (Lyle Ashton Harris, the artist, is Thomas's brother). By the middle of the film, we see that the filmmaker's experiences in Africa and recollections of his grandmother have helped him to recognize an inherited "second sight" that viewers are treated to through his camera taking in scenes of Black Brazil. All of this limns an unspoken but powerfully palpable homoerotic desire, which is fulfilled through the dense Black gay visual homopoetics of his film. *E minha cara* literally means "It's my face," but as a voice-over during the pivotal scene in which Thomas enjoys an intimate party with Brazilian friends and acquaintances explains, exclaiming "E minha cara!" is more like saying "That's me"—for example, describing an article of clothing that seems made for you or a new friend who feels immediately familiar and close. Thomas's film depicts a queer kind of relational multiple consciousness indeed. Like Nicole's, and that of a number of my friends, acquaintances, and respondents, and this author himself. At the climax of Thomas's film, his own face (cara) is recognized by a Black Brazilian boy who self-identifies with it as his face (E minha). In some ways resonant with Frantz Fanon's iconic "look, a *negre!*" moment, there is both a different purchase and outcome here. That famous scene of a young white French girl's doubled revulsion and fascination at seeing Fanon is archetypal misrepresentation: a white subject externalizing and projecting object status onto—or more precisely *as*—a negre. However, "E minha cara" is a form of self-recognition. Alas, this is not to say that this "projection" may not also prove to be mistaken, as we will see. Still, this is an intersubjective move. This consciousness does not make all the difference, but the difference is significant. And this difference has been mostly left unthought.

For the moment, we seek no truth claims, but rather to explore the space of what some common perceptions will tell us about relations among those who inhabit a category that too many see on the outside as monolithic or undifferentiated in their relations to various forms of power. How do we account for the common assumption, sometimes among Black folks themselves, of more intense homophobia among us? How *quare* does one have to be before seeming to become less Black?[8] How does one "act like" a Black woman crossing borders? For the sake of a more manageable scale and linguistic ease, a few conversations I engaged in the Anglophone Caribbean can index some examples. During a casual chat with a Jamaican hotel worker, I asked about different intensities and forms of heterosexism and homophobia that he had experienced in his travel around the region. Ralston's answer came swiftly and authoritatively: Bajans (Barbadians) were more likely to silently perjure "bullers" rather than to subject them to "the cutlass" because of the island's "close-knit," and in his view beloved and warm, colonial ties to Britain. "JamRock (Jamaica) is the most homophobic," he said. Oddly echoing northern rhetorics of cultural failure, this man who has sex with men nearly boasted as he explained that Jamaica's "intense" homophobia was a result of the "Nyabinghi warrior spirit" evidenced in both the Rastafari religion and everyday hooliganism on his native island. In Ralston's sociocultural imagination, tacit heterosexism is to spectacular violence as a rum shop in Bathsheba (Barbados) is to a bashment in downtown Kingston (Jamaica). Having both enjoyed a nice glass of Cockspur in the former and reveled in wining down in the latter, to me Ralston's assessment seems a correct analysis of the common sense. The resolutely appraising eyes in the rum shop make it seem as if the sotto voce "buller" that a visiting researcher might hear (or imagine hearing) would be the extent of the abuse that one would receive because he, a cisgender and appropriate-for-the-occasion-dressed man of a certain age, knows well the rules of polite West Indian greeting and playful banter. All these appraising ears can very clearly hear that this traveler is not *really* West Indian, and will certainly soon fly back *to foreign*. He is only temporarily enjoying the currency of his cultural competence for (a research trip that looks like) a holiday. Most significant is the fact that he will leave some hard currency on the island.

In Barbados, I asked the same questions of Natalie, a Bajan travel agent. Trinis (Trinbagonians) are more "slack," she says. "Sure. Of course." Because of what she tells me is the "godlessness" of the pluri-religious multiculturalism that "tolerates" and celebrates the licentiousness of Carnival, which, Natalie did not have to tell me, simply would never do at Crop Over in Barbados, the island popularly referred to as "Little England." Transnational Black relationality and comparative racial formation are also at work in the popular race talk of African (descended) immigrants to the United States. One may commonly hear folks who hold, or at least strategically deploy, many fascinating beliefs at once. For example, that race is unimportant and not discussed in their homelands (the two are in fact not the same thing) and that social class and racialization are "more complex" in their countries than in the United States. Compare this to the common Black US American retort that the *po-lice* do not recognize differences among various national, ethnic, religious, or sexual groups of people they interpellate as Black. *We*, this logic goes, are all therefore vulnerable to capricious state-sanctioned violence. Another migration narrative involves becoming Black (if at all) and encountering a lesbian, trans, or gay person only when one reaches the shores of urban North America. There are many sides to this. Observers hardly consider differences in internal migrations. That is, moving—from local rural spaces, provinces, or peripheries in which many things that exist are not named, are perhaps taken for granted, or are called by names that do not easily translate or reveal hierarchies outside of those particular contexts—to more populous or cosmopolitan places in one's own country, where folks find any number of new ways to identify and collect and refer to themselves and others.

Respondents in Kenya (Kenyan, Tanzanian, and Ugandan) offered no pushback to Black identification. Perhaps this reflects East African political genealogies in which pro-capitalist Jomo Kenyatta invoked Harambee in Kenya and Tanzanian socialist Julius Nyeri's Ujaama eschewed primary tribal identification in favor of the nation, region, and continent. This is certainly also aspirational ideology, but young East Africans seem to identify with their region, nation, and continent. Although there are many local variations, the common language of Kiswahili enables this. When I arrived in 2014, Kenyans had been spared some of the recent violent homophobic rhetorics endured by their Ugandan neighbors. Hate-mongering US Christian evangelicals and their African acolytes had less of a foothold in Kenya at that time. Still, there is plenty conservatism and what Binyavanga Wainaina called "thousand-year-old hate shit" to go around.[9] In Nairobi we were very careful at the local bar—even after a few bottles of Tusker—for one can scarcely tell when the friendliness of any particular "gay-friendly" establishment anywhere in the world will wear off, making one vulnerable to confrontation.

How might we reconcile the deeply held assertions of my respondent, Ben, with the neoliberal fantasy that all borders are made permeable by a platinum credit card or a stack of euros, regardless of race or gender? Ben punctuated his theorization with a dainty seafood fork as he reflected on his more than twenty-five years of experience "globe trekking," while we indulged in the gay middle-class American ritual of brunch on one excruciatingly beautiful afternoon in Miami. He told me, his fork aloft: "If you're a *Black* faggot, you're a faggot everywhere. . . . And a pig [police officer] is a pig is a pig." Judging this closely cropped, meticulously groomed CPA by his carefully creased Sunday chinos and perfectly pressed Brooks Brothers v-neck t-shirt and linen blazer, one might be tempted to call him "conservative." But Ben is a self-described "upper middle-class African-American gay man in his late fifties." He was making the point that Black masculinity is so surveilled, remarked upon, and prefigured as excessive "everywhere, and I have traveled to six continents, I know," he said, that a man who does not conform to stereotypes of hypermasculine performance will be hypervisible and in jeopardy of harassment and abuse—notably and most reliably by the police—everywhere he goes. Laughing, he let me know that he had "already done the research."

Months later, I reminded Ben of the disparate opinions of others in our brunch focus group—one of whom is a thirty-year-old who reported that he had felt "welcomed" and treated very well "as a gay traveler." He had dismissed Ben's point of view as a "radical Afrocentric" attitude. That day, with a raised eyebrow and a knowing aside, he said "cha" (child) in a way that we were all clear that he had decided to merely change the subject, but had not conceded the point. Ben offered another formulation of transnational Black relationality to me in private: "Sometimes when you go abroad and you don't understand the local dialect of racism, the only word you hear people saying is *fabulous!*" That is, the various itineraries followed here require careful translation and attention to anti-Black racism, transphobia, homophobia, and heterosexism as real, but also not necessarily transparent or identical from place to place. Ethnographic sensibility can also be a protective habit of mind, after all. Before moving on, allow me to offer one very Black and very gay popular reference, illustrating another key component of how we might try (and fail) to see one another and connect to one another. In an early scene of the 1975 film *Mahogany*, Diana Ross's character Tracey arrives in Rome to begin her ascent to supermodel status. Just as she exits her taxi, Tracey notices a Black man on the street. Or someone she interpellates as a Black man. Attempting to find her bearings, she calls out to him as if she were at home in Chicago, to ask directions. She says, "Hey, excuse me, brother!," and he continues to walk away as if he had not heard her hailing him. Tracey takes his lack of recognition in stride. As he walks away, Tracey mumbles and sucks her teeth at what seems a new realization for the first-time international traveler: "That ain't no brother," she says to herself. But there are other ways to see this failure to hail. For example, he may be a brother, in fact, but *non parlo inglese*.

"Can I Get a Window Seat? / Don't Want Nobody Next to Me"

With the recent circulation of erudite work founded upon the metaphorical abstraction of Black "social death," arguing enslavement as a paradigmatic condition, how can we (should we?) take seriously something as seemingly banal as Black travel? Here we take up more travel(ing) contradictions: what we might call *looking while Black*.[10] If *wherever you go, there you are*, are you Black and therefore socially dead everywhere, even on holiday or a field research assignment? Is this fatality reserved for Blacks from the US, or is it available to all descendants of the enslaved throughout the Americas? A good Black gay look at this requires both meditation on our humanity and on political-economic structuration to tease out "differential Black mobilities." Although "the gesture of recognition (indeed) stretches out her hand and utters the word, come . . . ,"[11] getting there is a trip.

Like Erykah Badu, Azia just wanted "a ticket out of town / to look around / and a safe touch down." The lyricist sings about desire for both acknowledgment and support on one hand ("I need someone to clap for me / I need your attention . . ."[12]) and, on the other, a need for a moment of distant respite: a break, perhaps from gendered and raced expectations of nonreciprocal giving of this sort of support and attention. This has come to be understood as "self-care." Whether you see this as merely a futile middle- or upper-class attempt at escape from hard political-economic or social realities or a radical praxis of (better than) *survival, pending revolution*, dear reader, this is what Azia was looking for as she hopped into a private car on her way to the airport to meet her evening flight to Morocco. Under her hand-printed silk head wrap were damp, newly shampooed dreadlocks and a freshly oiled scalp. Feeling fabulous, Azia told me that "the TSA nearly ruined [her] trip . . . with their demands to 'see what's under the turban.'" The drama escalated to a semiprivate area. TSA agents wanted to know "what's in her hair?" over Azia's protestation that the backscatter X-ray had not detected anything in her tight bun, so this was an unnecessary and embarrassing delay. This, before the barrage of questions and quizzed looks from the flight attendant to passengers who wondered aloud whether she had lost her way to Economy Class. Or had just cut an album in New York ("Isn't that that girl . . ."). Or is the lucky nanny for the adorable white family across the aisle. Cha. Perhaps TSA agents surmised, noting the passport stamps indicating frequent travel between the United States and various Caribbean and South American destinations and Mexico, and at least three or four European and African trips, that she was a "drug mule." Azia and I laughed, pitifully, sharing travel stories and musing on Zora Neale Hurston. She, an exemplar par excellence, of a Black woman traveling around the world alone and for her own purposes, had famously proclaimed the Black woman as "the mule of the world." Although in my own travel life I have been asked a series of questions and felt "profiled" by border agents on occasion, I do not believe that the profile was "mule." A drug "dealer" or "trafficker" perhaps— cisgender Black men are profiled as potential agents or runners, not as mute beasts carrying the burden of another.

If you had been watching at the hotel bar or the departure lounge or in line to exchange currency, you might wonder who among us is in fact the anthropologist. It is the horde of white folks on holiday, or business, or merely touring (seemingly carefree) who appear to always have their calipers at the ready and their own spyglasses aimed with laser focus—at me. They seem to need to survey, interview, measure, and observe the Black man with the fancy notebook who seems to know a few words of the language but with an (American?) accent. Fieldwork can look suspiciously like tourism. And here is yet another contradiction (in case you are counting, dear reader/ accountant) that we must find ways to hold. Being a Black person of any or no gender with a larger measure of material resources relative to your people at home and/or abroad means negotiating "authenticity" or solidarity against a modicum of exhalation. This is true even in cases in which those resources are leveraged in the form of research funding by the neoliberal university. The momentary exhalation is contingent and precarious. And it is also shallow—not at all a sustaining respiration. Maybe this too can be described as an ephemeral "gesture . . . stretching." Still, it is very nice to feel the slake of a lovely wine while admiring a serene landscape from a hotel balcony (which I am aware is privatized for the exclusive pleasure of travelers and "honoraries"). This may not be quite a "disavowal" but certainly is a problematic position or condition. Of course, there is violence here—both ambient and acute. But to suggest that class or gender makes no difference in experience would only dishonor everyone, especially those who labor daily in parts of the global plantation in which there is no letup.

Azia sighed heavily, reflecting on the levels and varieties of harassment that she and other Black women are subject to while traveling: "Can a sister just go and see something? Damn!"[13] To be sure, there are more-harrowing stories of other Black women-who-have-sex-with-women attempting to cross borders. Azia's banal Black bourgeois encounters with white entitlement and state surveillance are not spectacular. Not a sister raped or another murdered. Perhaps reporting cases of sex trafficking, physical abuse, or sexual harassment of cis and trans women here would more compellingly illustrate one end of the spectral violences that many Black women—especially those read as lesbians or gender nonconforming—experience at borders or in their attempts to reach them (after all, dear reader, is this not why many folks read ethnographic accounts of so-called Black bodies—to get their fill of culturally detailed tragedy?). Recalling this unexceptional experience of a Black woman being refused or paying heavy prices to simply move from Point A to a far-flung Point B that she feels may promise a perhaps lighter, or at least qualitatively different, load of accretive *misogynoir* is precisely our point. Can we not learn from this so-called kinder, gentler end of the spectrum? Are these aggressions not also worthy of some attention—perhaps as "lesser violence" all of a piece with other forms of harm that may be more spectacular (*all part of the same ki-ki*, Kevin Aviance might say), seemingly remarkable, or worthy of serious reflection?

Generally, my friends are more well traveled than I am. Across class statuses and incomes, curious librarians, artists, teachers, scholars, and attorneys (one with the heart of an archaeologist) understand travel to be essential to knowing themselves and the world in which they live, and they travel to every continent. This is the demand side. Like my middle-class Black gay respondents who shared their travel stories with me, they all deny being mere "consumers"—claiming and performing solidarity with their brothers and sisters throughout the world. For a view of another side of the equation—we can call this the supply side—let us return, briefly, to a conversation I had with Ramon many years ago (which I discussed in another way in an earlier work). Ramon—a Black sex worker I interviewed in Havana and was surprised to run into in Miami two years later—might ask, echoing Joe, "Where is my reflection" in the Black/queerpolis? How am I figured, and under what conditions do I enter global Black gay imagination? Today he would find his muscular, typically masculine mirror image mediated and monetized online on sites like Machofucker and ThugHunter and in a shower, go-go box, or "cage" in a gay bar in Madrid, New York, Paris, or elsewhere.

Years ago, when we met—before the advent of smartphone apps cut out the middleman to allow for direct payment—Ramon had quickly found a job as a stripper in addition to busing tables at a Miami Beach restaurant. Talk about immigrant industriousness! Untaxed tips, in cash. Today he might join increasing numbers of occasional sex workers and exhibitionists who receive tips from their private subscribers on entrepreneurial sites like OnlyFans—sort of Uber for exhibitionists, porn producers, and other sex workers—or simply set up a cash app for clients to pay directly for freelance sex work. Ramon's American dream was predicated on racialized objectification. He had learned at home in the tourist-sex-work economy of Havana what men in Rio, Bridgetown, Atlanta, and Montreal learn and exploit: *your trade is your stock*. During our last conversation many years ago, Ramon seemed, like many of the Cuban *pingueros* and *jineteras* that I had observed over the years, savvy about his role in the reproduction of exotic fantasies, both in Cuba and in his new home. The choices he and others made, at home and in countries to which they migrate, point to important differences in "integration" of LGBTQ individuals from the global South within much-celebrated so-called gay meccas of the North. Liberal legal protections do not always extend to migrants and refugees fleeing one form of violence, to experience another, and perhaps forced to make different sets of choices. San Francisco is not a universal queer haven for those who clean up after the Pride parade, for example. The terms of gay "freedom" must be rethought and recalibrated beyond the assumed subject. Paris is not so *gay* when prices and police violence in areas like the Marais drive Black and brown folks to the underresourced and hyper-policed *banlieue*, no matter how much they are celebrated at the periodic *Black blanc buerre* parties (BBB, noting Black and Arab men in attendance and entertaining, along with white customers) or are followed by would-be supplicants at La Mine. Of course, although most folks find occupations other than sex work, pre-scripted sexualization of Black folks' bodies remains. How do we face each other—Black/queer sistren, bredren, and kin—coming or going, here or there? Is the "gulf . . . too vast . . . heavy and double-edged," as Mr. Baldwin imagined as he strolled along the Seine—perhaps looking the other way after a perfunctory nod to avoid deeper engagement and confirmation of deep alienation from his African other/brother?[14] Or will he venture an *"excuse moi mon frère?"* How do we hold all of this with hands already full of souvenirs or wax print, or holding a hard-earned scholarship or student/working/expired visa? We shall see.

Sankofa Dancing, Naked, in the Surf

Your rum punch is in hand. And you hear that beat again. That canned techno-y Top 40 sound you remember from that Major Lazer/Beyoncé "Pon de Floor"/"Runs the World" mix that seemed to be everywhere in 2010. You find it tired and a bit sad, although your toes tap and that grenadine-drenched rum punch swills to the beat. Notwithstanding the toe tapping and mood lightening induced by the sun, sea, and bottomless drinks, to *really* feel it you need a soundscape carefully curated for the long-1980s club-educated ear, cultivated in New York and Chicago, with echoes of London, Kingston, Lagos, and Berlin. Real *real* dance music. Not merely "cute" but the music we *live for.* Cue the silky white powder that people of a certain age now risk expulsion from events for sprinkling on the dance floor. Facilitating balletic slides and gentle arabesque spins, the baby powder forms an impressionist *veve* on the dance-floor-as-altar. It serves as New World *efun*—cooling the transition as one straddles this world and the ether. But if the dance floor at Hedonism II in Negril, Jamaica, is an altar, *you already know* what gods are being worshipped here. The hotelier would like guests to believe it is Eros or Aphrodite calling you to beauty and pleasure, or Dionysus or Bacchus, who promise indulgence of appetites, all-inclusive style.[15] But this dance floor in Jamaica—not really "in Jamaica," in the same way that every Caribbean all-inclusive resort creates an extra-territorial enclave unto itself—is really consecrated to the invisible golden calf of global capital, headquartered elsewhere (perhaps in the *buy and buy*?). It reigns here. Still, Black folks enter with laughter, sensuality, and a particular air or heir of entitlement to this Caribbean space—acting (as if they are) free. "Bloomers" have come. The multiple gods and idols served by/for/within this group of mostly Black queer travelers blur too. Make no mistake: this trip must also generate income for the host, Olubode (Brown). So, in fine New World African fashion, there is powerful syncretism here. Soon, soon—before they can finish their third rum punch (and by then they have befriended the bartender, who reaches under the bar to pour the good rum for them)—the canned techno-y sound

8.1 Wave yuh flag! Advertisement for BLOOM Jamaica weekend, 2014.

of the resort DJ gives way. This time, it is house music that Phillip, Olu, and I programmed back in New Haven. Bass moves to her center. The absent tapping of the toe transforms to a languid head tilted back—eyes closed. A shoulder shimmy. A knowing smile. Now, you have arrived.

Red. Olu designed this party to represent the elemental energy of fire, and it is hot already. A warm night in which the evening breeze has faded away. The sea is still. The air is thick. Yes, just like the commercials, and descriptions in ethnographies and NPR stories—thick with the scent of night-blooming flowers and the sea. It is true. But instead of commercials peopled with smiling white folks, or even tales of poolside orgies that Hedonism likes to circulate (again, with all white folks), this tropical tableau is a study of browns and creams and blacks, in red. After nearly a year of observing while participating with the organizers of a historic and risky enterprise, I boarded a plane to Jamaica for the first time. I had traveled throughout the Caribbean region, but Jamaica was the place from which I had deliberately steered clear. There was something about the arrogance and banality of Jamaica's brand of homophobic violence, I had told myself. But in December I traveled to the (in)famous all-inclusive sex-positive resort Hedonism II, in Negril, to attend BLOOM Jamaica, a weekend party organized by Olubode (Olu) Brown, a gay Jamaican entrepreneur who has lived long term in the United States (see figure 8.1). An original member of Other Countries' Black Gay Men's Writing Workshop, a member of Gay Men of African Descent (GMAD), and a well-known entrepreneur in the community, Olu conceived the weekend party as one part of his "lifestyle" business—comprising specialty parties and weekly after-work soirees in New York City, an online magazine, books, and personal coaching. Olu and his partner at the time, Jason, wrote this:

> BLOOM | Jamaica is an offshoot of BLOOM | NYC—a party thrown by Jamaican-born SGL men who have spent their lives between the two countries. We are a celebration of the richness and diversity of our communities. We attract a broad range of guests of all sexualities and genders from North America, the Caribbean and from as far as Europe and Africa. It is because of the uniqueness and size of this group that Hedonism II in Negril, Jamaica invited us to have our celebration on the island. We're willing to engage people who are seriously looking to interact with an open mind. We believe there is more than one approach to liberation. Jamaicans are not a monolith and the situation on the island is more complex than meets the eye. Many Jamaicans support human rights for all and the situation on the island is slowly changing. The qualities that characterize the people who join us on this trip are fun, courageous, open-minded, intelligent, well-traveled, and having a strong sense of self and humor. This is not a group of activists. It is a trip for human beings who can find their fun in dealing with the fullness of their humanity while enjoying evolved, thrilling and adult experiences in a Jacuzzi or a room, on the beach, at one of our themed dance parties or at the bar.[16]

An illustrative conversation ensued on the BLOOM Jamaica Facebook page. The talking points repeated here were familiar to me, having accompanied my friends Olu and Jason to a number of marketing or recruiting opportunities (Black Gay Pride, Harlem Pride, and Fire Island Black/Out events) leading up to the December trip, as well as innumerable ad hoc exchanges—Olu was always recruiting. It is one of the most polite and effective of innumerable exchanges in which I witnessed Olu and Jason negotiate the reality of mediatized half-truths about Jamaica, its damnable violence, and the dangerous exceptionalism that allows us to ignore homophobic violences that fall outside of received racist and xenophobic frameworks of machete-wielding "natives," which occur regularly in the United States and elsewhere. Olu and Jason refined this approach through trial and error, including a few interactions that went poorly when they were challenged by would-be vacationers to "defend" their reasons for hosting the event in

Jamaica and at Hedonism II. The first commenter on Olu's Facebook page was enthusiastic about the trip and could not wait to start his adventure. However, it did not take long for those who were dubious to express their concerns. One of them, whom I will call "Mark," said, "Thanks for the invite BUT I can't support a country that is homophobic in their culture and official policy.[17] If I'm mistaken, please enlighten me." Primed for this sort of challenge, Olu responded with "Hey Mark, I understand your point of view. No debates here," then directed him to the "Why We Go to Jamaica" statement that he and Jason had prepared for just such conversations (or confrontations). A short time later, Mark seemed convinced by the persuasively argued statement. He thanked Olu for sharing the information, saying that "the perspective you shared with me puts Jamaica's homophobia in a different light." The first commenter returns to cosign. He posts that he had also held Mark's position before Olu had offered his perspective; with a wink, he then promised to save a dance for Mark, whose reservations about travel to Jamaica had precipitated this conversation. For his part, Mark said that this was an instance in which he "prefer[s] to be dead wrong." Jason then chimed in, reaffirming that a number of Bloomers who had been at first uneasy "took the plunge. They come back every year now and bring their friends. What we hear in the media here in the states is not even half the story." Finally, adopting one of the Jamaican Tourist Board's popular and affecting slogans, which promised that travelers to Jamaica gain privileged information that makes them want to return, Jason punctuated their case with "Once you go, you know!"

Popular tourism discourse does not recognize how and to whom violences are doled out in Jamaica and certainly seems uninterested in the socioeconomic roots of this. Olu and Jason's statement "Why We Go to Jamaica" is therefore a significant personal and political accounting. It begins, "We go to Jamaica because we are Jamaicans and know that it is just as safe for gay travelers on the island as it is for [other] travelers." To wit, they do not parse how "safe" Jamaica is for yardies, especially those who do not have class, color, or celebrity status, or family connections with which to negotiate protection. Here they are only referring to "travelers." Likewise, the chatter in gay online forums is focused on how comfortable or uncomfortable an openly gay traveler might be in the Caribbean, but the conversations on these sites hardly acknowledge the experiences of lesbian, gender-non-conforming, bisexual, or gay people who live in these societies. Nor have I seen would-be gay vacationers from the North ask citizens of these nation-states about their daily lives or where they might go for a good time in their hometown. Rather, would-be tourists turn to other northern travelers in these internet forums. Some important questions are glaringly missing: Friendly toward which gays? Is the "friendship" reciprocal or one-sided? The tourist assumption, it seems, is that the Caribbean is merely one large beach staffed with those whose purpose it is to cater to their holiday fantasies. Therefore, "islanders" do not occur to them as individuals but as part of the colorful fauna. Jason and Olu promise something different to Bloomers:

> We go home and bring our friends with us because we believe that engagement around a drink and a conversation (aka contact) is a powerful tool for social change. Each year, minds have been broadened because of this trip. Many who come each year had previously vowed never to spend dollars in Jamaica. Those guests have returned year after year and always bring more of their friends. Many form lasting friendships locally that keep them informed about what is really happening. After legislative change has been accomplished around the buggery laws, there has to be a cultural shift—that's the hard part, and this is where local engagement such as BLOOM | Jamaica will be important.[18]

The BLOOM manifesto "Why We Go to Jamaica" lays out an argument that is intended to clarify the complexity of Jason and Olu's experience as gay Jamaican men who live at the intersections of racial, national, sexual, and class boundaries that allow them privileged access to understand what others may see starkly in terms of "gay friendly" or "homophobic." With "We know and understand that there are specific historical reasons for violence on the island," they deliver a more nuanced and historically informed commentary than most. They continue: "The poor and marginalized among our friends and family on the island fend for themselves in a state traumatized by harmful colonial relics like sodomy laws instituted under British rule as well as devastating monetary policies . . . not only have we seen the documentaries, we live the reality." Of course, Olu and Jason's appeal that they "live the reality" of Jamaicans is a bit overstated. Although Olu spends significant time in Jamaica, his daily reality is not the same as his friends and family there. Those who emigrated from the island certainly know more intimately than outsiders, but as a Jamaican student in Kingston told me (riffing off Bob's lyric "who feels it knows it"), only those who live daily under the uncertainty and fear that many folks experience "lives it." Olu and Jason finish with this point in summary: "We at BLOOM know openly gay people who live happy and full lives on the island without harm or worry. We love our country and our people and we cherish the opportunity to share what Jamaica has to offer with our guests. We believe in taking our rightful place within our families and community and celebrating each other there. Because though shaming and boycotting are valid forms of protest we choose to engage Jamaica with our presence." Beyond its ambition to provoke "cultural change" when the colonial buggery laws inevitably end, it is really a promise of fun, friendship, and solidarity that BLOOM offers. This is what Puerto Rican critic Larry Fountain-Stokes missed when he visited Cuba. In his beautiful essay "De un Pajaro las Dos Alas: Travel Notes of a Queer Puerto Rican in Havana," Larry reports to his incredulous hosts that he "does not want to bed anyone, that this is not why [he] came," but also, on his first trip to the "other wing" of the bird that symbolizes his island's relationship to Cuba, Larry has "neither the money nor the condoms nor the place" and therefore feels "like a penniless child in an ice cream shop, and the treats are sharks on the prowl." Crying in his hotel room and lamenting the money-grubbing he experienced as a Latinx cultural tourist, "Havana has left [him] adrift between sexlessness and the fear of robbery. . . . You realize it was all for money, all just for a ride and a good time, while they made fun of your accent and didn't even look you in the face." What was to be a sort of literary and theater pilgrimage was therefore "not a *nido*/nest like Rodriguez de Tio but a site of grave anxiety" for him.[19]

By and large, northern queer activists and observers do not take up the historical background that conditions how particular societies have understood homosexuality and gender nonconformity. European sexualities were constituted through the stark, inhumane social structures of slavery and colonialism—not sealed off from the plantation or the colony but specifically enabled and activated by it, discursively and materially. Rape and massive widespread sexual abuse of youths and others, not only by white "slaveholders" but also by missionaries and clergy, colonial officials, functionaries, and tourists, were legal or otherwise statutorily permitted. Therefore, today local understanding of what it is to be queer is not only read through religion, where the surface analysis ends, but also through this long recursive history of racialized sexual abuse and colonial domination. Queerness is pathologized and understood in many cases as synonymous with pedophilia. Queerness therefore seems to recall lack of sexual autonomy and victimization more broadly—not only discourses of northern or "modern" personal liberty, therefore, but also of societal ruination. If they know and understand this history, queer rights advocates generally avoid historicizing the discourse. This is understandable. But we cannot understand the situation clearly without facing this context of a "traumatized state." The larger transnational controversy over northern gay activists' "murder music" campaign is one example. While "Black Lesbians and Gays against Media Homophobia" began work in 1992, later largely white groups called for a boycott of Jamaica because of homophobic violence and violent homophobic dancehall reggae lyrics like that of Buju Banton's infamous "Boom Boom Bye Bye" ("Boom bye bye / Inna batty bwoy head / Rude bwoy no promote no nasty man / Dem haffi dead").[20] In some instances, activists dramatically destroyed bottles of famous Jamaican exports Appleton rum and Red Stripe beer outside of bars in "gay villages" of the North. Many northern activists saw this as effective political theater, but this tactic was condemned by Caribbean and Caribbean-descended activists in London and elsewhere, and the Jamaican group J-FLAG, which opposed the boycott tactics. They understood the region's dependence on tourism and a small number of exportable products that are based on associations with tourism, and they saw the boycotting of an entire nation as a formidable threat to the economic well-being of their island and the region.

Further complicating the issue, at the same moment in which good rum and beer spilled into the gutters of New York's Chelsea and Greenwich Village, for example (reminding me of the scene in the film *Life and Debt* in which locally produced milk was wasted in order to maintain Jamaica's dependence on US-imported powdered milk), Buju and others were played loud and strong in Black gay clubs that I visited in the Bronx, Brooklyn, and Manhattan. Of course, New York has a large proportion of same-gender-loving and queer Caribbean folks and others who understood Jamaican patois lyrics better than others who were also enthusiastically wining down to the wicked riddims. I remember blue lights in a dark, thick-aired room above Flatbush Avenue, with dancehall, rockers, soca, and calypso all night, walls slick with sweat; and nimble bodies on the smaller dance floor of the Warehouse in the Bronx, where in the main room DJ Andre Collins gave us the closest thing to Better Days that New York had seen since the club closed in 1990; and upstairs at Octagon, where music from all over the Caribbean played, with house in the large room. These are not memories of fear or anger or violence. So many contradictions within epidemic time. I leave this to Javonte and others to parse with their own tools and sensibilities.[21] This should not be entirely surprising: even "conscious" US hip-hop groups such as Tribe Called Quest and Brand Nubians ("Punks Jump Up to Get Beat Down") were in harmony with the sophomoric homophobic violence evident in dancehall, although they were met with a deafening silence.[22] Whereas (for good reason, I believe) Buju became the poster child for "murder music," he is certainly not alone.[23] I echo Cheryl Clarke's astute 1983 assessment of our "failure to transform" in response to all this disrespect, disgust, violence, and contradiction (in dancehall and in hip-hop and beyond).[24] Black folks did not create the common sense of heteropatriarchy and racial capitalism that poses your sister as your enemy, then reifies that very structuration as your savior, but we can least afford it. Recall, if you will, dear sistren/bredren reader, the anonymous blogger who threatened Cleo Manago's life (and mine, and many of yours). It is in fact these brands of (racialized self-) hatred that truly constitute Babylon: kidnap, captivity, corruption, and ill-ease with one's humanity. Black/queerpolis is therefore one route to "Zion."[25]

9   "Black/Queer Mess" as Methodological Case Study

> Now I was hungry, not very comfortable, tired, beginning to be sweaty, seemingly untouched by the ecstasies, even the graces from which the others benefited. Just what was I doing there, and what was my capacity in that friendly, sincere community? How much of what I was doing was in the interest of science, how much was succumbing to the neurosis of the country, how much was seeking for knowledge, for a key to an unknown from which body and soul would benefit and with which doubt and fear would be dispelled? What did these people really think of me, one who could barely speak their tongue . . ? who turned—and still often does—to left instead of right in the salutes between houngan and hounci . . . ?[1]

Katharine Dunham's movements from place to place exemplify Afro-modernity. Her hybrid scholarly and artistic ethnographic fieldwork notating, then choreographing and re-creating African-derived Caribbean folk dances for popular and highbrow audiences alike, is revered as an exemplar of Black "transnational movement." Her dance scholarship, performance ethnography, choreographic notation, and performance choreography are only one aspect of what makes her a singular figure. Just as significantly, she brought these dances and her technique derived from them to underserved Black urban communities in the United States, where the discipline, pride, and cultural expression she modeled and demanded served youths who needed it. Still, Stephanie Batiste convincingly argues that at the same time, Ms. Dunham also "participated in an imperial process of identifying the native, appropriating culture, and reinvigorating a U.S. Black national identity" through this same Black transnational movement from global North to global South, and/ but returning north, a path familiar to contemporary anthropologists. Even as she provided "precious recognition and connection between Blacks across national borders," Stephanie quips that her classic anthropological work, *Island Possessed*, would be more aptly titled "Katharine Dunham Possessed."[2] Ms. Dunham's angsty confession above seems to corroborate this view.

Ms. Dunham and I are not alone, of course. Contemporary ethnographers are often likewise possessed or, more to the point, obsessed by our engagement with "the other" and the angst that accompanies this, especially when we see the other as a kind of "us." This is the second part of our consideration of the collisions that Black travelers engage in or precipitate, briefly addressing the dangerous straits that one must navigate when we insist on finding each other across *placed* discourses and boundaries, with the intention of not only *seeing* but also *saying* what we learned. Here we turn to query the limits of the project of transnational research and scholarship among those we understand as our people and in community. We take this risky trip because friendship and politics "in the field" are complex and deserve more critical consideration. At least I owe an elaboration of what I have called the "social erotics of love at work" and the problematics of inhabiting the space of sojourner/witness. Beyond obsession and possession, truly sincere, politically solidary fieldwork and friendship must begin with homework. Here I want to demonstrate doing some of my own—after John L. Jackson Jr., unpacking and offering another articulation of the "collision" of the sojourner/witness and a few of his far-flung fellow travelers. He writes:

> There is a need to think through that moment of contact itself . . . recognizing that the anthropologist is always a political actor in the everydayness of her practice (in a way that demands unpacking and explicit articulation) each and every time she sits at a community board meeting, watches a local rally, or asks the most idle of clarifying questions. The unit of analysis is not the anthropologist but instead the collision she is part of—whether intended or not.[3]

Here we will analyze the collision by thinking through methodologies of observant participation in terms of concepts of "cognate" and "stranger value." I want to join the conversation that Black anthropologists have already begun on the practice of Black-on-Black ethnography and how we might prepare ourselves to encounter and collaborate with research respondents who not only "inform" but are also informed colleagues, critics, and interlocutors in their own right. Here I ask (again) whether it is really our differences that preclude common political projects.

First, a quick word on "mess": I usually try to avoid it.[4] Still, at times our attempts to not be messy—that is, to always "keep it cute"—are ultimately unhelpful. I am learning this from young people. I am fascinated and excited, if not also at times frightened, by the ways that many of my young people seem to revel in *the ratchet*. They highlight Black joy and jouissance that can emerge from the messy or undone, the petty, and the slightly disreputable. Still, I have heard many young scholars, artists, and activists misapprehend the deep context of the phrase *respectability politics*—too often casually collapsing this with three distinct postures that should not be conflated: being hincty, and/or bourgie, and/or inauthentic—when what they are really describing may simply be an individual (self)possessed of a certain sense of deportment that may or may not emerge from class experience or class aspiration, and may be unconnected to whether anyone (authorizing whiteness) is watching. As for me, although I do not mind the fact of mess—of dirty laundry and tales out of school, for example—I certainly do not want to *heir* it. We the just slightly buttoned-up, the bourgie, the private, and/or the quiet can be forgiven for not wanting to publicly engage the pettiest and messiest mess, can we not? Everything Black folks do is already prescripted as riddled with a certain *candela*. Assumed to be appropriate for public consumption and amplified. Not only are our narratives always just arriving in academe, but they are also often read only for their color, sass, and seams—not for their epistemic brilliance (which some have been conditioned, wrongly, to see as exclusively emerging from the flawlessly composed and curated). Dear Kevin (Quashie) has already provided a beautifully wrought framework through which we can appreciate the choice to occupy the sovereign space of quiet as a mode of engagement and as a site from which to launch interventions.[5] Here is one methodological and ethnopoetic refraction of his formulation. Whereas I attempt here to re-narrate what talking about perceived differential power and positionalities, and perhaps at cross-purposes, can teach us about how to push beyond our current limits and toward grace and redemption within "all-kin" networks: no tea spilled here will stain. You will find the ethnographic details thinly circumscribed, by design.

Responding to a fiercely excoriating email, I wrote this to some *friends* who opposed an idea from Olu that I circulated for comment, proposing to invite regional LGBTQ and HIV activists to join his BLOOM party weekend in Jamaica to fete them and raise awareness and funds for their activist projects: "I own my position . . . not really an insider/outsider as Black anthropologists like to cast their positions, but really an outsider in (ruptured?) solidarity or kinship. I get it."[6] Although I suggested that I would step away and return afresh to the conversation later, this letter marked the end. I simply repaired to my study and my classroom—and there I remained. Moreover, since the initial ethnographic field research for this current work, I have shifted to keep more company with the words of the dead—their own shadiness and complex contradictions softened by time's hazy hagiography, or perhaps just the good manners to not speak ill of them. This is methodologically uncharacteristic for an ethnographer, of course. Our claim to textual authority most often begins with *I was there* and increasingly is expected to extend to *I helped.* In that email to my friends, I was reaching toward some future rapprochement—describing my position as more messily (un)composed than anthropologists before me had suggested—*an outsider in solidarity or in (ruptured) kinship.* My travel and fieldwork have been largely marked by connection and conviviality, but there have also been moments when the *lime* (in English-speaking Caribbean parlance, the casual good time or get-together) goes sour. That is the moment at which warm affect and positive flow of communication slows, courting bitterness. To make methodological sense of this, I will turn briefly to fellow travelers—many in both senses of the phrase—toward a fuller and perhaps reparative sense of the conundrum of being a Black "observant participator" or the position I described in other work as an "object, *looking*, like a subject" and claimed here as a *sojourner-witness(-scribe).*[7]

Brackette Williams argues that in the case of ethnographic fieldwork, if an anthropologist is to have any "stranger's value"—that is, the assumption of a naive, uninitiated, uninvested observer—that value must emerge from "the existence of a major power disparity between a position or positions that locate the anthropologist as translator and those that locate persons who are qualified to become the translator's translator."[8] This is of course at least troubled, if not completely undone, by the sort of deeply invested research in which Black anthropologists have engaged since the very early fieldwork by Caroline Bond Day.[9] Brackette holds that "these positionings create a type of subject-object that must continually do the homework of self-constructing by asking: 'what might the persons with whom I am interacting think me to be if I were not posing as an anthropologist?'" I will offer a few guesses as to who they thought me to be, later. In any case, it seems to me that my friends understandably rejected what they perceived as my taking on the role of translator and surely were not signing up to be the translator's translator. There is little need for this mediation in the transnational networks in which we live and work. So-called natives speak and write and circulate work quite independently. Brackette concludes that those whom Delmos Jones would call "native anthropologists" or others working in their "own society" among their own people never accrue "stranger value." This seems fair. However, Brackette shows the conundrum to be more complex later: "The identity of anthropologist as participant-observer could neither be constructed nor situated outside the double-edged, multifaceted question: 'who are you and what are you to me?'"[10] This is also inescapably a question of Black (un)belonging and perhaps the reason that their rebuff was so swift and biting: to them, I never belonged in their (Caribbean) (activist) kinship. This despite what they already knew about my persona background and politics before anthropology.

Brackette's elaboration of the Hurstonian distinction between "skinfolk" and kinfolk in this critique of "stranger's value" in anthropology provides useful formulations toward analyzing the "ambivalent, betwixt and between identity" of the Black anthropologist working with (or "among") African (descended) cultures.[11] Brackette offers that "such constructions do not begin with subjects' action in a place but rather with . . . the subject's possible identity configurations in a national and international order of status reckoning. . . ." Perhaps my friends could not avoid seeing me as enacting a major power disparity. Perhaps the disparity is unavoidably North/South. Our formation as Black anthropologists trained in North America—even radical, insider/outsider, engaged, decolonizing—still comes with the imprimatur of anthropology and its skeletons rattling around (sometimes literally)! I could not escape what I had become by being credentialed in what many of my people think of as the "colonial discipline."[12] Perhaps this goes with the territory. Moreover, I understand that supporting Olu's project, to organize a party to celebrate the region's activists in a problematic venue not ordinarily accessible to them or relevant to their work, is shaped by my gender, national, and class positions and may have been judged as "neoliberal" by my friends. Their threats to "expose" my association with the project idea may have been meant merely to incite a productive quarrel (that I refused).

Seizing Edward Baugh's metaphor of "the quarrel" in his seminal essay "The West Indian Writer and His Quarrel with History," Donette (Francis) suggests that "the quarrel is a Caribbean *condition* rather than a singular historical *event* . . . the mode of engagement in which subsequent generations . . . made their individual interventions. . . ."[13] With reflection and the benefit of Donette's tacit suggestion, I now realize that the quarrel is a strategic mode of engagement. Perhaps the upbraiding that I received was an invitation for me to pose a countering intervention: to quarrel back (and forth). Underscoring this in diasporic dimensions, I later understood that this could be read as an invitation to *bolekaja* (come down, let's fight!), an intellectual tradition that emerged among literary critics at Ibadan University.[14] I had indeed read phrases such as "fresh water interloper" and "colonial anthropology" as fighting words. But, it could be that calling me out (of my name)—which for me is clear evidence of *un falta de respeto* (lack of respect, a serious charge in Queens, where I come from, as well as in Havana, where I learned the phrase)—was not necessarily (or not only) interpellating me in the first paragraph of a breathlessly rebuking email as a colonizing tokenizing opportunist (and stupid to boot). There is more to learn here. In any case, I demurred. I imagine John (L. Jackson), in his AnthroMan© cape, would have continued to pursue the quarrel toward some important insight on (in)sincerity in the ethnographic project or Black (in)authenticity. He writes of his own quarrelsome (fascinating and certainly also insulting) Black US respondent Bill, who constantly scolded him and accused him of "sucking up wind under the white man. . . ." John confides: "All the while, of course, he continues reprimanding me for my many ignorances. I smile awkwardly as I listen, not always knowing what to do with my ethnographic face, and Bill even finds my smile disheartening, 'I don't know why you're smiling,' he censures. This is serious stuff. You don't even know how messed up and sick they have you. You can't even see it."[15] As for myself, this would not be the first time that I had entered a situation in which the modes of (familial) engagement and cultural "translation" may have been agreed upon and rehearsed before my arrival. My mind goes not only to many years of friendly acquaintance with two of the interlocutors, or friends, who wrote the email—what I read as our mutual respect and ease, sometimes peppered with teasing and side-eyes and steeups (chupse or teeth sucking), which kinship anthropologists would call "joking relations." Moreover, Donette's invocation of the quarrel as "a Caribbean *condition* rather" also recalled youthful miscommunication with my Barbadian grandfather, whom I thought of as quarrelsome, and a Guyanese cousin of my parents' age cohort whom I found especially taciturn. My mother—who, along with her siblings, always said "my father is" Bajan, never claiming Barbados for themselves over Brooklyn—explained their behavior as "how they are."

During her fieldwork in Guyana, Brackette, despite holding what she understood as a "shared historical connection," believed that she and the Guyanese people she worked with did not belong to the same Black identity. This is certainly understandable: these blacknesses are not the same. Brackette "did not expect the historical similarities or the ideology of Pan-Africanism to be of any constructive value" in Guyana.[16] In my own contexts I had. This project was hardly my first time "in the field." This had been the case in my Cuban fieldwork, and I enjoyed overwhelmingly warm welcomes among folks in the life in various locations around the world during my field research for *Disco Ball*. I had learned a great deal being the object of curiosity and initial skepticism as a US citizen getting in people's business in Cuba during my first ethnographic experience. Suspicion of being a CIA agent goes with the territory. And people tend to watch closely. But the reality of a revolutionary society in deep socioeconomic crisis presented opportunities to prove or disprove suspicions. The relative strength of socialist political solidarity and Black diasporic cultural connection over animosities between the United States and Cuban states was regularly tested in small ways and large ones. Demonstrable fidelity—not to the project of socialism, necessarily, but to human kindness and Black (and) queer solidarity—was scrutinized daily as my respondents and friends looked for ways "to resolve the difficulties" of Cuba's Special Period in Times of Peace. In the words of Delmos Jones, el pueblo was trying "to forge a solution." In 1970, at the leading edge of what we now understand as the decolonizing generation of anthropology, he offered that "a Black man in this century cannot avoid identifying with his people. I am an intrinsic part of the social situation that I am attempting to study. As part of the situation, I must also attempt to forge a solution."[17] I feel this profoundly. Still, Professor Jones was referring to fieldwork at home. Audre offers useful refinement of this, employing a different quality of light. You will recall that regarding the struggles she witnessed and reported on in Grenada, she parses her position this way: "I am a relative. . . ." Of course, *relative* can refer to "family," in cases, but also can mean merely "proximate." *Relative* can mean "to be compared," "in reference to," or "in relation" to something or someone else. I had perhaps been slow to recognize the crucial need to translate incisively when working closer to home, but still (only) (a) relative.

Among the homework errors that I made with my salty friends, perhaps the first was an error of translation. Proper language translation is necessary to determine true cognates or merely *faux amis* (*du traducteur*) or "false friends" (of the translator)." Both the ethnographer and the linguist must make the attempt: be willing to engage and to risk the humiliation of the wrong word, or gesturing "left instead of right in the salutes between houngan and hounci" and possibly missing "the graces from which the others benefited," perhaps producing (mis- or false) recognition.[18] In Black/queerpolity it is the expectation (my expectation?) of the extension of hospitality and the problematic management of familiarity that is the thing. That's *where it's at*, Pat may have said forty years ago, signifying in that US Black American English way of collapsing time and place and being. Perhaps this is the most crucial understanding of what Stuart indexes for us as a *placed* discourse. After all, the heart has its reasons. I ironically hear Paul (Gilroy) too, remixing the last line of Eric B and Rakim's "In the Ghetto." Rakim offers: "So much to say, but I still flow slow / I come correct, and I won't look back / Cause *it ain't where you're from, it's where you're at*."[19]

I turn to the notion of a *cognate ideal* here, making a brief and perhaps shallow etymological departure to offer a family of words whose mediations might have saved me some anguish: *cognate, cognoscence,* and *recognizance*.[20] Two different modes of attention operate here: one is John L. Jackson's exploration of ethnographic sincerity and authenticity, and the other is John Keene's linguistic/translation practice of "grace" work, in which no translations is perfectly consonant but sincere attempts are valid. *Cognate* is a noun, "one connected to another by ties of kinship . . . related in origin, traceable to the same source."[21] Rivers, remember! From Latin *cognatus* ("of common descent") from assimilated form of *com* ("together") and *gnatus*, the past participle of gnasci, older form of *nasci* ("to be born," "give birth, beget"), it is to be "allied by blood, connected or related by birth, of the same parentage, descended from a common ancestor."[22] That is, if they are not bredren, sistren, or bristers, our cognates are at least kissing cousins. Etymologically, *cognizance* (or *cognoscence*) refers at least to queer kith, if not kinfolk. The "knowledge, act or state of knowing," deriving from the Latin *cognoscere* ("to get to know, recognize"), it is likewise from *com* ("together") and *gno-* ("to know"). And are we not invested in knowing one another—our kin and kith? Of course, I am thinking of Jacqui (Alexander) here—insisting, after her friend Audre, that we invest in *knowing each other's histories*. What might Jacqui make of this mess? I wonder (but never asked her. I was too embarrassed by the whole affair). Now understood to mean "knowledge by observation or notice, understanding, information," to perhaps take this too far: *recognizance* is, from the French, "a bond acknowledging some obligation binding one over to do some particular act." That is, recognition—acknowledgment—provides the conditions for a bond that requires (ethical) action. We have heard this song before: "First, we must recognize each other," Audre insists, "in the fierceness of this now. . . ."[23] Thomas (Glave) told Essex-in-the-ether, those of us in the room, and you dear reader, all at once: "It is exactly the radical art and life-effort of conscientious remembrance that, against revisionism's erasures and in pursuit of *our* survival, must better become *our* duty. Memory in this regard becomes responsibility; as responsibility and memory both become *us*."[24] However, the rub is evidenced by my emphatic italicization of those pesky, vexing, sometimes personal and other times collective pronouns: *we, our, us*. All of this depends on how one understands who is included in *we, our, us*.

First, We Must Recognize Each Other

As we proceed upon the specific and difficult tasks of survival in the twenty-first century, we of the African Diaspora need to recognize our differences as well as our similarities. . . . We seek what is most fruitful for all people, and less hunger for our children. But we are not the same. . . . To successfully battle the many faces of institutionalized racial oppression, we must share the strengths of each other's vision as well as the weaponries born of particular experience. First, we must recognize each other.

—AUDRE LORDE, "SHOWING OUR TRUE COLORS"

In "Grenada Revisited: An Interim Report," first published by the journal *Black Scholar* in a special issue on the US invasion of Grenada, Audre Lorde writes that "the first time that I came to Grenada, I came seeking 'home' for this was my mother's birthplace and she had always defined it so for me."[25] But her first trip was not to the colony her mother had left nearly two generations before. Her first trip found revolutionary Grenada—just eleven months after the March 1979 triumph of the New Jewel Movement and the installation of the People's Revolutionary Government led by Maurice Bishop. "The second time," she reports, was soon after the extralegal invasion of the tiny island by US troops, merely four years later, on October 25, 1983, ordered by Ronald Reagan under the ruse of protecting medical students and other US citizens. For a more contemporary reference of "borrowed sameness," think fruitless searches for Iraqi WMDs and megaton bombings of empty Syrian barracks. But, it is Audre's understanding of recognition and her position *as a relative* in Grenada that we turn to for instruction here. She writes: "Grenada is their country. I am only a relative. I must listen long and hard and ponder the implications . . . or be guilty of the same quick arrogance of the US government in believing there are external solutions to Grenada's future."[26]

Audre "came in mourning and fear. . . . [Grenada] had been savaged, invaded, its people maneuvered into saying thank you to their invaders."

Connecting the 1983 US invasion of Grenada to the not-so-distant national memory of catastrophic defeat in Vietnam and racialized political unrest at home in the United States, she asks: "How better to wipe out the bitter memories of national defeat by Yellow people than with restoration of power in the eyes of the American public—the image of American Marines splashing through a little Black blood?"[27] Note how she nimbly shifts geographies, calling out connections so often ignored or obscured by other observers:

> In addition to being a demonstration to the Caribbean community of what will happen to any country that dares to assume responsibility for its own destiny, the invasion of Grenada also serves as a naked warning to thirty million African Americans. Watch your step. We did it to them down there and we will not hesitate to do it to you . . . the tactics for quelling a conquered people. No courts, no charges, no legal process. Welfare, but no reparations. . . .[28]

Here is an example of a relative who travels to visit often, then stays. Several years later, Audre's detailed reportage of disaster in the aftermath of Hurricane Hugo's 1989 devastation of the "US territory" of St. Croix, Virgin Islands, is distinct in part because here she writes as a "local" (not a native), bearing up against the manmade effects of a "natural" disaster. A close-up witness to the Anthropocene, she presciently writes: "And the next time you think choosing a rub-on deodorant instead of an aerosol is the only thing you can do to make a difference, just feel what kind of ecological violence it does to hurl forty tons of revolving plutonium up into the sky over our heads and call it scientific progress, which is what the U.S.A. has just done. In our name. With our money. And remember Hurricane Hugo."[29] On day three post-Hugo, Audre's report is eerily akin to eyewitness accounts of the aftermaths of hurricanes Harvey, Irene, and Maria (in Barbuda, Puerto Rico, and throughout the Caribbean); and of Katrina, in a New Orleans in which defective levees broke, causing massive death and destruction in Black communities of the Lower 9th Ward; and of 2010 post-earthquake and post-flood Haiti. There is more to say about how regarding one another via an ethic of intersubjectivity requires willingness *to see* that both includes and extends beyond our own breached levees and lack of (electrical) power, no matter the terrains we inhabit. For now, hear this:

> The promised help is a long time in coming. On the third day, the navy and the gunboats arrive in St. Croix. U.S. Marshals with M-16s they shove into anybody's face at the first hint of any disagreement with any of their orders. Army Military Police, Army Transport planes with command vehicles and

armored trucks, but no blankets, no cots, no emergency rations. . . . And think about the 60 percent of the rest of the world that live like this much of their lives. Some of whom still show up in the morning clean and well-combed and smiling at counters and kitchens every day in Johannesburg and New Delhi and Antigua and Tunica, Mississippi. . . . Day Fifteen. "Drawn guns": Holding old women at gunpoint in the airport, chatting with girls on the beach. St. Croix begins to remind me more and more of Grenada, 1983, another U.S. invasion of a Caribbean island.[30]

The long-awaited help that those whose noncitizen status or condition is underscored by lack of attention and criminalization of their subjectivities and needs is not only evident in the spectacularity of military invasion and disaster. AIDS, cancer, and violence had already begun their still-unrelenting assault on Black gay folks.

Relatively Out of Place

To be sure, it was more than personal heritage and study in Revolutionary/Special Period Cuba that conditioned my insistence on cognate relations with my research respondents, colleagues, and friends. I still believe that my incorrigible friends, and perhaps Brackette, rely too heavily on "critical analytic methods which privilege the nation-state and 'national' culture as . . . object[s] for comparative analysis" as opposed to, for example, the sort of Black-cosmopolitan outlook of my Brooklyn-born father, whose celebration of Black transnational cognizance I walk with as an anthropologist, traveler, and political subject.[31] To recognize common "culture" or cultural connectivity only within a specifically demarcated territory or limited to nation-state borders is incommensurable with notions of diaspora, pan-Africanism, and transnational blackness, as Charles Taylor argues in his "incorrigibility thesis."[32] It militates against what Michael (Hanchard) has aptly named "Afro-Modernity" and against my pan-African-minded father's gleeful recitation of the similarities between collard greens and *callaloo*; rice and peas, peas and rice; *bolinhos*, fish cakes, *bacalitos*, and fritters; along with his pride in my fluency and fluidity when the record changes from funk to calypso to salsa. Quarrelsome, incorrigible—and most of all, upsetting to my own possessive investment in a vision of my own cosmopolitan "Black Black Black" selfhood—the email I received from my friends posed me as if I were easily collapsible into or "not merely indistinguishable, but interchangeable" with Western projects and their disciplinary functionaries.[33] *Cha!*

Perhaps they are right. In any case, my "too bright" friends' critique is good to think with. Perhaps it is the very act of building one's career around asking questions of another (even one's cognate) that is perforce "internationalist," "disturbing," and "insulting" (their words) or at least dominating or assuming authority in ways that had not been previously agreed upon.[34] This points to a fundamental epistemological problem in the project of *decolonizing anthropology*, practiced by globetrotting Black researchers who are overwhelmingly from the North and largely middle class. "They"—our erstwhile cognates in the global South—can interpellate "us" as *gringos* even as "our" very reason for being *over there* (mostly uninvited) is to explore connections and demonstrate our willingness to be led to align with their projects, on which our own projects depend, and to foment (at least) collective recognizance. For recognition not only of our academic research and expressive culture, but in service of a larger political project of Afro-modernity. My critics were certainly correct to point out that my project (not just this book, but my larger intellectual commitment) reflects a Black framework looking for and finding resonance worldwide. You may turn me in to the Blackacademic authorities, dear reader! Or you may attempt to resign my analysis to the dustbin of "essentialism." But this would be an egregious misreading, capitulating to the tired, banal antiblackness that pervades academic discourse. This Black/gay habit of mind—to be Black in a way that recognizes skinfolk (not always as kinfolk, perhaps, but still *holding*) and incites or recruits cognoscence—is a political choice. Although elements of this are reflected, albeit in different ways, both in reparative and revindicationist streams of the Black intellectual tradition, it more precisely emerges from a radical Black lesbian feminist politics of recognition and the dogged attempt to reconstruct and repair "home."

Like Brackette, I expected that difference would be a challenge to maneuver throughout my multisited and multilingual research. But in contrast, my Black gay habit of understanding of difference as something to expect, honor, and explore had led me to understand that the differences between us could become points of productive conversation. I do not wish to "blur the intersections" as the "Yorùbá" pilgrim Kamari (Clarke) famously recounts in the preface to her *Mapping Yorùbá Networks*. You may recall that upon the triumphant Lagos arrival of a delegation from South Carolina's Òyótúnjí Village, one Òyótúnjí chief enthusiastically greets an inquisitive young Nigerian (Ègbá Yorùbá) child with "I'm from here . . . but a long time ago. . . ." Kamari says that the child, "pointing to [the chief's] light brown face and glancing at his clothing, [retorts] 'you are not Black like me. . . . Mama says you are a visitor, òyìnbó.'"[35] Children are among the sharpest critics and interlocutors! Recall, again, the Black Brazilian boy who claimed Thomas's face as his own (minha cara) and Fanon's disgusted and intrigued little French girl. Unlike the chief, whose faiths (in Ifa divination and in a certain brand of pan-Africanism) convince him and impel his appeal to the incredulous child to believe "we are the same," this witness/sojourner/scribe—your author—claims no sameness or Zionistic fervor for "return." Still, I must also part company for "a piece of the way" with a large cross-section of my Blackacademic kin who desire, following deconstructionist theory, to "explode all of the categories having to do with the very notion of 'Black community' and all of the inclusions and exclusions that come along with it."[36] I would rather engage in the conversation, in the struggle within the messy sticky space of what some of us still think of as Black community (among our other messy, sticky, contested affinities). Perhaps naively, and certainly contradictorily, I am unwilling to sacrifice what I have observed and experience as Black community/ies.

Audre's position had been that she was a "relative" to the Grenadians who were embroiled in their own fight, which was theirs to define and determine. We are not the same. I am not my sister. We must seek to know one another and find the productive parts of our interdependent differences. This bears repeating: "First, we must recognize each other."[37] I confess some consternation at how nearly completely the radical Black lesbian feminist praxis of working across differences within and beyond what they constantly reaffirmed as a dynamic Black community has fallen so nearly completely out of scholarly discourse since the ascension of elite Blackademe.[38] However, this complex, messy, sticky, interdependent, anthological stance of Black/queer-polity should not be categorized as merely one of alliance in which we have no personal-political investment. Nor should it be understood as necessarily altruistic or motivated by racial affect alone. Following Melvin Dixon, we ought not "mistakenly separate feeling from form and from their essential interaction. . . ."[39] Melvin was talking specifically about art and culture, to which we will turn again soon, but the lesson is more broadly applicable to transnational Black linkages. For Audre, this was not an altruistic position, one motivated only by heritable connections or good politics/ethics, but also because "self-preservation demands [it] . . . we gays and lesbians of color at a time in [this] country's history when its domestic and international policies, as well as its posture toward those nations with which we share heritage are so reactionary, must involve ourselves actively in those policies and postures."[40] That is, pointing out what she called the "borrowed sameness" of the strategies of empire: "the tactics for quelling (any) conquered people. No courts, no charges, no legal process. Welfare, but no reparations. . . ."[41] Incorrigibility would insist that we understand macheted gay men in Jamaican, raped South African lesbians, slaughtered Black (and) Latinx transwomen, dismembered Black gay men, exposed and neutralized bisexual politicians (and more) in the United States, and wrongly convicted queer Martiniquais in France, for example, as discrete occurrences to be understood only in particularized local contexts. This version of disaffiliation seems to reflect shallow analysis as well as shallow empathy.

Michael (Hanchard) suggests that we focus on "the production of locality"[42]—in other words, how hegemonic readings of historical and contemporary structuration construct a place as an "authentic" space complete with people who are naturalized as belonging, and of course others who are not and never could be. This is another shade of the healthy intellectual suspicion of "community" that Dwight (McBride) has argued. How might the position(s) of my friends, keeping the gate of what is and what is not acceptable in their region, shift if they were also asked to do some homework? Have my friends accepted the "US as a homology . . . superced[ing the] cultural, political, or ideological positions and distinctions" of (albeit "removed") Caribbean heritage, blackness, progressive politics, and our friendly acquaintance over many years?[43] There are classic contradictions here, of course, and much context and baggage that we will not unpack at the moment. It would have been productive to discuss, for example, whether—and if so under what conditions—there could ever be a translocal project in which people who do not live in the region (or do not currently live in the region) could participate, or to which they might provide/leverage resources. Would this be inherently "unlocal"? Remember that Jacqui famously revealed how vulnerabilities with respect to state power are intersectional, compounded, complex, and dynamic: "I am an outlaw in my country of birth: a national; but not a citizen," at once local and transnational.[44] Can this Black/queer time-space also become a fertile interstice for the constitution of new affinities and communities of support among gender and sexual "outlaws" across borders?

I am aware that some may accuse me of "fall[ing] prey to the conventions of race discourse" because of my (re)deployment of what many critics in the 1990s argued were essentializing gestures. To wit, this may also be a disciplinary conceit.[45] That the representation of lived cultural experience, so-called identity politics, and the discipline of anthropology all came under scrutiny during the long 1980s is no coincidence. Modernist regimes were rightly under revision and called into question ("called to the carpet" and asked to "come to Jesus!"). Still, the postmodern turn—falling perhaps too squarely on the French side of discursive deconstructive critique, rather than a brand of Marxist-inflected British critical cultural studies that accents experience and material analysis—often goes too far beyond the concrete experience of those who can least afford wholly "academic" criticism. One can speak from a particular "standpoint" or epistemic privilege or authority without claiming the mantle of official spokesperson or singular authority, or attempting to disprove or degrade other points of view. Can we not? What might we gain from thinking about all of this through sincere solidary politics rather than "authenticity" or localness? What else do we need to consider? What else is there to know or draw from contemporary archives of the living? Recently, Ryan (Jobson) and I opined that "decolonization is not what it used to be" and that the "West" "cannot be reduced to what it claims to be."[46] This asserts a political and intellectual point of view that is neither mainstream anthropological nor "native anthropology" per se. We wrote that as anthropologists we cannot passively or innocently exit the project of the West, yet we can generatively *disidentify* with it, as José (Esteban Muñoz) would say.[47] The social worlds and theoretical perspectives of Black folk from the crucible of "the West"—whom Faye (Harrison) has called "outsiders within"— provide a rich conceptual tool kit to apprehend the present epoch of capitalist proliferation and ecological crisis.[48] What I had hoped to add to the conversation with my critics runs parallel to this argument. That is, the assertion that my "mixed" US Black American and Caribbean heritage, elite academic training, political activism, and location and experience in Black/ queer communities might prove to be valuable in transnational conversation about the best ways to negotiate these "crises" (not the authoritative one and certainly not the only one). Perhaps understandably, however, when we North America–based academics and fieldworkers speak, many of our potential cognates or kinfolk (or "sisters and brothers") see only a ventriloquist act: US capital in the shape of the university, holding us firmly in its lap.

Perhaps it is therefore appropriate, and politically and intellectually generative, that all this goes with the territory. Had I asked, João (Vargas) certainly would have counseled me to not take on the anthropological mantle and its rattling white bones, and not to take my friendship crisis personally. I should have called him. He would not have framed the issue as one of sincerity, authenticity, translation, stranger's value, or repair, but as one of politics. To see this as a political issue, to be engaged head-on through self-critique and dialogue. Observant participation had, at first, found João regarded as a long-haired paper collector of indeterminate race and nationality among his neighbors in South Central Los Angeles. Perhaps a measure of his sincerity proved him not only (politically) Black to his friends, bandmates, collaborators, and neighbors, but, more specifically and pointedly, the evidence of his politics was demonstrated by working with the Coalition against Police Abuse and the care he showed this group.[49] Perhaps my friendship crisis and translational errors would have been different if I could have hewn closer to Ted's (Edmund T. Gordon's) activist stance. Certainly, more time and depth "in the field" might have more easily mitigated our clash rather than the decidedly "airplane" methods I had engaged in this project: moving quickly from one place to another and dashing off emails and drafts between teaching, publishing, and living my life, rather than languid liming or loud quarrels resolved by the day to day of life in proximity (as if my far-flung colleagues were not also likewise moving from here to there). Explicitly political in its intention and engagement with racialized Sandinista revolutionary policies and working daily for ten years on issues surrounding the everyday struggles of his neighbors, friends, and (eventually) family members in Bluefields, Nicaragua, Ted's context is different from those of us who traveled to pursue research questions as students or professionals. His "goals in Bluefields were to live as part of the community and to contribute to a political process"—as many of us sometimes claim reflectively but not as an original intention: "not to produce a commodified ethnographic account of the 'Other.'"[50] Therefore, his work was already one kind of *home* work, not typical "fieldwork." Still, Ted admits that his "head full of agendas" was shaped before he arrived—at first by his biracial Black Marxist upbringing and Black consciousness, which encouraged him to arm himself with practical skills to offer revolutionary struggle (in his case, as a fisheries expert). But he was also at first simultaneously "strange . . . and dangerous" to the Nicaraguans who would have to authorize his stay.[51] I too was/am strange, if not dangerous. Ensconced at a boutique hotel or Air BnB. Flying in for a short time for conversations that sought to canvass class, gender, and sexual subjects, while moving on to the next text, the next archive (and finally to the next essay, in which no problematic indicting, too-bright, back-chatting subjects appear).

10 Unfinished Work

I want to start an organization
to save my life.
...
I'm not concerned
about the attire of a soldier.
All I want to know
for my own protection
is are we capable
of whatever
whenever.
—ESSEX HEMPHILL, "FOR MY OWN PROTECTION"

BEGINNING IN THE 1970s, violence against women increased and went un-investigated or unsolved in urban areas such as Boston, precipitating the organizing of the Combahee River Collective and other groups. In South Africa the focus of Black activists was, understandably, ending apartheid, but without serious consideration of gender and sexuality before the emergence of leaders such as Simon Nkoli and Bev Ditsie, who fought on several fronts—against apartheid, against heterosexism in the anti-apartheid movement, and against racism within the gay and lesbian movement—toward a future liberation that no one else had articulated before. Jamaicans founded a freedom movement in 1977, claiming both gay existence since the Arawak and certain victory, with the resolution that it will require "a very long road." Soon after, Black Brazilians reanimated their inheritance of *quilombismo* to re-narrate a Black LGBT presence and *presente*.[1] Black gay is from the future because it must be. By the early 1980s, it was already *after the end of the world*. Once the HIV/AIDS pandemic began its unrelenting assault on Black communities, Black gay and bisexual men, Black lesbians, trans folks, and allies exponentially intensified the necessary work to save their own lives. There were no specific services to which Black trans, bisexuals, gays, and lesbians could turn—in the Americas or any other place in the world—before Black trans, bisexuals, gays, and lesbians did it for themselves. Neoconservatism emerged as a global conglomerate with the elections of Margaret Thatcher in the UK and Ronald Reagan in the US. Crack began its assault in Miami and spread throughout the United States and the world. As Marcus (Lee) offers, "The 1980s is often theorized as a period of Black political declination and deinstitutionalization—as a tragic lack—but, this view is tenable only if the framing excludes Black transgender, lesbian, bisexual, and gay male activists."[2] This is the context in which we should understand the reconstitution of Black communities and Black scholarship, here and there. US historians may continue to think of the period between the so-called Reconstruction era and World War I as the nadir of "race relations" in the United States, but if we look more closely at relations *between* Black people, we will see that the long 1980s represents a break that is likewise historically significant. As Cathy (Cohen)'s title avers, Black politics, as it was understood then, had reached "breakdown." The boundaries of what Black folks had taken for granted, identified by Michael Dawson as "linked fate"[3]—the understanding that Black political ideology and behavior remain consistent across class and other difference, the interests of each partisan of the group "linked" by the effects of racism and internal cohesion—were tested, and it failed to disastrous ends that we are still working through today.[4] Scholars have inadequately framed the question of contemporary Black politics, in large part because they have refused to account for the moment at which the frameworks of the past were ruptured and subsequently reconstituted by Black gay (lesbian, gay, bisexual, and transgender) activists, artists, and organizations. Cathy's signal work, *The Boundaries of Blackness: AIDS and the Breakdown of Black Politics,* empirically chronicles the consequences of this in the United States. But still, the intransigence persists, at great peril—

intellectually and materially. "You cannot go to your future, girl . . ."—Kevin
Aviance has already told us this—with a poor sense of historicity. We have
learned that we cannot depend upon politics that announces itself as Black,
any more than politics that announces itself as queer, to liberate us. Have
we not also learned that traditional disciplinary modes and attachments are
also inadequate to the urgent work still ahead of us?[5] Drawing both from
social science research and her experience working within organizations, including what would become the Audre Lorde Project, Cathy has incisively
challenged the "limits of the lesbian and gay political agenda based on a Civil
Rights strategy where assimilation into and replication of dominant institutions are the goals."[6] Moreover, she has incisively argued that traditional
modes of Du Boisian Black studies will have to be supplemented, and also
supplanted in some ways, by new research agendas.[7]

Today the stakes are, literally, life and death for African (descended) nonheteronormative and gender-variant individuals. But also it seems clear that
the project of creating an autonomous Black gay "political direction and
agenda" seems to have stalled out. This is a grave matter for me and many
fellow travelers. But barely a shrug registers for most folks. And we have not
defined whether a transnational agenda covering all of the ways homosexual, bisexual, transgender, gender-variant, gay, non-gender-conforming, lesbian, two-spirit, same-gender-loving . . . folks identify themselves in various
languages, and hold a number of ways of being and identifying as Black, is a
useful goal to aspire to reach. *Alluh* this—the far-flung locales and (dis)affilia-
tions, the shrugs, high stakes, and low investments, et cetera—leave us with
huge theoretical quandaries, nettlesome political problems, and ethical conundrums. Additionally, because I have committed to tell this story, for me
this constitutes a narrative challenge. Many of the scenes and many of the
people who made the still-significant long-1980s fierce have already passed,
of course. My preoccupation, pace Morrison, is that it seems they have also
been *passed on* in too many ways. Here, again, we invoke this "middle" moment at which Black gay explicitly emerges as belonging irreducibly to its
time, but exceeding this temporality. In the face of compounded vulnerabilities, yes: "against revisionism's erasures and in pursuit of our survival."[8]

You may think of the following conversation as a sort of ethnographic
glimpse of the current moment, pushing closer to our ambition to be "fluent
in each other's histories" and conversant in each other's freedom dreams,
dear reader.[9] Alternatively, you may choose to think of this as I did when
I began this research many years ago: *whither Black LGBTQ movement?* Having already demonstrated in previous chapters that the lack of an organized,

broad-based, global Black/queer political *movement* does not constitute a lack of Black/queer *politics*, this chapter follows a few still-unfolding far-flung political dramas, strategies, and imaginaries through various peregrinations, many of which appear fruitful and all of which are fraught. Our conversation takes us to the Caribbean—Guyana and Trinidad and Tobago—where activists are shaping a new agenda with familiar politics and affect. Then, we turn to East Africa, where we meditate on Afropolitanism, pan-Africanism, and the resolve to "free our imaginations." Engaging this juxtaposed transnational framework, as opposed to a formal "comparison" or "case study" in which the narrator's disciplinary expertise neatly solves what folks on the ground struggle with daily, may allow us to see in ways that "incorrigible" national discourses occlude. Before addressing this contemporary work, however, we necessarily turn to another re-narration: proposing possible futures through looking back closely at the long 1980s to reconsider the politics of Black gay movement in the United States. Recall that Jacqui has warned us that "crossings are never undertaken all at once or once and for all." This set of conversations crisscrosses danger and desires that we have visited previously.[10]

"For the embattled," radical thought and practice are indispensable to the project of staying alive with a bit of integrity, even with our myriad contradictions and challenges. There is no replacement for this, and reform will never be enough for those of us who live, barely, on the diminishing piers, bottoms, and gullies of the margin's margins. Before moving further in this meditation on our unfinished work, let me borrow the crystalline directness of the first generation of radical Black Lesbian feminist sistren whose work catalyzed the long 1980s: revolution is necessary for total liberation. And/but I hear the reminder that there is no Sierra Maestra in the urban United States. There is certainly no dense forest cover in the tony shops of Cape Town, the housing schemes of les banlieue, the archive or museum, the foundation, the press, the journal, or the university—although each can and must be transformed to foment greater humanity and higher consciousness. Toward these futures we ask ourselves: Why are we here? What sort of moment is this, now?

Another Dangerous Crossing

The evaporation of an autonomous Black gay "political direction and agenda" is multilayered, and some of the factors leading to this have become apparent only with the marvelous arithmetic of time and distance. Word on the (academic) street seems to be that the Black lesbian and gay movement and HIV/AIDS organizations of the long 1980s diminished in size, stature, and relevance because of the failure of "identity politics," the success of the mainstream gay rights movement, and better HIV/AIDS medications and combinations of medications that make HIV a manageable chronic disorder for people who can afford or otherwise have access to adequate medical care.[11] Although these factors are important, this view is incomplete. Global political-economic shifts that resulted in regentrification of urban space, the continuation of post–civil rights desegregation and concomitant disintegration of Black community spaces, and relatively easy access to communication technologies such as smartphone apps for dating and hookups (mitigating the need for gathering *at the club* and other places of communion), at the same time that heterosexual spaces became less exclusionary, have also all played important roles. Still, the fading of Black gay movement owes also to a failure of political imagination, as HIV/AIDS prevention work became its driver instead of one of the central objectives. The popular Silicon Valley metaphor of *building an airplane while in flight* begins to describe the context of wider Black gay movement and HIV/AIDS prevention and care in the long 1980s. However, hewing closer to the truth—imagine the genius necessary to build your aircraft while under rapid attack from the air and the ground. Your pilot, engineers, and navigators are dying, some after periods of painful disability and others very suddenly. Many onboard await their turn. The mission shifts. Soon, memory of how to build the craft is lost. The navigation becomes unclear: was there any point other than to become airborne?

AIDS policy and prevention advocates, many of them Black gay men, had not adequately examined the consequences of conflating the movement paradigm with (federally and charitably funded) AIDS prevention and shifting the focus to pathology and risk—rather than on more capacious radical formulations and dreams that had been offered by Joe, Essex, Assotto, and Marsha, for example, and the Black feminist lesbians from whom they learned and drew inspiration.[12] And these visions also require refinement and contextualization. As romantic and beautiful the initial step is, for example, we can now see that "Black men loving Black men" as an "autonomous agenda" can be carried out only within the context of a wider (intellectual, artistic, and activist) movement framework—like any other revolutionary paradigm. Recalling Pat's polite questioning of Black gay men's politics in not advocating for universal health care and our absence in fights against cancer, I wonder, What if? And, perhaps more usefully, What else? What have we forgotten or disavowed? AIDS services organizations (ASOS) "blew up" in size and support by the height of the long 1980s, and/but this is a good description of the unintended consequences of the shift from consciousness raising and political action to primarily HIV/AIDS prevention education and AIDS services. The nineties saw vast improvement from a few years earlier, when there were no viable treatment options. As a volunteer at AID Atlanta and Gay Men of African Descent (GMAD) in the early 1990s, I participated in "safer-sex" education and "outreach" to promote individual and group efficacy toward wellness and to decrease panic. This work is worthy and necessary. Had I arrived earlier, during the beginning of "the plague years," I hope that I would have had the courage and the stamina to fight and work as hard as many of my epidemic-dead brothers and sisters, and the living (still here), who fought and worked to stay alive and to save the lives of others.

Still, I am convinced by the evidence that Marcus Lee has marshaled, showing that early Black gay AIDS policy and prevention advocates authored an expedient but also potentially debilitating model, in which Black men who have sex with men (MSM) form the center of an exceptionally unruly tangle of pathology and HIV/AIDS vulnerability.[13] This is not easy. We are having this conversation toward helping to refine both how we fight *and for what*. From the late 1990s, for example, HIV testing became the holy grail—its public health intention to "identify and treat" meant to lower the collective viral load of particularly hard-hit places and reduce incidence of seroconversion. The sociocultural context of success—dramatically lowered HIV viral load of San Francisco, for example—ought to give us pause. This public health triumph is not just about new treatments, patient adherence, and the city's enviable HIV-care infrastructure. It is also a result of the dramatic rise in cost of living and aggressive policies pushing working-class and poor Black and other people of color—whose incidence of HIV is higher and whose access to treatment is lower and less dependable—out of the city.

In her *Virtual Equality: The Mainstreaming of Gay and Lesbian Liberation*, Urvashi Vaid extends Cathy's critical question—"What is this movement doing to my politics?"—likewise warning of the "mainstreaming" of the larger (read: largely white) LGBT and queer liberation movements, and advocating for the need to reach beyond what she termed "virtual equality."[14] Urvashi shows that the success of the larger LGB rights movement ("T" excluded here to reflect historical accuracy) is indicative of the appeal of "pragmatic politics: instead of doing the right thing, movements like ours do the expedient thing. . . ." The larger gay and lesbian movement made at least four strategic choices in the long 1980s that shape our current conjuncture: "degaying, desexualizing, and de-coupling AIDS-specific reforms from systemic reform and direct action. We used short-term, quick fix strategies that yielded dramatic but short-lived gains. As a consequence, we failed to tackle the underlying problems that still exacerbate the epidemic; the problems of homophobia and heterosexism, racism, sexism, classism and the dictates of a profit-driven health care system."[15] It is not my intention to compare the larger gay and lesbian rights movement's precipitous rightward shift to the stalling of (the) Black gay movement. Still, they are historically and ideologically related and entangled. Black HIV/AIDS activism reflects Urvashi's insightful assertion and proves Cathy's point about the need to distinguish progressive politics and movement praxis and to inaugurate a new (research) agenda. Crisis management must not be confused with movement agenda, political analysis, or good progressive scholarship, but the former can easily supplant each of these latter intentions. Focusing on expediency, Black gay men who led Black HIV/AIDS activism fashioned and perpetuated a notion of a particular and specific *Black homophobia* (rather than, for example, systemic racialized capitalist patriarchal heterosexism). They argued that this results in a pathological self-concept among Black men that leads to failure to comply with protective sexual behaviors during sex with men and nondisclosure of their sexual behaviors and history (and identity) with women sex partners, finding Black women to be unwitting victims of a reputedly rapacious mendacity. This is another iteration of Moynihan's "tangle of pathology" thesis, warmed over. A wide range of media promoted this idea in the long 1980s until it became our commonsense understanding of Black AIDS. Marcus's work on how Black men who have sex with men became subjects of—and *through*—social science and policy, and what Black gay men advocated as agents of policy and knowledge production, argues that this articulation of pathology/vulnerability, and the epistemic privilege of a vanguard of Black gay men to address it, was invented by Black gay men themselves. In any case, this proved to be a winning formulation—a successful tool for raising funds toward caring for people with HIV/AIDS and preventing more infections.[16]

By the 1990s, a brain drain ensued from on-the-ground movement work and artistry to other areas of endeavor. Some that had not existed, or had not been accessible, before the onset of the AIDS crisis, such as middle- and upper-level administration of ASOs, HIV outreach, education and public health positions, and academe. Your author is no exception. Sometimes, in the throes of crisis, essential questions go begging: What do we stand for? What sort of world do we envision? What sort of organizations, institutions, art, and individuals do we envision inhabiting this new world beyond this moment of crisis? What should each of us do to contribute, and where/how? Instructions from the ether show us ways forward, reminding us, as members of the Combahee River Collective quipped from a protest placard, "We cannot live without our lives." Please reconsider, for example, Pat Parker's questioning of the (bourgeois, or merely pragmatic?) politics of Black gay leadership evidenced by the narrow pursuit of increased funding for HIV and AIDS care within the established system and not for universal health care or socialized medicine. The former, of course, provides access to care only within existing so-called "free-market" structures of capitalism, in which some states or municipalities may offer those without financial resources life-sustaining medication if they qualify and can maintain the stamina to withstand what Dana-Ain Davis has, in the context of the (former) welfare system, called bureaucratic "ceremonies of degradation."[17] HIV/AIDS is necessarily suffused throughout our discussion of "an organization to save our lives." It is structuring even when not explicit and even though HIV is hardly the only monster currently stalking Black folks. Colin Robinson, who provides time-space traveling context, said:

> In my view, HIV has enabled or influenced much of the sexual rights work happening contemporarily. Its role has been to vastly expand public and institutional discourse about sexuality, to highlight homosexuals as a social group experiencing enhanced stigma and discrimination and to legitimate us as a target for strategic social and health programming. In the midyears of the pandemic, HIV emboldened GLBT advocates and created a sense of urgency and priority for both advocacy and sexuality, and helped strengthen sexual communities. HIV and HIV funding have helped give voice, infrastructure, access and often a framework or meaning to GLBT organizing and social activity. This has been the case in Trinidad and Tobago.

An undisputed leader in this realm in the United States during what he calls "midyears of the pandemic" and now having returned to the Caribbean, where, like much of the world, local LGBTQ organizing had focused largely on HIV among men who have sex with men and the creation of male social space, Colin notes that

> HIV has also had a distorting effect on MSM and GLBT community self-concept and priorities. HIV, its dominant discourse and the resources that follow it reframe organic community organizing, the nature of leadership and the substance of programmes and advocacy. MSM, and to an extent GLBT people, are seen primarily in terms of an infectious, disabling and stigmatising disease, and the legitimacy of GLBT representation, resource allocation and the decriminalisation of GLBT desire is justified in terms of disease, and often of preventing its costs or transmission to the population

at large, instead of in terms of the humanity or worth of GLBT people, the value of sexual autonomy or the legitimacy of desire and sexual pleasure.

CAISO (Coalition Advocating Sexual Orientation Inclusion), the Trinbagonian organization he currently helps to lead and to which we will soon turn, has been routinely called on by virtue of its being a GLBT group that engages with policy and planning issues related to HIV, and he says that the group has done so with ambivalence, recognizing the importance of "transforming HIV discourse to one which centres at first stigma, discrimination and vulnerability but ultimately autonomy and self-efficacy as core facets of sexual health." Still, it has also felt the need to push against the distorting and reductive impact of HIV on resource allocation, attention, and imagination with regard to other GLBT concerns and policy issues.

In 2012, after Cathy and Urvashi's fears had been borne out, Kenyon Farrow observed another "definite political move to the right by the LGBT equality movement, as well as the new alliance of national mainstream [read: white] LGBT organizations, Republican lawmakers, right-wing think tanks, and donors" that had been slowly coming together since the end of the long 1980s and emerged—or *metastasized*—during the centrist "gay-friendly" Obama administration.[18] I hear Audre warning of this future/tense in 1995: "And if we lose, someday women's blood will congeal upon a dead planet. If we win, there is no telling."[19] Who are the winners and losers today? What and who constitutes *we*? Citing the New York state same-sex marriage legislation, Kenyon argues that it was

> largely won by wealthy hedge fund managers and Tea Party sympathizers, who raised money for four Republican state legislators to provide the votes to ensure its passage. . . . Many of the gay donors who raise money, even for LGBT equality organizations, are "progressives" only because of marriage, and actually do not support most of what the rest of us would call a left agenda . . . (single-payer health care system, collective bargaining, public education, an end to massive imprisonment, reproductive justice, etc.). . . . But whatever we think about the mainstream equality movement, it is almost finished with its agenda, and thank goodness. Most of the policy issues that the mainstream LGB movement has made the central focus of its agenda are already won.[20]

This situation not only set the stage for the disastrous election of 2016 but also conditioned current lukewarm political opposition to the steady incremental rollbacks of these recent victories: their "cremation" or "evisceration,"

Melvin might say.[21] Summarizing the work of the New Queer Agenda editorial collective, Kenyon noted the inescapable out-of-timeness of the work of making good Black gay sense of dynamically reiterative, but also sometimes surprising and relatively rapidly shifting politics on the ground:

> When we began working on this collection, we were still in the midst of the Bush era . . . there was a sense of urgency at the time about articulating the limitations of single-issue politics and the focus on legislation and policy change as the sole path towards queer liberation. But, as this collection articulates, many queer and trans radicals critique the mainstream LGBT movement not just as a difference of form, but as *an actual dispute over essence*. . . . This collection represents a collective roar to the open skies: Can't we do better than equality?[22]

It is this "actual dispute over essence" that we likewise undertake here. Having achieved the "virtual equality" Urvashi warned against, some LGB organizations based in the North seemed to operate on the premise that systemic homophobia "at home" had been neutralized. It is as if these liberal advances and the abatement of AIDS deaths among urban, well-resourced, gay white men heralded their arrival to their full complement of citizenship. Mission accomplished. Therefore, we would be wise to attend to Cathy's more recent provocation about the rightward shift and attendant "performative solidarity" of gay rights groups in the wake of a series of video evidence of Black people being murdered by police and other vigilantes. These extrajudicial executions of a mounting list of Black girls, boys, women, and men in the US, the UK, and elsewhere; and the political assassination of Rio de Janeiro legislator Marielle Franco, who was killed allegedly by former police in 2018,[23] do not seem to figure prominently in the *calendar of loss* of the wider US LGBTQ or global gay rights movements beyond "thoughts and prayers" hashtags. Cathy points out that this "performative solidarity" of LGBTQ groups (i.e., statements of support and also frequent, unfortunate, and inaccurate narration of "parallels" between race and sexual identity) belies complicity with the same neoliberal policies that support the fact that "in fact, Black lives do not matter" (to them).[24]

Self-satisfied political insularity is not exclusive to this group, however. Nor is it exceptionally domestic. According to Black European observers and respondents, white neocolonial rescue fantasies in which Asian, Islamic, Latin American, and African (-descended) LGBTQ people are understood only as beneficiaries of the largesse of the European citizen subject who may deign to sponsor or "save" them mark interactions between racial groups. Meanwhile, Black LGBTQI activists in Cuba, the United States, the United

Kingdom, the Caribbean, Brazil, southern Africa, and eastern Africa have demonstrated that access to adequate health care, protection, and political recognition is far from a singularly "cultural" problem to be attributed to race, religion, or ethnicity.[25] These are political-economic issues with complex historical and spatial contexts, which are increasingly transnational. For example, the Southern Poverty Law Center showed that as gay and lesbian rights movements all over the North claimed important legislative, juridical, and cultural victories at the end of the Obama era, organized homophobic backlash and redoubled reactionary efforts intensified in the global South—financed by the erstwhile locally defeated organized foes of the US LGB movement such as fundamentalist Christian groups like Focus on the Family. Thus, the great shame of what some call "Global Gay" "Pride" is not that sisters and brothers in the global South are missing the rainbow-themed party as we parade shirtless and satisfied in the Castro, Le Marais, Soho, or Johannesburg's exclusive Melrose Arch, but that race (class and gender) remain largely unthought in gay international/global gay sexual rights work in local and translocal contexts. Like Black and other people of color in the global North, LGBTQIA folks in the global South struggle for access to adequate health care, education, and protection from violence and other vulnerabilities. However, among the most threatening of these vulnerabilities are often supported by well-heeled US-based fundamentalist Christian groups and the widespread common sense of (white) saviorship in which they traffic. In Nairobi, when I asked a group of East African activists what they would say to an audience of would-be US allies and supporters, one person jokingly said: "White Americans! Christian Americans! Gay Americans! Come get your people!" *Can't we do better than equality?*

In the passages that follow we ask what the most salient desires expressed by Black LGBTQ/SGL (sexual minority and/or gender-non-conforming) individuals and organizations are. How are politics of self—recognition, care, love/friendship, and erotic autonomy—enacted within these organizations and individuals? What are the most formidable obstacles to overcome? *For our own protection.*

Confronting "Homophobia" in Black/Queerpolis

Colin's poem "Unfinished Work" confronts "homophobia" differently than you might expect. He begins this poetic manifesto with memory, invoking a dear childhood friend, Michael, "dropping curtsey to / *Buller.*" The speaker says, "*I remember Michael's / thank you / neutering insult.*"[26] It is not direct conflict with a heterosexist social structure or individual "homophobe" that is at issue here. Rather, the collective, reiterative work of memory, resistance, *maroonage*, and *quilombo* building is the focus and urgent matter in this poetically distilled political philosophy. Quilombos, or Maroon societies, are settlements that the formerly enslaved created for themselves in Brazil that were not only destinations for escapees but also sites from which raids and other forms of opposition and resistance to the institution of slavery and the colonial state were launched. Maroon settlements arose throughout the Americas.[27] In Colin's poem the insult—"darkness of past wounds / . . . heels and / opened holes / of memory" that the speaker invokes later—is (merely) a structuring reality. What the speaker remembers and instructs is protracted, necessary work to "pervert / the language" together. Richly evoking the transnational, translinguistic space of Other Countries Black Gay Men's Writing Collective, rather than a mere one-way, no-return diaspora, like Melvin's poem "And These Are Just a Few," here Colin is "recollective"—remembering relationships, battles, places, and travels between people (and dedicating it "for Zola & for Shawn; for C-FLAG; for Rohan; and for Rohan"). He is also "prospective"—rehearsing what must happen in future (tense):[28]

> And from this quilombo
> I must still return . . .
> . . .
> Que griten
> they will call me
> *maricón*
> shout *buller*
> I will curtsy
> . . . [29]

Marlon Riggs's short film "Affirmation" (1990) also begins unexpectedly: not with a litany of "issues" or fierce righteous indignation, but with Sweet Honey in the Rock singing "Woke Up This Morning with My Mind Stayed on Freedom." Reginald Jackson unfolding a sweet story of sexual initiation. No snaps. No tears. Perched on a brownstone stoop on a sunny day while children play and cars go by, Reginald holds us in his thrall. The charming ordinariness of the story he tells—in a minor key and with a good bit of humor—is a striking complement to the drama and intensity of standard narratives of initiation and (non)belonging, and therefore a very fitting prelude to Marlon's important short film. Reginald's story unfolds under five titles taken from his memorable lines, beginning with "A sensitive man is *terrible* for your nerves," an account of meeting his first sexual partner, followed by "I didn't know if something was going to happen." During the "Lord, you start feeling things that you ain't never felt before!" portion, he says: "I didn't know you could feel these things, [much] less feel them on a regular basis. . . ." The next title, "Penetration is liberation," more explicitly responds to common pejoratives that equate a man being penetrated with "emascula-tion" (which in typical misogynist logic is read as dehumanization). Reginald continues: blushing, sometimes giggling, and other times looking over to the children playing nearby, who are presumably the reason for his coy language:

> At one point . . . feeling certain things, and . . . he sort of flipped one over and one went flying over, and before you knew it, one was experiencing many things of a personal nature! Shock and pain and everything at once. Then it stopped being shock and it stopped being pain . . . and, I think this was a different type of initiation . . . it said yes . . . penetration is liberation.[30]

The penultimate heading is, therefore "Lord, we sang praises to the Lord that day!" Reginald reports rushing to church to sing in his choir after *one was flipped over and experienced many things of a personal nature.* Eager to share his experience, he says to a choir mate who had warned him against this initiation: "It don't hurt. . . ."

"African American Freedom Day, Harlem" is the final heading, and two scenes of "Affirmation" form a climax that mirrors the opening of Colin's "Un-finished Work." A GMAD contingent marches along with African Ancestral Lesbians United for Societal Change (AALUSC), Minority Taskforce against AIDS, and other sibling organizations on a beautiful parade day in Harlem, complete with floats, drill teams, marching bands, and placards of Malcolm, Martin, (Elijah) Mohammad, and Marcus (Garvey) parading in front of ador-ing crowds. AALUSC rhythmically chants, exhorting folks to rise and fight "From Har-lem-to-So-we-to-!" Then, a smiling young man, seemingly sur-prised at the boldness of the GMAD contingent, shouts: "Homos!" Assotto—dressed in a white tank top and black biking shorts, carrying an African liberation flag and backed up by the GMAD contingent—enthusiastically answers this hail, without missing a beat of his dancerly stride. "Yes! Homos!" Assotto says, playfully pointing the small Black Liberation Flag at the young man in emphasis, *"cracking . . . lashing . . . free / like a whip."*[31]

. . .

Llamaron maricones
oímos cimarrones y viniendo

at this quilombo we arrived[32]
from different places
other countries
cities, villages. plantations
bantustans and ghettoes
other colonies and nations
old and new
from strange lands
but not strangers
we carried tongues like oil and
flames of Pentecost
that linked and licked
the darkness of past wounds
and heels and
opened holes
of memory
In passion whispered
buller batty baby
faggot maricón adodi
magic words
. . . [33]

Crowds continue to cheer. "The people / united / will never be defeated!" "We're Black, We're Gay. We won't have it no other way." There are also boos and hisses. Assotto is gazelle-like. Allen (dashing, as usual) chants along with other GMAD brothers: "*We're* Black-Black-Black-Black Gay-Gay-Gay-Gay. *We Won't Have It No Other Way!*" and "Hey-Hey. Ho-Ho: *Homophobia's Got to Go!*" Some, now listening more closely to the GMAD contingent, seem confused by what they are hearing: "*Gay-Gay-Gay-Gay. . . . Homophobia!*" Some continue to cheer. Others giggle or look bemused. Some boo and hiss. Marlon's lens catches one formerly enthusiastic onlooker fold his arms in apparent exasperation. At five minutes and thirty-seven seconds into the film, the march has stopped. Another sidewalk onlooker, whom I will call "Curly hair light-skinned trade," begins rudely yelling over the heads of giggling little girls, bemused elders, and interested, middle-aged Black women with fly 1990s eyewear. These women and girls stand, unwittingly, as a buffer between him and the GMAD contingent on the other side of the parade barricade. "Our children are out here!" Curly shouts. The parade has stopped momentarily, providing a prime opportunity for a standoff in front of the Greater

Refuge Temple on Adam Clayton Powell Boulevard and in the shadow of the Harlem State Office Building. Speaking, it seems, with full authority, as if he is the spokesperson for all African/Afrikan peoples everywhere for all time (ironically, even for those who would deny this brother full membership because of his physical features), Curly breaks the news that he seems at once eager and disheartened to give (there is such a strange look on his face, at once pleading and sardonic). Curly says, definitively, "You are not part of the African tradition!" In reply to GMAD's now-louder chants in response— "Hey-Hey Ho-Ho: Homophobia's Got to Go!"—he too escalates: "*You* got to go!" he shouts. "All of you got to go. . . . You still slaves!" he says, as the girls and women continue smiling, if not now also confounded, as they survey the gay men standing together on the streets of Harlem, USA.

Are these sisters standing at the crucial buffer zone recognizing *this type of gay*—loud and proud in many colors and styles, all at once—for the first time? GMAD members continue chanting, now focused on Curly. GMAD leaders motion for brothers to step back, avoiding or preparing for escalation. Nothing jumps off. There is no resolution to this climactic standoff, just rising action and irresolution. In the final sequence of the film, disembodied voices of GMAD members speak. A voice summarizes the fissure or boundary of Black solidarity and Black gay men's longing, reflecting on a moment before difference meant exclusion: "There [was] a Black consciousness. A Black awareness, you know . . . and people were there with a common thread. I think that common thread is in tatters at this point. I think that there should be some higher kinship there." Now, and then. Here, and there. Brothers talk about their dreams. They want recognition and (re)incorporation into Black publics "to nurture and be nurtured by other Black men" and "to be accepted enough to share our gifts," among which someone cites "how to treat women." Of course, Cheryl (Clarke), in her 1983 *Home Girls* essay "Homophobia in the Black Community: The Failure to Transform," had already famously excoriated the lack of any demonstrable kinship on the part of "Black macho intellectuals . . . who consistently or unwittingly have absorbed the homophobia of their patriarchal slave holders . . . and the Black woman intellectual . . . afraid to relinquish heterosexual privilege." This classic essay is a brilliant complement to her 1981 piece, "Lesbianism: An Act of Resistance," originally published in *This Bridge Called My Back: Writings by Radical Women of Color.* Cheryl had indeed called for a higher kinship: "That there is homophobia among Black people in America is largely reflective of the homophobic culture in which we live. . . . Yet we cannot rationalize the diseases of homophobia among Black people as the white man's fault, for to do so is to absolve ourselves of our core duty to transform ourselves."[34]

Black lesbian, gay, bisexual, transgender, and gender-non-binary folks in the long 1980s were offering everyone an opportunity to transform by rejecting homophobic poison: the "common sense" of the entire culture. This offer resonates today, for example, in the position of continental Africans who assert that it is homophobia and transphobia that are "un-African," not African homosexuals, bisexuals, and queers, or politics that support their rights, and by Caribbean activists fighting against colonial-era laws who point out that it is this set of laws, not LGBT inclusion, that is *from foreign*, against the nation, and/or anti-Black. Cheryl has already told us that we all have a duty to resist and transform ourselves and our communities, lest we find ourselves, as Curly would have it, *still slaves* to heteropatriarchy and racial capitalism. Essex's introduction to *Brother to Brother*, following up on Joe's elaboration of the contested "home" that Joe longed for and knew needed him but to which he "cannot go," echoes this longing and invitation to transform. Essex recognized the labor that this takes: to *work with* folks with whom we may stand at an impasse (I hear fam asking for a discount, or a special consideration: "can you *work with* me, sister/brother?"). Staring each other down on Malcolm X Boulevard, dancing and chanting in the street on our way to freedom. Likewise complexly contradictory, lacking easy resolution, and pragmatic even in its intimate heart-rending affect, Essex writes:

> We are a wandering tribe that needs to go home before home is gone. We should not continue standing in line to be admitted into spaces that don't want us there. We cannot continue to exist without clinics, political organizations, human services, and political institutions that we create to support, sustain and affirm us.... Our communities are waiting for us to come home.... They may not understand everything about us, but they will remain ignorant, misinformed, and lonely for us, and we for them, for as long as we stay away hiding in communities that really never wanted us, or the gifts we bring.... I am coming home. There is no place else to go that will be worth so much love and effort.[35]

"There is no place else to go that will be worth so much love and effort. No guarantees: but this discourse is placed (*at home*), and the heart has its reasons."[36] Nomadic *tribal* institution building is often lonely translational homework (I am aware that the foregoing is an awkwardly stated, dense contradiction, but that does not make it any less true or important to say). This, for the intents and purposes of the Black gay habits of mind we follow here, is our Unfinished Work—our *wuk* both here and there. Translating at a crossroad, which is also an intersection. Sometimes at impasse. With so much between us.

"Rights Coming!"

In 2014, while preparations for International Day against Homophobia Transphobia and Biphobia (IDAHOT) and Gay Pride celebrations began taking shape around the global North, President Yoweri Museveni of the East African nation of Uganda signed the nation's Anti-Homosexuality Act—among other restrictions and punishments, affirming that freedom of expression "can be validly restricted in the public interest." In neighboring Kenya, the National Gay and Lesbian Human Rights Commission was filing suit against the nation's NGO Coordination Board, which deemed their name "inappropriate." Actions like these by African governments impelled many to ask why Africa seemed to be bucking the global gay trend toward liberal rights, and many casual observers and commentators seem to think that they know the answer, boldly proclaiming the same analyses and platitudes on social media in righteous bursts of hashtag activism, "think pieces," and performative solidarity and expertise. The structure of the commentaries were consistent. Blame "African culture," then respond with shaking heads, hashtags, invectives against the offending national leaders, and calls for LGBTI Africans to sexile to "freedom" in the North. This is not only wholly insufficient but also willfully misplaces perhaps sincere empathy, concern, and activist solidarity. To be clear: the issue here is not African "backwardness" or a Black and/or brown wet blanket of "cultural pathology" spoiling the fabulous trajectory of worldwide gay/queer ascension (in the global South and among people of color in the North). It is, perhaps, not yet time to cue the glitter and Cher's "If You Believe," dear Pride reveler (no, this one is not disco). The work of African and Caribbean activists and scholars shows that access to adequate health care, protection, and political recognition is far from a merely "cultural" issue. These are complex political-economic problems with complex local historical contexts—the connections and roots of which are global. But the successful re-branding of the (radical) Queer Liberation movement as Gay Rights finds it so insular that it has all but erased political-economic power imbalance by class, race, nation, and gender, even though LGBTQ people—especially Black and other people of color, undocumented, unhoused, and poor people—continue to suffer under this regime.

On January 28, 2011, Caribbean sexual orientation inclusion and sexual health organizations issued a joint statement condemning the January 27 assassination of the gay Ugandan advocate David Kato. David had been publicly "outed" in a local newspaper a few months before he was murdered. The newspaper had existed for less than two months prior to the infamous headline, which sidelined news of impending war in Sudan and social disaster following a catastrophic landslide. It read, in color, "100 Pictures of Uganda's Top Homos Leaked." The subheading under David Kato's picture read "Hang Them."[37] David was bludgeoned to death with a hammer, in broad daylight, at his home. He died on his way to the hospital. The statement below from Caribbean activists pledged to redouble efforts toward "liberty, privacy, dignity and joy" despite "the continuing danger that sexuality, and the human rights defenders who work in this area, face in the Caribbean and elsewhere": "Were it not for advocacy late last year, thirteen Caribbean countries would have allowed 'sexual orientation' to be removed from an international statement of commitment to protect persons from unlawful killing because of who they are. . . . In places like Africa and the Caribbean, battles against slavery, colonialism, racism, apartheid, genocide, gender inequality and religious persecution ought to have taught us better lessons."[38]

The animating phrase, "in places like Africa and the Caribbean," refers to the common history of transatlantic racial capitalism—that is, slavery, colonialism, racism, indentureship, genocide—which inaugurated modernity itself and began to construct blackness. The "we" is constitutive of multiple blacknesses but also the aspirational pluricultural or multicultural Caribbean framework "out of many, one" or *alluh we* (all of us) that includes and exceeds blackness. The Caribbean, especially Guyana and Trinidad and Tobago, reflects a complex negotiation of difference (at least): urban/rural, regional/subregional/hemispheric, Christian/Hindu/Muslim, African/Asian/Middle Eastern descent, and racial and ethnic "mix." Colin puts it this way:

> Although Trinidad & Tobago shares a history of plantation slavery with other African American societies, in the century and a half since Emancipation we have become a multicultural country in which Afro [African descended] are enumerated as a statistical minority and the nation's second largest ethnic group (a few percentage points behind Indo [Indian descended], the plurality ethnic group, and ahead of people of mixed descent). Thus, CAISO's communities are not solely Black diaspora communities; our communities belong to the African, South Asian, Chinese and Middle Eastern diasporas.

According to Colin, their sociocultural visions are therefore not conceived through a prism of Black liberation alone. But to understand more holistically, we must not forget the historic tensions and postindependence political battles waged between Afro-Creole and Indo partisans, or the fact that these are live controversies today. I certainly heard this rhetoric play out on minibus rides through Laventile, a largely Black working-class area, during election season. As the solidarity statement Colin and other activists composed attests, one cannot disentangle global and historically structured antiblackness from Caribbean histories or present-day political-economic or sociocultural realities.

I have found a complex, contradictory reality in developing postcolonial nations, where the relationships of activists to the nation-state are generally built upon one of three general positions that emerge from important differences in the historical and lived experience of heterosexism and homophobia in imperial, national, and subregional contexts. Regarding the nonsovereign Caribbean, Vanessa Agard-Jones's work on the French overseas department of Martinique, for example, shows how sex education and HIV/AIDS prevention work on the island parallel Martinicans' strategic dependency on the French state, to which they belong.[39] In other examples, some organizations in the sovereign Caribbean, and a few individual LGBTQ asylees from Africa and the Caribbean who work as advocates but now live in the global North, appeal to northern rhetorics, strategies, and funding through discourses of the Caribbean and Africa as the "most homophobic" places in the world. However, the more widespread and growing trend—toward *sexual orientation inclusion*—is based on a shared lived experience of anticolonial struggle. "Homonationalism," Jasbir (Puar)'s formulation for the process by which the state and LGBTQ groups manufacture and promote nationalism—recruiting and (re)incorporating, for example, the most respectable eligible, white, cisgender, property-owning, or performing into state projects (like the military, or against so-called Muslim terrorists, for example)—provides a useful vocabulary to describe relatively new formations in and emerging from the United States and other settler colonial states such as Israel and Canada. Jasbir has called homonationalism "collusion between homosexuality and American nationalism" and has inveighed against attendant "pinkwashing," or the state's accommodation of a measure of gay and lesbian rights as a cover for systemic abuses of other groups.[40] But outside of the context of the French department and Dutch territories, there has been no pinkwashing, or homonationalist integration, in the Caribbean or Africa.[41] And of course, homonationalism and pinkwashing assume at least the cessation of open, state-sponsored violence toward homosexuals and transpeople, which is not the case in many sites. It is based on one's ability to appear eligible to attain not only legal status but also moral status as an appropriate citizen subject. In the Caribbean, those organizations with higher levels of intersectional commitment, working on behalf of vulnerable populations of many kinds, militate against homonationalist integration or "co-optation" by state interests. Their appeal cannot be described as "homonormative" inclusion but rather as negotiated recognition of difference. There are multiple ways to be silent, silenced, or "downpressed" that do not require a closet. Likewise, there are a number of modes of demanding recognition and representing (and making representations of) oneself that do not require rainbows, marches, tense family-dinner announcements, or the promise that "it gets better" if only one can manage to leave one's home in the bottom of a local community to arrive into full LGBTQ personhood in increasingly inaccessible high-priced gayborhoods or gay villages of San Francisco, Paris, São Paulo, or Johannesburg, for example.

SASOD

LGBTQ activism in the Caribbean is not insular. Activists and advocates work to decriminalize "buggery," "sodomy," and "cross-dressing" and to push forward their vision of "inclusion." Far from a single-minded focus on sexual rights, their politics are intersectional. Although like Black LGBTQ groups and advocates around the world, they strategically employ some of the language of international gay and lesbian rights activism, "sexuality inclusion" activism in the Caribbean eschews so-called global gay politics. The public advocacy appeals used by Guyana's Society against Sexual Orientation Discrimination (SASOD) and Trinidad and Tobago's Coalition Advocating Sexual Orientation Inclusion (CAISO) consciously deploy local idioms and institutions to win support of fellow citizens and national-level politicians and administrators. These sexual-inclusion advocates prefer a negotiated strategy in which public support is cultivated through an accent on local participation and coalition building with health, education, antiviolence, and youth advocacy groups, initiating cultural dialogue, for example, about sexuality in soca and calypso music and in local and international film, and a focus on issues of democratic access, fairness, and education.

On September 6, 2013, Chief Justice Ian Chang of the High Court of Guyana delivered his judgment in the case of Gulliver (Quincy) McEwan, Angel (Seon) Clarke, Peaches (Joseph) Fraser, Isabella (Seyon) Persaud, and the Society against Sexual Orientation Discrimination (SASOD) versus Attorney General of Guyana. McEwan, Clarke, Fraser, and Persaud, transgender women who are identified in local parlance as *dress-up girls*, were arrested, stripped, and ridiculed in police detention on an evening in 2009, after which they were fined for cross-dressing, then lectured from the bench by the chief magistrate to "give [their] lives to Jesus." Section 153 of Guyana's Summary Jurisdiction provision makes a criminal offense of "a man wearing female attire, and a woman wearing male attire, publicly, for any improper purpose," and the plaintiffs argued that this was discrimination inconsistent with the 1980 Guyana Constitution. In a partial victory, the chief justice found that the police had indeed violated the human rights of the four plaintiffs—by not informing them of the reason for their arrests. But his holding provided a disappointing nonanswer to other crucial facts of the case, and no immediate remedy. Justice Chang found that "it is not criminally offensive for a person to wear the attire of the opposite sex as a matter of preference or to give expression to or to reflect his or her sexual orientation. . . ." But the court also held that because of an 1893 law, predating Guyana's independence, "legislative rather than curial action is necessary to invalidate the provision." The judge thereby struck down the plaintiffs' claim altogether by punting to the legislative branch, as well as effectively invalidating the claim that the cross-dressing law amounted to discrimination on the basis of gender.

Justice Chang's ruling seems to misapprehend distinctions between gender and sexuality. It is not necessarily sexual orientation but gender identity or performance that is at issue here. Moreover, the court held that "cross-dressing in a public place is an offence only if it is done for an improper purpose." Gulliver McEwan, one of the plaintiffs and the director of Guyana Trans United (GTU), noted that "the Chief Justice was relatively clear that once you are expressing your gender identity, it's not criminal for a man to wear female attire." But Gulliver gets to the crux of the matter here: "The law really stifles us, because what could be an *improper purpose*? The trans community is very worried, and still fearful of arrests, in light of this decision."[42] The court also ruled that SASOD, the local LGBTQI organization, had no standing as a colitigant. SASODomites, the clever name by which members and supporters of Guyana's SASOD are called, have chosen film festivals, coalition work with HIV/AIDS and antiviolence organizations, and blogging as important strategies, along with their leadership in this court battle coordinated by legal scholars at the University of the West Indies, to overturn cross-dressing bans that effectively outlaw dress-up girls and transgender individuals. The cross-dressing ban case became a regional cause célèbre and has inspired the locally produced film and SASOD project "My

10.1 Logo of Trinidad and Tobago's Coalition Advocating for Inclusion of Sexual Orientation (CAISO), featuring carnival motif, voter's red-dyed finger, and the islands embedded in the palm.

COALITION
ADVOCATING
FOR INCLUSION OF
SEXUAL ORIENTATION

Wardrobe, My Right."[43] On November 13, 2018, the Caribbean Court of Justice (CCJ)—the regional high court newly established in 2001 to replace the Commonwealth's Judicial Committee of the Privy Council for an increasing number of Caribbean nations, and Guyana's final court of appeal—delivered its decision. McEwan and company prevailed against the attorney general of Guyana. The court ordered that Section 153(1)(xlvii) be struck.[44] But the project coordinator at Guyana Trans United, Alessandra Hereman, has said that despite this watershed victory against the ban on "cross-dressing" in Guyana, "stigma and discrimination persists and can lead to violence."[45]

CAISO is an acronym naming the organization's work (Coalition Advocating Sexual Orientation Inclusion) and honoring the importance and unifying appeal of the local Trinbagonian music form, calypso (locally "kaiso"). The organization's logo (see figure 10.1), prominently showing the index finger of one who has voted and with the twin islands indelibly imprinted on the palm, visually communicates CAISO'S local focus and commitment.

SASOD's regional "sibling" organization, Trinidad and Tobago's CAISO, stood in solidarity with SASOD and the plaintiffs, as did a number of regional organizations. Trinidad and Tobago has no cross-dressing ban but does have a colonial-era antisodomy (antibuggery) law, and CAISO had already successfully advocated for assurance of nonprosecution under this antibuggery statute but not for its abolition. Explaining this long-game strategy of engagement, Colin says that "my organisation is trying to build an LGBTI movement here that is strategic and imaginative. Although sodomy laws, even when unenforced, continue to fuel stigma and sanction discrimination, repealing them doesn't repeal the Bible or Qur'an."[46] When I asked why CAISO had sought assurance of nonprosecution of buggery laws rather than outright decriminalization, Colin told me that whereas he strongly supports the efforts of SASOD and the plaintiffs, it would be unwise and unimaginative to focus solely on litigation as a means of advancing sexual autonomy in the Caribbean. More work is necessary. Certainly, both SASOD and CAISO understand that juridical remedies alone are not sufficient to solve issues of sociocultural inclusion and protection. Several years after this conversation, the on-the-ground evidence seems clear: the recent CCJ ruling has not solved the issue of discrimination against gender-non-conforming and trans individuals in Guyana. Of course, South Africa's progressive constitution, which guarantees more protections than most others in the world, has not prevented the murders of Black lesbians any more than hate crime legislation in the US has in the US, as killing and assault of Black and Latinx trans women rise. Colin said that

> we have been talking in T&T a lot about "citizenship" in CAISO's work. We've also begun to talk about developing a culture of minority rights (though not in those words), e.g. in the context of the election we have begun advocating for protection of political opinion and affiliation from discrimination. But, like Guyana, we have this vital need to accommodate ethnic and religious difference for the society to work at all which we can draw on, but that other territories may not.

In a moment of renewed recognition of the deep antiblackness of the United States, these words ("need to accommodate ethnic and religious difference for the society to work") are chillingly resonant and chastening. In our original virtual conversation for *Black/Queer/Diaspora*, Colin said:

> CAISO's founders originally came together on Emancipation Day 2007, to meet with Kenny Mitchell, a gay, primary-school-educated taxi driver whose successful lawsuit for police harassment elicited widespread public sympathy and visible news coverage, in which he said he wanted to

speak out for gay rights for people who could not do so for themselves. The Mitchell case evidenced for GLBT people, media and national empathy with victims of discrimination, and substantiated the possibility of successful redress for discrimination for ordinary citizens. Efforts were made then, which fizzled, to form a novel cross-gender, cross-class advocacy organisation. CAISO itself formed on June 27, 2009, in response to a Cabinet announcement two days earlier that the proposed final version of a national Gender Policy [that had been the subject of noisy advocacy by evangelical Christians five years earlier over its inclusion of a handful of forward-thinking references to sexual orientation and termination of pregnancy] would expressly avoid dealing with sexual orientation.

Focused on interregional collaboration in the Caribbean and on the region's relationship with the rest of the world, Colin holds that "it's time for a strategic regional conversation where we enter as equals and talk about common interests and disagreements and the question of strategic political collaboration. My sense of past efforts is that they've been driven by power differences or by funding relationships that have had to balance political interests with others like HIV." Interviewed by a national newspaper, *TNT Times*, another of CAISO's leaders, Sharon Mottley, reflected on the founding of the organization:

> The minister's comments that there was no room for us in the gender policy sparked something . . . has shown us that unless we get up and say that we are here and that we want to be afforded the same rights and respect as anybody else it won't happen. . . . And so, I think this is an exciting time to be gay and lesbian in Trinidad and Tobago because we have young voices, we have powerful voices, we have a diversity of voices coming to the front and we're not stopping. We are ready to move.[47]

The interviewer asked Sharon and Colin, "On the spectrum of gay men being tortured and killed with impunity in Iraq, and Iceland appointing a lesbian prime minister and GLBT being allowed to marry in other parts of Europe, where do you think Trinidad and Tobago falls in terms of acceptance of homosexuality?" This framework of the interviewer—seemingly overdetermined by comparisons that unhelpfully collapse disparate cultural and geopolitical contexts—is not unusual. Many media outlets continue to plot LGBTQ rights on a stable bipolar trajectory, with ethnically more homogeneous and wealthier European societies with secure social welfare nets on one side and an unlikely triad of Iraq (standing in for the entire Islamic world), "Africa" (as if it were a country—and of course except South Africa), and Jamaica (imagined as the whole of the Caribbean) on the scandalous other.[48] Sharon says:

> GLBT citizens from other countries in the region . . . look very favourably on us. In Trinidad and Tobago, we have openly gay parties. We have our gay Mecca, our centre. This does not happen in other Caribbean islands. [People from] other Caribbean islands come to Trinidad and they're always in awe. And then at Carnival time you can have men dress up almost like women, leading [*mas* band] Island People's frontline section going down the road. That does not happen in other Caribbean countries. We have a long way to go, but to be able to sit here and comfortably say that I'm a lesbian woman, have this interview, I think that puts us ahead of a lot of other countries.[49]

Sharon is correct. The democratic traditions of Trinidad and Tobago make it a beacon for the rest of the region. Of course, it is not only the country's democratic traditions and Carnival but also its stable economy and functional state infrastructure supported by exploitation of the nation's oil and natural gas resources that make possible what often amounts to begrudging relative "live and let live" posture on the twin islands, compared to neighbors (if not always the popular chatter or legal statute). But Colin offers a more strategically usable response to the implicit hierarchical rhetoric underlying the reporter's question: "I'm always resistant to that whole quantification thing. I agree with everything that Sharon said, but I would also say that things are good enough here that there's hope for organizing, and I feel confident that we have the organising power to hold government accountable. But things are bad enough that people are still losing their lives and their ability to be free, and that always makes the work necessary."[50] At the end of the interview, he summarizes—recalling and rhyming with Marlon's films "Affirmation" and "Anthem," in which his poetic intervention "Unfinished Work" is central:

> It's about the affirmation. It's about community rituals. The same reason people go to mosques or to church. It can be really powerful, especially when you organise to do things that you can't do by yourself—that's the power of community: the power of people coming together to accomplish things—even if they don't like each other, to recognise that there are things we can accomplish by working together that we can't alone and that when we actually get those successes and we celebrate it's sweet. I've had some of those experiences already in CAISO. That's what makes the work worthwhile.[51]

Colin's strategy—and that which he and his colleagues in CAISO and CariFLAGS (Caribbean Forum for Liberation and Acceptance of Genders and Sexualities) follow—is to "build the values needed to sustain our embrace of sexual rights and the dignity of same sex sexuality."[52] Their focus is to build government capacity on gender and sexual orientation issues and to address vulnerabilities of sexual minority status, such as homelessness, school bullying, and stigma, which prove formidable barriers to access to health care and justice. I was able to experience this up close during a visit to Trinidad and Tobago in 2010. At the height of election season I canvassed Port of Spain neighborhoods and attended rallies with CAISOnians. The huge numbers of Trinbagonians out on the streets, in bars, and at campaign rallies of both major coalition parties met us with good-natured engagement. Months before, CAISOnians participated in a demonstration against a white US American "ex-gay" minister: Phillip Lee of "His Way Out Ministries." Lee had been invited to Trinidad and Tobago by a group of clergy to lecture at a youth sexual health seminar. The religious crowd and some advocates for youth and education policy reform, new to the coalition, were dubious about "gay rights," but CAISOnians won support with their open engagement and commitment to shared values with the youth and education advocates. The T-shirts that CAISOnians wore eloquently spelled out the tenor of the movement. As clever as a wry calypso, the shirt read: "The Homosexual Agenda: 1. Buy Crix [a popular local cracker brand] 2. Spend Time with Family 3. Work for Equality." This lighthearted T-shirt with an incisive and sophisticated political message typifies this stream of work underway in nations of the Caribbean, in which advocates for *sexual orientation inclusion* build local alliances and depend primarily on their localness, national belonging, and regional cooperation. They highlight the fact that restrictive gender and sex laws are vestiges of the colonial past that mirror the present neocolonial vision of US-based religious fundamentalist groups, which fund and propagandize homo hatred. At the same time, in *Decolonising Sexual Citizenship*, in which he lays out conditions for engagement by would-be Commonwealth allies, Colin asserts that seeking redress in that body would erroneously pose the buggery laws as a "British colonial problem" requiring a British solution. Rather than engage in what he calls "polarizing national debates over still misunderstood and misrepresented sexualities" that can easily foreclose other gains and opportunities to deepen "shared values of non-discrimination . . . and fairness," CAISO has focused on local coalition building and advocacy for local and subregional solutions, supported by "international solidarity, South–South dialogue and North–South listening."[53]

In terms of differences in strategy and relative reliance on the global North, Colin admits that

> in the past, regional voices in critique of local strategies (mine has been one) haven't been pitched too sensitively or been heard as generous. But strategic decisions made locally in Jamaica have regional impacts, since Jamaica still has a disproportionate impact on regional popular culture.... Sometimes the way to make change in Jamaica may be through levers elsewhere; and there are places to do so within the region without the baggage of Global North engagements.... How are we collaborating in shifting the terms of engagement on sexual diversity and citizenship in the region as a whole?[54]

Though often challenging, South–South dialogue has been ongoing, through various organs such as CariFLAGS, but the international solidarity and North–South listening pieces—burdened with perhaps deeper mistrust and power asymmetries—are much less developed.[55] Colin's *Decolonising Sexual Citizenship* points to a number of northern LGBT rights strategies commonly in practice, which he argues are ineffective—or, more generously, cannot support long-lasting broad-based support. This includes "public scolding" of politicians, use of HIV as a convenient entry point to transform sexual health policies, and what he calls "silken suit" fund-raising. He writes, "If Global North advocates wish to be part of the movement to end 'sexual apartheid' they must resist temptation to take the reins. They must engage in genuine North-South dialogue and international solidarity. They need to get behind Global South initiatives and push in the direction carved out by Southern activists."[56] Colin has spoken forcefully against those who he says

> feel license to speak like abolitionists on behalf of the GLBT interests of the [Caribbean] region ... distort[ing] organizing strategies ... at the expense of nurturing local political alliances, of building ownership of GLBT issues by other sexual rights stakeholders, of developing strategic power domestically, of building a local base to which leadership is accountable, of developing appeals and legitimacy in the currency of domestic and traditional values and frameworks, or simply of being politically innovative in response to local conditions.[57]

Speaking in the broader context of "global gay" politics during our roundtable, he said that

> the most dangerous impact of the "spread" of Western GLBT politics ... is not that certain understandings and assumptions about how GLBT

politics is practiced in the North are being exported to us. The larger danger instead is that ideas about how GLBT politics should be practiced in the Global South, quite differently from in the North . . . are being conceived in, and spread from, the North. . . . Because of the assumptions that civil and political rights frameworks are weak, enlightened governance is not yet achieved, and GLBT communities are relatively powerless in Global South states, there is the expectation that GLBT liberation politics will rely on external advocates and look for moral authority to international covenants and arbitrating bodies rather than engaging in domestic political work.

"I Am Not an Afropolitan; I Just Dress Like One!"

Binyavanga Wainaina's *One Day I Will Write about This Place* was published to critical acclaim in 2011, years before releasing what he called his "lost chapter" of the memoir, "I Am a Homosexual, Mum," in January of 2014. With this, the founding editor of the influential literary journal *Kwani?* joined local LGBTQI activists and advocates in Kenya and throughout the continent who had been actively working to ensure the safety and inclusion of LGBTQI people in Africa. Binyavanga's "lost chapter" added sexuality as another facet of itinerancy and displacement to his crucial work, provoking readers past diaspora, pan-Africanism, and Afropolitanism to something that looks to me like what we signal with "Black/Queerpolis." In the memoir "this place" refers not only to his native Kenya but also to all of Africa, given his long residence in South Africa, extended visits in Nigeria, and references to places all over the continent (and throughout the world). Still, before the addition of the lost chapter, *One Day I Will Write about This Place* was silent about homosexuality, including Binyavanga's own. In a tender and poignant turn of Black/queer time, although the lost chapter is addressed to his mother, he wrote and published the essay years after she and his father had already passed to the ether. The "lost chapter" imagines a conversation that never was. It begins:

11 July, 2000.
This is not the right version of events.
Hey mum. I was putting my head on her shoulder, that last afternoon before she died. She was lying on her hospital bed. Kenyatta. Intensive Care. Critical Care. There. Because this time I will not be away in South Africa, fucking things up in that chaotic way of mine. I will arrive on time, and be there when she dies.

. . .

"I have never thrown my heart at you mum. You have never asked me to."

Only my mind says. This. Not my mouth. But surely the jerk of my breath and heart, there next to hers, has been registered? Is she letting me in?

Nobody, nobody, ever in my life has heard this. Never, mum. I did not trust you, mum. And. I. Pulled air hard and balled it down into my navel, and let it out slow and firm, clean and without bumps out of my mouth, loud and clear over a shoulder, into her ear.

"I am a homosexual, mum."[58]

Binyavanga had held his public silence until the confluence of the concurrent rise of the "Kill the Gays" bill in neighboring Uganda, similar legislation and increased media attention to violence in Nigeria, and the death of Carlota, one of the author's close friends, compelled him to speak. One of the most important contemporary African cultural figures, he stepped into this politically fraught moment with humor and seemingly very few fucks to give—knowing that this could have potentially cost him dearly. In a Facebook post commemorating the release of "I Am a Homosexual, Mum" two years later, and commenting on the intentional publication politics of local African outlets, Binyavanga's friend, scholar/activist Neo Musangi, wrote:

> Today, in 2014, "I Am a Homosexual, Mum . . ." was published by the almighty Chimurenga and later taken up by Africasacountry.com, of course before the Americans got to see it. That essay, like the six-part video series ["We Must Free Our Imaginations"], shifted and re-shaped many conversations, not only around sexuality, but also around religion, Black consciousness and stupidity, on this continent. So, today I want to thank you sweetheart and to thank your beautiful mum and the smiley Baba for you. I am grateful to the Universe for your continued healing and strength.[59]

Later, Neo posted a photo of Binyavanga by photographer Msingi Sasis, titling it "Photographing the Photograph." Here he returns the gaze of the viewer twice. This exuberant portrait of Binyavanga frames him against a brilliant cerulean blue wall, with huge blue flowers in what looks like a floor-sized vase to the left of the tufted green wing chair in which he is seated—wearing a flowered wax-print jacket—while also appearing in another pose, leaning on the chair, above his own shoulder. A yellow sunflower appears as one sun above the vase as light streams through a window on the other side of the tableaux. Tagging Binyavanga, who was convalescing after one of a number of strokes, Neo wrote, cheekily: "Original photo credit: Msingi Sasis/ Model: Binyavanga Wainaina/ Dressed by: All of West Africa via Dutch Capitalists/ Make-up: The Universe."[60] Earlier that year, acknowledging his Twitter and Instagram feeds replete with check-ins from Nairobi to Dakar just before the celebrated Dakar Biennale, from Johannesburg to London (to New Haven—where we were fortunate to host him at Yale!), and featuring gorgeous West African (and, yes also Dutch[61]) wax prints, custom shoes, and art from Senegal during his extended stay there, Binyavanga the trickster quipped with characteristic cleverness and self-deprecation: "I am not an Afropolitan; I just dress like one!" recalling his much-discussed plenary lecture titled "I Am a Pan-Africanist, Not an Afropolitan."[62]

Achille Mbembe's rendering of "Afropolitanism" is not a "perfect fit" with Black/queerpolis, to be sure. Here we follow Black/queer artists, activists, and people every day to offer a dynamic, textured, enduring feeling of common union among African (descended) peoples that is not only and not merely a condition of biopower, history, global political economy, or common vulnerabilities. Here we see this unfold as transnationalism and globalization played in a minor key. And pragmatic politics also driven by desire. A libidinal drive to (re)construct family and new futures with what Binyavanga might call "our own new sci-fi things." However, the point is not to pull off a seamless and elegant suture to Achille's brand of Afropolitanism but rather to make the "failure" (thanks, Jack!) or "irresolution" (thanks, Matt!) or intersection or *agencement* more generative and more interesting: to see new horizons and to explore the pleasures and potential efficacy of it all.[63] Here I offer an enticement to read reparatively and also, again, for resonance across blacknesses. After all, rocking with the polyphonic rhythms of Black/queerpolis (of course, I hear Wumi now[64]), Achille's poetic, hybrid, transcontinental definition turns on the following:

> Awareness of the interweaving of the here and there, the presence of the elsewhere in the here and vice versa, the relativisation of primary roots and memberships and the way of embracing, with full knowledge of the facts, strangeness, foreignness and remoteness, the ability to recognize one's face in the face of [one's Black/queer other] . . . and make the most of the traces of remoteness in closeness, to domesticate the unfamiliar, to work with what seems to be opposites—it is this cultural, historical and aesthetic sensitivity that defines the term "Afropolitanism."[65]

Calling for "broad-mindedness" and arguing against a "nativistic reflex" in the face of Africa's "worlds of movement," Achille has averred that "the cultural history of the continent can hardly be understood outside the paradigm of itinerancy, mobility, and displacement."[66] This goes equally for the entire Black world. And not only for Black subjects already authorized in scholarly and popular literatures and film, such as global petro-billionaires, high-flying heads of state, internet scammers, Nollywood producers, Oprah and her high-achieving girls. For example, think about transcontinental networks that include Black gay South African flight attendants whose multiple cultural competencies and cosmopolitan Black consciousness, grounded in the local experience of post-apartheid South Africa, show that this notion of broad-mindedness does not come only from well-to-do professionals, artists, or intellectual elites. These men and women constitute another current of contemporary "worlds in motion." Think too of those fleeing war and certain rape, famine, and/or ethnic, sexual, or religious persecution over land and on the high seas. Remember flickers of African disco ball luminescence: flashes at the bottom of the ocean.

Binyavanga turns us ruthlessly toward a continental view of our current conjuncture. Likewise addressing the familial and local, and deeply resonant with US Black gay writing from the long 1980s, Binyavanga's video essay "We Must Free Our Imaginations" lays out an analysis of current issues and a future vision for the continent of Africa. Binyavanga seeks a "muscular secular space" that will bring (back) the "oxygen" of democratic discourse and governance—like others in Kenya and throughout the continent, in the Caribbean, and increasingly in the United States and other places where reactionary political projects (often in the guise of religious fundamentalism) drive public discourse and policy. His vision is focused on the expansion and liberation of Africans' imagination and capacity for innovation. LGBTQ rights and recognition, like many other issues, are inevitably a part of achieving this. Focused on eradicating "shit from a thousand years ago hate" kept in place and reinvigorated by "middle classes that have been trained not to imagine," "We Must Free Our Imaginations" starts abruptly, with a stark white background and simple black tilting that reads: "One: Bring Me the Obedient Children." Binyavanga begins:

> I want to live a life of a free imagination. I want to work with people around this continent, to make new exciting things. To make sci-fi things and to make stories and to make pictures. I want this generation of young parents to have their kids see Africans writing their own stories, printing their own stories. That simple act; I think that is the most political act one can have. I want to see a continent where every kind of person's imagination doesn't

have to look for being authorized. Me, I'm an African, and I'm a Pan-Africanist. I want to see this continent change.[67]

This resonates with Sharon's affirmation—"We are here"—speaking and working on the other side of the reflective, faceted Atlantic (or is it a disco ball, as Wura claims?). Binyavanga repeats the same phrase in his video—"We are here"—adding with a conspiratorial giggle, "So you just deal."[68] Regarding Caribbean activists invoking the disco-ball–like array of "places like Africa and the Caribbean . . . battles against slavery, colonialism, racism, apartheid, genocide, gender inequality and religious persecution . . . ,"[69] Binyavanga seems to agree with this cognate analysis of borrowed sameness of (British) colonial remnants of sodomy laws. As he says,

> When you take that set of laws. . . . The word *sodomy* is the most Victorian word ever. . . . Me, I'm just saying. What is the word for "sodomite" in [African] languages? That word *sodomite* came because the most anal people in the world, the Victorians, came and said *these Africans have many queer behaviors. They just married 12 people; and then tomorrow they're going to worship. . . . Then, they are just dancing endlessly. And I'm sure, in the middle of the night, they are performing sodomy!* The only countries in the world where there are antisodomy laws are countries that were colonized by the Victorians. Nigeria, Kenya, India—same place. Where people inherited that . . . idea. So now, mysteriously (homophobes say) *"It was never African."* And I'm like, no! They put that law because they were expecting that you were. Whether you are or not.[70]

Binyavanga asserts that before colonialism there were no laws against same-sex sexual behavior or gender expression in Africa. Likewise, before the recent missionary reincursion of so-called evangelical Christians to the global South, homophobia in East Africa did not include the vile homicidal rhetorics of the likes of American preacher Scott Lively, from the United States, who incited and paid Ugandans to fight against what the demagogue called a "genocidal" and "pedophilic" gay movement. A new colonial or missionary zeal is sweeping the continent, in which foreigners have effectively spread a new "gospel" among preachers and politicians willing to be their mouthpieces. Antihomosexual hatred is good for business. And religious expressions of homophobia that are redeployed by opportunist politicians are convenient. During election season this can be used as a means to "unite" Christian and Muslim fundamentalists, and others who would otherwise be divided along religious or ethnic/tribal lines, under the banner of homo hatred and transphobia. The film *God Loves Uganda* tracks the genealogy of the "Kill the Gays" bill and the partnership between Ugandan LGBT activists and advocates and the Center for Constitutional Rights, in the United States, which filed a historic federal lawsuit in the United States against Lively on behalf of Sexual Minorities Uganda (SMUG).[71] The "straw queer" is an opportune figure to blame for any number of unrelated economic conditions and social ills. As neoconservative regimes disguised as populism rise in the United States, the United Kingdom, Brazil, the Philippines, and elsewhere, with similar maneuvers of disinformation and targeting of minority populations, this tactic also seems good for electoral popularity among those tired of watching their domestic affairs be dictated from London, Washington, or Brussels. Worldwide, homo hate and transphobia are apparently easily disguised as local "tradition." Organizations such as East African Sexual Health and Rights Initiative (UHAI-EASHRI), Gay and Lesbian Coalition of Kenya (GALCK), and Kenya's National Gay and Lesbian Human Rights Commission (NGLHRC) have developed keen contextual analyses of their issues. Rather than external solutions, they should be able to count on our willingness to acknowledge their leadership on their issues and our support in expanding their analysis and work. I'm just saying—*Sasa nina-chojaribu kusema ni*—Binyavanga asks, "How many lives will be destroyed?" Although the "we" in "We Must Free Our Imaginations" is clearly read as *Africans*, and "this place" in *One Day I Will Write about This Place* is Africa, it is *Black/queer-political* in its broad-mindedness. In a pivotal moment in the video essay's first chapter, Binyavanga summarizes: "I believe Africa is rising. I am an African and I am here to stay. . . . But you see, the thing is that we're just here. Me, I'm not going away. I'm here. So you deal."[72] I hear this contradictory, difficult transnational *wuk* harmonizing with Essex and with GMAD: "There is no place else to go that will be worth so much love and effort," "Yes, Homo!," and "Black! Black! Black! Black! Gay! Gay! Gay! Gay! We Won't Have It No Other Way!"

Having heard it at Tracks, New York, back in the day, preserved and reedited in Marlon's film, and at a mall bookstore in Port of Spain, Colin's poetic refrain plays on in my head. The interpellation of difference as abjection offered in the slur also sounds like a recognition of the fact that something else is needed here. That we must bring something else to move us all far beyond our colonized grammars, and come as Maroon. Freewoman. Free. Marooned among "bristren"—brothers and sisters, cis, trans, and otherwise, who are

working to be psychically free from "shit from a thousand years ago hate."
It ain't always pretty here. We and it are yet unfinished. Colin invites/com-
mands us *when they shout faggot*, "pervert the language." We hear Cimarrón:

> . . .
> rewrite history
> redecline the past
> and conjugate a future
> reinvent etymology
> grow new roots
> . . . [73]

III

Conclusion
lush life (in exile)

Here we are again, dear reader—friend—stumbling out of the club into the light of dawn. It seems wrong to "conclude." My practice is to stay a piece, to continue to read and talk—hopefully going further up or down the road with you. Perhaps rediscovering old paths or forging new ones. We have argued for and within Black gay time and aliveness here. Yet I know that to advance our exchange I must bring this trip to a close, even with an ellipsis still open for the entry of your stories (laid side by side). I want to read your margin notes. To hear your response and your call, following your generous act of reading. "Concluding" is not how I want to understand the practice we are engaged in in these last pages. Because even "coda" is too narrowly disciplined for our engagement, please allow me to spin a few important cuts: traveling music to resonate in your ear and mind until we begin the dance again, together. First, a word on exile and expatriation, followed by glances to Havana and Harlem, and my final love letter to a glamorous New Afrikan who has finally come home, free. Finally, I will offer a short note on grace and the project of Black studies.

"I Used to Visit All the Very Gay Places..."

As a youngster who read everything James Baldwin had written and imagined for himself a future likewise constantly jetting off here and there, I projected myself, like Mr. Baldwin, living in what I imagined as glamorous Black "exile" somewhere other than here. Taking tea in Tunis. Sipping pastis in my courtyard in St. Paul de Vence (thank you, Jordan, for scaling the walls in 2009 to bring me a precious keepsake). In my Afrocentric fancy the geography eventually shifted. I imagined that like the latter Du Bois—Black social democrat, citizen of Ghana Du Bois, whom Black studies scholars talk about the least—I would eventually take up residence *on the continent*. It is not that I thought that this was my home, but rather a place from which I could contribute and where I might breathe freer without the choke of ambient racism. Later, when the opportunity (to fly away to work in a Central African refugee camp) came, via Cary Alan Johnson, he explained to me what being away from family and friends in the United States during the height of the AIDS pandemic had cost him. I imagined my loneliness and estrangement. It was clear to me that this would not be my path. But Richard Wright had made it all seem both romantic and radical. *Tres chic.* Wright's class and gender privilege is apparent in his essay "I Choose Exile," in which he gives his account of being "fed up" with American racism. The last straw—being denied the chance to buy an idyllic Connecticut country house. As a result, he "announced to [his] wife: 'This is the first of April. We are leaving America on the first of May. Take the child out of school. Put the furniture in storage. Buy tickets for Paris. We're through here.'" I can see his arms sweeping, his chest swelling. Head high in umbrage and patriarchal pride. Positively cinematic. Wright found the "mellow influence of a deeply humane culture" in France immediately following World War II.[1] This writer, who had been afflicted with the "FB Eye Blues" in the United States, found upon arrival to France that "irony of ironies! When I descended from the boat-train in Paris in May, 1946, not only was Gertrude Stein on hand to greet me, but the United States Embassy had sent its public relations man with two sleek cars to aid me. I found that abroad the United States government finds it convenient to admit that even Negroes are Americans! (Read between the lines!)."[2]

Billy Strayhorn knew that only escape from the United States—("A week / in Paris) would ease the bite of it." Even polyamorous pleasures of new lovers—"a trough full of hearts," after all, "could only be a bore." This seventeen-year-old already knew something about the pattern of a certain type of gay life and queer ennui, which not only obtained in the thirties when he wrote the song but perhaps has transformed only in scale, not qualitative intensity. It is the condition of estrangement, loneliness, and perhaps perpetual "expatriation." Citing a planned escape to the clubs, bars, and boîtes of the Quartier Pigalle, in which Mr. Strayhorn would eventually spend extended periods, the speaker in his timeless jazz standard "Lush Life" opines: "I used to visit all the very gay places, those come-what-may places, where one relaxes on the axis of the wheel of life. . . ."[3] Those bars where the girls throw back "12 o'clock 'tails." Not just any "sad and sullen" girls; today the lyrical genius might admit plainly that the "distingué" (distinctive, strange, or alluring) "traces" of those bar denizens were marks of their trans or lesbian and/or gay identities. Of course, today these "gay, come-what-may" spaces have been transformed by gentrification and commoditization of the lush gay life created some thirty years after this song was first recorded. To what shores can we expatriate for a lush life these days?

Before my arrival in Cuba in 1998, I had misread expatriation as exile. The sort of so-called exile in which the State Department sends a car to escort you to your fabulous Left Bank pied-à-terre, allows you to pass from one port to another in bohemian vagabondage, or follows your own righteous denunciation of nationality is one thing. One particularly masculine thing, it seems. Expatriation is not the same as exile. Even to be wrongly deported into exile from one's naturalized home in the United States for exercising your rights of expression, as revolutionary Claudia Jones was, is another thing. Rightly, her case became a cause célèbre, and prominent radical intellectuals wrote about Jones and rallied around her as she prepared to go to the United Kingdom, where she continued her livelihood of radical journalism and transnational Left community organizing work. This is not the exile I encountered in Cuba toward the end of the twentieth century during its "Special Period." To be actively pursued and terrorized while fleeing to preserve your freedom and continue your unpaid and largely thankless work while living in a small apartment in a run-down microbrigade on the outskirts of Havana, extended at the pleasure of an embattled Cuban government, is exile. To be unable to see your family, which has borne the weight of your particular political commitments, is exile. I learned this from my sister, Nehanda.[4]

Our other beloved and more well-known sister (whom I will refer to here as "Sister") had referred to their shared condition as that of "a 20th century escaped slave" living in "one of the largest, most resistant and most courageous Palenques [Maroon camps] that has ever existed": Cuba.[5] Nehanda and her New Afrikan comrades know this well. Dedicated to bringing together what they conceive of as the nation of New Afrikans (Black folks) within the

C.1 Nehanda Isoke Abiodun. A freedom fighter contemplates a monument celebrating another freedom fighter: Carlota, leader of the Triumvirato Rebellion of enslaved Africans. Matanzas, Cuba, 2000. Photo by author.

bounds of the United States to live autonomously, they understand all Black people, or "New Afrikans," as hostages to the illegitimate slaveocracy of the United States, and our de-territorialization as a condition that can be solved only through an independent nation-state. Nehanda herself said that "going to prison frightens me, but living as a neo-slave terrorizes me. That's why I struggle."[6] It now occurs to me that her story (at least the parts of it that I am, or feel, authorized to tell) constitutes another necessary theater—a story to pass on as I try to impart a different "quality of light" by which we may be able to read the failures of our liberation movements as something other than proof positive of the failure of our living (and failure of our precious and valiant dead). Something alively complicated and Blackfull.

A Glamorous New Afrikan Comes Home, Free

Nehanda Isoke Abiodun—also known as Cheri Dalton, Cherry, Nia, and once also called LaVerne—was a freedom fighter (see figure C.1). And she got it honest. Nehanda learned from her paternal grandmother that her ancestors had been maroons on St. Croix. Her father, who had joined the Nation of Islam during the "plague time" of heroin and despair in Harlem, grew disillusioned with the Nation just before Malcolm's assassination and turned to other forms of Black militancy. He had passionately debated with his (step)brothers and other family members about the right methodology toward Black freedom. Nehanda herself believed that

New Afrikans have a responsibility to themselves. It is necessary to build our own institutions and look to the government as little as possible for solutions. At different times in our struggle, demonstrations and sit-ins have made it possible to bring about certain changes in the United States, and without a doubt there comes a time in all struggles when negotiations are necessary. However, I feel for us to ultimately achieve full equality, an independent nation is the only answer.[7]

Upon her arrival in Cuba, two Babalawos (Santeria priests) told her in brilliant detail that her deceased father was her "protector and had cleared many dangerous paths so [she] could go safely through them . . . act[ing] as [her] Ellegua," or opener of the way. But she also said that

I do not think that being free in Cuba and not in some prison—or worse yet, dead because of the bullet of some FBI agent—is because of Divine intervention. I am free today because of some very heroic disciplined individuals. Most of whom the history books will probably never tell about. And I continue to be free because of people who believe in an independent New Afrika . . . as well as individuals dedicated to the ending of oppression wherever it exists.[8]

Here she was too humble to count herself as her own "heroic and disciplined individual." That is left for us to say—to tell in this history book, at least. Nehanda made herself free and kept herself free; and her sacrifices cut her and her family deeply. Nehanda preferred to be out and about in Havana: lecturing to visiting groups about international Black struggle, hip-hop, Cuban history, and other topics. She had to, I later understood. Otherwise, *they* would have won. Still, I sometimes annoyed Nehanda with my abundance of caution. After all, although I was honored to step in and imagine myself as her own personal rum-swilling, ethnographic note-taking, temporary FOI (Fruit of Islam, the famously bow-tied and disciplined security detail of Nation of Islam) when in Cuba; she was, of course, eminently qualified to take care of herself and certainly did not need my so-called protection. One day in La Habana Vieja gave form to my fears. A fit, middle-aged white man briefly overheard Nehanda and me speaking in English at the outdoor café of the Hotel Inglaterra and came to our table. We were clear that he was up to something more than looking for cut-rate cigars. I had already seen the reissue of the FBI Wanted List, and I understood that if a term paper that found its way to the internet could impel the New Jersey governor to put a new, higher bounty on our Sister's head, anything was possible. Both were targets and "wanted," but Sister is more well known and therefore in heightened jeopardy. On a few occasions, while waiting for her, it became clear that plans and location had to be changed or canceled. Security is a constant concern. It was chilling to hear the white man from the United States utter our Sister's name, likely to test our reactions. We registered none. I am proud of the way our quickly improvised subterfuge, complete with fake Caribbean accents, composed a short, noncommittal, dismissive story for the annoying Yuma. This extemporaneous performance art allowed us to slip out of his sight, with Nehanda quickly on the phone to report this. A few days later, we heard that Cuban police had apprehended an American in a fishing boat packed with electrical tape, rope, and chloroform.

The 1960 struggle between Harlemites and Columbia University over its efforts to build an effectively segregated gym in Morningside Park, where young Cheri (Nehanda) played, was her first political battle. Although the long-term experience "strengthened [her] convictions about the futility of working within the system . . . [she also recognized that] these types of community organizations are necessary, without them our conditions would be worse." Nehanda recognized protest politics and grassroots organizing as "in many aspects . . . our first line of defense." She volunteered with the West Harlem Community Organization from the time she was a child until she began college—fittingly poetic, at Columbia. "The university was a major contributor to my radical [politics, and now she would] use the institution to teach [her] how to better defeat its efforts to oppress our people," she said.[9] Nehanda and I talked about Harlem a lot. It is where she grew up and where I lived after my first research trip to Cuba while a graduate student at Columbia. Foreshadowing the current moment in which the university has executed its long-awaited Harlem plan—sprawling in each direction— she said that "what I didn't know then, but was to discover in time, was that the building of the gym was the first step in an attempt to retake Harlem by large real estate developers."[10] What she may not have been aware of then was that Columbia University (like New York University) is one of the largest real estate holders in New York City and has contributed mightily to its transformation (or regentrification). Returning to Harlem for Nehanda's memorial service in the winter of 2019 again collapsed time and place for me. After a long period out of contact, I had been scheduled to travel to Havana in February, when Nehanda was to be publicly honored for her tremendous contributions to Black Cuban culture (through her work as the doula and "godmother of Cuban hip-hop"), to US medical students, and to women who needed "uplift."[11] She loved the young people whom she tutored in Black history, Black consciousness, and Black gender and sexuality politics. She kept their secrets and worked with them to have fewer secrets. She fought and strategized and finessed to resolve the material problems and dramas of their daily lives. Nehanda was our ambassador in Cuba. Finding resources where there were none. Supporting others when she had so little. Spearheading Black August and her annual Anti-Colonial Thanksgiving. She took her role as "Mama Nehanda" seriously as an extension of her revolutionary New Afrikan work. My sister Nehanda had been ill and seemed to be recovering when she died and passed to the ether on January 30, 2019. I would not see her again in this life. Out of time.

A Final Love Letter. "Siempre, Hasta Victoria"

(Harlem, Feb. 15, 2019)

The Cecil is one of the places I'd dreamed of bringing you, Nehanda (I almost wrote Nia, I am so used to it). I tried on a few occasions to interpret gentrified Harlem for you, as you might understand it, and not how social scientists might focus on what we have lost and are losing. I wanted to emphasize how we were and are still Us. Doing how we do. Even as they encroach. We are still us, on the corners that remain, and the bourgie of us still enjoy a glass or two of Barolo with our perfectly grilled lamb chops! I risk embarrassing myself as my eyes well up at The Cecil. The 90s R&B is too loud for dining, but I am grateful for the interruption of my post-memorial service reverie. Chinganji and V modeled that regal restraint that you would have insisted upon, at your service (even though you would have been boo-hooing the entire time, like I did—with dignity, of course!). At the next table, I hear that Black woman laughter that you had perfected. I can hear your cackle (and wheeze) now. This laughter is balm and prophylaxis for me. The sisters and I share a few words. Then, leaning on the other side of the sisters' table, the inevitable brother arrives, cheesing, to be playfully indulged only until their food starts to cool, and then must be respectfully dismissed with an "a'ight now, brother. . . ." Seamless, elegant. Serious Blackfullness. Brunch and dinner at new restaurants, and old ones you would not recognize, are packed with white folks who have miraculously materialized regular garbage pick-up and street sweeping in Harlem! The po-lice keep watch, digitally occupying from towers with bright lights suspended above the avenues, making night like day in a strange time-space. Remember my mentioning "the panopticon" when we visited that plantation in Matanzas and saw the overseer's watchtower from which he would watch Africans cut and process sugar cane? Like that. There are a lot of white folks around these days—even more than when I lived there, and scandalized you and Sister with my story of the white lady pushing her own white baby in a carriage as I crossed the court-yard of the Manhattanville projects on my way to class early one morning. A sure sign of "the end," we had all observed. But, this is still ours in a way you would recognize and celebrate, Nehanda. Harlemites have not ceded the cultural territory. You wrote to your childhood friend "Word is we grew up in an underprivileged, deprived neighborhood. It's true that when Adam Clayton Powell was the congressman . . . he held hearings and they designated our block as the worst block in the United States."[12] But, of course, you agreed with Nikki that they would not understand: "Black love is Black wealth."[13]

There is a large party celebrating a birthday, a few tables away. If you had been here, Nehanda, we certainly would have been over there to greet the birthday girl, before our next course. That broughtupsy and cu-riosity that Large Marge instilled in you. Grace and glamour. Intelligent, self-possessed and charming, you are the one I would send if I had been in charge of fundraising and garnering support for the movement: the tall, beautiful, persuasive Harlem girl would be the one. The men and the women, the wealthy and the poor, would not resist that laugh . . . those eyes that had already analyzed and decided. Your people are interrupting my post-memorial reminiscing again. Instead of the standard birthday song, or even Stevie's version, they are playing Rihanna. Loudly: "Cake! Cake! Cake! Cake!" and the dining room goes up. I love my people. This feels, in flashes, a bit like the Black "champagne socialism" we talked about. I am laughing now, remembering the look of surprise on that brother's face, years ago. He was shocked and confused that you were eat-ing (black market) lobster and drinking the oldest rum we could find in Havana for that celebration. You summed up Black champagne socialism when you said "I don't think there's anything intrinsically wrong with a Mercedes, I just think everyone ought to have one" (Yes, you said it! I remember this distinctly, and wrote it in my notes). A romantic would-be revolutionary with hands softer than mine, and a raised eyebrow of youthful judgment that he had good sense enough to keep to himself; that brother could not see the many days and months in which you had (and would have) nothing—before going underground, and certainly after. Nada. No hay. No visit to el shopping for chicken or cooking oil, because you had no US dollars. Nothing except paltry Cuban rations, and whatever you could barter or borrow from neighbors, as you all tried to stay afloat. The Cubans are metaphorically "exiled" from the rest of the world—cut off by the heartless and senseless US Embargo; and you were doubly exiled—suffering the same deprivations of *el pueblo* without the comfort of your own family or your neighborhood, or *your* people. To-night, on this *isla* (Manhattan), after the last sips of Calvados are drained from my glass, there's a hefty bill to be paid. And of course, it is brick out-side these doors: so cold. Only a few can get in here. This ain't nowhere near socialism of any kind.

I am remembering our long nights laughing as Havana Club and La Mulata (lesser brands, only if we had no more money) filled our glasses and accompanied our long laughter and our tears. One after the other in no particular order or categorization—all the same profound love. Whether in the form of parental guilt, political frustration, personal dif-ficulties; our grief, mourning, hope or fear for the future, and our resolve; or the antics of the day as we gossiped about folks who were "stuck on stupid," no matter. There was always laughter (and always will be). "Ay, no hay que llorar. . . ." Isaac Delgado had just recently covered Celia's "la vida es un carnaval" when we met. At first, it can feel like some sappy bullshit, but once you begin dancing to it, you know it can be true, if you let it be. Momentarily. Even in exile. *Que la vida es una hermosura / Hay que vivirla / . . . / Que en la vida no hay nadie solo / Oh, there's no need to cry (Do not cry) / Que la vida es un carnaval* ("Life is beautiful / it must be lived / . . . / in life no one is alone / There is always someone . . ."). I want this to be true. I can hardly bear to admit that exile is defined by perpetual loneliness, but it is. Still, *Hay que vivirla*—it must be lived. I will not bore you with how that simple truth is now in such controversy in Black studies.

I broke the rule. ¡Estoy llorando! Again, without you. Just another sip. A few more laughs with Black folks reveling in the Blackfullness of Har-lem. I met Uncle N at the memorial, and several of your stories of him, and of Large Marge, whooshed into my head at the same time. And now, in the company of the Ancestors, when you meet mommy and daddy and aunt Natalie (and uncle Milton, just a month before you), you will see that I did not make up a thing—they are likely still carrying on the same conversations, the same shtick they had entertained each other with over more than seventy years together. On my way to your memorial service, I went by Large Marge's building—where she fell in love with my Phillip, in 1999. She had sneered at my African name, gleefully approved of "(Prince) Phillip's," and greeted us both with the warmth and love of family. Pretending to struggle with the name Jafari, your beautiful mother playfully snapped "you must be one of them!" And I quickly and clearly answered her that I was not a member of y'all's New Afrikan People's party! With the quickness. But I did also say that I love and respect your aims and your sacrifices for our people. Of course, she rolled her eyes—then poured each of us a drink. Fed us. We had a great time talking about you and how much you love her and your children, and about all the changes happening in Harlem up to then (so much has happened since). The truth is, I might have joined the Party, or other cadres, since my twenties had been spent doing similar work. But so-called "revolutionaries" and Black nationalists of various sorts had already scarred me. I would not give them another chance. And now, I confess that I also resent their inability—our inability, really, as this is a failure of the entire Black left—to protect you and other freedom fighters from exile, or imprisonment. I know this is unfair. As Large Marge told me about Black militancy, it is "like fighting a nuclear bomb with a slingshot." She thought it was stupid, but I cannot help but celebrate the courage, commitment and effort. Still, too many of the folks that I met in the US who claimed to represent "revolution" were misguided ideologues, comfortably wrapped in impotent homophobia and misogynoir. The opposite of revolutionary, in fact. Thanks to you and Sister, I witnessed, up close, what Ché had said: ". . . The true revolutionary is guided by a great feeling of love. It is impossible to think of a genuine revolutionary lacking this quality. . . ." It is not lost on me that Ché began this passage saying "At the risk of seeming ridiculous. . . ."[14]

Fugitivity means facing the possibility that you may one day be captured. At your memorial, V told the story of your "go bag." You had no James Bond type accoutrement, but if you had been fated to, you were sure enough not going to be caught without some lipstick on, and your outfit together. At the service, V joked that you had been underground so long that your fly go bag outfit was now very out of style. Did you ever update it? We had laughed about this before—the prayer you wrote: "God I don't want to be caught, but if I am, please give me that strength not to talk, allow me to carry myself with the dignity of those who have resisted before me; and please don't let the pictures that will be printed in the newspapers have me looking like a gorilla instead of a guerilla." I am still giggling behind this.[15] Although you were likely deep underground then, you must have seen the *New York Daily News* cover photo of Sister when they captured her. Somehow, her afro was on point—a penumbra, a crown, and an indestructible halo. Beautiful skin impossibly glowing. Sister's hands, though shackled, like her ankles, are elegantly posed in benediction, like that of an icon—Jesus of Queens, Christed One of North Carolina. But we are not indestructible, not one of us. *Black may not crack*, but oh my God, our insides! Only her defiant, gleaming eyes, staring down those who were vapidly gazing at her newspaper image over a morning cup of coffee—in "double-breasted mourning" and "domestic bacteria," Sister Sonia might call this condition—gave any indication of the degradation, beatings and torture she had endured at the hands of the police.[16] How she had been and continues to be maligned, both by lies about what happened on the New Jersey Turnpike; and like you, by not being accorded the customary respect that any valiant combatant in a long complicated war should be extended. When someone in a student group visiting Cuba asked why you fled the US—that is, asking what you were accused of, it was important to remind them that you had never been captured and therefore never had your day in court. Still, what you were accused of—conspiring to "expropriate" or "liberate" or "steal" money from an armored car, which reportedly found its way to clinics and freedom fighters in Africa and around the world, and conspiring to get our Sister to Cuba, left me agreeing with the position I heard you tell innumerable student groups. Of course, never giving any details, and speaking hypothetically and academically on your political position and ethical commitment, you said: "If I had done these things, I would be proud." I am proud to love you. Siempre (Always).

Siempre. That was the benediction at your homegoing service—your "homecoming"—ain't that the way with us, always at once coming and going? "Siempre . . ." (Always). Stevie Wonder entitled the song "As," and it is a whole spiritual philosophy in itself.[17] I remember it as "Always" because it is his refrain that you cannot let go of once you hear it. That note that runs up and down leaving everyone but Stevie breathless. Chinganji was the first up to dance. She had invited me to sit up front with she and Mukungu, and I was honored to be there, listening to Josey and Kathryn, Hannah, Cathyryn, Mukungu and Chinganji, V, and E with your beautiful grandchildren—everyone gave such loving tributes. Still, at this point in the service I was ready for a good long ugly cry over a glass of aged brown liquor, solo—not to do the bus stop with hundreds of people, standing room only, at the National Black Theater. I am glad that Chinganji is smarter than me, and that I dared not disobey her invitation to dance. In her earlier remarks, she had recalled how you two brought the electric slide to Cuba, at the afternoon matinee disco (or, y'all's *claim* to have brought it)! According to Chinganji, the two of you introduced the electric slide a year or two before I first arrived, only to be outdone by the sisters and brothers who added rumba moves to it (these days we have the cha-cha slide—which could be another transnational circuit). The matinee was so much fun, and so disorienting—to be dancing to classic 70s and 80s R&B early in the afternoon, in that dark, windowless disco in El Vedado that had not been remodeled since the 70s, at the end of the 1990s. I was there with you two at the matinee one afternoon when we were nearly overrun on the second go round of electric slide—shoulders and asses shaking *en clave*, and footwork a lo Cubano. You can't outdo us, even when it is *us* outdoing doing us! But then, sister, we will always have "Love Is the Message" at your 50th birthday party. Daughter of Oshun, you were resplendent in gold. Appropriate, since you were our glittery Ambassador of New Afrika. Messenger of the new world to come. Light flickered in the warm glow of Caribbean sunset, and we all lit up the darkest part of the night, until sunrise—time did not stand still, but neither did we. Between us, *luz de mi vida,* there will always be a disco ball.

Love break Love break Love break. Love break[18]

"But We Held Out Our Eyes Delirious with Grace"

A *between* can be a space of tension: an unanswered or open question.[19] Perhaps also an unanswered phone or an open wound. It can be an adhesive kiss. But between is also always shared space. Interstitial. The intersection meets, between. It is what we share. Not only are the Atlantic and other seas and landmasses "between us," but we also share an ecology. *Between* is in the stroke (/) that articulates closely and is a synapse for exchange. A spark, a catalyst, or perhaps a suture—*stitches, darling!*—but not glue. There is so much between us. We must not dishonor or discard any of it. Marcus had asked for a "Black/gay normative theory." This book is as close as I can get, in my own way and as honestly as I can manage, to sketch for him and for others one vision. I have tried to make good Black/gay sense of the current moment, attempting to re-member a Black gay politics that may be necessary for all our futures.

It seems clear now—belatedly, perhaps, that the anthological habits of mind and quality of analysis of radical Black lesbian feminists undergird a politics of accomplice that might have made us (all) free. Precisely not "presupposing a horizon of overcoming . . . and pictur[ing] a past and present that secures its plausibility," which revolutionary romance had promised.[20] Black gay offered (only) friendship/love, constant struggle, paths toward personal and group autonomy and moments of respite, a strident expression of dramatic sibilance, and a clear path to understanding and working with and within difference. Death—whether by cancer, AIDS, or violence—was recognized as a constant specter. It was fought against, along with the commitment to not be "double cremated"—that is, not only dead/buried but eviscerated as well—as if you had never existed. (Do you see now why the lack of attention to this work is so "personal"?) But we could not describe this as pessimistic.

What we offer here will not satisfy everyone (or anyone, entirely). I can understand that some critics and individuals would have wanted a more certain, less messy, sexier, "clearer," denser, more standard, or more au courant theorization. I hear them clamoring—some elegantly and convincingly. Some of your margin notes, dear reader/friend, are already prefigured in pencil. Some of *yuh vex*! For one, some of you threaten to scream if you have to read that five-letter name once more—I get it. But (deep breath, darling) *A-u-d-r-e* warned us against "drug[ging] ourselves with dreams of new ideas. . . ." Here we have offered newly considered (re)narrativizations of what she called "old and forgotten ideas, new combinations, extrapolations and recognitions from within ourselves, along with the renewed courage to try them out."[21] And it ain't easy. This is one creative response to the "And if we lose?" question assayed in the first pages of our conversation. It chats back to those who say that we have already lost. And to those who (want us to) believe there is no "us" to lose anything at all and/or who wish to annihilate an "I" that might contribute to the reproduction of a "we" with an actively alive connection to our (wronged and/or failed) dead. We are advocating a practice of dynamic sociality that involves, among a few things, tarrying with/for the dead and being alive to our messy and difficult-to-translate Blackfull nows. This work extends an invitation to see and hear beyond the schools or camps that we are used to finding in neat opposition, and to tune in to polyphonies that urge a different dance, begun again. I do not offer this as a refutation.

In fact, the vantage of inside/outside or "ruptured kinship or solidarity" that Black anthropologists have offered moves precisely against the logic of one view supplanting the other or insisting that several things cannot be "true" or useful or usable at the same time. As opposed to a winner-takes-all game, the readings here are reparative and include the possibility of failure. The conversation we enjoin is open to revision, multiplicity, and extension. After all, this is how Black gay life is lived and imagined, variably, across and within different space-times, beyond any area (studies), discipline, or theoretical framework.

Finding themselves already untimely and almost out of time, the "epidemic dead and the living" of the long 1980s built the tradition that *Disco Ball* follows. Anthologized themselves into spaces of multiplicity and productive, messy, sexy, difference—not fracture. Not disengagement or disaffiliation. Not nonbeing. And/but this is never easy "nor neat, or pretty, or quick," as Pat has already told you.[22] To be anthologized is to be called and culled together under one cover. The title may not fit easily for each of us or each of our genre choices, styles, or languages. But we consent to gather together to at least explore our common through-lines, hoping for generative connections between our individual projects, toward *something* else.[23] One way to describe this something else is via Tina Campt's "grammar of Black feminist futurity."[24] In her language, *There's a Disco Ball Between Us: A Theory of Black/Gay Life* can be described as seeking to articulate a "grammar of possibility ... beyond a simple definition of the future tense ... striv[ing] for the tense of possibility grammarians refer to as the future real conditional [*that which will have had to happen*] and reflecting an attachment to a belief in what *should* be true, which impels us to realize that aspiration."[25] As Barbara (Ransby) reminds us, we have our own work to do in the now. We revisit and re-narrativize because we still do not know enough or know deeply enough. We are looking for the techniques, strategies, and spells to make it through what scholars have called "afterlife of slavery" or "wake(s)" or "break(s)"— and what I have tried to illustrate as the kaleidoscopic time space of the disco ball: here/now/there/then, simultaneously.[26]

Today, the children are turning it. They are turning inveterate politics and strategies on their heads, literally snatching the mic from stalwart crusaders who are by now perhaps too comfortably adjacent to power. The children are seizing the worldwide stage that the internet provides, and they are turning civil rights songs and spirituals into a *vogue*. In response, radical feminist Black gays—lesbians, trans folks, gay men, and bisexuals of the anthological generation—might simply say, "You're welcome." Practices of #BlackLives-

Matter, the Movement for Black Lives, and allied movements have taken up their mantle of intersectionality, anti-normativity, refusal to perform respectably, deployment of the sexy and the fun alongside the very real possibility of imminent death and, plainly and finally, the lack of fucks to give. Picture another conjuncture: the formation of Black studies. Whereas the intention of the Ford Foundation and university presidents may have been one thing—*come to college rather than burning our cities.... Imbibe the Liberal tradition and put down Cabral and Mao and Rodney and Fanon*—the intention of the students, those with the pens and rocks and keys to the trustee boardrooms in their hot sweaty hands, was quite another. Still, there was a conjuncture of interests that brought them together and that, I daresay, brings nearly every one of us to Black studies and Black/queer studies today. These days, I ask myself to imagine how to cultivate fortuitous mash-ups and conjunctures without getting the politics and the love pulverized into a mere plaque on the wall, or a Disneyfied caricature of my intention, reading: "Here sat a Black fag in a fierce Tom Ford Suit. Books by Duke. Eyewear Japanese. Prefers his rum *bastante añejo* and food from farm to table." We are worth so much more than *Project Tenure, America's Next Top Full Prof,* or *Survivor: Towers of Ivory.*

"The thing is, I just don't want people to think I am a naive optimist," Tina admits confiding to her friend while they powerwalk and talk about writing.[27] You will recognize this anxiety, of course, as one of my own. One that I had to release (or, more likely, lean into) to complete this work (then reiterate/revise, complete again, repeat, then edit at least once more). Ché resounds in my mind's ear (*A riesgo de parecer ridículo*), impelling me to try: "At the risk of seeming ridiculous...."[28] Today, there is certainly little to evince a rosy view. Still, I hope that you will acknowledge the unthought facileness of our common articulation of naive (and/to) optimist and the converse assumption of sophisticated pessimism, even generations after the formulation of necessary and indivisible *pessimism of the intellect and optimism of the will* in times and circumstances such as ours.[29] There is so much more to consider beyond pessimism *or* optimism.

I find much resonance with the best of the set of works glossed as Afropessimist. It seems to me that the legion of graduate students parroting their smart, dire passages with pornographic glee, and their discontented critics frustrated by the airless depressive erudition of their argumentation, have both missed an essential piece of this work, which, as Vanessa (Agard-Jones) reminded me, emerges from the author's own experiences of organized political struggle and engagement with Black politics on the ground. I read the best of this stream of work extending Orlando Patterson's notion of social death of the slave as more evidence of profound Black radical fatigue after the failure of Black politics and facing (another) *after the end of the world*. *This time*, they seem to be saying, *embrace it*. Whereas various acolytes read or pose this work as proof positive of "impossibility" as they reduce Black folks to "bodies" that do not dance or fuck or laugh or fight back, I read the best of it as refined intellectualization of frustrated work toward improving the condition of Black folks. I do not agree, but I hear them saying "better to pose social death to prevent more dead ends." But I hear another trend gaining saliency in Black studies that has not received much attention, perhaps because its roots are so deeply entangled. I hear theorists I will call *disaffiliates*, saying "Let the dead bury their dead." In my crystal (disco) ball (which is also a high-fidelity speaker), I already hear them groaning loudly in these margins, "Enough already with the conscientious critical remembrance!" They might say give it up already and move on to something that might actually "work" to make more *liberty*. . . . They want to "indulge the passing dreams of choice" that she said we could not do—those of us who "sit at the shores of decision / crucial and alone."[30] Theorists of many stripes mistake that position at the edge of decision as a permanent one and fail to see it as a crucial locus of enunciation meant to highlight and enable those within the most dangerous crosshairs. They read a shoreline as an insignificantly small place, not a continent whose ebbs and flows beget other continents and from which sisters and brothers have already changed the world for the better. They misread "alone," not understanding that the final lines of the poem— "It is better to speak . . . remembering . . ."—give us precisely the incantation to transform alone to community: speech/action that instantiates an us/we. "*Siempre. Hasta* . . . ," "like bread in our children's mouths."[31]

This is not pathological. No "melancholy" in this historicism but rather mourning, anger, love, and aliveness.[32] This is a condition of blackness. Thus, the position of disaffiliates is alarming. And it is hurtful to me, which is part of their argument, in fact. That (this ain't none of my business, not necessarily, and) I would not feel hurt if I were to disaffiliate or at least hold a cool, disciplined academic distance. Not be so sentimental (and I cannot help also hearing: *act like a man!*). But "my grace" came in the form of the words and action of the epidemic dead and the living of the long 1980s, who provided the conjure medicine of space-time projection. They created a crucial prefiguration of who I (am) (could) becom(ing), therefore not only what and whom I see but, more precisely and importantly, also *how I see*: a Black/gay habit of mind. David (Scott) offers the important formulation of "generational vantage" in terms of coming of age within a particular time frame and therefore with a particular relation to understanding of specific discourses within a conjunctural "problem space." Still, I am not only referring to the white hair in my beard and slight/bop twist habitus. At a 2019 panel reflecting on Black Nations/Queer Nations?, Jacqui (M. Jacqui Alexander) once again clarified for me the conjunctural questions I need to ask myself, not only to define the problem space but also to engage intellectual/activist visions as blackprints for building *something else* (here's that "normative theory" piece that is so unfashionable). She described this Black/gay theory of living by insisting that we all grapple with a deceptively simple set of questions: "Who Are You? Why Did You Come? Who Do You Walk With?"[33] I have elliptically argued here that in the current moment we are all various sorts of conscripts of the *"epidemic living* and the dead." This does not guarantee or place us in any trajectory for final overcoming or failure. This finds us alive, acting, choosing or being forced to choose, working and wuking and werking through and within various "wakes" and "holds" that occur simultaneously and that flow not only from the Middle Passage but also from various waves of subjectification. The generational vantage of Black gay habit of mind does what David has called for: "In a present in which that revolutionary horizon of overcoming evaporates as a future we can aspire to . . . [I have tried to illumine, through a methodology as queer as cat bones, a re-] narrative that connects past, present, and future in other ways than does the revolutionary romance."[34] Melvin had already offered this. Audre had already offered this. The epidemic living and the dead have already told you. This is a remixed, long play. Shall we dance?

acknowledgments

This book is a sort of extended acknowledgment of my bonds with and thanks to conversation partners, ancestors, and friends here and there. *Thank you.* I hope that you can feel my deep gratitude on every page—in every riff and quotation, reformulation, wink and nod throughout. The following notes acknowledge contributions to this book, not my unbounded gratitude to a long list of people not mentioned here. This too will be incomplete, and idiosyncratic to this moment of recollection. I apologize for both.

There's a soundtrack to this too (of course). We begin with "Umi Says" by Yasin Bey (Mos Def):

> Put my heart and soul into this song
> I hope you feel me
> From where I am, to wherever you are
> I mean that sincerely

On July 21, 2007, my friend Ana-Maurine Lara wrote a seven-line poem for me at the Fire & Ink/RedBone Press retreat in Austin. It has been pinned above my desks in three different cities. It is never far from Jimmy Baldwin's Provence key, from Jordan Rogers, or the paper cutout of embracing Black arms made for me by Lidia Marte. Ana-Maurine's first line is "Listen." This work is made possible because I believed her—and everyone who shared that space at our magical retreat on the lake. I have tried to listen carefully, even when there was a lot of static. My students at four institutions (and counting) have been my generous and effective teachers. My writing and thinking practice was deepened and expanded by a set of truly gifted colleagues and friends, some of whom were once my students. A return to my alma mater, Morehouse College, to lend my hand in the present served to reconcile my past, and more importantly gave me clear visions of brilliant Black futures being crafted by those emerging. Teaching "Black LGBTQ Genealogies" at Morehouse realigned me in the best ways, right on Black gay time. This impelled a significant perspective shift in my research and my writerly voice. Thank you to all of my AUC students, especially the triumvirate—Fatima Jamal, Kenny Pass, and Marcus Lee—and to Alexandria (Lexi) Smith. After an intense graduate seminar, filmmaker and Yale AfAm/American studies doctoral student Wills Glasspiegel shared his stunning video interviews with the indefatigable Kevin Aviance, which reorganized and reignited my thinking, not just in the shape of a disco ball, but also its ineffable flicker/flash and the force of the ether that keeps turning it. My friend Wura Natasha Ogunji generously lent not only her magnificent artwork to be reproduced but also the book's name (*There's a Disco Ball Between Us*). An artistic visionary and expert draughtswoman, Wura and her visual and poetic work gave shape to my own inchoate impressions, helping me to see my field notes, persistent memories, and ways of being as a single composition.

Let me acknowledge two classroom scenes. In Hazel Carby's "Racial Formations" class, a brilliant group of first-year African American studies doctoral students read *¡Venceremos?* deeply, finely, and generously, making connections beyond my words to the depth of the conversations between my respondents and me and to my writerly intentions. It was the sort of time-traveling, discipline-traversing, border-crossing conversation that I have tried to engender in *Disco Ball*. I still think about how Hazel worked in her classroom: seemingly effortless but also intensely attentive, incisive, and potentially encyclopedic (never ostentatious, but with her vast facilities always at the ready). (Now Drs.) Ashley James and Andrew Dowe elegantly showed me how my first book could also point to so much more that there is left to say. And the hospitality mirrored what I was experiencing "in the field" in the early days of *Disco Ball* research. I shall never forget the generosity that Hazel and our students showed me—intellectually, and by mixing mojitos with beautiful Martiniquais rum as a Caribbean *brindis* in the middle of the day in the Gordon Parks Conference Room. A couple years later, during my visit to his "Americanist Scholars" course, Michael Denning catalyzed, at (what I now know was) precisely the right moment, the first of a few crucial shifts I would make to complete this book. What I had written was on the verge! And under pressure. It could have simply become a big book of easily assimilable transnational ethnographic case studies that the Yale Social Science Divisional Committee may have wanted for promotion to full professor (but that nobody else needed and nobody—other than the committee, perhaps—had asked for). Comparing ¡Venceremos? to what would become this book, Michael observed that this work is not the ethnography of any particular place—"it is an ethnography of an idea." I remain grateful for his timely intervention and for brilliant comments by Daphne Brooks, Matthew Jacobson, and Inderpal Grewal, who attended the session and engaged so generously. These scenes were extraordinary but not surprising as a feature of intellectual life during that brief moment at Yale African American studies. Our leader, Elizabeth Alexander, offered a vision of an expansive and engaged critical Black studies that I hold close and try to cultivate. She opened our semesters like a true headmistress, her gold charm bracelet dangling and diction crisp as she recited our succinct, time-honored marching orders from the poetry of Gwendolyn Brooks, Audre Lorde, or Robert Hayden . . . at the start and end of each semester. Elizabeth reached into our great poetic ether to invoke occasion at 81 Wall Street. Thank you to my dear colleagues in African American studies; American studies; anthropology; ethnicity, race, and migration; and women's, gender, and sexuality studies who reminded me that our work, if it is sincere, endures and expands beyond any institution's imprimatur (read also: "brand"). My profound thanks also go to the smartest person at 10 Sachem Street, Kamari Clarke. Kamari mentored me, then was one of the first, of many, to show us how to make a principled and poised exit. Cue: mash-up between Sister Nancy and Chaka Demus & Pliers' versions of "Bam Bam."

This truth cannot be discounted: transnational research, writing, and engagement require more money and time than most institutions invest. I am very grateful for the vote of confidence and material support of generous research funds and faculty leaves afforded me by Yale University, and grants from Yale's MacMillan Center for International Studies and Whitney Humanities Center. The University of Miami supported the final publication subvention and future translation, for which I am very grateful. Without this material support, this book would not have been possible. Moreover, I will say again: *no one is able to do ethnography without people who share.* My gratitude goes to those who opened their mouths to tell their own truths and to those who opened doors to archives to find other voices and images.

If these acknowledgments were just about my "personal" thanks, I could simply write a nice list of names of usual suspects without this *too bright* interruption. But I remember. And I am still listening. I must therefore also acknowledge the deafening silences and stunned faces with which this work and I have been met. (Having read the book, you may understand why.) I chat back here because silences and erasures still proliferate in academic reading practices, faculties, curricula, admission, hiring committees, office hours appointments, and publication: threatening my students and others emerging. Versions of a few chapters of *There's a Disco Ball Between Us* were out on the stroll over many years. I am grateful for all of my lecture audiences, co-panelists, and students. I learned to listen carefully—both to discern who my actual conversation partners and primary "audiences" for this book might be and to recognize the variety of registers that constitute those otherwise deafening silences.

Early on, in "How to See and Say, Here and Now"—a 2013 University of Pennsylvania Department of Anthropology colloquium lecture—I was trying to work out a methodology for ethnographic engagement, after *¡Venceremos?* and before the notion of "ethnography of an idea" catalyzed my shift to highlight my own meaning making as an intellectual and political strength rather than as an ethnographic failure. I remember this as the intensification of mostly silent Q&As. It was as if I had presented something too far *beyond the pale* in anthropology. But, as usual, Deborah Thomas, John Jackson, and Kamari Clarke rigorously and warmly engaged and encouraged, brilliantly pushing me on the "here-and-there" comparative framework and crucially asking for an accounting of scale, distinction, and stakes. A few other key lectures at departments of anthropology also proved clarifying for my writing and revisions. Among these I must note (at least) a few: Bayo Holsey, Lorand Matory, and Charles Piot invited me to give a joint anthropology and African American studies lecture at Duke University, where African American Studies Department colleague Wahneema Lubiano shared among the most cogent and generous analyses of the work I had heard. Instantly, I was happily in *her* seminar during the Q&A furiously jotting her crystalline questions and comments. Having already written that Black queer studies serve as a space in which one might experience freedom in the form of pedagogical and epistemological pleasure, Wahneema instantiated this for me that day, and Bayo and Randy extended this mode of generous engagement. This constitutes an important low-key ethnographic scene and salient epistemological position that centrally informs this work: for me, our Black (queer) studies conversations—sometimes within the prevailing disciplinary bounds, and/but always pushing against them—were always the most urgent and sophisticated and compelling. Still, my account should not be read as a "community" account any more than an academic one authorized by a particular discipline. Having mourned missed opportunities for fuller conversations, and perhaps quarrel, with my folks, I am thankful to the Black Gay Research Group (2003, 2012) and Black Gay Men's Network (2010) for inviting me to present my work-in-progress, even when my earnest enthusiasm, nerdiness, and my (perhaps annoying) insistence on questioning the politics and efficacy of exclusive male space may have gotten in the way of productive conversation and "translation."

The Queering Anthropology Conference at Yale, organized by my Department of Anthropology colleague Karen Nakamura, brought GLBT and queer anthropology folks together, providing me with the thrill of finally meeting Gloria Wekker and to offer a response to her superb keynote, as well as hearing fascinating keynote talks by Martin Manalansan and Don Kulick, and the chance to debate the shallows and depths of queer anthropological ties with conversation partners including Karen, Vanessa Agard-Jones, Christa Craven, Naisargi Dave, Nesette Falu, Lyndon Gill, Shaka McGlotten, Scott Morgensen, Marcia Ochoa, Margot Weiss, and Mary Weismantel. I remain haunted by Mary's keen invocation in that space of police/vigilante execution of Black youths as an unexamined aspect of "reproductive failure." The symposium was my first opportunity to thank Tom Boellstorff in person for his deeply invested and generous three-page, single-spaced revise/resubmit response to my article submission when he was editor of *American Anthropologist* (surprise: I did not initially receive this as the gesture of care and commitment that it was). Later, after a rejection from *AA*, Inderpal Grewal tutored me in her home over a lovely bottle of Sancerre. She said: "I see the problem. You have written a beautiful essay. But the assignment is to write a good anthropology article." I received this savvy analysis as a choice. Not only did my immediate mission to revise become crystal clear, but my own resolve shifted. After following Tom and Inderpal's advice, the piece was accepted immediately at *American Ethnologist*. The invitation to return to UT-Austin to deliver a talk and workshop this work with Lyndon Gill, Xavier Livermon, Dora Santana, Omise'eke Natasha Tinsley, and Matt Richardson came at a fortuitous moment. I am thankful to this important (again, brief) Black queer diaspora formation and to long-term UT friends and colleagues Juliet Hooker, João Vargas, Ted Gordon, Charlie Hale, Shirley Thompson, Steve Marshall, Jenifer Wilks, and others for their engagement. Special thanks go to Lyndon for pushing me on the question of historicity.

I am grateful for my "Black Erotics: New Theories on Race and Porn" co-panelists Nicole Fleetwood, Mireille Miller-Young, Jennifer Christine Nash, and Carla Williams. We each presented work that elicited pearl-clutching in the packed house at the Black Portraiture(s): The Black Body in the West conference in 2013. I am indebted to Deborah Willis for the invitation, the engagement, and her unflappability. Reading the room, I asked Deb's permission before showing the slide of "Brother with No Suit"—impressively protuberant and playful, projected on the beautiful floor-to-ceiling screen of the Musée du Quai Branly. CAAR 2011 Paris: "Black States of Desire: Dispossession, Circulation, Transformation" was productive and important, less because of scholarly exchange between Black queer studies scholars and our heterosexual Blackademic kin (sadly there was very little, as usual) than our fellowship with Black/queer colleagues from here and there, including the sublime party in that dark basement club in the Marais. After all, as Kassav sings, "Zouk-la sé sèl médikaman nou ni" (Zouk is the only medicine we have). Ana-Maurine Lara and colleagues at University of Oregon WGS, Anthropology, and Latin American studies provided among the earliest interlocutors for my understanding of "ethnography of an idea," which proved to be very productive, and conversation with Ana and Alai Reyes-Santos among the deep green of the Willamette Valley (and its pinot noir I have grown to adore) was especially restorative. In 2016, two important lectures and sets of conversations—delivering the Miranda Joseph Endowed Lecture at University of Arizona's Gender and Women's Studies and a keynote at Illinois State's Women's and Gender Studies—were especially helpful and engaging. Thank you to the wonderful colleagues at both institutions, including Susan Stryker, Miranda Joseph, and Erin Durban-Albrecht, and to the keen historian in the audience who pushed me to define and delimit "my 1980s." Thanks also to Antke Engel and Jule Jakob Govrin for their invitation to ICI Berlin/Institute for Queer Theory and especially to Serena Dankwa, my incisive and kind conversation partner for "Desire, Friendship, and Intimacy across the Black World." Days later, the highlight in Vienna was certainly fellowship with members of "Black Women's* Space," Vienna. Their clear-sighted, imperative DIY creation of a VIP section of Black community members in the first few rows of one of the whitest spaces I have ever experienced—the baroque lecture hall at Vienna University, Academy of Fine Arts—(with engaged and kind folks) inspired improvisations in my presentation that I carried with me to new revisions and new fieldwork encounters. And speaking of Black women resolutely making space, many thanks to Criola Organização de Mulheres Negras, in Rio de Janeiro; Universidade do Estado do Rio de Janeiro; and my brother João Costa Vargas for inviting me to participate in the International Graduate Seminar: "Resistance in Black/

African Diaspora" in 2012, and most recently "in Rio" via videoconferencing and Raquel DeSouza's seamless translation, which she executed *com muito plenenegritudade* (with much Blackfullness). Jordan had offered me the word *plenenegritude* as a translation for "Blackfull" months before, and I was proud to tell him that this recognized expert and former UT PhD student also employed this neologism. Once again, Criola presented us with the challenge of multiple genealogies, multiple languages, and multiple ways of understanding, and grappling with what João called "invitations to containment." This odd acknowledgments section is one small gesture toward making good on principled resistance to containment—spilling over conventions that may limit what is necessary to convey—at least gesturing toward some "risk" following the Criola conversation. *Obrigada/o*. I look forward to the challenge of translating this work.

Toward the end of this long journey, my 2017 Theory Workshop presentation at the University of Chicago Center for Race, Culture, and Politics was an important indication of how the best of political theorists might respond to my differently disciplined handling of (what I think of as) questions of politics and my account of HIV/AIDS in the long 1980s. Close engagement by Cathy Cohen (whose voice I hear in my head while writing), Adom Getachew, Marcus Lee, Ray Noll, and sociologist Kenny Pass helped me to rethink and reorder my evidence (which awaits correction and refinement by Marcus's account of Black gay politics in his dissertation to come). Thanks also to Cathy, Michael Hanchard, David Scott, Joy James, and the late Richard Iton for sterling examples of political theory that evidence capacious reading practices and extend across geographic and disciplinary borders. If I have not cited bell hooks in every chapter, it is only because I have already assimilated so much of her work in my own thinking. Thank you to her for exemplifying the most eminently teachable Black critical cultural studies.

In 2018 Columbia Anthropology welcomed me back to deliver the Franz Boas lecture in the same conference room/lounge in which, as a graduate student, I had witnessed numerous academic knife fights on occasions like these. It meant a great deal to see a few of my former professors, such as Steven Gregory, who taught my first anthropology of race course at NYU (he must have been a teenager) and thankfully held me to his own high standard as a member of my dissertation committee at Columbia years later. Two wonderful things happened that evening. First, David Scott asked a searing question about my conception of "after revolution/before freedom," then generously reframed my provisional answer, compelling my rethinking, rereading, and rewriting. Next, another faculty member assayed a weighty comment/question, which I received as an accusation—that the synopsis of this book that I offered represented a "normative project." This is quite an indictment in Franz Boas's house! I may have stammered. Walking backward to the lectern to print the note on my text in block letters, it occurred to me (and I couldn't help but say aloud) that she was probably right. If normative means that the point of this book is to perform and propose a could/should have/*will be* in that Black feminist tense of possibility, yes. This would become another key insight that would set my re-revisions and final reiterations flowing—now free of disciplinary propositions that are not my own (at least not all of the time, not in every work) and do not further my intellectual intentions, ethical warrants, or commitments.

One day I will write an intellectual history of a few related streams of end-of-the-century Black intellectual tradition and Black studies, exemplified by leaders whom I have had the honor to observe up close. For now, I will merely cite their names in the order I first found them and was transformed by their scholarly, artistic, and institutional capacity-building work. I include them here because this book writes to and through a Black studies tradition that they have mightily helped me to find, know, and assert my place within. First and foundationally, as an undergraduate: Drs. Johnnetta Cole, Gloria Wade-Gayles, Beverly Guy-Sheftall. As a graduate student: M. Jacqui Alexander, Cathy Cohen (as community intellectuals—I had not yet read a word of their scholarship), Manthia Diawara, and Manning Marable. I am grateful to have been mentored by Carole Boyce-Davies, Ted Gordon, Omi (Joni) Jones, and Cathy (again, but this time coming to terms with her transformative scholarship) in my first years in the professoriate, reminding me what I had come here to do in the first place. And toward crystallizing my own unique contribution *here, in this place*: Elizabeth Alexander, Cathy (again), and E. Patrick Johnson, whose work as an oral historian, editor, anthologist, and theorist has shaped Black queer studies and lovingly obliged me to sharpen my own tools. I also recall Farah Jasmine Griffin, whom I met for the first time as the panel chair of one of my first scholarly presentations, at "The Future of African American Studies" conference at Harvard in 2000 (alongside Marlon Bailey and Xavier Livermon, and where I first met Dagmawi Woubshet and Salamishah Tillet, who were members of the W. E. B. Du Bois Graduate Society, which organized the conference). My paper was "unconventional," perhaps, and (as there is in this book) there was a house-music score to the whole thing. I was a ball of nerves presenting autoethnographic US-based work (as opposed to my Cuban research in process, which felt more formally authorized), until I saw Farah *listening*. I could feel the engagement of someone I admired from afar and whose scholarship had already taught me so much (even before *If You Can't Be Free, Be a Mystery!*). This was an early lesson in pedagogy. When I am tired, I remember this. I adjust my attitude and resolve to speak kindly—pay attention—to the children (as she did that day). This affirmation carries.

With great care and an eye toward engendering lively, important conversations across disciplinary borders, Ken Wissoker has done a mighty work at Duke! My profound thanks go to you, for your eyes and your heart, and your belief in this project, Ken. My sincere thanks also go to Assistant Editor Joshua Gutterman Tranen, whose equanimity and care speak to wisdom beyond his years. Project Editor Annie Lubinsky created a seamless and facilitative process—conjuring order during a very stressful period—and the copy editor was serious, and gentle with my voice. The art department listened to my perhaps unusually specific and deeply felt ideas for what the book should look like, and Jim ChuChu generously lent his stunning image (*Pagans IX*), which seems to illustrate the embodied world-making the book meditates on and traces. His figure pulls from a gaseous ether—a fissure in the plane of regular space/existence. Not an on-the-nose disco ball, Erica James (who suggested Jim's work) offered that this one may have "shattered into magical dust as the subject vogues."

The index is your finding aid in this conversation and beyond. Who but Steven G. Fullwood could produce a document so resonant with these sets of conversations? Thank you, friend. My thanks also go to Jordan Rogers and Jovanté Anderson for their kind assistance with often eleventh-hour requests for art permissions, bibliography, and secondary translation. I have had a secret weapon throughout this long journey: my friend and writing accountability partner, Tricia Anne Matthew, whose keen intellect and work ethic are matched by her sensitivity and generosity. I am very grateful to "Our Heroine," Tricia.

Anonymous reviewers One and Two are truly friends of my mind. They demonstrated their enthusiastic support of this book from the start through the clarity of their deep commitment to meticulous work in two sets of reviews. I am truly grateful to each of them. The remaining foibles are exclusively mine to own. I wish for every serious writer what Robert Reid-Pharr and Kevin Quashie gave to me. I showed up to our time together (my "manuscript seminar") with huge oaktag Post-its and markers, tabs identifying problematic or controversial parts of the manuscript, anxiety that I had already taken so long to write, and an expectation that this work would be misunderstood. They showed up with their finely closely read copies of the work (as it was, then—less three or more chapters to come), experience writing multiple brilliant monographs of their own, and with open arms and among the deepest study practices and quickest wits in the game. They listened, asked a few difficult questions, quickly told me what they loved and what might best hit the editing floor. Then they extended permission/direction to complete the book that I wanted to write, with no throat clearing and no apologies. Kevin told me, from memory, precisely what page the book *really* began on: a reordering that catalyzed the final transformation of this work; and Robert, in a way so matter-of-fact that he and Kevin were stunned when I began to cry, said, "You've written a theory of Black gay life." Like the anonymous friends of my mind, they clocked my deep unspoken desire— ever so lovingly and incisively. And the book found a new subtitle. Even after Robert, Kevin, and Reader Two (Round One) had already wisely warned me about the likely consequences, it was Donette Francis who, after reading chapter 9, offered a key citation that saved me from publishing completely all up in my feelings (there are important distinctions between *in* and *all up in* that must be maintained, after all), restoring close criticality. Donette has also given me the incalculably valuable gift of an invitation to mutual accomplice, building on uncertain shores: "marooned in Miami." Steven suggested I find the wherewithal to share at least parts of this work with at least a couple people who fill these pages. It occurred to us that Cary Alan Johnson and Colin Robinson might not know how profoundly their work has shaped Black gay culture, and that it has made my work possible. So I told them by sending the manuscript. Their affirmation of this work means the world to me. Mos Def again:

> I ain't no perfect man
> I'm trying to do, the best that I can
> With what it is I have.

I am grateful that my friends have remained my friends over many years: lending encouragement and full belly laughs, and reminding me that my value to them resides in the love and loyalty between us. That this true friendship includes scholars, artists, and community workers, many of whom I have already mentioned in these pages, is an embarrassment of riches that I will continue to try to pay forward. My parents, Geraldine L. Allen and James Herbert Allen, Sr., are still a constant and unwavering foundation of support, even from the ether. Thank you to my family and extended family:

my four siblings; aunts, and uncles, nibblings, grand nibblings, goddaughter, cousins. *Mojuba* to all of my ancestors, known and unknown.

Cue "Just Us" (Two Tons of Fun):

> Reachin'. Touchin'. Holdin'. Laughin'.
> There is more
> That i can hope for.
> Livin', lovin' in your arms.

Ten years ago, I wrote that without Phillip, huge parts of this work, and my own sensibilities, would have perished long ago under a terrifying mound of grief, drafts, anxieties, drywall, and dishes. Well, the terrifying mound grows—compounded by more loss, moving boxes, administrivia, preventable pandemics, serial murders, casual violence, and and . . . yet I remain undrowned, largely because his love is my buoy, my lighthouse, and my mooring. Most days, I enjoy the splash of all the aliveness and foolishness because he is here to share it. Phillip K. Alexander and I are still here and still happy. Making our own little revolutionary statement, for ourselves, each day for twenty years and counting. Essex and Joe already dreamed us, my love: "Long may we live to free this dream."

An Invitation

1 "The duppy, loosely translated from Jamaican patois, refers to the specter or the ghost that emerges when one has failed to properly bury or dispose of the deceased: therefore, emancipation is haunted by slavery, independence by colonialism, and apparent civil rights victories by Jim Crow." See Richard Iton, *In Search of the Black Fantastic*, 135. See also Gilmore, *Golden Gulag*, 247.

2 In a 1990 interview with Charles Rowell (published a decade later), Audre Lorde offered the neologism *Blackfullness*, which captures the space of possibility and belonging beyond any particular place (although she found it for herself in the Virgin Islands), which we reach for and return to throughout this work. Audre said, "Here in the Virgin Islands is where I've chosen to live. I feel that the strength, the beauty, the peace of life in St. Croix is part of my defense kit; it's a part of what keeps me alive and able to fight on. Being surrounded by Black people's faces, some of whom I like, some of whom I don't like, some of whom I get along with, some of whom I don't get along with, is very affirming. Basically, there is a large and everpresent Blackfullness to the days here that is very refreshing for me, although frustrating sometimes, because as in so many places, we have so many problems with how we treat each other. But that's part and parcel of learning to build for the future." See Charles Rowell, "Above the Wind," 56.

3 You have got to be ready. Ms. Georgia Louise Turner, the grandmother of my love (Phillip), gave sterling clarity to this idea one day in a conversation in which Phillip was startled to hear a crucial piece of a family story that he had not heard before. He asked why she hadn't previously told him this key information.

He assumed that she also didn't know about the story. Ms. Louise replied, matter-of-factly, "Well. You have to ask the right questions. . . ."

4 Kevin Quashie extolled the virtue of "completing the line" in a conversation we had about studying with care. My anthropologically disciplined ear also hears this as a form of ethnographic "thickness": striving to tell the story holistically. Here, fragments abound! Still, most find completion of the line throughout the work (and in your margin notes). For a sterling example of a new critical ethnographic holism that reveals the conceit of "thickness" for what it is and demonstrates "slic[ing] into a world from different perspectives, scales, registers, and angles," see John L. Jackson, *Thin Description*, 16. For another brilliant example of the scholarly and writerly rigor that our conversation reaches toward, see Kevin's *The Sovereignty of Quiet*.

5 Lorde, "Smelling the Wind."

6 Here I am also of course invoking Melvin Dixon, who wrote "this poem is for Joseph, remember Joe?" in his poem "And These Are Just a Few."

7 I owe this framing to Melvin's "And These Are Just a Few," which ends "This poem is for the epidemic living and the dead," refracting the first line: "This poem is for the epidemic dead and the living."

8 "I can't become a whole man simply on what is fed to me: watered-down versions of Black life in America. I need the ass-splitting truth to be told, so I will have something pure to emulate, a reason to remain loyal." See Hemphill, *Ceremonies*, 65.

9 Lorde, "Dear Joe."

10 Donette Francis theorizes "antiromance" in her *Fictions of Feminine Citizenship*.

11 See Lorde, "Age, Race, Class, and Sex."

Introduction

1 Trouillot, *Silencing the Past*, 15.

2 Ogunji quoted in Free, "Personal Ties."

3 Brand, *A Map to the Door of No Return*.

4 See Manalansan, "Race, Violence, and Neoliberal Spatial Politics."

5 Kevin Aviance interview in Glasspiegel, dir., "Icy Lake." I am very thankful to Wills, a former student in African American studies at Yale, who shared clips of his interviews with Kevin Aviance while his short film was in production.

6 See Moten, *In the Break*; and Sharpe, *In the Wake*.

7 Moving beyond what she has named "qualitative collapse," Michelle Wright argues in her *Physics of Blackness* for a multidimensional and dynamic conception of blackness that is at once material and phenomenological. Hers is one of a number of formulations helpful for the archival, ethnographic, and narrative time-space turns and leaps we are invested in executing here. She writes, for example, that "when a linear spacetime epistemology begins, as many Black diasporic epistemologies do, with object status—being enslaved, relocated and so on—the laws of cause and effect make it difficult to reverse the binary that is set in place, because oppression is asserted as the cause of

all historical events (effects) in the timeline, excepting those events that are caused by a Black (resistant) reaction. . . . Yet because it is a reaction to an action, we are again returned to a weird and dismally fixed race-ing of the Black physics, in which whiteness always retains the originary agency and, because origins dominate a linear narrative, white racism is always the central actor in Black lives condemned to the status of reactors." It seems to me that Stephen Best is centering whiteness/white racism in this way. Best's work argues vigorously not only against recovery of a "we" at the point of our violent origin but also advocates disaffiliation from a "we." Moreover, I believe he misses or deemphasizes the politics and potential of the projects of Saidiya Hartman, Vincent Brown, NourbeSe Philip, Toni Morrison, and other scholars of the archival turn. I worry about the politics of his pathologizing move—why melancholia and disaffiliation? What does disaffiliation do, and for whom? See M. Wright, *Physics of Blackness*, 116; and Best, *None Like Us*.

8 Reginald Harris, personal communication, 2007. See also G. Winston James, "At the Club."

9 Kevin hosted ArenA, a weekly event produced by celebrity DJ Junior Vasquez, at the Palladium: New York City's massive Greenwich Village dance club billed as "the gay man's pleasure dome" in 1985 by owners Steve Rubell and Ian Schrager (of Studio 54 fame). ArenA was one of the most popular parties in New York City in the mid- to late nineties. The gay men to whom Rubell and Schrager catered were white, but ArenA also drew crowds of Black, Latinx, and other mostly but not exclusively LGBTQ men and women of color from the island of Manhattan and beyond on Saturday nights and Sunday mornings.

10 Kevin Aviance in Wills Glasspiegel, dir., "Icy Lake."

11 Fanon, *Black Skin, White Masks*, 13. As Fanon famously averred, "I belong irreducibly to my time." For him, "the present" is to be considered "in terms of something to be exceeded."

12 Lorde, "A Litany for Survival."

13 Ové, dir., *Baldwin's Nigger*.

14 Halberstam, *In a Queer Time and Place*, 6.

15 Loose Joints, "Is It All over My Face?," 1980.

16 Hemphill, "The Tomb of Sorrow."

17 Allen, "For 'the Children,'" 311.

18 Glave, *Words to Our Now*, 25.

19 Lorde, "A Litany for Survival."

20 Notes on nomenclature are important here. First, Assotto Saint as grammarian holds that "Afrocentrists in our community have chosen the term 'Black gay' to identify themselves. As they insist, Black comes first. Interracialists in our community have chosen the term 'gay Black' to identify themselves. As they insist, 'gay comes first.'" Both groups' self-descriptions are ironically erroneous: "It's not which word comes first that matters but rather the grammatical context in which those words are used—either as an adjective or as a noun. An adjective is a modifier of a noun. The former is dependent on the latter."

Assotto is certainly correct, technically, although his bright line between "interracialists" and "Afrocentrists" overstates the case. We will explore this in the next chapter. *Disco Ball* employs the convention of "Black gay." See Saint, *The Road before Us*, xix. Also, since the 1950s *gay* has been widely accepted among women, with gay girls, gay women, and lesbian used sometimes interchangeably. In other cases *lesbian* (and capitalized, *Lesbian*) denoted and still denotes a particular politics of autonomy and visibility. The explicit statement was necessitated by gay men's attempts to silence and invisibilize women. *Bisexual* and *transgender* do not seem to emerge strongly as identity positions distinct from gay until the end of the long 1980s and early aughts, respectively. Although the long-1980s Black gay formulation progressively gestured toward community adhesion of all nonheteronormative Black folks, the lack of consistent feminist and trans allyship and accomplice by cisgender gay men constrained the emergence of a movement that truly reflected this.

21 See Muñoz, *Cruising Utopia*.

22 Of course there is: the work work wuk wuk wuk wuk of it all! Tremendous labor. A number of these were published by Kitchen Table Press. In the next chapter we will turn to Lisa C. Moore's RedBone Press, which began publishing just outside of the long 1980s, but it must be noted here that RedBone (and Steven Fullwood's Vintage Entity Press) continues the crucial work of serious Black lesbian and gay publishing—not only with respect to award-winning single-author works but also the anthologies that carry on the tradition in the best ways. As both a prime example of this and evidence of the work of Black LGBTQ publishing at the time of publication, see especially Fullwood, Harris, and Moore, *Carry the Word*.

23 M. Walker, "I Want to Write."

24 M. Walker, "For My People."

25 E. Alexander, "Ars Poetica #100: I Believe."

> Poetry, I tell my students,
> is idiosyncratic. Poetry
>
> is where we are ourselves,
> (though Sterling Brown said
>
> "Every 'I' is a dramatic 'I'")
> digging in the clam flats
>
> for the shell that snaps,
> emptying the proverbial pocketbook.
>
> Poetry is what you find
> in the dirt in the corner,
>
> overhear on the bus, God
> in the details, the only way
>
> to get from here to there.
> Poetry (and now my voice is rising)

is not all love, love, love,
and I'm sorry the dog died.

Poetry (here I hear myself loudest)
is the human voice,

and are we not of interest to each other?

26 Lorde, "Poetry Is Not a Luxury," in her *Sister Outsider*, 25.
27 Here Sylvia Wynter is arguing against an othering "ethnos" in which one must be estranged from historical and material particularities of intersubjective humanity. See Wynter, "Ethno or Socio Poetics," 78.
28 Césaire, "Calling the Magician."
29 Saint, "Why I Write," 3.
30 Yes, another anthological work—in film. Riggs, dir., *Tongues Untied*.
31 Baldwin, *Just above My Head*, 512.
32 Hartman, "Venus in Two Acts," 13.
33 I borrow the notion of a writerly work from Roland Barthes. See Barthes, *S/Z*, 5. See also Keep, McLaughlin, and Parmar, "Readerly and Writerly Texts." Sherry B. Ortner, who was my graduate advisor, had a wonderful (and only slightly shady) way of bracketing poststructuralist French theory in the classroom. This is not to say that the backhand wave that went along with her utterance of "the French" was a dismissal of this important work or a collapse of their differences. See her masterful reformulation of Bourdieu and Foucault in the refinement of her own theory of practice in, for example, *Anthropology and Social Theory* and her classic "Theory in Anthropology since the Sixties."
34 These largely follow Eve Kosofsky Sedgwick. See her "Paranoid Reading and Reparative Reading." Other examples include Ahmed, "Happy Objects"; Cvetkovich, *An Archive of Feelings*; and Halberstam, *The Queer Art of Failure*.
35 This is not to diminish the important scholarly contributions of Herskovits, Mintz, and others who follow these foundational anthropologists, such as Richard and Sally Price, and John Szwed. The politics of their various citational practices is another matter—related, but not my aim to parse at this time. Here I am drawing the crucial distinction in perspective and politics between antecedent Afro-American anthropology and the decolonizing and/or Black anthropology that has emerged since the 1980s. See Allen and Jobson, "The Decolonizing Generation."
36 Harrison, *Outsider Within*.
37 See Magubane and Faris, "On the Political Relevance of Anthropology"; E. Gordon, "Anthropology and Liberation"; and Jobson, "The Case for Letting Anthropology Burn."
38 Boellstorff, "Queer Studies in the House of Anthropology," 26.
39 Cohen, "Deviance as Resistance."
40 Brooks, "I Am a Black."
41 Paul Gilroy wrote this in 1993: "My point here is that the unashamedly hybrid character of these Black Atlantic cultures continually confounds any simplistic

(essentialist or anti-essentialist) understanding of the relationship between racial identity and racial non-identity, between folk cultural authenticity and pop cultural betrayal. . . . Black identity is not simply a social and political category to be used or abandoned according to the extent to which the rhetoric that supports and legitimizes it is persuasive or institutionally powerful. Whatever the radical constructionists may say, it is lived as a coherent (if not always stable) experiential sense of self. Though it is often felt to be natural and spontaneous, it remains the outcome of practical activity: language, gesture, bodily significations, desires. We can use Foucault's insightful comments to illuminate this necessarily political relationship. They point towards an anti-anti-essentialism that sees racialized subjectivity as the product of the social practices that supposedly derive from it." See Gilroy, *The Black Atlantic*, 99, 102.

42 See Gates, *The Signifying Monkey*; and Shakespeare, *Macbeth*.

43 Trouillot, *Global Transformations*, 47.

44 In parts 2 and 3 we will return to my perhaps not-so-subtle suggestion to mind Black radical feminist insistence on embodiment and community engagement. One example is the sort Stephanie Mills commands/invites in her 1979 hit "Put Your Body in It": "Don't be afraid . . . and if it takes you all night long / I'll see you through / put your body in it!"

45 I am grateful to Cheryl Roberts, Yolanda M. Martinez-San Miguel, Pat Saunders, Vickie Greene, LaShaya Howie, Ana-Maurine Lara, "Felicidades Gris," and Jackie Brown (who was the first to advise "some things ain't got no words") for engaging my last-minute efforts to Facebook crowd-source "a word" to describe this action I describe here. Many thanks also to Aimee Cox, Maya Berry, and Juana Maria Rodriguez, who encouraged me to abandon the search for the right word and keep the description! Cheryl offered "waltz" to name this action I had described. This resonated most: I pictured the side shuffle of the feet, with one hand in the air (holding a drink?) and the other on the side of another dancer.

46 Boyce-Davies, *Black Women, Writing and Identity*, 47.

47 This is riffing off of Stuart Hall, of course. But it is recursive in another way. Here I am posing the same question I asked in our special "Black/Queer/Diaspora" issue of *GLQ* precisely to push beyond that collection to include responses to it and the longer historicity in which it is embedded.

48 Lorde, "Poetry Is Not a Luxury," 36.

49 Rodney, *The Groundings with My Brothers*.

50 C. L. R. James, *Every Cook Can Govern*.

51 Following movements of "Third World" peoples, women, and LGBTQI folks, anthropology attempted a few corrective turns in the long 1980s. Decolonizing/Black anthropology is likely the most enduring of these, alongside moves toward reflexivity, experimentation, and attention to writing. More recently, there seems to have been a disavowal of this, leading to what George Marcus has termed a "crisis of reception (of ethnography)." See Harrison, *Decolonizing Anthropology*. See also Marcus, "On the Problematic Contemporary Reception of Ethnography," 199.

52 Allen and Jobson, "The Decolonizing Generation."

53 Ferguson and Gupta, "Beyond 'Culture'"; Clifford and Marcus, *Writing Culture*.

54 See Christian, "The Race for Theory."

55 Césaire, "Calling the Magician," 121.

56 See Agard-Jones, "What the Sands Remember"; and E. Alexander, "Ars Poetica #100."

57 M. Alexander, "Not Just (Any) Body Can Be a Citizen," 5.

58 Christian, "The Race for Theory," 68.

59 Allen, "For 'the Children,'" 322.

60 Hartman, "Venus in Two Acts," 2.

61 Dixon, "And These Are Just a Few," 71.

62 Spillers, "Interstices," 154.

63 See Halberstam, *The Queer Art of Failure*.

64 Lorde, "Age, Race, Class, and Sex," 114.

Chapter One. The Anthological Generation

1 Black/gay is nomadic. Although there are territories that it might and sometimes strategically does claim, the realm it holds is de-territorialized. The nomad is a way of being in the middle or between points. It is characterized by change. To be nomadic in this way is the condition of being unsettled. What people of conscience can be settled with all that is de-territorializing, deracinating, and striated in seemingly enclosed sedimented political realities of our lives (and deaths) today? Of course, nomadism is also about (self-)naming. Recall Hortense Spillers's admonition to attend to how and what we are called. Whom, what—and where—are the children naming today? And to what uses have they put their lineages? What unsettles them and sets them flowing again?

2 *Tabanca* is a Trinbagonian word used to express the painful, depressed state following a breakup or (perhaps temporary) loss of an authentic heartfelt article. Carnival tabanca is the way I have most often heard this latter sense. For example, one of my respondents, in an interview recalling her recent trip "home" to Trinidad, expressed "some serious-serious tabanca" and displayed a forlorn affect regarding having to leave Trinidad and Tobago to return to the United States, where she has lived for most of her life.

3 Crystal Waters, "100% Pure Love," 1994.

4 Agard-Jones, *Body Burdens*.

5 Glave, *Words to Our Now*, 25.

6 "Womanist is to feminist as purple is to lavender." See A. Walker, *In Search of Our Mothers' Gardens*, xi. Walker notably drew the distinction of her coined term *womanism*, poetically recognizing the resonance but incompleteness for Black women of a feminism without their perspectives and full inclusion. Still, there is no doubt that the work that she has done over more than fifty years as a writer, advocate, scholar, and activist qualifies her as one of the most important figures of Black feminism (as well as its sister, womanism).

7 David Scott, *Omens of Adversity*, 120. The music? I hear Barrington Levy.

8 I hear also: nothing as constitutive of who we are today than the dead and their ideas. See Woubshet, *The Calendar of Loss*, ix. The quotation in the heading is from Dixon's "And These Are Just a Few." As Dag parses Melvin's poem, from which this movement borrows its title, it is "recollective (it remembers past deaths) and prospective (it hails imminent deaths, including his own)" (7). In addition to synchronizing a unique timeline of loss, the poem also takes a tally of the dead, and each loss builds on the loss that precedes it. According to Dagmawi, the dead become a collection of "'language,' 'lore' peeled off pages, puns, and meter," each loss manifested as a text within a larger text of loss (7).

9 Lorde, "For Each of You."

10 Kenan, *Let the Dead Bury the Dead*.

11 Lemmons, dir., *Eve's Bayou*.

12 Ogunji, dir., "Sweep." Wura sweeps his Nigerian compound as if it were a Zen garden after embedding her fetal-positioned body in the red earth of his motherland.

13 Hemphill, "Loyalty."

14 This seeming departure to the world of Lemmons's gorgeous Black classic *Eve's Bayou* is not to argue that it is a "queer text" or that its characters are. Death, sex, class differences, and generational antagonisms and silences are not exclusive to people in the life. We do not need to proclaim the singularity of Black LGBTQ experience and art to rightly claim its importance and significance.

15 "And far as the eye of God could see / Darkness covered everything, / Blacker than a hundred midnights / Down in a cypress swamp." See J. Johnson, "The Creation."

16 This refrain was a common one during the long 1980s. The truth of the statement is detailed in Cathy Cohen's tour-de-force *The Boundaries of Blackness*. Moreover, this was reiterated in the 2005 report of the Black AIDS Institute, detailing then-new data showing that in several US cities nearly one in two Black men who had had sex with men were infected with HIV.

17 C. Harris, "I'm Going Out Like a Fucking Meteor," 208.

18 Reid-Pharr, "Stronger, in This Life," 66.

19 At HBCUs (historically Black colleges and universities) it is our practice to show respect and deference to our beloved professors by emphasizing the hard-earned doctorate: so (Beverly), Dr. Guy-Sheftall it is! See Guy-Sheftall, *Words of Fire*. It is difficult for me to refer to Dr. Guy-Sheftall as Beverly, as she has recently insisted. I now know her as an eminent senior colleague, but I still remember her as a beloved teacher at Spelman College who would greet me warmly on campus—a stalwart Black feminist presence on innumerable raucous student panels on everything from Shahrazad Ali to Spike Lee during those tumultuous days. And colleague of the brilliant scholar, teacher, poet, and archivist of Black women's voices Dr. Gloria Wade-Gayles, my local maternal figure at school and my first Black women's studies teacher ("Images of Black Women in Media").

20 Barbara Smith in K. Taylor, *How We Get Free*, 30. See Morris and Hockley, *We Wanted a Revolution*, the catalog of the eponymous 2017 Brooklyn Museum exhibit. The past tense ("wanted") seems appropriate because although present-day radical Black feminists would agree that this was the original goal, it is not perfectly clear to me whether today "revolution" is a serious goal among more than a few. Has revolution slipped completely out of the frame, as radicality seems to have shifted precipitously to the right, toward neo-radicalism, as Joy James identified in her "Radicalizing Feminism"?

21 See Hill Collins, *Black Feminist Thought*, 221.

22 However, I will note just a few who wrote during the long 1980s and on whom I most centrally call in *There's a Disco Ball Between Us*: Barbara Smith, Hortense Spillers, and Barbara Christian. Foundational and indispensable examples of this work also prominently include bell hooks's *Feminist Theory from Margin to Center*; Beverly Guy-Sheftall's magisterial introduction to *Words of Fire*; and Anne duCille's cogent assessment of academic Black women's studies in her article "The Occult of True Black Womanhood."

23 Nash, "Feminist Originalism," 12.

24 This recent text conversation with Marcus Lee illustrates my point:

> MARCUS: Wow. Cathy is really a sage.
>
> ME: Yes! What has the Oracle saged?
>
> [Then he recounts to me that he is reading a recent book that poorly engages themes that Cathy Cohen has already elucidated in her work.]
>
> MARCUS: [The author] can't see it [in the way that Cathy does in "Deviance as Resistance"].
>
> ME: Ah. Can't, or won't see it? given the literature that's already out
>
> MARCUS: Yes. [He bullet points the claims.] [The author] loses so much analytic purchase . . . by not contending with their sexed dimensions! Cathy warned you about this in '04, sis!
>
> It's really interesting. What's up with that?
>
> ME: Cathy is sage. And brilliant. And righteous. And/but what she's saying isn't magical, but rather emerges from an intellectual tradition and habit of mind that these people keep discounting and ignoring, at their own peril.
>
> This is stuff that should have been in the "settled argument" file since her series of articles right before and immediately following AIDS & The Breakdown. . . .
>
> And if a white man had written it in French, it would be.
>
> MARCUS: Yup.
>
> [Then, as I have now learned to expect from this young one, and thus why the transcript finds its way here, the clamshell snaps when Marcus offers the following.]

MARCUS: I wonder how it feels to be lauded, but ignored!

ME: I have not been able to name that space. I'mma try a little bit this Friday.

(I tried to cull some of my thoughts on the anthological women in my presentation "Notes on the 'Anthological Generation,' Or, How 'Bulldaggers' Can Save Black Studies from Itself" at Columbia University's April 2019 conference "To Be Free. Anywhere in the Universe.")

25 Shange, *For Colored Girls Who Have Considered Suicide, When the Rainbow Is Enuf*, 65.

26 Beal, *Black Women's Manifesto*; Crenshaw, "Demarginalizing the Intersection of Race and Sex"; Spillers, "Interstices."

27 Spillers, "Interstices," 155.

28 Combahee River Collective, "Combahee River Collective Statement."

29 See, for example, B. Smith, "Ain't Gonna Let Nobody Turn Me Around"; and B. Smith, "Doing Research on Black American Women."

30 Ware, *Woman Power*. See also Sloan, *Black Feminism*.

31 P. Robinson and colleagues, "Poor Black Women's Study Papers," 189.

32 P. Robinson and colleagues, 189.

33 K. Taylor, *How We Get Free*, 48.

34 It is instructive to note that the particular combination of antiblackness and misogyny deployed against Black women is so particular and invidious that it required a specific term. Moya Bailey and Trudy coined this term in "On Misogynoir."

35 Nash, "Feminist Originalism," 5.

36 Quoted in K. Taylor, *How We Get Free*, 177.

37 See Foucault, *The Archaeology of Knowledge* and *The Order of Things*. Regarding conjunctures, see Hall, "Gramsci and Us." I wonder what we could make of an honest assessment of "What/who is this woman in Black women's studies?" following Hall's probing "What Is This 'Black' in Black Popular Culture?"

38 See duCille, "The Occult of True Black Womanhood."

39 At a University of Miami lecture, Christina mentioned that Hazel Carby had noted that Christina is a "forensic etymologist." This is one instantiation of this, and a practice I have found illuminating for my own analysis. See Sharpe, *In the Wake*, 29.

40 Combahee River Collective, "Combahee River Collective Statement."

41 Quoted in K. Taylor, *How We Get Free*, 44.

42 Lorde, "Turning the Beat Around," 73.

43 Higashida, *Black Internationalist Feminism*, 2.

44 Parker, "Revolution," 240.

45 Parker, "Tour America."

46 Bambara, "Foreword," *This Bridge Called My Back*, viii.

47 Quoted in B. Smith, *Home Girls*.

48 Imagine this logic being reinvigorated today: the measure of our intellectual worth taken as a function of what the work does and how it reflects and

conjures refractions of new and better futures. One of Marvin K. White's prophetic poetic interventions shared on social media in fall 2019 summarizes this point: "My humanity longs for the word to become published, but my soul longs for the word becoming flesh."

49 Reprints from other publications in *The Black Woman* are not only a testament to Toni Cade Bambara's consciousness of creating a capacious anthological statement and archive but also demonstrate connections that these works make between perhaps disparate audiences. A version of Pat Robinson and colleagues' "Working Papers" (see above) had been previously published in the Women's Liberation Front (read: white women's . . .) journal *Lilith*. Abbey Lincoln's essay originally appeared in *Negro Digest* (which became *Black World* in 1970), the monthly literary highbrow Johnson Publications property that preceded its legendary and ubiquitous *Jet* and *Ebony* magazines. It announced on the masthead in fine Du Boisian fashion: "Knowledge is the key to a better tomorrow." Léopold Sédar Senghor's address to the opening of Dakar's Collo-quium of Negro Arts and Culture, "The Defense and Illustration of Negri-tude," appeared in this same issue—complete with a state photo of the writer and scholar, who had recently begun his twenty-year tenure as president of Senegal.

50 One of the most salient examples in these anguished letters to the editor in response to Ms. Lincoln were with respect to straight Black men's putative obsession with white women.

51 Renita Weems also answers Lincoln, echoing radical Black women artists singing in chorus: "The Black Woman Artist Will Revere the Black Woman" in her *Conditions Five: The Black Women's Issue*, and her *Home Girls* essay "Artists without Art Form." As a clergywoman and scholar of womanist and feminist theology, Weems writes in the *Conditions Five* essay that "the Black woman writer has insisted upon recording the tragic and the fortunate of her lot. And in so doing she answers the question posed by actress/activist Abbey Lincoln some twelve years ago in her essay titled, 'Who Will Revere the Black Woman?' The black woman artist will revere the black woman. For it is her duty to record and capture with song, clay, strings, dance and, in this case, ink, the joys and pains of Black womanhood. And the person who is sane, secure and sensitive enough to revere her art is the same person who will revere her life. Sojourner Truth, a poet in her own way, knew all of this when she told her mostly white audience, 'I suppose I am about the only colored woman that goes about to speak for the rights of colored women'" (50). This critical tradition of attention, assessment, and even celebration is now also evidenced in a number of works, beginning in the 1970s and mostly in an-thologies and journal articles but also in monographs. And it is international. A number of important Black feminist critics (and artists as critics) have de-voted illustrious careers to the work of other Black women. Fortunately, there are too many to note without the risk of insult by mistaken exclusion, so I will not attempt a list here. I will restrict my citation to four earlier indispens-able works: Boyce-Davies, *Black Women, Writing and Identity*; Carby, *Cultures*

in Babylon; Griffin, *Beloved Sisters and Loving Friends*; and Wall, *Women of the Harlem Renaissance*. I will also note that Black gay men have also contributed to this critical tradition (and reverence). Among these, see Quashie, *Black Women, Identity, and Cultural Theory*.

52 The frontispiece of the issue reads "Conditions, a magazine of writing by women with an emphasis on writing by lesbians, is regularly edited by Elly Bulkin, Jan Clausen, Irena Klepfisz, and Rima Shore."

53 Lorde, Parker, and Sullivan, *Sister Love*, 65.

54 Lorde, Parker, and Sullivan, 88. See also Lorde, "Eye to Eye"; and DeVeaux, *Warrior Poet*, 290–95.

55 Not exactly the same. The epigram reads "If you have ever . . . ," not "And in case you have. . . ." See Lorde, *Chosen Poems*.

56 Lorde, "Dear Joe."

57 The quotation in the heading is from Parker, "The 1987 March on Washington," 276.

58 For a cogent discussion of the neoradical streams within discourse and movements uncritically understood as radical, see J. James, "Radicalizing Feminism."

59 Parker, "The 1987 March on Washington," 276.

60 In this regard, see some especially sterling works, for example, Carbado and Weise, *Time on Two Crosses*; Delany's indispensable *Times Square Red, Times Square Blue* and *The Motion of Light in Water*; Holcomb, *Claude McKay, Code Name Sasha*; Mumford, *Not Straight, Not White*; and Bost, *Evidence of Being*; nearly everything by James Baldwin.

61 Dixon, "I'll Be Somewhere Listening for My Name," 73.

62 Of course, most prominently James Baldwin, but also a number of Harlem Renaissance writers and artists before the long 1980s. It is also important to note, with disappointment, that proponents of the discourse self-identified as (straight) "Black male feminist" have not, in fact, sought to investigate or honor the Black gay intellectual origins of this discourse but instead construct themselves as "firsts."

63 Notwithstanding actual events, I understand the formulation of "crisis" as particularly and conjuncturally manufactured, after Stuart Hall and colleagues: *Policing the Crisis*.

64 Among a number of fine historiographic and sociocultural critiques, see especially Mullings, "African-American Women Making Themselves"; and Mumford, "Untangling Pathology."

65 Stuart Hall et al., *Policing the Crisis*.

66 The emergence, or boom, in the study of Black masculinity in the Caribbean in the 1990s was likewise borne out of an understanding of "Black masculinity marginalization," the severity of which was obviated by statistics of low educational achievement and high incidence of sexual and domestic violence and incarceration. Rhoda Reddock has done tremendous work to analyze this and provide new frameworks for Caribbean masculinities. See Reddock, *Interrogating Caribbean Masculinities*; and L. Lewis, "Caribbean Masculinity."

67 Sadly, important works on Black masculinity that avoid this pathologizing move often perhaps protest too much—bifurcating Black men into too simply drawn sociological "types."

68 Regarding "beached whale," "awaiting their verb," foundational theorization of Black gender drama, psychoanalysis, and family tropes, pushing beyond the racism and misogynoir of Moynihan, see Spillers, "Mama's Baby, Papa's Maybe," 65. For important exceptions to the hegemonic dichotomous Black masculinity discourse, see hooks, *We Real Cool*; and E. Gordon, "Cultural Politics of Black Masculinity," which accents a wider "repertoire" of individual behaviors and identifications that include both "respectability" and "reputation." See also Allen, *¡Venceremos?* (the chapter "De Cierta Manera . . . Hasta Cierto Punto [One Way or Another . . . Up to a Certain Point]").

69 Carl et al., "Black Gay Men Expressing Themselves in Print."

70 Carl et al.

71 Carl et al.

72 Baldwin, *Just above My Head*, 512. See also Other Countries, "Preface," in *Voices Rising*, xi.

73 Silvia Rivera, "Y'all Better Quiet Down." I first encountered this video via the now-deleted Vimeo page of artist, archivist, and activist Tourmaline (fka Reina Gossett).

74 Kenyatta Ombaka Baki, in Blackheart Collective, *Blackheart 2: The Prison Issue*.

75 Ngulu wrote in the May issue of *B&G* magazine of another silenced constituency among Black gay men: those who do not reveal their sexual desires and practices with other men, often reviled as "in the closet" or "DL." Lauding a supportive editorial in the nationally circulated zine, he congratulates *B&G* editors for "a meritori[ous] April editorial in the GMAD tradition of 'Finding Community in Diversity.'" He incisively informs readers that he had organized "brothers of color who are privately homosexual/bisexual/gay and aware that there is more than a singular definition of 'Silence = Death.'" He said that "no one else was doing it, so I took it upon myself." He wrote: "In our anonymity, B-men have actively supported, publicized, participated in numerous political, health and cultural community activities—the least and most publicly effective of which was the donation of the red, black and green liberation flags to the brothers of color contingency in last year's Gay Pride March." (These flags make an appearance in the next section of this chapter.) That men who were unwilling or unable to publicly march found this way to participate is a potent example of community diversity. Ngulu ends with this fabulous line: "As I've said so many time before, 'my clothes are in my "closet"—I am in my bed with my Black love.'"

76 Wynter offers this important footnote in her "Towards the Sociogenic Principle": "These include Ronald Judy who writes, 'The title that Fanon gave to the fifth chapter of Peau noire, masques blancs was "L'expérience vécue du Noir" which Charles Lam Markmann translated as "The Fact of Blackness." . . . What is cut away completely is the focal concern with experience. L'expérience vécue is conflated into "the fact" so that the adjective becomes the substantive.

Although vécue can be rendered in English, as something like "factual" it is the very nature of the referenced factuality that is vexing. Is the factual that which is in-itself independent of consciousness or is it that which is in-itself-for consciousness? With vécue, we are thus brought to ponder experience.'" See Judy, "Fanon's Body of Black Experience," 53.

77 Sun Ra and the Intergalactic Research Arkestra, 1970. I was reminded of this Afro-futurist prophecy by Vanessa Agard-Jones's invocation of it in her rethinking of the Anthropocene (personal communication with author).

78 Blackheart Collective, *Blackheart 2: The Prison Issue*.

79 Blackheart Collective, *Blackheart 2: The Prison Issue*.

80 Beam, "Brother to Brother," 230–42.

Chapter Two. "What It Is I Think They Were Doing, Anyhow"

This chapter title riffs on a riff. See Hull, "What It Is I Think She's Doing Anyhow." See also the original: Bambara, "What Is It I Think I'm Doing Anyhow." I have added a comma where Akasha Hull placed a period. You may have noticed, dear reader, that I use lots of commas (and em dashes and semicolons). There seems to be so much to say and so much causally connected, not running on but intersecting, perhaps dramatized by a semicolon or made perhaps more definite by a dash. Periods are relatively rare. Perhaps this style of conversation reflects my desire to mark, hold, and make room for others to say what they think folks were doing. I wanted to provide a sketch or framing in advance of a more focused and deeply researched exposition of our literatures and politics (but isn't that what we have been waiting for, for so long?). Fortunately, important new work has emerged by Darius Bost (see *Evidence of Being*) and others to fulfill this promise—I am grateful. However, at some point in perhaps the end of the eighth year of my research and writing process, I decided to focus on writing rather than keeping up with new work. That is, I have unfortunately not consulted Darius's celebrated work yet, although I eagerly await learning from him and others I have missed in what appears to be a rich period of publishing. My apologies if this proves to have been a poor choice.

1 "Nobody here will lean too heavily on your flowers / nor lick the petals of a lavender gladiola / for its hint of sweetness." Lorde, "Dear Joe."

2 Barbara Smith quoted in Fullwood and Stephens, *Black Gay Genius*, 23.

3 Cohen, "Deviance as Resistance," 28.

4 Barbara Smith quoted in Fullwood and Stephens, *Black Gay Genius*, 23.

5 Robinson quoted in Fullwood and Stephens, *Black Gay Genius*, 75.

6 Cohen, "Deviance as Resistance," 28.

7 Reid-Pharr, "Stronger, in This Life," 69.

8 Hemphill, "Introduction," xxxvi.

9 Hemphill, "Introduction"; Richardson, *The Queer Limit of Black Memory*.

10 This is close to what I meant when I used the term *Black gay genius* in a conversation with Charles Stephens nearly twenty years ago. I meant to describe what I saw emanating from Charles himself, years before he coedited *Black*

Gay Genius and created the Counter Narrative Project, an organization that is a glittering instantiation of this genius.

11 Joe could not have predicted the Open-24-Hours Tower of Babel that is the internet-mediated market of ideas and images today. And then, of course, there is the issue of the intentions of the multitudinous representations. Whom do we ask? Who will account for the quality of representations of LGBTQ Black folks? We must account for the intentions and politics of the representations and not presume that they are all progressive, transgressive, or revolutionary. Time has already taught us.

12 Dixon, "And These Are Just a Few."

13 Ransby, quoted in K. Taylor, *How We Get Free*; Reid-Pharr, "Stronger, in This Life."

14 Barbara Smith quoted in Fullwood and Stephens, *Black Gay Genius*, 35.

15 The following short exchange between Toni Cade Bambara and her interviewer, the poet Kalamu Ya Salaam, is instructive in this regard. The two writers were discussing a call she made to unite our wrath, our visions, and our powers in her novel *The Salt Eaters*, through the work of the Seven Sisters, a multicultural and multimedia arts troupe: "Kalamu asks: 'Do you think that fiction (and more generally, literary work) is the most effective way to do this?' Toni says 'No. The most effective way to do it, is to do it!'" See T. Lewis, *Conversations with Toni Cade Bambara*, 24.

16 McBride and Joyce, *A Melvin Dixon Critical Reader*, ix.

17 Christian, "The Race for Theory."

18 Dixon, "I'll Be Somewhere Listening for My Name."

19 Dixon, "Rivers Remembering Their Source," 30.

20 Dixon, 33.

21 Dixon, 48.

22 Dixon.

23 Baldwin, "Encounter on the Seine," 89.

24 Baldwin. This is to say nothing, at this time, of the "deliberate" self-isolation from other Black Americans that Mr. Baldwin reports and "the wariness with which he regards his colored kin" (85, 86).

25 See especially Pierre, *The Predicament of Blackness*; and Vargas, *The Denial of Antiblackness*.

26 Perhaps had Mr. Baldwin and Mr. Ellison interacted with Caribbean and African intellectuals more regularly, or had lived for extended periods in Africa, as Melvin had, their point of view might have shifted. I should not be coy here—there is clearly at least ambivalence here, and likely disdain. While "Encounter on the Seine" paints a (beautiful but) awfully dim picture of the prospects for diaspora sociality, the history of Présence Africaine (literally and in terms of the journal) characterized by pan-African and Caribbean Francophone exchange is clear. It seems that Alioune Diop, Jean Price-Mars, Aimé Césaire, Léopold Sédar Senghor, Cheikh Anta Diop, and them were all chilling together on rue des Écoles, in the Latin Quarter. Was Jimmy Baldwin not invited, as Richard Wright was? More in part 2.

27 To wit, this would be different in the context of Dutch, Spanish, and French territories before the confederation of colonies or incorporation in the United States and, of course, cultural practices among, for example, French Creoles and Arcadians (Cajuns).

28 Ové, dir., *Baldwin's Nigger*.

29 One example of this can be found in this interview with M. Aimé Césaire: "What we [he and Senghor] hold in common is the obstinate refusal to be alienated, to lose our attachment to our countries, our peoples, our languages. Moreover, in my case it was the careful cultivation of Africans that protected me culturally. That contact counter-balanced the influence of European culture. Senghor, with whom I lived in the Latin Quarter for practically ten years before the war, held considerable sway over my personal life. . . . [Creole] is neither a patois nor a dialect. I was among the first in the French West Indies to consider it [Creole] a language: at one and the same time neo-French and neo-African. . . . A white skin perhaps, but certainly a Black soul. In other words, in order to shoulder his total reality the Martinican has a bilingual vocation. This must be the approach then: to proceed from the experience of using two tongues to the acceptance of a true bilingual status, over paths that have yet to be charted." Decraene, "Aimé Césaire: Black Rebel," 64.

30 Baldwin, "The Preservation of Innocence"; Dixon, "This Light, This Fire, This Time." In other works, such as his commentary on Gayl Jones's Corregidora, Melvin takes up orality once again as he analyzes her use of "Black speech as an aesthetic device" and he probes the definition and form of Black aesthetics and the uses of memory, which other Black literature scholars began to take up more readily between the late aughts and the present.

31 Dixon, "This Light, This Fire, This Time," 35.

32 Dixon, "Rivers Remembering Their Source," 33.

33 Here 1979 emerges again as a pivotal beginning of the long 1980s! The publication of James Baldwin's *Just above My Head* inaugurated the form of "the Black gay novel." Soon after came Larry Duplechan's *Eight Days a Week*, published in 1985, and his four subsequent novels, among them *Blackbird*, which was recently adapted for a film, and Steven Corbin's *Fragments That Remain*. I voraciously devoured these in the late 1980s and 1990s. Of course, the widespread commercial appeal of E. Lynn Harris's *Invisible Life*—self-published and successfully sold by the author in 1991—was unprecedented, establishing his significance even before he went on to pen a dozen novels and other works, inspiring a number of writers' and filmmakers' exploration of Black gay experiences and imaginations before his untimely passing. By the end of the long 1980s, Darieck Scott published *Traitor to the Race*, a writerly, imaginative, and sober portrait in which themes of violence and white supremacy serve as the backdrop for the fantastical imagination of the Black gay male protagonist, and are reminiscent of Melvin's masterpiece, *Vanishing Rooms*. In subsequent chapters we will turn again to the problematique of what and who enters Black gay consciousness and the literary "canon."

34 McBride and Joyce, *A Melvin Dixon Critical Reader*, xiii.

35 Mr. Baldwin writes, "Well . . . I looked around me and could see that the reason that they would be so tolerant—as they thought—was because they didn't have any niggers in Paris. . . . And it was very good for me in a way; except, my momma didn't raise any fools. I realized almost at once that the Algerian was the nigger in Paris . . . the same thing that was happening at home was . . . happening in France. . . . The same thing that's going on in the US is going on in European cities—and for the same reasons." See Baldwin, "James Baldwin: The Black Scholar Interviews," 39.

36 Dixon, "I'll Be Somewhere Listening for My Name," 148.

37 "No population in the developed world has been as heavily affected by HIV as Black men in the U.S. who have sex with other men (MSM). Indeed, one could study the entire world and have difficulty finding another group in which the HIV burden is greater than among Black MSM." See "Back of the Line."

38 Dixon, "I'll Be Somewhere Listening for My Name," 152.

39 Lofton, dir., "O Happy Day."

40 Huey P. Newton, "A letter from Huey to the revolutionary brothers and sisters about the women's liberation and gay liberation movements," 1970.

41 See, for example, A. Nelson, *Body and Soul*; and Spencer, *The Revolution Has Come*.

42 Hayes, "Theme from *Shaft*" (Enterprise, 1971). Note also that according to a *New York Times* article, "The opening of Gordon Parks's detective movie 'Shaft' contains 15 seconds of rare documentation [as this now-classic opening theme plays]—in Metrocolor, no less—of a Gay Activists Alliance protest march, just a year and a half after Stonewall." www.nytimes.com/2017/03/09 /insider/1971-ostriches-a-six-foot-tall-gay-duck-and-john-shaft.html.

43 "You allow him to degrade you constantly by uncle-tomming him to death," one of the boys says to Bernard about the "friend" who quipped the pickaninny comment, then corrected Bernard about using "boy" as he talked to Mrs. Dahlbeck. Bernard replies, "He can do it . . . I do it to myself, and I let him do it because it is the only thing that makes him an equal." Femme identification and performance are equated in this odd defense.

44 It is also notable that this scene in *Shaft* is a ruse. On the telephone at a bar in front of henchmen sent to kill him, Shaft is actually calling police, who will arrive to arrest them as they eavesdrop on his call: "He's a complicated man . . . (John Shaft)."

Chapter Three. Other Countries

This chapter is certainly not the book-length social history of the "Other Countries" Black gay men's writing collective that the organization and our current literary and political practices need and deserve. It does not take up Other Countries at all. Steven has indicated in the index notes where to find archives helpful in this process. Here I have borrowed the name to indicate and honor its sense of Black gay men's diversity—which Daniel Garrett critically assessed with (auto)ethnographic sensibility in his brilliant essay "Other

Countries: The Importance Difference" in Other Countries' first publication (*Black Gay Voices*). "Other Countries" perhaps also signifies the distance from one another that many of us keep, and the individual sovereignty that many of us seek.

1 Chaka Khan, "Naughty," lyrics Gregg Diamond (Burbank, CA: Warner Bros. Records, 1980).

2 Khan.

3 Allen, "For 'the Children.'"

4 The toll continues to mount: "Since the beginning of the epidemic, 76 million people have been infected with the HIV virus and about 33 million people have died of HIV/AIDS. Globally, 38.0 million [31.6–44.5 million] people were living with HIV at the end of 2019. An estimated 0.7% [0.6–0.9%] of adults aged 15–49 years worldwide are living with HIV, although the burden of the epidemic continues to vary considerably between countries and regions. The WHO African region remains most severely affected, with nearly 1 in every 25 adults [3.7%] living with HIV and accounting for more than two-thirds of the people living with HIV worldwide." See Global Health Observatory, "HIV/AIDS."

5 Woods, "We Be Young."

6 Somehow, I have taken possession of Marvin (K. White)'s reading copy of *The Road before Us*. In this copy, Assotto Saint, the editor and publisher of the poetry anthology, wrote to him: "Marvin: I will forever hold you to keep delivering wonderful poems like 'Last Rights' to the world. Keep writing, keep polishing your craft, and always dare to be more"—Yves ("Yves" is encircled in a heart). It is our great privilege that Marvin followed Yves/Assotto's advice. Here is acknowledgment of Marvin's calling and inheritance. Thumbing through to Carlos's poem, I noticed that Marvin's book contains the same inscription on page 120 found in my own copy (the whereabouts of which I imagine I will learn in an endnote one day), which I purchased that night in 1991: Carlos Segura's home address, on Ashland Place, written on the second page of his poem "Classifieds." The only difference from the "personal" inscription in my copy is that Marvin's version includes explicit A train directions, since the Oaklander was out of his BART comfort zone. I am not shocked that I was not the only one who wanted a private reading.

7 C. Johnson, "Hey Brother, What's Hap'nin'?," in *Brother to Brother*. Cary was the director of the Amnesty International Washington, D.C., office when he accomplished two crucial mentoring activities that deeply affected my life. First, he recommended me for the Ralph Bunche Human Rights Fellowship, where I worked in the Southeast Regional office of Amnesty in Atlanta, and he introduced me to dear Marques, the first man whom I would love in a romantic relationship. (Not Joe, but quite close, in fact. He had been a student activist at Howard University at the same time that I did similar work at Morehouse.) Cary—a senior Africanist human rights professional and a founding member of Other Countries and GMAD—contributed poetry and short stories to *The Road before Us, Brother to Brother, In the Life*, and the Other

Countries anthologies *Black Gay Voices*, which were singular in their depiction of African and US Black/continental African relationships and diaspora longing.

8 Another club scene: It occurred to me only belatedly that folks steering me to Atlanta's Loretta's (and later Traxx) and not the Marquette Club on Fair Street (known as "the queasy 'Quette") was a gender and class hail. The 'Quette was a "low bar" (although, truth be told, Loretta's was not much higher), in which, as Sharon Bridgforth might describe, "a whole lotta shit is libal to happen," reminding me of her fictional juke joint (see *love conjure/ blues*). At the 'Quette a magnificent array of gender and working-class aesthetics was celebrated. At Loretta's, the only presiding "queen," the HIV/AIDS activist Madam Edna Brown, held a college degree, worked at an HBCU, and served in the music ministry of local mainstream Black churches. One evening, amid her announcements of the upcoming club events, she interrupted the merriment by delivering an a capella one-line blues riff as a retort to some remark from the crowd, but looking at Doug, Marlon, and me. She sang: "Get You Some Business Baby (and Leave Mine Alone)." All praises to Madam Edna, who was killed in 1991. (See Z. Z. Hill, "Get You Some Business," lyrics George Jackson and Grady Parnell [Malaco Records, 1983].)

9 Of course, we cannot control how we are seen or what purposes others see us fulfilling. Recently, Steven (Fullwood) and I shared some of our (often hilarious) youthful experiences around desire, cultural work, political work, and mentorship (and pederasty) in our community. We compared notes on our experiences with a brother who is older than us and known to (still) trade his vast knowledge for sexual attention from younger men (younger than Steven and I are now) and who had been disappointed by the older experienced man seeming to propose a relationship of quid pro quo. Having heard this since we were the age of the young men speaking, Steven, speaking for both of us, said, "I never had a problem with him because he never wanted to fuck me."

10 I share this note here to provide a counternarrative to the legion of educated and accomplished Black folks who cite a litany of injuries at the hands of Black folks who they claim are jealous or limited (thus forcing their disaffiliation and/or antiblackness). One night during an early-1990s GMAD forum discussing contemporary Black gay art, a long-standing, well-loved activist member of the community quipped at me: "You are the last white woman, aren't you?" He had overheard me as I excitedly turned to a friend while the speaker was making their presentation, to say how much the work reminded me of Matisse and gush about the use of color. The activist was doing a few things at the same time, all of which must be read in a deeply contextual and reparative frame. Certainly, he was being shady as he amplified my European high art citation, relative to the Black gay art/ist being discussed, and perhaps also my deportment (and wont to enjoy using words like deportment in everyday speech and endnotes!). At the same time, the senior brother's view of "the last white woman" does not solely ascribe art loving/knowledge to white folks. The target of his correction was the impertinence of whiteness.

He was admonishing my chatter while others were speaking. The lesson here is that had I not been outta pocket (inappropriate, rude) in that instant, perhaps I would not have gotten read (please note, dear reader, to my knowledge, this was the first and last time this epithet was assigned to me). This insight will become useful when we turn to debates around (dis)affiliation in Black studies in the conclusion and in my forthcoming work. The "acting white" epithet is put in context by Prudence Carter, "Intersecting Identities."

11 E. Johnson, *Sweet Tea*, 442.

12 Oddly, I have not talked to any of those whom I know and could actually speak to today—not about this. What brand of ethnographic refusal is this? Part 3 will offer some clues. A planned memoir project may find analysis.

13 McBride, "Can the Queen Speak?," 366.

14 Hemphill, "Black Machismo," 130.

15 Hemphill, "Heavy Breathing," 6.

16 Hemphill, "American Wedding," 171.

17 Isaac Jackson quoted in Joseph Beam, "Leaving the Shadows Behind," xxii. After this quotation Joe begins the next paragraph: "In 1985, we are still radicals." Later in *In the Life*, Joe offers his now-famous remix: "Black men loving Black men is the revolutionary act of the eighties." Beam, "Brother to Brother," 191.

18 "No one conceptualizes me, I am the concept." See Gamson, *The Fabulous Sylvester*, 155.

19 White, "Second Read: From the Queen James Bible," unpublished manuscript, 2018.

20 See "To Be Real," III, Essex's enthusiastic commentary on *Paris Is Burning*. The occasion of the ball scene gives him the opportunity to discuss cultural appropriation (for example, by Madonna), race, class, and the concept of "realness." He speaks respectfully about Octavia St. Laurent and the "clarifying voice" of Dorian Corey, as well as the pragmatism of Pepper LaBeija, regarding their own trans identity and others' choice of gender affirmation (fka "sex change"). Still, today Essex's use of "he" to describe each of these individuals seems odd, at best, and insensitive, given our more informed understanding of gender fluidity, identity, and pronoun usage.

21 Roberta Flack, *First Take* (Atlantic Records, 1969).

22 Nina Simone, *Nina Simone at Town Hall* (Colpix Records, 1959).

23 Hemphill, "HOMICIDE: For Ronald Gibson."

24 Asked "What about the term 'drag queen'? People in STAR prefer to use the term 'transvestite.' Can you explain the difference?" Marsha replied: "A drag queen is one that usually goes to a ball and that's the only time she gets dressed up. Transvestites live in drag. A transsexual spends most of her life in drag. I never come out of drag to go anywhere. Everywhere I go I get dressed up. . . . When you're a transsexual, you have hormone treatments and you're on your way to a sex change. . . ." The interviewer follows up, perhaps leading the witness to an anticipated answer: "You'd be considered a pre-operative transsexual then? You don't know when you'd be able to go through the sex

change?" And Marsha answers, "Oh, most likely this year. I'm planning to go to Sweden. I'm working very hard to go." See E. Young, "Rapping with a Street Transvestite Revolutionary," 115.

25 Tourmaline (fka Reina Gossett), 2014.

26 E. Young, "Rapping with a Street Transvestite Revolutionary." "The assimilation imperative became so overwhelming that trans people were kicked off the protected identities list in the anti-discrimination bill in hopes that it would pass New York City Council more quickly. As Sylvia put it in an 1992 interview with Randy Wicker on the Christopher Street Pier, Marsha P Johnson, Bubbles Rose Marie, and other street queens catalyzed the movement for gay liberation only to be violently kicked out & exiled 'when drag queens were no longer needed in the movement!' This violence continues today through the historical erasure of the many contributions of Sylvia & Marsha, sex workers, homeless people, people of color and poor trans people from the riots at Stonewall." www.reinagossett.com/crunkfeministcollective-happy-birthday -marsha.

27 Saint, "Miss Thing/For Marcia Johnson."

28 Assotto was an accomplished modern dancer, poet, editor, essayist, playwright, producer, and New Wave pop musician. See Saint, *Spells of a Voodoo Doll.* The heading I have chosen, "Does the Haitian Queen Speak?"(Èske Ayisyen Rèn nan pale), over two better Kreyol phrases, rhymes better with my meaning. Both go to important axes of Gayatri Spivak's original argument and Dwight's clever appropriation: Èske larenn lan kapab pale? (Is the queen able to speak?); Èske larenn lan pèmèt yo pale? (Is the queen permitted to speak?). See Dwight McBride, "Can the Queen Speak?"

29 See McBride, "Can the Queen Speak?," 365. Parentheses mine. I cannot help but hear Nina Simone in Dwight's insistence—"I mean this critique quite specifically"—here. His line in the sand is reminiscent of Simone's aside "And I mean every word of it!" in a live performance of her "Mississippi Goddamn." The full passage reads: "As a community of scholars who are serious about political change, healing Black people, and speaking truth to Black people, we must begin the important process of undertaking a truly more inclusive vision of 'black community' and of race discourse. As far as I am concerned, any treatment of African American politics and culture, and any theorizing of the future of Black America, any black religious practice or critique of black religion that does not take seriously the lives, contributions and presence of Black gays and lesbians (just as we take seriously the lives of Black women, the Black poor, Black men, the Black middle-class, etc.) or any critique that does no more than to render token lip-service to Black gay and lesbian experience is a critique that not only denies the complexity of who we are as a representationally 'whole people,' but denies the very 'ass-splitting truth' which Essex Hemphill referred to so eloquently and so very appropriately in *Ceremonies.*"

30 Saint, "The Impossible Black Homosexual."

31 Robinson in Riggs, dir., "Anthem," reading an excerpt from his poem "Unfinished Work." Assotto's works were in English. Erin writes that "Saint's

archives suggest that he did not pursue Haitian venues as outlets for his creative work, and explanations of Haitian references in his pieces seem to confirm that he did not create this work with even a diasporic audience in mind." See Durban-Albrecht, "The Legacy of Assotto Saint," 238.

32 Colin describes himself using the West Indian term too bright (rude) in "An Archaeology of Grief," 76. Elizabeth Alexander, a classmate, remembers Colin and his grand cape fondly. Colin never mentioned Yale to me.

33 Among other works, see especially C. Harris, "I'm Going Out Like a Fucking Meteor." In the special section, Craig Harris thanked authors who "due to deadlines and space limitations" were not included, announcing that works by James S. Tinney, D. Marie S. Walker, Gwendolyn Rogers, Joseph Beam, John E. Bush, and Guy Weston "meant for inclusion in this supplement, will appear in the next few issues of The Native." Moreover, although editor Patrick Merla concedes in a note adjacent to the introduction that "Craig G. Harris, supplement editor, and many of his contributors have presented strong arguments . . . insisting upon, among other things, the capitalization of 'b' when referring to the Black nation, its peoples, or its institutions," Merla had decided to "enforce our policy on editorial style."

34 Augustin-Billy, "Ayiti Pa Lakay Ankò." I am indebted to her for generously sending me an electronic copy of the full essay while I was traveling. As Erin Durban-Albrecht's astute understatement avers in the same special issue of the *Journal of Haitian Studies*, the abridgment of the essay "reduced the complexity of the transnational critiques fiercely presented by this historical figure in his lifetime." See "The Legacy of Assotto Saint," 236.

The republished version of "Haiti: A Memory Journey" has circulated without any details of its original publication in a problematic radical gay newspaper's series on Black lesbian and gay diaspora, alongside key Black lesbian and gay figures writing on gay life in Africa, tensions between largely white gay organizations and Black activists in the United States, gender differences in Black lesbian and gay collaboration, and the film adaptation of *The Color Purple*.

35 Saint, "Haiti: A Memory Journey," 33–34.

36 Saint, "Haiti: A Memory Journey." Emphasis mine.

37 McAllen Detention Center, in Puerto Rico, also began operating in 1981, detaining Haitian refugees. By 1983, the Reagan administration had composed its "Mass Immigration Emergency Plan," requiring that ten thousand immigration detention beds be located and ready for use at any given time.

38 Assotto was educated in French in Haiti.

39 Morisseau-Leroy, "Mèsi papa Desalín."

40 Saint, "Haiti: A Memory Journey," 35.

41 Saint.

42 Morisseau-Leroy, "Mèsi papa Desalín."

43 Hemphill, "Does Your Mama Know about Me?," 42.

44 Saint, "Haiti: A Memory Journey," 35. I'm calling on all homophobic Haitians to remember that one who has been oppressed should not in turn oppress others. We must forgive, yet never forget, so that the bloodshed, the violent

and too-often-fatal persecution of ex-tons tons macoutes without due process of law will come to an end. We must never be guilty of the same crimes committed to us. We should all renew our energies for the struggle ahead and move beyond the boundaries. We will be heroes: heroes of our own making, heroes to ourselves, heroes to Haiti.

45 Saint, "Haiti: A Memory Journey," 33.

46 Saint, "'Going Home Celebration' for Donald Woods," 135.

47 Woubshet, *The Calendar of Loss*, 14.

48 Marlon Ross, quoted in Woubshet, 70.

49 I include this as an example of how brilliant and well-meaning people spoke (and speak) past one another. In an otherwise exceptionally positive review in the weekly Gay Community News (GCN), Cary raised the question of the slippage between Marlon's filmic avatar and the contemporary experience of the artist (see below). Essex escalated in his reply (see Essex Hemphill, "Choice"), arguing that "Johnson's comments about Riggs' personal relationship are blatantly intrusive and cannot be justified in the context of a brief arts review." Essex sets readers against the critic: "Johnson seems to believe that the sum total of Riggs' Black gay journey—as it is depicted in *Tongues Untied* is somehow not credible simply because Riggs' lover is white." But I do not see this belief, or "the suggestion that a Black gay man can only love a Black man to be authentically Black," in Cary's review. I read Essex's response as defensive personal clapback on behalf of his friend. In Marlon Riggs's correspondence (in the Stanford archive) a note that Essex wrote him on March 3, 1990, included a draft of his GCN response asking he and Jack (Essex's partner) to offer feedback. The film became a lightning rod for these discussions. Ron Simmons's commentary on his friendships with Marlon and Essex (and Joe) is particularly enlightening regarding this dynamic. See Simmons, "Joe, Essex, Marlon, and Me." See also Marlon's interview with Lyle Ashton Harris, "Cultural Healing: An Interview with Marlon Riggs."

Cary's review said: "This is the film we've been waiting for, the Black Gay Official Story. It's a work which should be screened in Sexuality 101 classes: an early '90s show and tell. It's the film you'd show to any straight person you wanted to understand you. It presents our lives not through any rose-colored vision of ourselves as ever-masculine, always healthy, and forever connected in loving couples. It shows us as we are: often angry, sometimes confused but always persevering. *Tongues Untied* is a picture we can live with."

After more praise, in the last paragraph he continues:

"My discovery after seeing the film, that Marlon Riggs has a white lover struck me as ironic and may leave some feeling cheated. I do not fault Riggs here for his choice of a partner, only for what I see as a deception. Despite his obvious talent and the positive vibe of the film one can't help but ask, does he really believe any of this? If Black men loving Black men is truly 'the revolutionary act' as he states at the film's conclusion, then why isn't he acting? And why are we led to believe that his fixation with white men was a phase through which he passed? Certainly there are many different ways to love Black men, but 'coming home' as it is presented in the film, features our primary intimate couplings with other Black men. Clearly, the journey back to ourselves is a process, not an event. Nevertheless, *Tongues Untied* is a Black gay time capsule. It is Marlon Riggs' gift to our community, and the culture it embodies is our collective gift to the double brothers of tomorrow." From C. Johnson, "Not in Knots."

50 An untenured friend sent this line from an imaginary essay they were inspired to write about interracial relationships, which they admit they will likely never write, given the controversy and silencing (which, in their case, is working). Note that the title of this section is drawn from L. Jordan, "Black Gay v Gay Black."

51 In US gay parlance, "dinge queen" is used to denote a white man who prefers to date Black men. Dinge, according to Etymology Online: "1736, in Kentish dialect, 'dirty, foul,' a word of uncertain origin, but perhaps related to dung. Meaning 'soiled, tarnished, having a dull, brownish color' (from grime or weathering) is by 1751; hence 'shabby, shady, drab' (by 1855). The noun dinge 'dinginess' (1816) is a back-formation; as a derogatory word for 'black person, Negro,' by 1848. Related: Dingily; dinginess." www.etymonline.com/search?q=Dinge, accessed March 2021.

52 See Darieck Scott, "Jungle Fever?"; Reid-Pharr, "Dinge"; and McBride, "It's a White Man's World."

53 McBride, "It's a White Man's World," 88.

54 Lorde, *Zami, a New Spelling of My Name*.

55 Saint, "The Impossible Black Homosexual."

56 See Stanford, "Yeah, Baby." To honor the author's intentions, provide clues to its oral performance, and preserve this rare and out-of-print work, the poem is printed here using the original spacing, line breaks, and punctuation found in the original chapbook. Meta Du Ewa Jones taught me the word prosody (rhythm, intonation, stress, and musicality that is printed/expressed on the page in various ways, including line breaks and nonstandard punctuation), and the relationship between textuality and prosody, over a dining room table as she described the paper she was writing in which Meta "focus[es] on the visual performance of jazz-influenced texts as indicative of poets' unique approaches to scripting African-American musical and verbal sound." See M. Jones, "Jazz Prosodies: Orality and Textuality." If I had my druthers (and, mostly, if I had the requisite skill to write it!), I would insist that *There's a Disco Ball* be printed with line breaks, spaces, and (lack of) punctuation that would better express the voices of the author and his conversation partners: our music. Today, these special gestures will have to do.

57 Saint, "Preface," xix. Here Assotto quotes L. Jordan, "Black Gay v Gay Black," 25.

58 Cary Alan Johnson, quoted in McGruder, "To Be Heard in Print," 53.

59 Perhaps this is a revelatory example. An otherwise lovely colleague—single, gay, Black, and only a few years younger than I—sat at my dinner table and told my partner and me that he finds Black men "ugly." This putatively sophisticated elite academic chose the category "Black men"—presumably any shape,

size, color, nationality, or temperament of Black—as the catchall for ugliness. Why was he able to say this—essentially that his hosts and their family and most of their friends are unattractive to him? Because the rules of liberal (i.e., also) "civil" academic speech dictate that this is merely his "choice," which should be left uninterrogated and to which my response should be to move on from the risotto to the next course without recrimination. Imagine!

60 Julien, "Confessions of a Snow Queen," 125.

61 Morrow, "An Interview with Isaac Julien," 410.

62 Morrow.

63 Julien, "Confessions of a Snow Queen," 125.

64 Isaac said: "We have all grown up as snow queens—straights, as well as white queers—Western culture is in love with its own [white] image." See Julien, 126.

65 A 2016 NIH report averred that "if current HIV diagnoses rates persist, about 1 in 2 Black men who have sex with men (MSM) . . . in the United States will be diagnosed with HIV during their lifetime, according to a new analysis by researchers at the Centers for Disease Control and Prevention (CDC)." See "Lifetime Risk of HIV Diagnosis," February 23, 2016, www.cdc.gov/nchhstp /newsroom/2016/croi-press-release-risk.html.

66 For example, after Marlon's death his lover, Jack Vincent, confided this poignant extra-filmic moment to the *San Francisco Examiner*: "From his hospital bed, Riggs tells the camera that he knows there will come a day when he will go home, 'and I want my mother and my grandmother and Jack to be there to hold my hand and rub my head and feet and let me die.' When he first watched the movie, Jack Vincent recalls thinking, 'Who's Jack? I mean, you've met big mama, you've met mama. Which one's Jack?' Vincent, who was Riggs's partner for fifteen years and principal caretaker throughout Riggs's illness, does not appear in *Black Is . . . Black Ain't*. 'I guess it depends on how you see the theme of the film,' Jack said. 'One point of view is that it is a film by and about Black people. If it's a film about Blacks, then I'm not Black. But it is also a film about Marlon and Marlon's life. And he was in a relationship. When they filmed in the hospital, where do you suppose I was? I was there. I was taking care of Marlon.'" See Erika Milvy, "White Ain't . . . ," *SFGate*, May 8, 1995, www.sfgate.com/style/article/White-ain-t-3147227.php.

67 The cover of the 1983 collection *Black Men/White Men*—of a Black man and a white man embracing—comes to mind as an alternative image. The collection is a sad illustrative foil to the Black gay anthological tradition in works edited by Joe, Essex, Blackheart, and Other Countries. Whereas these offer cross-sections of Black gay life and thought, *Black Men/White Men* traffics in tired objectification of Black men and rehearsal of only the most trite fantasies of Black abjection and white heroism in taking on Black lovers.

68 Perhaps in contradistinction to Ian Patrick Polk's *Noah's Arc*, which Rikki directed for the US cable channel LOGO.

69 See, for example, Olusoga, *Black and British*; and Carby, *Imperial Intimacies*.

70 "White boys are so pretty" is a line from "White Boys/Black Boys" in the film version of *Hair*, which premiered off-Broadway at the Public Theatre in

1967, went to Broadway the next year, and was brought to the screen in 1979: the beginning of the long 1980s. It provides a sharp, wonderfully performed sendup of interracial desire in the context of exploitation of a multiracial group of young people by the US state and the sort of masculinist vampirism that the Vietnam War required and enabled. There are two parts to the scene: in one, two groups of women are in Central Park—one white and the other Black (led by the magnificently formidable talent Nell Carter)—and in the other, two separate panels of men in medical army uniforms inspect a steady line of undressed Black and white male recruits. Marvelous fun—and this is transgressive.

71 To wit, I am not saying that "Tar Beach" is one of the biomythic parts of the story, as opposed to a bio-portion. I am saying that these divisions are not immaterial to understanding the whole work, or the form of biomythography. Neither makes this landmark book, or her methodological innovation, less significant. The narrative is self-consciously crafted, regardless of how much described "actually happened." See Lorde, *Zami, a New Spelling of My Name.*

72 Lorde, 177. The conversation is differently configured among and about Black women's interracial desire. We remember Audre in the context of her long-term relationship with Gloria Joseph and not her long- and short-term relationships with white women lovers or with her white husband and father to her two children. For biographical information to complement *Zami,* see DeVeaux, *Warrior Poet.*

73 Lorde, "Tar Beach," 12–13.

74 Bethel, in *Conditions Five: The Black Women's Issue.* This was written, she says, while traveling to the First Annual Third World Lesbian Writers Conference in 1979.

75 Bethel, "what chou mean *we* white girl?"

76 Cheryl Dunye's early short films are especially demonstrative in this regard, including "The Potluck and the Passion," "An Untitled Portrait," "Vanilla Sex," "She Don't Fade," and "Janine," which are collected in the anthological video *The Early Works of Cheryl Dunye.*

77 Eve writes, in brackets, "From 1977, when he was 16, to the end of his life, Gary Fisher kept a journal and a number of corollary notebooks. What follows are selections, ordered consecutively, from the thousands of pages of these journals and notebooks." Eve says that she and Gary settled on the book's title, *Gary in Your Pocket,* which has remained, "well or ill-advisedly." This section's title is a gesture of re-narrativization. I want to release Gary from the confines and strictures of your pocket, and invoke his poem "I Hope He Smiles." See Fisher, *Gary in Your Pocket,* 121, 286, 17.

This reader finds the book difficult in a few ways. I trust that this is legally authorized. But I wonder, ethically, whether Gary—a dying graduate student who longed to be published but could not gather himself to do it in his lifetime (because of illness, but also just because of whatever limitations we each own)—could have really consented in the ways we would each hope for ourselves and our own works. I wonder about my own professional ethics—what should be my stance on retelling? Don Belton writes a heartbreaking and incisive introduction to *Gary in Your Pocket*, noting, for example, the seemingly simple truth of publishing: "The young, Black gay writer is too easily rejected, and therefore too easily compromised by our society." More discursive and material effects of antiblackness resound in a few examples. First, I hear this compounded by Gary's adolescent wish-craft that this reader did not find resolved—willing himself white because he is "not a stereotype"—as if "that's all that matters." Moreover—and fault me if you will, dear reader, but—I cannot help but read Gary alongside and at times conflated with Belton's tragic end at the hands of a former white lover, and I cannot help but hear the title of Belton's review essay "How to Make Love to a White Man" as a rereading of Gary's journal entries.

78 Fisher, *Gary in Your Pocket*, 94; McBride, "It's a White Man's World." 94.

79 Fisher, *Gary in Your Pocket*, 281.

80 See Delany, *The Mad Man* and *Hogg*. See Reid-Pharr, "The Shock of Gary Fisher," 148.

81 Here I am not centrally concerned with what Robert called "the more subtle, more perverse, more radical aspects of Fisher's aesthetic" in his "The Shock of Gary Fisher" (138). Moreover, I am not criticizing the fact of (violent) s/m kink or "play" here. However, I do wonder who's really playing here. And I am questioning the materiality of this aesthetic.

82 Hemphill, *Ceremonies*, 96.

83 Hemphill, 99.

84 Quashie, "Queer. Caribbean. Miami. Boy," 4.

85 Quashie. And Kevin's imagination in retelling goes to Sula, as Nel and Sula encounter a "flock of young Black men, including Ajax who . . . utters a phrase that has no clear dictionary meaning but that is nonetheless exact: 'Pigmeat.' Wanton and still too compelling to avoid." Thirty-something years later, he still melts.

86 More than twenty years later, walking to the college dining hall with Troy and them after class—one student gingerly asks about my husband. I thought, "Stay out of my business." But we lived on campus, Phillip and I. We three were hypervisible in that tiny fishbowl. Many of the students had already seen us temporarily occupying space on that mostly white campus with our big friendly brown dog (Billy Strayhorn). Just as I choose not to do the forensics of partner choice for literary figures, friends, and colleagues, I want to claim this dignity or privilege or privacy for myself. But recently, a young brother admonished us for keeping our relationship too private for young Black gay men to easily see and imagine the option that they find diminishing: it matters. I do not want to reify the tired old camps of interracialists and Afrocentrists, Black gays and gay Blacks, as if that mistaken grammar always and unproblematically predicts where we stand in relation to loving and supporting Black students. But Black men who plan, pledge, or "end up" in short- or long-term relationships with Black men do not escape the spyglass. Black Black Black! is far from an unproblematic "escape" from white supremacy. What is it we are doing—socially, politically, economically, psychically, and

epidemiologically—when we do each other? Our choices—to the degree that they are "choices" for particular individuals—condition something that is far from utopic: "but beautiful" (I hear Nancy Wilson sing).

Chapter Four. Disco

Alas, I am not a poet; I just play one—uneconomically, in long-ass prose, looking for "the clam that snaps / God in the details / the dust in the corner" of the sociopolitical. See E. Alexander, "Ars Poetica." So I lean on my brister, Marvin, for this epigram. See Marvin K. White, "Theology of the Discopocene," forthcoming.

1 "Time has been lost in trying / We have been left outside / Looking at passions dying / Emotions grow strong all the time / But it's alright, we can still go on." Cymande, "Bra," 1972. The band was made up of nine self-taught Caribbean-born, London-based musicians/singers.

2 Hall, "Race, Articulation and Societies Structured in Dominance."

3 Funkadelic, *Free Your Mind and Your Ass Will Follow* (Westbound, 1970).

4 See, especially, Gilroy, *Empire Strikes Back*.

5 This will be my working definition of neoliberalism: retreat of the welfare apparatus of the state—health care, education, housing, and education—with exponential expansion of privatized policing of various "crises" targeting poor (and) Black folks and other poor people of color. Neoliberalism is always corporate, for the retreats and expansion are filled and forced by private business interests that are often multinational. This is related to, but not the same as, "neo-liberal," which I use in other contexts to denote a political or ethical stance associated with a classic liberal point of view, which has shifted to the right since the dawning of the long 1980s.

6 June Tyson, featured singer in Sun Ra and His Intergalactic Research Arkestra, *It's after the End of the World (Live at the Donaueschingen and Berlin Festivals)* (MPS Records, 1972). I thank Vanessa Agard-Jones for a stirring invocation of this in terms of the Anthropocene.

7 David Scott, *Omens of Adversity*, 2.

8 Hall, "Race, Articulation and Societies Structured in Dominance," 341.

9 For local examples, see Dunn, *Black Miami in the Twentieth Century*; Gregory, *Black Corona*; and Vargas, *Catching Hell in the City of Angels*.

10 Cohen, *The Boundaries of Blackness*, 79.

11 See Webb, *Dark Alliance*; and Blum, "The CIA, Contras, Gangs, and Crack."

12 See "A Brief History of the Drug War."

13 Here's the first exchange between Press Secretary Larry Speakes and journalist Lester Kinsolving in 1982, after nearly a thousand people had died from AIDS:

> LESTER KINSOLVING: Does the president have any reaction to the announcement by the Centers for Disease Control in Atlanta that AIDS is now an epidemic in over 600 cases?

LARRY SPEAKES: AIDS? I haven't got anything on it.

KINSOLVING: Over a third of them have died. It's known as "gay plague." [press pool laughter] No, it is. It's a pretty serious thing. One in every three people that get this have died. And I wonder if the president was aware of this.

SPEAKES: I don't have it. [press pool laughter] Do you?

KINSOLVING: You don't have it? Well, I'm relieved to hear that, Larry! [press pool laughter]

SPEAKES: Do you?

KINSOLVING: No, I don't.

SPEAKES: You didn't answer my question. How do you know? [press pool laughter]

KINSOLVING: Does the president—in other words, the White House—look on this as a great joke?

SPEAKES: No, I don't know anything about it, Lester.

See German Lopez, "The Reagan Administration's Unbelievable Response to the HIV/AIDS Epidemic," December 1, 2016, www.vox.com/2015/12/1/9828348 /ronald-reagan-hiv-aids.

14 David Scott, *Omens of Adversity*, 36.

15 Parker, "Revolution," 254.

16 Bridgforth, *love conjure/blues*, 9. Emphasis mine. I invoke Sharon's exquisite juke-joint theoretic here again to bring into sharper focus what a sincere politics of Black inclusion could look like. She sets the scene:

> work/and play hard
> and do the jernt be packed!
> mens womens some that is both some that is neither/be
> rolling all up and between the sounds/laying up in
> them rent rooms/and dancing off all bettye's home
> cooking
> anyway

17 Ashford and Simpson, "Bourgie Bourgie" (Warner Music, 1977). This gorgeous instrumental groove remained preferred in the clubs, although by 1980, Ashford and Simpson added (catchy critically sharp/shady and funny) lyrics for the popular hit they produced for Gladys Knight and the Pips: "Livin' the life / You're a jet-setter / Livin' the life / You've got it all together / Hold the pose, turn the nose. / Some fancy struttin' / It's a fact you from across the tracks / You said you wasn't. [Then the infectious hook.] Everybody wants to be / Bourgie Bourgie. . . ." See Gladys Knight and the Pips, "Bourgie Bourgie," on *About Love* (Columbia Records, 1980).

18 Do yourself a favor—watch or rewatch *The Wiz*. Appropriately, the Emerald City scene was the most expensive ever filmed at the World Trade Center,

including three costume changes and twenty-two playback speakers, in order for all four hundred dancers (choreographed by Louis Johnson) to hear the music simultaneously. See Charlie Smalls, *The Wiz* (original motion picture soundtrack, 1978). And yes, as Junior LaBeija assesses in *Paris Is Burning*, the category here is "O-p-u-l-e-n-c-e. Opulence. You own everything. Everything is yours!" See Livingston, dir., *Paris Is Burning*.

19 Chic, "Good Times" (Atlantic Records, 1979).

20 Wilson and Rodgers, "Black-White Wage Gaps Expand with Rising Wage Inequality," 6.

21 More shocking is their convincing and bracing evidence that even those measures that we know to be marginally effective to keep individual Black families afloat, such as "greater educational attainment," increasing Black home ownership, buying and banking Black, Black people saving more, entrepreneurship, and greater financial literacy, will also not close the enormous racial wealth gap. See Darity et al., "What We Get Wrong about Closing the Racial Wealth Gap," 6–65.

22 Salsoul Orchestra, "Ooh, I Love It (Love Break)" (Salsoul Records, 1983). To hear a version closer to what you would have heard on WBLS radio station or at the Paradise Garage in the long 1980s (or indeed what Pray Tell insisted on hearing in the *Pose* episode), see MFSB—"Love Is the Message" (extended version), www.youtube.com/watch?v=p4wpRkcV9Ds, accessed March 2021.

23 Several months before I dared to go to the Garage for the first time alone, James took me to Better Days. I have not been the same since. The Paradise Garage closed in 1987.

24 Sister Sledge, "He's the Greatest Dancer."

25 Giovanni, "Nikki-Rosa."

26 Carl Bean, "I Was Born This Way" (Motown, 1977).

27 Campt, "Black Feminist Futures and the Practice of Fugitivity."

28 See Campt.

29 J. Jordan, "Poem about My Rights." Emphasis original. See https://www .youtube.com/watch?v=XUSTxhYu7-4.

30 I send it to my friend Tricia. She replies "Oh Lush Life . . . oh, especially sitting out in this glorious summer heat. Thank you. That's a song for those who have loved through deep longing. . . . I know the song well and he transforms it." See Andy Bey, "American Song" (Minor Music, 2005). Not sibilance and stridence, but breath too, breath! See Billy Strayhorn, "Lush Life" (Tempo Music, 1949).

31 Change (featuring Luther Vandross), "Searchin'" (Warner/RFC Records, 1980).

32 Evelyn "Champagne" King, "Shame" (RCA and Big Break Records, 1977).

33 Diana Ross, "Love Hangover" (Motown Records, 1976).

34 Salsoul Orchestra Featuring Loleatta Holloway, "Run Away" (Salsoul Records, 1977).

35 Grace Jones, "Nightclubbing" (Island Records, 1981).

36 See Lawrence, *Hold On to Your Dreams*.

37 Lorde, *Zami, a New Spelling of My Name*, 22.

38 The section heading is from Bean, "I Was Born This Way."

39 Hemphill, "Loyalty."

40 Carl Bean, "I Was Born This Way" (Motown, 1977).

41 Sylvester, *Living Proof* (Fantasy Records, 1979).

42 Sylvester, "Over and Over" (Fantasy Records, 1977).

43 Anzaldúa, *Borderlands/La frontera.*

44 M. Alexander, *Pedagogies of Crossing*, 283.

45 See Crawley, *Blackpentecostal Breath.*

46 E. Johnson, "Feeling the Spirit in the Dark."

47 Sylvester, "Over and Over."

Chapter Five. Black Nations Queer Nations?

1 See Fatima Jamal, "The Thrill and Fear of 'Hey, Beautiful,'" *New York Times*, June 30, 2017, www.nytimes.com/2017/06/30/opinion/trans-sexual-assault -black-women.html.

2 As documented in the film, Jacqui extended a welcome at the opening plenary of the 1995 Black Nations/Queer Nations? Lesbian and Gay Sexualities in the African Diaspora: A Working Conference, with members of the planning committee from the Black and queer activist and scholarly community in New York. A number of these folks were part of the original organizing committee, which changed over time: M. Jacqui Alexander, Hamilton College; Kenn Ashley, activist; Cheryl Clarke, poet, Rutgers University; Cathy Cohen, Yale University; Martin Duberman, the Graduate Center, City University of New York, and director of the Center for Lesbian and Gay Studies; Cheryl Dunye, filmmaker; Shari Frilot, filmmaker; El Gates, Yeshiva University, Benjamin N. Cardozo School of Law; Jackie Goldsby, Yale University; Peter Kwan, Columbia University; Wahneema Lubiano, Princeton University; Kagendo Murungi, Rutgers University; Charles Nero, Bates College; Robert Reid-Pharr, City College of New York; Colin Robinson, Gay Men of African Descent; Kendall Thomas, Columbia University; Dr. Sacha Vington; Anthony Williams, the Graduate Center, City University of New York.

3 Frilot, dir., *Black Nations/Queer Nations?* Unless otherwise indicated, all following quotations in this section will refer to this film.

4 Woodard, "Just as Quare as They Want to Be," 1281.

5 Frilot, dir., *Black Nations/Queer Nations?*

6 Lorde, "The Transformation of Silence into Language and Action," 81. Quoted in Frilot, dir., *Black Nations/Queer Nations?*

7 Frilot.

8 Frilot.

9 Another brilliant Trinbagonian is relevant here, of course, and will find more resonance in part 2: "Black/Queerpolis." In her masterful *Map to the Door of No Return*, Dionne Brand writes that "too much has been made of origins. All origins are arbitrary. This is not to say that they are not also nurturing, but they are essentially coercive and indifferent. Country, nation, these concepts are of course deeply indebted to origins, family, tradition, home. Nation-states

are configurations of origins as exclusionary power structures which have legitimacy based solely on conquest and acquisition." See Brand, *A Map to the Door of No Return*, 64.

10 Boyce-Davies, *Black Women, Writing and Identity*, 42.

11 Eric Williams, "'Massa Day Done,'" address delivered on March 22, 1961, at the University of Woodford Square.

12 Boyce-Davies, *Caribbean Spaces*.

13 M. Alexander, "Not Just (Any) Body Can Be a Citizen," 5.

14 See, for example, Gilroy, *Against Race*.

15 I explored this in "Discursive Sleight of Hand: Race, Sex, Gender" in *¡Vencer-emos?*, 41–73.

16 Staple Singers, "I'll Take You There" (Berkeley, CA: Stax, 1972).

17 Aya Institute, the community organization that community psychiatrist (and not only incidentally my partner at the time) Dr. Sacha Vington and I had founded, had been running weekly drop-in group sessions at the Audre Lorde Project, along with consulting and training for a few LGBTQ+ and HIV services groups in the city. But as I had observed in earlier work in Atlanta, although Aya argued that mental health and spiritual clarity were prerequisite to effective activist work as well as individual well-being, most folks were understandably more focused on the urgent everyday work of keeping their lifesaving organizations open. Like a number of groups around the world, we had taken the name of our institute from West Africa. We borrowed Aya (the fern)—an ndinkra symbol from the Akan of what is now Ghana, which means "I am not afraid of you. I am independent of you."

18 E. Johnson, "'Quare' Studies."

19 "PanAfrikans Beware: The Faggits Are Coming!!" Posted on April 1, 2013. Link no longer active.

20 "PanAfrikans Beware."

21 When I cited this in a talk at the American Anthropological Association meetings in 2013, a few important senior anthropologists found this less than funny or enlightening. Of course, the material well-being and rights of real people in real places and the scholarly framing of their lives are nothing to play with, as Jack certainly knows. Jack was referring to the feudal practices of LGBT and queer studies scholars, not "the folk" that these scholars might imagine. But they were having none of it—from the moment I invoked Jack! Instead, they aggressively invited me to "bend the knee" to an anthropological kingdom that eschews the use of "queer" altogether, perhaps in service to autochthonous nomenclature and/or merely to teach those upstart humanities theorists a lesson! I had unwittingly stepped into a skirmish—to "queer or not to queer"—in which I have steadily lost interest. See Halberstam, "Game of Thrones: The Queer Season." Jack has also tried to model ways for (white) queer theory to be in conversation with Black and queer-of-color work, and how to advance a refreshed and relevant form of queer studies. See especially Halberstam, "Shame and White Gay Masculinity."

22 Muñoz, *Cruising Utopia*, 1.

23 Moten, *In the Break*.

24 Walcott, "Somewhere out There," 33.

25 Editorial note: This book was written over many years, before the Zoom application and OnlyFans "won" the pandemic.

26 Mauss, *The Gift*.

27 Just a few years before *Black Nations/Queer Nations?*, Essex had embarked on his second tour of the United Kingdom, hosted by Ajamu Ikwe-Tyehimba (now also known as Ajamu X), Kobena Mercer, and others, during which he deepened his connections to Black British artists and activists. Essex was speaking out of his own US context. Still, that sites of racialized shame, cruelties of slavery, and ghettos are not only US phenomena also shows, once again, the "borrowed sameness" that Audre had identified. So the "I" that Hemphill employs here is both personal/specific and what I believe he would have us appreciate as "universal" to a Black male subject. Quotations transcribed by author from Essex's panel address at Black Nations/Queer Nations? Conference, in Frilot, dir., *Black Nations/Queer Nations?*

Photos of Essex wearing a similar polyester three-piece suit—his head intact on his shoulders, imitating Milton Moore's pose, and zippered up for a G rating—await analysis in the Marlon Riggs archive. I would suggest careful consideration of Black feminist theorization and historical contextualization (alongside his own words and other photo representations) through a Wynterian "deciphering practice" to render a fuller picture of Essex's complex understanding of his buttoned-up-polyester-suit redux. See Wynter, "Rethinking 'Aesthetics.'" Questions of "discretion" and/or "respectability politics" and/or "dissemblance" are fraught. See, for example, Clark Hine, "Rape and the Inner Lives of Black Women in the Middle West"; and Higginbotham, *Righteous Discontent*. I thank Joshua Gutterman Tranen for sharing his archival photos. The photographer is a well-known Chicago activist and zine creator, Scott Free.

28 See Ntozake Shange, "Foreword," in Robert Mapplethorpe, *The Black Book*.

29 See Xandre Rodríguez, "Mapplethorpe & Me," *Dazed*, March 25, 2014, www.dazeddigital.com/fashion/article/19356/1/mapplethorpe-me.

30 Hemphill, "Introduction," xl.

31 See Sarah Cascone, "Robert Mapplethorpe's Controversial 'Man in Polyester Suit' Photo Sells for $478,000," *Artnet*, October 8, 2015, https://news.artnet.com/market/robert-mapplethorpe-polyester-suit-sells-338631.

32 This can also be found, along with other writing inspired by visual artworks, in Shange, *Ridin' the Moon in Texas*.

33 Shange, "Foreword," ii.

34 Shange, "irrepressibly bronze, beautiful, and mine," in "Foreword," i. Also published in Shange, *Ridin' the Moon in Texas*.

35 Quotations from Essex's panel address at Black Nations/Queer Nations? Conference, in Frilot, dir., *Black Nations/Queer Nations?*

36 Of course, this is not a cure, nor are drugs universally available and information about them equally shared and known. Moreover, some patients do not tolerate the cocktail well, leaving fewer options to combat HIV.

37 Lorde, "A Litany for Survival."

38 Lorde.

39 McKay, "If We Must Die."

40 Sharpe, *In the Wake*, 132.

41 Juana has likewise asked us to consider the politics of queer bonds, queer sex, and community in what she calls the violent "political ambiance" that typifies the sociocultural spaces that we inhabit today. See Rodríguez, *Sexual Futures, Queer Gestures, and Other Latina Longings*, 280.

42 Brand, *In Another Place, Not Here*, 1.

43 Sharpe, *In the Wake*.

II. Black/Queerpolis

1 Hall, "Cultural Identity and Diaspora," 223.

Chapter Six. Bonds and Disciplines

Barbara Christian's title, "But What Do We Think We Are Doing Anyway," is a riff on Gloria T. Hull's "What It Is I Think She's Doing Anyhow."

1 Johnson and Henderson, *Black Queer Studies*, 6.

2 M. Alexander, "Danger and Desire," 160. See Iton, *In Search of the Black Fantastic*, 38. This is a high barre for Black intellectual and artistic perseverance and thriving, within what Richard Iton called "post 89/90 life." See Iton, "Still Life," 38.

3 Allen, "Black/Queer/Diaspora at the Current Conjuncture," 230.

4 M. Alexander, "Danger and Desire," 160.

5 Tinsley and Allen, "After the Love."

6 Allen, "Black/Queer/Diaspora at the Current Conjuncture," 217.

7 Christian, "The Race for Theory," 77.

8 Lorde, Parker, and Sullivan, *Sister Love*.

9 Allen, "Black/Queer/Diaspora at the Current Conjuncture," 214.

10 Tinsley, *Thiefing Sugar*.

11 Allen, *¡Venceremos?*

12 Tinsley, *Ezili's Mirrors*.

13 Sharpe, *In the Wake*, 51.

14 Earth, Wind & Fire, "After the Love Has Gone" (ARC/Columbia Records: 1979).

15 Allen, "Black/Queer/Diaspora at the Current Conjuncture," 237.

16 Morrison, *Beloved*, 89.

17 Today, I wonder how my current disavowals will be read. What we will learn from your penciled margins? Who will invite me to dance again? How will the magnificent arithmetic of distance add up?

18 Working on the United States does not preclude this, but these participants were among the folks that I understood to be focused on making interventions in a transnational conversation at the time: Natalie Bennett, Fatima El-

Tayeb, Lyndon Gill, Rosamond S. King, Ana-Maurine Lara, Xavier Livermon, Graeme Reid, Matt Richardson, Colin Robinson, Omise'eke Natasha Tinsley, Rinaldo Walcott, and Michelle Wright. Vanessa Agard-Jones, whose essay appears in the special issue, was doing dissertation fieldwork in Martinique at the time. Steven G. Fullwood joined us for the first day of the symposium.

19 Roderick A. Ferguson, *The Reorder of Things*, 36.

20 See Allen and Tinsley, "A Conversation 'Overflowing with Memory.'"

21 See Lara, *Queer Freedom, Black Sovereignty*; *Streetwalking*; and *Kohnjehr Woman*.

22 Focusing on the archipelago across language and political formation, Rosamond's book constitutes an important contribution to this conversation that insists both on local and regional specificities and diasporic connection. See R. King, *Island Bodies*.

23 See Livermon, *Kwaito Bodies*.

24 See Reid, *How to Be a Real Gay*.

25 Walcott, "Somewhere out There," 30.

26 Dixon, "This Light, This Fire, This Time," 39.

27 M. Alexander, *Pedagogies of Crossing*, 294.

28 See Jacqui Alexander, quoted in Frilot, dir., *Black Nations/Queer Nations?*

Chapter Seven. Archiving the Anthological at the Current Conjuncture

Barbara Smith and Beverly Smith, "'I Am Not Meant to Be Alone and without You Who Understand,'" 63. I encountered this statement in Alexis Pauline Gumbs's essay "Seek the Roots" before reading the original more recently (both now in heavy rotation in my Black feminism classes). "Seek the Roots" is typical of Alexis's crucial work: it provides another important ruttier to find (one's way) home(s) and to connect ancestral inheritances to bright manifold futures.

1 Richardson, *The Queer Limit of Black Memory*, 5. Matt is riffing on Derrida. (See *Archive Fever*.) For more regarding French archive fever, see Foucault, *The Archaeology of Knowledge*. This passage from his "Of Other Spaces" is provocative for our exploration: "There are heterotopias of indefinitely accumulating time, for example museums and libraries . . . have become heterotopias in which time never stops building up and topping its own summit. . . ." Foucault, "Of Other Spaces," 26.

2 The following passage citing my original endnote on this project is found in Colin Robinson's "The Work of Three-Year Old CAISO—Reflections at the MidPoint" (note 1), in which he published a portion of his responses and the questions that Matt and I put to colleagues. "Originally conceived of as a panel on comparative sexual rights, erotic autonomy, and 'Archives and Politics "For My Own Protection,"' my intention was to include in this issue a roundtable discussion featuring a few individuals whom I admire for the pathbreaking work they are doing to document/archive and improve black queer life and culture in a number of sites around the world (Steven G. Fullwood, Black Gay & Lesbian Archive, 'Fire & Ink'; Zethu Matebeni Forum for

the Empowerment of Women; Colin Robinson, Coalition Advocating Inclusion of Sexual Orientation; Selly Thiam, None on Record; Ajamu X, Sharing Tongues; Rukus!). For a variety of reasons, this did not work out. These projects that propose to 'save' culture, share tongues, and put on record provide a very differently configured and no less 'political' politics, which the working group is committed to engaging. One of our immediate forthcoming projects, therefore, will be to reconvene, revise, and publish this important conversation." Allen, "Black/Queer/Diaspora at the Current Conjuncture," n. 16.

3 See, especially, Hazel's earlier works during the long 1980s, including "White Woman Listen!"; *Reconstructing Womanhood*; and *Race Men*. There is much more to say, and this critical habit is certainly not limited to Hazel or her students.

4 See Carla Kaplan, *Zora Neale Hurston: A Life in Letters*. Speaking of the high crime of attempted evisceration, you may recall that after the initial commercial failure of the now-classic *Their Eyes Were Watching God*, after a number of works had been rejected by publishers, and after a false accusation of child molestation, sensationalized by Black newspapers, Hurston returned to Central Florida destitute and depressed. After her death and her burial in a grave in which her name was misspelled, paid for by a group of her neighbors, nearly all of her personal letters, books, scrapbooks, and clippings were burned. Now, reconsider, if you will, her 1945 proposal to Du Bois in the note directly following.

5 On June 11, 1945, Zora Neale Hurston made an elaborate and beautiful proposition to W. E. B. Du Bois, the vision of which may help us to envision the ether, the archive, and the best of Black memory. She wrote in part: "Why do you not propose a cemetery for the illustrious Negro dead. . . . Something like Pere la Chaise in Paris? . . . On 100 acres of land in Florida . . . because it lends itself to decoration easier than any other part of the United States . . . magnolias, bay, oaks, pines, palms . . . hibiscus, crotons. . . . Let there be a hall of meeting, and let the Negro sculptors and painters decorate it with scenes from our own literature and life. Mythology and all. . . . Let no Negro celebrity, no matter what financial condition they might be in at death, lie in inconspicuous forgetfulness . . . as much as 100 acres to prevent white encroachment . . . and space for an artist colony. . . ." See Hurston, "Letter to W. E. B. Du Bois."

6 Richardson, "No More Secrets, No More Lies."

7 Section ii begins "Jameel was what he preferred to be called / even though his mother still called him Glenn / pronouncing both 'n's / . . . ." Exceptionally talented and intimately part of the central cohort of the Black gay 1980s, Craig G. Harris is certainly "somewhere listening for his name." See C. Harris, "Hope against Hope."

8 Allen, "Crucial Palimpsest," xv.

9 D. Taylor, *The Archive and the Repertoire*.

10 Charlene is the living witness. And she is most certainly entitled to her full experience and narration. I have no quarrel or intention to ask her to defend her prerogative. I want to know more and deeper, to be able to understand

and re-narrate from other vantages. If I read Charlene correctly, the covering mercy at the center of her faith insists, in repayment, that she preach against a woman's right to choose, against marriage equality, against LGBTQ rights, and against trans recognition, for example. See Cothran, "Redeemed!"

11 Hartman, "Venus in Two Acts," 2. The work of this chapter is also in gratitude to (and impossible without) the scholars—Saidiya prominent among them— who have radically reshaped our relationship to archives, along with the Black trans and queer archivists themselves.

12 Philip, quoted in Saunders, "Defending the Dead, Confronting the Archive," 68–69.

13 Hartman, "Venus in Two Acts," 2.

14 Gumbs, "Seek the Roots," 17.

15 The intentions of Drs. Johnetta Cole and Beverly Guy-Sheftall in convincing Audre to keep her significant collection at Spelman, an institution dedicated to educating Black women, is resonant with the work our cohort is doing. Toni Cade Bambara's papers are also at Spelman.

16 David Scott, "Introduction," 7.

17 See Gramsci, *Selections from the Prison Notebooks of Antonio Gramsci*.

18 Lorde, "A Litany for Survival."

19 David Scott, "Introduction," 1.

20 Before the BGLA, there were two archival projects that specifically focused on collecting Black queer materials: the Gay & Lesbian Collection at the Auburn Avenue Research Center on African American Culture and History, Atlanta-Fulton Public Library; and the Shango Project, the National Archives for Black Lesbians and Gay Men, a project created by Bill Stanford Pincheon. The Black Gay and Lesbian Archive (then BGLA, now the In the Life Archive—ITLA) was formally donated in 2004 to the Schomburg Center for Research in Black Culture, a research library of the New York Public Library.

21 David Scott, "Introduction," 2. There are a number of folks we will turn to who do this work with no less commitment and meticulous vigilance. I highlight Steven not only because he has been doing this work longer than most but also because of the profound contributions he has made to the conception and research and production of this book (and to me as a friend).

22 Ajamu X, Campbell, and Stevens, "Love and Lubrication in the Archives, or Rukus!," 293.

23 As Ajamu told us in his response to the round table, "rukus! Federation is an artist led organisation and was launched in 2000 by Ajamu (Photographer and Community Activist) and Topher Campbell (Film Maker and Theatre Director). We are an award winning Company, which is known for its long-standing and successful programme of community-based work. The communities we serve are African, African-Caribbean and Black British who identify as Lesbian, Gay, Bisexual, Trans, Queer artist, activists and cultural producers, locally, nationally and internationally. Our work has a reputation for being dynamic and participative, and includes one off events, screenings, workshops, debates and exhibitions. Prior to the formation of rukus! (*Rukus!*

is a derivative of the word *raucous* and an African American Porn star) Both Topher and I have been active with the arts, theatre and cultural sector. At the heart of our practice is a commitment to bringing artistic and philosophical concepts and creativity to our work." Email correspondence, 2012.

24 Ajamu X, Campbell, and Stevens, "Love and Lubrication in the Archives, or Rukus!," 293.

25 Steven, responding to Colin in the virtual roundtable. He continues: "Currently I am hoping to work with organizations in their early stages to put it in their mission statements that they will save their records and work with appropriate repositories to collect and archive their remarkable histories. This effort might help change the dynamics of organizing as we currently know it."

26 Ajamu X, Campbell, and Stevens, "Love and Lubrication in the Archives, or Rukus!," 286.

27 Musila, "Navigating Epistemic Disarticulations," 696.

28 This account is taken from eyewitnesses and from my own viewing of the scene on YouTube: "LGBT Activists Disrupt Joburg Gay Parade 2012."

29 Ajamu X, email correspondence, 2012.

30 Ajamu X, Campbell, and Stevens, "Love and Lubrication in the Archives, or Rukus!," 282.

31 Silva Santana, "Transitionings and Returnings," 182.

32 Sharpe, *In the Wake*.

33 Hannah Nelson, one of Gwaltney's interviewees in *Drylongso*, said that "the difference between Black people and white people is that Black people know when we are just playing." Nelson gets at the soul of ethical satire and camp performance here. But not "just playing" pays better: "'No you better don't,' Miss Ru!"

34 More tensions and understandable suspicion arise with invocations of the "popular." So I must say this plainly even if controversially: I love *Pose!* (the first two seasons—I will be watching carefully to see what is next!). It set out a very challenging goal to represent a largely unknown group of people and moment that would telescope their significance while keeping a large number of viewers tuned in. Although this is clearly not one of the beloved PBS shows of the long 1980s that shaped my prepubescent years and eschewed ratings and viewer shares for educative content and representation, *Pose* has a good sense of this that makes it heart-filled, entertaining, and precious. For me, this was likewise true of *Metrosexuality*.

35 Campbell X, quoted in R. Lewis, "'At the Site of Intimacy,'" 193.

36 Campbell X, dir., "Desire."

37 *The Aggressives* (2005) shares similar subject matter with these films and unfortunately also betrays its outsider framing—among the first and still one of the most widely distributed, it betrays the fashion industry "street scout" "culture vulture" sensibilities of its white cisgender director.

38 Ellison, Green, Richardson, and Snorton, "We Got Issues," 162.

39 Snorton, *Black on Both Sides*, 7.

40 Silva Santana, "Transitionings and Returnings," 187.

41 Tourmaline, dir., "Atlantic Is a Sea of Bones." See also Clifton, "Atlantic Is a Sea of Bones."

42 Nyong'o, "Atlantic Is a Sea of Bones."

43 Morrison, *Beloved*, 1.

44 Muholi, "Mapping Our Histories," 4, 13.

45 Matebeni, "Intimacy, Queerness, Race," 404..

46 Muholi, "Mapping Our Histories," 19.

47 Muholi, 18.

48 Tourmaline, "On Untoreli's 'New' Book."

49 Gumbs, "Seek the Roots," 18. Of course, Alexis would agree that books can constitute an archive as well. Some must. In addition to publications previously cited, these include, most prominently, the indispensable annotated bibliography edited by Fullwood, Harris, and Moore, *Carry the Word*. More-recent anthologies are Johnson and Henderson, *Black Queer Studies*; E. Johnson, *No Tea No Shade*; NEST Collective, *Stories of Our Lives*; Glave, *Our Caribbean*; Tamale, *African Sexualities*; E. Johnson, *Black. Queer. Southern. Women*; Opoku-Gyimah, Beadle-Blair, and Gordon, *Sista!*; Gordon and Beadle-Blair, *Black and Gay in the UK*.

50 Hall, "Constituting an Archive," 89.

51 Colin had poetically offered a similar point of view, which we will turn to in chapter 10, "Unfinished Work," which borrows its title from the poem in which he insists we speak/confess/remember. See C. Robinson, "Unfinished Work."

52 Allen and Tinsley, "A Conversation 'Overflowing with Memory,'" 251.

53 Philip, quoted in Saunders, "Defending the Dead, Confronting the Archive," 70.

54 Hartman, "Venus in Two Acts," 2.

55 Philip, quoted in Hartman, "Venus in Two Acts," 3. See also Philip, *Zong!*, 7.

56 Lorde, "Poetry Is Not a Luxury," 82.

57 Gumbs, *M Archive*. Following Jacqui's *Pedagogies of Crossing*, Alexis explains that her *M Archive: After the End of the World* imagines another form, speculative documentary, "which is not ancestrally co-written but is also written in collaboration with the survivors, the far-into-the-future witnesses to the realities we are making possible or impossible with our present apocalypse."

58 Hartman, "Venus in Two Acts," 3.

59 See Wynter, "Rethinking 'Aesthetics,'" 245.

60 McKay, "If We Must Die."

61 Gumbs, *M Archive*, xi.

62 Chandan Reddy, personal communication, 2019.

Chapter Eight. Come

1 Lorde, "A Litany for Survival."

2 Bridgforth, *Delta Dandi*.

3 Allen, "For 'the Children,'" 314.

4 Rodriguez, *Sexual Futures, Queer Gestures, and Other Latina Longings*, 138. See also hooks, *Belonging*. As I have written before, "homespace" is my friendly amendment to bell hooks's "homeplace." I want to emphasize the fact that the spaces we create are not necessarily sited in a particular "place" but rather made or assembled through our interactions within it.

5 Here I refer to the 2007 Baile Funk version by DJ Sandrinho. Still, I cannot resist noting the recursivity of the earlier Astrud Gilberto version: "O dinheiro de quem não dá É o trabalho de quem não tem" ("The money of the one who does not give, comes from the one who works but does not receive it").

6 Mary Louise Pratt asks, "What do people on the receiving end of Empire do with metropolitan modes of representation? . . . What materials can we study to answer those questions?" She proposes "anti-conquest" as a "strategy of innocence . . . constructed in relation to older imperial rhetorics of conquest . . . the main protagonist [being] 'the seeing-man' . . . white male subject of European landscape discourse—he whose Imperial eyes passively look out and possess." See Pratt, *Imperial Eyes*, 7–8, 9. See also Caren Kaplan, *Questions of Travel*. See especially M. Alexander, "Erotic Autonomy as a Politics of Decolonization"; and Puar, "A Transnational Feminist Critique of Queer Tourism." Honor Ford-Smith cites "representational practices" of the tourism industry's recycling of images of "colonial domination," which she argues "reproduce new forms of institutional and cultural racism," in Ford-Smith, "Come to Jamaica and Feel Alright." Ford-Smith holds that the Euro-American tourist is both a consumer and a creator, for the impressions formed on short visits will mediate how the person processes information later on. But of course this is true of all visitors. Still, there is the assumption of a white cisheterosexual male gaze in each of these fine works. What changes? Is there a significant difference if we show Black travel to Black spaces? Or parse distinctions and connections through ethnography?

7 Brand, *In Another Place, Not Here*.

8 See E. Johnson, "'Quare' Studies."

9 See Wainaina, "We Must Free Our Imaginations."

10 The quotation in the section heading is from Erykah Badu, "Window Seat" (Universal Motown Records, 2010). This looking while Black rhymes with the Elizabeth Alexander essay "Can You Be BLACK and Look at This?," reprinted in her luminous book of essays, *The Black Interior*.

11 Rodriguez, *Sexual Futures, Queer Gestures, and Other Latina Longings*, 138.

12 Badu, "Window Seat."

13 Puar asks, "The dearth of lesbian tourist accounts and research could be linked to differences in gendered relations to globalization and tourism. . . . Does queer tourism itself, as an industry, a practice, and a spatial understanding of capitalism and identity, reinscribe lesbian invisibility . . . how do lesbians travel, and which lesbians travel?" See Puar, "A Transnational Feminist Critique of Queer Tourism," 114.

14 Baldwin, "Encounter on the Seine," 124.

15 The old decor recalled pleasure grottos out of Hollywood's imagination of classic Greek and Roman excess. The resort has since been renovated, but the rationalization of space to conjure this structure of (imagined) feeling remains.

16 BLOOM Jamaica 2014. Olubode Brown, www.facebook.com/events/d41d8cd9/bloom-jamaica-2014/717009714984148, accessed 2020.

17 I have changed the names of the commentators to preserve their likely expectation of privacy in that semipublic space.

18 Olubode Brown, "Why We Go to Jamaica." Statement circulated in 2014. Internet link currently unavailable.

19 La Fountain-Stokes, "De un Pajaro las Dos Alas," 13–14.

20 Banton composes a vision of diasporic violence and terroristic control of gender roles. Just two stanzas of this vile lyric is enough: "Boom bye bye / Inna batty bwoy head / Rude bwoy no promote no nasty man / Dem haffi dead / . . . All a di New York crew / Dem no promote Batty man / Jump an dance / Unno push up unno hand. / All di Brooklyn girl / Dem no promote batty man . . . / Canadian gals dem no like batty man / If yuh are not one / Yuh haffi push up." Buju Banton, "Boom Bye Bye" (Penthouse Records, 1992). See Desire Thompson, "Buju Banton Explains Why He Removed Controversial Song 'Boom Bye Bye' from Catalog," *Vibe*, March 2019, www.vibe.com/music/music-news/buju-banton-why-he-removed-boom-bye-bye-from-catalog-641251. It is not hard to imagine that fifteen-year-old Banton rhetorically deploys instruments of violence readily at hand, holding no distinction between the gay man and the pedophile, and exacting murder fantasies in a political setting in which there is no hope for something that looks like justice or community repair or individual restoration to the boy who had been harmed. But Buju did not come to this realization at twenty or twenty-one. It was only after the financially damaging Murder Music campaign that he made his canned apology. The larger issue, as Deborah Thomas has already averred, is the confluence of general acceptance of homhatred (in this case, in Jamaica specifically), cultural "authenticity," and transnational markets. See Thomas, *Exceptional Violence*.

To be sure, although crusaders for decency and against sexual objectification in the United States saw themselves as working for the protection of children in their protests against 2 Live Crew and other groups, they very likely had not considered the fact that it was the improvised dance-floor call and response and chants of children themselves who had invented or "written" much of (what sufficed as) the lyrics of popular dance music in Miami bass, rap, and dancehall. Michele Wallace, following bell hooks, who had been a central voice attempting to make good Black feminist sense of the complex problem of sexism in rap, warned that "with the failure of our urban public schools, rappers have taken education into their own hands . . . the end result emphasizes innovations in style and rhythm over ethics and morality . . . rap lyrics can be brutal, raw and, where women are the subject, glaringly sexist." She quotes bell hooks, whom she says "sees the roots of rap as a youth rebellion against all attempts to control Black masculinity, both in the streets and in the home." See Wallace, *Dark Designs and Visual Culture*, 134–37.

21 Among other things, Javonte Anderson's dissertation project "seeks to explore how queer Jamaicans reappropriate the violence of the genre (of dancehall) to experience erotic agency. In this current conjuncture of rights-oriented justice and state-sponsored liberation encroaching on the island . . . this understudied choreography of bodies can reveal . . . fraught meanings of late modern freedom in the Caribbean." Personal communication, 2020.

22 See Cannick, "Hip-Hop's Homophobia and Black Gay America's Silence."

23 Buju Banton and his dancehall colleagues Elephant Man, Beenie Man, Bounty Killer, Capleton, and TOK (whose version of the gay-snuff fantasy song "Chi Chi Man" was adopted by Jamaica's Labour Party in 2001, according to a number of sources) engaged in a sort of one-upmanship of antigay and anti-lesbian sentiment reminiscent of how Christian pastors whip their congregations into frenzy with homophobic pronouncements from their pulpits. Still, among the transnational throng Buju is the only one reportedly charged with a case of actual—not rhetorical or "artistic"—gay bashing, cited by Amnesty International and Human Right Watch. See Amnesty International, *Amnesty International Report 2006—Jamaica*. Regarding TOK, see L. Nelson, "Jamaica's Anti-gay 'Murder Music' Carries Violent Message."

24 C. Clarke, "The Failure to Transform."

25 Bob Marley and the Wailers, "Exodus" (Tuff Gong, 1977).

> Open your heart, uh! And look within
> Are you satisfied
> With the life you're living?
> We know where we're going
> We know where we're from
> We're leaving Babylon
> We're going to the Father's land
> In this exodus
> Movement of Jah people
> Exodus
> The movement of Jah people
> . . .
> Jah come to break down pressure
> Rule equality, yeah, yeah, yeah, yeah
> Wipe away transgression
> Set the captives free. . . .

Of course, more Bob is necessary here. See also "Kinky Reggae" on *The Fabulous Wailers*, in which various forms of sex are playfully narrated (Island Records, 1977). And Trinbagonian calypso, from the start, also has numerous examples of playful and/or slightly naughty lyrics that emerge from clever wordplay—of course this attitude of live and let live flourished pre-AIDS, and before the concretization of virulent fundamentalist white US evangelicalism imported to the Caribbean.

Chapter Nine. "Black/Queer Mess" as Methodological Case Study

1 Dunham, *Island Possessed*, 127.
2 Batiste, "Dunham Possessed," 9.
3 Jackson, "On Ethnographic Sincerity," S285. I am grateful to the growing cohort of anthropologists of the Black world whose contributions to this conversation refine and upend and sometimes threaten to explode the conventions of the guild. A number of them are invoked here. The centrality of John's thinking on this reminds me that much of the conversation about Black-on-Black anthropology also derives from work done "close to home." For a more recent exemplar, see Aimee Meredith Cox's award-winning *Shapeshifters*.
4 Thank you to the anonymous reader who in the first draft of this work warned me to avoid "Black queer mess," steering me in the new direction the chapter would take and unwittingly giving it a new title.
5 Quashie, *The Sovereignty of Quiet*.
6 I realize now that I did not "get it" at that moment. My reply email begins: "Dear Friends: You will find, below, a lot of yes, thank you; some gee, I didn't think of it; a plea to see the idea as innovative if not also flawed; a couple moments of taking great umbrage; and a place of sincere contrition. I am exhausted! Most of all you will find this response characterized by an attitude of 'well, this is why I brought this to your attention.' I have begun at the end. Please let me begin with your helpful suggestions, as they provide a way forward—even forward/away from this particular event if need be. Following this, please find my comments set off under your original comments, and in blue."
7 Allen, *¡Venceremos?*, 22.
8 B. Williams, "Skinfolk, Not Kinfolk," 77, 84.
9 Professor Day drew respondents for her study from her extended family and community networks in and around Washington, D.C. She was among the first Black scholars to earn a graduate degree in anthropology (master's, 1932). Another physical anthropologist, William Montague Cobb, was the first to earn the doctorate (1932). See Day, *A Study of Some Negro-White Families in the United States*.
10 B. Williams, "Skinfolk, Not Kinfolk," 77, 84.
11 B. Williams. Ms. Hurston had, of course, famously declared "All my skinfolk ain't kinfolk"—now a popular aphorism drawing a bright line between oneself and folks of one's own race or ethnicity whose political or other sensibilities or behaviors are not aligned with one's own. I would be remiss if I did not point out the fact that Hurston used this anecdote as a distancing mechanism to draw distinction between herself and loud, ill-mannered Black people on the train. Here she was not referring to a critical political difference but

respectability, in fact. Unlike several of my Black feminist anthropology kin, I can go only so far down the road with this brilliant forbear. Her forcefully argued views, intellect, and unmatched wit make her a fabulous intellectual figure who is much too complex to be uncritically apotheosized.

12 The fact that I was situated at Yale—with its own old, literal skeletons—exacerbated the matter.

13 In her introduction to the ten-year anniversary issue of *Anthurium*. Francis, "Intellectual Formations," 1. See also Baugh, "The West Indian Writer and His Quarrel with History."

14 "Bolekaja intellectualism" was popular while Carole Boyce-Davies was a student at Ibadan and has endured and expanded. The word is Yorùbá and recalls the tense mass-transit buses of urban Nigeria. See Boyce-Davies, "Pan-Africanism, Transnational Black Feminism and the Limits of Culturalist Analyses in African Gender Discourses," 85.

15 Jackson, *Real Black*, 7.

16 B. Williams, "Skinfolk, Not Kinfolk," 85.

17 D. Jones, "Toward a Native Anthropology."

18 I do not mean to paint my friendly professional acquaintances with the broad brush of "false friendship." I mean *faux amis* in its linguistic register. For the quotation, see Dunham, *Island Possessed*, 127.

19 Eric B and Rakim's "In the Ghetto" (MCA Records, 1990). See Gilroy, "It Ain't Where You're from, It's Where You're At."

20 Christina mentioned, in an aside during a 2018 lecture at the University of Miami, that Hazel Carby had called her methodical attention to the words "forensic etymology." It occurred to me that this would be a generative moment to employ this mode of attention.

21 See Online Etymology Dictionary, www.etymonline.com/search?q=cognate &ref=searchbar_searchhint.

22 Online Etymology Dictionary.

23 Lorde, "Showing Our True Colors," 69.

24 Glave, *Words to Our Now*, 25.

25 Lorde, "Grenada Revisited," 21.

26 Lorde, 29.

27 Lorde, 24.

28 Lorde, 26. We must also note that soon after, during the Clinton regime, even "welfare" was reduced, creating an even tighter squeeze.

29 Lorde, "Of Generators and Survival," 82.

30 Lorde, 74.

31 Hanchard, "Acts of Misrecognition," 6.

32 See C. Taylor, *Philosophical Papers*, 2.

33 Hanchard, "Acts of Misrecognition," 7.

34 Unpublished letter from anonymous group of interlocutors/friends.

35 See K. Clarke, *Mapping Yorùbá Networks*, xi–xiii.

36 A number of others have made this point, but Dwight's is among the most cogent articulations and keenly assesses a number of angles of the anthological

generation's methodologies and formulations on how/why to "see" and "say" that I attempt to take up in this work. My admiration for and wider engagement with Dwight's astutely argued works throughout *Disco Ball* make his the irresistible exemplar to reconsider belonging, speech, (and authority) in the context of Black gay sensibilities. See McBride, "Can the Queen Speak?"

37 Lorde, "English Introduction to Farbe bekennen."

38 One of my incisive and generous anonymous readers asked in the penultimate revision of this work, "Who constitutes . . . elite Black academics?" "Elite Blackademe" includes everyone I cite in this work (and others): folks who are employed by any university or college and/or who hold an advanced degree, who are routinely read and cited by their colleagues, who are often asked to weigh in on peer review, and who are invited to present their work to colleagues. These folks (we) circulate in relatively small and rarified professionally mediated conversations, some that overlap with other scholarly and nonscholarly conversations, and others that do not. I do not mean "elite" only in terms of those who work at top-rated and/or wealthy schools, although there is, increasingly, significant overlap. (I will leave it to other authors to parse that "overlap.") For a sterling conjunctural analysis of Black presence in elite academe at the moment that it was emerging, see Hazel Carby's "The Multicultural Wars," which begins, "As a Black intellectual, I am both intrigued and horrified by the contradictory nature of the Black presence in North American universities." This is still true for me too. Carby, "The Multicultural Wars," 7.

My invocation of "part(ing) company" for "a piece of the way" with a large cross-section of my elite Blackacademic kin attempts to draw attention to what I understand as the hegemonic intellectual position to discursively deconstruct categories of experience. I want to raise questions for Black studies about what I see as a precipitous rightward shift, not necessarily or only a turn toward conservatism, per se, but certainly to deployment of neoliberal norms. The dramatic preponderance of this orientation was not always the case. See J. James, "Radicalizing Feminism," for a crucial and cogent article about nearly imperceptible shifts and slippages, and Marable, "Introduction."

39 Dixon, "Rivers Remembering Their Source."

40 Lorde, "Turning the Beat Around," 73.

41 Lorde, "Grenada Revisited," 26.

42 See Hardt and Negri, *Empire*, 45. Signee One: a former longtime resident of the United States born in the Caribbean; Signee Two: US born and resident with Caribbean and continental African parents; Signee Three: Caribbean national who remains in their nation of birth; Signee Four: Caribbean-born person with higher education and residence in United States and the Caribbean.

43 Hardt and Negri, 8. There are classic contradictions here, of course, and much context and baggage that we will not unpack. We will merely repeat what Michael Hanchard offered in his response to critics: we should avoid "political ethnocentrism [in which] the politics of nation-states are privileged

and the mobilization of non-state actors are neglected and, when identified, poorly understood." Hanchard, "Acts of Misrecognition," 7.

44 M. Alexander, "Not Just (Any) Body Can Be a Citizen," 5.

45 McBride, "Can the Queen Speak?," 372. Autochthonous categories, deeply held personal and cultural understandings, and affective ties need and deserve something more and something other than Derridean deconstruction and critique, which has become a blunt instrument. This is not a completely novel reading, of course, but akin to others made in a number of ways and contexts, and from different political positions and disciplines. To wit, both "anthropologize" and "essentialist" emerged through poststructuralist and postmodern turns in the long 1980s. Here I want to think critically about—and take issue with—how contemporary anthropology is too often flatly read (or dismissed) even after various turns and reassessments and attempted corrections. Although some critics understandably deploy the term anthropologizing as a pejorative, given the discipline's horrendous complicity with colonialism, and make the mistake of reading historic particularity and cultural specificity as "essentializing," for example, we must be more careful, and we must also initiate discourses of disciplinary decolonization in other fields and disciplines as anthropologists continue to engage.

46 Allen and Jobson, "The Decolonizing Generation," 144.

47 Muñoz, Disidentifications.

48 Allen and Jobson, "The Decolonizing Generation."

49 Vargas, Catching Hell in the City of Angels.

50 E. Gordon, Disparate Diasporas, viii.

51 See the multiple levels of contradiction and de-territorialization in this short passage by Ted: "I was a gringo without clear institutional ties. Who is this Black hippie? Does he really have these degrees? He sure doesn't look like it. What is he doing here? Whom is he really working for? The African Peoples Socialist Party from the United States? He wants to go to the Atlantic Coast? Nobody in their right mind wants to live there." E. Gordon, Disparate Diasporas, 8.

Chapter Ten. Unfinished Work

1 See C. Smith, "Towards a Black Feminist Model of Black Atlantic Liberation"; and Nascimento, "Quilombismo." The Black Brazilian group Quimbanda Dudu, founded in 1981, has a racially complex origin story that we will narrate in future publications. Dora Santana parsed the ways that the Portuguese word presente denotes both being here when called upon and calling on ancestors.

2 Marcus Lee, personal communication, 2018.

3 Dawson, Behind the Mule.

4 See Dawson, Behind the Mule; T. Johnson, "Can the Democratic Party Retain Its Hold on Black Voters?"; and Lopez Bunyasi and Smith, "Do All Black Lives Matter Equally to Black People?"

5 The academic project is not a project of liberation or one to "save (your) life." That some of the tools and habits of scholarship can be and have been very helpful to describe, correct, and prescribe via the Black intellectual tradition (à la Manning Marable) is not to say that the larger academic project is here for any of this. Quite the contrary—Manning writes his classic essay on Black studies and the Black intellectual tradition precisely because he finds that a number of his contemporaries seemed to be unaware of the politics of the Black radical intellectual tradition as the foundation of contemporary Black studies. See Marable, "Introduction." Sylvia Wynter later elucidates this in another way in "On How We Mistook the Map for the Territory." Joy James takes a long historical view, critically interrogating the historicity and ethics of the "talented tenth" ideology on which much of Black elite striving (including some scholarship) affectively rests. See *Transcending the Talented Tenth*. Of course, Cathy's "Deviance as Resistance" is resonant with this work and puts a finer point on new directions to follow.

6 In 1997 Cathy Cohen called for "a politics where the non-normative and marginal positions of punks, bulldaggers, and welfare queens" are the basis for progressive transformational coalitional work. See Cohen, "Punks, Bulldaggers and Welfare Queens," 437. By 2004, Cathy had developed this into a new research agenda for Black studies, in which the central theoretic marshals "deviance as resistance." See Cohen, "Deviance as Resistance."

7 Cohen, "Deviance as Resistance."

8 Glave, *Words to Our Now*, 25.

9 M. Alexander, "Remembering This Bridge, Remembering Ourselves," 91.

10 M. Alexander, "Danger and Desire."

11 The quotation in the section heading is from M. Alexander, "Danger and Desire."

12 National and local ASOs have been perpetually plagued by lack of resources, in some cases woeful mismanagement, and mostly single-mindedness, perhaps being uninterested in being informed by intellectuals and artists, and "inspired" only by the categories of prevention dictated by the funding agencies that make their work possible.

13 Marcus Lee, "Black Gay Identity in Known Quantities," dissertation chapter, forthcoming, University of Chicago.

14 Cohen, "What Is This Movement Doing to My Politics?" See also Vaid, *Virtual Equality*.

15 Vaid, *Virtual Equality*, 4, 74.

16 Lee, "Black Gay Identity in Known Quantities."

17 Davis, *Battered Black Women and Welfare Reform*, 68.

18 Farrow, "Afterword," 3.

19 You will recall that 1995 is the year that we close out the long 1980s. See Lorde, "Age, Race, Class, and Sex," 23. See also Spillers, "All the Things You Could Be by Now If Sigmund Freud's Wife Was Your Mother."

20 Farrow, "Afterword," 3. Editorial collective: Joseph N. DeFillipis, Lisa Duggan, Kenyon Farrow, and Richard Kim.

21 This was written before the worldwide uprisings around Black lives and police/prison abolition, at the onset of the COVID-19 pandemic. Obviously, these explosive events and rhetorics that unfolded alongside the contentious US elections have heated political discourse in general. Still, the elements of a Left agenda that Kenyon cites still await their "hot" mass political moment. Moreover, it remains to be seen whether the structural or policy impacts of this historic moment will equal the dramatic and cacophonous performances of (ahem) "wokeness" by non-Black people who needed to have their attention focused by a pandemic to recognize that the extrajudicial execution of a(nother) Black person by the police in the streets indicates a problem that is systemic and worthy of address.

22 Farrow, "Afterword," 3, emphasis mine.

23 Councilwoman Franco self-described as "woman, Black, mother, lesbian, from the favelas, open about sexuality and Rio's problems, and on top of all this, a human rights activist."

24 See "Cathy Cohen Remarks upon Receiving the Kessler Award, '#DoBlacklives matter, #DoBlackLivesMatter? From Michael Brown to CeCe McDonald,'" On Black Death and LGBTQ Politics, Center for Lesbian and Gay Studies (CLAGS), Elebash Auditorium, Graduate Center, CUNY, Friday, December 12, 2014.

25 Of course, I do not mean to suggest here that the projects of all LGBTQIA organizations in these disparate cultural historical contexts are the same.

26 "Unfinished Work" appeared in *Voices Rising* and *Our Caribbean* before being published in Colin's beautiful debut book of poetry, *You Have You Father Hard Head*. My interpretation of Colin's work here is slightly different from the author's, and it reflects an ongoing conversation between us. Whereas Colin emphasizes the politics of what he calls "fundamental anti-essentialism," my position is certainly anti-antiessentialist. These positions find perhaps tense reiteration and conversation here.

27 Although the most famous are quilombos like Palmares in Brazil, Palenques of Colombia and Cuba, or Maroon societies of Jamaica and other spaces, Maroons were also found in the swamps of the eastern US and other sites in the Americas. Brilliantly practicing her hashtag activist insistence to "#Cite BlackWomen" in scholarship, Christen Smith introduces English-only readers to Beatriz Nascimento, who she writes "defined quilombo as a multi-sited material and symbolic territorialization of Black space from the favela (urban working class shantytowns), to the baile blacks (Black dance parties), to the terreiro (African-Brazilian religious houses associated with the practice of candomblé), and actual 'remnant quilombo communities' (contemporary maroon societies)." See Nascimento, "Quilombismo." For her, "quilombo is not just a place, culture or community, but also a verb—the ideological practice of encampment and resistance against the oppression of slavery. . . . She identifies racialized poverty, the disparagement of Black aesthetics, urban segregation, and the erasure of history as contemporary legacies of the conditions of slavery." See C. Smith, "Towards a Black Feminist Model of Black

Atlantic Liberation." See also Guridy and Hooker, "Corrientes de pensamiento sociopolitico Afrolatinoamericano," 256. Contemporary scholars have also seized on Maroon/Quilombo to express both historical forms and scales of the widespread practice of both full-scale maroonage and what they call petit marronage, which include work stoppages and other forms of resistance. Regarding philosophical understandings of quilombo/maroon, see Neil Roberts, *Freedom as Marronage*.

28 As Dagmawi parses, Melvin's poem "And These Are Just a Few" is "recollective (it remembers past deaths) and prospective (it hails imminent deaths, including his own)." He continues: "In addition to synchronizing a unique timeline of loss, the poem also takes a tally of the dead, and each loss builds on the loss that precedes it." See Woubshet, *The Calendar of Loss*, 7. Colin's "Unfinished Work" and much of his other writing likewise tallies, synchronizes, compounds, and serializes loss as a Black gay man who has not only seen his closest friends and a huge number of his contemporaries die but also a significant number of others "lost" to him (or he to them) to seemingly insurmountable resentment, shared grief, distrust, perceived tyranny, terror, and what he often described as treachery. This too is a central reality of the politics of quilombo building. See C. Robinson, *You Have You Father Hard Head*. I will explore this further in future work.

29 C. Robinson, "Unfinished Work."

30 See Riggs, dir., "Anthem," along with two other important Riggs short films, "Affirmations" and "Non, je ne regrette rien."

31 Those on the street that day who may not have made it to Traxx, the Gay and Lesbian Center, or even the Harlem State Office Building to see Assotto and Colin and the men of Other Countries perform their work might have had only this potent yet carnivalesque popular reference for what they saw: Antonio Fargas's "Lindy" in *Car Wash*. The 1976 film is not ideal, and we would expect more today. Dressing down a homophobe in African robes, Lindy reads with a gender-queer acuity that theorists would not begin to approach for thirty years, when Lindy says (with dignity and resolve): "I am more man than you will ever be, and more woman than you will ever get!" That is humanely and "levelly human," as the Combahee River Collective had insisted upon, "more" levelly human, in fact, while presently occupying the moral high ground!

32 "Faggot! / When they shout faggot / I hear Maroon . . . they called us faggots and we heard maroons and coming / to this space of freedom to which we have escaped." Page 52.

33 C. Robinson, "Unfinished Work."

34 I hear Cheryl in this essay and in "Lesbianism: An Act of Resistance," remixed with Ron Simmons's searing and formative "Some Thoughts on the Challenges Facing Black Gay Intellectuals" and Charles Nero's erudite and brave criticality in "Toward a Black Gay Aesthetic," together prefiguring the thematic and critical concerns and foundation of Black queer studies to come—the impact of these intellectuals and their works are suffused throughout. Each,

of course, was published in anthologies. See C. Clarke, "The Failure to Transform," 205, and "Lesbianism," 128; Nero, "Toward a Black Gay Aesthetic," 229; Simmons, "Some Thoughts on the Challenges Facing Black Gay Intellectuals," 211.

35 Hemphill, "Does Your Mama Know about Me?," 42.

36 Hall, "Cultural Identity and Diaspora," 223.

37 Uganda's *Rolling Stone* newspaper had been publishing for only two months when this occurred, and it was ordered to cease publication two months later. BBC News reported that the twenty-two-year-old avowed Christian editor Giles Muhame offered this defense of his newspaper: "We want the government to hang people who promote homosexuality, not for the public to attack them." See "Uganda Gay Rights Activist David Kato Killed," BBC News, January 27, 2011, www.bbc.com/news/world-africa-12295718.

38 "Caribbean Groups Join International Community in Saluting Murdered African Human Rights Worker."

39 Agard-Jones, "Le jeu de qui?"

40 See Puar, "Mapping US Homonormativities," 71.

41 Moreover, in the North the potential effectiveness of homonationalist integration of Black queer people is constrained by tensions between dueling civil rights discourses and policy battles (the reductive accounting forcing false dichotomies of sexual or racial justice, for example) and the realities of profound antiblackness (you will recall, aimed at the president of the republic, for example), stretching this to incoherence. This incisive theorization therefore may seem beside the point to those who are Black and/or undocumented and/or gender nonconforming and/or poor. In fact, many of course want inclusion and incorporation, and would likely sign up for flag waving and linking up against "common enemies" if this meant finally, for the first time, garnering the full benefits of state provision and protection and cultural inclusion (to wit, this hegemony adheres even without these benefits). There is so much more to say.

Notwithstanding the progressive sexual orientation and gender protections of the South African constitution, governments have not attempted to ingratiate, "collude" with, or accommodate homosexual groups. Quite the contrary in many cases, demonstrating that the new constitution was significantly more forward looking than the politics of the day.

42 "Constitutional Court Rules That Cross-Dressing Is Not a Crime If Not for Improper Purpose—Rights Groups Plan Appeal on Dubious Decision," emphasis mine.

43 See Marks, dir., "My Wardrobe, My Right."

44 Please see *Caserta, S. McEwan and Others v. Attorney General of Guyana* (C.C.J.), http://doi.org/10.1017/ilm.2019.14 2018.

45 See Patoir, "Despite CCJ Ruling on Cross-Dressing, Transgender People Still Face Violence, Discrimination."

46 C. Robinson, *Decolonising Sexual Citizenship*, 6.

47 See Sharon Mottley, "It's Our Time Now," www.socawarriors.net/forum/index.php?topic=46872.0.

48 Mottley.

49 Mottley.

50 Mottley.

51 Mottley.

52 Robinson, personal communication, 2010.

53 C. Robinson, *Decolonising Sexual Citizenship*, 4.

54 Robinson, personal communication, 2010.

55 CariFLAGS is a regional nonprofit based in Trinidad and Tobago made up of leading LBGTI NGOs across the Caribbean. CariFLAGS staff and leadership are based across the region—in St. Lucia, Jamaica, Trinidad and Tobago, the Dominican Republic, Belize, Grenada, Guyana, and Suriname.

56 For example, as the Human Dignity Trust's CEO Jonathan Cooper said in the Guardian on September 14, 2011, "We will fundraise, and there is something rather charming that you can say to somebody: 'If you give us £50,000, I can more or less guarantee that you will have decriminalized homosexuality in Tonga.' And actually, you know, that's great." See Zoe Williams, "Gay Rights: A World of Inequality," September 13, 2011, www.theguardian.com/world/2011/sep/13/gay-rights-world-of-inequality.

57 C. Robinson, "The Work of Three-Year Old CAISO—Reflections at the MidPoint."

58 Wainaina, "I Am a Homosexual, Mum."

59 Neo Musangi, public Facebook post, January 18, 2016.

60 Musangi.

61 See P. Young, "Ghanaian Woman and Dutch Wax Prints." See also her dissertation, "Cloth That Speaks: African Women's Visual Voice and Creative Expression in Ghana (West Africa)."

62 Binyavanga Wainaina, lecture given at 2012 UK African Studies Association. See also Santana, "Exorcizing Afropolitanism."

63 See Jack Halberstam on "queer failure": Halberstam, The Queer Art of Failure. See Matt Richardson on "irresolution": Richardson, *The Queer Limit of Black Memory*.

64 Wunmi, "Keep It Rocking" (Jellybean Soul, 2008).

65 Mbembe, "Afropolitanism," 28.

66 Mbembe, 27.

67 Wainaina, "We Must Free Our Imaginations."

68 Wainaina, "We Must Free Our Imaginations," part 3, "The Devil Next Door," @4:04, www.youtube.com/watch?v=AmiO1EJ-ru8.

69 "Caribbean Groups Join International Community in Saluting Murdered African Human Rights Worker."

70 Wainaina, "We Must Free Our Imaginations," part 4, "A Thousand Years of Hate," @00:16, www.youtube.com/watch?v=TcZ_pkYH-DQ. Although Binyavanga's position here is technically not completely correct—there are in fact some countries that were not colonized by Victorians that have or have had antisodomy laws—the influence of British imperialism, its discontents (as other civilizations responded to it), and its sequelae (like Americanism) cannot

be overstated. His point is well taken. Moreover, one should remember that sodomy does not have a clear and transferrable legal definition. Courts often regard as sodomy any sexual act that it or the community deems "unnatural."

71 The Massachusetts District Court validated SMUG's claims that Lively "aided and abetted a vicious campaign of repression against LGBTI Ugandans" but also dismissed the case on jurisdictional grounds. A note on Lexis states "Following the dismissal of an association's claims against an individual under the Alien Tort Statute, 28 U.S.C.S. § 1350, the court dismissed the individual's appeal in part because it lacked jurisdiction to entertain the individual's request for removal of unflattering comments from the district court's opinion; . . . [3] The court lacked jurisdiction to consider an order denying the individual's motion to dismiss as it never ripened into a judgment and had no effect on the outcome of the case." See https://advance.lexis.com/open/document /lpadocument/?pdmfid=1000522&crid=dXJuOmNvbnRlbnRJdGVtOjVUMF QtOTBQMS1GQkZTLVMyNFYtMDAwMDAtMDA&pddocfullpath=%2Fs hared%2Fdocument%2Fcases%2Furn%3AcontentItem%3A5ToT-90P1-FBFS -S24V-00000-00&pdcomponentid=6385.

72 Wainaina, "We Must Free Our Imaginations," part 3, "The Devil Next Door."

73 C. Robinson, "Unfinished Work."

Part III. Conclusion

1 Mr. Wright was sadly mistaken in his confidence that "the deep contrast between French and American racial attitudes demonstrated that it was barbarousness that incited such militant racism in white Americans." He falls prey to commonsense liberal thinking in the United States, which conveniently reads "racism" very narrowly, placing it solely at the feet of the unsophisticated and uneducated. Moreover, he is understandably pleased with the improvement in the way he is treated in France and is enamored of André Gide, whose overblown sense of French curiosity and tolerance brings us this statement: "The more uncivilized a white man, the more he fears and hates all those people who differ from him. With us in France, the different, the variant is prized; our curiosity to know other people is the hallmark of our civilized state. In America it is precisely the variant, the different who is hounded down by mobs and killed. The American is a terribly socially insecure man who feels threatened by the mere existence of men different from himself." R. Wright, "I Choose Exile."

2 R. Wright.

3 Billy Strayhorn, "Lush Life" (Tempo Music, 1949).

4 A microbrigade was one of the self-help projects of the Cuban Revolution wherein local citizens were trained in building trades and built their own dwellings. Nehanda is anonymized in my book ¡Venceremos? as "Nia," and the book is dedicated to her. Moved by the role that a very elementary internet search played in the intensification of federal and New Jersey efforts to capture Assata Shakur, I chose to not place her name, or Nehanda's, in easily

searchable main text as a (perhaps naive) very small measure of privacy. I have maintained this gesture for our Sister: citing her name in endnotes only.

5   Shakur, "An Open Letter from Assata Shakur."

6   Abiodun, "Letters to the World," unpublished manuscript. I am not sure of the date of its production. Nehanda gave this to me sometime between late 1998 and the end of 1999.

7   Abiodun.

8   Abiodun, "Dear Kayla Imani," in "Letters to the World."

9   Abiodun.

10 Abiodun.

11 Nehanda organized regular donations for Cuban women of good-quality foundation garments, which are hard to come by on the island. These donations were enabled by what she called her own "greedy list" of things she needed from visitors to Cuba. It was always modest—not greedy. And most of the things she requested from "home" were to be shared, like Black books and *Essence* magazines. One of the few perennial items that was not shared was Lawry's seasoning salt.

12 Abiodun, "Letters to the World."

13 Giovanni, "Nikki-Rosa."

14 "At the risk of seeming ridiculous, let me say that the true revolutionary is guided by a great feeling of love. It is impossible to think of a genuine revolutionary lacking this quality. Perhaps it is one of the great dramas of the leader that he or she must combine a passionate spirit with a cold intelligence and make painful decisions without flinching. Our vanguard revolutionaries must idealize this love of the people, of the most sacred causes, and make it one and indivisible." See Guevara, "From Algiers, for Marcha," 225.

15 Abiodun, "Letters to the World."

16 Sonia Sanchez and Sweet Honey in the Rock, "Stay on the Battlefield, for Sweet Honey in the Rock" (EarthBeat!, 1995). Reflecting on Sister's "together" look, even in custody, our thanks must be extended to the prison guard or employee of the illegitimate state (likely a sister) who aided this representation of dignity. Complicated, yes?

17 Stevie Wonder, "As" (1976).

18 See MFSB, "Love Is the Message," mixed with the Salsoul Orchestra, "Ooh, I Love It (Love Break)," 12" Original Remix, Shep Pettibone (Salsoul Records, 1982).

19 Section titles from Sanchez, "For Sweet Honey in the Rock."

20 David Scott, quoted in Hall, "David Scott by Stuart Hall."

21 "Sometimes we drug ourselves with dreams of new ideas. The head will save us. The brain alone will set us free. But there are no new ideas still waiting in the wings to save us as women, as human. There are only old and forgotten ones, new combinations, extrapolations and recognitions from within ourselves, along with the renewed courage to try them out. And we must constantly encourage ourselves and each other to attempt the heretical actions our dreams imply and some of our old ideas disparage." See Lorde, "Poetry Is Not a Luxury," 83.

22 Parker, "Revolution."

23 I can still hear my Aunt Natalie saying to me, or about me, "That boy is something else!," hearing deep love, concern, and exasperation all at once, and I am inextricably tethered to a resolve to see this "something else" through. This is how I first understood Roderick Ferguson's generative invocation of "something else" in his path-clearing *Aberrations in Black*.

24 Campt, *Listening to Images*, 17.

25 This quotation is in her book. See Campt, *Listening to Images*, 17. In her talk there is a perhaps slightly more sanguine elocution. I hear: "in turn realizes that aspiration." See also Campt, "Black Feminist Futures and the Practice of Fugitivity."

26 See Hartman, *Lose Your Mother*; Moten, *In the Break*; and Sharpe, *In the Wake*.

27 Campt. This aside was crucial and affirming for me. Although her main content is captured in her *Listening to Images*, Campt's conversational quality here in the inaugural talk of her chairship of the Barnard Center for Research on Women—asides, in-the-moment restatements, and evident abundance of feeling—is priceless and beautiful.

28 Guevara, "From Algiers, for Marcha," 225.

29 Gramsci is customarily credited with coining "pessimism of the intellect, optimism of the will," but he apparently attributed the original formulation to Romain Rolland, who wrote "whoever lives in times of great struggle must achieve this intimate alliance . . . of pessimism of the intelligence, which penetrates every illusion, and optimism of the will." See Rolland, "Review of Roland Lefebvre's 'Le Sacrifice D'Abraham.'" See also Gramsci, *Selections from the Prison Notebooks of Antonio Gramsci*.

30 Lorde, "A Litany for Survival."

31 Lorde. Also feeling resonance and reference to the Cuban revolutionary rhetoric of protracted struggle: Siempre. Hasta—"Always, Until (Victory)."

32 Regarding "melancholy historicism," see Best, *None Like Us*.

33 I remember now that many years ago, at a panel discussion that I moderated between Jacqui and Chela Sandoval, one of the additional key animating questions for both of these foundational senior scholars was "Who sent you?" This too is key. Chela talked about her Chican@ community, which "sent" her to take advantage of the new educational opportunities that affirmative action had offered, at a crucial moment in US history; Jacqui talked about being from Trinidad and Tobago, "sent" to study abroad. These are not stories of self-aggrandizement but of multigenerational support and direction. "Black Nations/Queer Nations" panel: Kendall Thomas (Columbia Law School), moderator; M. Jacqui Alexander; Cathy Cohen; Chandan Reddy; Rinaldo Walcott. The panel took place during Queer Disruptions III, sponsored by the Institute for the Study of Women, Gender, and Sexuality at Columbia University, February 2019.

34 David Scott, quoted in "David Scott by Stuart Hall."

Abiodun, Nehanda. "Letters to the World." Unpublished manuscript, circa 1998–1999.

Agard-Jones, Vanessa. "Bodies in the System." *Small Axe* 17, no. 3 (2013): 182–92.

Agard-Jones, Vanessa. *Body Burdens: Toxic Endurance and Decolonial Desire in the French Atlantic* (forthcoming).

Agard-Jones, Vanessa. "Le Jeu de Qui? Sexual Politics at Play in the French Caribbean." *Caribbean Review of Gender Studies* 3 (2009): 1–19.

Agard-Jones, Vanessa. "What the Sands Remember." *GLQ* 18, nos. 2–3 (2012): 325–46.

Ahmed, Sara. "Happy Objects." In *The Affect Theory Reader*, edited by Melissa Gregg and Gregory J. Seigworth, 29–51. Durham, NC: Duke University Press, 2010.

Ahmed, Sara. *Strange Encounters: Embodied Others in Post-coloniality*. Abingdon, UK: Routledge, 2000.

Ajamu X, Topher Campbell, and Mary Campbell Stevens. 2010. "Love and Lubrication in the Archives, or Rukus! A Black Queer Archive for the United Kingdom." Special issue, *Archivaria* 68 (2009): 271–94. Accessed May 3, 2019. https://archivaria.ca/index.php/archivaria/article/view/13240/14558.

Alexander, Elizabeth. "Ars Poetica #100: I Believe." In *American Sublime*, 26. St. Paul, MN: Graywolf, 2005.

Alexander, Elizabeth. *The Black Interior*. Minneapolis, MN: Graywolf, 2004.

Alexander, Elizabeth. "Can You Be BLACK and Look at This? Reading the Rodney King Video(s)." *Public Culture* 7, no. 1 (1994): 77–94.

Alexander, M. Jacqui. "Danger and Desire: Crossings Are Never Undertaken All at Once or Once and for All." *Small Axe* 11, no. 3 (2007): 154–66.

Alexander, M. Jacqui. "Erotic Autonomy as a Politics of Decolonization: An Anatomy of Feminist and State Practice in the Bahamas Tourist Economy." In *Feminist Genealogies, Colonial Legacies, Democratic Futures*, edited by M. Jacqui Alexander and Chandra Mohanty, 63–100. New York: Routledge, 1997.

Alexander, M. Jacqui. "Not Just (Any) Body Can Be a Citizen: The Politics of Law, Sexuality and Postcoloniality in Trinidad and Tobago and the Bahamas." *Feminist Review* 48, no. 1 (1994): 5–23.

Alexander, M. Jacqui. *Pedagogies of Crossing: Meditations on Feminism, Sexual Politics, Memory, and the Sacred*. Durham, NC: Duke University Press, 2006.

Alexander, M. Jacqui. "Remembering This Bridge, Remembering Ourselves: Yearning, Memory, and Desire." In *This Bridge We Call Home: Radical Visions for Transformation*, edited by Gloria E. Anzaldúa and AnaLouise Keating, 81–103. New York: Routledge, 2002.

Allen, Jafari. "Black/Queer/Diaspora at the Current Conjuncture." *GLQ* 18, nos. 2–3 (2012): 211–48.

Allen, Jafari Sinclaire. "Crucial Palimpsest: Re-reading *Brother to Brother*." In *Brother to Brother: New Writings by Black Gay Men*, edited by Essex Hemphill, xiii–xxxii. Washington, DC: RedBone, 2007. First published 1991.

Allen, Jafari Sinclaire. "For 'the Children': Dancing the Beloved Community." *Souls* 11, no. 3 (2009): 311–26.

Allen, Jafari Sinclaire. *¡Venceremos? The Erotics of Black Self-Making in Cuba*. Durham, NC: Duke University Press, 2011.

Allen, Jafari Sinclaire, and Ryan Cecil Jobson. "The Decolonizing Generation: (Race and) Theory in Anthropology since the Eighties." *Current Anthropology* 57, no. 2 (2016): 129–48.

Allen, Jafari S., and Omise'eke Natasha Tinsley. "A Conversation 'Overflowing with Memory': On Omise'eke Natasha Tinsley's 'Water, Shoulders, into the Black Pacific.'" *GLQ* 18, nos. 2–3 (2012): 249–62.

Amnesty International. *Amnesty International Report 2006—Jamaica*. May 23, 2006. www.refworld.org/docid/447ff7ac16.html.

Anderson, Elijah, and Tukufu Zuberi, eds. "The Study of African American Problems: W. E. B. Du Bois's Agenda, Then and Now." Special issue, *Annals of the American Academy of Political and Social Science*, 2000.

Anzaldúa, Gloria. *Borderlands/La frontera*. Madrid: Capitán Swing, 2016. First published 1987.

Augustin-Billy, Andia. "Ayiti Pa Lakay Ankò: Assotto Saint's Search for Home." *Journal of Haitian Studies* 22, no. 1 (2016): 82–105. http://doi.org/10.1353/jhs.2016.0026.

"Back of the Line: The State of AIDS among Black Gay Men in America." Black AIDS Institute, 2012. Accessed June 2019. https://blackaids.org/wp-content/uploads/2020/09/Back-of-the-Line-The-State-of-AIDS-Among-Black-Gay-Men-in-America-BAI-Report-2012.pdf.

Bailey, Moya, and Trudy. "On Misogynoir: Citation, Erasure, and Plagiarism." *Feminist Media Studies* 18, no. 4 (2018): 762–68. http://doi.org/10.1080/14680777.2018.1447395.

Baker, Houston A., Manthia Diawara, and Ruth H. Lindeborg, eds. *Black British Cultural Studies: A Reader*. Chicago: University of Chicago Press, 1996.

Baldwin, James. "Encounter on the Seine: Black Meets Brown." In *The Price of the Ticket: Collected Nonfiction, 1948–1985*, 35–39. New York: St. Martin's, 1985. First published 1948.

Baldwin, James. "James Baldwin: The Black Scholar Interviews." *Black Scholar* 5, no. 4 (1973): 33–42.

Baldwin, James. *Just above My Head*. New York: Dial, 2000. First published 1979.

Baldwin, James. "The Preservation of Innocence." *Zero* 1, no. 2 (1949).

Baldwin, James. "Princes and Powers." In *The Price of the Ticket*. New York: St. Martin's/Marek, 1987. First published 1951.

Bambara, Toni Cade, ed. *The Black Woman: An Anthology*. New York: Washington Square, 2005. First published 1970.

Bambara, Toni Cade. "Foreword." In *This Bridge Called My Back: Writings by Radical Women of Color*, edited by Cherríe Moraga and Gloria Anzaldúa. New York: Kitchen Table: Women of Color Press, 1981.

Bambara, Toni Cade. "What Is It I Think I'm Doing Anyhow." In *The Writer on Her Work: Contemporary Women Reflect on Their Art and Their Situation*, edited by Janet Sternberg, 153–78. New York: Norton, 1980.

Barthes, Roland. *S/Z*. Translated by Richard Miller. Malden, MA: Blackwell, 2006.

Batiste, Stephanie. "Dunham Possessed: Ethnographic Bodies, Movement, and Transnational Constructions of Blackness." *Journal of Haitian Studies* 13, no. 2 (2007): 18–22.

Baugh, Edward. "The West Indian Writer and His Quarrel with History." *Small Axe* 16, no. 2 (2012): 60–74. First published 1977.

Beadle-Blair, Rikki, dir. *Metrosexuality*. TLA Releasing, 2001.

Beal, Frances M. *Black Women's Manifesto; Double Jeopardy: To Be Black and Female*. New York: Third World Women's Alliance, 1969. http://www.hartford-hwp.com/archives/45a/196.html.

Beam, Joseph. "Brother to Brother: Words from the Heart." In *In the Life: A Black Gay Anthology*, 230–42. New Orleans: RedBone, 2007. First published 1986.

Beam, Joseph, ed. *In the Life: A Black Gay Anthology*. New Orleans: RedBone, 2007. First published 1986.

Beam, Joseph. "Leaving the Shadows Behind." In *In the Life: A Black Gay Anthology*, xxii. New Orleans: RedBone, 2007. First published 1986.

Bell, Derrick. *Faces at the Bottom of the Well: The Permanence of Racism*. New York: Basic, 1992.

Belton, Don. "How to Make Love to a White Man." Review of *The Masculine Marine: Homoeroticism in the U.S. Marine Corps*, by Steven Zeeland. *Transition* no. 73 (1997): 164. http://doi.org/10.2307/2935452.

Best, Stephen. *None Like Us: Blackness, Belonging, Aesthetic Life*. Durham, NC: Duke University Press, 2018.

Bethel, Lorraine. "what chou mean *we* white girl? or, the cullid lesbian feminist declaration of independence (dedicated to the proposition that all women are not equal, i.e. identical/ly oppressed)." In *Conditions Five: The Black Women's Issue*, 1979.

Bethel, Lorraine, and Barbara Smith, eds. *Conditions Five: The Black Women's Issue*, 1979.

Blackheart Collective. *Blackheart 2: The Prison Issue*. New York, 1984. https://archive.org/stream/blackheart_2/blackheart_2_djvu.txt.

Blum, William. "The CIA, Contras, Gangs, and Crack." Institute for Policy Studies, 1996. Accessed August 15, 2020. https://ips-dc.org/the_cia_contras_gangs_and_crack.

Boellstorff, Tom. "Queer Studies in the House of Anthropology." *Annual Review of Anthropology* 36 (2007): 17–35. http://dx.doi.org/10.1146/annurev.anthro.36.081406.094421.

Bost, Darius. *Evidence of Being: The Black Gay Cultural Renaissance and the Politics of Violence*. Chicago: University of Chicago Press, 2018.

Boyce-Davies, Carole. "Beyond Unicentricity: Transcultural Black Presences." *Research in African Literatures* 30, no. 2 (1999): 96–109.

Boyce-Davies, Carole. *Black Women, Writing and Identity: Migrations of the Subject*. Abingdon, UK: Routledge, 2002.

Boyce-Davies, Carole. *Caribbean Spaces: Escapes from Twilight Zones*. Urbana: University of Illinois Press, 2013.

Boyce-Davies, Carole. "Pan-Africanism, Transnational Black Feminism and the Limits of Culturalist Analyses in African Gender Discourses." *Feminist Africa* 19 (2014): 78–93.

Brand, Dionne. *In Another Place, Not Here*. New York: Grove, 1997.

Brand, Dionne. *A Map to the Door of No Return: Notes to Belonging*. Toronto: Vintage Canada, 2002.

Bridgforth, Sharon. *Delta Dandi: A Conjure*. Long Center Rollins Studio Theatre. University of Texas–Austin, 2009.

Bridgforth, Sharon. *love conjure/blues*. Washington, DC: RedBone, 2004.

"A Brief History of the Drug War." Drug Policy Alliance. www.drugpolicy.org/issues/brief-history-drug-war.

Brooks, Gwendolyn. *The Essential Gwendolyn Brooks*. Edited by Elizabeth Alexander. New York: Library of America, 2005.

Brooks, Gwendolyn. "I Am a Black." In *The Essential Gwendolyn Brooks*, edited by Elizabeth Alexander, 128–29. New York: Library of America, 2005.

Campbell X, dir. "Desire." http://thirdhorizonfilmfestival.com/films/desire.

Campt, Tina. "Black Feminist Futures and the Practice of Fugitivity." The Helen Pond McIntyre '48 Lecture. Barnard Center for Research on Women. YouTube, October 21, 2014. www.youtube.com/watch?v=2ozhqw84oPU.

Campt, Tina. *Listening to Images*. Durham, NC: Duke University Press, 2017.

Cannick, Jasmyne A. "Hip-Hop's Homophobia and Black Gay America's Silence." *Between the Lines*, April 20, 2006. https://pridesource.com/article/18369.

Carbado, Devon W., and Donald Weise, eds. *Time on Two Crosses: The Collected Writings of Bayard Rustin*. New York: Cleis, 2015.

Carby, Hazel. *Cultures in Babylon: Black Britain and African America*. London: Verso, 1999.

Carby, Hazel. *Imperial Intimacies: A Tale of Two Islands*. Brooklyn, NY: Verso, 2019.

Carby, Hazel. "The Multicultural Wars." *Radical History Review* 54 (1992): 7–18.

Carby, Hazel. *Race Men*. Cambridge, MA: Harvard University Press, 1992.

Carby, Hazel. *Reconstructing Womanhood: The Emergence of the Afro-American Woman Novelist*. Oxford: Oxford University Press, 1987.

Carby, Hazel. "White Woman Listen! Black Feminism and the Boundaries of Sisterhood." In *The Empire Strikes Back: Race and Racism in 70s Britain*, edited by Paul Gilroy et al., 212–35. Abingdon, UK: Routledge, 1994.

"Caribbean Groups Join International Community in Saluting Murdered African Human Rights Worker." SASOD, 2011. Accessed August 15, 2020. www.sasod .org.gy/sasod-blog-caribbean-groups-join-international-community-saluting -murdered-african-human-rights.

Carl, Fred, et al. "Black Gay Men Expressing Themselves in Print." Accessed March 2020. https://structures-of-feeling.tumblr.com/About. First published 1983.

Carter, Prudence. "Intersecting Identities: 'Acting White,' Gender, and Academic Achievement." In *Beyond Acting White: Reframing the Debate on Black Student Achievement*, edited by Erin McNamara Horvat and Carla O'Connor, 111–32. Lanham, MD: Rowman & Littlefield, 2006.

Césaire, Aimé. "Calling the Magician: A Few Words for a Caribbean Civilization." In *Refusal of the Shadow: Surrealism and the Caribbean*, edited by Krzysztof Fijałkowski and Michael Richardson. London: Verso, 1996. First published 1944.

Christian, Barbara. "But What Do We Think We're Doing Anyway: The State of Black Feminist Criticism(s) or My Version of a Little Bit of History." In *New Black Feminist Criticism, 1985–2000*, by Barbara Christian. Edited by Gloria Bowles, M. Giulia Fabi, and Arlene R. Keizer, 5–19. Urbana: University of Illinois Press, 2007. First published 1989.

Christian, Barbara. "The Race for Theory." *Feminist Studies* 14, no. 1 (1988): 67–79.

Clark Hine, Darlene. "Rape and the Inner Lives of Black Women in the Middle West: Preliminary Thoughts on the Culture of Dissemblance." *Signs* 14, no. 4 (1989): 912–20.

Clarke, Cheryl. "The Failure to Transform: Homophobia in the Black Community." In *Home Girls: A Black Feminist Anthology*, edited by Barbara Smith, 190–201. New Brunswick, NJ: Rutgers University Press, 2000. First published 1983.

Clarke, Cheryl. "Lesbianism: An Act of Resistance." In *This Bridge Called My Back: Writings by Radical Women of Color*, edited by Cherríe Moraga and Gloria Anzaldúa, 128–37. New York: Kitchen Table: Women of Color Press, 1981.

Clarke, Kamari Maxine. *Mapping Yorùbá Networks: Power and Agency in the Making of Transnational Communities*. Durham, NC: Duke University Press, 2004.

Clifford, James, and George E. Marcus, eds. *Writing Culture: The Poetics and Politics of Ethnography*. Berkeley: University of California Press, 1986.

Clifton, Lucille. "Atlantic Is a Sea of Bones." In *Next: New Poems*. Brockport, NY: BOA, 1987.

Cohen, Cathy. *The Boundaries of Blackness: AIDS and the Breakdown of Black Politics*. Chicago: University of Chicago Press, 1999.

Cohen, Cathy J. "Deviance as Resistance: A New Research Agenda for the Study of Black Politics." *Du Bois Review: Social Science Research on Race* 1, no. 1 (2004): 27–45.

Cohen, Cathy J. "Punks, Bulldaggers, and Welfare Queens: The Radical Potential of Queer Politics?" In *Black Queer Studies: A Critical Anthology*, edited by E. Patrick Johnson, 21–51. Durham, NC: Duke University Press, 2005. First published 1997.

Cohen, Cathy. "What Is This Movement Doing to My Politics?" *Social Text* 61 (Winter 1999): 111–18.

Combahee River Collective. "Combahee River Collective Statement." In *Home Girls: A Black Feminist Anthology*, edited by Barbara Smith, 272–82. New York: Kitchen Table: Women of Color Press, 1983.

"Constitutional Court Rules That Cross-Dressing Is Not a Crime If Not for Improper Purpose—Rights Groups Plan Appeal on Dubious Decision." *Feminist Conversations on Caribbean Life*, September 9, 2013. https://redforgender .wordpress.com/2013/09/09/constitutional-court-rules-that-cross-dressing -is-not-a-crime-if-not-for-improper-purpose-rights-groups-plan-appeal-on -dubious-decision.

Cooper, Brittney C. *Beyond Respectability: The Intellectual Thought of Race Women*. Urbana: University of Illinois Press, 2017.

Corbin, Steven. *Fragments That Remain: A Novel*. Boston: Alyson, 1995.

Cothran, Charlene E. "Redeemed! 10 Ways to Get Out of the Gay Life, if You Want Out!" Evidence Ministry. www.theevidenceministry.org/redeemed-10 -ways-to-get-out-of-the.

Cox, Aimee Meredith. *Shapeshifters: Black Girls and the Choreography of Citizenship*. Durham, NC: Duke University Press, 2015.

Crawley, Ashon T. *Blackpentecostal Breath: The Aesthetics of Possibility*. Philadelphia: Temple University Press, 2016.

Crenshaw, Kimberlé. "Demarginalizing the Intersection of Race and Sex: A Black Feminist Critique of Antidiscrimination Doctrine, Feminist Theory and Antiracist Politics." *University of Chicago Legal Forum*, 1989, article 8.

Cvetkovich, Ann. *An Archive of Feelings*. Durham, NC: Duke University Press, 2003.

Darity, William, Jr., Darrick Hamilton, Mark Paul, Alan Aja, Anne Price, Antonio Moore, and Caterina Chiopris. "What We Get Wrong about Closing the Racial Wealth Gap." Samuel DuBois Cook Center on Social Equity, Insight Center for Community Economic Development, 2018. Accessed August 15, 2020. https:// socialequity.duke.edu/wp-content/uploads/2019/10/what-we-get-wrong.pdf.

Davis, Dana-Ain. *Battered Black Women and Welfare Reform: Between a Rock and a Hard Place*. Albany: State University of New York Press, 2006.

Dawson, Michael C. *Behind the Mule: Race and Class in African-American Politics*. Princeton, NJ: Princeton University Press, 1995.

Day, Caroline Bond. *A Study of Some Negro-White Families in the United States*. Cambridge, MA: Peabody Museum of Harvard University, 1932.

De Shields, André. "His (Blues) Story." In *The Road before Us: 100 Gay Black Poets*, edited by Assotto Saint, 30–31. New York: Galiens, 1991.

Decraene, Philippe. "Aimé Césaire: Black Rebel." *Callaloo* 17 (1983): 63–69.

Delany, Samuel. *Hogg*. Normal, IL: Black Ice, 1995.

Delany, Samuel. *The Mad Man*. Ramsey, NJ: Voyant, 2002. First published 1994.

Baker, Houston A., Manthia Diawara, and Ruth H. Lindeborg, eds. *Black British Cultural Studies: A Reader*. Chicago: University of Chicago Press, 1996.

Baldwin, James. "Encounter on the Seine: Black Meets Brown." In *The Price of the Ticket: Collected Nonfiction, 1948-1985*, 35-39. New York: St. Martin's, 1985. First published 1948.

Baldwin, James. "James Baldwin: The Black Scholar Interviews." *Black Scholar* 5, no. 4 (1973): 33-42.

Baldwin, James. *Just above My Head*. New York: Dial, 2000. First published 1979.

Baldwin, James. "The Preservation of Innocence." *Zero* 1, no. 2 (1949).

Baldwin, James. "Princes and Powers." In *The Price of the Ticket*. New York: St. Martin's/Marek, 1987. First published 1951.

Bambara, Toni Cade, ed. *The Black Woman: An Anthology*. New York: Washington Square, 2005. First published 1970.

Bambara, Toni Cade. "Foreword." In *This Bridge Called My Back: Writings by Radical Women of Color*, edited by Cherríe Moraga and Gloria Anzaldúa. New York: Kitchen Table: Women of Color Press, 1981.

Bambara, Toni Cade. "What Is It I Think I'm Doing Anyhow." In *The Writer on Her Work: Contemporary Women Reflect on Their Art and Their Situation*, edited by Janet Sternberg, 153-78. New York: Norton, 1980.

Barthes, Roland. *S/Z*. Translated by Richard Miller. Malden, MA: Blackwell, 2006.

Batiste, Stephanie. "Dunham Possessed: Ethnographic Bodies, Movement, and Transnational Constructions of Blackness." *Journal of Haitian Studies* 13, no. 2 (2007): 18-22.

Baugh, Edward. "The West Indian Writer and His Quarrel with History." *Small Axe* 16, no. 2 (2012): 60-74. First published 1977.

Beadle-Blair, Rikki, dir. *Metrosexuality*. TLA Releasing, 2001.

Beal, Frances M. *Black Women's Manifesto; Double Jeopardy: To Be Black and Female*. New York: Third World Women's Alliance, 1969. http://www.hartford-hwp.com/archives/45a/196.html.

Beam, Joseph. "Brother to Brother: Words from the Heart." In *In the Life: A Black Gay Anthology*, 230-42. New Orleans: RedBone, 2007. First published 1986.

Beam, Joseph, ed. *In the Life: A Black Gay Anthology*. New Orleans: RedBone, 2007. First published 1986.

Beam, Joseph. "Leaving the Shadows Behind." In *In the Life: A Black Gay Anthology*, xxii. New Orleans: RedBone, 2007. First published 1986.

Bell, Derrick. *Faces at the Bottom of the Well: The Permanence of Racism*. New York: Basic, 1992.

Belton, Don. "How to Make Love to a White Man." Review of *The Masculine Marine: Homoeroticism in the U.S. Marine Corps*, by Steven Zeeland. *Transition* no. 73 (1997): 164. http://doi.org/10.2307/2935452.

Best, Stephen. *None Like Us: Blackness, Belonging, Aesthetic Life*. Durham, NC: Duke University Press, 2018.

Bethel, Lorraine. "what chou mean *we* white girl? or, the cullid lesbian feminist declaration of independence (dedicated to the proposition that all women are not equal, i.e. identical/ly oppressed)." In *Conditions Five: The Black Women's Issue*, 1979.

Bethel, Lorraine, and Barbara Smith, eds. *Conditions Five: The Black Women's Issue*, 1979.

Blackheart Collective. *Blackheart 2: The Prison Issue*. New York, 1984. https://archive.org/stream/blackheart_2/blackheart_2_djvu.txt.

Blum, William. "The CIA, Contras, Gangs, and Crack." Institute for Policy Studies, 1996. Accessed August 15, 2020. https://ips-dc.org/the_cia_contras_gangs_and_crack.

Boellstorff, Tom. "Queer Studies in the House of Anthropology." *Annual Review of Anthropology* 36 (2007): 17–35. http://dx.doi.org/10.1146/annurev.anthro.36.081406.094421.

Bost, Darius. *Evidence of Being: The Black Gay Cultural Renaissance and the Politics of Violence*. Chicago: University of Chicago Press, 2018.

Boyce-Davies, Carole. "Beyond Unicentricity: Transcultural Black Presences." *Research in African Literatures* 30, no. 2 (1999): 96–109.

Boyce-Davies, Carole. *Black Women, Writing and Identity: Migrations of the Subject*. Abingdon, UK: Routledge, 2002.

Boyce-Davies, Carole. *Caribbean Spaces: Escapes from Twilight Zones*. Urbana: University of Illinois Press, 2013.

Boyce-Davies, Carole. "Pan-Africanism, Transnational Black Feminism and the Limits of Culturalist Analyses in African Gender Discourses." *Feminist Africa* 19 (2014): 78–93.

Brand, Dionne. *In Another Place, Not Here*. New York: Grove, 1997.

Brand, Dionne. *A Map to the Door of No Return: Notes to Belonging*. Toronto: Vintage Canada, 2002.

Bridgforth, Sharon. *Delta Dandi: A Conjure*. Long Center Rollins Studio Theatre. University of Texas–Austin, 2009.

Bridgforth, Sharon. *love conjure/blues*. Washington, DC: RedBone, 2004.

"A Brief History of the Drug War." Drug Policy Alliance. www.drugpolicy.org/issues/brief-history-drug-war.

Brooks, Gwendolyn. *The Essential Gwendolyn Brooks*. Edited by Elizabeth Alexander. New York: Library of America, 2005.

Brooks, Gwendolyn. "I Am a Black." In *The Essential Gwendolyn Brooks*, edited by Elizabeth Alexander, 128–29. New York: Library of America, 2005.

Campbell X, dir. "Desire." http://thirdhorizonfilmfestival.com/films/desire.

Campt, Tina. "Black Feminist Futures and the Practice of Fugitivity." The Helen Pond McIntyre '48 Lecture. Barnard Center for Research on Women. YouTube, October 21, 2014. www.youtube.com/watch?v=20zhqw840PU.

Campt, Tina. *Listening to Images*. Durham, NC: Duke University Press, 2017.

Cannick, Jasmyne A. "Hip-Hop's Homophobia and Black Gay America's Silence." *Between the Lines*, April 20, 2006. https://pridesource.com/article/18369.

Carbado, Devon W., and Donald Weise, eds. *Time on Two Crosses: The Collected Writings of Bayard Rustin*. New York: Cleis, 2015.

Carby, Hazel. *Cultures in Babylon: Black Britain and African America*. London: Verso, 1999.

Carby, Hazel. *Imperial Intimacies: A Tale of Two Islands*. Brooklyn, NY: Verso, 2019.

Delany, Samuel. *The Motion of Light in Water: East Village Sex and Science Fiction Writing, 1960–1965.* Boulder, CO: Paladin, 1990.

Delany, Samuel. *Times Square Red, Times Square Blue.* New York: New York University Press, 1999.

Derrida, Jacques. *Archive Fever: A Freudian Impression.* Translated by Eric Prenowitz. Chicago: University of Chicago Press, 1995.

DeVeaux, Alexis. *Warrior Poet: A Biography of Audre Lorde.* New York: Norton, 2006.

Dixon, Melvin. "And These Are Just a Few." In *Love's Instruments* 71–73. Chicago: Tia Chucha, 1995.

Dixon, Melvin. "I'll Be Somewhere Listening for My Name." In *A Melvin Dixon Critical Reader*, edited by Dwight A. McBride and Justin A. Joyce, 147–52. Jackson: University Press of Mississippi, 2010. First published 2000.

Dixon, Melvin. *Love's Instruments.* Chicago: Tia Chucha, 1995.

Dixon, Melvin. "Rivers Remembering Their Source." In *A Melvin Dixon Critical Reader*, edited by Dwight A. McBride and Justin A. Joyce, 30–51. Jackson: University Press of Mississippi, 2010.

Dixon, Melvin. "This Light, This Fire, This Time." *Out/Look* 6 (Fall 1989): 38–45.

Dixon, Melvin. *Vanishing Rooms.* New York: Dutton Adult, 1991.

Drake, St. Clair. *Black Folk Here and There: An Essay in History and Anthropology.* Los Angeles: Center for Afro-American Studies, 1987.

Duberman, Martin. *Hold Tight Gently: Michael Callen, Essex Hemphill, and the Battlefield of AIDS.* New York: New Press, 2014.

duCille, Anne. "The Occult of True Black Womanhood: Critical Demeanor and Black Feminist Studies." *Signs* 19, no. 3 (Spring 1994): 591–629.

Duneier, Mitchell. *Slim's Table: Race, Respectability, and Masculinity.* Chicago: University of Chicago Press, 1994.

Dunham, Katherine. *Island Possessed.* New York: Doubleday, 1969.

Dunn, Marvin. *Black Miami in the Twentieth Century.* Gainesville: University Press of Florida, 1997.

Dunye, Cheryl, dir. *The Early Works of Cheryl Dunye.* First Run Features, 2008.

Duplechan, Larry. *Blackbird.* Vancouver: Arsenal Pulp, 2015.

Duplechan, Larry. *Eight Days a Week: A Novel.* Boston: AlyCat, 1995.

Durban-Albrecht, Erin. "The Legacy of Assotto Saint: Tracing Transnational History from the Gay Haitian Diaspora." *Journal of Haitian Studies* 19, no. 1 (2013): 235–56.

Ellison, Treva, Marshall (fka Kai) Green, Matt Richardson, and C. Riley Snorton. "We Got Issues." *TSQ* 4, no. 2 (2017): 162–69. http://doi.org/10.1215/23289252-3814949.

El-Tayeb, Fatima. *European Others: Queering Ethnicity in Postnational Europe.* Minneapolis: University of Minnesota Press, 2011.

Fanon, Frantz. *Black Skin, White Masks.* Translated by Charles Lam Markmann. New York: Grove, 1967.

Farrow, Kenyon. "Afterword: A Future beyond Equality." "A New Queer Agenda," edited by Joseph N. Defilippis, Lisa Duggan, Kenyon Farrow, and Richard Kim. Special issue, *Scholar & Feminist Online* 10.1–10.2 (2012). http://sfonline.barnard.edu/a-new-queer-agenda/afterword-a-future-beyond-equality.

Ferguson, James, and Akhil Gupta. "Beyond 'Culture': Space, Identity, and the Politics of Difference." In *The Cultural Geography Reader*, edited by Timothy S. Oakes and Patricia L. Price, 72–79. Abingdon, UK: Routledge, 2008.

Ferguson, Roderick A. *Aberrations in Black: Toward a Queer of Color Critique.* Minneapolis: University of Minnesota Press, 2003.

Ferguson, Roderick A. *The Reorder of Things: The University and Its Pedagogies of Minority Difference.* Minneapolis: University of Minnesota Press, 2012.

Fisher, Gary. *Gary in Your Pocket: Stories and Notebooks of Gary Fisher.* Edited by Eve Kosofsky Sedgwick. Durham, NC: Duke University Press, 1996.

Ford-Smith, Honor. "Come to Jamaica and Feel Alright: Tourism, Colonial Discourse and Cultural Resistance." In *Reordering of Culture: Latin America, the Caribbean and Canada in the Hood,* edited by Alvina Ruprecht and Cecilia Taiana, 379–96. Ottawa: Carleton University Press, 1995.

Foucault, Michel. *The Archaeology of Knowledge.* Translated by A. M. Sheridan Smith. London: Routledge, 1969.

Foucault, Michel. "Of Other Spaces." *Diacritics* 16, no. 1 (1986): 22–27.

Foucault, Michel. *The Order of Things: An Archaeology of the Human Sciences.* London: Pantheon, 1970.

Francis, Donette A. *Fictions of Feminine Citizenship: Sexuality and the Nation in Contemporary Caribbean Literature.* New York: Palgrave Macmillan, 2010.

Francis, Donette A. "Intellectual Formations: Locating a Caribbean Critical Tradition." *Anthurium* 10, no. 2 (2013). http://doi.org/10.33596/anth.229.

Free, Brian. "Personal Ties: Wura-Natasha Ogunji at MASS Gallery." Accessed May 25, 2017. https://newamericanpaintings.com/blog/personal-ties-wura-natasha-ogunji-mass-gallery.

Frilot, Shari, dir. *Black Nations/Queer Nations? Lesbian and Gay Sexualities in the African Diaspora.* New York: Third World Newsreel, 1996.

Fullwood, Steven, Reginald Harris, and Lisa C. Moore. *Carry the Word: A Bibliography of Black LGBTQ Books.* New York: Vintage Entity, 2007.

Fullwood, Steven G., and Charles Stephens, eds. *Black Gay Genius: Answering Joseph Beam's Call.* New York: Vintage Entity, 2014.

Gamson, Joshua. *The Fabulous Sylvester: The Legend, the Music, the Seventies in San Francisco.* New York: Holt, 2005.

Garrett, Daniel. "Other Countries: The Importance Difference." In *Other Countries: Black Gay Voices; a First Volume.* New York: Other Countries, 1998.

Gates, Henry Louis, Jr. *The Signifying Monkey: A Theory of African American Literary Criticism.* Oxford: Oxford University Press, 2014. First published 1989.

Gill, Lyndon. *Erotic Islands: Art and Activism in the Queer Caribbean.* Durham, NC: Duke University Press. 2018.

Gilmore, Ruth Wilson. *Golden Gulag: Prisons, Surplus, Crisis, and Opposition in Globalizing California.* Berkeley: University of California Press, 2007.

Gilroy, Paul. *Against Race: Imagining Political Culture beyond the Color Line.* Cambridge, MA: Harvard University Press, 2001.

Gilroy, Paul. *The Black Atlantic: Modernity and Double Consciousness.* Cambridge, MA: Harvard University Press, 1993.

Gilroy, Paul, ed. *Empire Strikes Back: Race and Racism in 70s Britain.* Abingdon, UK: Routledge, 1994.

Gilroy, Paul. "It Ain't Where You're From, It's Where You're At . . . The Dialectics of Diasporic Identification." *Third Text* 5, no. 13 (1991): 3–16.

Giovanni, Nikki. "Nikki-Rosa." In *Black Feeling, Black Talk, Black Judgement.* New York: William Morrow, 1971.

Glasspiegel, Wills, dir. "Icy Lake." 2014. YouTube. www.youtube.com/watch?v =xxi8kbgxxcI.

Glave, Thomas, ed. *Our Caribbean: A Gathering of Lesbian and Gay Writing from the Antilles.* Durham, NC: Duke University Press, 2008.

Glave, Thomas. *Words to Our Now: Imagination and Dissent.* Minneapolis: University of Minnesota Press, 2007.

Global Health Observatory. "HIV/AIDS." February 9, 2021. www.who.int/data /gho/data/themes/hiv-aids#:~:text=Global%20situation%20and%20 trends%3A%3A,at%20the%20end%20of%202019.

Gordon, Edmund T. "Anthropology and Liberation." In *Decolonizing Anthropology: Moving Further toward an Anthropology of Liberation*, edited by Faye V. Harrison. Arlington, VA: Association of Black Anthropologists, American Anthropological Association, 1997.

Gordon, Edmund T. "Cultural Politics of Black Masculinity." *Transforming Anthropology* 6, nos. 1–2 (1997): 36–53.

Gordon, Edmund. *Disparate Diasporas: Identity and Politics in an African-Nicaraguan Community.* Austin: University of Texas Press, 1998.

Gordon, John R., and Rikki Beadle-Blair, eds. *Black and Gay in the UK: An Anthology.* London: Angelica Entertainment, 2014.

Gordon, Lewis R., T. Denean Sharpley-Whiting, and Renée T. White, eds. *Fanon: A Critical Reader*. Oxford: Blackwell, 1996.

Gramsci, Antonio. *Selections from the Prison Notebooks of Antonio Gramsci.* New York: International, 2008.

Gramsci, Antonio. *Selections from the Prison Notebooks of Antonio Gramsci.* Edited by Quintin Hoare and Geoffrey Nowell Smith. New York: International, 1973.

Gregory, Stevens. *Black Corona: Race and the Politics of Place in an Urban Community.* Princeton, NJ: Princeton University Press, 1999.

Griffin, Farah Jasmine, ed. *Beloved Sisters and Loving Friends: Letters from Rebecca Primus of Royal Oak, Maryland, and Addie Brown of Hartford, Connecticut, 1854–1868.* New York: One World/Ballantine, 2001.

Grossberg, Lawrence. "On Postmodernism and Articulation: An Interview with Stuart Hall." *Journal of Communication Inquiry* 10, no. 2 (Summer 1986): 45–60.

Guevara, Che. "From Algiers, for Marcha. The Cuban Revolution Today." In *The Che Reader: Writings on Politics and Revolution*, 2nd ed., edited by David Deutschmann, 212–30. North Melbourne, Australia: Ocean, 2005.

Gumbs, Alexis Pauline. *M Archive: After the End of the World.* Durham, NC: Duke University Press, 2018.

Gumbs, Alexis Pauline. "Seek the Roots: An Immersive and Interactive Archive of Black Feminist Practice." *Feminist Collections* 32, no. 1 (2011): 17–20.

Guridy, Frank, and Juliet Hooker. "Corrientes de pensamiento sociopolitico af-rolatinoamericano." In *Estudios Afrolatinoamericanos: Una introducción*, edited by Alejandro De la Fuente and George Reid Andrews, 291–68. Buenos Aires: CLACSO, 2018.

Gwaltney, John Langston. *Drylongso: A Self-Portrait of Black America*. New York: New Press, 1993. First published 1980.

Guy-Sheftall, Beverly. "The Evolution of Feminist Consciousness among African American Women." In *Words of Fire: An Anthology of African-American Feminist Thought*, 1–22. New York: New Press, 1995.

Guy-Sheftall, Beverly, ed. *Words of Fire: An Anthology of African-American Feminist Thought*. New York: New Press, 1995.

Halberstam, Jack. "Game of Thrones: The Queer Season (House of Nemo)." April 8, 2013. *Bully Bloggers*. https://bullybloggers.wordpress.com/2013/04/08 /game-of-thrones-the-queer-season-by-jack-halberstam-house-of-nemo.

Halberstam, Jack. *In a Queer Time and Place: Transgender Bodies, Subcultural Lives*. New York: New York University Press, 2005.

Halberstam, Jack. *The Queer Art of Failure*. Durham, NC: Duke University Press, 2011.

Halberstam, Jack. "Shame and White Gay Masculinity." *Social Text* 23, nos. 3–4 (2005): 84–85.

Hall, Stuart. "Constituting an Archive." *Third Text* 15, no. 54 (2001): 89–92.

Hall, Stuart. "Cultural Identity and Diaspora." In *Identity: Community, Culture, Difference*, edited by Jonathan Rutherford, 222–37. London: Lawrence and Wishart, 1990.

Hall, Stuart. "David Scott by Stuart Hall." *Bomb* 90, Winter 2005. https:// bombmagazine.org/articles/david-scott.

Hall, Stuart. "Gramsci and Us." In *Antonio Gramsci: Critical Assessments of Leading Political Philosophers*, edited by James Martin, 227–38. Abingdon, UK: Routledge, 2002.

Hall, Stuart. "1980: Race, Articulation and Societies Structured in Dominance." In *Sociological Theories: Race and Colonialism*, 305–45. Paris: UNESCO, 1980.

Hall, Stuart. "What Is This 'Black' in Black Popular Culture?" In *Black Popular Culture: A Project by Michele Wallace*, edited by Gina Dent, 21–33. Seattle: Dia Art Foundation and Bay Press, 1992.

Hall, Stuart, Robert Reiner, Chas Critcher, Tony Jefferson, John Clark, and Brian Roberts. *Policing the Crisis: Mugging, the State, and Law and Order*. London: Macmillan, 1978.

Hanchard, Michael. "Acts of Misrecognition: Transnational Black Politics, Anti-imperialism and the Ethnocentrisms of Pierre Bourdieu and Loic Wac-quant." *Theory, Culture & Society* 20, no. 4 (2003): 5–29.

Hanchard, Michael. "Afro-modernity: Temporality, Politics, and the African Dias-pora." *Public Culture* 11, no. 1 (1996): 245–68.

Hardt, Michael, and Antonio Negri. *Empire*. Cambridge, MA: Harvard University Press, 2001.

Harris, Craig G. "Hope against Hope." In *Brother to Brother: New Writings by Black Gay Men*, edited by Essex Hemphill, 182–89. Washington, DC: RedBone, 2007. First published 1991.

Harris, Craig G. "I'm Going Out Like a Fucking Meteor." In *Sojourner: Black Gay Voices in the Age of AIDS*, edited by B. Michael Hunter, 208–22. New York: Other Countries Collective, 1993.

Harris, E. Lynn. *Invisible Life*. New York: Anchor, 1991.

Harris, Lyle Ashton. "Cultural Healing: An Interview with Marlon Riggs." *After Image* 11 (March 1991).

Harris, Thomas Allen, dir. *É minha cara = That's My Face*. Brooklyn, NY: Chimpanzee Productions, 2001.

Harrison, Faye V., ed. *Decolonizing Anthropology: Moving Further toward an Anthropology of Liberation*. Arlington, VA: Association of Black Anthropologists, American Anthropological Association, 1997.

Harrison, Faye. *Outsider Within: Reworking Anthropology in the Global Age*. Urbana: University of Illinois Press, 2008.

Hartman, Saidiya. "Venus in Two Acts." *Small Axe* 26 (June 2008): 1–14.

Hemphill, Essex. "American Wedding." In *Ceremonies: Prose and Poetry*, 170–71. San Francisco: Cleis, 1992.

Hemphill, Essex. "Black Machismo." In *Ceremonies: Prose and Poetry*, 130. San Francisco: Cleis, 1992.

Hemphill, Essex, ed. *Brother to Brother: New Writings by Black Gay Men*. Washington, DC: RedBone, 2007. First published 1991.

Hemphill, Essex. *Ceremonies: Prose and Poetry*. San Francisco: Cleis, 1992.

Hemphill, Essex. "Choice." *GCN*, May 6–12, 1990: 11, 13.

Hemphill, Essex. "Does Your Mama Know about Me?" In *Ceremonies: Prose and Poetry*, 37–42. San Francisco: Cleis, 1992.

Hemphill, Essex. "For My Own Protection." In *In the Life: A Black Gay Anthology*, edited by Joseph Beam, 174. New Orleans: RedBone, 2007. First published 1986.

Hemphill, Essex. "Heavy Breathing." In *Ceremonies: Prose and Poetry*, 344. San Francisco: Cleis, 1992.

Hemphill, Essex. "HOMOCIDE: For Ronald Gibson." In *Ceremonies: Prose and Poetry*, 144–45. San Francisco: Cleis, 1992.

Hemphill, Essex. "Introduction." In *Brother to Brother: New Writings by Black Gay Men*, edited by Essex Hemphill, xxxv–lviii. Washington, DC: RedBone, 2007. First published 1991.

Hemphill, Essex. "Loyalty." In *Ceremonies: Prose and Poetry*, 63. San Francisco: Cleis, 1992.

Hemphill, Essex. "To Be Real." In *Ceremonies: Prose and Poetry*, 111–21. San Francisco: Cleis, 1992.

Hemphill, Essex. "The Tomb of Sorrow." In *Brother to Brother: New Writings by Black Gay Men*, edited by Essex Hemphill, 93–103. Washington, DC: RedBone, 2007. First published 1991.

Higashida, Cheryl. *Black Internationalist Feminism: Women Writers of the Black Left, 1945–1995*. Urbana: University of Illinois Press, 2017.

Higginbotham, Evelyn Brooks. *Righteous Discontent: The Women's Movement in the Black Baptist Church, 1880–1920*. Cambridge, MA: Harvard University Press, 1993.

Hill Collins, Patricia. *Black Feminist Thought: Knowledge, Consciousness, and the Politics of Empowerment.* Boston: Unwin Hyman, 1990.

Holcomb, G. E. *Claude McKay, Code Name Sasha: Queer Black Marxism and the Harlem Renaissance.* Gainesville: University Press of Florida, 2007.

hooks, bell. *Belonging: A Culture of Place.* Abingdon, UK: Routledge, 1991.

hooks, bell. *Feminist Theory from Margin to Center.* Boston: South End, 1984.

hooks, bell. *We Real Cool: Black Men and Masculinity.* New York: Routledge, 2004.

hooks, bell, and Cornell West. *Breaking Bread: Insurgent Black Intellectual Life.* New York: Routledge, 2016.

Hull, Akasha (Gloria). "What It Is I Think She's Doing Anyhow: A Reading of Toni Cade Bambara's *The Salt Eaters.*" In *Home Girls: A Black Feminist Anthology*, edited by Barbara Smith, 124–42. New York: Kitchen Table: Women of Color Press, 1983.

Hurston, Zora Neale. "How It Feels to Be Colored Me." *World Tomorrow*, May 1928.

Hurston, Zora Neale. "Letter to W. E. B. Du Bois, June 11, 1945." *Credo.* University of Massachusetts Amherst. https://credo.library.umass.edu/view/full/mums312-b106-i184.

Iton, Richard. *In Search of the Black Fantastic: Politics and Popular Culture in the Post–Civil Rights Era.* Oxford: Oxford University Press, 2011.

Iton, Richard. "Still Life." *Small Axe* 17, no. 1 (2013): 22–39.

Jackson, John L. "On Ethnographic Sincerity." *Current Anthropology* 51, no. S2 (October 2010): S279–S287.

Jackson, John L. *Real Black: Adventures in Racial Sincerity.* Chicago: University of Chicago Press, 2005.

Jackson, John L. *Thin Description: Ethnography and the African Hebrew Israelites of Jerusalem.* Cambridge, MA: Harvard University Press, 2013.

James, C. L. R. *Every Cook Can Govern: A Study of Democracy in Ancient Greece.* Detroit: Bewick, 1992. First published 1956.

James, G. Winston. "At the Club." In *The Damaged Good.* New York: Vintage Entity, 2006.

James, Joy. "Radicalizing Feminism." In *The Black Feminist Reader*, edited by Joy James and T. Denean Sharpley-Whiting, 239–58. Malden, MA: Blackwell, 2000.

James, Joy. *Transcending the Talented Tenth: Black Leaders and American Intellectuals.* Abingdon, UK: Routledge, 2013.

James, Joy, and T. Denean Sharpley-Whiting, eds. *The Black Feminist Reader.* Malden, MA: Blackwell, 2000.

Jobson, Ryan Cecil. "The Case for Letting Anthropology Burn: Sociocultural Anthropology in 2019." *American Anthropologist* 122, no. 2 (2020): 259–71.

Johnson, Cary Alan. "Hey Brother, What's Hap'nin'?" In *Brother to Brother: New Writings by Black Gay Men*, edited by Essex Hemphill, 105–6. Washington, DC: RedBone, 2007. First published 1991.

Johnson, Cary Alan. "Not in Knots: TONGUES UNTIED Is the Black Gay Official Story." GCN, February 25–March 3, 1990, 11.

Johnson, E. Patrick, ed. *Black. Queer. Southern. Women: An Oral History.* Chapel Hill: University of North Carolina Press, 2018.

Johnson, E. Patrick. "Feeling the Spirit in the Dark: Expanding Notions of the Sacred in the African-American Gay Community." *Callaloo* 21, no. 2 (1998): 399–416.

Johnson, E. Patrick, ed. *No Tea No Shade*. Durham, NC: Duke University Press, 2016.

Johnson, E. Patrick. "'Quare' Studies, or (Almost) Everything I Know about Queer Studies I Learned from My Grandmother." *Text and Performance Quarterly* 21, no. 1 (2001): 1–25.

Johnson, E. Patrick, ed. *Sweet Tea: Black Gay Men of the South: An Oral History*. Chapel Hill: University of North Carolina Press, 2008.

Johnson, E. Patrick, and Mae G. Henderson, eds. *Black Queer Studies: A Critical Anthology*. Durham, NC: Duke University Press, 2005.

Johnson, James Weldon. "The Creation." In *God's Trombones*, 15–20. New York: Penguin, 2008. First published 1927.

Johnson, James Weldon. *God's Trombones*. New York: Penguin, 2008. First published 1927.

Johnson, Theodore R. "Can the Democratic Party Retain Its Hold on Black Voters?" *Atlantic*, September 7, 2015. www.theatlantic.com/politics/archive/2015/09/the-changing-outlook-for-black-voters/403975.

Jones, Alethia, and Virginia Eubanks, eds., with Barbara Smith. *Ain't Gonna Let Nobody Turn Me Around: Forty Years of Movement Building with Barbara Smith*. Albany: State University of New York Press, 2014.

Jones, Delmos. "Toward a Native Anthropology." *Human Organization* 29 (1970): 251–59.

Jones, Gayl. *Corregidora*. Boston: Beacon, 1987.

Jones, Meta Du Ewa. "Jazz Prosodies: Orality and Textuality." *Callaloo* 25, no. 1 (2002): 66–91. http://doi.org/10.1353/cal.2002.0022.

Jordan, June. *Directed by Desire: The Collected Poems of June Jordan*. Edited by Jan Heller Levi and Sara Miles. Port Townsend, WA: Copper Canyon, 2007.

Jordan, June. "Poem about My Rights." YouTube. www.youtube.com/watch?v=XUSTxhYu7-4.

Jordan, June. *Naming Our Destiny: New and Selected Poems*. New York: Basic, 2005.

Jordan, June. "Poem about My Rights." In *Directed by Desire: The Collected Poems of June Jordan*, edited by Jan Heller Levi and Sara Miles, 309–12. Port Townsend, WA: Copper Canyon, 2007.

Jordan, L. Lloyd. "Black Gay v Gay Black." *BLK*, June 1990, 25.

Judy, Ronald A. T. "Fanon's Body of Black Experience." In *Fanon: A Critical Reader*, edited by Lewis R. Gordon, T. Denean Sharpley-Whiting, and Renée T. White, 53–73. Oxford: Blackwell, 1996.

Julien, Isaac. "Confessions of a Snow Queen: Notes on the Making of 'The Attendant.'" *Critical Quarterly* 36, no. 1 (1994): 120–26.

Julien, Isaac, dir. *This Is Not an AIDS Advertisement*. San Francisco: Frameline, 1987.

Kaplan, Caren. *Questions of Travel: Postmodern Discourses of Displacement*. Durham, NC: Duke University Press, 1996.

Kaplan, Carla, ed. *Zora Neale Hurston: A Life in Letters*. New York: Doubleday, 2002.

Kasino, Michal, dir. *Pay It No Mind: The Life and Times of Marsha P. Johnson*. Frameline Films, 2012. https://youtube/rjN9W2KstqE.

Kay, Jackie. *Trumpet*. London: Pan, 1998.

Keep, Christopher, Tim McLaughlin, and Robin Parmar. "Readerly and Writerly Texts." *Electronic Labyrinth*. www.sas.upenn.edu/~struck/barthes.pdf.

Kenan, Randall. *Let the Dead Bury the Dead*. Boston: Mariner, 1993.

King, Deborah K. *Multiple Jeopardy, Multiple Consciousness: The Context of a Black Feminist Ideology*. Chicago: University of Chicago Press, 1988.

King, Rosamond S. *Island Bodies: Transgressive Sexualities in the Caribbean Imagination*. Gainesville: University Press of Florida, 2014.

La Fountain-Stokes, Lawrence M. "De un Pajaro las Dos Alas: Travel Notes of a Queer Puerto Rican in Havana." *GLQ* 8, no. 1 (2002): 7–33.

Lara, Ana-Maurine. *Kohnjehr Woman*. Washington, DC: RedBone, 2017.

Lara, Ana-Maurine. *Queer Freedom, Black Sovereignty*. Albany: State University of New York Press, 2020.

Lara, Ana-Maurine. *Streetwalking: LGBTQ Lives and Protest in the Dominican Republic*. New Brunswick, NJ: Rutgers University Press, 2021.

Lawrence, Tim. *Hold On to Your Dreams: Arthur Russell and the Downtown Music Scene, 1973–1992*. Durham, NC: Duke University Press, 2009.

Lee, Marcus. "Black Gay Identity in Known Quantities." PhD diss. chapter, University of Chicago. Forthcoming.

Lemmons, Kasi, dir. *Eve's Bayou*. Chubbco Films, 1997.

Lewis, Linden. "Caribbean Masculinity: Unpacking the Narrative." In *The Culture of Gender and Sexuality in the Caribbean*, edited by Linden Lewis, 94–128. Gainesville: University Press of Florida, 2003.

Lewis, Reina. "'At the Site of Intimacy': An Interview with Campbell X, January 2015." *Fashion, Style & Popular Culture* 3, no. 2 (2016): 193–207. http://doi.org/10.1386/fspc.3.2.193_1.

Lewis, Thabiti, ed. *Conversations with Toni Cade Bambara*. Jackson: University Press of Mississippi, 2012.

"LGBT Activists Disrupt Joburg Gay Parade 2012." YouTube. www.youtube.com/watch?v=Hnxip-T_Hnw.

Livermon, Xavier. *Kwaito Bodies: Remastering Space and Subjectivity in Post-apartheid South Africa*. Durham, NC: Duke University Press, 2020.

Livingston, Jennie, dir. *Paris Is Burning*. Art Matters, 1990.

Lofton, Charles, dir. "O Happy Day." San Francisco: Frameline, 1996.

Lopez Bunyasi, Tehama, and Candis Watts Smith. "Do All Black Lives Matter Equally to Black People? Respectability Politics and the Limitations of Linked Fate." *Journal of Race, Ethnicity, and Politics* 4, no. 1 (2019): 180–215. http://doi.org/10.1017/rep.2018.33.

Lorde, Audre. "Age, Race, Class, and Sex: Women Redefining Difference." In *Sister Outsider: Essays and Speeches*, 114–23. Berkeley, CA: Crossing, 1984.

Lorde, Audre. *The Black Unicorn: Poems*. New York: Norton, 1978.

Lorde, Audre. *Chosen Poems*. New York: Norton, 1982.

Lorde, Audre. *The Collected Poems of Audre Lorde*. New York: Norton, 1978.

Lorde, Audre. "Dear Joe." *Callaloo* 14, no. 1 (1991): 47–48.

Lorde, Audre. "English Introduction to Farbe bekennen: Afro-deutsche Frauen auf den Suren ihrer Geschichte." In *I Am Your Sister: Collected and Unpublished Writings of Audre Lorde*, edited by Rudolph P. Byrd, Johnnetta B. Cole, and Beverly Guy-Sheftall. Oxford: Oxford University Press, 2009.

Lorde, Audre. "Eye to Eye." In *Sister Outsider: Essays and Speeches*, 145–75. Berkeley, CA: Crossing, 1984.

Lorde, Audre. "For Each of You." In *The Collected Poems of Audre Lorde*. New York: Norton, 1978.

Lorde, Audre. "Grenada Revisited: An Interim Report." *Black Scholar* 15, no. 1 (1984): 21–29.

Lorde, Audre. "A Litany for Survival." In *The Black Unicorn: Poems*, 31–32. New York: Norton, 1995.

Lorde, Audre. "Of Generators and Survival—Hugo Letter." *Callaloo* 14, no. 1 (1991): 72–82.

Lorde, Audre. "Poetry Is Not a Luxury." In *Sister Outsider: Essays and Speeches*, 81–84. Berkeley, CA: Crossing, 1984.

Lorde, Audre. "Showing Our True Colors." *Callaloo* 14, no. 1 (1991): 67–71.

Lorde, Audre. "Sister, Morning Is a Time for Miracles." In *The Collected Poems of Audre Lorde*, 347–48. New York: Norton, 2000. First published 1982.

Lorde, Audre. "Smelling the Wind." In *The Marvelous Arithmetics of Distance: Poems*, 3. New York: Norton, 1993.

Lorde, Audre. "Tar Beach." In *Afrekete: An Anthology of Contemporary Black Lesbian Writings*, edited by Catherine E. McKinley and L. Joyce DeLaney, 1–18. New York: Anchor, 1995. First published 1982.

Lorde, Audre. "The Transformation of Silence into Language and Action." In *Sister Outsider: Essays and Speeches*, 81–84. Berkeley, CA: Crossing, 1984.

Lorde, Audre. "Turning the Beat Around: Lesbian Parenting." In *A Burst of Light: And Other Essays*, 30–39. New York: Ixia, 2017. First published 1986.

Lorde, Audre. *Zami, a New Spelling of My Name: A Biomythology*. Bloomsbury, UK: Persephone, 1982.

Lorde, Audre, Pat Parker, and Mecca Jamilah Sullivan. *Sister Love: The Letters of Audre Lorde and Pat Parker 1974–1989*. Edited by Julie R. Enszer. Dover, FL: Sinister Wisdom, 2018.

Magubane, Bernard, and James C. Faris. "On the Political Relevance of Anthropology." *Dialectical Anthropology* 9 (1985): 91–104.

Mambety, Djibril Diop, dir. *Touki Bouki*. Kino Video, 1996.

Manalansan, Martin F. "Race, Violence, and Neoliberal Spatial Politics in the Global City." *Social Text* 23, nos. 3–4 (2005): 141–55.

Mapplethorpe, Robert. *Robert Mapplethorpe—The Black Book*. München: Schirmer/ Mosel.

Marable, Manning. *How Capitalism Underdeveloped Black Africa: Problems in Race, Political Economy and Society*. Boston: South End, 1999. First published 1983.

Marable, Manning. "Introduction: Black Studies and the Racial Mountain." In *Dispatches from the Ebony Tower: Intellectuals Confront the African American*

Experience, edited by Manning Marable, 1–28. New York: Columbia University Press. 2000.

Marcus, George E. "On the Problematic Contemporary Reception of Ethnography as the Stimulus for Innovations in Its Forms and Norms in Teaching and Research." *Anthropological Journal on European Cultures* 11 (2002): 191–206.

Marks, Neil, prod. "My Wardrobe, My Right." YouTube. www.youtube.com/watch?v=kiUq2UwgBOE.

Matebeni, Zethu. "Intimacy, Queerness, Race." *Cultural Studies* 27, no. 3 (2013): 404–17.

Mauss, Marcel. *The Gift: The Form and Reason for Exchange in Archaic Societies*. Abingdon, UK: Routledge, 2002. First published 1925.

Mbembe, Achille. "Afropolitanism." In *Africa Remix: Contemporary Art of a Continent*, edited by Simon Njami, 26–30. Johannesburg, South Africa: Jacana Media, 2007.

McBride, Dwight. "Can the Queen Speak?" In *Why I Hate Abercrombie & Fitch: Essays on Race and Sexuality*, 201–26. New York: New York University Press, 2005. First published 1998.

McBride, Dwight. "It's a White Man's World." In *Why I Hate Abercrombie & Fitch: Essays on Race and Sexuality*, 88–131. New York: New York University Press, 2005.

McBride, Dwight. *Why I Hate Abercrombie & Fitch: Essays on Race and Sexuality*. New York: New York University Press, 2005.

McBride, Dwight A., and Justin A. Joyce, eds. *A Melvin Dixon Critical Reader*. Jackson: University Press of Mississippi, 2010.

McDowell, Deborah E. Review of *Conditions: Five*, by Lorraine Bethel and Barbara Smith. *Black American Literature Forum* 16, no. 2 (1982): 77–79. http://doi.org/10.2307/2904140.

McGruder, Kevin. "To Be Heard in Print: Black Gay Writers in 1980s New York." *Obsidian III* 6, no. 1 (2005): 49–65.

McGuire, Danielle. *At the Dark End of the Street: Black Women, Rape, and Resistance—A New History of the Civil Rights Movement from Rosa Parks to the Rise of Black Power*. New York: Alfred A. Knopf, 2011.

McKay, Claude. "If We Must Die." *Liberator* 2, no. 17 (July 1919): 21.

McKay, Claude. *Selected Poems of Claude McKay*. New York: Harcourt Brace Jovanovich, 1953.

McKinley, Catherine E., and L. Joyce DeLaney, eds. 1995. *Afrekete: An Anthology of Contemporary Black Lesbian Writings*. New York: Anchor, 1995.

Moraga, Cherríe, and Gloria Anzaldúa, eds. *This Bridge Called My Back: Writings by Radical Women of Color*. New York: Kitchen Table: Women of Color Press, 1981.

Morisseau-Leroy, Félix. "Mèsi papa Desalín." In *Haitiad and Oddities*. Miami: Pantaléon Guilbaud, 1991. https://thelouvertureproject.org/index.php?title='Mési_Papa__Desalin'_poem_by_Morriseau-Leroy.

Morris, Catherine, and Rujeko Hockley. *We Wanted a Revolution: Black Radical Women, 1965–85: A Sourcebook*. Durham, NC: Duke University Press, 2017.

Morrison, Toni. *Beloved*. London: Vintage, 2016.

Morrow, Bruce. "An Interview with Isaac Julien." *Callaloo* 18, no. 2 (1995): 406–15.

Moten, Fred. *In the Break: Aesthetics of the Black Radical Tradition*. Minneapolis: University of Minnesota Press, 2003.

Muhanji, Cherry. *Her: A Novel*. San Francisco: Aunt Lute Foundation, 1990.

Muholi, Zanele. "Mapping Our Histories: A Visual History of Black Lesbians in Post Apartheid South Africa." MFA thesis, Ryerson University, 2009.

Mullings, Leith. "African-American Women Making Themselves: Notes on the Role of Black Feminist Research." *Souls* 2, no. 4 (Fall 2000): 18–29.

Mumford, Kevin J. *Not Straight, Not White: Black Gay Men from the March on Washington to the AIDS Crisis*. Chapel Hill: University of North Carolina Press, 2016.

Mumford, Kevin J. "Untangling Pathology: The Moynihan Report and Homosexual Damage, 1965–1975." *Journal of Policy History* 24, no. 1 (2012): 53–73.

Muñoz, José Esteban. *Cruising Utopia: The Then and There of Queer Futurity*. New York: New York University Press, 2009.

Muñoz, José Esteban. *Disidentifications: Queers of Color and the Performance of Politics*. Minneapolis: University of Minnesota Press, 1999.

Musila, Grace A. "Navigating Epistemic Disarticulations." *African Affairs* 116, no. 465 (October 2017): 692–704. https://doi.org/10.1093/afraf/adx031.

Nascimento, Abdias. "Quilombismo: An Afro-Brazilian Political Alternative." *Journal of Black Studies* 11, no. 2 (1980): 141–78.

Nash, Jennifer C. "Feminist Originalism: Intersectionality and the Politics of Reading." *Feminist Theory* 17, no. 1 (2016): 3–20.

National Advisory Commission on Civil Disorders (Kerner Commission). "Report of the National Advisory Commission on Civil Disorders: Summary of Report." www.eisenhowerfoundation.org/docs/kerner.pdf.

Nelson, Alondra A. *Body and Soul: The Black Panther Party and the Fight against Medical Discrimination*. Minneapolis: University of Minnesota Press, 2013.

Nelson, Leah. "Jamaica's Anti-gay 'Murder Music' Carries Violent Message." Southern Poverty Law Center, February 27, 2011. www.splcenter.org/fighting -hate/intelligence-report/2015/jamaicas-anti-gay-murder-music-carries -violent-message.

Nero, Charles. "Toward a Black Gay Aesthetic: Signifying in Contemporary Black Gay Literature." In *Brother to Brother: New Writings by Black Gay Men*, edited by Essex Hemphill, 263–88. Washington, DC: RedBone, 2007. First published 1991.

NEST Collective, ed. *Stories of Our Lives: Queer Narratives from Kenya: From an Archive of Stories Collected for the "Stories of Our Lives" Research Project*. Nairobi, Kenya: Nest Arts, 2015.

Nyong'o, Tavia. "Atlantic Is a Sea of Bones." *ASAP Journal*, 2018. Accessed April 20, 2019. http://asapjournal.com/b-o-s-6-2-atlantic-is-a-sea-of-bones-tavia-nyongo.

Ogunji, Wura-Natasha, dir. "Sweep." 2001. https://wuraogunji.com/artwork /2233005_Sweep.html.

Olusoga, David. *Black and British: A Forgotten History*. Basingstoke, UK: Pan Macmillan, 2016.

Opoku-Gyimah, Phyll, Rikki Beadle-Blair, and John R. Gordon, eds. *Sista! An Anthology of Writing by Same Gender Loving Women of African/Caribbean Descent with a UK Connection*. London: Team Angelica, 2018.

Ortner, Sherry B. *Anthropology and Social Theory: Culture, Power, and the Acting Subject*. Durham, NC: Duke University Press, 2006.

Ortner, Sherry B. "Theory in Anthropology since the Sixties." *Comparative Studies in Society and History* 26, no. 1 (January 1984): 126–66.

Other Countries. "Preface." In *Voices Rising: Other Countries III*. Washington, DC: RedBone, 2007.

Ové, Horace, dir. *Baldwin's Nigger*. Infilms, 1969.

Parker, Pat. "The 1987 March on Washington: The Morning Rally." In *The Complete Works of Pat Parker*, edited by Julie R. Enszer, 272–77. Dover, FL: Sinister Wisdom, 2016. First published 1989.

Parker, Pat. "Revolution: It's Not Neat or Pretty, or Quick." In *The Complete Works of Pat Parker*, edited by Julie R. Enszer, 254–59. Dover, FL: Sinister Wisdom, 2016. First delivered 1983.

Parker, Pat. "Tour America." In *The Complete Works of Pat Parker*, edited by Julie R. Enszer, 77. Dover, FL: Sinister Wisdom, 2016.

Patoir, Isanella. "Despite CCJ Ruling on Cross-Dressing, Transgender People Still Face Violence, Discrimination." *News Room*, November 27, 2019. https://newsroom.gy/2019/11/27/despite-ccj-ruling-on-cross-dressing-transgender-people-still-face-violence-discrimination.

Perry, Imani. *May We Forever Stand: A History of the Black National Anthem*. Chapel Hill: University of North Carolina Press, 2018.

Philip, Marlene NourbeSe. *Zong!*, as told to the author by Setaey Adamu Boateng. Middletown, CT: Wesleyan University Press, 2008.

Pierre, Jemima. *The Predicament of Blackness: Postcolonial Ghana and the Politics of Race*. Chicago: University of Chicago Press, 2012.

Pratt, Mary Louise. *Imperial Eyes: Travel Writing and Transculturation*. London: Routledge, 1991.

Puar, Jasbir K. "Global Circuits: Transnational Sexualities and Trinidad." *Signs* 26, no. 4 (2001): 1039–65.

Puar, Jasbir K. "Mapping US Homonormativities." *Gender, Place & Culture* 13, no. 1 (2006): 67–88.

Puar, Jasbir K. "A Transnational Feminist Critique of Queer Tourism." *Antipode* 34, no. 5 (2002): 935–46.

Quashie, Kevin. *Black Women, Identity, and Cultural Theory: (Un)becoming the Subject*. New Brunswick, NJ: Rutgers University Press, 2004.

Quashie, Kevin. "Queer. Caribbean. Miami. Boy: A Personal Geography." *Anthurium* 16, no. 1 (2020). http://doi.org/10.33596/anth.367.

Quashie, Kevin. *The Sovereignty of Quiet: Beyond Resistance in Black Culture*. New Brunswick, NJ: Rutgers University Press, 2012.

Reddock, Rhoda, ed. *Interrogating Caribbean Masculinities: Theoretical and Empirical Analyses*. Kingston, Jamaica: University of the West Indies Press, 2004.

Reid, Graeme. *How to Be a Real Gay: Gay Identities in Small-Town South Africa*. Scottsville, South Africa: University of Kwazulu-Natal Press, 2013.

Reid-Pharr, Robert F., ed. *Black Gay Man: Essays*. New York: New York University Press, 2001.

Reid-Pharr, Robert F. "Dinge." In *Black Gay Man: Essays*, edited by Robert F. Reid-Pharr, 85–98. New York: New York University Press, 2001.

Reid-Pharr, Robert F. "The Shock of Gary Fisher." In *Black Gay Man: Essays*, edited by Robert F. Reid-Pharr, 135–49. New York: New York University Press, 2001.

Reid-Pharr, Robert. "Stronger, in This Life: Loving the Genius of Essex Hemphill and Joseph Beam." In *Black Gay Genius: Answering Joseph Beam's Call*, edited by Steven G. Fullwood and Charles Stephens, 65–74. New York: Vintage Entity, 2014.

Richardson, Matt. "No More Secrets, No More Lies: African American History and Compulsory Heterosexuality." *Journal of Women's History* 15, no. 3 (2003): 63–76.

Richardson, Matt. *The Queer Limit of Black Memory: Black Lesbian Literature and Ir-resolution*. Columbus: Ohio State University Press, 2013.

Riggs, Marlon, dir. *"Anthem," "Affirmations," and "Non, Je Ne Regrette Rien (No Re-gret)": 3 Short Films by Marlon T. Riggs*. San Francisco: Kanopy Streaming, 2015.

Riggs, Marlon, dir. *Tongues Untied*. California Newsreel, 1989.

Rivera, Sylvia. "Y'all Better Quiet Down." Original authorized video by LoveTapes Collective, 1973 Gay Pride Rally, New York City. https://vimeo.com/234353103.

Roberts, Neil. *Freedom as Marronage*. Chicago: University of Chicago Press, 2015.

Robinson, Colin. "An Archaeology of Grief: The Fear of Remembering Joe Beam." In *Black Gay Genius: Answering Joseph Beam's Call*, edited by Steven G. Fullwood and Charles Stephens. New York: Vintage Entity, 2014.

Robinson, Colin. *Decolonising Sexual Citizenship: Who Will Effect Change in the South of the Commonwealth?* London: Commonwealth Advisory Bureau, 2012.

Robinson, Colin. "Unfinished Work." In *You Have You Father Hard Head*. Leeds, UK: Peepal Tree, 2016.

Robinson, Colin. "The Work of Three-Year Old CAISO—Reflections at the MidPoint." Activist Report (Trinidad and Tobago). *Theorizing Homophobias in the Caribbean—Complexities of Place, Desire & Belonging*, 2012. www.caribbeanhomophobias.org/colinrobinson.

Robinson, Colin. *You Have You Father Hard Head*. Leeds, UK: Peepal Tree, 2016.

Robinson, Pat, and colleagues. "Poor Black Women's Study Papers." In *The Black Woman: An Anthology*, edited by Toni Cade Bambara, 189–97. New York: Signet, 1970.

Rodney, Walter. *The Groundings with My Brothers*. London: Bogle-L'Ouverture, 1969.

Rodney, Walter. *How Europe Underdeveloped Africa*. London: Verso, 2018. First published 1972.

Rodríguez, Juana Maria. *Sexual Futures, Queer Gestures, and Other Latina Longings*. New York: New York University Press, 2014.

Rolland, Romain. "Review of Roland Lefebvre's 'Le Sacrifice D'Abraham.'" *L'humaníte* (1920).

Rowell, Charles. "Above the Wind: An Interview with Audre Lorde." *Callaloo* 23, no. 1 (Winter 2000): 52–63.

Saint, Assotto. "Going Home Celebration (for Donald Woods)." In *Spells of a Voodoo Doll: The Poems, Fiction, Essays and Plays of Assotto Saint*, 135–36. New York: Masquerade, 1996.

Saint, Assotto. "Haiti: A Memory Journal." In *Spells of a Voodoo Doll: The Poems, Fiction, Essays and Plays of Assotto Saint*, 229–34. New York: Masquerade, 1996.

Saint, Assotto. "The Impossible Black Homosexual (Or Fifty Ways to Become One)." In *Spells of a Voodoo Doll: The Poems, Fiction, Essays and Plays of Assotto Saint*, 169–72. New York: Masquerade, 1996.

Saint, Assotto. "Miss Thing/For Marcia Johnson." In *Spells of a Voodoo Doll: The Poems, Fiction, Essays and Plays of Assotto Saint*, 209–12. New York: Masquerade, 1996.

Saint, Assotto, "Preface." In *The Road before Us: 100 Gay Black Poets*, edited by Assotto Saint, xvii–xxv. New York: Galiens, 1991.

Saint, Assotto, ed. *The Road before Us: 100 Gay Black Poets*. New York: Galiens, 1991.

Saint, Assotto. *Spells of a Voodoo Doll: The Poems, Fiction, Essays and Plays of Assotto Saint*. New York: Masquerade, 1996.

Saint, Assotto. "Why I Write." In *Spells of a Voodoo Doll: The Poems, Fiction, Essays and Plays of Assotto Saint*, 3–8. New York: Masquerade, 1996.

Sanchez, Sonia. "For Sweet Honey in the Rock." In *Shake Loose My Skin: New and Selected Poems*, 148–50. Boston: Beacon, 1999.

Santana, Stephanie Bosch. "Exorcizing Afropolitanism: Binyavanga Wainaina Explains Why 'I Am a Pan-Africanist, Not an Afropolitan' at ASAUK 2012." *Africa in Words Blog*, February 8, 2013. https://africainwords.com/2013/02/08/exorcizing-afropolitanism-binyavanga-wainaina-explains-why-i-am-a-pan-africanist-not-an-afropolitan-at-asauk-2012.

Saunders, Patricia. "Defending the Dead, Confronting the Archive: A Conversation with M. NourbeSe Philip." *Small Axe* 12, no. 2 (2008): 63–79.

Scott, Darieck. "Jungle Fever? Black Gay Identity Politics, White Dick, and the Utopian Bedroom." *GLQ* 1, no. 3 (1994): 299–321.

Scott, Darieck. *Traitor to the Race*. New York: Plume, 1996.

Scott, David. *Conscripts of Modernity: The Tragedy of Colonial Enlightenment*. Durham, NC: Duke University Press, 2005.

Scott, David. "Introduction: On the Archaeologies of Black Memory." *Small Axe* 26, no. 10 (2008): 1–16.

Scott, David. *Omens of Adversity: Tragedy, Time, Memory, Justice*. Durham, NC: Duke University Press, 2014.

Sedgwick, Eve Kosofsky. "Paranoid Reading and Reparative Reading, or, You're So Paranoid, You Probably Think This Introduction Is about You." In *Touching Feeling: Affect, Pedagogy, Performativity*. Durham, NC: Duke University Press, 2003.

Shakur, Assata. *Assata: An Autobiography*. Brooklyn, NY: Lawrence Hill, 1987.

Shakur, Assata. "An Open Letter from Assata Shakur." *Canadian Dimension* 32, no. 4 (July 1998): 17, 21.

Shange, Ntozake. *For Colored Girls Who Have Considered Suicide, When the Rainbow Is Enuf: A Choreopoem*. Oakland, CA: Shameless Hussy, 1975.

Shange, Ntozake. *Ridin' the Moon in Texas: Word Paintings*. New York: St. Martin's, 1987.

Sharpe, Christina Elizabeth. *In the Wake: On Blackness and Being*. Durham, NC: Duke University Press, 2016.

Silva Santana, Dora. "Transitionings and Returnings: Experiments with the Poetics of Transatlantic Water." *TSQ* 4, no. 2 (2017): 181–90.

Simmons, Ron. "Joe, Essex, Marlon, and Me." In *Black Gay Genius: Answering Joseph Beam's Call*, edited by Steven G. Fullwood and Charles Stephens, 53–64. New York: Vintage Entity, 2014.

Simmons, Ron. "Some Thoughts on the Challenges Facing Black Gay Intellectuals." In *Brother to Brother: New Writings by Black Gay Men*, edited by Essex Hemphill, 263–88. Washington, DC: RedBone, 2007. First published 1991.

Sloan, Margaret. *Black Feminism: A New Mandate*. New York: Ms. Magazine, 1974.

Smith, Barbara. "Aint Gonna Let Nobody Turn Me Around." *Black Scholar* 22, no. 12 (1992): 90–93. http://doi.org/10.1080/00064246.1992.11413019.

Smith, Barbara. "Doing Research on Black American Women." *Radical Teacher* 3 (1976): 25–27.

Smith, Barbara, ed. *Home Girls: A Black Feminist Anthology*. New Brunswick, NJ: Rutgers University Press, 2000. First published 1983.

Smith, Barbara, and Beverly Smith. "'I Am Not Meant to Be Alone and without You Who Understand': Letters from Black Feminists 1972–1978." *Conditions Four* 2, no. 1 (Winter 1979): 62–77.

Smith, Christen Anne. "Towards a Black Feminist Model of Black Atlantic Liberation: Remembering Beatriz Nascimento." *Meridians* 14, no. 2 (2016): 71–87. http://doi.org/10.2979/meridians.14.2.06.

Smith, Faith, ed. *Sex and the Citizen: Interrogating the Caribbean*. Charlottesville: University of Virginia Press, 2011.

Snorton, C. Riley. *Black on Both Sides: A Racial History of Trans Identity*. Minneapolis: University of Minnesota Press, 2017.

Spencer, Robyn C. *The Revolution Has Come: Black Power, Gender, and the Black Panther Party in Oakland*. Durham, NC: Duke University Press, 2016.

Spillers, Hortense. "'All the Things You Could Be by Now If Sigmund Freud's Wife Was Your Mother': Psychoanalysis and Race." *Critical Inquiry* 22, no. 4 (Summer 1996): 710–34.

Spillers, Hortense J. "Interstices: A Small Drama of Words." In *Black, White and in Color: Essays on American Literature and Culture*, edited by Hortense Spillers, 152–75. Chicago: University of Chicago Press, 2003.

Spillers, Hortense J. "Mama's Baby, Papa's Maybe: An American Grammar Book." *Diacritics* 17, no. 2 (Summer 1987): 64–81.

Spillers, Hortense J. "Toward an Intramural Protocol of Reading." In *Black, White, and in Color: Essays on American Literature and Culture*, 277–300. Chicago: University of Chicago Press, 2003.

Stanford, Adrian. "Yeah, Baby." In *Black and Queer*, 9. Boston: Good Gay Poets, 1977.

Staples, Robert. *Black Masculinity: The Black Male's Role in American Society*. San Francisco: Black Scholar, 1986.

Tamale, Sylvia, ed. *African Sexualities: A Reader*. Oxford: Pambazuka, 2011.

Tatem, Darnell. "A System of Slavery in the Real." *Blackheart 2: The Prison Issue* (1984), 34–37.

Taylor, Charles. *Philosophical Papers 2*. Cambridge: Cambridge University Press, 2005.

Taylor, Diana. *The Archive and the Repertoire: Performing Cultural Memory in the Americas*. Durham, NC: Duke University Press, 2003.

Taylor, Keeanga-Yamahtta, ed. *How We Get Free: Black Feminism and the Combahee River Collective*. Chicago: Haymarket, 2017.

Thomas, Deborah A. *Exceptional Violence: Embodied Citizenship in Transnational Jamaica*. Durham, NC: Duke University Press, 2011.

Tinsley, Omise'eke Natasha. *Ezili's Mirrors: Imagining Black Queer Genders*. Durham, NC: Duke University Press, 2018.

Tinsley, Omise'eke Natasha. *Thiefing Sugar: Eroticism between Women in Caribbean Literature*. Durham, NC: Duke University Press, 2010.

Tinsley, Omise'eke Natasha, and Jafari Allen. "After the Love: Remembering Black/Queer/Diaspora." GLQ 25, no. 1 (2019): 107–12. https://doi.org/10.1215/10642684-7275586.

Tourmaline (fka Reina Gossett), dir. "Atlantic Is a Sea of Bones," 2017.

Tourmaline (fka Reina Gossett). "On Untoreli's 'New' Book," 2013. https://thespiritwas.tumblr.com/post/45275076521/on-untorellis-new-book.

Trouillot, Michel-Rolph. *Global Transformations: Anthropology and the Modern World*. New York: Palgrave Macmillan, 2003.

Trouillot, Michel-Rolph. *Silencing the Past: Power and the Production of History*. Boston: Beacon, 1995.

Vaid, Urvashi. *Virtual Equality: The Mainstreaming of Gay and Lesbian Liberation*. New York: Anchor, 1996.

Vargas, João Costa. *Catching Hell in the City of Angels: Life and Meanings of Blackness in South Central Los Angeles*. Minneapolis: University of Minnesota Press, 2006.

Vargas, João Costa. *The Denial of Antiblackness: Multiracial Redemption and Black Suffering*. Minneapolis: University of Minnesota Press, 2018.

Wainaina, Binyavanga. "I Am a Homosexual, Mum." *Africa Is a Country*, January 19, 2014. https://africasacountry.com/2014/01/i-am-a-homosexual-mum.

Wainaina, Binyavanga. *One Day I Will Write about This Place: A Memoir*. Minneapolis, MN: Graywolf, 2013.

Wainaina, Binyavanga. "We Must Free Our Imaginations." YouTube, January 21, 2014. www.youtube.com/watch?v=8uMwppw5AgU&t=41s.

Walcott, Rinaldo. *Black Like Who? Writing Black Canada*. Toronto: Insomniac, 2003.

Walcott, Rinaldo. *Queer Returns: Essays on Multiculturalism, Diaspora and Black Studies*. Toronto: Insomniac, 2016.

Walcott, Rinaldo. "Somewhere out There: The New Black Queer Theory." In *Blackness and Sexualities*, edited by Michelle Wright and Antje Schuhmann, 29–40. Berlin: Lit Verlag, 2007.

Walker, Alice. *In Search of Our Mothers' Gardens: Womanist Prose*. New York: Harcourt, 1983.

Walker, Margaret. "For My People." *Poetry* 51, no. 2 (1937): 81–83.

Walker, Margaret. "I Want to Write." In *This Is My Century: New and Collected Poems*, 113. Athens: University of Georgia Press, 1989.

Wall, Cheryl, ed. *Changing Our Own Words: Essays on Criticism, Theory, and Writing by Black Women*. New Brunswick, NJ: Rutgers University Press, 1989.

Wall, Cheryl. *Women of the Harlem Renaissance*. Bloomington: Indiana University Press, 1995.

Wallace, Michele. *Dark Designs and Visual Culture*. Durham, NC: Duke University Press, 2004.

Ware, Cellestine. *Woman Power: The Movement for Women's Liberation*. New York: Tower, 1970.

Warren, Calvin L. *Ontological Terror: Blackness, Nihilism, and Emancipation*. Durham, NC: Duke University Press. 2018.

Webb, Gary. *Dark Alliance: The CIA, the Contras, and the Crack Cocaine Explosion*. New York: Seven Stories Press, 2014.

Weems, Renita. "Artists without Art Form: A Look at One Black Woman's World of Unrevered Black Women." In *Home Girls: A Black Feminist Anthology*, ed. Barbara Smith, 94–105. New Brunswick, NJ: Rutgers University Press, 2000. First published 1983.

Weems, Renita. "The Black Woman Artist Will Revere the Black Woman." In *Conditions Five: The Black Women's Issue*, edited by Lorraine Bethel and Barbara Smith, 1979.

West, Cornel. *Race Matters*. Boston: Beacon, 1993.

White, Marvin K. "Last Rights." In *The Road before Us: 100 Gay Black Poets*, edited by Assotto Saint, 158–62. New York: Galiens, 1991.

White, Marvin K. *Last Rights*. Washington, DC: RedBone, 2002.

White, Marvin K. "Second Read: From the Queen James Bible." Unpublished manuscript, 2018.

White, Marvin K. "Theology of the Discopocene." Unpublished manuscript, 2018.

Wilderson, Frank, III. "Gramsci's Black Marx: Whither the Slave in Civil Society?" *Social Identities* 9, no. 2 (2003): 225–40.

Williams, Brackette F. "Skinfolk, Not Kinfolk: Comparative Reflections on the Identity of Participant-Observation in Two Field Situations." In *Feminist Dilemmas in Fieldwork*, edited by Diane L. Wolf, 72–95. New York: Routledge, 1996.

Williams, Eric Eustace. "'Massa Day Done.' Public Lecture at Woodford Square, 22 March 1961." *Callaloo* 20, no. 4 (1997): 725–30. http://doi.org/10.1353/cal .1997.0085.

Williams, Stereo. "Hip-Hop's Most Anti-gay Lyrics." *rollingout*, February 5, 2013. https://rollingout.com/2013/02/05/lord-jamar-calls-kanye-west-queer -conscious-hip-hops-10-most-homophobic-lyrics/2.

Wilson, Valerie, and William M. Rodgers, III. "Black-White Wage Gaps Expand with Rising Wage Inequality." Economic Policy Institute, 2016. Accessed August 15, 2020. www.epi.org/publication/black-white-wage-gaps-expand -with-rising-wage-inequality.

Woodard, Vincent. "Just as Quare as They Want to Be: A Review of the Black Queer Studies in the Millennium Conference." *Callaloo* 23, no. 4 (2000): 1278–84.

Woods, Donald. "We Be Young." In *The Road before Us: 100 Gay Black Poets*, edited by Assotto Saint, 158–62. New York: Galiens, 1991.

Woubshet, Dagmawi. *The Calendar of Loss: Race, Sexuality, and Mourning in the Early Era of AIDS*. Baltimore: Johns Hopkins University Press, 2015.

Wright, Michelle M. *Becoming Black: Creating Identity in the African Diaspora*. Durham, NC: Duke University Press, 2004.

Wright, Michelle M. *Physics of Blackness: Beyond the Middle Passage Epistemology*. Minneapolis: University of Minnesota Press, 2016.

Wright, Richard. "I Choose Exile." Unpublished essay. Department of Special Collections and Archives, Kent State University, 1951.

Wynter, Sylvia. "Ethno or Socio Poetics." *Alcheringa: Ethnopoetics* 2, no. 2 (1976): 78–94.

Wynter, Sylvia. "On How We Mistook the Map for the Territory, and Reimprisoned Ourselves in Our Unbearable Wrongness of Being, of Desêtre: Black Studies toward Human Project." In *Not Only the Master's Tools: African-American Studies in Theory and Practice*, edited by Lewis Gordon and Jane Anna Gordon, 107–72. Boulder, CO: Paradigm, 2006.

Wynter, Sylvia. "Rethinking 'Aesthetics': Notes towards a Deciphering Practice." In *Ex-iles: Essays on Caribbean Cinema*, edited by Mbye B. Cham, 237–79. Trenton, NJ: Africa World, 1992.

Wynter, Sylvia. "Towards the Sociogenic Principle: Fanon, Identity, the Puzzle of Conscious Experience, and What Is Like to Be 'Black.'" In *National Identities and Sociopolitical Changes in Latin America*, edited by Mercedes F. Dúran-Cogan and Antonio Gómez-Moriana, 30–61. Abingdon, UK: Routledge, 2013. First published 2001.

Young, Allen. "Rapping with a Street Transvestite Revolutionary: An Interview with Marcia Johnson." In *Out of the Closets: Voices of Day Liberation*, edited by Karla Jay and Allen Young, 112–20. New York: New York University Press, 1992. First published 1971.

Young, Paulette. "Ghanaian Woman and Dutch Wax Prints: The Counter-appropriation of the Foreign and the Local Creating a New Visual Voice of Creative Expression." *Journal of Asian and African Studies* 51, no. 3 (2016): 305–27. https://doi.org/10.1177/0021909615623811.

index

Page numbers in italics refer to figures.

of University of Rio de Janeiro, 222; *Tongues Untied*, 347n49; at Yale, 97–98, 172, 314–15; 359n

Poe, Watufani, 211

pornography, xvi, 157, 158, 227; porn, xv, xvii, xviii, 72, 74, 155, 156, 158, 160, 161, 236, 317, 362n23; erotica, xvii, 161

Pose, 126, 130, 210, 354n22, 362n34

prison, 55–59, 145, 298, 299, 372n12, 377n16, 378n29

Puar, Jasbir, 279, 364n6

"quare," see E. Patrick Johnson

quarrel, 66, 79, 249, 250, 255, 317, 360n10. See also "Bolekaja intellectualism"

Quashie, Kevin, 114, 247, 321, 326, 336n51

queer, 152–53. See also Black gay time; Black gay temporality; Black Nations, Queer Nations?; Black/queer; Black queer diaspora; Black/Queerpolis; Black queer studies

quilombo, 272, 274, 373n28; *quilombismo*, 262, 370, 372–73n27. See also maroon/ marronage; palenques

Ransby, Barbara, 38, 39, 64, 308

Reddock, Rhoda, *Interrogating Caribbean Masculinities*, 336n66

Reddy, Chandan, 220, 363, 378

Reid, Graeme, xviii, 186, 359n18

Reid-Pharr, Robert, 88, 99, 321, 348, 355n2; "Stronger In This Life," 33, 62, 332, 338, 339; "The Shock of Gary Fisher," 351n81

relationality, 17, 64, 168, 231, 232. See also sociality

respectability, x, 45, 53, 247, 337n68, 357n27, 368n11

revolution, 11, 20, 35, 44, 46, 57, 64, 65, 72, 74, 86, 95, 98, 111, 119, 120, 121, 122, 123, 148, 152, 196, 212, 233, 264, 304, 319, 333n20, 341, 378

revolutionary, 11, 43, 51, 58, 60, 64, 72, 81, 83, 84, 85, 86, 93, 120, 121, 122, 123, 124, 161, 196, 216, 251, 253, 255, 260, 265, 297, 301, 303, 304, 307, 311, 323, 339n11, 341n40, 344n17, 345n24; Cuban, 376n4; Grena-

dian (New Jewel Movement), 122, 122, 253; sexual, 119

Richardson, Len, 78, 80

Richardson, Matt, xviii, xix, 63, 169, 170, 172, 173, 175, 176, 180, 181, 182, 184, 185, 186, 192, 193, 198, 205, 211, 219, 290, 317; "No More Secrets, No More Lies," 194; *Queer Limit of Black Memory*, 338, 359n18; "We Got Issues," 362

Riggs, Marlon, xix, 58, 63, 64, 65, 73, 83, 87, 97, 103, 104, 106, 108, 109, 115, 196, 200, 207, 272, 293, 347n49, 349; *Affirmation*, 106, 272, 273, 285; *Anthem*, 106, 212, 285, 345, 373n30; *Tongues Untied*, xviii, 12, 65, 83, 84, 97, 106, 109, 177, 329. See also Marlon Riggs Papers at SU.

Rivera, Sylvia, xvii, 55, 57, 216, 345n26; Street Transgender Action Revolutionaries (STAR), 56

Robinson, Colin, xviii, xix, 30, 62, 69, 76, 78, 88, 95, 177, 181, 187, 189, 190, 193, 198, 203, 204, 212, 268, 272, 278, 279, 283, 284, 285, 286, 293, 294, 322, 346n32, 355n2, 360n2, 362n25; "Decolonising Sexual Citizenship," 287; *Think Again*, 218; "Unfinished Work," 271, 373nn28, 31; 363n51, 372n26, 373n31; "The Work of Three-Year Old CAISO—Reflections at the MidPoint," 359n18. See also Colin Robinson Papers at SCRBC.

Robinson, Phillip, 60

Rodríguez, Juana Maria, 36, 330n45, 358n41

Rogers, Jordan, 211, 313, 321

Ross, Diana, xviii, 4, 131, 233; "Love Hangover," 131

Ross, Marlon, 97

Rustin, Bayard, 382. See also Bayard Rustin Papers at LOC.

Saint, Assotto (Yves Francois Lubin), xvii, 11, 64, 84, 87, 88, 97, 274, 327n20, 345n28, 346n31, 348n57, 373n31; "Haiti: A Memory Journey," 89; *The Road Before Us: 100 Black Gay Poets*, 342n6; *Spells of a Voodoo Doll*, 88. See also Assotto Saint Papers at SCRBC.